BUNKER HILL

ALSO BY NATHANIEL PHILBRICK

The Passionate Sailor

Away Off Shore: Nantucket Island and Its People, 1602–1890

Abram's Eyes: The Native American Legacy of Nantucket Island

Second Wind: A Sunfish Sailor's Odyssey

In the Heart of the Sea: The Tragedy of the Whaleship Essex

Sea of Glory: America's Voyage of Discovery;
The U.S. Exploring Expedition, 1838–1842

Mayflower: A Story of Courage, Community, and War

The Last Stand: Custer, Sitting Bull, and the Battle of Little Bighorn

Why Read Moby-Dick?

Nathaniel Philbrick

BUNKER HILL

A City, a Siege, a Revolution

VIKING

VIKING
Published by the Penguin Group
Penguin Group (USA) Inc., 375 Hudson Street,
New York, New York 10014, USA

USA | Canada | UK | Ireland | Australia | New Zealand | India | South Africa | China

Penguin Books Ltd, Registered Offices: 80 Strand, London WC2R ORL, England
For more information about the Penguin Group visit penguin.com

Illustration credits appear on pages 379–80.

Maps by Jeffrey L. Ward

Art on pages iv–v: View of Long Wharf and Part
of the Harbor of Boston in New England, America (detail).
Courtesy of the Bostonian Society, Object Collection

LIBRARY OF CONGRESS CATALOGING IN PUBLICATION DATA
Philbrick, Nathaniel.
Bunker Hill : a city, a siege, a revolution / Nathaniel Philbrick.
pages cm
Includes bibliographical references and index.
ISBN 978-0-670-02544-2
1. Bunker Hill, Battle of, Boston, Mass., 1775.
2. Boston (Mass.)—History—Revolution, 1775–1783. I. Title.
E241.B9P48 2013
973.3'312—dc23
2013001534

Printed in the United States of America
1 3 5 7 9 10 8 6 4 2

Designed by Francesca Belanger
Set in Photina MT Std

To my mother,
Marianne Dennis Philbrick

Boston has been like the vision of Moses: a bush burning but not consumed.

—the Reverend Samuel Cooper, April 7, 1776

Contents

Preface: The Decisive Day   *xiii*

Part I: **Liberty**   *1*

CHAPTER ONE: **The City on the Hill**   *3*

CHAPTER TWO: **Poor Unhappy Boston**   26

CHAPTER THREE: **The Long Hot Summer**   44

CHAPTER FOUR: **The Alarm**   61

CHAPTER FIVE: **The Unnatural Contest**   84

Part II: **Rebellion**   107

CHAPTER SIX: **The Trick to See It**   109

CHAPTER SEVEN: **The Bridge**   132

CHAPTER EIGHT: **No Business but That of War**   161

CHAPTER NINE: **The Redoubt**   188

CHAPTER TEN: **The Battle**   208

Part III: **The Siege**   231

CHAPTER ELEVEN: **The Fiercest Man**   233

CHAPTER TWELVE: **The Clap of Thunder**   264

EPILOGUE: **Character Alone**   292

Acknowledgments   *297*

Notes   *301*

Bibliography   *357*

Illustration Credits   *379*

Index   *381*

Preface: The Decisive Day

On a hot, almost windless afternoon in June, a seven-year-old boy stood beside his mother and looked out across the green islands of Boston Harbor. To the northwest, sheets of fire and smoke rose from the base of a distant hill. Even though the fighting was at least ten miles away, the concussion of the great guns burst like bubbles across his tear-streaked face.

At that moment, John Adams, the boy's father, was more than three hundred miles to the south at the Continental Congress in Philadelphia. Years later, the elder Adams claimed that the American Revolution had started not with the Boston Massacre, or the Tea Party, or the skirmishes at Lexington and Concord and all the rest, but had been "effected before the war commenced . . . in the minds and hearts of the people." For his son, however, the "decisive day" (a phrase used by the boy's mother, Abigail) was June 17, 1775.

Seventy-one years after that day, in the jittery script of an old man, John Quincy Adams described the terrifying afternoon when he and his mother watched the battle from a hill beside their home in Braintree: "I saw with my own eyes those fires, and heard Britannia's thunders in the Battle of Bunker's hill and witnessed the tears of my mother and mingled with them my own." They feared, he recounted, that the British troops might at any moment march out of Boston and "butcher them in cold blood" or take them as hostages and drag them back into the besieged city. But what he remembered most about the battle was the hopeless sense of sorrow that he and his mother felt when they learned that their family physician, Dr. Joseph Warren, had been killed.

Warren had saved John Quincy Adams's badly fractured forefinger from amputation, and the death of this "beloved physician" was a terrible blow to a boy whose father's mounting responsibilities required that he spend months away from home. Even after John Quincy Adams had grown into adulthood and become a public figure, he refused to attend all anniversary celebrations of the Battle of Bunker Hill.

Joseph Warren, just thirty-four at the time of his death, had been much more than a beloved doctor to a seven-year-old boy. Over the course of the two critical months between the outbreak of hostilities at Lexington Green and the Battle of Bunker Hill, he became the most influential patriot leader in the province of Massachusetts. As a member of the Committee of Safety, he had been the man who ordered Paul Revere to alert the countryside that British soldiers were headed to Concord; as president of the Provincial Congress, he had overseen the creation of an army even as he waged a propaganda campaign to convince both the American and British people that Massachusetts was fighting for its survival in a purely defensive war. While his more famous compatriots John Adams, John Hancock, and Samuel Adams were in Philadelphia at the Second Continental Congress, Warren was orchestrating the on-the-ground reality of a revolution.

Warren had only recently emerged from the shadow of his mentor Samuel Adams when he found himself at the head of the revolutionary movement in Massachusetts, but his presence (and absence) were immediately felt. When George Washington assumed command of the provincial army gathered outside Boston just two and a half weeks after the Battle of Bunker Hill, he was forced to contend with the confusion and despair that followed Warren's death. Washington's ability to gain the confidence of a suspicious, stubborn, and parochial assemblage of New England militiamen marked the advent of a very different kind of leadership. Warren had passionately, often impulsively, tried to control the accelerating cataclysm. Washington would need to master the situation deliberately and—above all—firmly. Thus, the Battle of Bunker Hill is the critical turning point in the story of how a rebellion born in the streets of Boston became a countrywide war for independence.

This is also the story of two British generals. The first, Thomas Gage, was saddled with the impossible task of implementing his government's unnecessarily punitive response to the Boston Tea Party in December 1773. Gage had a scrupulous respect for the law and was therefore ill equipped to subdue a people who were perfectly willing to take that law into their own hands. When fighting broke out at Lexington and Concord, militiamen from across the region descended upon the British stationed at Boston. Armed New Englanders soon cut off the land approaches to Boston. Ironically, the former center of American resistance found itself gripped by an American siege. By the time General William Howe replaced Gage as the British commander in chief, he had determined that New York, not Boston, was where he must resume the fight. It was left to Washington to hasten the departure of Howe and his army.

The evacuation of the British in March 1776 signaled the beginning of an eight-year war that produced a new nation. But it also marked the end of an era that had started back in 1630 with the founding of the Puritan settlement called Boston. This is the story of how a revolution changed that 146-year-old community—of what was lost and what was gained when 150 vessels filled with British soldiers and American loyalists sailed from Boston Harbor for the last time.

Over the more than two centuries since the Revolution, Boston has undergone immense physical change. Most of the city's once-defining hills have been erased from the landscape while the marshes and mudflats that surrounded Boston have been filled in to eliminate almost all traces of the original waterfront. But hints of the vanished town remain. Several meetinghouses and churches from the colonial era are still standing, along with a smattering of seventeenth- and eighteenth-century houses. Looking southeast from the balcony of the Old State House, you can see how the spine of what was once called King Street connects this historic seat of government, originally known as the Town House, to Long Wharf, an equally historic commercial center that still reaches out into the harbor.

For the last three years I have been exploring these places, trying to get a fix on the long-lost topography that is essential to understanding how Boston's former residents interacted. Boston in the 1770s was a land-connected island with a population of about fifteen thousand, all of whom probably recognized, if not knew, each other. Being myself a resident of an island with a year-round population very close in size to provincial Boston's, I have some familiarity with how petty feuds, family alliances, professional jealousies, and bonds of friendship can transform a local controversy into a supercharged outpouring of communal angst. The issues are real enough, but why we find ourselves on one side or the other of those issues is often unclear even to us. Things just *happen* in a way that has little to do with logic or rationality and everything to do with the mysterious and infinitely complex ways that human beings respond to one another.

In the beginning there were three different colonial groups in Massachusetts. One group was aligned with those who eventually became revolutionaries. For lack of a better word, I will call these people "patriots." Another group remained faithful to the crown, and they appear herein as "loyalists." Those in the third and perhaps largest group were not sure where they stood. Part of what makes a revolution such a fascinating subject to study is the arrival of the moment when neutrality is no longer an option. Like it or not, a person has to choose.

It was not a simple case of picking right from wrong. Hindsight has shown that, contrary to what the patriots insisted, Britain had not launched a preconceived effort to enslave her colonies. Compared with other outposts of empire, the American colonists were exceedingly well off. It's been estimated that they were some of the most prosperous, least-taxed people in the Western world. And yet there was more to the patriots' overheated claims about oppression than the eighteenth-century equivalent of a conspiracy theory. The hyperbole and hysteria that so mystified the loyalists had wellsprings that were both ancient and strikingly immediate. For patriots and loyalists alike, this was personal.

Because a revolution gave birth to our nation, Americans have a tendency to exalt the concept of a popular uprising. We want the whole world to be caught in a blaze of liberating upheaval (with appropriately democratic results) because that was what worked so well for us. If Gene Sharp's *From Dictatorship to Democracy*, the guidebook that has become a kind of bible among twenty-first-century revolutionaries in the Middle East and beyond, is any indication, the mechanics of overthrowing a regime are essentially the same today as they were in the eighteenth century. And yet, given our tendency to focus on the Founding Fathers who were at the Continental Congress in Philadelphia when all of this was unfolding in and around Boston, most of us know surprisingly little about how the patriots of Massachusetts pulled it off.

In the pages that follow, I hope to provide an intimate account of how over the course of just eighteen months a revolution transformed a city and the towns that surrounded it, and how that transformation influenced what eventually became the Unites States of America. This is the story of two charismatic and forceful leaders (one from Massachusetts, the other from Virginia), but it is also the story of two ministers (one a subtle, even Machiavellian, patriot, the other a punster and a loyalist); of a poet, patriot, and caregiver to four orphaned children; of a wealthy merchant who wanted to be everybody's friend; of a conniving traitor whose girlfriend betrayed him; of a sea captain from Marblehead who became America's first naval hero; of a bookseller with a permanently mangled hand who after a 300-mile trek through the wilderness helped to force the evacuation of the British; and of many others.

In the end, the city of Boston is the true hero of this story. Whether its inhabitants came to view the Revolution as an opportunity or as a catastrophe, they all found themselves in the midst of a survival tale when on December 16, 1773, three shiploads of tea were dumped in Boston Harbor.

Part I

LIBERTY

Liberty is all very well, but men cannot live without masters. There is always a master. And men either live in glad obedience to the master they believe in, or they live in a frictional opposition to the master they wish to undermine. In America this frictional opposition has been the vital factor. It has given the Yankee his kick.

—D. H. Lawrence, *Studies in Classic American Literature*, 1923

Resentment is a passion, implanted by nature for the preservation of the individual. Injury is the object which excites it. Injustice, wrong, injury excites the feeling of resentment, as naturally and necessarily as frost and ice excite the feeling of cold, as fire excites heat, and as both excite pain. A man may have the faculty of concealing his resentment, or suppressing it, but he must and ought to feel it. Nay he ought to indulge it, to cultivate it. It is a duty. His person, his property, his liberty, his reputation are not safe without it. He ought, for his own security and honor, and for the public good to punish those who injure him. . . . It is the same with communities. They ought to resent and to punish.

—Diary of John Adams, March 4, 1776

The tumult of the people is very properly compared to the raging of the sea. When the passions of a multitude become headstrong, they generally will have their course: a direct opposition only tends to increase them; and as to reason, one may as well expect that the foaming billows will hearken to a lecture of morality and be quiet. The skillful pilot will carefully keep the helm, and so steer the ship while the storm continues, as to prevent, if possible, her receiving injury.

—Samuel Adams, March 25, 1774

CHAPTER ONE

The City on the Hill

M ore than five thousand people waited inside the Old South Meetinghouse, the largest gathering place in Boston. On that evening in the
middle of December 1773, they were impatient to hear what Governor Thomas
Hutchinson had to say about the three ships bearing East India tea currently
tied up to Griffin's Wharf. After several unsatisfactory meetings, in which
they debated about how to respond to the governor's stubborn insistence that
the tea must be landed, many of them, particularly those who had traveled
from towns outside Boston, wanted to go home. It was then, just as frustration
and exhaustion began to push increasing numbers of people out the door,
that the most eloquent lawyer in this town of eloquent lawyers rose from his
seat in the east gallery and was given permission to speak.

Josiah Quincy Jr. was only thirty-one years old and dying of tuberculosis.
He was cross-eyed and pale and yet burned with a frightening ferocity in the
cold air of the unheated meetinghouse. He'd just returned from a tour of the
colonies that had taken him from South Carolina to Rhode Island (suggested
by his physician, Dr. Joseph Warren, who had hoped the milder temperatures
might improve his rapidly deteriorating health). Quincy knew firsthand that
a surprising consensus was emerging among the inhabitants of British North
America—a consensus that was bound to have astounding and yet frightening consequences.

He began by referring to the way their cumulative breaths rose like smoke
toward the ceiling several stories above their heads. He called it "the spirit
that vapors within these walls" and warned that it would take more than hot
air—"popular resolves, popular harangues, popular acclamations, and popular vapor"—to "vanquish our foes." Given Great Britain's military strength,
it behooved them all to think carefully about what they were about to do: "Let
us weigh and consider before we advance to those measures which must
bring on the most trying and terrific struggle this country ever saw."

If anything, Quincy was calling for caution, but the mere mention of a possible war with the mother country was enough to prompt the staunch loyalist Harrison Gray to warn "the young man in the gallery" that he risked being prosecuted for treason for his "intemperate language." Quincy, who along with John Adams had successfully defended the British soldiers on trial after the Boston Massacre three years before, responded, "If the old gentleman on the floor intends, by his warning to 'the young man in the gallery' to utter only a friendly voice in the spirit of paternal advice, I thank him. If his object be to terrify and intimidate, I despise him. Personally, perhaps, I have less concern than any one present in the crisis which is approaching. The seeds of dissolution are thickly planted in my constitution. They must soon ripen. I feel how short is the day that is allotted to me."

At that moment, some men disguised as Indians could be seen through the meetinghouse windows heading down Milk Street toward the wharves. The bitter rain that had been falling most of the day had stopped, and a bright moon shone in the darkening sky. The words that followed were so eerily prescient that they were still being repeated almost eighty years later by a Bostonian who'd been there that day in the east gallery. "I see the clouds which now rise thick and fast upon our horizon," Quincy said, "the thunders roll, and the lightnings play, and to that God who rides on the whirlwind and directs the storm I commit my country."

The last decade had been a time of growing discord and anxiety. Many looked to the passage of the Stamp Act in the summer of 1765 as the start of all their troubles, but it went back much further than that. From the very first, with the arrival of the original Puritan settlers in 1630, the inhabitants of Boston had seen themselves as an exceptional and essentially independent people. Their projected "city on a hill" was to be a shining example of what could be accomplished when men and women lived according to the true dictates of God beyond the reach of the Stuart kings and their bishops.

There had been complications along the way: internal religious controversies, conflicts with other settlements, a revolution back home in England, and in 1675, the outbreak of a ruinous war with the Indians; but through it all the colonists of Massachusetts had clung to the conviction that they constituted an autonomous enclave. In 1676, in the midst of King Philip's War, the British agent Edward Randolph traveled to Boston and spoke with Massachusetts governor John Leverett. Even though his colony had been decimated by the ongoing struggle with the Indians, Leverett, whose blood-soaked leather battle jacket still exists, insisted that Massachusetts was, in essence, independent. "He freely declared to me," Randolph wrote to King Charles II, "that the laws made by your Majesty and your Parliament obligeth them in nothing . . . , that your Majesty ought not to retrench their liberties, but may enlarge them if your Majesty please." A hundred years before the Declaration of Independence, the governor of Massachusetts boldly insisted that the laws enacted by the colony's legislature superseded those of even Parliament.

Leverett may have talked as if his colony were free to do whatever it wanted, but the truth proved quite different. It soon became apparent that the two-year war with the Indians had devastated Massachusetts. A third of its towns had been burned to the ground; only after decades would the colony's median income level approach the prewar level. Having virtually annihilated their closest Indian allies, the New Englanders now lacked a buffer to protect them from the French and *their* Indian allies to the north. Over the course of the next century, an unrelenting series of brutal wars forced Great Britain to take an active part in the defense of the colony. Within a decade of King Philip's War, the colony's original charter had been revoked, and Massachusetts became a royal province ruled by a governor holding office at the pleasure of the king. In the confusion surrounding Britain's Glorious Revolution of 1688, Bostonians took the opportunity a year later to jail Governor Edmund Andros and his hated customs surveyor Edward Randolph, the same official who thirteen years earlier had complained about Governor Leverett's audacity. With the eventual arrival of a new charter and a new governor in 1692, an uneasy sense of order was reestablished in Massachusetts, even if the colonists never became reconciled to a governor whose first loyalty lay with Great Britain instead of them.

And always, it seemed, there was another war—a bloody business at which the New Englanders excelled. In 1690, the colony participated in the first of the assaults that would eventually turn the peninsular portion of French Acadia into British Nova Scotia. In 1745, Massachusetts mounted the New World equivalent of a crusade into Canada when an army of 4,200 provincial soldiers sailed from Boston in a fleet of ninety ships against the French fortress at Louisbourg. Despite receiving just token assistance from the British military, the colonial soldiers triumphed, only to see the fortress returned in subsequent treaty negotiations between Great Britain and France. After the eventual conquest of Canada in 1763, during which the provincials helped retake the fortress they had first won more than a decade before, the New Englanders turned their attention from the enemy to the north to anyone who might meddle in their affairs.

For most of the early eighteenth century the American colonies had enjoyed the benefits of a policy later known as "salutary neglect." Left to do pretty much as they pleased, the colonies had been free to pursue economic growth unhindered by the onerous taxes paid by most British subjects. But by the end of the French and Indian War in 1763—a war fought, in large part, on the colonies' behalf that had saddled Great Britain with a debt of about $22.4 billion in today's U.S. currency—the ministry determined that it was time the colonies began to help pay for their imperial support.

Even the colonists admitted that they must contribute in some way to maintaining the British Empire. The question was how to go about raising the money. Well before the slogan "No taxation without representation" became a battle cry in America, the New Englanders' Puritan ancestors had used the same logic to object to the early Stuarts' attempts to increase taxes. But the colonies had more than just a principle behind their reluctance to be dictated to by the British ministry. They had three thousand miles of ocean between them and the mother country, along with seemingly limitless prospects for growth on a continent that stretched another three thousand miles to the Pacific Ocean. Rather than propose a means of raising revenue that they deemed fair, the colonials were more than happy to direct their considerable energies toward opposing whatever plan the British ministry put forward. When the old Puritan sense of certainty was combined with New England's proven ability to put up a fight, it was not surprising that Massachusetts confronted the taxation question with a pugnacity reminiscent of the backwoods battles of the previous century.

In 1765 Parliament passed the Stamp Act, a bill that required colonists to purchase special paper embossed with a revenue stamp for legal documents, newspapers, journals, and other printed materials. Whereas the British government saw the act simply as a way for the colonists to begin paying for their keep, the colonists viewed the Stamp Act as a violation of their basic liberties. What surprised almost everyone was the violence the act inspired, particularly in Boston, where a mob ransacked the house of then lieutenant governor Thomas Hutchinson. Parliament quickly repealed the hated act in 1766, but not without insisting on its future right to tax the colonies. A year later, with the passage of the Townshend Acts, Parliament tried taxing only paper, paint, lead, glass, and tea imported from England. The revenues from these taxes were to be used to pay the salaries of colonial governors and judges, which the colonial legislatures had formerly paid with funds raised through locally administered taxes. Although in this instance the act relieved the province of a financial burden, it increased the likelihood that the officials would act in the best interests of the crown instead of the colonies. Boston merchants responded by refusing to import British goods, and by the spring of 1768 the Massachusetts legislature had sent out a circular letter encouraging the other colonies to support a nonimportation agreement.

Even more significant to relations with Britain was the creation of the American Customs Board to facilitate the collection of customs duties, monies that not only went toward paying the colonies' collective tab back in Great Britain but also helped pay the salaries of the customs officers. The board's five commissioners were headquartered in Boston and came to embody the loathsome "innovations" being insisted upon by the British ministry. Armed with what were known as "writs of assistance," the officers did not have to obtain a warrant before searching ships, shops, and homes for smuggled goods. As early as 1761 the lawyer James Otis had argued that because these writs violated English constitutional rights, they were illegal. Otis lost the case in court, but New Englanders continued to insist upon their rights. In 1768 a riot erupted when officials seized John Hancock's merchant vessel *Liberty*—an outbreak of violence that contributed to the decision by the British government to send several regiments of troops, known as the regular army, to Boston.

With the arrival of the regulars, the focus shifted from the issue of taxation to the evils of a military occupation. Patriot leaders began keeping a journalistic diary of the many abuses the townspeople supposedly suffered at the hands of the soldiers. On the night of March 5, 1770, escalating tensions climaxed in what came to be known as the Boston Massacre. An angry crowd of sailors, artisans, apprentices, and boys surrounded a small group of regulars, who in the confusion of the moment fired their muskets. When the fusillade ceased, five people lay dead or mortally wounded. Outrage swept through the city's unlit network of convoluted streets as hundreds and then thousands of Bostonians surged into the center of town. With the people threatening to attack the soldiers, Lieutenant Governor Thomas Hutchinson appeared on the balcony of the Town House and promised that "the law should have its course." The crowd reluctantly dispersed. After several rancorous town meetings, the regulars were withdrawn from Boston.

The trial of the British soldiers was delayed until the fall, but several months before that, in late June 1770, a comet appeared in the night sky. John Greenwood, then ten years old, remembered that more than just a comet had blazed over Boston. "Armies of soldiery had been seen fighting in the clouds overhead," he wrote; "and it was said that the day of judgment was at hand, when the moon would turn into blood and the world be set on fire." The regiments of soldiers were gone, but the sense of foreboding was stronger than ever. "For my part," he remembered, "all I wished was that a church which stood by the side of my father's garden would fall on me at the time these terrible things happened, and crush me to death at once, so as to be out of pain quick."

Due in large part to the brilliance of Josiah Quincy and John Adams, the accused soldiers were either found not guilty or were convicted of manslaughter, which entailed the comparatively minor punishment of branding on the base of the thumb. With a partial repeal of the Townshend Acts, a period of calm settled across New England. And then, in the summer of 1773, more than three years after the Massacre, Bostonians learned of the passage of the Tea Act.

The British ministry had a problem. The crown-chartered East India Company was burdened with too much tea. To eliminate that surplus, it was decided to offer the tea to the American colonies at the drastically reduced price of two shillings per pound—a third less than the original price. Unfortunately and unwisely, Parliament included in the reduced price a tiny tax of three pence per pound. This gave the patriots ideological grounds on which to object to an act that might otherwise have been viewed as a windfall for the colonial consumer. The ministry made the additional tactical error of allowing only a handful of privileged "consignees" (all of them loyalists) to act as agents for the East India Company. The patriots were able to claim that the legislation was a thinly veiled attempt to impose a London-centered commercial monopoly on the colonies, and Bostonians followed New York and Pennsylvania in strongly opposing the Tea Act.

Other, less noble reasons motivated the patriots. Many Boston merchants sold illegal Dutch tea procured from the Caribbean island of St. Eustatius (known today simply as Statia). Since the low-priced East India tea would undersell the smuggled Dutch tea, the merchants stood to lose significant income. Then there was the grudge that a leading Boston merchant had with the island of Nantucket.

New England, unlike the southern colonies and the British islands of the Caribbean, did not have a staple crop such as tobacco or sugar. It did have, however, whale oil, which accounted for more than half the region's exports to Great Britain, at least in terms of their value. Since much, if not most, of the whale oil was shipped directly to England from the tiny, largely loyalist island of Nantucket, Boston merchants had been relegated to the margins of this lucrative trade. This had not prevented John Hancock from spending the last decade—and a significant portion of the fortune he had inherited from his uncle—trying to corner the whale oil market by buying up available supplies and controlling their delivery to London. Nantucket's wily Quaker merchants, however, had managed to frustrate his every move.

Two of the three ships tied up to Griffin's Wharf in Boston on December 16, 1773, were Nantucket vessels that had taken on East India tea after unloading their shipments of whale oil in London. Hancock, who had emerged as the preeminent public figure associated with the patriot cause, now had at long last a way to make at least one of the islanders defer to his wishes. It was all in the name of patriot ideals, of course, but for Hancock it must have been a form of sweet revenge to watch as one of his hated rivals, the Nantucket merchant prince Francis Rotch (pronounced "Roach"), stood trembling before the gathering at the Old South Meetinghouse.

The chronology of what occurred after Rotch returned from making his desperate appeal to Governor Hutchinson is hazy, but we do know that once he explained to the crowd in the meetinghouse that the governor had refused to allow his ship the *Dartmouth* to leave Boston Harbor without unloading the tea, shouts erupted that could be heard several blocks away. At some point, people began to pour out into the streets, and soon enough, more than a hundred Bostonians disguised as Indians were dumping chests of tea into the harbor.

Unfortunately, the tide was out. The tea leaves heaped in the shallows surrounding the ships, requiring that boys scamper across the mudflats and try to scatter the clumps with their hands and feet. By the next morning the swirling tide and wind had created an undulant cat's cradle of tea: crisscrossing lines of brown-flecked spindrift that reached from the docks and shipyards of Boston's South End toward Castle Island, three miles to the east. It was to here, at what was known simply as the Castle, where a fort and a regiment of British soldiers provided them with protection, that the half-dozen or so tea consignees had fled to escape the angry crowds back in Boston.

If the patriots had their way, that was where they would stay. But as Admiral John Montagu reminded several townspeople soon after what came to be called the Boston Tea Party, someday the piper had to be paid.

Almost a month later, on the morning of January 15, 1774, as a city waited with mounting dread for word of how the British government was going to respond to the outrage committed at Griffin's Wharf, a mysterious costumed defender of the people's liberties announced his presence amid the cold, windblown streets of Boston. In tribute to the Puritans' revolutionary past, he called himself Joyce Junior after Cornet George Joyce, an officer in the parliamentary New Model Army of the English Civil War. Joyce had been credited with capturing King Charles; he had also been present when the British sovereign was beheaded. By adopting the name of a notorious regicide, Joyce Junior was evoking the memory of a time when English subjects had dared to do the unthinkable: overthrow and execute their king.

In a handbill that appeared in "the most public spaces" of Boston that Saturday, Joyce Junior vowed to punish any of the tea consignees who tried to leave Castle Island, exhorting his "Brethren and Fellow Citizens" to help him give the consignees "such a reception as such vile ingrates deserve." What that reception might entail was suggested by the title Joyce Junior ascribed to himself at the bottom of the handbill: "Chairman of the Committee for Tarring and Feathering."

The appearance of this particular character was a recent phenomenon, but the persona—that of a shadowy enforcer—was nothing new to Boston. Some version of the upstart regicide had been part of the annual celebration known as Pope Night. Every November 5, two rival gangs of boys and apprentices from the city's North and South Ends (divided by the creek that flowed from Mill Pond to the harbor) marched behind carts that displayed the figures of the pope and the devil. The ultimate object of Pope Night was to seize the opponent's cart, and the inevitable battle resulted in untold broken bones and in 1764 even a boy's death. Based on the British tradition of Guy Fawkes Day, which celebrated the foiling of a 1605 plot to blow up Parliament and the king, Pope Night emphasized not the miraculous salvation of royal government but Congregational New England's long-standing hatred of the Catholic Church. Presiding over the bare-knuckled tumult of Pope Night appears to have been a Joyce Junior–like figure wearing a white wig, red cloak, large boots, a sword, and what was described as a "horrible" mask.

Yet another version of Joyce Junior was spotted during the uproar that preceded the Boston Massacre in 1770. A "tall man in a red cloak and white wig" was seen haranguing the crowd at Dock Square before the townspeople headed toward the center of town for the final encounter with the British soldiers. This may have been the same shadowy figure that at least one witness claimed was standing behind the beleaguered regulars, exhorting them to fire.

Although Joyce Junior wore a mask, many in Boston undoubtedly knew the identity of the man who claimed to be the chairman of the committee of tarring and feathering. He threatened and boasted like a seasoned sailor from the rough-and-tumble world of the Boston waterfront, but Joyce Junior was in actuality the twenty-six-year-old son of Harvard professor John Winthrop, whose great-great-grandfather of the same name had been a founder of the Massachusetts Bay Colony. Professor Winthrop's son (also named John, and thus a junior on two accounts) had been publicly admonished while an undergraduate at Harvard "for making indecent tumultuous noises in the college." By 1773 he was a merchant with a general store on Treat's Wharf. Just before the Tea Party, he was part of a group charged with preventing the East India tea from being landed from the ships. Now he was doing everything in his power to make sure the streets were free of tea consignees and other "traitors to their country."

The appearance of Joyce Junior in January 1774 appears to have been part of an effort by patriot leaders to control the aftermath of the Tea Party. Unwieldy mob eruptions such as the one that provoked the Boston Massacre inevitably made for bad publicity in both America and England. In an effort to depict the destruction of East India tea as an act of principle rather than of rage, the Tea Party had been minutely choreographed from the start. Joyce Junior was continuing this attempt to channel if not contain the violence.

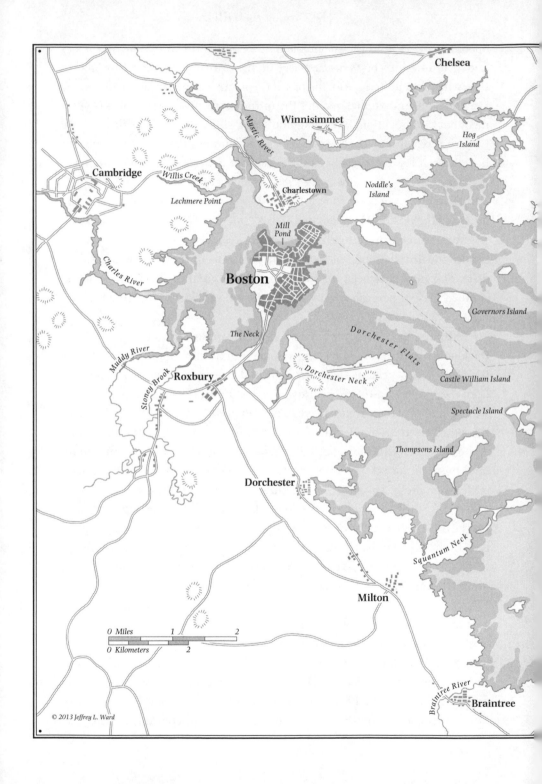

Chelsea

Winnisimmet

Hog
Island

Mystic River

Charlestown

Noddle's
Island

Cambridge

Willis Creek

Lechmere Point

Mill
Pond

Boston

Charles River

Governors Island

The Neck

Dorchester Flats

Muddy River

Stoney Brook

Roxbury

Dorchester Neck

Castle William Island

Spectacle Island

Thompsons Island

Dorchester

Squantum Neck

Milton

0 Miles   1   2

0 Kilometers   2

Braintree River

Braintree

© 2013 Jeffrey L. Ward

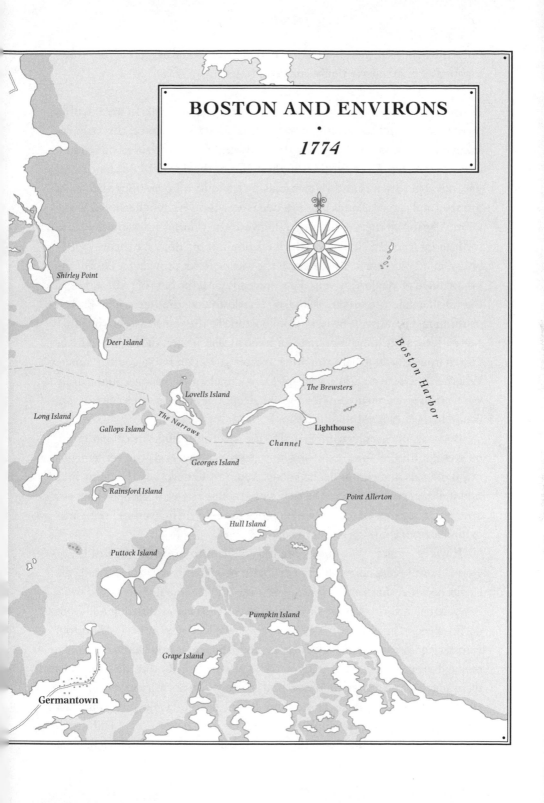

BOSTON AND ENVIRONS
·
1774

Shirley Point

Deer Island

Boston Harbor

Lovells Island

The Brewsters

Long Island

The Narrows

Gallops Island

Lighthouse

Channel

Georges Island

Rainsford Island

Point Allerton

Hull Island

Puttock Island

Pumpkin Island

Grape Island

Germantown

But as all of Boston was about to learn, there were some aspects of this growing insistence on liberty that no one controlled.

Boston had always been a town on tiptoe. Just a square mile in area, with a
mere sliver of land connecting it to the mainland to the south, this tadpole-
shaped island was dominated by three towering, lightly settled hills and a
forest of steeples. From Boston's highest perch, the 138-foot Beacon Hill, it
was possible to see that the town was just one in a huge amphitheater of
humped and jagged islands that extended more than eight and a half miles to
Point Allerton to the southeast. To the west, the Charles River reached into
the interior from the shallows of the Back Bay, linking Boston to nearby Cambridge and Watertown. To the north the Mystic River provided access to the
inland town of Medford even as the waterway, with the help of Willis Creek to
the west, made almost an island of Charlestown, another whale-backed
drumlin just a half mile by ferry from Boston. To the southeast, on the other
side of the equally hilly outcropping known as Dorchester, the Neponset River
flowed from Milton, where Hutchinson, now governor, had a country home.
Whether it was from a hill, a steeple, or a cupola, Bostonians could plainly
see that they were surrounded by two deep and endless wildernesses: the
ocean to the east and the country to the west.

Boston's topography contributed to the seemingly nonsensical pattern of
its streets. Rather than following any preconceived grid, the settlement's
original trails and cart paths had done their best to negotiate the many hills
and hollows, cutting across the slopes at gradual angles to create a concave
crescent of settlement within which more than fifty wharves and shipyards
extended from the town's eastern edge.

It was in winter that this city of hills came into its own—at least if you
were a boy. Streets normally crowded with people, horses, oxcarts, and carriages became, thanks to a coating of snow and ice, magical coasting trails
down which a youngster on his wooden sled could race at startling and wonderful speeds. On January 25, 1774, at least two feet of snow covered Boston.
Runner-equipped sleighs glided across roads that carts and chaises had once
plodded over, moving so silently across the white drifts that tinkling bells
were added to the horses' halters so that the people of Boston could hear them
coming. The boys in their sleds did not have this luxury, however, and that
afternoon a child approaching the end of his run down Copp's Hill in the
North End slammed into the fifty-year-old customs officer John Malcom—at

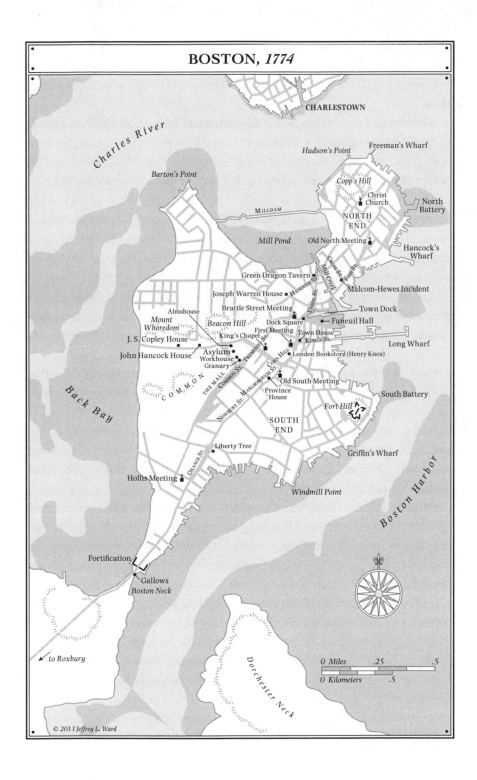

BOSTON, *1774*

CHARLESTOWN

Charles River

Barton's Point

Hudson's Point

Freeman's Wharf

Copp's Hill

Christ
Church

North
Battery

MILLDAM

NORTH
END

Mill Pond

Old North Meeting

Hancock's
Wharf

Cross St.

Mill Creek

First St.

Green Dragon Tavern

Malcom-Hewes Incident

Joseph Warren House

HANOVER ST.

UNION ST.

Town Dock

Brattle Street Meeting

Almshouse

Dock Square

Faneuil Hall

*Mount
Whoredom*

Beacon Hill

First Meeting

Town House

J. S. Copley House

King's Chapel

KING'S ST.

Long Wharf

John Hancock House

Asylum
Workhouse
Granary

London Bookstore (Henry Knox)

CORN HILL

TREMONT ST.

COMMON ST.

C O M M O N

THE MALL

MARLBOROUGH ST.

Old South Meeting

Province
House

South Battery

NEWBURY ST.

Fort Hill

SOUTH
END

Liberty Tree

ORANGE ST.

Griffin's Wharf

Hollis Meeting

Back Bay

Windmill Point

Boston Harbor

Fortification

Gallows
Boston Neck

← to Roxbury

Dorchester Neck

0 Miles	.25	.5
0 Kilometers	.5	

© 2013 Jeffrey L. Ward

least, according to one account. Another version has Malcom falling into an argument with the boy when the child complained that Malcom had ruined the coasting run that passed by his front door by throwing woodchips on the snow.

Malcom, as his vocation might suggest, was a loyalist; he also had a reputation for losing his temper. Raising his cane in the air as if to strike the boy, he shouted, "Do you talk to me in that style, you rascal!" It was then that George Hewes, a shoemaker, came upon them standing at the mouth of Cross Street.

Hewes had recently participated in the Tea Party and was known to be a patriot. But at this point, political beliefs were of little concern to him; worried that Malcom might injure the defenseless boy, he told the customs agent to leave the child alone.

Malcom turned to Hewes and accused him of being a "vagabond" who should not presume to speak to a gentleman such as himself. Besides commanding a host of coasting vessels, Malcom had served as an officer in several campaigns during the French and Indian War; he'd also fought more recently in what was known as the War of Regulation in North Carolina, where he'd assisted royal governor William Tryon in brutally suppressing an uprising of citizens who objected to the taxation system then prevalent in this section of the South. Malcom claimed to have had two horses shot out from underneath him in North Carolina and later wrote in a petition to the king that "none could go further in the field of battle when the bullets flew thickest, he was then in his element."

Malcom's love of combat had recently gotten him into some serious professional trouble. Earlier that fall, while serving in the customs office in Falmouth (now Portland, Maine), he'd seized a ship and her thirty-man crew under the slimmest of pretexts. His pompous and overbearing manner had so angered the sailors that they'd relieved him of his sword and provided him with a "genteel" coat of tar and feathers—genteel in that they'd left his clothes on to protect his skin from the hot tar. Malcom had been humiliated but apparently not hurt, and even his superior officer at the customs office had had little sympathy for him. By that snowy day in January, Malcom was back home in Boston arguing with not only a surly boy with a sled but this prying shoemaker as well.

Hewes was unimpressed by Malcom's claims of social superiority, especially given what had happened to the customs agent in Maine, a story that had been repeated with great relish in Boston's many newspapers. "Be that as it will," Hewes replied to Malcom's rebuke, "I never was tarred and feathered anyhow."

This was too much for Malcom, who took up his cane and smashed Hewes in the head, ripping a two-inch gash in his hat and knocking him unconscious. When Hewes came to his senses, a Captain Godfrey was admonishing Malcom, who soon decided to beat a hasty retreat to his home on Cross Street.

All that afternoon word of the incident circulated through the streets of Boston. By eight o'clock in the evening, an angry crowd had assembled outside Malcom's house. By that time Hewes had visited Dr. Joseph Warren, just across the Mill Bridge on nearby Hanover Street. Both a physician and a distant relative, Warren had told him that if it weren't for his extraordinarily thick skull, Hewes would be a dead man. On Warren's advice, Hewes applied to a town official for a warrant for Malcom's arrest, but it now seemed that a different kind of justice was about to be served.

Earlier in the evening, Malcom had taken a manic delight in baiting the crowd, bragging that Governor Hutchinson would pay him a bounty of twenty pounds sterling for every "yankee" that he killed. His undoubtedly long-suffering wife, the mother of five children (two of whom were deaf), opened a window and pleaded with the townspeople to leave them alone. Whatever sympathy she had managed to gain soon vanished when Malcom pushed his unsheathed sword through the window and stabbed a man in the breastbone.

The crowd swarmed around the house, breaking windows and trying to get at the customs official, who soon fled up the stairs to the second story. Many Bostonians served as volunteer firemen, and men equipped with ladders and axes were soon rushing toward the besieged house on Cross Street. Even Malcom appears to have realized that matters had taken a serious turn, and he prepared "to make what defense he could."

Nine years before, this section of the city had been the scene of one of the most notorious acts of violence ever directed against an official in colonial America. On August 26, 1765, as outrage over the Stamp Act swept across the colonies, a mob of several hundred Bostonians attacked the home of Lieutenant Governor Thomas Hutchinson, breaking windows, beating down doors, and destroying the house's elaborate furnishings. Hutchinson was also a historian, and countless manuscript pages were found scattered in the street—a fact that moved the lawyer Daniel Leonard to suggest that the crowd had acted not out of anger over the Stamp Act but to prevent the publication of yet another ponderously written volume of Hutchinson's history of Massachusetts.

Collective violence had been a long-standing part of colonial New England, a trait the English settlers had brought from the mother country. Crowds tended to intervene when government officials acted against the interests of the people. In 1747 a riot had broken out in Boston when a naval press gang seized several local sailors. Twenty-three years later, anger over the depredations of yet another press gang contributed to the *Liberty* Riot of 1768, triggered by the seizure of John Hancock's ship of the same name by Boston customs officials. In that the crowds were attempting to address unpunished wrongs committed against the community, they were a recognized institution that all Bostonians—no matter how wealthy and influential they might be—ignored at their peril. But as John Malcom was about to find out on that frigid night in January 1774, and as Thomas Hutchison had learned almost a decade before him, the divide between a civic-minded crowd and an unruly and vindictive mob was frighteningly thin.

Malcom and his family huddled in their home's second floor. A locked door stood between them and the angry crowd down below. They heard the thud of the ladders against the sides of the house and the cries of the men and boys as they climbed up to the second-story windows and punched through the glass. It was then that "a Mr. Russell," perhaps William Russell, an usher (or teaching assistant) at a school on Hanover Street, appeared inside the house. Smiling broadly, he assured Malcom that he came in friendship and shook the customs officer's hand. He then asked if he could see Malcom's sword. Desperate for whatever assistance he could find, Malcom reluctantly handed over the weapon, only to watch as Russell (who, if he indeed was William Russell, had participated in the Tea Party) called out to the others in the house that Malcom was now unarmed. "They immediately rushed in," Malcom wrote, "and by violence forced your memorialist out of the house and beating him with sticks then placed him on a sled they had prepared." One can only wonder what Mrs. Malcom and her sons and daughters were thinking as they watched him disappear into the unlit streets.

After a stop at a nearby wharf to pick up a barrel of tar (at some point, down-filled pillows, perhaps taken from Malcom's own house, were also collected), the crowd, which now numbered more than a thousand people, hauled Malcom through the snowy streets to the center of town, where after three "Huzzas," they loaded him into a cart parked in front of the Customs House. Almost four years before, this had been the site of the Boston Massacre, and as a consequence the building was now referred to as Butchers' Hall. Bonfires were common in this portion of King Street, a sixty-foot-wide plaza-like space in front of Town House paved with seashells and gravel where the stocks and whipping post were also located. One of these fires may have been used to heat the stiff and sludgy pine tar (a distillation of the bituminous substance that bubbled from a smoldering pine tree) into a pourable black paste.

It was one of the bitterest evenings of the year. Boston Harbor had frozen over two nights before. Malcom was undoubtedly trembling with cold and fear, but this did not prevent the crowd from tearing off his clothes (dislocating his arm in the process) and daubing his skin with steaming tar that would have effectively parboiled his flesh. Once the feathers had been added, Malcom was clothed in what was known at the time as a "modern jacket": a painful and mortifying announcement to the world that he had sinned against the collective mores of the community. Tarring and feathering went back centuries to the time of the crusades, and was also applied to the effigies used during Pope Night; a few Boston loyalists before him had been tarred and feathered, but none could claim the level of suffering that Malcom was about to endure.

Soon the crowd began pushing Malcom's cart up King Street toward the Town House, the cupola-topped brick building emblazoned with the king's seal that was the home of the colony's legislature. Once past the Town House, they turned left onto Boston's main thoroughfare, known in this portion of the city as Cornhill. With the three-story brick edifice of Boston's first Congregational meeting, referred to as the Old Meeting, on their right, they made their way through a gauntlet of tightly packed buildings of varying heights. Lights flared in the windows as they passed, the crowd's shouts and whistles washing across the brick and clapboard facings and echoing up into the hills to the right, where the almshouse, the asylum for the "disorderly and insane," the workhouse, and the granary overlooked the rolling forty-five-acre sweep of the common.

Cornhill had become Marlborough Street by the time they reached the block containing the governor's official residence, Province House. On the cupola of this stately three-story brick structure was a copper weathervane depicting an Indian with an arrow in his bow. When the wind was from the east, the Province House Indian seemed to be aiming at the even higher weathercock on the spire of the Old South Meetinghouse, just across the street. The crowd stopped between these two soaring buildings and ordered Malcom to curse Governor Hutchinson (who was safely ensconced at his country house ten miles away in Milton that night) and "say he was an enemy to his country." Malcom steadfastly refused.

On they proceeded through the freezing darkness, the cart's wheels crunching through the snow. They were now in the heart of the South End, the more affluent side of town, where Marlborough turned into Newbury Street. At the corner of Essex on their left, they stopped at the huge old elm known as the Liberty Tree. A staff rose above the topmost portion of the tree, on which a flag was often flown. This was where the first protests against the Stamp Act had been held back in 1765, and in the years since, the Liberty Tree had become a kind of druidical, distinctly American shrine to the inherent freedoms of man and that Enlightenment sense of "the state of nature" that exists before a people willingly submit to the dictates of a government of their own choosing. On this cold night, the people of Boston were directing their anger against a man who resolutely, even fanatically, insisted that they must defer to a distant king and a legislature that no longer respected their God-given rights, that obedience must be paid not only to their royal sovereign but to a man like John Malcom: a bitter and grasping underling whose world was crumbling beneath him. Malcom stood in the cart below the tree's bare winter branches and once again refused to curse the governor.

They continued down Newbury to where it became Orange Street. Soon they were approaching the town gate at Boston Neck, more than a mile from the Town House. The old brick fortification dated back to King Philip's War, when Boston had become a refuge for those attempting to escape the Indians, and once through the gate, they were out onto the thin strand of wave-washed earth that connected Boston to the town of Roxbury. On either side of them, the icy marshes and shallows extended out into darkness. On the left, just past the gate, was the gallows.

They placed a rope around Malcom's neck and threatened to hang him if he would not do as they'd previously ordered. By this time the tar had congealed into a frozen crust; his body's inner core had probably become so chilled that he no longer had the ability to tremble. Once again, he refused to curse the governor, but this time he asked that they would "put their threats into execution rather than continue their torture."

They took the rope off Malcom's neck, pinioned his hands behind his back, and tied him to the gallows. Then they began to beat him with ropes and sticks "in a most savage manner." According to one account they even threatened to cut off his ears. At last, he said he would do "anything they desired." They untied him and made him curse the governor and the customs board of commissioners. But his sufferings were not over.

For several more hours they continued to parade Malcom through the streets of Boston. Not everyone shared in the crowd's pitiless delight; a few people, including the man whose intervention had started this horrifying concatenation of events, the shoemaker George Hewes, were so appalled by Malcom's treatment that they attempted to cover him with their jackets.

By the time the crowd reached Copp's Hill near Malcom's home in the North End, he must have passed out, for he makes no mention of this final stop, which is described in several newspaper accounts. Here, in the cemetery near the summit of the hill, was the grave of Malcom's younger brother Daniel. Daniel appears to have had the same fiery personality as his brother. Whereas John became a customs agent, Daniel sided with the opposite, more popular camp, famously barricading himself in *his* house in 1766 to prevent the crown's agents from finding the smuggled wine he had supposedly hidden in his cellar. When Daniel died in 1769 at the age of forty-four, he was a patriot hero, and the inscription on his gravestone described him as "a true son of Liberty / a Friend to the Publick / an Enemy to oppression / and one of the foremost / in opposing the Revenue Acts / on America."

Daniel had been celebrated for breaking the laws of his day. That night in January 1774, his loyalist brother John sat slumped in a chair that someone had placed inside the cart. It was true that he was obnoxious and impulsive, that he'd virtually invited the treatment he'd received. But the fact remained that this "enemy of the people" had been scalded, frozen, and beaten to within an inch of his life not because he'd taken a swipe at a shoemaker but because he upheld the unpopular laws that his brother had scorned. It had been a brutal, even obscene display of violence, but the people of Boston had spoken.

Around midnight, the crowd finally made its way back to Malcom's house on Cross Street, where he was "rolled out of the cart like a log." Once he'd been brought back into the house and his frozen body had begun to thaw, his tarred flesh started to peel off in "steaks." Although he somehow found the strength to make a deposition five days later, it would be another eight weeks before he could leave his bed.

The John Malcom incident had created a problem for Joyce Junior. Despite having declared himself to be the chairman of the committee of tarring and feathering, he had had nothing to do with what had happened to Malcom. In fact, he and other patriot leaders disapproved of this spontaneous and entirely unscripted outbreak of violence. In an attempt to clarify this potentially embarrassing situation, he issued yet another proclamation, this one disavowing any association with the incident. "Brethren and fellow citizens!" the handbill read. "This is to certify, that the modern punishment lately inflicted on the ignoble John Malcom was not done by our order—We reserve that method for bringing villains of greater consequence to a sense of guilt and infamy."

Over the course of the next few months, Joyce Junior posted more announcements (one of which appeared in the *Boston Gazette* over John Winthrop Junior's advertisement for a new shipment of flour) in which Winthrop's alter ego continued to issue threats against the tea consignees and their associates. One night in April, the painter John Singleton Copley awoke to discover that his house on Beacon Hill (just down the street from the Hancock mansion) was surrounded by a raucous mob that wanted to know if a Mr. Watson from Plymouth was staying with him. At thirty-five, Copley had long since established himself as the foremost painter not only in New England but all America. A largely self-taught genius and purposefully apolitical, Copley had painted the portraits of many loyalists and of many patriots. He had an unmatched ability when it came to creating a sense of his subject's presence. When you looked at a Copley portrait, you felt as if the subject was *there* for all time, frozen in an eternal now. If there was anyone of whom all of Boston should have been proud, it was Copley. But as far as the patriots were concerned he could not be trusted since he was married to the daughter of a tea consignee.

George Watson, a merchant from Plymouth, was part of the extended loyalist family into which Copley had married. Copley explained to those gathered outside his house that it was true that Watson had visited him earlier in the day, but he had long since departed. In a letter to his brother-in-law, Isaac Winslow Clarke, still marooned on Castle Island, he recounted how the mob threatened that "my blood would be on my own head if I had deceived them; [that] if I entertained him or any such villain for the future [I] must expect the resentment of Joyce."

Copley had long since decided that he owed it to his talent to cross the Atlantic and see for himself the masters of Europe, and by the middle of June, he would be on his way to London, never to return. The irony was that Copley privately expressed his sympathies for the patriot cause. In years to come, his paintings of the 1760s and 1770s became the visual icons with which future generations of Americans celebrated Boston's revolutionary past. But in April 1774 Copley, a self-made artist who stared into the eyes of his subjects and somehow found a way to convey their imperishable essence, was being threatened by the thuggish minions of an overeducated trader who was the great-great-great-grandson of the colony's Puritan founder.

Copley wasn't the only artist in Boston who had an uneasy relationship with the city's patriots. Boston's most widely known poet was a twenty-one-year-old African enslaved woman named Phillis Wheatley, whose first volume of poems had been published in England just the year before and was now being sold in the city's many bookshops. Not only a precocious literary talent, Wheatley had used her growing fame during a recent trip to London to gain access to some of the foremost cultural and political figures of the day, including the secretary of state for the colonies, Lord Dartmouth (for whom the college in New Hampshire had been named), and Benjamin Franklin. She'd also used that fame to leverage a promise from her master, Daniel Wheatley, to grant her freedom.

For the citizens of Boston, whose love of liberty did not prevent one in five families from owning slaves, Wheatley's celebrity caused difficulties. In a letter that was reprinted in the Boston press that March, she wrote to the Mohegan preacher Samson Occom about the patriot cause's inherent duplicity. "For in every human breast," Wheatley wrote, "God has implanted a principle, which we call love of freedom; it is impatient of oppression, and pants for deliverance. . . . God grant deliverance in his own way and time, and . . . [punish] all those whose avarice impels them to countenance and help forward the calamities of their fellow creatures. This I desire not for their hurt, but to convince them of the strange absurdity of their conduct whose words and actions are so diametrically opposite. How well the cry for liberty, and the reverse disposition for the exercise of oppressive power over others agree I humbly think it does not require the penetration of a philosopher to determine."

On the road from Cambridge to the ferry landing in Charlestown was a landmark that spoke to the legacy of slavery in New England. In 1755 the slave Mark had been executed for conspiring to poison his abusive master. Whereas his female accomplice had been burned to death, Mark had been hanged; his body was then stuffed into an iron cage that was suspended from a chain at the edge of the Charlestown Common, where the corpse was left to rot and be picked apart by birds. Long after the physical remains of the executed slave had disappeared, the place where "Mark was hung in chains" continued to be a much commented-on part of the landscape surrounding Boston. Slavery was more than a rhetorical construct for the city's white residents; it was an impossible-to-ignore reality in a community where African men, women, and children were regularly bought and sold and where anyone taking the road into or out of nearby Charlestown had no choice but to remember what had happened in 1755 when a black man threatened to overthrow his oppressor.

One of Boston's great collective fears during the recent occupation by British regulars in the year and a half leading up to the Boston Massacre was that the soldiers might foment the city's slaves into a rebellion against their patriot owners. A 1768 petition signed by the merchants John Hancock and John Rowe accused a captain of His Majesty's Fifty-Ninth Regiment of having encouraged "certain Negro slaves in Boston . . . to cut their master's throats, and to beat, insult, and otherwise ill treat their said masters, asserting that now the soldiers are come, the Negroes shall be free, and the Liberty Boys slaves—to the great terror and danger of the peaceable inhabitants of said town."

For years, members of Boston's black community had been signing petitions requesting that the province's General Court find a peaceable way to address their plight. In the spring of 1774 legislators voted on yet another unsuccessful petition presented by "a great number of blacks of this province who by divine permission are held in a state of slavery within the bowels of a free and Christian country." As these petitioners knew all too well, what Phillis Wheatley called the "strange absurdity" of American slavery was not limited to the South.

The truth was that the righteous and coercive certainty of patriots such as John Winthrop Jr., aka Joyce Junior, had more in common with the increasingly autocratic and shortsighted policies promulgated by British prime minister Frederick North than either side would have cared to admit. They had drastically different agendas, but they went about achieving those agendas in essentially the same way. Both shared an indignant refusal to compromise. Neither had much to do with a democratic or popular will.

As it turned out, Joyce Junior's ominous and blustering announcements in the local press did more than even the tarring and feathering of John Malcom to create the impression in England that a brutish vigilantism reigned in the streets of Boston. In early March, as Parliament debated what to do in response to the Boston Tea Party, Joyce Junior's January 15 broadside was reprinted in the London papers. With the words of the "chairman of the committee for tarring and feathering" having come to the public's attention, even America's friends in Parliament felt that they must account in some way for this disturbing practice. On March 28, one member of the House of Commons acknowledged that "the Americans were a strange set of people, and that it was in vain to expect any degree of reasoning from them; that instead of making their claim by argument, they always chose to decide the matter by *tarring and feathering*." With the examples of both Joyce Junior and John Malcom before them, an almost unanimous consensus emerged in Parliament: Boston must suffer the worst of all punishments for its collective and apparently ongoing sins.

But if Joyce Junior and other patriot leaders regretted the tarring and feathering of John Malcom, the object of all this furor appears to have taken a different view. Malcom was proud of his sufferings. Later that year he sailed for London with a wooden box containing the ultimate trophy: a withered hunk of his own tarred-and-feathered flesh.

On January 12, 1775, Malcom attended the levee at St. James's, where he knelt before King George III and handed His Majesty a petition. What Malcom wanted more than anything else, he informed the king, was to return to Boston and resume his duties as a customs official—but not as just any customs official. He wanted to be made "a single Knight of the Tar . . . for I like the smell of it."

CHAPTER TWO

Poor Unhappy Boston

O n Friday, May 13, 1774, a British sloop-of-war approached the lighthouse at the entrance to Boston Harbor. She was the *Lively*, twentyeight days from England, with a notable passenger: Lieutenant General Thomas Gage, commander in chief of the military in North America and soon to be the new royal governor of Massachusetts.

Gage, fifty-four, had spent much of the last decade stationed in New York City, but in his youth he had seen more than his share of death on the battlefields of Europe and the New World. At twenty-five he was at Fontenoy (in what is today Belgium), where after politely conferring across a narrow divide about when to begin the fighting, opposing British and French armies killed or wounded about fifteen thousand of one another. A year later, in 1746, he witnessed the brutal suppression of the Scottish Highland clans at Culloden. Nine years after that, he was in Pennsylvania with a young provincial officer named George Washington at the onset of the French and Indian War. Both Gage and Washington served under General Edward Braddock during the disastrous Battle of the Monongahela near modern Pittsburgh. As the British army marched through the dense American wilderness, a deadly barrage erupted from unseen French and Indian forces. Bullets riddled Gage's coat and grazed his eyebrow and stomach and wounded his horse, but somehow, like Washington, he survived. Applying some of the lessons learned in that humiliating defeat, Gage helped to establish a regiment of light infantry whose dress and tactics were better adapted to the guerilla-style fighting of the frontier. But all of this innovation went for naught when in 1758 Gage's superior officer, General James Abercromby, ordered an ill-advised assault on a fortified French position at Fort Ticonderoga that resulted in two thousand needless casualties.

Once given his own command, Gage showed a reluctance to fight. In 1759, while his good friend James Wolfe died in glorious triumph at Quebec,

Gage dithered in Albany, apparently oblivious to orders to march on a French fort at the headwaters of the St. Lawrence. Despite talk of a censure, his close friend the commander in chief General Jeffrey Amherst had him installed as military governor of Montreal.

By that time Gage had married the beautiful Margaret Kemble of New Jersey. Her grandfather had been a merchant in Turkey; her grandmother had been Greek. Add some French and English blood, and it was no wonder that she radiated a bewitching exoticism, a sad and contemplative hauteur that is still discernible in the portraits of her that have survived. Gage, her senior by fourteen years, personified the English gentleman. With a straight and elegant nose on a slender face, he was a most upright and world-weary man. His friends were devoted to him, but no one matched the loyalty of his older brother, William, the famously absentminded viscount whose influence within the British ministry had helped to elevate Gage to the highest military rung in America.

For the last ten years Gage's duties as commander in chief had kept him in New York, where he and Margaret had lived in what was described as "conjugal felicity." By the spring of 1773 their two eldest sons, Harry and John, were enrolled at Gage's alma mater, Westminster School in London; in June, Gage and Margaret, who was once again pregnant, sailed with the rest of the family for England. It was Gage's first trip home in seventeen years.

He was disturbed to discover that London had changed almost beyond recognition while he'd been in America. In a letter to General Frederick Haldimand, who was serving in his stead in New York, he compared London to Constantinople or "any city I had never seen." The bureaucracy that had evolved during the last decade and a half as Britain attempted to maintain control over its expanding empire was not only large; it was appallingly inefficient. Gage spent his days in "a perpetual hunt," trying to find officials who were just as assiduously trying to find him. No wonder the ministry had appeared so vacillating and indecisive in its dealings with the Americans. No one seemed to be in charge.

In welcome contrast to all this troubling change were his family's two ancestral estates—Highmeadow on his mother's side in Gloucestershire and Firle on his father's side in Sussex. Both were still the inviting retreats they'd been when he was a boy, and it was at Highmeadow that their sixth child, Charlotte Margaret, was born in the summer of 1773. By the end of the year,

Gage appears to have decided that it was time to make England his family's permanent home. Then, in January 1774, came word of the Boston Tea Party, and Gage was wanted in London for his expertise in colonial affairs.

On January 29 Gage attended a hearing at the Cockpit, an octagonal room in Whitehall Palace that had once served as a cockfighting arena for Henry VIII and later, renovated by the architect Inigo Jones, as a small theater. The Cockpit now served as the judicial chamber for the king's Privy Council, and with tensions between Britain and the American colonies approaching a crisis, this was where Benjamin Franklin, agent for Massachusetts, presented a petition from the province's legislature requesting the removal of Governor Thomas Hutchinson.

A year before Franklin had leaked some letters written by Hutchinson and other colonial officials to patriot leaders in Boston. That the letters were private and had been acquired through undoubtedly nefarious means did nothing to quell the outrage they incited among the people of Massachusetts. According to Samuel Adams, the letters provided incontrovertible proof that the governor had been assisting the ministry "in their designs of establishing arbitrary power."

Franklin, no keen revolutionary, had originally hoped that the letters would demonstrate that Hutchinson, not the British government, was responsible for Boston's troubles. With Hutchinson serving as the scapegoat, relations between the colonists and Britain might begin to improve. Franklin, however, had made a catastrophic miscalculation.

Representing the ministry at the hearing in the Cockpit was Solicitor General Alexander Wedderburn. Wedderburn had a reputation for eloquence and mockery, and the privy councillors had invited a large number of spectators sympathetic to the crown who, along with Thomas Gage, had packed themselves into this intimate, theatrical space for what promised to be the political equivalent of a blood sport.

For the next hour, Franklin, silent and stone-faced, endured an unceasing stream of abuse from Wedderburn as many of those surrounding the two men laughed and applauded. Franklin was, according to Wedderburn, not only a deceitful thief; he was the "first mover and prime conductor" of all the unrest in Boston and even had secret ambitions to succeed Hutchinson as governor.

Gage had known Franklin since the Braddock campaign back in 1755, when the Boston-born Philadelphian had helped to assemble the many horses and wagons necessary to transport the troops and provisions into the Pennsylvania wilderness. The general seems to have been both fascinated and troubled by the spectacle of the sixty-eight-year-old polymath in an antiquated wig being ridiculed by a bellowing lawyer and a crowd of Britain's most influential politicians. "The Doctor was so abused," Gage wrote, "his conduct and character so cut and mangled, I wonder he had confidence to stand it; and the whole audience, which was humorous, to a man against him." No matter what anyone thought of Franklin's role in the controversy, the encounter did not bode well for the future of British-American relations.

On February 4 Gage was admitted into the inner sanctum of the British Empire: the small, richly furnished room known as the King's Closet at St. James's Palace, where he found himself in the presence of George III. For the colonists in America, the king represented their most cherished link to Britain. George III, it was said, remained steadfast in his love for his American subjects. It was the king's advisers in the ministry who were the problem. Several years before, the Boston lawyer James Otis had given voice to the fantasy that would have solved everything: If only England "was sunk in the sea so that the king and his family were saved" and brought to America. With England gone, the colonies could have their beloved king all to themselves, without the bother of that conniving and corrupt ministry and Parliament.

But as quickly became clear to Gage, the king was no uninvolved figurehead. With bulging, heavily lidded eyes, the king questioned him closely about Boston and Massachusetts. The general, not normally the most assertive of men, seems to have been temporarily intoxicated by his proximity to ultimate power. "He says," George III reported to Lord North, "they will be lions, whilst we are lambs, but if we take the resolute part they will undoubtedly prove very meek." Gage maintained that only four regiments of soldiers were "sufficient to prevent any disturbance." The king urged North to meet with Gage and "hear his ideas as to the mode of compelling Boston to submit to whatever may be thought necessary."

Gage left the king with the impression that he was ready "at a day's notice" to return to America and implement whatever "coercive measures" were required. In actuality, he had deep reservations about returning to the colonies, particularly when it came to Massachusetts. "America is a mere bully," he'd written back in 1770, "from one end to the other, and the Bostonians by far the greatest bullies." He might talk tough to the king, but he was by nature a kind and forgiving man. For a military officer, he had an unusual abhorrence for confrontation and, in his mid-fifties, with a total of three children attending schools in England, ample reason not to return to America.

His wife, however, felt differently. After only half a year in England, Margaret already missed her native land. She may have wanted her new child to meet her family back in America. Given the growing sense of urgency surrounding Britain's response to the Tea Party, Gage eventually decided that between the demands of his country and his wife, he had no choice but to return to America as military commander and royal governor of Massachusetts.

Once the *Lively* had sailed past the lighthouse set amid the cluster of little islands called the Brewsters (which the Pilgrims had named 153 years before for their lay minister William Brewster), the twenty-gun sloop-of-war headed north between Lovells Island to starboard and Georges Island to port. Up ahead, past Thompson, Spectacle, and Long islands to the west, was the cliff-faced oval of Castle William, where the British flag with its red St. George and blue St. Andrew crosses flew above the stone walls of a fort. About three miles beyond that Gage could see the rounded eminence of Boston's Beacon Hill, surrounded by a bristle of spires and ship masts.

For the next four days, Gage remained at the Castle, where he learned what he could from the tea consignees, whose confinement to the fort's living quarters was now approaching six months. Also present at the Castle was Governor Thomas Hutchinson, who was soon to leave for London. Hutchinson, sixty-two, had come to represent all that the patriots claimed was wrong with the British Empire. In reality, he was far more sympathetic to the plight of provincial Massachusetts than his enemies ever allowed. Back in 1765 he had privately criticized the Stamp Act; he had also had reservations about many of the ministry's subsequent actions. But rather than constantly challenge Parliament's right to dictate policy, as the patriots insisted on doing, he felt it was in the colony's best interests to work through proper governmental channels. At his house in Milton he had created his own version of an English country estate, where he watched in increasing bewilderment as the inhabitants of the province he loved above all else came to view him as a grasping and scheming traitor.

Hutchinson and the tea consignees reported that Boston was in turmoil. Word of the Port Act, the first of several measures Gage was to enforce over the course of the next few months, had preceded the general by three days.

The town was to be sealed off from almost all commercial activity until such time as "peace and obedience to the laws shall be so far restored." By June 1, no ships requiring customs oversight were to enter Boston Harbor. By June 15, no ships were allowed to leave. With a fleet of British naval vessels patrolling a twenty-five-mile swath of coastline extending from Point Shirley to the north and Point Allerton to the south, Boston, the third largest port in North America, would be effectively cut off from the rest of the colonies and the world. Vessels were to go instead to Marblehead, twenty miles to the north, with nearby Salem becoming the new seat of provincial government as Boston was left to contemplate the enormity of its transgressions. Only after its citizens had repented of their sins and paid for the destroyed tea would the king and his ministers allow prosperity to return.

Bostonians were stunned by the severity of the act. An entire community had been punished for the actions of a hundred or so rabble-rousers. Contrary to Britain's own laws, Bostonians had been tried and condemned without having even been accused of a specific crime. By May 13 Josiah Quincy Jr., the lawyer who had warned back in December that desperate times were ahead, had already written a passionate response to the Boston Port Act that ended by quoting the Athenian statesman Solon. It was far better, Solon had said, "to repress the advances of tyranny and prevent its establishment." But once tyranny had managed to assert itself, there was only one alternative: "Demolish it."

The loyalists surrounding Gage insisted that this heated rhetoric indicated that the Port Act was doing exactly as Parliament had intended. "I hear from many," he reported to Secretary of State Lord Dartmouth, "that the act has staggered the most presumptuous." What the patriots needed, Gage felt, was a chance for the consequences of the act to set in. "Minds so enflamed cannot cool at once," he wrote Dartmouth, "so it may be better to give the shock they have received time to operate." But as it turned out, time was not on Gage's side.

On the very day that Gage arrived at the Castle, a town meeting was convened at its usual place on the second story of Boston's Faneuil Hall on Dock Square, just a block to the north of King Street. Hanging from the walls were portraits of Peter Faneuil, the wealthy merchant of Huguenot descent who paid for the building's construction in the 1740s; of former Massachusetts governor William Shirley; and of Isaac Barré, one of the patriots' most outspoken friends in Parliament (even if he had voted in support of the Port Bill). On the ground floor beneath the hall, which was said to accommodate upward of 1,500 people, were the stalls of the town market. Swinging in the sky above the building's cupola was a grasshopper weathervane (similar to that on London's Royal Exchange) fashioned by Deacon Shem Drowne, the same coppersmith who had made the Indian archer above Province House.

For the patriots, this "spacious hall" was a "noble school . . . where the meanest citizen . . . may deliver his sentiments and give his suffrage in very important matters, as freely as the greatest lord in the land." For the loyalists, the town meetings at Faneuil Hall were closer to "a pandemonium than a convocation," since any attempt to oppose the patriots was often met with shouts and even physical intimidation. All agreed that the last decade of political unrest had taken its toll on patriots and loyalists alike. But it wasn't just the fisticuffs in the streets and the tarring and feathering. Something was going on inside all of them—a painful, almost cellular metamorphosis—as they struggled to define what it was to be an American in the British Empire.

What the patriots were proposing, once the Enlightenment rhetoric and sanctimonious evocation of their forefathers had been pushed aside, was exactly what Governor Leverett had insisted on back in 1676: that Parliament had no say in what happened in Massachusetts. And as Thomas Hutchinson had pointed out just the year before, this was, in essence, a demand for independence—a word that these self-styled "conscience patriots" insisted was not yet part of their vocabulary. And as is often the case when someone is unable or unwilling to acknowledge the true implications of his or her beliefs, many of the patriots were plagued by periods of psychic and physical torment.

James Otis was generally credited with initiating this remorseless quest for liberty back in 1761, by objecting to the British government's right to search private premises without a warrant. Since then, the passionate attorney (whom John Adams dubbed the patriot's Martin Luther) had dared to wonder out loud whether he'd been right. Otis's mood swings and rants had become so extreme in recent years that he had been placed under the care of a family outside Boston. But Otis was only the most visible casualty of the tortured ambivalence that went with being a patriot. After representing the British soldiers involved in the Boston Massacre alongside Josiah Quincy in the fall of 1770, John Adams suffered a breakdown that required him to retreat temporarily to his ancestral home in Braintree. Two years later, he was distressed to discover that "my constitutional or habitual infirmities have not entirely forsaken me." At a social gathering in Boston he lost control of himself when the subject turned to politics. In a violent verbal outburst he uttered the unspeakable truths that were on all their minds: "I said there was no more justice left in Britain than there was in hell—that I wished for war. . . . Such flights of passion, such starts of imagination, though they may [impress] a few of the fiery and inconsiderate, yet they lower, they sink a man."

They were a high-strung group of what we would call today overachievers—"ambitious beyond reason to excel," as one of their descendants described them—and just about every leading patriot seemed to have some sort of psychosomatic complaint. The Reverend Samuel Cooper, whose dual role as a patriot and minister of the most affluent congregation in Boston led to the accusation that "silver-tongued Sam" possessed a "ductility quite Machiavellian," suffered from what was said to be an addiction to snuff. John Hancock's gout had a way of incapacitating him at times of greatest stress; and the lawyer Joseph Hawley, to whom John Adams deferred when it came to matters of political policy, was so racked by depression that he would one day take his own life. Even Josiah Quincy, who burned with a seemingly quenchless indignation, acknowledged, on occasion, that the loyalists might have a point.

There was, however, one man who did not let the ambiguities upset him; who was so in sync with the great ideological engine driving the patriot movement that he transcended all the potential paradoxes and denials; and at 11:00 a.m. on May 13, the imperturbable Samuel Adams was chosen as moderator of the Boston town meeting.

He was fifty-one, but with his gray hair and trembling hands, he seemed much older. He had a resonant singing voice, a distrust of horses, and a giant Newfoundland dog named Queue that hated British soldiers. He had failed at every business venture he had ever attempted, but he had one extraordinary talent: he understood, in a deeply historical sense, the future.

America had been founded by immigrants who, little thanks to their mother country, had made a life for themselves in a distant land. And now the mother country wanted to assert her right to control the descendants of those immigrants. But there was a blatant absurdity attached to this claim.

England was a tiny island on the other side of the Atlantic Ocean. America was a vast continent, with a population that doubled every twenty years and that would soon include more English people than lived in all of Britain. No matter how strong the ties between America and England, this fundamental fact could not be ignored.

Samuel Adams lived and inhabited this truth. He invested it with the spiritual fervor of his Puritan ancestors but with an essential difference. Where the Puritans had seen God's will lurking behind the seeming disorder of daily life, Adams, thanks to the Enlightenment, also saw a human hand. There were no unintended consequences in the eighteenth century. If something bad happened, someone had caused it to happen, and Boston was now the victim of a more-than-decade-old plot on the part of the British ministry to enslave America, to drain this bounteous land of all her resources so that England, an island lost to luxury and corruption, could sustain the fraudulent lifestyle to which it had become accustomed.

Nothing could sway Samuel Adams from these beliefs. No personal antagonism (and there were plenty) was enough to make him lose sight of the struggle for American liberty. He'd labored for more than a decade writing articles and letters and attending meeting after meeting, but not until the fall of 1772, with the creation of the twenty-one-member Boston Committee of Correspondence, did he find a way to link the fate of Boston to the entire province and, ultimately, to all the colonies.

Massachusetts (which then included what is today Maine) had more than 250 towns and a total population of about 300,000. By sending out open letters that were then discussed in town meetings across the colony, Boston patriots transformed what had once been a purely local form of government into a forum on the issues that affected everyone. Instead of worrying about repairing roads or bridges, citizens were now using the town meeting to debate the proper response to the Tea Act. This meant that even before Governor Hutchinson had a chance to issue his latest official pronouncement, the inhabitants of what were called the "country towns" of Massachusetts were talking among themselves, forming a consensus, and, more often than not, cheering Boston on its rebellious stand against British tyranny. Through the medium of the Committees of Correspondence, Samuel Adams and his compatriots had created what was, in essence, an extralegal, colony-wide network of communication that threatened to preempt the old hierarchical form of government.

In the fall of 1772 the Boston committee announced its presence with the publication of the "Boston Declaration," a kind of tutorial on why natural law superseded anything that Parliament could devise. To the committee members' pleasant surprise, towns that had never before shown an interest in earlier political controversies responded warmly to Boston's invitation to weigh in on the need to defend Massachusetts's long-held liberties. Gorham (about ten miles inland of modern Portland, Maine) was one of seven townships granted to the veterans of King Philip's War and their descendants in the early eighteenth century. During an Indian raid in 1746 that many town inhabitants still vividly remembered, five people had been killed and three abducted. For the citizens of Gorham, the fight for liberty was not about the current frustrations with Parliament; it was about the terror, anger, and violence that went with colonizing this ancient and blood-soaked land. "Our eyes have seen our young children weltering in their gore in our own houses, and our dearest friends led into captivity," they wrote to the Boston Committee of Correspondence in January 1773. "We . . . have been used to earn our daily bread with our weapons in our hands. Therefore we cannot be supposed to be fully acquainted with the mysteries of court policy, but we look upon ourselves as able to judge so far concerning our rights as men. . . . We look with horror and indignation on the violation of them. . . . Many of our women have been used to handle the cartridge, and load the musket, and the swords which we whet and brightened for our enemies are not yet grown rusty."

In town after town, colonists took Boston's statement of natural rights and made it their own. And as the citizens of Gorham had made unmistakably clear, they were more than willing to fight for those freedoms.

Governor Hutchinson was so alarmed by the committee's inroads throughout the province that he responded with a tutorial of his own. On January 1773 he delivered a lecture to both chambers of the General Court in which he pointed out the fallacies behind the committee's assertions in the Boston Declaration. Instead of convincing the patriots of the errors of their ways, however, Hutchinson's response only added to the growing momentum. Much to the governor's apparent surprise, the Massachusetts House of Representatives quickly replied with a detailed treatise (written by members of the Committee of Correspondence) that laid the philosophical and legal groundwork for future thoughts about independence.

In the months ahead, Hutchinson watched helplessly as the once lackadaisical pace of events in the colony seemed to accelerate into a disastrous rush. Soon after suffering through the storm ignited by his ill-conceived response to the Boston Declaration, Hutchinson found himself engulfed in the controversy surrounding the packet of letters leaked by Benjamin Franklin. Even before that began to die down in the fall of 1773, he was embroiled in the maneuverings that culminated in the Boston Tea Party. Through it all, the Boston Committee of Correspondence had been sending out letters that gave each controversy an impact and resonance it otherwise never would have had.

The turnaround was remarkable. In the fall of 1772, Hutchinson had been congratulating himself on the contented calm that had settled over the colony. Then came the Committee of Correspondence, and within a year and a half, the governor's reign was over—a downfall that had been hastened, if not scripted, by Samuel Adams and his junta of unelected committee members.

On the afternoon of May 13, 1774, in Faneuil Hall, the town meeting elected an eleven-man committee "to write a circular letter to the several towns of this province and to the several colonies, acquainting them with the present state of our affairs." In addition to Samuel Adams, the committee included many members of the Committee of Correspondence, such as John Adams, Dr. Joseph Warren, Josiah Quincy Jr., and the mercurial and outspoken merchant William Molineux. But there were some surprising additions to the committee, most notably the politically amibiguous John Rowe, whose ties to the loyalists were as strong as, if not stronger than, his allegiance to the patriot cause.

By naming Rowe and the others, Samuel Adams shrewdly addressed a potentially thorny problem. Boston had divided over the proper response to the Port Act. Many merchants were convinced that there was a simple and sensible solution to the crisis, so sensible, in fact, that Benjamin Franklin had thought of it back in London soon after learning about the Tea Party. Why not simply pay for the tea? Rather than sit there and watch as commerce withered to nothing and the city filled up with British soldiers, why not swallow their collective pride and come up with the 9,660 pounds sterling (about $850,000 in today's U.S. currency) required to put this whole sad affair behind them and move on with their lives?

This was not what Samuel Adams and his compatriots wanted to hear. Rather than approaching the act as a problem to be solved, they saw it as an opportunity to be exploited. They argued that to capitulate now would only encourage even harsher measures in the future. And besides, given the haziness of the act's wording, it was difficult to determine whether reimbursing the East India Company would be enough to convince the British Parliament to repeal the act. Instead of compliance, they wanted nothing less than a complete boycott of British goods—not just in Boston and Massachusetts but throughout all thirteen colonies.

With the creation of the new committee containing Rowe and other merchants operating as a smoke screen, Adams proceeded to do exactly as he wanted. A motion was passed that the Committee of Correspondence should "dispatch messengers with all possible speed to the other colonies and the several towns in this province, charged with the letters [that] they have wrote relative to shutting up this harbor." Then came the coup de grace: a motion was passed in support of the assertion that a boycott of British imports and exports "will prove the salvation of North America and her liberties."

Rowe assumed that the motion simply stated the mood of the meeting, and in the days ahead he worked with the committee to articulate what was supposed to be the town's official response to the Boston Port Act. But it was all for nothing—the committee never delivered a recommendation. In the meantime, the Boston Committee of Correspondence's May 13 letters stating the need for a boycott had long since been sent. The impression broadcast throughout Massachusetts and America was that Boston unanimously supported a boycott and expected the other colonies to follow suit. Bostonians, however, were far from agreed as to what to do about the Port Bill.

At noon on Tuesday, May 17, four days after his arrival at Castle Island, Lieutenant General Thomas Gage landed at Boston's Long Wharf. A third of a mile long, lined with more than fifteen warehouses and shops (one of which had once been the boyhood home of the painter John Singleton Copley), Long Wharf was a wide and inviting platform of commerce that gestured toward the harbor and the ocean beyond like an opened hand.

Five and a half years before, during the fall of 1768, Long Wharf had been the arrival point of the soldiers that had ultimately made the Boston Massacre an inevitability. Now, with the arrival of General Gage and the knowledge that at least four regiments of British soldiers were on the way, the town was being forced to relive that nightmare even as it prepared to suffer an altogether new ordeal.

But there was at least one consolation. Governor Thomas Hutchinson, the most reviled man in all of Massachusetts, was to depart soon for England, and General Gage was said to be a most reasonable man, with an American wife.

Gage was met at Long Wharf by a delegation that included the upper chamber of the General Court, known as His Majesty's Council; the town selectmen; and a host of other officials, including the province's secretary, Thomas Flucker. Preceding this august group were the Independent Company of Cadets, the elite of Boston's militia, who were responsible for accompanying the royal governor at official functions. Dressed in red coats with blue facings, patterned on the uniforms worn by the British Foot Guards, the cadets were the governor's official bodyguards and were commanded by John Hancock.

If Samuel Adams was the guru of the patriot cause, Hancock, thirty-seven, was its uncrowned king. Handsome, with the stubble of a beard visible on his clean-shaven cheeks, he'd recently scored a major success in March with a surprisingly well-delivered Massacre Day Oration, an annual event held in the Old South Meetinghouse that provided Bostonians with a stirring reminder of the evils of a standing army. No one in America had lived a more privileged life than John Hancock, and yet there was a profound difference between him and the man whom it was now his sworn duty to protect, Lieutenant General Thomas Gage. Gage's family had lived on their estate in the Sussex town of Firle since the fifteenth century. His status as British gentry was something that he and everyone he knew took for granted. Hancock's wealth, on the other hand, was only a generation old. His uncle, who had adopted him when he was a boy, had amassed much of his fortune selling arms and provisions to the British army during the French and Indian War. John Hancock's inherited wealth had provided him with a beautiful house on Beacon Hill, an ornate carriage, fashionable clothes, and a nasty case of gout, but it had not won him the sense of entitlement that the landed aristocracy in England enjoyed. As anyone in the colonies could see, fortunes could be lost even more quickly than they could be made, and as a consequence, the wealthy in America tended to be (relative to their counterparts in Britain, at least) an insecure and touchy lot.

Much has been said in both his and our own time to malign Hancock's intelligence and temper, but not even Samuel Adams proved as adept at responding to the mood swings of the American people. After his uncle's death, he purposely changed the direction of the family business to include a variety of house and shipbuilding projects that came to employ, his lawyer John Adams estimated, at least one thousand Boston families. In the 1770s, as his wealthy peers throughout New England became the objects of envy, suspicion, and open ridicule, Hancock became ever more popular. He served diligently both as a selectman and as a moderator at town meetings. Whereas the idealistic fervor of Samuel Adams could rub even patriots the wrong way, Hancock had the charismatic flair required to attract a loyal popular following, and it was little wonder that Hutchinson had once tried to bring him into the loyalist fold. To the end, however, Hancock remained his own man. He declined to serve on Samuel Adams's Boston Committee of Correspondence, and as Thomas Gage was about to discover, Hancock had a talent for the deftly delivered stab in the back.

Cannons were fired from Admiral Montagu's flagship, HMS *Captain*, and from the batteries in the North End and on Fort Hill to the south. Gage had brought with him both his chariot and his coach, and it's more than likely that at least one of these vehicles was used to transport him and his retinue up Long Wharf to King Street. Here he received a standing salute from the companies of militia, artillery, and grenadiers before reaching the Town House, whose red bricks had recently been painted gray to resemble stone. Once he'd stepped from his carriage to the entrance of the Town House, he climbed the stairs to the council chamber, where he presented his commissions from the king to the upper house of the General Court. After taking the required oaths, he appeared on the balcony overlooking King Street and read a proclamation directing all militia officers to maintain their commissions until receiving further orders, which prompted three volleys from the companies on the street below. A vast crowd had assembled on the square that had formerly been the scene of the Boston Massacre and the tarring and feathering of John Malcom, and on that afternoon in May they gave their new governor three rousing cheers.

Once he'd had a chance to be introduced to a large number of Boston's leading citizens, Gage was again escorted by Hancock and the cadets, this time to Faneuil Hall, where he enjoyed what was described as an "elegant dinner," even if his toast to his predecessor Governor Hutchinson elicited a prolonged hiss. At some point, Gage presented Hancock with his personal flag, featuring the Gage family coat of arms.

Inevitably, Hancock, the young and arrogant darling of the patriot movement, ran afoul of Thomas Gage. Later in the summer, Gage accused Hancock of not paying the proper respect as he passed between the cadets' lines at the entrance to the governor's residence at Province House. When Gage angrily called for Hancock's dismissal, the cadets responded by returning Gage's flag and refusing to serve under another commander. Hancock had lost his command, but Gage had been robbed of his personal guards. Once again, Hancock had found a way to elevate his standing among the people of Boston.

On May 25, the new royal governor suffered through an Election Day sermon at the First Meeting based on the scriptural proverb "When the righteous are in authority, the people rejoice: but when the wicked beareth rule, the people mourn." Later that day he was presented with a slate of twenty-eight candidates for his own governor's council that was filled with patriots. As was his right, he rejected thirteen of them, including John Adams and Harvard professor John Winthrop. He also reminded both houses of the General Court that as of June 1 they would be meeting not in Boston but, as the Port Act required, in Salem. Instead of living in Province House, Gage needed to be based near the new temporary capital, and over the course of the next few days he made arrangements to stay in a mansion in the little town of Danvers, just a few miles from Salem.

On May 29, Admiral Montagu began setting up the blockade that would prevent all shipping from reaching or leaving Boston Harbor. Given the size of the anchorage, it was no easy matter. The *Magdalen* was placed at Point Shirley at the harbor's extreme northeastern corner, the *Mercury* fourteen miles to the south at Point Allerton, and the *Tamar* hovered near the harbor entrance at the Brewsters. Six other vessels took up positions throughout the inner harbor, with the largest and most conspicuous of the warships, the admiral's flagship *Captain*, placed between Long and Hancock's wharves, the entire Boston waterfront comfortably in range of her guns.

On June 1 John Rowe recorded in his diary, "This is the last day any vessel can enter this harbor until this fatal act of Parliament is repealed. Poor unhappy Boston. God knows only thy wretched fate. I see nothing but misery will attend thy inhabitants."

But the Boston Port Act was only the beginning. The very next day, word reached the city that a vessel had arrived in Marblehead with a draft of another bill that would be referred to in the months ahead as the Massachusetts Government Act. Not content with sealing off Boston, Parliament had decided to strip the colony of the essence of its royal charter, which dated back to 1692. With the exception of one pro forma annual gathering to elect town officials, regular town meetings, the lifeblood of the patriot movement, were to be forbidden. Instead of being nominated by the House of Representatives, subject to the governor's veto, the upper chamber of the General Court was to be handpicked by the king through what was called a writ of mandamus (Latin for "we command").

It now seemed as if everything Samuel Adams had predicted was about to come true. By August, when the Government Act went into effect, every town in Massachusetts would be deprived of its liberties.

John Rowe received the disturbing news while attending a meeting of fellow Boston merchants. Rowe was a moderate, a man doomed to see both sides of the situation and to reserve judgment; he loved the mother country, but he also cared deeply about the town of Boston. Back in December he appears to have gotten so caught up in the excitement surrounding the Tea Party that he was heard to shout, "Who knows how tea will mingle with salt water?" It was an exclamation he had come to regret as he struggled to play both sides of the political fence. "The people have done amiss [with the Tea Party]," he wrote in his diary, "and no sober man can vindicate their conduct, but the revenge of the ministry is too severe."

Samuel Adams seems to have taken the Government Act as a kind of goad. It was time, he and the Boston Committee of Correspondence decided, to circumvent the merchants and their attempts to pay for the tea and appeal directly to the farmers of the country towns. Since the merchants' livelihood was based on trade with London, they would always be wary of anything that might endanger that profitable relationship. It was the "yeomanry" of the country—people like the farmers of Gorham who kept their muskets at the ready even when plowing their fields—who could be counted on to do the right thing. "Is it not necessary," Samuel Adams wrote on May 30, "to push for a suspension of trade with Great Britain as far as it will go, and let the yeomanry (whose virtue must finally save this country) resolve to desert those altogether who will not come into the measure?" Perhaps if England's merchants were made to suffer at least a portion of the economic misery inflicted on Boston, the British ministry might begin to see the error of their ways.

On June 2, the committee began drafting what it melodramatically titled

"The Solemn League and Covenant." In the tradition of Joyce Junior, this was a startlingly direct reference to the English Civil War and the 1643 agreement by which Parliament combined with Scotland against the Royalists. As its title suggested, the Solemn League and Covenant was all about commitment and coercion. By signing this agreement, New Englanders were pledging not only to boycott all British goods but to spurn and vilify any of their countrymen who dared to do differently.

On June 8 the committee quietly sent out copies of the Solemn League and Covenant to towns throughout Massachusetts over the signature of the town clerk, William Cooper. It took only a few days for word of the covenant to make its way back to the merchants in Boston. As was to be expected, they were outraged. In what was nothing less than a barefaced act of intimidation, the committee was attempting to precipitate a boycott by creating the false impression that Bostonians had already agreed to the measure and then, once they'd used that lie to get the country towns on their side, force the merchants into line.

Like John Rowe, John Andrews was a merchant who had always been cautiously supportive of the patriot cause; but this underhanded move by Adams and his committee was simply too much. The patriots' reckless disregard for the principles they were supposedly working to uphold might, in Andrews's view, serve the purposes of the British ministry by fracturing the city into two warring factions. "Those who have governed the town for years past . . . seem determined to bring total destruction upon us . . . ," he wrote his brother-in-law in Philadelphia. "I am afraid we shall experience the worst [of] evils, *a civil war.*"

By this time, transports containing the promised regiments of soldiers had begun to arrive in the harbor. On June 14, Lieutenant Colonel George Maddison and the Fourth Regiment disembarked at Long Wharf and after marching up King Street pitched their tents on the Boston Common, near the livestock pound. John Rowe reported that there were "a number of spectators to see them." The following day, the Fourth Regiment was joined by Major Clerk and the Forty-Third, who set up camp near the workhouse to the northeast. Traditionally, the common had been a bucolic oasis, where lovers liked to stroll at dusk along the tree-lined path known as the Mall; with the arrival of hundreds of soldiers, it was becoming an open-air barracks and training ground. The troops had displaced the town's sizable herd of cows, many of which attempted to return to their old grazing grounds ("where the richest herbage I ever saw abounds," marveled one officer) until driven away by stones thrown by the regiments' sentries.

In the meantime, the waterfront, normally a center of nonstop commotion, had grown eerily silent. Goods and provisions were still allowed to enter Boston, but because of the Port Bill they had to be first off-loaded at Salem then transported overland by wagon to Boston—a trip of almost thirty miles that one merchant claimed cost even more than the freight from England. Even worse, Boston's stevedores, sailors, and mechanics—indeed, anyone who relied on the once-constant influx of shipping at the city's docks—no longer had a way to support themselves.

On Sunday, Rowe went for a walk along the wharves. In the past he would have seen ship after ship lined up along the waterfront with their sails drying in the late-spring sun as well as an anchorage full of coasting schooners and merchant ships. Boston Harbor was now shockingly empty; what vessels remained belonged, for the most part, to the British navy. "'Tis impossible to describe the distressed situation of this poor town," he wrote, "not one topsail merchantman to be seen."

CHAPTER THREE

The Long Hot Summer

By mid-June it seemed certain that an angry showdown between the merchants and the Boston Committee of Correspondence was about to erupt in Faneuil Hall. But matters were also coming to a head in Salem, where the province's legislative body, the General Court, went into session on June 7. Reaction to Boston's call for a boycott had been mixed, but sympathies for the town's plight remained strong throughout the colonies. As indicated by letters received by the Boston Committee of Correspondence from committees in Rhode Island, Pennsylvania, New York, and Virginia, the time was considered right for a meeting of representatives from all thirteen colonies to work out a coordinated response to the ministry's attempts to limit colonial rights, for "an attack upon one colony was an attack on all." It was time, Samuel Adams and his coterie of patriots decided, for the Massachusetts House of Representatives to select the delegates to represent the colony at what would come to be called the First Continental Congress in Philadelphia.

Each year, the Massachusetts House chose a committee to draw up a report on the state of the province. This year it was secretly decided that the nine members of this committee should be the ones to come up with a slate of delegates for the Continental Congress. Unfortunately a loyalist had made his way onto the committee. Daniel Leonard was a lawyer descended from a family of Taunton ironmongers. Up until recently he had distinguished himself for his wit, style, and criticism of the administration; in fact, he had been the one who joked back in 1765 that Thomas Hutchinson's house had been destroyed because of what Leonard judged to be his poorly written history of Massachusetts. That winter, however, Leonard had grown increasingly disaffected with the patriots. At some point in the spring he became a committed loyalist, a transformation that the residents of Taunton attributed to Thomas Hutchinson, who was seen speaking to Leonard on the town green beside what came to be known as the Tory Pear Tree.

Whether or not Leonard had been seduced by Hutchinson, he was a most dangerous opponent to have on the committee. Not only was he still highly respected among the members of the House, but he might report the committee's discussions to General Gage. It was decided that two committee meetings must be held each evening after the adjournment of the General Court. The first was to be a sham meeting in which the committee pretended to discuss the Port Bill, with Samuel Adams giving the impression that he might be open to paying for the tea. One of the committee members was another Taunton lawyer named Robert Treat Paine, who counted Leonard as a good friend. Paine marveled at how convincingly Adams strung Leonard along at these meetings. "It would be hard to describe," Paine later wrote, "the smooth and placid observations made by Mr. S. Adams, saying that it was an irritating affair, and must be handled cautiously; that the people must have time to think and form their minds, and that hurrying the matter would certainly create such an opposition that would defeat the matter and many observations of this kind, all tending to induce Mr. Leonard . . . to think that matters would terminate in obedience to the Port Bill." Each meeting ended quite abruptly, with Adams insisting that since it was so hot and they had been attending court all day, "it was unprofitable to sit any longer" and time to go to bed. Once the meeting had been adjourned, however, all the members except Leonard "immediately repaired to a retired room . . . , shut their doors and entered freely and fully on all the subjects of grievances."

After three nights of these clandestine meetings, Adams and his fellow committee members had come up with a slate of candidates for the Continental Congress that included Samuel Adams, John Adams, and Robert Treat Paine. But they still had a problem. When it came time to make their report to the House of Representatives, Leonard would instantly know that he had been tricked. He might even succeed in blocking their efforts to elect representatives to the Continental Congress. He must not attend the meeting of the House on Friday, June 17. But how to get him out of Salem?

Paine had an idea. The Court of Common Pleas was to sit in Taunton on Tuesday, June 14. He would convince Leonard that the two of them should attend that session with the understanding that they would get back to Salem in time "to attend all important business." So on Saturday, June 11, the two lawyers set out on the fifty-five-mile journey to Taunton. A week later on Saturday, June 18, they were on the road back to Salem when they heard the news that forever ended their friendship.

With Leonard out of the way, the committee had been free to make their report, but not before a motion was heard to clear the galleries and lock the House chamber doors. By this time Gage had gotten word that something treasonous was afoot, and he immediately dispatched the provincial secretary Thomas Flucker with a proclamation dissolving the General Court. Finding the door locked, Flucker had no choice but to read the proclamation from the courthouse steps, a brief two-sentence directive that ended with the words, "God Save the King." By that time, the House of Representatives was in the midst of approving the delegates for the First Continental Congress. Samuel Adams and the other committee members were jubilant, and that night a celebratory dinner was held in Boston at the home of Dr. Joseph Warren on Hanover Street.

Warren had a most unusual household. A recent widower with four children between the ages of two and eight, he was not only a leading patriot but also had one of the busiest medical practices in Boston. He had two apprentices living with him on Hanover Street, and he sometimes saw as many as twenty patients a day. His practice ran the gamut, from little boys with broken bones, like John Quincy Adams, to prostitutes on aptly named Damnation Alley, to his good friend the tubercular Josiah Quincy. He was so frequently asked to visit the sick—even on a Sunday, when the normally busy streets of Boston were almost completely deserted—that he'd chosen a pew at the Reverend Samuel Cooper's Brattle Street Meeting opposite a side door, "for the prevention of disturbance when abruptly called on for medical aid." He had what doctors call "the touch," that ability to put patients at ease—a particular challenge in the eighteenth century, since many of the accepted medical treatments of the day did more physiological harm than good.

Warren's portrait by John Singleton Copley presents a man with gray-blue eyes; a full, sensuous mouth; and an aura of vivacious engagement. According to one account, "The ladies judged him handsome," and his first child seems to have been conceived well before he and his wife, Elizabeth Hooten, just seventeen, were married. Elizabeth died in 1772, and by the spring of 1774 Warren, thirty-three, was one of the most eligible widowers in Boston. The night after the election of the delegates to the First Continental Congress, amid a euphoric assemblage of the city's leading patriots, Warren may have struck up the romantic relationship that was to be the most important of what remained of his abbreviated life.

Warren recorded in his ledger book that just the month before he had seen a patient named Mercy Scollay. Thanks to a poem that appeared in a magazine edited by Isaiah Thomas, publisher of the notoriously radical newspaper the *Massachusetts Spy*, we have reason to suspect that Scollay was at Warren's house on June 17.

Mercy Scollay was thirty-three and dangerously close to becoming a spinster. She was later described by a Warren family member as "a woman of great energy and depth of character." If the painting by Copley that has been associated with her is indeed Mercy Scollay, she had penetrating and intelligent eyes and an ironic twist to the mouth, not unlike that of her forceful father, John, who was also painted by Copley, and as chair of the town's selectmen was about to lead Boston through some of its most difficult days.

In a prefatory paragraph to a poem that appeared in the June 1774 issue of the *Royal American Magazine*, Isaiah Thomas recounted how he had recently attended a patriot social gathering during which a gentleman asked a lady what she considered to be "the necessaries of life" given the demands of the boycott associated with the Solemn League and Covenant. The woman responded a day or so later with a flirtatious poem of 114 lines titled "On Female Vanity" that Thomas published anonymously. In the poem, the woman argues that character and intellect, not physical beauty, are what really matter in a woman, particularly in such challenging times. According to the poet, "those modest antiquated charms that lur'd a Brutus to a Portia's arms" will always trump the "gauze and tassels" of a younger, extravagantly dressed woman. Expertly combining private and political spheres, "On Female Vanity" reads like a love letter cloaked in the issues of the day.

Sixteen years later, the noted patriot author Mercy Otis Warren claimed credit for writing the poem at the prompting of Harvard professor John Winthrop. But that was not what Bostonians chose to believe in 1774. According to John Winthrop's wife, Hannah, the gossipmongers insisted that the author was "Miss Mercy Scollay and the gentleman who requested [the poem] Dr. Warren." In the summer of 1774, Scollay and Warren were, apparently, the couple to watch.

By the end of June, letters of support were pouring in to the Boston Committee of Correspondence from all over America. With the prospect of the Continental Congress in September, Samuel Adams's attention was already beginning to shift from Boston to Philadelphia. But first he and the other members of the Committee of Correspondence had to face the furor created by their handling of the Solemn League and Covenant.

The morning of Monday, June 27, the day of the town meeting that was to address these issues, proved to be quite hot, and "with many people just idle enough to attend," Faneuil Hall was filled to overflowing. Samuel Adams was once again chosen moderator of the meeting. It was moved that all the letters written by the committee since the receipt of the Port Bill be read aloud. Faneuil Hall was so crowded that those standing at the back of the room had difficulty hearing what was being said and kept shouting, "A little louder!" Finally it was decided that given the heat and the crowd, they needed to move to the much larger Old South Meetinghouse.

They reconvened at 3:00 p.m. with the reading of the many letters written by the committee, culminating in the Solemn League and Covenant. Once the controversial document had been read, the loyalist John Amory launched into a prepared speech that concluded with a motion to "censure and annihilate" the Committee of Correspondence, which was immediately seconded. Samuel Adams responded by moving that he be replaced as moderator so that he could defend himself and the committee. With the patriot Thomas Cushing taking over as moderator, the debate began.

Speaking on behalf of the committee were not only Adams but also fellow members Joseph Warren, Josiah Quincy, Dr. Thomas Young, and William Molineux. The merchants were represented by the province's treasurer, Harrison Gray, the same elderly loyalist who had objected to Josiah Quincy's treasonous words prior to the Tea Party back in December, along with a host of others. But it was Samuel Eliot who most impressed fellow merchant and brother-in-law John Andrews. Speaking with a "freedom and manliness peculiar only to himself," Eliot explained that since New York, Rhode Island, and Philadelphia had so far proved reluctant to join the boycott, it made no sense to punish Boston's own merchants, who were already reeling from the effects of the Port Bill and its insistence that their imported goods come via Salem. Many of these merchants were expecting shipments from England that would not arrive in Salem until after August 31, the date by which the Solemn League and Covenant insisted that all trade must stop. Not only would the covenant ruin the local merchants, it would serve no greater purpose. By attacking the covenant rather than the committee, Eliot kept the focus on the issues instead of the personalities, and his remarks received,

Andrews wrote, "a universal clap." The debates continued until long past 8:00 p.m., and as it was growing dark, the meeting was adjourned until the next morning.

Bells were ringing throughout the town when the meeting reconvened at Old South. After more still-heated debate, it was finally moved to vote on the motion "for censuring and annihilating" the Committee of Correspondence. If, like Samuel Eliot, the merchants had kept to the covenant rather than the committee, they might have succeeded. But they had, like Samuel Adams before them, overreached. The motion was defeated by "a great majority." But this wasn't enough for the Committee of Correspondence. A motion was then made that the town "approve the honest zeal of the Committee of Correspondence and desire that they would persevere with their usual activity and firmness, continuing steadfast." John Rowe estimated that the motion carried by a margin of at least four to one.

Samuel Adams and his committee had prevailed on the town floor, but their Solemn League and Covenant ultimately proved a failure. Bostonians never approved the measure, which was adopted by only half a dozen or so towns throughout the province. A lesson had been learned: the committee worked well when spreading news and generating public opinion, but the committee could not set policy—that was up to the people of Massachusetts. And as the long hot summer ahead would prove, the people, 95 percent of whom lived in the country towns beyond Boston, had minds of their own.

Gage had had such high hopes for the loyalists of Boston. With regiments of soldiers arriving on an almost weekly basis throughout the month of June, he had anticipated that supporters of government in Boston and other towns in Massachusetts would gladly step forward with the evidence he needed to round up the most notorious of the patriots and try them for treason. But this did not prove to be the case. In a letter to Lord Dartmouth, he told of hearing "many things against this and that person, yet when I descend to particular points and want people to stand forth in order to bring crimes home to individuals by clear and full evidence, I am at a loss." This "timidity and backwardness" on the part of the loyalists was attributed to the fear that the British ministry would soon do as it had always done after a crisis in America: repeal the offending acts and leave the loyalists "to the mercy of their opponents and their mobs." Given what had happened to John Malcom and others, you could hardly blame them.

Even Gage's own soldiers were already giving him problems. Occasional confrontations between the regulars and the locals, particularly at night, were to be expected. What Gage hadn't anticipated was how quickly his men began to desert, encouraged by a series of broadsheets that began to appear in June. "The country people are determined to protect you and screen you from any that may attempt to betray you to your present slavery . . . ," one tract promised. "Being in a country now where all are upon a level you may by one push lay the foundation of your own good living in a land of freedom and plenty and may make the fortunes of your posterity."

The British army had been succumbing to this siren song for decades. Even Gage, with his American wife, had partially surrendered to the pull that the continent exerted on an Englishman: a beckoning promise of new beginnings combined with a sense of the old, almost primeval Britain of their ancestors. Over the course of the next two months, the regiments stationed in Boston would lose more than two hundred soldiers to desertion. Gage seems to have quickly realized that despite his assurances to the king back in February, his mission was doomed from the start. He should never have accepted this wretched post.

By the beginning of summer, he'd decided that his current misery was his wife's fault. On June 26 he wrote Margaret that he was "ready to wish he had never known her." Thomas Hutchinson was visiting the Gage estate in Sussex when this extraordinary letter arrived in August. By that time, Margaret had long since left to join her husband in America, but this did not apparently prevent other family members from reading the letter and sharing its contents. "[Gage] laments," Hutchinson recorded in his diary, "his hard fate in being torn from his friends after the difficulty of crossing the Atlantic in the short time of nine months [in England], and put upon a service in so disagreeable a place, which, though he had been used to difficult service, he seemed to consider as peculiarly disagreeable; wishes Mrs. Gage had stayed in England as he advised her; for though it was natural she should desire to see her friends at New York, etc., yet she could have no sort of satisfaction in New England amidst riots, disorders, etc." Hutchinson knew firsthand what the patriots of Boston could do to a magistrate trying to uphold the sovereignty of the crown, and he was deeply troubled by the revelation. "The whole letter," he wrote, "discovers [i.e., discloses] greater anxiety and distress of mind than what appears from all the accounts we have received concerning him."

On July 1 Gage learned that Admiral Montagu's replacement, Admiral Samuel Graves, had arrived in Boston Harbor in his flagship *Preston* along with
several transports bearing the Fifth and Thirty-Eighth Regiments. Commanding the Fifth was Earl Hugh Percy, the future second Duke of Northumberland, and on July 6, Gage returned to Boston to meet with Percy at
Province House.

Percy, just thirty-one years old, had served in Europe during the Seven
Years War. He was cadaverously thin, nearsighted, and had a big bulbous
nose. But he was also impeccably bred, immensely wealthy, and a talented
soldier, and Gage entrusted the young general with stewardship of the forces
gathered in Boston while he attended his duties in Salem.

Boston was known for its love of liberty, its piety, and its prostitutes. In the
town's hilly northwestern corner was a lightly settled neighborhood that the
soldiers dubbed Mount Whoredom. One afternoon at the end of July at an establishment known as "Miss Erskine's," fifteen British officers "committed,"
John Andrews wrote, "all manner of enormous indecencies by exposing their
anteriors, as well as their posteriors, at the open windows and doors, to the
full view of the people . . . that happened to pass by." By dusk, the party at
Miss Erskine's had begun to break up. Andrews, who happened to be walking
nearby, saw two of the officers make their rampaging way through an old
woman's apple shop, "turning over all [her] things," before assaulting two
men with "their fists in their faces and damning them." A few minutes later a
group of five officers, all of them with their small swords drawn, came upon
the wine cooper Abra Hunt and his wife. Abra was, according to Andrews,
whose letters provide a rich and detailed portrait of a city under occupation,
"a well-built, nervous fellow," and when the soldiers began to comment on his
wife, Abra took up his hickory walking stick and laid open one of the officers'
heads. A small crowd gathered, and before he could kill the officer with another blow, several of his fellow citizens restrained him. In the meantime, the
rest of the soldiers began flourishing their swords and soon cleared the street
of pedestrians, with the exception of Samuel Jarvis, Samuel Pitts, a chair
maker named Fullerton, and "a negro fellow." Pitts found himself fending off
two of the officers with his cane, and might have been seriously wounded if a
sword hadn't struck the fence he was standing against. As it was, three of his
knuckles were bloodied before he subdued the two soldiers, and the other Bostonians succeeded in disarming the remaining three officers.

When informed of the disturbance, Percy was quick to promise the town's selectmen that all the offending officers would be held accountable for their actions. For their part, Bostonians knew that it was important that they, too, do everything they could to keep their fellow citizens in line. Many of the soldiers looked to bait the townspeople into doing something that might be interpreted as an act of insurrection. "I hope the *strict* observance of a steady and peaceable conduct will disappoint their views," John Andrews wrote, "for [I] am persuaded there is nothing they wish for more than an opportunity to deem us rebels; but God forbid they should ever be gratified."

With so many people put out of work by the Port Bill, the town selectmen worried that many of Boston's poorer residents would no longer be able to feed themselves. But by early August, donations from across the country began to flood into the city. Eleven carts of fish came from Marblehead; two cargoes of rice from Charleston, South Carolina; and one thousand bushels of grain from Weathersfield, Connecticut. A Committee of Donations was formed to thank the towns for their gifts, and the letters, many written by Samuel Adams and Joseph Warren, followed the pattern established by the Committee of Correspondence in establishing personal lines of communication among the communities.

The Bostonians had objected to paying a tax on British tea, but they were more than willing to fund an expensive public works project if it helped the town get through the crisis. Under the direction of the town's selectmen, municipal funds were used to hire jobless mechanics, artisans, and dockworkers to build ships, clean up the wharves, and repair roads. John Andrews complained that while the poor had the town to relieve them and the rich had their savings and rents, small merchants such as himself had nothing. "[The] burden falls heaviest, if not entirely, upon the middle people among us," he wrote. And yet, despite all these anxieties, Andrews was amazed by how well his fellow citizens were holding up. "[There is] ease, contentment, and perfect composure in the countenance of almost every person you meet in the streets," he marveled, which "much perplexes the governor and others."

On August 6, the *Scarborough* arrived with the much-anticipated Massachusetts Government Act. Gage's already tormented world suddenly became much worse. As part of the act, the king and the ministry had named thirty-six mandamus councillors—all of them loyalists—and on August 8, Gage assembled as many of them as he could in Salem. A disturbing number either did not respond to the summons or downright refused to accept their positions on the council, knowing that to be a mandamus councillor was to invite the kinds of abuses that the patriots had formerly directed against the tea consignees and John Malcom. The Massachusetts Government Act also made provisions for the selection of jurors in the superior courts, and talk was already circulating through the western parts of the province about preventing the courts from sitting. And then there was the issue of town meetings, which had been declared all but illegal.

As if the Government Act wasn't enough, Parliament had passed three additional pieces of legislation: the Administration of Justice Act, which the patriots branded "the Murderer's Act" because it allowed governors to move the trials of royal officials accused of a crime to a venue outside their own colony (and thus "get away with murder"); the Quartering Act, which provided for housing British soldiers in a colony's unoccupied buildings; and finally the Quebec Act, which, besides allowing French Canadians to practice Catholicism (not a popular provision among New England's papist-hating Congregationalists), expanded that province all the way to the Ohio River to the south and to the Mississippi to the west. Many leading colonists, especially in Pennsylvania and Virginia, such as Benjamin Franklin and George Washington, had applied for land grants in this huge swath of territory, which included modern Ohio and Illinois. By effectively prohibiting western expansion, Parliament had found a way—unrelated to the unrest in Boston— to anger and frustrate not just the citizens of Massachusetts but virtually all of colonial America.

Instead of making the colonists think about repentance, what were collectively referred to as the Coercive Acts had the opposite effect. Massachusetts's patriots were more resolved than ever to persevere in their insistence on liberty while the loyalists were finding it increasingly difficult to defend the ministry's overbearing measures. In the meantime, the undecided, whom John Andrews described as "the lukewarm that were staggering," were moving ever closer to becoming confirmed patriots. But no matter what camp they were in, all agreed that the ministry had made a mess of the situation. Everywhere in Boston, Andrews claimed, Lord North was cursed "morn to noon and from noon to morn by every denomination of people."

Joseph Warren was about as busy as a doctor could be in Boston, but that did not prevent him and his fellow Committee of Correspondence members from composing countless letters to towns throughout New England and beyond, thanking them for their donations or their letters and resolutions of support. Thirteen of these letters were received in a single day, and Thomas Young reported that he and the others convened "every day or two" to make sure all the correspondence was answered in a timely manner.

From the first, Warren saw himself and all New England in a mythic quest that united the here and now of the present generation with the travails of their glorious ancestors. As far back as 1765 he had distinguished himself as an effective political writer when he began writing newspaper articles under a variety of pseudonyms. He had the polemicist's talent for emotional overstatement. Instead of Joyce Junior's sneering insistence on submission, Warren saw himself as part of a rapturous convergence of past, present, and future that required everything a person could give: "When I perceive the impending evil . . . , I cannot hold my peace. In such a case no vehemence is excessive, no zeal too ardent. . . . Trace the renown of your progenitors and recollect the stands, the glorious stands they have often made against the yoke of thralldom." In the spring of 1774 he composed a song that served as a rousing anthem for the patriot movement, and that summer, as he wrote letter after letter, his was one of the most recognizable and unabashedly passionate voices coming out of Boston.

He was bright, articulate, and multifaceted, but Warren was also something of a spendthrift. His now deceased wife had reportedly been worth a considerable amount of money at the time of their marriage, but by her death in 1772, Warren seems to have worked his way through most, if not all, of those resources. His straitened circumstances may have contributed to the intense activity of his medical practice in 1774 and 1775. Financial considerations also probably influenced his decision to embark that summer on what appears to have been his version of a get-rich scheme: a twenty-one-year partnership with a group of physicians (which included a surgeon with one of the regiments currently stationed in Boston) to build smallpox hospitals in Boston and Philadelphia.

That Warren entered into a long-term agreement with a British army surgeon in July 1774 might seem incredible, given what we know today about what was to occur in the coming months. The evidence seems clear, however, that in the summer of 1774 not even Warren's farsighted mentor, Samuel Adams, was convinced that war was imminent. The patriots had been opposing Britain's policies for the last decade, but this did not mean they anticipated a permanent rupture. "Nothing is more foreign from our hearts," Warren had written that spring, "than a spirit of rebellion. Would to God they all, even our enemies, knew the warm attachment we have for Great Britain, notwithstanding we have been contending these ten years with them for our rights!" Boston's patriots (who still referred to England as "home") were not trying to reinvent the world as they then knew it; they were attempting to get back to the way it had been when they were free from imperial restraint.

In the meantime, Warren's relationship with Mercy Scollay appears to have progressed. That month, Mercy's sister Priscilla, who at nineteen was fourteen years younger than Mercy, married the merchant and Tea Party participant Thomas Melvill, twenty-four. Thomas Melvill and Warren traveled in the same patriot circles, and it's possible that the wedding helped to bring Warren and Melvill's new sister-in-law ever closer. We will never know the details of how matters stood between the two of them, but we do know that Scollay became increasingly intimate with Warren's children and that by the spring of the following year, she and Warren had, according to several accounts, agreed to marry. This did not mean, however, that their private lives settled into a comfortable and predictable course. In this time of tumultuous, often catastrophic change, nothing could be counted on for long.

Almost two months before, the delegates to the Continental Congress had been chosen behind locked doors at the courthouse in Salem. On August 10, those four delegates gathered in the home of Thomas Cushing on Bromfield Street in Boston. Over the course of the previous weeks, the patriots had taken it upon themselves to ensure that their famously threadbare leader, Samuel Adams, was properly prepared for his trip to Philadelphia. Arrangements were made to repair his house and barn; he'd been measured for a new suit of clothes; he'd received a new wig, a new hat, six pairs of shoes, and some spending money. Back in June, many in Boston had been embittered by Adams's handling of the Solemn League and Covenant, but now, thanks in large part to the Coercive Acts, he was once again viewed as the stalwart defender of the colony's rights. There had been rumors circulating throughout July and August that he was about to be arrested and sent to England for trial. Despite being urged "to keep out of the way," Adams had continued to walk the streets of Boston and write his letters in the Selectmen's Office, which served as headquarters for the Committee of Correspondence, and the people loved him for it. "They value him for his *good* sense, *great* abilities, *amazing* fortitude, *noble* resolution, and *undaunted* courage," John Andrews wrote to his brother-in-law.

Cushing, Samuel Adams, his cousin John Adams, and Robert Treat Paine boarded a yellow coach pulled by four horses with two white servants in front and four African Americans in back. Even though five British regiments were encamped in plain view, the delegates made a point of making "a very respectable parade" along the periphery of the common as they headed out that morning toward Watertown and, ultimately, Philadelphia.

It was a proud and exciting moment for Boston's patriots, but a disturbing one as well. How could they possibly fill the void left by even the temporary absence of Samuel Adams?

In early August, a celebrity arrived in Boston. Lieutenant Colonel Charles Lee, forty-two, was not only a famous British army officer who, in addition to serving with distinction in America during the French and Indian War, had fought in both the Polish and Portuguese armies; he was one of Lord North's most virulent critics. Although still technically a member of the British army, he had grown disillusioned with his professional prospects and was considering a permanent move to Virginia. He was now in the midst of a kind of exploratory tour of the Atlantic seaboard. Everywhere he went he praised the colonies as "the last asylum" of British liberty while leaving the distinct impression that if ever, God forbid, there should be a war between the mother country and her colonies, he was the natural choice to lead the Americans to victory.

Lee decided to stay at the wooden two-story tavern on School Street called the Cromwell's Head. In addition to being a notorious patriot gathering place, it was where, almost twenty years before, the young George Washington had stayed during his one and only trip to Boston. Washington had served with both Gage and Lee during the Braddock campaign back in 1755, and if Lee had a native-born rival for command of the colonial forces, it was George Washington.

Winningly uncouth and eccentric, Lee was also highly intelligent and impulsive. He considered the novelist Laurence Sterne, author of *Tristram Shandy*, a good friend but had also spent several years amid the wilds of Pennsylvania and New York. The Indians had given him the name "Boiling Water," and he was reported to have had two children by the daughter of a Mohawk chief. This was just the military figure to capture the imaginations of the city's patriot leaders, and on August 6 Lee sent his old friend Thomas Gage a letter.

Lee made the paradoxical claim that it was the "warm zeal and ardor" of his affection for Gage that had prevented him from making any effort to visit him. He then proceeded to inform the new royal governor that he had been duped by the British government.

> I believe, Sir, I have had an opportunity of knowing the way and tricks of the cabinet better than you. I make no doubt but they have been all played off upon you. May fortune or some God extricate you from . . . their clutches. I cannot pretend to say whether or not the Americans will be successful in their struggles for liberty, but from what I have seen in my progress through the colonies, from the noble spirit pervading all orders of men from the first estate and gentlemen to the poorest planters, I am almost persuaded they must be victorious and most devoutly wish they may; for if the machinations of their enemies prevail, the bright goddess liberty must fly off from the face of the Earth.

For Gage, who was then trying to implement the Coercive Acts from his temporary seat in Salem, it must have been maddening to know that Lee was in Boston doing everything he could to make him look like a fool. And then, on August 15, yet another colorful veteran of the French and Indian War, Colonel Israel Putnam, fifty-six, from Pomfret, Connecticut, arrived in Boston with a herd of 130 sheep for the town's poor. Like Lee, Putnam was an outsize, almost mythological character. The citizens of Pomfret told the story of how he had rid the town of its last remaining wolf. With a musket in one hand and a torch in the other and with a rope tied around his feet in case he needed to be quickly extricated, he had climbed into the wolf's den and dispatched the snarling mother and her cubs. During the war with France, he had been a member of the famed Rogers's Rangers and might have been burned to death by the Caughnawaga Indians if not for a fortuitous shower of rain.

Charles Lee was delighted to see the old warrior, and the two of them had the temerity to visit the regiments camped on the common, where they traded stories with friends. Inevitably the British officers asked whether Lee and Putnam had come to Boston to fight. The patriot Thomas Young assured Samuel Adams that both soldiers left the impression that should matters come to a head, the colonials—not the British regulars—could count on their support. Young also reported that when Lee finally left Boston on August 17, "Never man parted from us with a more general regret than General Lee."

By the end of August, Gage was getting unsettling reports from the western portion of the province. Safely removed from the regiments collected in Boston and Salem, the country towns were making sure that the Coercive Acts were, in the words of John Andrews, "a blank piece of paper and not more." It had started as early as June, when sixty representatives from several towns in Berkshire County met at Stockbridge and came up with a series of resolutions that became the model for counties throughout the province. In addition to demanding a boycott of British goods, the delegates meeting at Stockbridge drew up a declaration of rights along with a pledge to maintain their own form of local government. A month later, Worcester held a similar convention. Whereas the people of the Berkshires had emphasized the need for maintaining order, those in Worcester County were more concerned that each town maintain a company of well-trained and well-armed militia.

Instead of the Port Bill, it was the arrival of the Massachusetts Government Act in August that pushed the province into a state of what Gage deemed open rebellion. One after the other, in town after town, mandamus councillors were forced to either resign or flee to the safety of Boston. On August 23, Daniel Leonard began to realize that it was no longer safe for him in Taunton and quietly slipped away for Boston. The following day two thousand men assembled on the Taunton town green and would have pulled down Leonard's house if not for the pathetic pleas of his aged father. In Great Barrington, 120 miles to the west, citizens shut down the local courts. In Salem, Gage found himself in a standoff with the Committee of Correspondence, which had dared to call a town meeting even though the gathering was now, according to the Government Act, illegal. Gage had the offending committee members arrested and threatened to jail those who refused to put up bail. When it began to look as if about three thousand militiamen might forcibly "rescue the committee," Gage had no choice but to call off his regulars and forget the matter.

A few days later, the residents of Danvers, which now served as Gage's adopted home, also called a town meeting. John Andrews gleefully reported that the meeting was continued for several needless hours just "to see if [the governor] would interrupt them." When Gage was told of the town's outrageous behavior, he was reported to have cried, "Damn 'em! I won't do anything about it unless his Majesty sends me more troops."

The following day, Gage traveled to Boston to ensure that the superior court was allowed to sit. Although the judges made an appearance, the jurors refused to cooperate, and the session proved an embarrassing failure. "Civil government is nearly [at] its end," Gage wrote Lord Dartmouth, "the courts of justice expiring one after the other. . . . We shall shortly be without either law or legislative power. . . . Nothing that is said at present can palliate. Conciliating, moderation, reasoning [are] over."

In just about every town outside Boston it had become impossible to support, publicly at least, the British government. A unanimity unlike anything ever experienced in the previous hundred years had swept across Massachusetts. Up until this point, internal division and unrest had been a long-standing part of colonial life. The Salem witch trials were only the most notorious example of how rumor, superstition, and personal animosities could overtake a town. Disagreements over monetary policy, banking schemes, and smallpox inoculation had divided the colonists. As the province's population continued to climb, many towns, particularly those surrounding Boston, had begun to run out of land, creating tensions within families that forced many younger inhabitants to relocate to the hinterlands to the west, north, and east to what we now know as Maine. And then there was the perennial issue of religion.

In the 1740s the itinerant English minister George Whitefield had aroused an evangelical fervor throughout the colonies that emphasized the individual's emotional experience of God. Later referred to as the Great Awakening, this upsurge of religious feeling divided communities across Massachusetts into two groups: the "old lights," who dismissed Whitefield as a sensationalist, and the "new lights," who embraced the sense of the dramatic that Whitefield and his followers brought to the pulpit. In 1750 the future patriot leader Joseph Hawley led a bitter battle to remove the brilliant and controversial new-light minister Jonathan Edwards from the meeting at Northampton. In the years after Edwards's ouster, passions remained so high in Northampton that Hawley felt compelled to issue a public apology for having sought the minister's dismissal. That had been in 1760, and now, almost a decade and a half later, all these old divisions had been largely forgotten as colonists united in their opposition to the policies of the British ministry. It was more than a little ironic: an incipient rebellion had pulled these once-warring New Englanders together.

There were exceptions, of course. All across the province there were those who chose to remain faithful to the crown. Financial considerations motivated many of the loyalists, particularly those who were employed by the king or had won commissions for their military services during the French and Indian War. Some were simply contrarians who couldn't help but object to the patriots' coercive demand for unity. Others, such as Daniel Leonard, had been lied to once too often to see much nobility in the clarion call for liberty. Josiah Quincy's older and much less volatile brother, Samuel, shared Leonard's disillusion with the patriot leaders. But that did not prevent him from loving his outspoken brother. "Our notions both of government and religion may be variant," he wrote Josiah, "but perhaps are not altogether discordant." Neither of them suffered from "a defect of conscience or uprightness of intention," he insisted. They simply had different views of what was best for their country.

On the evening of August 30, John Andrews went for a walk along the mall of Boston Common. He spotted Governor Gage coming up a nearby street surrounded by a retinue of six officers, three aides-de-camp, and eight orderly sergeants. Gage's entourage was stopped by a recently arrived mandamus councillor from Bridgewater, "a mere plow-jogger to look at," scoffed Andrews. Once the governor had conferred with the newly exiled councillor, he continued to the head of Winter Street, where Brigadier Percy had rented a home beside the common. The two officers had matters to discuss, and "while [Gage] went in," Andrews wrote, "his attendants of high and low rank stood in waiting at the gate like so many *menial slaves*." Unknown to Andrews, and to just about everyone else in Boston, Gage had a plan that would soon have the entire province in an uproar.

CHAPTER FOUR

The Alarm

Each town in Massachusetts had its own militia. Historically these companies of amateur soldiers had defended New England's settlements from attacks by Native Americans, which had climaxed a hundred years before with King Philip's War and the destruction of a third of the region's English settlements. Although that conflict remained the high-water mark of violence in New England, clashes with the Indians had persisted throughout the eighteenth century. "I have seen a vessel enter the harbor of Boston," the loyalist Peter Oliver wrote, "with a long string of hairy Indian scalps strung to the rigging, and waving in the wind." The Indians had been the New Englanders' traditional foe, but by the middle of the century the militiamen's attention had shifted.

During the French and Indian War, colonial and British soldiers had fought side by side against a common enemy. But as Oliver also observed, "Savage is a convertible term." Even before the Boston Massacre, the anger that had once been directed toward the Indians had been transferred to the British regulars. And it wasn't just the army; the British navy, which had a history of abducting colonists for service on its warships, was also a perennial source of outrage and anxiety. In 1769 a harpoon-toting sailor on a vessel from Marblehead stabbed the leader of a British impressment gang in the neck. For a variety of reasons—not the least of which was the people's hatred of impressment—the sailor was acquitted and released. Fears of the marauding British remained so high in coastal New England that townspeople who lived within twenty miles of the sea routinely brought the same muskets to Sunday meeting that their ancestors had once used against the Indians. The colonists were still fighting for their liberties, but now it was their supposed allies, the soldiers and sailors of the British Empire, who had become the enemy.

By the end of August 1774, as the possibility of an armed conflict between the New Englanders and the British regulars became increasingly likely, attention turned to the black granular mixture of saltpeter, charcoal, and sulfur known as gunpowder. Notoriously difficult to manufacture, gunpowder was almost exclusively produced in Europe. Assuming Britain was about to ban the exportation of gunpowder to Massachusetts (a ban that did, in fact, occur that fall), the militiamen's firearms would be rendered useless if an alternative supply were not soon found. Gage, on the other hand, could depend on a steady supply of gunpowder from Britain. It was still in his best interests, however, to acquire all available stores in the province, and both sides began a desperate rush for gunpowder.

By law, each town was allotted its own reserve of powder, which was stored in a regional magazine. In Boston, large quantities had already been taken from the powderhouse on the common as the many towns surrounding the city withdrew their reserves. For his part, Gage wanted to make sure that nothing happened to the powder that belonged to the crown and had begun to move those stocks to the security of the Castle. As part of this effort, he wrote William Brattle (who despite being a major general in the Cambridge militia was always referred to by his alliterative earlier rank as Brigadier Brattle) about the status of the reserves at a powderhouse on Quarry Hill in modern Somerville. Brattle reported that the only remaining powder at the arsenal was the 250 half-barrels belonging to the crown.

If Brattle had simply answered Gage's question, all might have remained well with the doughty brigadier. But Brattle, who like Daniel Leonard and Samuel Quincy had started out as a patriot but was now a committed loyalist, chose to relay a conversation he'd had with a militia officer from Concord. The officer, Brattle wrote, had complained of being pressured by local patriots to prepare his company "to meet at one minute's warning equipped with arms and ammunition." Brattle recounted how he'd warned the officer that to comply with this policy—which was clearly intended to hasten the militia's response to a possible incursion by British regulars—was to risk being "hanged for a rebel." Brattle ended the letter by assuring Gage that "the king's powder . . . shall remain [at Quarry Hill] as a sacred depositum till ordered out by the Captain General." The clear implication was that Gage should act quickly to prevent the patriots from stealing the powder.

Four days later, on Wednesday, August 31, Gage was making his way up Boston's Newbury Street toward the residence of an officer who lived in a house near the Liberty Tree. Whether it was by accident or (as John Andrews

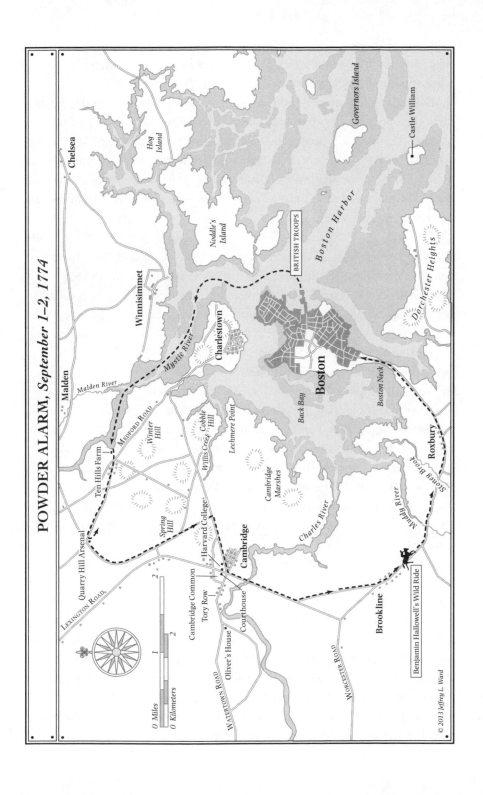

POWDER ALARM, *September 1–2, 1774*

Chelsea

Hog
Island

Governors Island

Castle William

Noddle's
Island

Boston Harbor

BRITISH TROOPS

Winnisimmet

Malden

Charlestown

Dorchester Heights

Malden River

Mystic River

Boston

Back Bay

Boston Neck

MEDFORD ROAD

Ten Hills Farm

Winter
Hill

Willis Creek Cobble
Hill

Lechmere Point

Roxbury

Stoney Brook

Quarry Hill Arsenal

Spring
Hill

Harvard College

Cambridge
Marshes

Charles River

Muddy River

LEXINGTON ROAD

Cambridge Common
Tory Row
Courthouse

Cambridge

Benjamin Hallowell's Wild Ride

WATERTOWN ROAD

Oliver's House

Brookline

WORCESTER ROAD

0 Miles   1   2

0 Kilometers   1   2

© 2013 Jeffrey L. Ward

believed) by design, Brigadier Brattle's unfortunately long-winded letter slipped from the governor's pocket onto the surface of the street, where someone sympathetic to the patriot cause eventually discovered it.

Bostonians had already noticed some unusual activity among the soldiers encamped on the common. Earlier that afternoon, a group of several hundred regulars had been culled from the various regiments. After being provided with a day's provisions, the soldiers were told to be prepared to march early the next morning. "Various were the conjectures respecting their destination," John Andrews wrote, but not even the regulars knew where they were headed.

Shortly after 4:00 a.m. in the predawn darkness of Thursday, September 1, a battalion of about three hundred soldiers under the command of Lieutenant Colonel George Maddison was assembled on the common and marched to Long Wharf, where a fleet of thirteen boats was waiting for them. They were soon being rowed across the harbor to the mouth of the Mystic River along the northern edge of Charlestown.

About three miles up the river, past the point where the Mystic was joined by the smaller Malden River, was Ten Hills Farm. Originally owned by Governor John Winthrop, this beautiful property had been named for the mini–mountain range that rose up along the Mystic River's western shore, providing panoramic views of the harbor from Cobble, Winter, and the highest of them all, Prospect Hill. Just a mile west from the landing at Ten Hills Farm was the Quarry Hill arsenal, where Sheriff David Phipps had eight wagons waiting to be loaded with the king's powder. Sprouting protectively from the top of the conical stone structure was one of Benjamin Franklin's lightning rods.

Gunpowder in the eighteenth century was much more volatile than it later became. Shoes with any metal on the soles that might cause a spark on the powderhouse's stone floor had to be removed, and since a flame of any kind was forbidden, the soldiers were forced to wait for daybreak, when it was light enough to begin removing the barrels and loading up the wagons. As the powder was transported to the boats waiting on the Mystic River, Sheriff Phipps led a small detachment of soldiers to Cambridge. Once they'd borrowed some horses from a local tavern keeper, they hauled off two of the province's fieldpieces and headed across the bridge at the Charles River and marched the eight miles through Roxbury to Boston. In the meantime, the rest of the regulars transported the gunpowder by boat down the Mystic River to the Castle in Boston Harbor.

By then, word of Brigadier Brattle's letter had already spread through Boston and beyond. As Gage perhaps intended, Brattle, not the governor, became the object of the people's scorn once it became known that the king's powder and some fieldpieces had been removed by several hundred British soldiers. A crowd began to assemble in Cambridge and soon made its way to the group of seven magnificent homes known as Tory Row. Situated about a mile from the Cambridge Common on the road to Watertown, these houses enjoyed grand views of the Charles River. The children of the original owners had intermarried to the point that Tory Row had become one of the most exclusive, closely knit communities in America. Brigadier Brattle lived in the house closest to the common, and it's likely that even before the crowd arrived, he had mounted his horse and fled for Boston, where he quickly decided that he had no choice but to retreat all the way to the Castle.

By that afternoon and evening, the crowd in Cambridge had surrounded the house of the province's attorney general, Jonathan Sewall. Sewall had also left for Boston, but someone inside the house fired a warning shot. Some windows were broken, but for the most part the crowd, made up of "some boys and negroes," according to one account, showed little interest in pressing the matter and eventually disbanded.

At some point, however, a rumor was started: when the British soldiers arrived in Cambridge to take the powder, it was claimed, the local militia had opposed them. A skirmish ensued, and the regulars killed six militiamen.

The news of six dead militiamen astounded everyone who heard it, and by midnight the rumor had reached almost forty miles west to Worcester. Even as the rumor headed west, it spread to the north and east to New Hampshire and to Maine; it also headed south to Rhode Island and Connecticut. By early that Friday morning, virtually every town within a fifty-mile radius of Boston was in a tumult as its militiamen prepared to march to the "relief of their brethren." Soon about twenty thousand, some said as many as forty thousand, men were streaming toward Boston.

On the night of September 1 a merchant named McNeil was staying at a tavern in Shrewsbury, Massachusetts, about thirty-eight miles from Boston. Around midnight he was awakened by a violent rapping on the tavern door. He heard the tavern keeper being told "the doleful story that the powder was taken, six men killed, and all the people between there and Boston arming and marching down to the relief of their brethren."

Within a quarter of an hour, fifty men had assembled at the tavern in Shrewsbury. Those who weren't writing messages to be sent on to towns even farther to the west were preparing their weapons and provisions. Soon they were all on their way to Boston. By the time McNeil set out that morning, the only man left in the entire town was the elderly tavern keeper.

It took most of the day for McNeil to press on to Boston. "He said he never saw such a scene before," recounted the minister Ezra Stiles, who spoke with McNeil several weeks later. "All along were armed men rushing forward, some on foot, some on horseback, at every house women and children making cartridges [paper packets of gunpowder], [casting] bullets, baking biscuit, crying and bemoaning and at the same time animating their husbands and sons to fight for their liberties, though not knowing whether they should ever see them again." Just as their ancestors had once rallied to protect their families from the Indians, this new generation of New Englanders was preparing to confront the British regulars.

Ezra Stiles asked McNeil whether any of the militiamen on the morning of September 2, 1774, "appeared to want [i.e., lack] courage." "No, nothing of this," McNeil replied, "but a firm intrepid ardor, [a] hardy, eager, and courageous spirit of enterprise, a spirit for revenging the blood of their brethren and rescu[ing] our liberties." All along the road to Boston McNeil saw women who had already armed and supplied their own men now offering handfuls of cartridges and bullets to those who continued to pass by. McNeil claimed "the women surpassed the men for eagerness and spirit in the defense of liberty by arms. . . . They expected a bloody scene, but they doubted not success and victory."

Throughout the morning and afternoon McNeil rode in "the midst of the people" as they made their way to Boston. Over and over again, it was "positively affirmed" that six men had been killed by the regulars. Not until he was within two miles of Cambridge did he hear the first contradictory report. Soon he was approaching a crowd of several thousand people. Instead of confusion, there was, he remembered, "an awful stillness."

Earlier that morning in Boston, Dr. Joseph Warren received word that "incredible numbers were in arms, and lined the roads from Sudbury to Cambridge." Warren had taken over from Samuel Adams as leader of the Boston

Committee of Correspondence, and citizens in both Charlestown and Cambridge asked that he do something "to prevent the people from coming to immediate acts of violence."

This was a different kind of role for the committee, whose previous activities had been limited to the written word. Warren was now needed, not as a writer, but as a mediator in what sounded like a highly volatile situation. As it turned out, this was just the leadership role to which Warren's talents were suited.

Whereas Samuel Adams was part political boss, part ideologue, Warren, close to two decades younger, possessed a swashbuckling personal magnetism. He'd been born in the nearby town of Roxbury, just across from Boston Neck, and as a boy he was often seen wandering the streets of Boston, selling milk from the family farm. The eldest of four brothers, Warren was recognized as an unusually gifted boy, and when he was fourteen he began his studies at Harvard. In the fall of that year his father was picking apples from the top of a tall ladder when he fell and broke his neck. Warren's youngest brother, John, had been just two years old at the time of this tragic event, and one of his first memories was of watching his father's lifeless body being carried away. With the financial help of family friends, Warren was able to continue at Harvard and later served as a kind of surrogate parent for his brothers, particularly for John, who had recently finished his medical apprenticeship with Warren and was now a doctor in Salem.

At Harvard, Warren's talent for pursuing a dizzying variety of extracurricular activities was soon evident. Early on, he staged several performances of the popular politically themed play *Cato* in his dorm room. The French and Indian War was then in full swing, and he joined the college's militia company. A classmate later told the story of how Warren responded to being locked out of a meeting of fellow students in an upper-story dormitory room. Instead of pounding at the door, he made his way to the building's roof, shimmied down a rainspout, and climbed in through an open window. Just as he was making his entrance, the rotted spout collapsed to the ground with a spectacular crash. Warren simply shrugged and commented that the spout had served its purpose. For a boy who had lost his father to a fatal fall, it was an illustrative bit of bravado. This was a young man who dared to do what should have, by all rights, terrified him.

It was at Harvard that Warren showed an interest in medicine. The great challenge for medical students in the eighteenth century was finding human cadavers for dissection. It's likely that Warren was a member of the Spunkers: a club of medical students (of which we know his younger brother John and Warren's apprentice William Eustis were members) who regularly raided graveyards, jails, and poorhouses in search of bodies. Illegal, yet all in the name of a higher good, this grisly game of capture the corpse was the perfect training ground for a future revolutionary.

In 1764 an epidemic of smallpox ravaged Boston. Warren, just twenty-three and a new doctor, served on a team of physicians that inoculated approximately five thousand people—a third of the entire population of Boston—who'd been quarantined on Castle William. Over an intense three-month period, Warren treated John Adams, the children of Thomas Hutchinson, the customs agent Benjamin Hallowell, the province's secretary, Thomas Flucker, John Singleton Copley's father-in-law, Richard Clarke, along with a host of the town's poor, prostitutes, slaves, and sailors.

Around this time, Warren burst on the political scene with several controversial newspaper articles about then governor Francis Bernard. Although Warren always looked to Samuel Adams for guidance, he quickly established his own identity as a political leader, becoming in 1772 the moving spirit behind the North End Caucus, a group quietly organized to handpick the candidates for key positions in town and provincial government. Warren had that rarest of talents: the ability to influence the course of events without appearing to assert his own will—what one contemporary described as "the wisdom to guide and the power to charm." There were other patriot leaders who believed they were calling the shots, another contemporary later remembered, but it was really Warren through the North End Caucus—an organization that most Bostonians didn't even know existed—who controlled "the secret springs that moved the great wheels."

Warren's influence extended to the St. Andrew's Lodge of Masons, the society that came to serve as the clandestine nerve center of the patriot cause. Warren was the lodge's grand master and presided over meetings at the Green Dragon Tavern on upper Union Street near the Mill Pond in the North End, where, it was claimed, the details of the Boston Tea Party had been worked out in December 1773. In the fall and winter to come, the Green Dragon was where Paul Revere and other lodge members oversaw the surveillance of the British troops, yet another patriot activity in which Warren was deeply involved. Whether it was as leader of the St. Andrew's Masonic Lodge, the North End Caucus, or now the Boston Committee of Correspondence, Warren had become one of the most influential patriot leaders in Boston.

On the morning of Friday, September 2, 1774, with thousands of militiamen gathering on the other side of the Charles River in Cambridge, he sent out a messenger to notify his fellow Boston Committee of Correspondence members that he needed them for an impromptu meeting. So as to prevent a possible panic in the occupied city, he chose not to inform the messenger of the reason for the meeting. As a consequence, committee members were in no great rush to attend to Warren's summons, and once only a handful of members had assembled, Warren and his associates left for Cambridge.

Instead of taking the longer land route through Roxbury, as Brigadier Brattle had done the previous afternoon, they made their way to Hudson's Point in Boston's North End, where they took the ferry to Charlestown, less than half a mile away. From there it was just four miles on a road that after passing Breed's and Bunker's Hills on the right and Charlestown's Mill Pond on the left, skirted the edge of Charlestown Common (where the gibbeted remains of the slave Mark had once hung in chains) and headed west to Cambridge.

They found about four thousand people—almost three times Cambridge's entire population—gathered in the large open field that served as the town's common. Once the farmers heard that the rumors about the six dead militiamen were false, they had agreed to leave their weapons in Watertown before proceeding to Cambridge. With no regulars to fight, they turned their attention to making sure Cambridge's mandamus councillors renounced their posts. At that moment, all eyes were turned to the steps of the courthouse, where two of the councillors stood in the hot summer sun. One of these was the physician and alchemist Samuel Danforth, who previously claimed to have discovered the secret to immortality known as the philosopher's stone. The discovery had apparently not enabled the seventy-eight-year-old councillor to speak in anything other than a barely audible rasp, and Warren's fellow committee member Thomas Young marveled that "not a whisper interrupted the low voice of that feeble old man from being heard by the whole body." Judge Joseph Lee also renounced his position as mandamus councillor and later remarked that "he never saw so large a number of people together and preserve so peaceable order before in his life." But the quiet was not to last.

Around noon, a gentleman in a chaise came upon the crowd gathered on the Cambridge Common. He was on his way from Salem to Boston, and since the road along the common was filled with people, he was forced to pause before continuing on to the bridge across the Charles River. This happened to be Benjamin Hallowell, fifty-four, a member of the customs board who was almost as despised as former governor Thomas Hutchinson. Hallowell had insisted, it was said, that ships with provisions for Boston's poor be banned from entering the harbor, even though the Port Act did not technically forbid them to. In his youth he'd been a noted privateer captain and had accumulated enough prize money during the French and Indian War that he'd built a big and sumptuous house on Hanover Street. He'd married into the well-to-do Boylston family, and as his role as customs officer made it dangerous to live in Boston, his wife Mary used some of her inheritance to purchase a house in the portion of Roxbury known as Jamaica Plain. Brash and hotheaded (John Adams described him as a "Hotspur"), he believed it was time Gage used the regulars to teach these seditious people a lesson. But even Hallowell seems to have been taken aback by the prospect of passing through a crowd of four thousand patriot militiamen.

He soon realized that these were mostly farmers from the outlying country towns and therefore unaware of his reputation in Boston. He became hopeful of making it to the river without incident. But then someone recognized him.

Isaiah Thomas, the patriot writer and editor who in June had published the poem attributed to Mercy Scollay, was in Cambridge that day. According to Hallowell, Thomas cried out, "Damn you, how do you like us now, you Tory son of a bitch" as he made it known to anyone who would listen that Hallowell was "an enemy to the country." Soon about 160 men on horseback were on his trail, "having taken," Hallowell wrote, "a resolution to destroy me."

Joseph Warren and his fellow committee members realized that the pursuit of Hallowell could very well ruin what had so far been an exemplary demonstration of the people's "patience, temperance, and fortitude." Thomas Young and others jumped on their own horses and did their best to dissuade those at the head of the posse that "the shedding of one man's blood would answer no good purpose." Most of the riders gave up the chase, but a group of eight or ten refused to turn back.

Hallowell had succeeded in crossing the Charles and putting about three miles between him and Cambridge when the group of enraged horsemen caught up to him and his black servant, who was following the chaise on a horse. A man named Bradshaw was in the lead and told him to stop so that he could speak with him. When Hallowell refused, Bradshaw rode up beside the horse that was pulling the chaise and began to beat the animal over the head as he tried to grab its reins. By this time, Hallowell had a pistol in his hand, and whenever Bradshaw or the others approached, he aimed the weapon at them till they moved away. Bradshaw later claimed that at one point Hallowell even pulled the trigger, but the pistol failed to fire.

The road to Boston took them through several different villages in Roxbury, and Bradshaw kept repeating the cry, "Stop the murderer, the Tory murderer, he has killed a man!" "This hue and cry," Hallowell wrote, "occasioned a sallying forth of the people from the houses . . . ; others upon the road joined in the cry—all endeavoring to stop me."

After about a mile of this frenzy, the horse pulling the chaise began to give out. Hallowell ordered his servant to give him his saddled horse, which turned out to be "a fleet one," and after tying the reins together and dropping them on the horse's neck, Hallowell continued on with a pistol in each hand. By the time he approached Boston Neck, he estimated that he was surrounded by about a hundred people, "all endeavoring to seize me," as he "ran the gauntlet" toward the town gate. Just as he reached the guard at the entrance, his horse began to fail. Hallowell leaped to the ground and ran the rest of the way into Boston.

The city was soon alive with rumors of its own. The country people, it was said, planned to "fling in about 15,000 by the way of the Neck, and as many more over the ferry." Once the provincials secured a foothold in the city, they would, John Andrews reported, "come in like locusts and rid the town of every soldier."

Gage placed a guard at the powderhouse on the common; he also doubled the guard on the Neck while dispatching soldiers dressed as sailors to gain intelligence of what was really happening across the river in Cambridge. To his credit, he did not send any armed regulars. "Had the troops marched only five miles out of Boston," Joseph Warren wrote, "I doubt whether a man would have been saved of their whole number."

The hurly-burly with Hallowell also had an inevitable effect on the country people gathered in Cambridge. Anticipating a possible attack by the regulars, some of them rushed back to Watertown to retrieve their muskets and swords. Soon they were converging on the home of Lieutenant Governor Thomas Oliver. It was time to make the magistrate admit the full magnitude of his sins against the people.

Oliver, forty, had been born in Antigua, where the family's sugar plantation helped fund the huge mansion called Elmwood he had built at the end of Tory Row. Up until his recent appointment to lieutenant governor, Oliver had steered clear of politics and was well respected throughout the province. Even the notorious patriot firebrand Josiah Quincy Jr. counted him as a friend, and if not for Gage's impatient insistence that he accept the posts, Oliver would have declined the appointments to both the lieutenant governorship and the governor's council. The patriots weren't angered that he'd accepted his position as lieutenant governor; it was that he had agreed to serve as a mandamus councillor. Just as Lee and Danforth had been forced to disavow their commissions, Lieutenant Governor Oliver must resign as a mandamus councillor.

Earlier in the day, Oliver had succeeded in convincing the crowd gathered around his house that it would be in their best interests if he traveled to Boston, spoke with Governor Gage, and reported back to them later in the day. True to his word, he had returned to his house on Tory Row. However, as Gage had predicted, it now looked as if he was about to fall into "the snare." The people were becoming "unmanageable," and Oliver, perhaps remembering what had happened to the house of former Lieutenant Governor Thomas Hutchinson, decided that he had better get himself back to Boston. He had just climbed into his carriage when "a vast crowd advanced and in a short time my house was surrounded by 4,000 people, and one-quarter of them in arms." He retreated back into his house, unsure of what to do next.

Oliver reluctantly agreed to allow Warren and four other members of the Boston Committee of Correspondence inside his house, where they informed him that they had been delegated to "demand my resignation as councillor." Oliver refused. In the meantime, people began to "press up to my windows," Oliver wrote, "calling for vengeance." He could hear his wife and children crying in the next room. "I cast about to find some means of preserving my reputation," he wrote to Lord Dartmouth, and "proposed that the people should take me by force." The committee advised against it, and Oliver finally scribbled on the resignation letter they thrust before him, "My house being surrounded by 4,000 people, in compliance with their commands I sign my name Thomas Oliver."

McNeil, the trader from Connecticut who had spent the previous night in Shrewsbury, watched as Oliver's signed declaration was "handed along the lines and read publicly at proper distances till the whole body of the people were made to hear it." Soon, McNeil recalled, "the solemn silence" was replaced by "a cheerful murmur or general universal voice of joy." It was about six in the evening, an hour before sunset, and as the people scattered in various directions, the thunder rolled and it began to rain.

That what came to be called the Powder Alarm did not live up to the rumors it inspired stands as a tribute to Warren's ability to mediate a most challenging and potentially explosive situation as well as to the steadiness of the country people who traveled to Cambridge on that Friday in September 1774. Their refusal to indulge in violence, and the almost surreal sense of courtesy that underlay that resolve, speaks to the complexity of the emotions that the events of the past spring and summer had evoked among them. At least at this stage, they were not willing to fire the first shot.

As became clear in the weeks ahead, much remained to be done if the provincials had any hope of successfully meeting the threat presented by Gage's ever-growing army in Boston. They needed a better intelligence network so that they could anticipate the regulars' next move before it happened. They also needed to restructure the militia. Many of the older officers were loyalists who had no interest in opposing the British regulars. Changes needed to be made in the officer corps in almost every town's militia; new systems for training and outfitting the militiamen also had to be implemented.

But perhaps the most important lesson learned in the aftermath of the Powder Alarm was that even if Boston had first opposed British tyranny, the country people outside the city were the ones now leading the resistance movement. Instead of feeling as if the resolute crowd had threatened his own authority as a political leader, Joseph Warren embraced this most recent development as evidence of a new and exciting era. In a letter to Samuel Adams at the Continental Congress, Warren reported that what he'd witnessed at Cambridge had inspired in him "the most exalted idea of the resolution and intrepidity of the inhabitants." This ability to maintain his poise within the ineluctable pull of seemingly chaotic events would serve him well in the months ahead.

Samuel Adams and the other three delegates from Massachusetts quickly realized that many at the Continental Congress in Philadelphia did not trust them.
New Englanders, it was said, were "intemperate and rash," and secretly lusted for
"a total independency"—not just from Great Britain but from the rest of the colonies as well. Once the mother country had been defeated, it was asserted, the
New Englanders would then declare war on the colonies to the south and establish themselves as the brutal sovereigns of all America. To counteract this concern, Samuel Adams realized that it was absolutely essential that his colony
remain on the defensive. Massachusetts must remain the victim, no matter what.

And then, on Tuesday, September 6, came word of the Powder Alarm.
Traveling from town to town along the eastern seaboard, the rumor had
made it to Philadelphia in a mere five days. In Connecticut, a letter written by
Israel Putnam falsely claiming that in addition to the six provincials killed,
Boston was being bombarded by British artillery as tens of thousands of colonial militiamen marched toward the burning city, was copied and carried all
the way to Philadelphia.

Philadelphians reacted much as the New Englanders had done. "All is
confusion," reported Silas Deane, a delegate from Connecticut. "Every tongue
pronounces revenge. The bells toll muffled, and the people run as in a case of
extremity, they know not where or why." Delegates who had been divided
into two camps—those who wanted to repair the breach with Britain and
those who favored the continued push for colonial liberties—found themselves speaking with a single voice. "War! war! war! was the cry," John Adams wrote, "and it was pronounced in a tone which would have done honor
to the oratory of a Briton or a Roman."

It took two days, but eventually the delegates learned the truth. Boston
was not under attack. The regulars had taken some powder, but no one had
been killed. It was back to the business of deciding how to respond to the Coercive Acts. And then, a week later, on September 17, Paul Revere arrived
from Boston with a document known as the Suffolk Resolves.

The Government Act had made town meetings illegal in Massachusetts, but it
had said nothing about the counties. Throughout the summer and fall, town
representatives gathered at county conventions all across Massachusetts,
and on September 9, 1774, at Vose's Tavern in Milton, Joseph Warren stood
before the delegates of Suffolk County (which included Boston and towns to

the west and south and included modern Norfolk County) and read them what he'd been working on for the last three days: nineteen resolves in which he had tried to capture the sense of their previous two meetings. Not only did Warren declare that "no obedience is due" to the Coercive Acts, since they were "the attempts of a wicked administration to enslave America"; he set forth a blueprint by which Massachusetts might successfully win back her liberties. Each town must elect militia officers, who should muster the militia at least once a week; that said, the militia was "to act merely upon the defensive, so long as such conduct may be vindicated by reason and the principles of self-preservation, but no longer." If, as threatened, Gage were to seize any patriot leaders, they would respond by taking loyalist hostages of their own. Following the lead of the Solemn League and Covenant, they vowed to "abstain from the consumption of British merchandise and manufactures." In order to fill the void left by Gage's dismissal of the General Court, a "provincial congress" was to convene in Concord in October that would "pay all due respect and submission" to anything passed by the Continental Congress. During these perilous times, all "routs, riots, and licentious attacks" must cease at once. Lastly, it was determined to create a system of couriers by which the towns might be alerted "should our enemies, by any sudden maneuvers, render it necessary to ask the aid and assistance of our brethren in the country."

That day at Vose's Tavern, Warren read each resolve several times so that all the delegates knew exactly what they were voting on. It must have been a scene of intense excitement as the delegates gave their unanimous consent "paragraph by paragraph." Resolve 17 insisted that "renewing harmony and union between Great Britain and the colonies [is] earnestly wished for by all good men." Overall, however, this was a radical document—but not uniquely so, given what other conventions had already or were about to produce—by which the inhabitants of Suffolk County declared their intention to make preparations for possible war.

What made the Suffolk Resolves ultimately so significant was the impact the document had on the Continental Congress in Philadelphia on September 17 and 18. Warren had appended a preamble that poetically evoked the historical importance of the present moment. Before launching into a passionate account of the colony's hazardous situation, he told how Massachusetts had witnessed "the power but not the justice, the vengeance but not the wisdom of Great Britain." The surging rhythms of Warren's prose gave the document an emotional force that succeeded in cutting across the cultural and ideological differences of those gathered in Philadelphia, who voted unanimously to endorse the Suffolk Resolves. John Adams was ecstatic. "The esteem, the affection, and the admiration for the people of Boston and . . . Massachusetts which were expressed yesterday," he wrote, "and the fixed determination that they should be supported, were enough to melt a heart of stone. I saw tears gush into the eyes of the old grave pacific Quakers of Pennsylvania."

Owing to the combined effects of the Powder Alarm and the Suffolk Resolves, the Continental Congress had gotten off to a surprisingly militant start. In the weeks and months ahead, a certain amount of retrenchment inevitably occurred as passions began to cool among the delegates. But if nothing else, the endorsement of the Suffolk Resolves proved that, contrary to what the North administration had predicted, the disparate colonies of British North America could indeed act as one.

By September 24, Paul Revere was back in Boston with the good news from Philadelphia about the endorsement of the Suffolk Resolves. In an age when communication between the colonies could take days and even weeks, Revere provided the patriots with a decided advantage over the less nimble British. But the peripatetic silversmith was much more than the colonial equivalent of a Pony Express rider. Since he was a close friend of Joseph Warren and others, he knew as much as anyone about the patriot movement in Boston and as a consequence could speak with some authority when he carried messages to Philadelphia or, in the months ahead, to towns closer to home.

Revere soon learned that in the two weeks since he departed for Philadelphia, Gage had been working steadily to prepare the town for a possible onslaught from the country. For reasons of safety, all vestiges of the provincial government that had formerly been in Salem (as well as Gage's personal headquarters in Danvers) were moved back to Boston, which was now, for all intents and purposes, a city under siege. Six fieldpieces were rolled out to the Neck, and a dozen larger cannons planted at the town entrance. Warships were repositioned around the city. A more long-term project was the transformation of the crumbling fortifications at the town gate into what the patriots complained was an unnecessary "fortress." The Fifty-Ninth Regiment, formerly stationed in Salem, was ordered to entrench themselves on either side of the Neck, where they provided a daunting gauntlet for anyone coming into or out of Boston.

The country people, however, remained defiant after their staggering show of strength during the Powder Alarm. John Andrews told of the huge farmer who marched proudly into Boston between the ranks of soldiers lining the Neck, "looking very sly and contemptuously on one side and the other, which attracted the notice of the whole regiment." The giant farmer stopped and addressed the regulars around him. "Ay, ay," he crowed, "you don't know what *boys* we have got in the country. I am near nine feet high and one of the smallest among 'em." Another visiting farmer joined a group of soldiers engaged in target practice on the common. After astonishing them with his accuracy, he bragged, "I have got a boy at home that will toss up an apple and shoot out all the seeds as it's coming down."

The country people were having their fun with the soldiers, but their bravado was not without a basis in truth. Native New Englanders (thanks to a healthier diet and living conditions) were statistically two inches taller than their European counterparts. For the regulars, confined to a mile-square island that had recently been surrounded by thousands upon thousands of militiamen, the ministry's confident talk of the overwhelming power of the British military must have seemed more than a little hollow.

The regulars represented one of the greatest armies in Europe, but this did not change the fact that the last time any of them had been in combat was more than twelve years before; indeed, most of them had never seen any action. It was true that the New England militia was made up, for the most part, of farmers, but many of them were farmers who knew how to fight. One patriot told of how two veterans of the 1745 Siege of Louisbourg dismissed the new fortifications on the Neck as "mud-walls in comparison with what they have subdued." If at some point the country people had to storm the ramparts Gage had constructed at the town gate, these old-timers claimed that "they would regard them no more than a beaver-dam."

With an army of several thousand British regulars holding Boston, the town of Worcester, forty miles to the west, became the unofficial center of the provincial resistance movement. A county convention had emphasized the need to strengthen the preexisting system of town militias, which were soon mustering once, sometimes twice a week. What were known as "Minute

Men"—elite groups culled from the towns' militias—were created to be ready for battle in a minute's notice. Not a new concept, the Minute Men dated back to the French and Indian War and were just one example of how the colonists' experience in that earlier conflict had prepared them for what would become the American Revolution.

Along with gunpowder, the provincial militiamen needed guns, and it was to Boston, where local merchants and gunsmiths possessed large stockpiles of weapons, that many of the country people came to secure muskets and other small arms. Since martial law had not yet been declared in Massachusetts, there were limits to what Thomas Gage could legally do to oppose the patriots' efforts to prepare for war, and in the weeks after the Powder Alarm, John Andrews estimated the outflow of muskets and pistols from Boston to be no less than a hundred per day.

What the patriots really needed if they had any hope of one day opposing the British army and navy were cannons similar to the ones that currently loomed from the fortifications and ships in and around Boston. However, many town militias did not yet have adequate supplies of muskets, let alone fieldpieces and larger artillery. The one exception was Boston's "train," an artillery company within its militia regiment, under the command of Major Adino Paddock, a loyalist who was not about to let the company's brass fieldpieces fall into patriot hands.

Two of the brass cannons were stored in a newly built British gun house at the edge of the common. On September 16, several Bostonians had the audacity to approach the house in broad daylight and, as the guards stepped outside, liberate the cannons, each weighing around five hundred pounds. After being lugged across a small yard, the artillery pieces were temporarily hidden in the wood bin of the nearby South Writing School before being smuggled out of the city. The British sergeant guarding the gun house was overheard to exclaim, "I'll be damned if these people won't steal the teeth out of your head while you're on guard!"

One of the Bostonians who helped carry the cannons was the tanner William Dawes, who had a button on the cuff of his shirt jammed deep into his wrist by the weight of the brass barrel. After attempting to ignore the increasingly painful injury for several days, he finally visited Dr. Joseph Warren.

"Dawes," Warren asked, "how and when was this done?"

When Dawes proved reluctant to answer him, Warren said, "You are right not to tell me. I had better not know."

One night later that fall, several old and very rusty iron cannons were secretly placed on a flat-bottomed boat and floated into the North End's Mill Pond. The plan was to row them out into the harbor and up into a creek in Cambridge, where they could be transported into the interior of the province. Unfortunately the boat became trapped by the outgoing tide and was abandoned on the mudflats. The next morning, Admiral Graves confiscated the cannons, but this did not prevent the patriot owner from suing for their return, and in a surprise decision, the Admiralty Court determined that the navy "had no right by virtue of the Port Bill to stop or molest any boats carrying merchandise."

For Gage, the patriots' complaints about British tyranny seemed utterly absurd since British law was what allowed them to work so assiduously at preparing themselves for a revolution. Never before (and perhaps since) had the inhabitants of a city under military occupation enjoyed as much freedom as the patriots of Boston.

One of Gage's biggest concerns was providing winter quarters for an army that by the end of the fall was approaching three thousand men. He had originally planned to build barracks on the common. At first the town selectmen had approved of the idea, since the barracks would mean the soldiers did not have to take over houses in town, while the building project would provide much-needed work for the city's carpenters. What the selectmen had not taken into account were the country people.

As had become clear during the Powder Alarm, the most radical patriots were no longer in Boston; they were in the towns outside the city. Many of these country people believed that Boston should be abandoned by its inhabitants so that they could attack the soldiers and loyalists who remained. Perhaps not surprisingly, the country people did not agree with the Boston selectmen's decision to cooperate with General Gage in the building of barracks, and a committee of representatives from the outlying towns convinced both the Boston selectmen and the Committee of Correspondence that the barracks should not be built. Andrews reported that Gage was heard to complain that "he can do very well with the Boston Selectmen but the damn country committees plague his soul out."

In desperation, the general was forced to reach out to John Hancock for help in convincing Boston's carpenters to ignore the dictates of the various committees and resume work on the barracks on the common. For Gage, it was the ultimate humiliation. After having dismissed the arrogant merchant for the disrespect he had shown him as commander of the cadets, he was now reduced to pleading for Hancock's assistance, which the patriot leader quite gladly refused.

Making Gage's position all the more untenable was the distressing lack of living quarters in Boston. Many patriot families had already left the city, but with the arrival of so many loyalist refugees, there were, Andrews judged, not even half the number of homes needed to house the soldiers and their families. Out of desperation, empty warehouses on the wharves and even rum distilleries, filled with the awful stench of the decaying organic matter left after fermenting molasses, were converted into barracks.

As the fall turned to winter, those still confined to their tents on Boston Common, which included many of the soldiers' wives and children, began to die. A new graveyard was established at the far corner of the common, and in only a few months' time more than one hundred people had been buried. By December the soldiers had moved into their winter quarters, but that did not prevent disease from taking a terrible toll, and by January the regulars were dying at the rate of three to four a day. The ready availability of cheap rum, which the patriots were happy to foist on the regulars, was also killing its share of men. "Depend on it . . . ," wrote one British commander, "[rum] will destroy more of us than the Yankees will."

Desertion had always been a problem, but now outright mutiny had become a genuine possibility. Already, one deserter had been executed on the common, his bullet-riddled body laid out on top of his coffin for all the regulars to see, and many soldiers were so brutally flogged that their ribs were laid bare—a horribly painful injury that often led to kidney problems and death. A cannon was moved into the center of town in the event, John Andrews claimed, of an uprising on the part of the troops—an irony that was not lost on anyone in this city, where the Boston Massacre was still vividly remembered.

Gage now realized that his earlier claim that he could contain Massachusetts with a mere four regiments had been nothing but a deluded boast. By the end of October, he was writing Lord Dartmouth that no less than twenty thousand soldiers were required to retake New England. He knew this might seem like an absurd figure to the ministry back in London, but he assured Dartmouth that such a large army "will in the end save Great Britain both blood and treasure."

The country people had succeeded in shutting down the colony's legislature and courts. Trapped in Boston, Gage was powerless to exert any control beyond the borders of the city. Each town had its own selectmen to manage local affairs, but some kind of colony-wide political body had to be created, or the patriot movement would grind to a disorganized halt. If Gage decided to break out of Boston and seize more of their munitions, it might be necessary to defend themselves from the British soldiers. Each town had its own militia, but at some point the colony might need to raise its own provincial army. The soldiers would need to be paid; provisions and equipment would need to be purchased, and for that to happen taxes needed to be collected. An extralegal government of some sort must be created, and in October a new era arrived in Massachusetts with the sitting of the first Provincial Congress in Concord.

Representatives from throughout the province, many of them former members of the General Court, traveled to Concord, where they convened at the town's meetinghouse. "You would have thought yourself in an assembly of Spartans or ancient Romans," Joseph Warren enthused in a letter to a patriot friend, "had you been a witness to the ardor which inspired those who spoke upon the important business they were transacting."

In truth, however, the 260 members of the Provincial Congress were deeply divided. Some thought they should revert to Massachusetts's original charter from 1629, which would allow them to elect their own governor. It would be a way to get the colony functioning again without declaring independence from Britain. Others saw this as a needless ruse—why not simply create a new government out of whole cloth and get on with it? The debates were kept in secret, so there is no direct evidence of what was being said, but we do know that Warren and the other Boston delegates (which included John Hancock, who served as the Congress's president) found themselves "by far the most moderate men." In several letters to Samuel Adams in Philadelphia, Warren asked for his mentor's advice. They must, Adams responded in so many words, refrain from doing much of anything; otherwise they ran the danger of causing the other colonies to think twice about supporting Massachusetts. In the meantime, Warren remained "rapacious for the intelligence" that might provide the guidance he so desperately needed.

Warren's sense of isolation only increased when his good friend Josiah Quincy left at the end of September for London. It was time that a patriot from Boston challenged the version of events that former governor Thomas

Hutchinson and other loyalists were promulgating in England, and Quincy was just the man to do it. There was, however, the issue of Quincy's health. Back in February 1773, Warren had witnessed his friend's most recent will and testament, and with both the patient and his doctor hoping for the best, Quincy departed in secret from Salem.

Quincy's was just one of several departures by noted patriots that fall. Dr. Thomas Young, a transplant from Albany, New York, was one of Boston's most passionate patriots, and he had already suffered two near-fatal beatings in the streets of Boston. The physician seemed unfazed by the incidents, but it was another matter for his wife, who began to weep whenever Young left the house. When Gage began building the fortifications at the town gate, she became so "enveloped [in] constant terrors" that she took to her bed and appeared, Young wrote to Samuel Adams, "as inanimate as a corpse." Young decided he must "seek an asylum for her," and in the middle of September he abruptly moved his family to Providence, Rhode Island.

About a month later, the patriot William Molineux, whom John Rowe described as "the first leader of dirty matters," died after a brief illness. The loyalists gossiped that Molineux had actually killed himself (with laudanum provided by Joseph Warren) when it was discovered that he'd been embezzling money from the owner of the wharf he managed. In any event, Warren was suddenly without three of the movement's most active members.

He inevitably began to rely more on the physician and Committee of Correspondence member Dr. Benjamin Church. Whereas Warren was known for his openhearted pursuit of liberty, Church had a talent for withering sarcasm. Like Warren, he had composed at least one patriot song, but unlike Warren he had also written a loyalist parody of his own composition. That Church got away with such unsettling behavior was a tribute to his arrogant brilliance, and Paul Revere later maintained that since the patriots "needed every strength, they feared, as well as courted him." For his part, Warren "had not the greatest affection for [Church]," according to Revere. One wonders, however, if Warren had had much enthusiasm for the dirty trickster Molineux. Then as now, just because two people were of the same political affiliation did not mean that they necessarily liked each other.

On November 9, the delegates from the Continental Congress in Philadelphia finally returned to Boston, and the church bells were ringing till midnight. The Congress had agreed to an intercolonial commercial boycott of British goods, but in the interests of maintaining unanimity among the colonies at this critical moment, the delegates had refrained from sanctioning the creation of a full-fledged alternative government in Massachusetts. Any additional measures would have to wait until the second Continental Congress in the spring. Until then, the province must remain in a tense state of limbo—unless, of course, someone, whether it be Gage or the patriots, made the first move.

The Unnatural Contest

During the second week in December, the Boston Committee of Correspondence learned that Gage was about to retrieve the powder stored in New Hampshire's version of the Castle—Fort William and Mary, situated on a small island near Portsmouth. Paul Revere was sent to warn the town's citizens, and on December 14 several hundred men assaulted the poorly defended fort. The handful of British soldiers stationed there were quickly subdued, and soon the fort's powder was in patriot hands. Just to make sure, the next day another group returned to take the fort's cannons. As soon as he heard of the theft, Gage ordered Admiral Graves to dispatch two ships for Portsmouth, which after pounding through a brutal winter storm, arrived too late to be of any help.

But as it turned out, the patriots had been misinformed. Gage had not yet decided to provoke another powder alarm in Portsmouth. If New Hampshire governor Wentworth was to be believed, many local patriots began to regret the haste with which they'd responded to Revere's alarm as the magnitude of what they'd done started to sink in. If Gage had been so inclined, the two warships now anchored beside Portsmouth could have destroyed the town with their cannons.

It was a change of heart that was detectable throughout New England in the early winter of 1775. All fall the patriots had been on a violent spree as angry crowds forced mandamus councillors to renounce their crown-appointed positions. To be fair, some of the crowds' actions were largely symbolic. In the town founded by the Pilgrims in 1620, the famed Plymouth Rock (or at least a piece of it) was extracted from the waterfront and placed in a spot of honor on the town's main street. In Taunton, a flag that read "Liberty and Union" was hoisted on a 112-foot liberty pole (a branchless alternative to Boston's Liberty Tree that had become popular throughout the colonies). But there were also more than a few instances of needless cruelty.

In the fall of 1774, a thirty-one-year-old farmer named Jesse Dunbar made the mistake of buying an ox from a mandamus councillor in Marshfield named Nathaniel Ray Thomas. Soon after Dunbar had slaughtered the ox at his farm in Plymouth, he was visited by a committee of patriots. Claiming that he had violated the boycott against buying British goods, the patriots loaded the dead ox on a cart and stuffed Dunbar into its eviscerated body. The patriots proceeded to take Dunbar and the ox on a tour of the surrounding towns. By the time they reached Kingston, Dunbar was having difficulty breathing inside the fetid carcass. When he was allowed to walk beside the cart, however, the crowd accused him of intentionally tripping a child and stuffed him back into the ox. In Duxbury, the crowd pushed the animal's slippery innards in Dunbar's face before finally dumping him and the ox in front of Thomas's house in Marshfield.

By the winter, as the once-raging fires of patriot anger began to die down, a backlash of sorts commenced. On December 22, 1774, Timothy Ruggles, a veteran of the French and Indian War and a mandamus councillor from Hardwick, sent a proclamation to the newspapers calling for a loyalist resistance movement among the patriot-dominated towns outside Boston. What he called the "Association" included the pledge, "We will upon all occasions, with our lives and fortunes, stand by and assist each other in the defense of life, liberty, and property whenever the same shall be attacked or endangered by any bodies of men, riotously assembled upon any pretence, or under any authority not warranted by the laws of the land." The Taunton lawyer Daniel Leonard began a series of articles under the byline Massachusettensis that so effectively questioned the legitimacy of the patriot movement that John Adams, just back from the Continental Congress, felt compelled to respond as Novanglus. In a January 18, 1775, letter to Lord Dartmouth, Gage claimed that thanks to Leonard "the absurdity of the resolves of the Continental Congress [had been] exposed in a masterly manner." Now that the people had had the "leisure of reflection and think seriously of their danger," they had become, Gage reported, "terrified at what they have done."

Nine days later, Gage was pleased to inform Dartmouth "that the towns in this province become more divided, notwithstanding the endeavors used to keep up their enthusiasm." In Marshfield, the home of Nathaniel Ray Thomas, the mandamus councillor who had sold Jesse Dunbar the ox, and one of the few towns in Massachusetts where there were more loyalists than patriots, the citizens requested that Gage send a battalion of regulars to defend them from the militiamen of the surrounding towns. Gage gladly dispatched one hundred soldiers under the command of Captain Nesbitt Balfour, who took up residence in the buildings associated with Thomas's large estate, and Marshfield became one of the few loyalist outposts beyond Boston in Massachusetts.

Even in once-belligerent Worcester, the patriot movement was showing distressing signs of infighting and waning momentum. "[We] are in a most lamentable situation . . . ," Ephraim Doolittle wrote John Hancock. "Our Tory enemies using all their secret machinations to divide us and break us to pieces. . . . I fear if we are not soon called to action we shall be like a rope of sand and have no more strength."

By the beginning of the new year, Gage had long since been joined by his wife Margaret and the rest of their extended family, which included his adjutant and brother-in-law Stephen Kemble. The extraordinarily capable engineer Captain John Montresor helped oversee the building of the fortifications at the town entrance, which by January had been finished off with a coat of whitewash. One of Gage's most trusted associates was the Swiss-born General Frederick Haldimand, who had recently arrived from New York and taken up residence in a house near the common.

In an incident that started in a way reminiscent of what had proved to be John Malcom's undoing, Haldimand was approached by a "committee" of boys who complained that his servant had thrown ashes on the coasting, or sledding, path that ran past his house. Slipping into the patriot rhetoric of the day, the boys explained that "their fathers before them had improved it as a coast from time immemorial" and requested that the snow and ice in front of the general's house be returned to its former state. Haldimand was happy to oblige, and when he later told Gage of the encounter, his commander wearily responded that "it was impossible to beat the notion of liberty out of the people, as it was rooted in 'em *from their childhood*."

Gage received much criticism that winter from both sides. Many of the patriots viewed him as the hated tool of the North administration, while his own officers dismissed him as "an old woman" who pandered unnecessarily to the townspeople. Gage realized that the simmering tension between the soldiers and Bostonians could explode at any moment into a bloody act of violence that might spark a war. Since he could always discipline his own troops, the townspeople were his chief concern, and he made every effort to address their demands, however irritating and seemingly inconsequential. Since this took up a disproportionate amount of his time, he proved less available to the many mandamus councillors who had been forced to take up residence in the city. John Andrews commented that while Gage was "always ready to attend to" the selectmen and other community leaders, "the poor refugee councilors are obliged to walk the entry [of Province House] for hours before they can be admitted to audience." Inevitably contributing to Gage's coolness to the councillors was their reluctance to testify against the patriot leaders, and Andrews was convinced that Gage secretly "despises them from his heart."

Gage's relationship with Admiral Graves was also less than ideal. The frosty decorum that existed between the two commanders in the summer quickly degenerated in December with the arrival of several hundred marines under the command of Major John Pitcairn. The marines existed in a kind of jurisdictional netherworld between the army and the navy (John Andrews claimed they exemplified the worst attributes of both), and Graves, who was as volatile and outspoken as Gage was courteous, objected to the general's insistence that the marines remain under his sole control. When later in the winter Graves's blockade turned away a vessel with much-needed supplies for the soldiers stationed in Boston, even the mild-mannered Gage had difficulty controlling his temper.

Some observers attributed the acrimony between the two leaders to their wives, who, like their husbands, vied for dominance within the increasingly circumscribed world of Boston. In addition to being beautiful, Margaret was reported to be strong-willed, and one British officer even claimed that Thomas Gage "was governed by his wife." Another officer reported that a ball held on January 11 was the result of a subscription scheme "proposed by Mrs. Gage and carried into execution by her favorites by which she enjoyed a dance and opportunity of seeing her friends at no expense." Despite the plight of thousands of British soldiers and sailors who suffered from insufficient supplies of food and terrible living conditions, the officers continued to enjoy the finer things in life.

On February 27 both the Gages and the Graveses attended a ball to which "a great number of the gentlemen and ladies of the town" were also invited. This may have been the event described late in life by Bostonian Hannah Mather Crocker, who had vivid memories of the women's sumptuous clothes as they glided across the dance floor to the rhythm of a minuet or rigadoon: "Two or three tiers of ruffles on the gown and works of lace and muslin, long ruffles double or triple, the hair powdered white. . . . And all was harmony and peace as the tiptoe step [of the ladies] was scarcely heard, so lightly did they skim along the floor. . . . The gentlemen's dress . . . was neat and elegant: a white broadcloth coat with the silver basket button [and] silver vellum trimmed buttonhole on blue cloth with gold vellum, satin waistcoat and small cloths with gold or silver knee bands. . . . A handsome worked ruffle around the hand formed a fop complete." For Crocker, who as a little girl had witnessed the destruction of her relative Thomas Hutchinson's house in the North End, what she called "The Last Queen's Ball" marked the sad and inevitable end of an era.

The previous fall, the Provincial Congress had formed the Committee of Safety, which in the absence of a governor assumed many of the province's executive responsibilities as Massachusetts prepared for possible war. John Hancock was the committee's chairman, but Joseph Warren quickly distinguished himself as its most active member. One of the committee's immediate concerns was creating an adequate stockpile of military stores for a projected army of fifteen thousand men. That winter, large amounts of goods and materials made their way to the town of Concord: 4 brass fieldpieces, 2 mortars, 15,000 canteens, 1,000 tents, 10 tons of lead balls, 300 bushels of peas and beans, 20 hogsheads of rum, 20 hogsheads of molasses, 1,000 hogsheads of salt, 150 quintals of fish, 1,000 pounds of candles, 20 casks of raisins, 20 bushels of oatmeal, 1,500 yards of Russian linen, 15 chests of medicine, and 17,000 pounds of salt cod. John Andrews ascribed the high food prices in Boston that winter to the incredible amount of provisions stored not just in Concord but "in every town in the country."

Since the colony's inhabitants were not about to donate these supplies, funds had to be collected to finance their purchase. In the fall, the Provincial Congress had appointed a treasurer to collect the taxes that would have otherwise been paid to a crown-supported government. To no one's surprise, the collection of funds lagged well behind what they had previously been. It was to be a persistent problem: everyone wanted liberty, it seemed, but far fewer were willing to pay for the army that might be required to win that liberty.

In the winter of 1775, Joseph Warren was in desperate need of funds to purchase the provincial army's medical supplies. Despite having a flourishing medical practice, he was, he admitted, "much in need of cash." So he approached his three brothers about donating "a large portion of their small paternal estate" to the cause. That apparently not being enough, Warren had no qualms about approaching his younger brother John, who owed him money for his medical education. John had just started practicing medicine in Salem, and despite the fact that he was barely making ends meet, his older brother asked him to take out a loan for the not-inconsiderable sum of two hundred pounds. Unlike Joseph Warren, who had a history of running through vast sums of money, John had an "abhorrence of debt" and balked at the request. That did not prevent Warren from not so gently asking once again, and in April he purchased from the Boston apothecary John Greenleaf five chests of medical supplies at fifty pounds each with cash that may or may not have come from his younger brother John.

Warren was not a man of moderation; everything in his astoundingly varied life—from his family and loved ones, to his medical practice, to being grand master of the St. Andrew's Masonic Lodge—had become caught up in the push for American liberty. By that winter, what was already for Warren a somewhat injudicious intermingling of private and public worlds became even more complicated when it was revealed that one of the people they all trusted was a spy.

As early as November, Paul Revere was approached by someone whom he described as having "connections with the Tory party but was a Whig at heart." This unnamed patriot with ties to the loyalists was, in all probability, the twenty-four-year-old bookseller Henry Knox, who had recently married the dark-haired and beautiful Lucy Flucker, daughter of the province's secretary, Thomas Flucker. Knox's marriage to a member of Boston's loyalist aristocracy may have given him access to the inner workings of the Gage administration, but there was also his bookstore on Cornhill. Frequented by officers of both the British army and navy, the London Bookstore reflected Knox's personal interest in military matters (he was an officer in the town's artillery company), and Knox often found himself in conversation with some of Gage's intimates. At one point he overheard a naval officer revealing that the sailors aboard His Majesty's ships in Boston "were grown so uneasy and tumultuous, that it was with great difficulty they could govern them." The army officer he was talking to responded that they were having, if anything, even more trouble with the soldiers. By January, this tidbit of information was being repeated by patriots throughout Boston and beyond.

That fall, the patriots had formed a secret committee composed of around thirty men—mostly artisans and mechanics and including Paul Revere—who kept a watchful eye on the movements of the British. The mechanics met regularly at the Green Dragon Tavern and reported their findings to Warren, Hancock, Samuel Adams, Benjamin Church, and a handful of others. Knox informed Revere that the "meetings were discovered," and as proof, repeated almost word for word what had been said during a meeting at the Green Dragon just the night before. Revere and the others tried changing the venue of their meetings, but soon discovered that "all our transactions were communicated to Governor Gage."

Knox also revealed that even the supposedly secret proceedings of the Provincial Congress were known to his father-in-law. "It was then a common opinion," Revere wrote, "that there was a traitor in the Provincial Congress, and that Gage was possessed of all their secrets." The question was who.

By the winter of 1775 the core group of patriot leaders had spent an intense, emotionally exhausting decade together; they were markedly different sorts of people, but they were all part of a political brotherhood that had come to define their lives. None of them appears to have wanted to face the possibility that there was a Judas in their midst.

They knew that Gage (as had Hutchinson before him) had made overtures to just about all of them. Joseph Warren appears to have genuinely liked the general, and in a letter written to Josiah Quincy in late November even admitted to having had several "private conversations" with Gage, whom he described as "a man of honest, upright principles, and one desirous of accommodating the difference between Great Britain and her colonies in a just and honorable way." If this was true, wasn't it possible to claim that leaking supposed secrets to the British might actually work to the patriots' advantage if the information allowed the two sides to come to a mutually beneficial resolution?

Back in 1768, as master of the St. Andrew's Masonic Lodge, Warren had shown a willingness to reach out to the British regulars who had recently arrived in Boston. Up until that point, Warren's efforts to elevate St. Andrew's to grand lodge status had been stymied by Boston's older and more well-to-do St. John's Masonic Lodge, whose members had shown nothing but scorn for the upstart rival. By forming a temporary alliance with the British soldiers who were masons, Warren was able to gain the support he needed to put his own lodge on an equal footing with St. John's. Never losing sight of his ultimate goal, Warren had forged a successful partnership with those who, by all rights, should have been his enemies.

Eight years later, Warren demonstrated a similar pragmatism in his willingness to confide in Thomas Gage. In fact, after events came to a violent head at Lexington and Concord, Warren wrote to Gage and essentially apologized for not having told him more. "I have many things which I wish to say to your Excellency," he wrote, "and most sincerely wish I had broken through the formalities which I thought due to your rank, and freely have told you all I knew or thought of public affairs; and I must ever confess, whatever may be the event, that you generously gave me such an opening as I now think I ought to have embraced." In the winter of 1775 Gage and the patriots were not yet at war; they were in the midst of a most problematic swirl of ever-changing events, and no one knew where they were headed. For those such as Warren, who honestly wanted relations between the colonies and the mother country to be set right, speaking openly with the other side was not necessarily wrong, and this may have, in part, contributed to their unwillingness to identify the traitor among them.

The fact remained, however, that there *was* a traitor, and his name was Dr. Benjamin Church.

Church's profession was perfectly suited to being a spy. Only a doctor could meet with a nonstop parade of people from all walks of life without creating suspicion. He was one of the few physicians in New England who had been trained in Europe, and he possessed a cosmopolitan haughtiness that he seems to have used to good effect amid the stodgy provincials of Boston. When asked why he socialized with so many loyalists, he claimed to be using them for his own political purposes. The force of Church's judgmental, often audacious personality seems to have put almost everyone on the defensive and allowed him to meet regularly with those who could have easily provided Gage with Church's detailed reports.

His father of the same name was one of Boston's foremost auctioneers; his great grandfather of the same name had been a famous Indian fighter during King Philip's War. The original Benjamin Church had mastered the strategy of using captured Indian warriors against their own people. In his narrative of the war, which had been recently reissued with engravings by Paul Revere, Church insisted that he'd followed the only course that could have turned the conflict around for the English. He also admitted to having qualms about what he'd done. One wonders whether his great-grandson was ever troubled by similar concerns about the morality of his actions.

Dr. Benjamin Church may not have been the most likable of men, but when one reads the reports he filed with Gage, one is impressed not by the cagey duplicity of the writer but by the objectivity—even honesty—of his observations. Indeed, he almost seems to have been performing the exact service that Joseph Warren later wished *he* had provided. And since no transcripts are known to exist of the debates of the Provincial Congress, Church's reports, which remained among Gage's personal papers for close to 150 years before they were finally discovered in the archives of the Clements Library in Ann Arbor, Michigan, are the best record we have of what the patriots were thinking in the winter of 1775.

On March 4, Church wrote, "A disposition to oppose the late parliamentary measures is become general. The parent of that disposition is a natural fondness for old custom and a jealousy [i.e., suspicion] of sinister designs on the part of the administration." He attributed the "irresolute" workings of the Provincial Congress to "the discordant sentiments of their oracular leaders, partly from the weakness of the executive power of that body and partly from an inadequate knowledge in conducting their novel enterprise." Various proposals to assume the old charter or form a military government had been rejected because "it would amount to a declaration of independency and revolt and thereby preclude the possibility of a peaceable accommodation." The other concern was that such potentially radical actions "might produce a schism or rather give encouragement to some lukewarm brethren in other provinces to detach themselves from the present combination." Church reported that the delegates had appointed generals to lead a possible provincial army and that if hostilities should commence, "the first opposition would be irregular, impetuous, and incessant from the numerous bodies that would swarm to the place of action and all actuated by an enthusiasm wild and ungovernable." That said, the militiamen could be counted on, Church wrote, to fight with a lethal effectiveness: "The most natural and most eligible mode of attack on the part of the people is that of detached parties of bushmen who from their adroitness in the habitual use of the firelock suppose themselves sure of their mark of 200 [yards]." These remarkably prophetic words were written a month and a half before the first shots were fired at Lexington Green.

That Gage was reading these espionage reports, which included dispatches from several other spies, is indicated by the fact that in February he sent a battalion of troops under the command of Lieutenant Colonel Alexander Leslie to capture the cannons that were reported to be in Salem. As in the earlier Powder Alarm, the soldiers were transported by water, but unlike that operation, the effort of Leslie's battalion was unsuccessful, not because of misinformation on the part of Church or the other informants, but because the quick-witted locals used a raised drawbridge to delay the regulars' arrival in Salem until the armaments had been moved.

Gage also employed his own soldiers as spies. At the end of February he sent out two officers disguised as surveyors to scout out the roads to Worcester. Equipped with reddish handkerchiefs, brown-colored clothes, and sketch pads, they created maps and drawings of the countryside. They observed the militia practicing on the town common in Framingham. They found occasional respite in the households of a handful of loyalists, but for the most part they were under almost constant scrutiny by the many suspicious patriots they encountered and in several instances were forced to flee for their lives. When they returned to Boston after a night at a loyalist's tavern in Weston, some of the first British officers they saw were Generals Gage and Haldimand and their aides-de-camp, inspecting the fortifications on the Neck. The two spies had so effectively adapted themselves to the alien world of patriot New England that not until they had reintroduced themselves did Gage and even some of their close friends finally recognize who they were.

Josiah Quincy Jr. was engaged in another kind of reconnaissance. For most Americans, England was an abstraction: a mythical homeland that despite its geographic distance from America remained an almost obsessive part of their daily lives. Quincy, along with many other patriot leaders, had been under the impression that the mother country was bloated, dissolute, and weak with rot. Almost immediately upon his arrival in Plymouth, however, he was distressed to discover that he had completely underestimated the strength of the British Empire. "My ideas of the riches and powers of this great nation," he wrote in his diary after a tour of the naval docks, "are increased to a degree I should not have believed if it had been predicted [to] me." When he reached London on November 17, he wrote, "The numbers, opulence &c, of this great city far surpass all I had imagined. My ideas are upon the wreck, my astonishment amazing."

On November 19, after meeting Benjamin Franklin, who became an intimate friend over the course of the next few months, Quincy found himself in the presence of Lord North. Quincy was one of Boston's foremost lawyers and had been part of the patriot inner circle for years, but he was an ingenue when it came to the British ministry. North was as seasoned and artful a politician as the Empire possessed, and he spoke with Quincy for two hours. Ingratiating and surprisingly respectful, North succeeded in getting Quincy to speak his mind even as the prime minister conveyed his determination "to effect the submission of the colonies." When Quincy blamed the current problems on "gross misrepresentation and falsehood" on the part of former governor Thomas Hutchinson, North replied that "very honest [men] frequently gave a wrong state of matters through mistake, prejudice, prepossessions and bypasses of one kind or other." Quincy, who wrote of how "much pleasure" his conversation with the prime minister gave him, seems to have failed to realize that North's statement could also apply to himself. In a subsequent conversation with Hutchinson, who was also in London at the time, the prime minister described Quincy as "designing to be artful without abilities to conceal his design."

North seems to have underestimated the young American lawyer. Quincy may have lacked the polish of a ministry veteran, but he demonstrated a refreshing ability to listen and learn as he sometimes fumbled his way through the complex and essentially foreign world of the British political system. On November 24, he spoke for an hour and a half with Lord Dartmouth; on November 29, he witnessed the grand procession of the king ("I was not awestruck with the pomp," he wrote); on December 16, he went to the House of Commons (where he "heard Lord North explain what he meant when he said he would have America at his feet"); on January 1, he conversed with Colonel Isaac Barré, who despite being a friend to America had voted for the Port Bill and was offended by some of Quincy's remarks; and on January 20, in what proved to be the highlight of his trip to London, he attended the debates in the House of Lords and watched as Lord Chatham (whom Quincy compared to "an old Roman Senator") spoke eloquently on the colonies' behalf. All the while, Quincy was in discussions with a host of patriot-sympathizers, many of whom insisted that it was time for Massachusetts to act.

Quincy, along with just about all political observers of the time, including Benjamin Franklin, was unaware of the extent to which Lord North had moved beyond the hard-line posturing of the last few months. It was true that on February 2, he had declared in Parliament that Massachusetts was now in a state of rebellion. He was also pushing forward yet another Coercive Act directed at shutting down the coastal fishery upon which New England depended. But he also had hit upon a seemingly counterintuitive idea that he believed would solve everything. Britain should refrain altogether from directly taxing America and allow each colony to determine on its own how to pay for the costs associated with its defense and civil government. Known as his "Conciliatory Proposition," this plan represented a way for Britain to offer America an important concession without completely compromising its own authority. Thomas Hutchinson was so encouraged by the proposal that on February 22 he wrote his son back in Massachusetts, "I hope peace and order will return to you before the summer is over, and that I shall return before winter."

Parliament, however, was in no mood for conciliation. Many members were confused and frustrated by North's sudden change of direction and gave the proposal little credence. But perhaps the biggest obstacle to finding a solution was the communication lag between Britain and her colonies. A ship took about a month to cross the Atlantic with news from America. When combined with the time required for the king and his ministry to work out a Parliament-approved response to each new development in Massachusetts, plus the extra month required to get that response back to America, misunderstandings between the British Empire and her increasingly indignant colonies were unavoidable. After a decade of building tension, Britain and Massachusetts had been reduced to shouting at each other across a vast and storm-tossed sea.

By the end of February, Quincy had decided that he must return home to Boston and communicate everything he had learned to Samuel Adams and Joseph Warren. Back in December, he had begun to spit up blood, and Franklin feared that his "zeal for the public . . . will eat him up." Franklin was also troubled by Quincy's growing conviction that war had become the only alternative. In early March, after the two talked long into the night, Franklin succeeded in convincing Quincy that caution, not a reckless need for action, was the best policy. "I was charmed," Quincy recorded. "I renounced my own opinion. I became a convert to his. . . . This interview may be a means of preventing much calamity and producing much good to Boston and the Massachusetts Bay, and in the end to all America." Although more than three thousand miles away in London, Quincy was being whipsawed by the same opposing opinions that were then being voiced on the floor of the Provincial Congress in Concord.

The day before his departure, Quincy had one last interview with Franklin, who asserted, "By no means take any step of great consequence (unless on a sudden emergency) without advice of the Continental Congress." As long as Massachusetts was able to avoid outright violence for the next year and a half and America adhered to the nonimportation agreement, Franklin believed that Parliament must be forced to relent and "the day is won."

On March 4, suffering from "fever and spasms" and still spitting up blood, Quincy sailed for New England. Throughout his stay in London he had been writing to his wife Abigail, who had given birth to a daughter just before he left for England. Their son Josiah had turned three in February. If all went well, Quincy would be in Boston by the middle of April.

March 5, the fifth anniversary of the Boston Massacre, was a Sunday, so the annual oration was delayed to Monday. Almost everyone in Boston—including Gage, who put the regiments on alert that day—expected trouble. The already harassed regulars were inevitably going to resent an oration whose very purpose was, in the words of Samuel Adams, "to commemorate a massacre perpetuated by soldiers and to show the danger of standing armies." Even though he had already delivered a Massacre Day Oration three years ago, Dr. Joseph Warren was asked to do it again. If there was trouble, Samuel Adams wanted someone of Warren's experience and resolve in the pulpit.

March 6 was exceptionally warm, with the temperature in the mid-fifties. At 10:00 a.m., Bostonians began to file into the Old South Meetinghouse, and before long the pews were crowded with people, some of them British officers. Expecting them "to beat up a breeze," Adams invited the officers to sit in the pews directly in front of the pulpit so that they "might have no pretence to behave ill, for it is a good maxim in politics as well as war to put and keep the enemy in the wrong." This put the soldiers uncomfortably close to the many leading patriots in attendance, which included Samuel Adams (the meeting's moderator), John Hancock, Benjamin Church, town clerk William Cooper (brother of the minister Samuel Cooper), and the Boston selectmen. The estimated thirty to forty British officers were not only sitting in pews; some, it was said, were seated on the steps leading up to the pulpit, which had been draped in black cloth. Surrounding the officers and town dignitaries were at least five thousand townspeople. A soldier claimed that every man in this immense crowd held "a short stick or bludgeon in his hand." "It is certain both sides were ripe for it," First Lieutenant Frederick Mackenzie recorded in his diary, "and a single blow would have occasioned the commencement of hostilities." "Every person was silent," another witness remembered, "and every countenance seemed to denote that some event of consequence might be expected."

Around eleven o'clock, a one-horse chaise containing Warren and a servant could be heard clattering down Cornhill to Marlborough Street. Rather than immediately entering the meetinghouse, they disappeared into the apothecary's across the street. One observer noticed that the servant held a bundle in his hands.

A few minutes later, Warren emerged, dressed in what was described as a "Ciceronian toga." It was an outrageous act of dramatic symbolism. A toga— a twenty-foot-long piece of cloth that is folded and wrapped around the wearer's body, its outer edge draped over the left shoulder—was what was worn by a citizen of Rome and distinguished him from a soldier and a slave. At Harvard, Warren had performed the play *Cato* with his classmates. In that play, Cato, the devout republican who courageously opposes Caesar's tyranny, speaks inspiringly of the sacredness of liberty. On March 6, 1775, Warren, clad in a toga, was about to perform before both his fellow townspeople and the soldiers who had made Boston a city of occupation.

Since the aisles of the meetinghouse were jammed with people, Warren was taken around to the back of the building, where he was able to access the pulpit from a rear window, making an entrance almost as dramatic as when he had burst through the open window of a Harvard dorm room. He stood before his audience in "a Demosthenian posture," a loyalist reported, "with a white handkerchief in his right hand, and his left hand in his breeches." For the vast majority of those present, Warren's evocative histrionics intensified the already surging emotions of the moment. For those who did not share in his point of view, however, Warren's antics were downright juvenile, and he was, the loyalist wrote, "groaned at by people of understanding." Warren began to speak with the high-pitched nasal delivery that had been a staple of New England ministers since the early seventeenth century, and one loyalist commented derisively on his "true puritanical whine."

But the speech that might have been an incendiary taunt directed at the British soldiers turned out to be surprisingly respectful of all those present. When Warren talked about what had happened on March 5, 1770, he did not dwell on the savagery of the soldiers; instead he focused on the agony and despair of the families who had lost loved ones that night. As many of those gathered there in the Old South Meetinghouse knew, Warren had lost a father in his youth, and he seems to have drawn upon the traumatic memories of his younger brothers when he told of a widow and her children witnessing the final death throes of a husband and parent. "Come widowed mourner," Warren melodramatically intoned, "here satiate thy grief; behold the murdered husband gasping on the ground, and to complete the pompous show of wretchedness, bring in each hand thy infant children to bewail their father's fate. Take heed, ye orphan babes, lest, whilst your streaming eyes are fixed upon the ghastly corpse, your feet glide on the stones bespattered with your father's brain." This was a scene made not from the empty political rhetoric of the day but from the darkest collective memories of the Warren family.

When he did mention the soldiers, he was sure to offer them a backhanded compliment that also served as a kind of warning. Just as Peter the Great had learned "the art of war" from King Charles of Sweden, only to use that knowledge to defeat his former mentor, so were the people of Boston taking careful note of the soldiers' exercises on the common. "The exactness and beauty of their discipline," he said, no doubt with a nod to the officers assembled around him, "inspire our youth with ardor in the pursuit of military knowledge."

At one point during the speech, a captain of the Royal Welch Fusiliers who was seated on the stairs near the pulpit responded with a warning of his own. He held up his hand; arranged on his open palm were several lead bullets. Not missing a beat, Warren dropped his white handkerchief onto the officer's hand.

It was the ideal time for Warren to launch into a paragraph he appears to have added at the last minute. "An independence of Great Britain is not our aim," he insisted. "No, our wish is that Britain and the colonies may, like the oak and the ivy, grow and increase in strength together." What they all wanted was that this "unnatural contest between a parent honored and a child beloved" result in long-lasting peace. "But if these pacific measures are ineffectual," Warren cautioned, "and it appears that the only way to safety is through fields of blood, I know you will not turn your faces from your foes, but will, undauntedly, press forward, until tyranny is trodden under foot, and you have fixed your adored goddess Liberty . . . on the American throne."

Not until after Warren had finished did the excitement begin. Once the applause had died down, Samuel Adams rose from his seat and, standing beside the pulpit, proclaimed that the thanks of the town should be extended to Warren "for his elegant and spirited oration and that another oration should be delivered on the fifth of March next to commemorate the bloody massacre of the fifth of March 1770." The use of the word *massacre* immediately drew a response from the officers, many of whom began to hiss while others shouted, "Oh fie! Oh fie!"

Bostonians in the eighteenth century had a decidedly different accent from the British, especially when it came to the pronunciation of the letter *r*. Instead of "Fie!" they heard the officers shouting "Fire!" Mistakenly fearing that the meetinghouse was about to be consumed in flames, they began to run for the doors as others leaped out the first-story windows. Adding to the "great bustle" inside the church was the sudden appearance of the Forty-Third Regiment, its fife and drums blaring, outside the front door. Many of the patriot leaders gathered around the podium became convinced that the regulars had come to arrest them and hurriedly joined the general exodus out of the meetinghouse.

As it turned out, the soldiers had just returned from a brief march into the countryside and had no interest in what was going on inside the Old South. As the regiment continued down the street and the people inside the meetinghouse came to the realization that there was no fire, Samuel Adams called them back to order. After conducting what little business remained, the meeting was adjourned.

As had occurred in Cambridge during the Powder Alarm in September, at Fort William and Mary in Portsmouth in December, and in Salem as recently as February, when Lieutenant Colonel Leslie attempted to seize the patriots' cannons, an outbreak of deadly violence had somehow been averted. One could only wonder when and where the next crisis might arise.

Instead of bloodshed, the British officers chose to respond to Warren's Massacre Day Oration with ridicule. On Thursday, March 9, Thomas Ditson, a farmer from the town of Billerica, tried to buy a musket from one of the soldiers. After cheating him out of his money, the regulars did unto the patriot yokel what the patriots had been doing to the loyalists. They seized Ditson, coated him with tar and feathers, and to the outrage of the inhabitants, paraded him through the streets of town. Soon after, a delegation from Billerica complained to Gage, who pretended, at least, to be equally upset.

Almost a week later, on Wednesday, March 15, the day of the much-ballyhooed publication of Warren's speech, the regulars countered with an oration of their own. What John Andrews described as "a vast number of officers" assembled on King Street, where they conducted a mock town meeting that chose a moderator and seven selectmen. This group of dignitaries then proceeded into the nearby British Coffee House, where they soon appeared on the balcony overlooking the street. Among them was the orator, who instead of a white toga, wore "a black gown with a rusty grey wig and fox tail hanging to it." This was the loyalist physician Thomas Bolton from Salem, who began to read an oration that may have been written by the turncoat Benjamin Church, who is one of the handful of patriot leaders not mentioned in this biting and contemptuous screed.

Where Warren had started his oration by insisting that his own words could not match those of the previous Massacre Day orators—"You will not now expect the elegance, the learning, the fire, the enrapturing strains of eloquence which charmed you when a Lovell, a Church, or a Hancock spake," he had humbly begun—Bolton immediately went for the jugular. "I cannot boast the ignorance of Hancock," he sardonically insisted, "the insolence of Adams, the absurdity of Rowe, the arrogance of Lee, the vicious life and untimely death of Molineux, the turgid bombast of Warren, the treason of Quincy, the hypocrisy of Cooper, nor the principles of Young."

The oration was a masterwork of character assassination. Hancock was "resolved to make a public attempt to become a monarch." He was also a notorious ladies' man, whose numerous paramours included the "cook maid Betty Price." William Molineux, Bolton claimed, had "through the strength of his own villainy and the laudanum of Doctor Warren . . . quitted this planet and went to a secondary one in search of liberty." Warren was such a boring speaker, Bolton insisted, that most of his listeners were asleep by the time he had finished his oration. Thomas Young was an atheist, and Dr. Samuel Cooper, besides "prostituting his religion" by preaching rebellion instead of "holy writ," was guilty of adultery. The patriots might claim they were on the side of righteousness, but in actuality they were conniving, carnal, and egotistical.

Bolton lampooned John Rowe for having speculated about how tea and salt water might mix, and Rowe was indignant. "This day an oration was delivered by a dirty scoundrel . . . ," he recorded in his diary, "wherein many characters were unfairly represented and much abused and mine among the rest." Even normally even-tempered John Andrews was miffed: "A person must [be] more than a stoic to prevent his irascibility rising."

In truth, the patriots were no different from any group of people. All of them were flawed, and all of them had something to hide. Benjamin Church, who may or may not have had a hand in writing the mock oration, was doing his best to conceal that he was financially overextended and had at least one mistress—not to mention the fact that he was a spy for the British. That winter Isaiah Thomas, publisher of the *Massachusetts Spy*, suffered the indignity of watching his wife, Mary, conduct a very public affair with the young and dashing Major Benjamin Thompson. In addition to being an already married officer in the New Hampshire militia, Thompson, like Benjamin Church, later proved to be a spy for Thomas Gage. Perhaps using the affair as a way to learn more about the patriots' increasingly clandestine activities, Thompson took Mary Dill Thomas on a trip to Portsmouth and back in which they spent no less than five nights together in as many taverns and guesthouses. In divorce papers he filed two years later, Thomas recounted how his wife had defiantly told him that she "would roast in hell rather than give [Thompson] up."

The affair was unsavory and no doubt embarrassing for Thomas, but at least he could claim that he had done nothing wrong. Such was not the case, however, when it came to the carefully guarded secret held by Dr. Joseph Warren.

March 30 was sunny and very cold, with a few showers of wispy snow, as noted by Dr. Nathaniel Ames of Dedham in his diary. He also recorded that he traveled to Boston that day to visit his good friend Joseph Warren. Whether on March 30 or a week or so later in early April, Ames returned to the tavern he owned with a new boarder, whom he described in his account book as Warren's "fair *incognita pregnans*." The girl's name was Sally Edwards, and she was about six months pregnant. If two letters Mercy Scollay later wrote, in which she refers to Edwards as a "little hussy" and a "vixen," are any indication, Scollay did not have much sympathy for the woman's plight. Given that Sally Edwards ended up living with the same family that took in Warren's oldest daughter, Betsy, it's possible that Edwards had been a nanny for Joseph Warren's children.

There is also the possibility that Sally Edwards had become pregnant by another man, and that Warren was providing her with a discreet safe haven. In all likelihood, however, in mid- to late September 1774, when Warren was caught up in the excitement of the Powder Alarm and the Suffolk Resolves, he got a young woman named Sally Edwards pregnant.

When Mercy Scollay learned of this indiscretion is an open question. Warren's account book reveals that he treated Scollay several times in September 1774, including two visits in a single day, during which he treated her with ipecac, an emetic used until quite recently to induce vomiting after a poisonous substance has been ingested. In the eighteenth century, however, ipecac had an additional use based on the ancient belief that disease was the result of an imbalance in four essential humors: blood, phlegm, choler (or yellow bile), and black bile. Too much of any one humor created physical as well as emotional problems. For example, too much black bile meant that you suffered from melancholy; too much phlegm and you were stolid or phlegmatic. It was up to the doctor to restore the balance in the humors. Bleeding was one popular way to bring the levels back in sync, as was purgation, and ipecac was used to reduce the levels of choler through vomiting. This meant that about the time Warren may have had sexual relations with Sally Edwards, he was treating Scollay for excessive anger and irritability.

Scollay's last recorded visit to Warren's office was on March 19, 1775, and within a few weeks' time, Sally Edwards was safely tucked away at the Ames tavern in Dedham. By then, or soon after, Joseph Warren and Mercy Scollay had agreed to marry.

On March 30, the same sunny, unseasonably cold day that Dr. Nathaniel Ames traveled from Dedham to Boston, General Hugh Percy led the First Brigade on a march into the countryside. All winter, Gage had been sending the soldiers on brief forays out of Boston. They provided much-needed exercise for the regulars and accustomed the surrounding towns to having soldiers in their midst. This might prove beneficial to Gage when he launched a truly decisive move against the patriots. Lulled into a state of relative placidity by the previous exercises, the country people wouldn't realize that the operation was the real thing until it was too late.

But on March 30, that all changed when at six in the morning, Percy marched across Boston Neck with the one thousand soldiers under his command in the First Brigade. Lieutenant John Barker recorded in his diary that "it alarmed the people a good deal. Expresses were sent to every town near." What Joseph Warren described as "great numbers, completely armed" appeared on the roads around Boston. At the bridge at Cambridge, the boards were pulled up to prevent the soldiers from crossing the Charles River. At Watertown, the next town on the river beyond Cambridge, two pieces of artillery were positioned at the bridge in anticipation of the troops' arrival. No trouble occurred, however, and by 11:00 a.m., after five hours of marching through the countryside, Percy and his brigade were back in Boston. The march had been only an exercise, but given the size of the British force it could have easily turned into something much more dangerous.

At ten the next morning, the Boston Committee of Correspondence sponsored a meeting of what was known as the "little Senate," the committee representing the towns neighboring Boston, in the selectmen's chamber in Faneuil Hall to discuss the issues raised by Gage's most recent move. This meant that even as Warren was attempting to arrange matters for Sally Edwards, he was helping to formulate the policy that would govern what happened the next time Gage sent a brigade into the country.

The committee decided that since Percy's men were "without baggage or artillery," the regulars had not been out "to destroy any magazines or abuse the people" and did not therefore pose a significant threat. If the country people had attacked Percy's brigade on March 30, they might have been judged guilty of exactly the kind of reckless act of aggression that the patriot leadership wanted to avoid. So as to prevent such an "unnecessary effusion of blood," the Provincial Congress responded to the committee's recommendation by passing the following resolve: "That whenever the army . . . to the number of 500, shall march out of the town of Boston with artillery and baggage, it ought to be deemed a design to carry into execution by force the late acts of Parliament . . . [and] ought to be opposed; and therefore the military force of the province ought to be assembled, and an army of observation immediately formed, to act solely on the defensive so long as it can be justified on the principles of reason and self-preservation."

No one—neither the provincials nor Gage and his army—wanted to be judged guilty of initiating what might very well become a bloody war. Massachusetts risked losing the support of the other colonies; the king and the North administration risked losing the support of Parliament and the British people. And yet both sides were under pressure to do something more than simply wait it out. Many of the patriots feared that if nothing happened soon, an unsatisfactory compromise might be the result, and they'd be right back to where they started. Gage had spent the fall and winter doing his best to prevent an explosion of violence and was now awaiting word from

Lord Dartmouth on how he should proceed. In the meantime, even his most politically moderate officers had lost all patience with these upstart provincials. As a Whig, General Percy had been predisposed to sympathize with the New Englanders; by the winter, however, all sympathy had been lost. "The people here are the most designing, artful villains in the world," he wrote to a relative back in England. "They have not the . . . least scruple of taking the most solemn oath on any matter that can assist their purpose, though they know the direct contrary can be clearly and evidently proved in half an hour."

Percy's accusation of duplicity was about to meet a critical test. As of early April, the Provincial Congress had determined that the Committee of Safety could not issue an alarm unless the battalion of regulars was equipped with baggage and artillery. Since February, members of the Provincial Congress, most notably the lawyer Joseph Hawley, had expressed concern that an undue amount of power had been granted to the committee respecting this important issue. Given what had happened back in September with the Powder Alarm, they knew that if a battalion of soldiers ventured from Boston and another regionwide alarm was sounded, a commencement of hostilities was almost guaranteed. "When once the blow is struck," Hawley wrote to Thomas Cushing, "it must be followed, and we must conquer, or all is lost forever. . . . I beg you, therefore, as you love your country to use your utmost influence with our Committee of Safety, that the people be not mustered, and that hostilities be not commenced, until we have the express, categorical decision of the continent [i.e. the rest of the colonies] that the time is absolutely come that hostilities ought to begin."

Even Hawley realized that gaining the consent of the other colonies might prove impractical given the possible suddenness of a move on the part of Gage. To help prevent any individual or small coterie of individuals on the Committee of Safety from co-opting the agenda of the patriot movement and prematurely starting a war, Congress had already determined that the vote of five members of the Committee of Safety was required before issuing the alarm. As a further safeguard, Congress also decided that not more than one of these five members could be from Boston, thus requiring that a meeting of those members who lived outside the city be convened before the trigger was pulled. And so the Committee of Safety had its orders. Before the alarm could be sounded, three conditions must be met: first, the British force must exceed five hundred men; second, the soldiers must be equipped with baggage and artillery; third, five members of the committee must vote in favor of the alarm.

Thanks to Benjamin Church, Gage quickly learned of the Provincial Congress's resolve. Gage now knew that as long as the next group of regulars to leave Boston had no artillery or baggage, the patriots could do nothing—according to their own legislature—to oppose them. It remained to be seen whether the patriots would obey their representatives.

Part II

REBELLION

———◆———

Here's fine revolution,
an we had the trick to see 't.

—William Shakespeare, *Hamlet*

We cannot make events. Our business is wisely to *improve* them.

—Samuel Adams to the Reverend Samuel Cooper, April 30, 1776

Should the whole frame of nature round him break,
In ruin and confusion hurled,
He, unconcerned, would hear the mighty crack,
And stand secure amidst a falling world.

—Joseph Addison's translation of Horace's *Odes,* book 3, ode 3

CHAPTER SIX

The Trick to See It

On April 2, Joseph Warren received a letter from Arthur Lee, an American in London who had become a close friend of Josiah Quincy Jr. Lee had encouraged Quincy at the end of March to believe that war between America and Great Britain was inevitable. Lee's letter to Warren (written back on December 21, 1774) sounded a similarly alarmist note. In December, both houses of Parliament had voted in support of the ministry's conviction that Massachusetts was now in "actual rebellion." What's more, additional regiments were on their way to reinforce Gage's already considerable army of almost three thousand regulars. Warren seized upon the news as a reason to send out the call to the members of the Provincial Congress, many of whom had returned home, to reconvene in Concord. After a troubling winter of infighting and irresolution, this was just the news to shake the delegates out of what Warren called "that state of security into which many have endeavored to lull them."

Warren still hoped for a reconciliation with Great Britain, but this had not prevented him from doing everything possible to prepare the province for war. As a member of the Committee of Safety, he had led efforts to assemble military stores in Worcester, Concord, and other towns throughout the province. He also worked to provide some organization to the provincial "army of observation" that would take the field in the event of an incursion by the British. What's more, he had begun to prepare *himself* for a possible conflict. He might be trained as a doctor, but if it should come to war, he intended to fight.

By one account, Warren had spent the last "several years . . . preparing himself by study and observation to take a conspicuous rank in the military arrangements which he knew must ensue." His father had once told him, "I would rather a son of mine were dead than a coward," and he seems to have taken that parental directive to heart. Rather than oversee the medical side of the provincial army, he ultimately hoped to be "where wounds were to be made, rather than where they were to be healed." If glory was to be won in this possible conflict with the mother country, the place to do it was not in the Provincial Congress (of which he was now a member) or even the Continental Congress; it was on the battlefield.

Warren's biggest obstacle to achieving this goal was his own outsize talent. His seemingly limitless capacity for work, along with his unmatched ability to adapt his own actions to meet the demands of the moment, meant that as the speed of events began to increase in the days ahead, he was inevitably looked to as the person to keep the patriot cause together. Given that he was now an influential member of the Provincial Congress and of the perhaps even more powerful Committee of Safety, most assumed that his role was in government. But that is not where Warren ultimately wanted to be. He knew that if he was going to alter the preconceptions people had about him, he must prove himself as a soldier, and so in the weeks ahead he not only continued his leadership role in the Congress and the Committee of Safety: he would be present in the ranks at virtually every encounter between colonial and British forces.

Accompanying this shift in vocation was a dramatic change in attitude. In the fall Warren had worked to soothe the outrage of the country people. By the spring, he was desperately attempting to inject some life into what had become a dangerously listless Provincial Congress. "Such was his versatility," one observer recorded, "that he turned from . . . lectures of caution and prudence to asserting and defending the most bold and undisguised principles of liberty, and defying in their very teeth the agents of the crown." When one night his medical apprentice William Eustis warned him that some British officers were lurking suspiciously near his house, he announced, "I have a visit to make to a lady in Cornhill this evening and I will go at once; come with me." Warren placed two pistols in his pockets, and they went about their rounds. In another instance, Warren and Eustis overheard some officers speaking condescendingly about the military skills of the New Englanders. "These fellows say we won't fight," Warren erupted. "By heavens! I hope I shall die up to my knees in blood!"

What Eustis and other patriots took to be Warren's natural and laudatory adjustment to the increasingly perilous times was seen by the loyalists as part of a highly calculated strategy. Since it was the quickest way to achieve their secret goal of independence, Warren and his mentor Samuel Adams had been, the loyalists insisted, hoping for a war from the very beginning. Thomas Hutchinson claimed that "as [Warren] discovered a great degree of martial as

Three views of Boston drawn in 1764, the year before the passage of the Stamp Act.

Looking north from Boston's Beacon Hill across the many ropewalks at Barton's Point, with Charlestown beyond.

Looking south from Beacon Hill across Boston Common and the Back Bay, with Boston Neck curving to the right toward Roxbury.

Looking north from Long Wharf toward Boston's North End.

The cross-eyed Josiah Quincy Jr., the most articulate lawyer in Boston and a passionate patriot, died of tuberculosis before he could report on the results of a diplomatic mission to London during the winter of 1775. This portrait was painted posthumously by Gilbert Stuart. (Photograph © Museum of Fine Arts, Boston)

Some of the forceful intensity that made Samuel Adams such an effective revolutionary leader is evident in this portrait painted by John Singleton Copley soon after the Boston Massacre.
(Photograph © Museum of Fine Arts, Boston)

Sometimes referred to as "King Hancock," John Hancock had the highest public profile among Boston's patriots. This portrait was painted by Copley circa 1770–1772.

The Reverend Samuel Cooper led Boston's most affluent congregation at the Brattle Street Meeting; he was also one of Boston's leading patriots and maintained a correspondence with Benjamin Franklin in London.

King George III in 1771, four years before the eruption of violence at Lexington and Concord.

In 1771, John Singleton Copley traveled to New York, where he painted this portrait of General Thomas Gage, future royal governor of Massachusetts.

Margaret Gage's much-commented-on beauty is evident in this portrait by Copley, which the artist considered one of his finest.

Joseph Warren, dressed in the traditional black of a physician, leans on an anatomical drawing in this portrait painted by Copley in the mid-1760s. (Photograph © Museum of Fine Arts, Boston)

A Lady in a Blue Dress was painted by Copley in the early 1760s and may depict Joseph Warren's future fiancée, Mercy Scollay.

The silversmith Paul Revere, painted by Copley in 1768, the year British troops first arrived at Long Wharf.
(Photograph © Museum of Fine Arts, Boston)

The Green Dragon Tavern in Boston's North End was the home of the St. Andrew's Masonic Lodge and an important center of patriot activities in the 1770s.

Captain John Montresor was the highly skilled British engineer who oversaw the construction of the many defensive works around Boston and on the Charlestown peninsula during the siege.

The fighting at Lexington Green, the first in a series of four engravings issued by Amos Doolittle in 1775 based on interviews with eyewitnesses and careful study of the terrain.

The newly arrived British officers Colonel Francis Smith and Major John Pitcairn stand on the hill overlooking the town of Concord, studying the militiamen on Punkatasset Hill to the north.

Militiamen and British regulars collide at the North Bridge in Concord.

The flag that militiamen from the town of Bedford reputedly flew during the fighting at the North Bridge.

The fighting along the road from Lexington to Charlestown.

Some claimed that if Captain Timothy Pickering of Salem had shown the proper spirit, he and his militia company might have cut off General Percy's British regulars before they reached Charlestown.

Artemas Ward of Shrewsbury was forty-seven and suffering from an attack of kidney stones when he took command of the provincial forces after the fighting at Lexington and Concord.

John Trumbull's *Death of General Warren at the Battle of Bunker's Hill.* When Abigail Adams first saw this painting in 1786, she claimed that "my blood shivered."
(Photograph © Museum of Fine Arts, Boston)

Abigail Adams, circa 1766, ten years before she witnessed the reading of the Declaration of Independence at the State House in Boston.

Despite having been raised as a Quaker, the Rhode Islander Nathanael Greene quickly distinguished himself as one of Washington's most promising young generals. This portrait was painted by Charles Willson Peale in 1783.

OPPOSITE: Charles Willson Peale painted this portrait of George Washington around 1780. According to one observer, "There is not a king in Europe that would not look like a valet de chamber by his side."

RIGHT: By successfully transporting sixty tons of artillery from Fort Ticonderoga to Cambridge (a journey of three hundred miles), Henry Knox justified his appointment to colonel of the Continental Army's troubled artillery regiment.

The British officer J. F. W. Des Barres made this sketch of the British lines at Boston Neck in 1775.

A view of Boston from Willis Creek in Cambridge by Des Barres.

Another Des Barres sketch, showing the islands of Boston Harbor from the city's Fort Hill.

Boston from Dorchester Heights by Des Barres.

The minister Mather Byles was an unrepentant loyalist who chose to remain in Boston after the evacuation of the British. A noted punster, he called the soldier who was ordered to guard him his "observe-a-Tory."

The immense crowd that gathered on June 17, 1843, to celebrate the completion of the Bunker Hill Monument.

well as political courage," he wanted nothing less than "to become the Cromwell of North America." Peter Oliver agreed. "Conquer or die were the only alternatives with him, and he publicly declared that 'he would mount the last round of the ladder or die in the attempt'"—a particularly evocative attribution, given the fate of Warren's father.

We will never know for sure how much personal ambition influenced Warren's role in initiating the chaotic rush of events to come. But if there was anyone with the political and social skills to prosper amid the collective trauma of a revolution, it was Joseph Warren.

Upon hearing the news that more troops were headed their way, many Bostonians began to panic. Rumors flew about the city. General Percy reported that the country people planned to "set [Boston] on fire and attack the troops before reinforcement comes."

It was as if the fear that had first incapacitated Dr. Thomas Young's wife in the days after the Powder Alarm in September had lain dormant over the fall and winter and was only now, with the arrival of spring, reclaiming Boston's inhabitants. It was an extraordinary and terrifying epiphany. All the rhetoric about taxes and representation, about liberty and freedom, about the sovereignty of Parliament, was about to incite an all-consuming war that might very well start here, in the city they called home. Like Lot and his family, they had no choice but to abandon everything that they once held dear and flee for their lives.

On Tuesday, April 11, John Andrews reported that "all [is] in confusion . . . , the streets and Neck lined with wagons carrying off the effects of the inhabitants, who are either afraid, mad, crazy, or infatuated . . . , imagining to themselves that they shall be liable to every evil that can be enumerated if they tarry in town."

On Sunday, April 9, in the midst of religious services at the Brattle Street Meeting, Joseph Warren was seen conferring tensely with the Reverend Samuel Cooper. The British ministry, it was rumored, had ordered Gage to arrest Boston's leading patriots, and Cooper, who corresponded regularly with Benjamin Franklin in London, was in danger. Cooper broke off his conversation with Warren to baptize a child, but by Monday, April 10, Cooper and his wife had left Boston for a friend's house in Weston.

Samuel Adams and John Hancock were already safely removed from Boston, spending their days at the Provincial Congress in Concord and their nights at the Clarke parsonage in the nearby town of Lexington. Even though he knew Gage had the equivalent of a warrant for his arrest, Warren was determined to remain in Boston for as long as possible. In the meantime, he hastily made arrangements for Mercy Scollay, whom he now considered part of his "family," and his four children to live in Worcester, about forty miles from Boston. In a brief letter to a Dr. Dix, he explained that his furniture had already been moved to his mother's house in Roxbury, where the doctor could send some wagons to retrieve both the furniture and his loved ones for transportation to Worcester. Warren also seems to have been involved in getting both Isaiah Thomas and his printing press to the same safely removed town. It was during this period of turmoil that Warren's college friend Dr. Nathaniel Ames began billing Warren's account for boarding Sally Edwards at Ames's tavern in Dedham.

Looking back over two centuries later, we know that the patriot movement ultimately led to independence, but such an end result was by no means inevitable in the spring of 1775, when many still believed that the British government must eventually do as it had always done in response to past colonial protests and withdraw the offending legislation. At the root of the patriots' misguided optimism was their continued confidence in George III. The fiction they all clung to was that once the king saw for himself how his ministers had misled him, he would withdraw the troops and the demand for unjust taxes and allow New England to remain forever free. But, in actuality, the king was hardly the colonies' great ally, and in fact he saw more clearly than they did the possible results of their current actions. As early as November 18, 1774, he'd written Lord North, "The New England governments are in a state of rebellion. Blows must decide whether they are to be subject to this country or independent."

The last thing most patriots wanted was a war, and more than a few Bostonians now felt that they would have never willingly embarked on this journey if they had known where they were headed. His newspaper opponent John Adams might be loath to admit it, but Daniel Leonard had expressed the sentiments of many inhabitants when he compared the city's political leaders "to a false guide, that having led a benighted traveler through many mazes and windings in a thick wood, finds himself at length on the brink of a horrid precipice, and, to save himself, seizes fast hold of his follower, to utmost hazard of plunging both headlong down the steep, and being dashed in pieces together against the rocks below." This sense of disorientation and betrayal—

How did we get here in the first place?—was what many were feeling as they stuffed whatever goods would fit in a wagon and joined the long line out of Boston.

Like Joseph Warren, John Andrews resolved to remain in Boston. In recent weeks Andrews's wife Ruthy had been hard at work on a landscape sketch that Andrews proudly claimed was "equal to any copper plate that I ever saw." The drawing had even garnered praise from General Percy, "who expressed his very great admiration of it." The town might be in turmoil, but life went on in Boston, and in a letter to a relative Percy wrote of the weather. Although the last three weeks had been "cold and disagreeable, a kind of second winter," the previous months had been for the most part remarkably warm. "Thank God, I still continue to enjoy my health perfectly," Percy wrote, "and have very much surprised the inhabitants here by going constantly all winter with my bosom open without a great coat. . . . I think I have felt it colder in England."

The king had long since decided that "blows must decide" the current crisis, but not so the members of the Provincial Congress in Concord. On April 7 the spy Benjamin Church reported to Gage that the delegates were in "great consternation" and were considering a recess "to consult with their constituents." Church asked Gage whether that would be a good development from his perspective. "It would prevent their taking any hasty steps," he pointed out, while Gage waited for "his dispatches" from the ministry. Clearly, Church was well acquainted with the inner workings of both Congress and General Gage's staff. He also had some advice: "A sudden blow struck now or immediately on the arrival of the reinforcements from England should . . . overset all their plans." On April 9, he reported that despite the fact that the "people without doors are clamorous for an immediate commencement of hostilities," Congress appeared incapable of taking any "decisive measures." On Saturday, April 15, he reported that the deadlock continued and that the one item the Congress could agree on was that they should officially encourage the inhabitants of Boston to leave the city. On Tuesday, April 18, he reported that Congress was now in recess until May and that with Samuel Adams soon to leave for the Second Continental Congress in Philadelphia, Adams had left "particular directions" with Joseph Warren on "how to act."

Whether or not Church's April 7 suggestion lay behind it, Gage had begun to make preparations "for a sudden blow" as early as April 11, when the

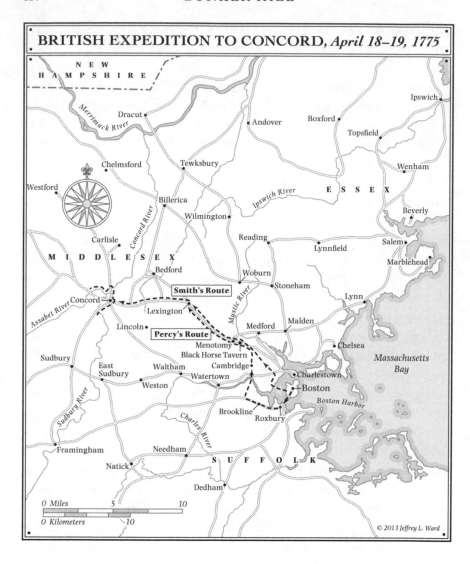

BRITISH EXPEDITION TO CONCORD, *April 18–19, 1775*

warship *Somerset* was moved up the harbor so that she lay between Boston and Charlestown, "exactly in the ferry way between the two towns." And then, on April 14, Gage finally received the long-awaited orders from Secretary of State Lord Dartmouth.

The letter had been written back on January 27, when the saber rattling of the North administration had been at its height. Although Dartmouth qualified his statements in half a dozen ways, his overall message was clear: the time had come for Gage to *do* something, since "the king's dignity and honor and safety of the empire require that . . . force should be repelled by force." If a conflict was inevitable, let it begin now, before Massachusetts entered "a riper state of rebellion." Dartmouth reported that both the king and the ministry felt that "the first and essential step" was to "arrest and imprison the principal actors and abettors" in the Provincial Congress. That said, he realized that "in a situation where everything depends so much upon the events of the day and upon local circumstances your conduct must be governed very much by your own judgment and discretion."

The irony is that by the time Gage received Dartmouth's letter, the anger of the ministry, along with that of many Massachusetts patriots, had cooled. If Gage had done nothing that spring, the patriot leaders, already beset by growing discord within their own ranks, would have had even more trouble maintaining a united front. The ministry had played perfectly into the radicals' hands when Gage finally chose to act on a letter based on information and instructions that were several months old.

But perhaps the greatest irony was that a suggestion from a British spy, not the letter from Dartmouth, seems to have initiated the series of decisions that was to have such a momentous historical impact. In the end, Gage didn't do as Dartmouth had recommended and arrest the leaders of the Provincial Congress, which would have almost certainly led to the seizure of many loyalist leaders (a response recommended in the Suffolk Resolves drafted by Joseph Warren back in September). Instead, Gage proceeded with plans to secure and destroy the military stores in Concord, which had become, thanks to being a town at the crossroads between Boston and the many settlements to the west and north, a major gathering point for patriot weapons and provisions. Church and Gage's other spies assured him that large amounts of military supplies (including the valuable brass cannons that had been spirited out of Boston back in the fall) had been accumulated in Concord; the town, about twenty miles outside of Boston, was also close enough for a detachment of regulars to march there and back in a single day—an important consideration, given the hostility of the country people. And besides, the likelihood that a company of poorly trained militiamen had the gumption to stand up to the regulars—let alone fire on them—seemed remote at best.

On April 15, the day the Provincial Congress adjourned, Gage ordered that the two elite companies of his regiments—the grenadiers (the bigger and more powerful men) and the light infantry (who were faster and more agile)—be relieved of their duties "till further orders." The supposed reason for the order was so that the soldiers might learn new "exercises and evolutions," but Lieutenant John Barker rightly guessed that "this . . . is by way of a blind. I dare say they have something for them to do."

Gage's officers were not the only ones to take notice. The patriots had been keeping careful watch on the regulars' movements since the fall and quickly realized that something was afoot. The next suspicious development was the midnight launching of boats from the decks of the transports anchored in the harbor. These were the type of small rowing vessels that had been used to take the troops up the Mystic River back in September, and the next morning they could be seen clustered at the sterns of the men-of-war. From his house on Hanover Street, Warren directed Paul Revere to ride to Lexington, where Samuel Adams and John Hancock were still living in the town's parsonage, and inform them of these ominous developments. On the way back to Boston, Revere stopped in Charlestown, where he made arrangements with the local patriots that if the troops did indeed march out of the city, he would make sure that signal lanterns were placed in the belfry of Christ Church, whose steeple was, at 191 feet, the tallest in Boston, taller, in fact, than even Beacon Hill. One lantern would mean the regulars were taking the land route out across the Neck into Roxbury; two lanterns would mean the boats had been used to row the soldiers across the Charles River to either Charlestown or Cambridge.

In an espionage report written on Tuesday, April 18, Gage received detailed information about where the stores were located in Concord. Many of the provisions were hidden in houses in the center of town; most of the military supplies were at a farmhouse on the other side of the Concord River. By the end of the day, Gage had completed the second draft of his orders for Colonel Francis Smith, who was to take a force of about seven hundred grenadiers and light infantry to Concord, destroy or capture the stores (what both sides wanted most were the cannons), and return to Boston. The soldiers were to leave that night in boats brought to the shore along the western edge of the common, and they were to be without both baggage (usually transported in wagons) and artillery. If all went well, they would be back in their barracks before nightfall of the following day.

Joseph Warren was one of the last patriot leaders still in Boston on the night of April 18. Around nine o'clock, just as the regulars began to assemble in the remote reaches of the common, he is said to have received word of the impending expedition and decided to alert the countryside that British troops were headed for Concord. The question is who told Warren where the soldiers were headed.

Gage did not inform General Percy of the expedition until that night. After his meeting with Gage, Percy was passing a group of Bostonians gathered on the common when he overheard one of them say, "They will miss their aim."

"What aim?" Percy asked.

"The cannon at Concord."

Percy turned abruptly around, rushed back to Province House, and told Gage that his supposedly clandestine mission was no longer a secret. The general was thunderstruck, claiming that besides Percy he had told only one other person.

Many have speculated as to who that person may have been. Margaret Kemble Gage is often looked to as the most likely candidate, even though there is no tangible evidence to support the supposition. The story goes that she and her husband grew apart after the events of April 1775, and Gage quickly sent her packing on a ship back to London. In fact, Margaret Gage did not leave Boston until the late summer and was soon followed by her husband. Hardly estranged from one another, the Gages would have two more children together.

In all likelihood there was no shadowy informant. Boston was too compact and crowded a town for much of anything to happen without a good portion of its residents knowing about it. Traditions have come down to us of someone who overheard a conversation between two officers on Long Wharf, of someone else who saw a battle-ready light infantryman in a Boston shop, and of yet another who spoke with a groomer in the stables of Province House who told him of the expedition. All of these things—or some versions thereof—might have happened. Earlier that afternoon about a dozen mounted officers wearing long blue coats to conceal their scarlet uniforms had left via the Neck and enjoyed a dinner at a tavern in Cambridge. Later that night, when the British officers began to take up positions on the various roads leading to Concord (so as to prevent any messengers from alerting the countryside), the ever-vigilant patriots had added evidence of where the regulars were headed. With the exception of the soldiers themselves, just about everybody in Boston seemed to know where the troops were headed that night.

Much more significant than the identity of Warren's informant is the reason Warren decided to alert the countryside. In early April the Provincial
Congress had determined that a column leaving Boston must be equipped
with baggage and artillery before it constituted a threat to the province. Congress had also determined that a vote of five members of the Committee of
Safety (only one of them being from Boston) was required before the alarm
could be sounded. Earlier that day, the committee had met at the Black Horse
Tavern in the town of Menotomy (now known as Arlington) on the way to
Concord from Cambridge. At that moment three committee members were
staying at the Black Horse, and two others were at their homes in nearby
Charlestown. Warren could have crossed the harbor, just as Paul Revere was
soon to do, and after consulting his fellow committee members helped make
what would have been, even with the committee's unanimous consent, a
controversial decision given the expedition's absence of artillery and baggage. Warren opted instead to send out the tanner William Dawes (of the
cannon-compressed shirt button) by Boston Neck and then called for Revere
and directed him to row across the harbor for Charlestown. Even before the
regulars had arrived in the marshes of Cambridge and set out for Concord,
the alarm was being sounded in towns to the west and north of Boston.

This was exactly the scenario that Joseph Hawley and the other moderates in the Provincial Congress had hoped to avoid: one influential committee
member had ignored proper protocol and set into motion the process that
made a confrontation between British regulars and the militia almost inevitable. Knowing that Samuel Adams had employed essentially the same strategy back in June when he attempted to circumvent the opposition to the
Solemn League and Covenant, one can only wonder whether he had sent an
earlier message to Warren via Paul Revere, urging him to issue the alarm
even if the criterion demanded by the Provincial Congress was not met. It's
even more probable that Warren's decision to send out the alarm was like
most decisions made during a crisis—a spontaneous reaction to a seemingly
confused rush of unexpected events. Even if the troops crossing the Charles
River were without baggage or artillery, they exceeded the five-hundred-man
threshold imposed by Congress. The possibility that Smith's troops were after
not just the military stores in Concord but also Samuel Adams and John Hancock was another concern.

What Warren did was technically wrong, but at least he had made a
decision—something the hypersensitive Gage had been struggling to do now

for weeks. Whether premeditated or spur of the moment, or a mixture of both, Warren's decision to send out Dawes and Revere rendered the debates at the Provincial Congress moot. After more than four months of preparing for the eventuality, Warren was about to have his war.

Paul Revere reached Lexington around midnight. As a precaution, a guard headed by the militia sergeant William Munroe had been posted around the house in which Samuel Adams and John Hancock were staying. Munroe and his men had been given orders to be as quiet as possible so that those inside could sleep, and when the sergeant admonished the newly arrived messenger for making too much noise, Revere erupted, "Noise! You'll have noise enough before long! The regulars are coming out!" By this point both Adams and Hancock were awake. "Come in, Revere," Hancock ordered. "We are not afraid of you."

Revere explained that he'd managed to elude two of the officers Gage had sent out to guard the road to Concord, and when Dawes arrived soon after, the patriot leaders could rest assured that the alarm these two messengers had helped to start was now—according to the system that had been previously organized by the Committee of Safety—being carried from town to town throughout Massachusetts and beyond. Warren had been concerned that in addition to the stores in Concord, the regulars were out to arrest Hancock and Adams, but as the Reverend William Gordon later related, the leaders had convinced themselves that Concord was the real aim of the British expedition.

It was a short walk from the Clarke parsonage to the Lexington Common, or Green, a crude triangle of lumpy grass formed by the intersection of the road from Boston to the east, the road to Concord to the west, and the road to Bedford to the north. In addition to some chest-high stone walls, which would later remind the regulars of the hedgerows back in England, the green was bounded by the houses of Jonathan Harrington and Daniel Harrington to the west, that of Marret Munroe to the south, and Buckman's Tavern to the east. Within the eastern tip of the green was the Lexington Meetinghouse. Rather than a bell-equipped spire, the congregation had opted for a more economical stand-alone belfry, which stood fifty yards or so to the west of the meetinghouse. Soon the bell was ringing, and by 2:00 a.m. approximately 130 members of the 144-man Lexington militia had assembled on the green under the leadership of forty-six-year-old Captain John Parker. Parker was six feet, two inches tall and the father of four girls and three boys, all between the ages of four and fourteen. He was also a veteran of the French and Indian War and had been at the Siege of Louisbourg in 1758 and with Wolfe when he had taken Quebec. He was now a farmer who lived about two miles from the center of town, and like Josiah Quincy Jr., he was dying of tuberculosis. He had had trouble sleeping the night before, and it looked as if he was going to get even less sleep tonight.

As was true in all the town militias throughout Massachusetts, this group of men knew each other intimately. Parker, it was said, was related to at least a quarter of the men gathered there that night. Of the militia's 144 members, 14 of them were Munroes, 11 were Harringtons, 10 were Smiths, 7 were Reeds, and 4 were Tidds. They lived in a tightly knit, largely self-contained community that was profoundly different from what was to be found in a typical village in England. They voted in town meetings that instilled the assumption that they had a direct say in how their government worked. Their sense of self-worth was determined not by ancient notions or protocols of class but by their ability to farm, hunt, and fight. At the center of all their lives was the Lexington Meeting, whose black-robed minister Jonas Clarke assured them that just as God had approved of their forefathers' battles with the Indians and the French, their current insistence on liberty was also divinely sanctioned. In keeping with this melding of spiritual and martial concerns, the meetinghouse—unheated and safely removed from other structures near the green—served as the town's powderhouse.

Years later, one of the militiamen who participated in the events of that day insisted that it wasn't the Tea Act or the Boston Port Bill or any of the Coercive Acts that made them take up arms against the regulars; no, it was much simpler than that. "We always had been free, and we meant to be free always," the veteran remembered. "[Those redcoats] didn't mean we should." It was a sense of freedom strengthened by the knowledge that to the west and north, and to the east in Maine, lay a wilderness that their children could one day go to as their forefathers had done when they first sailed for the New World. Nothing like this was available to the future generations of Europe. It was a sense of promise that made the militiamen's resolve to oppose these troops all the more powerful.

But to say that a love of democratic ideals had inspired these country people to take up arms against the regulars is to misrepresent the reality of the revolutionary movement. Freedom was for these militiamen a very relative term.

As for their Puritan ancestors, it applied only to those who were just like them. Enslaved African Americans, Indians, women, Catholics, and especially British loyalists were not worthy of the same freedoms they enjoyed. It did not seem a contradiction to these men that standing among them that night was the thirty-four-year-old enslaved African American Prince Estabrook, owned by town selectman and justice of the peace Benjamin Estabrook.

While Gage had honored the civil liberties of the patriots, the patriots had refused to respect the rights of those with whom they did not agree, and loyalists had been sometimes brutally suppressed throughout Massachusetts. The Revolution, if it was to succeed, would do so not because the patriots had right on their side but because they—rather than Gage and the loyalists—had the power to intimidate those around them into doing what they wanted. As one of Gage's officers observed, "The argument which the rebels employ to oblige everyone to do what they wish, is to threaten to announce them to the people as Enemies of Liberty, and everyone bends." Not since the Salem witch trials had New Englanders lived with such certainty and fear, depending on which side of the issues they found themselves.

It was cold that night on the Lexington Green, and after one of the scouts whom Parker had sent down the road to Boston reported that there was no sign of the British, the militia captain dismissed his men, telling them to be ready to reassemble at the beat of a drum. Those who lived close to the green went home, but most of them, including Parker, retired to the convivial warmth of Buckman's Tavern.

There they would remain for the next three hours. At some point, we know that John Hancock made his way to the green. At that time, Hancock was Massachusetts's leading political celebrity. Samuel Adams might be looked to as the mastermind, but Hancock was the public face of the patriot movement and would be later referred to that day as "King Hancock." He was both president of the Provincial Congress and chairman of the Committee of Safety. He also had strong ties to Lexington. Not only had he been living here for the last few weeks, his grandfather had built the house in which he was staying, and some of his youth had been spent in Lexington.

Hancock was a leading merchant and political figure, but like Joseph Warren he harbored his own military ambitions. He'd been the colonel of the Independent Company of Cadets, and after talking with the militiamen on the green (and perhaps in Buckman's Tavern), he returned to the parsonage on the road to Bedford and began sharpening his sword. According to Hancock's fiancée, Dorothy Quincy, who was also staying at the Clarke parsonage that night along with Hancock's aunt, he spoke as if he intended to join the militiamen when they reformed on the green. Adams, however, patted him on the shoulder and insisted, "That is not our business; we belong to the cabinet." When Hancock reluctantly agreed that they must "withdraw to some distant part of town," he made one final proclamation that Sergeant William Munroe still remembered fifty years later. "If I had my musket," he claimed, "I would never turn my back upon these troops."

By five in the morning, Hancock and Adams—minus Dorothy and Hancock's aunt—were in Hancock's carriage and rumbling toward a safer location. Meanwhile, Captain Parker had gotten startling news. The regulars were just minutes away.

Not until well after midnight had Colonel Francis Smith managed to get all seven hundred or so of his men across the Charles River. They'd been forced to wade from the boats to shore, and after once again wading across a small tidal river so as to prevent the soldiers' leather-soled shoes from alerting the countryside as they pounded across a wooden bridge, they'd started up the road through Cambridge.

The chilly spring air glowed with the gray light of the full moon as the grenadiers in their tall bearskin caps and the light infantrymen in their close-fitting black leather helmets trudged up the road, each footfall magnified hundreds of times into a single booming step that sounded like a giant striding out of Boston in the dark. One woman looked out her window and was astonished to see the soldiers' gun barrels glinting in the moonlight like a river of flowing silver. The widow Rand watched the soldiers pass and then went looking for her neighbor, whom she found casting bullets in a shed behind his house. When she told him of what she'd seen, he refused to believe her. Only after he'd seen the many nearly identical footprints in the road did he realize that the old woman had been telling the truth.

In the town of Menotomy, between Cambridge and Lexington, Colonel Smith began to realize that his attempts at secrecy had gone for naught. Signal guns could be heard in the distance up ahead. He ordered his men to halt and sent back a messenger to General Gage, requesting reinforcements. In addition to the grenadiers and light infantry, Gage had included a battalion of marines in the expedition, and Smith ordered Marine Major John Pitcairn to push ahead with six companies of light infantry and secure the two bridges that provided access to the town of Concord from the north.

The Black Horse Tavern was in Menotomy, and the sound of the regulars awakened the three Committee of Safety members who were staying there— Jeremiah Lee, Azor Orne, and Elbridge Gerry, all from Marblehead. In a panic, Gerry rushed for the front door, only to be stopped by the tavern keeper, who directed the three officials to escape out the back. Gerry proceeded to trip and fall facedown in the stubble of a cornfield, where he was soon joined by the two others, who lay trembling in the damp cold until the regulars had moved on toward Lexington.

Pitcairn sent ahead an advance guard led by Marine Lieutenant Jesse Adair. Accompanying Adair were several loyalist guides, one of whom, Daniel Bliss from Concord, would be of immense help when it came to accomplishing their primary objective. As they pushed on through the night, they surprised several unsuspecting travelers, including Asahel Porter and Josiah Richardson from Woburn, who were quickly captured and forced to march with the column.

Around 3:30 a.m., about five miles from Lexington, they were approached by a group of horsemen. They were the officers whom Gage had sent out the previous day to guard the road to Concord. Led by Major Edward Mitchell, they had recently captured Paul Revere, who after alerting Samuel Adams and John Hancock had continued with William Dawes toward Concord. Revere had brazenly informed the officers that Smith's troops "had catched aground in passing the river" and that since he had alarmed the countryside there would soon be as many as five hundred militiamen gathered in Lexington. As Mitchell's group approached the town green with their captive, they heard a volley of musketry—probably warning shots intended to rouse the town—"which," Revere later reported, "alarmed them very much." Mitchell decided he had no choice but to release Revere and warn Smith that "the whole country" knew what they were about.

In his conversation with Smith's advance guard, Major Mitchell claimed that he and his fellow officers had been forced to "gallop for their lives" out of Lexington, where the militiamen were already awaiting the arrival of the troops. Seeming to corroborate Mitchell's overheated assertions were the sounds of bells and signal guns. Beacon fires could be seen flickering in the distant hills. A well-dressed gentleman in a small carriage approached with the news that no less than six hundred militiamen had gathered on the Lexington Green; next came a wagon filled with cordwood for Boston. The driver said there were now one thousand men in Lexington.

On they pushed through the early-morning darkness, and by 4:00 a.m., with dawn approaching, they began to detect a "vast number of country militia" moving across the boulder-strewn fields on either side of them toward Lexington. The regulars wore heavy red coats and white breeches, their chests crisscrossed by belts burdened with cartridge boxes, swords, and bayonets. The country people posed a very different picture of the "soldier" in their floppy-brimmed hats, baggy, dark-colored coats, gray homespun stockings, and buckled cowhide shoes as they strode through the dim light with their powder horns slung from their shoulders. The only significant similarity between the regulars and these militiamen was that they all carried muskets.

Accompanying Adair in the advance guard was Lieutenant William Sutherland, who with Adair's help was able to capture one of these militiamen— thirty-one-year-old Benjamin Wellington of Lexington, whom they relieved of his musket and, unusual for a militiaman, his bayonet. Soon after, a group of horsemen appeared in the road ahead. One of them shouted, "You had better turn back for you shall not enter the town." As the horsemen began to gallop away, a lone rider turned and raised his musket. A soundless flash of light flared from the base of the barrel. The militiaman had pulled the trigger and ignited the weapon's priming powder, but for some reason the main charge in the barrel had failed to detonate—what was known as a "flash in the pan." The militiaman's intent was unmistakable, but so far no ball had whistled in the regulars' direction.

A report was made to Major Pitcairn, who ordered his six companies of light infantrymen to halt. If at least one Yankee was willing to fire upon the king's troops, he had no choice but to prepare his men for the worst as they marched into Lexington. He ordered them to load. Each soldier had a cartridge box full of paper-wrapped charges of powder and ball. After ripping open one of the cartridges with his teeth and pouring the contents into the barrel of his musket, each man threw away the top of the cartridge. Later that day, William Munroe counted approximately two hundred scraps of cartridge paper scattered on the road.

They could hear a drum beating the militiamen to arms. Around a slight

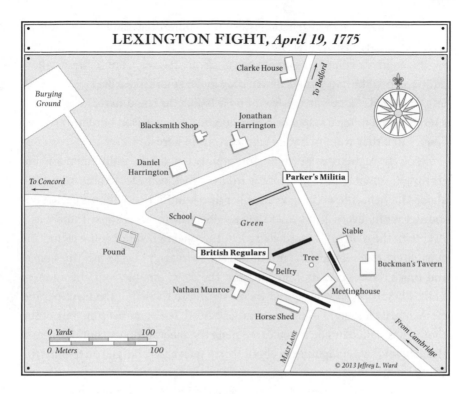

LEXINGTON FIGHT, *April 19, 1775*

Clarke House
To Bedford
Burying Ground
Jonathan Harrington
Blacksmith Shop
Daniel Harrington
To Concord
Parker's Militia
School
Green
Stable
Pound
British Regulars
Tree
Belfry
Buckman's Tavern
Nathan Munroe
Meetinghouse
Horse Shed
0 Yards   100
0 Meters   100
MALT LANE
From Cambridge
© 2013 Jeffrey L. Ward

bend in the road they got their first glimpse of the Lexington Green. Immediately ahead was the three-story-high meetinghouse, with the belfry beside it, clanging away. Buckman's Tavern was on their right, and in the distance, partly obscured by the meetinghouse, were two lines of militiamen. They estimated there were two hundred, possibly three hundred men ahead of them.

In reality, there were barely seventy militiamen on Lexington Green. After three hours of waiting, they had assembled in a poorly organized, possibly alcohol-debilitated rush. Those who hadn't yet gotten their powder were in the meetinghouse filling their powder horns. Men were still filtering in from all sides of the common. At the moment the British appeared, Paul Revere and Hancock's secretary John Lowell staggered past the militiamen with Hancock's trunk of official papers, which they had just retrieved from the attic of Buckman's Tavern and were now trying to conceal before the marauding British could get hold of it. Revere heard Parker say to his men, "Let the troops pass by. Don't molest them, without they being first." As had been said over and over again in instructions from the Committee of Safety, the militia-men were not to fire the first shot.

Pitcairn's six companies amounted to about 250 men, but to these callow militiamen in the half-light of dawn, they looked more like a brigade of 1,500. One man said, "There are so few of us it is folly to stand here." Parker was later reported to have responded, "Stand your ground. Don't fire unless fired upon. But if they want to have a war let it begin here."

Soon the regulars were advancing rapidly toward the militiamen and be-ginning to shout. At the head of the infantrymen was Lieutenant Adair and Major Mitchell, still seething with anger and humiliation after his earlier en-counter with Revere. Just before they reached the meetinghouse there was a fork, with the road to Concord going left, the road to Bedford going right. The most direct route toward the militia was to swing right of the meetinghouse, and that's the way Adair, Mitchell, and the six companies of light infantry went. Pitcairn, who was behind them, swung to the left of the meeting and momentarily lost sight of the companies ahead. For some reason, four of the companies halted beside an oak tree near the meetinghouse, but Adair and Mitchell and two companies of about thirty men each charged on toward the militiamen.

For many months now, the regulars had endured the taunts and outright maliciousness of not just the Bostonians but also country people just like these. It was the country people who had refused to allow the barracks to be built that might have saved the lives of the soldiers' comrades and loved ones who were now buried at the edge of Boston Common. For the regulars this was personal, not political. If any of these farmers dared to fire their muskets, a British volley was sure to follow.

One officer, perhaps Mitchell, shouted, "Damn them, we will have them!" About seventy-five yards from the militiamen, the two companies were or-dered to form a line of battle, an interlocking formation of three lines, stag-gered in such a way that the men behind were able to fire over the shoulders of those ahead of them. Crying "Huzza! Huzza!," the regulars shouted so loud that orders were impossible to hear. There were three officers on horses posi-tioned just ahead of the regulars, and at least one of them was having a vir-tual tantrum, shouting "Throw down your arms, ye villains, ye rebels, damn you, disperse!"

With dozens of British muskets pointed in their direction, Parker decided that they had no choice but to do exactly as the officer was telling them to do, so he ordered his men to disperse. Some of the militiamen were immediately on the move; others, perhaps not able to hear Parker, stood either stubbornly or in catatonic fear and held their ground. Some of the militia claimed one of the mounted officers fired his pistol. The British regulars claimed that it was the provincials who fired first—not those gathered on the green, but someone behind a stone wall to their right or perhaps standing at a doorway or window of Buckman's Tavern. Major Pitcairn was riding toward the two companies, shouting, "Soldiers, don't fire, keep your ranks, and surround them." At some point, his horse was hit by two balls fired from the sidelines. One soldier was hit in the leg; another in the hand. Soon the two companies of light infantry were firing without orders. The first volley was ragged and indistinct but was then followed by a "continual roar."

The smoke was so thick that the only evidence of the enemy the militiamen could see were the heads of the officers' horses. At first, John Munroe was convinced that the regulars were firing only warning blanks, since no one seemed to be getting hit by any balls. But when the man beside him— another Munroe by the name of Ebenezer—got slammed in the arm by a ball, they knew otherwise. Despite his wound, Ebenezer shouted, "I'll give them the guts of my gun," and blasted away into the acrid cloud of dark gray smoke. Ebenezer later testified that the air was so thick with whizzing musket balls that "I thought there was no chance for escape and that I might as well fire my gun as stand still and do nothing." John Munroe was one of the few militiamen to get off two shots. Unfortunately, he overcharged his musket the second time, and "the strength of the charge took off about a foot of my gun barrel." Captain Parker's cousin Jonas had placed his hat full of musket balls and flints on the ground between his feet and vowed he would "never run." He was hit on the second volley, and as he lay on the ground, struggling to reload his gun, the infantrymen ran up and stabbed him to death with their bayonets.

Most of the militiamen, however, never even fired their guns. Several were killed while sprinting for cover. Jonathan Harrington lived on the west side of the common and was shot down as he ran for the safety of his house. His horrified wife and children watched as he crawled across the dusty road and died on their doorstep. Asahel Porter and Josiah Richardson, the two men from Woburn who had been captured earlier that night by the British advance guard, were released on the Lexington Green. Both were warned to walk and not run as they made their way to safety. Richardson did as ordered and survived, but Porter panicked and was gunned down as he ran from the British troops. Several horses were spooked by the blast and crackle of gunfire and carried their riders—including Lieutenant Sutherland—on wild rides around the green and beyond. In the meantime, Major Pitcairn, whom a patriot minister described as "a good man in a bad cause," tried desperately to put a stop to the chaos and "struck his . . . sword downwards with all earnestness" as a signal to cease fire.

Order wasn't restored until Colonel Smith and the grenadiers finally caught up to the light infantry. With the help of Lieutenant Sutherland, Smith found a drummer, whom he commanded to sound the beat to arms, which was the signal for the men to regroup into ranks. According to Sutherland, this did not prevent a few more shots from being fired by the provincials in Buckman's Tavern. Now that most of the militiamen had been sent "scampering off," the infuriated infantrymen were about to turn their attention to the tavern and the meetinghouse. Smith wrote that the soldiers were "much enraged at the treatment they had received, and having been fired on from the houses repeatedly were going to break them open to come at those within." If something was not done quickly, anyone still in those buildings was sure to be killed. What Smith and the regulars didn't know was that in the attic of the meetinghouse, the militiaman Joshua Simons waited with the barrel of his musket thrust into a keg of powder. If the soldiers attacked, he was going to make sure that none of them lived to claim the town's powder.

Luckily, Colonel Smith succeeded in "putting a stop to all further slaughter of those deluded people." The infantrymen reluctantly fell into line and after firing a victory salute gave three rousing huzzas. Besides Pitcairn's twice-wounded horse and two soldiers who had received minor injuries, all the casualties had been suffered by the provincials, with eight dead and ten wounded, including Prince Estabrook, who became the first African American casualty of the Revolution since the death of the black sailor Crispus Attucks at the Boston Massacre.

From the standpoint of the British, the skirmish at Lexington had been a disaster. For a frighteningly extended period of time, Colonel Smith and his officers had lost control of their men. Even after the infantrymen had been induced to stop firing their muskets, it took a while to calm them down. "We then formed on the Common," Lieutenant John Barker wrote in his diary, "but with some difficulty, the men were so wild they could hear no orders."

Part of the problem had to do with Gage's decision to put together an expedition made up of grenadiers and light infantrymen rather than go with one of the three brigades that made up the force he had in Boston. Although these seven hundred men represented the elite in his army, they had never trained together and were unfamiliar, for the most part, with the officers who were now commanding them. The trust and cohesion that went with a group of men who had been training and living together for several years did not exist among Smith's expedition. Throughout the long day ahead, orders given by the British officers were either misinterpreted or ignored, an inevitable result of unfamiliarity in a time of crisis.

Compounding the difficulty was the fact that they were already fourteen miles into what they now knew was enemy territory. The prospect of the march back to Boston through a countryside that was rapidly filling up with militiamen was daunting, to say the least. In fact, when shortly after the incident at Lexington, Colonel Smith revealed for the first time the purpose of their mission, several of his officers advised him to turn back. "From what they had seen . . . ," Lieutenant Frederick Mackenzie wrote, "they imagined it would be impracticable to advance to Concord and execute their orders." Colonel Smith simply told them that he was "determined to obey the orders he had received," and they continued on to Concord.

The encounter at Lexington was just as disastrous for the town's militiamen, who suffered what might be termed the country equivalent of the Boston Massacre. It apparently made no difference that, unlike the Bostonians, who had been armed with only clubs, rocks, and snowballs, the militiamen were equipped with muskets. Once the king's troops had been goaded into firing their weapons, the Lexington militia suffered casualties that were as lopsided as those suffered by the crowd in Boston in 1770. Just as determining who was at fault became a hotly contested political issue in the aftermath of the Boston Massacre, so was what happened at Lexington about to spark a controversy that persists to this day as to who was the first to discharge his musket or pistol.

The real question was not who fired the first shot, but why were Parker and his men on the Lexington Green in the first place? Seventy or so militiamen had no chance of stopping an advance guard of more than two hundred British regulars. Instead of spending much of the early-morning hours drinking at Buckman's Tavern and then stubbornly lingering on the green, the

Lexington militia should have already been in Concord, where they could have helped hide and ultimately defend the military stores. As it was, they had almost called attention to what few kegs of powder they had hidden in the town's meetinghouse. What purpose was to be served by standing out there on the grass as the soldiers marched by?

Years later, General William Heath, who was about to join with Joseph Warren and play an important role in subsequent events that day, commented that by standing so near the road, Parker and his men had been guilty of "too much braving for danger [since] they were sure to meet with insult, or injury, which they could not repel." If they were intent on engaging the British, they should have been where many of them ended up: behind a stone wall.

Some have speculated that Samuel Adams may have been responsible for the militia being on the Lexington Green. Since Adams had a reputation for stage-managing events, whether it was the selection of the province's delegates to the Continental Congress in June or Warren's Massacre Day Oration in March, perhaps he accompanied John Hancock to the Lexington Green and convinced Captain Parker to make a stand against the British. However, Hancock, not Adams, was Lexington's local hero, and he had been the one who, according to William Munroe, proclaimed just minutes before the skirmish, "If I had my musket, I would never turn my back upon these troops." Parker may very well have had Hancock's words in mind when he initially told his men to stand their ground.

Thanks to Reverend William Gordon's account of the events of that day, we know that as Adams and Hancock beat a hasty retreat from Lexington, Adams proclaimed, "Oh, what a glorious morning is this!" Hancock missed his meaning entirely and thought his companion was talking about the weather. "I mean," Adams insisted, "this is a glorious day for America."

Hancock was not as thickheaded as Samuel Adams, who apparently recounted the exchange to Gordon, seemed to imply. Being a businessman, Hancock possessed a practical sense of the human resources required to get a job properly done. Adams was more of a theorist, a man who always had his eye on the bigger picture and who never seems to have allowed the paltry concerns of individuals to interfere with his pursuit of American liberty. For him, any event that furthered the cause—even a confused and heartrending event such as the Boston Massacre—was "glorious." Hancock, on the other hand, had seen for himself the men who were about to face the British at Lexington, and he appears to have been less taken with the patriotic possibilities of what was about to unfold. According to his fiancée, he described the militia-men as "but partially provided with arms and those they had were in most miserable order." He may have quite rightly suspected that he and Adams were leaving a slaughter in their wake.

Hancock, in the end, had the wisdom not to take the field at Lexington Green. In just a few hours' time, Joseph Warren was about to make a very different decision.

CHAPTER SEVEN

The Bridge

The morning of April 19, 1775, marked the beginning of a beautiful spring day in New England. The unusually warm winter meant that the trees and flowers were ahead of themselves that April, and the foliage dotting the surrounding fields was hazed with blossoms and the bright green buds of emerging leaves. Now that the column's presence was no longer a secret, Colonel Francis Smith ordered the fifers and drummers to strike up a tune during the six-mile march to Concord.

Mary Hartwell lived in the town of Lincoln, just to the west of Lexington. Her husband Samuel was a sergeant in the local militia, but that did not prevent her from appreciating what she saw that morning when she looked out her window. "The army of the king was coming up in fine order," she later told her grandchildren, "their red coats were brilliant, and their bayonets glistening in the sunlight made a fine appearance; but I knew what all that meant, and I feared that I should never see your grandfather again."

Colonel Smith seems to have made a special effort to instill a renewed sense of discipline among his troops that morning. The British army had a long and distinguished tradition to uphold, and Smith later claimed that despite being shot at twice from the surrounding woods, his men marched from Lexington to Concord "with as much good order as ever troops observed in Britain or any other friendly country."

The fact remained, however, that they were not in a friendly country. But was this truly enemy territory? Twenty years before, the regulars had been looked to as the allies, if not the saviors, of the New Englanders as they marched together over these same country roads on their way to battle the French and Indians. Now that the enemy in that war had been defeated, the New Englanders were acting as if the New World of their Puritan ancestors was theirs and theirs alone. It was left to Colonel Smith and his regulars to remind these people that this was still British soil.

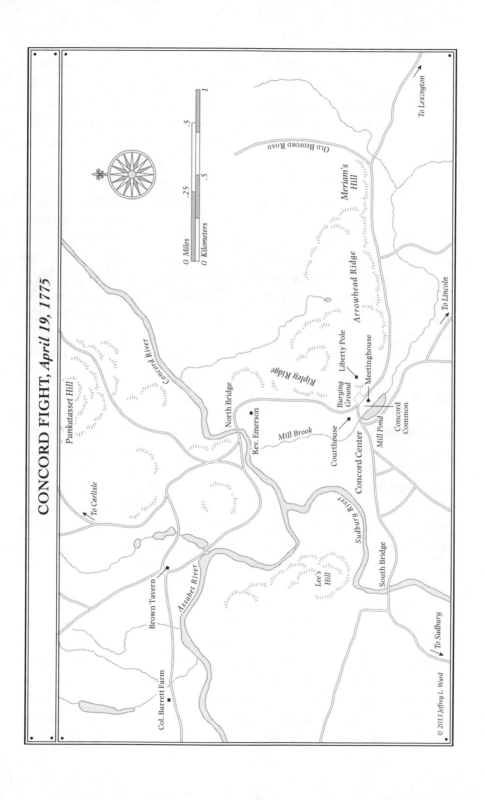

CONCORD FIGHT, *April 19, 1775*

To Lexington

Old Bedford Road

Meriam's Hill

Arrowhead Ridge

Punkatasset Hill

Concord River

Ripley Ridge

Liberty Pole

Meetinghouse

Burying Ground

To Lincoln

North Bridge

Rev. Emerson

Mill Brook

Courthouse

Concord Center

Mill Pond

Concord Common

To Carlisle

Sudbury River

Lee's Hill

Brown Tavern

Assabet River

South Bridge

To Sudbury

Col. Barrett Farm

0 Miles   .25   .5   1
0 Kilometers   .5

© 2013 Jeffrey L. Ward

Concord is a town surrounded by hills. In 1775, it was also a town where open fields, crisscrossed by stone walls, predominated. This meant that the small group of militiamen gathered on Meriam's Hill at the intersection of the road to Concord and the road to Bedford, about a mile from the center of Concord, had plenty of time to watch the long line of British troops approaching from the east. And like Mary Hartwell before them, they were transfixed by the spectacle of seven hundred British regulars marching through the clear morning air. "The sun was rising and shined on their arms," the magnificently named Thaddeus Blood remembered, "and they made a noble appearance in their red coats."

Unlike what had happened just a few hours before in Lexington, when in the dim light of dawn the troops had burst upon the green in a terrifying rush, the people of Concord had ample, if not too much, time to contemplate what these colorfully dressed soldiers were about. Definitive word of what had happened at Lexington had not yet reached Concord. Since the militiamen had been directed *not* to fire the first shot, there were to be several tense and agonizing hours to come as the militia's leaders, full of hesitancy and indecision, tried to figure out what to do.

On a hill overlooking the town's meetinghouse, which just the week before had been the temporary home of the Provincial Congress, stood most of Concord's militia along with a group of civil, military, and religious leaders. Near this collection of elders was a liberty pole topped by a flag, which like the flag in Taunton may have read "Liberty and Union." One of the youngest members of this distinguished group was the minister William Emerson, thirty-two. All winter and spring he had been encouraging the town's residents to resist British attempts to limit their God-given liberties. "Let us stand our ground," he insisted that morning. "If we die, let us die here!"

Others, such as Colonel James Barrett, sixty-five, a veteran of the French and Indian War whose house on the other side of the Concord River was where many of the most critical military stores were now hidden, had less enthusiasm for forcing a confrontation. The debate continued even as the advance guard of militia that had been monitoring the British rushed into town with the regulars at their heels. Finally they decided to abandon their position beside the liberty pole and retreat with the town's women and children across the North Bridge to the militias' prearranged meeting place at Punkatasset Hill, about a mile from the town center, where they could monitor the British and yet be out of the regulars' immediate reach.

It irked them to watch as the soldiers marched into the almost empty town, cut down the liberty pole, and began searching for the cannons, ammunition, and other military equipment that Gage's spies had reported to be hidden in the inhabitants' homes. Most alarming for Colonel Barrett was the sight of seven companies of light infantrymen heading for the North Bridge in the direction of his farm. Once at the bridge, the commander of the British detachment, Captain Lawrence Parsons, left three companies to guard the crossing in anticipation of his eventual return as he pushed ahead with four companies toward the Barrett homestead, about two miles from the bridge. By that time Colonel Barrett had left Punkatasset Hill and was on his way to warn his wife and family that the regulars were coming.

The Barretts had spent the previous day and night preparing for this eventuality. Barrett's fourteen-year-old grandson, James, had led a team of oxen towing a cart full of military supplies to a nearby swamp, where he and his companions hid the stores under pine boughs. South of the barn, others plowed up a thirty-foot-square section of field and, instead of sowing it with seed, laid muskets in the trenches. Some of the cannons were laid under a bed of sage; other pieces of artillery were buried beneath a mound of manure.

As soon as he arrived that morning, Barrett encouraged his wife, Rebeckah, to flee. "No," she replied. "I can't live very long anyway, and I'd rather stay and see that they don't burn down the house and barn." While her husband returned to Punkatasset Hill by a back route through the woods, she and her family made some final preparations in anticipation of the soldiers' arrival.

Captain Parsons was led to the Barrett farm by Ensign Henry DeBerniere, one of the two British spies that Gage had sent out that winter into the New England countryside. Upon meeting Mrs. Barrett, Parsons immediately realized that this was not going to be easy. She expected, she sternly informed him, that he and his men would "respect private property." Once he assured her that this was the case, she proceeded to shadow his every move, repeatedly reminding him of his promise and in several instances providing enough of a distraction to steer his men away from hidden caches of bullets and other stores. By 8:00 a.m., they'd managed to find only a few wooden gun carriages, which they burned on the road near the corn barn after Mrs. Barrett insisted that they move them away from the larger barn near her house.

Tired, frustrated, and hungry, Captain Parsons requested something to eat. Mrs. Barrett obliged, and the soldiers enjoyed a meal of brown bread and milk in the same large room the colonel used to muster and organize the Concord militia. When the soldiers insisted she take some coins as payment, Mrs. Barrett replied, "This is the price of blood."

By the time Colonel Barrett returned to Punkatasset Hill, the number of militiamen had increased significantly as companies continued to arrive from towns to the west and north of Concord. At the beginning of the morning, the British column of seven hundred men had possessed an overwhelming numerical advantage, but now with the arrival of additional militia companies and with the division of Smith's force into several isolated battalions, the situation had changed dramatically. At present only about a hundred regulars were at or near the North Bridge, waiting for Captain Parsons's return from the Barrett house. The militia leaders assembled on Punkatasset Hill began to contemplate moving their force of somewhere between three and four hundred men closer to the regulars near the bridge.

Accompanying Colonel Barrett were Major John Buttrick, forty-three, leader of the local regiment of minutemen, as well as five Concord company captains, three of whom were related by blood or marriage to Colonel Barrett. Not all the officers present that morning were inclined to agree with Colonel Barrett; for example, Lieutenant Joseph Hosmer, thirty-nine, already had a well-established reputation for making the lives of the town elders uncomfortable. Instead of deferring to rank when making decisions, these New Englanders followed, in the tradition of the town meeting, a more consensual approach. Eventually they decided that the time was right to make a move toward the North Bridge.

About three hundred yards to the northwest of the bridge was a low, flat-topped hill on which one of the companies of British troops was positioned. Leaving the women and children and dogs on Punkatasset Hill, the American militiamen began marching toward the British position, about a thousand yards away. The New Englanders were relieved to watch the company of regulars hurriedly abandon their initial position and join the other company closer to the bridge.

For the next hour, the American militia and the British regulars stood at ease watching each other, with only a few hundred yards between them. The Concord River flooded each spring, and the road leading down to the North Bridge had to curve around an inlet of seasonal marshland, where a causeway connected the road to the bridge. A cool westerly breeze surged across the surrounding meadow. According to tradition, the militia company from nearby Bedford carried a crimson flag (which still exists) depicting an armored arm reaching out of the clouds with a sword clenched in its fist. The Latin phrase "Vince aut Morire" (Conquer or Die) was emblazoned around this forbidding, celestial-looking appendage, which, thanks to the wind direction, would have been clearly visible to the regulars on the bridge, especially if one of the officers had a spyglass.

Flags such as this had been carried into battle during the English Civil War; they'd also accompanied the militiamen's forefathers during King Philip's War, when the region's Wampanoags, Nipmucks, and Narragansetts had been reviled by the English as the literal children of Satan. Now that New England's original inhabitants had been defeated, this most recent generation of colonists looked back on the struggles of the past with some nostalgia. Rather than despise the foes of their ancestors, they had begun to invoke and even honor their memory. Whether they disguised themselves as Mohawks during the Boston Tea Party or had come to recognize the tactical advantages of what their forefathers had once dismissed as the Indians' "skulking way of war," these men had moved in directions that would have been inconceivable to the Puritans of the past. After generations of adapting to their surroundings, they had become a people who were profoundly different from the British regulars watching them tensely from the North Bridge.

At least one militiaman, however, was a relative newcomer to Massachusetts. At some point, James Nichols, the owner of a farm in Lincoln and recently emigrated from England, handed his musket to one of his townsmen. "I will go down and talk to them," he said. He walked to the bridge and struck up a conversation with the British officers. After a while, he returned to the hill. Nichols, who was described as a "good droll fellow and a fine singer," clearly had no heart for what was about to transpire. It was time, he said, to head home. With gun in hand, James Nichols walked away.

The alarm had reached the town of Acton around 3:00 a.m. Thanks to the thirty-year-old gunsmith Isaac Davis, Acton had one of the best-equipped militia companies in the province. Not only did Davis have a beautiful musket of his own manufacture but he had equipped each of the men in his company with a bayonet. They were also well practiced, having met at Davis's home twice a week since November 1774.

But on the morning of April 19, as he prepared to lead his men to Concord, about six miles to the southeast, Davis was, according to his wife, "anxious and thoughtful." Several of their four children were suffering from scarlet fever. By about seven o'clock, more than twenty militiamen had collected at the Davis house, and Isaac decided they must leave. His wife believed that he had "something to communicate" as he took up his musket and cartridge box, but, unable to find the words, he simply said, "Take good care of the children," and walked out the door.

They marched quickly past the Acton Meetinghouse and, soon after that, past Brooks Tavern, where they were greeted by handkerchiefs waving from the windows and doorway. All the while additional members of their company kept catching up to them and falling into line until they eventually comprised thirty-eight men, close to the entire company.

After following the road for several miles, they took a shortcut along a woodland path and two miles later found themselves at the edge of a field overlooking the home of Colonel Barrett. They could see Captain Parsons and his men moving about the property, looking for stores. Staying off the main road and marching on a direct line through the fields, they passed a tavern kept by the widow Brown, about a mile from the North Bridge. Thirteen-year-old Charles Handley was living at the tavern then; years later he would remember hearing Davis's fifer play "The White Cockade," a bouncy Scottish tune that memorialized Bonnie Prince Charlie's doomed attempt to overthrow the British king. During that 1745 uprising the prince had placed a white rose on his bonnet, and thus the "white cockade" became an emblem of rebellion. With the fife and drum playing this song of defiance, Captain Isaac Davis and his men marched toward the North Bridge of Concord.

By about nine that morning, somewhere between four and five hundred militiamen had assembled on the flat-topped hill overlooking the river. In addition to those from Concord, Lincoln, and Bedford, officers and men had arrived from Carlisle, Chelmsford, Groton, Littleton, and Stow, including Lieutenant Colonel John Robinson, who had just arrived ahead of his militia companies from Westford. At some point, they were joined by Captain Davis's company from Acton.

As they had been doing for several hours now, Colonel Barrett and his officers were discussing what to do next. Then someone pointed out that smoke had begun to rise from the center of Concord. This was the opportunity for which Lieutenant Hosmer had been waiting all morning.

Hosmer had a history of taking adversarial positions at town meetings. He was also a militant patriot, and he'd probably grown increasingly impatient with Colonel Barrett's reluctance to engage the British. As billows of smoke continued to rise into the windy sunshine, he turned to Barrett and said, "Will you let them burn the town down?"

Colonel Smith and Major Pitcairn had fared no better than Captain Parsons in their search for military stores in Concord's town center. The townspeople were, Colonel Smith later reported to General Gage, "sulky," and in one instance a man even attacked Major Pitcairn, who scored one of the few successes that morning when he came upon three rusty cannon barrels. As the burly grenadiers moved about the houses, some of the officers sat in the sun on chairs that they'd temporarily confiscated, sipping hard cider.

As at the Barrett farm, the regulars came upon a few wooden gun carriages, which they burned in the road along with some other wooden objects, including the town's liberty pole. When the wind took hold of the flames and the conflagration spread to the nearby Town House, local matron Martha Moulton urged the officers to put out the fire. When they equivocated, saying, "Oh, Mother, don't be concerned," Moulton took up a pail of water and shamed them into helping her. Soon a bucket brigade had succeeded in extinguishing the flames, creating the cloud of smoke that the militiamen saw from the hill on the other side of the Concord River. The regulars weren't burning the town; they were doing their best to save it.

All of this was lost, however, on the militiamen and their officers. As far as they were concerned, Concord was about to be burned to the ground by the regulars. Colonel Barrett reluctantly decided that they must challenge the soldiers at the bridge and rescue the town. If they got lucky, the regulars would let them pass unmolested. If not and the bridge became a scene of brutal fighting, the company leading the militiamen must have bayonets. Other captains volunteered, but their companies were not as well equipped as the men from Acton, and Isaac Davis was given the honor of leading them toward the regulars gathered at the North Bridge. "I have not a man that is afraid to go," he assured the other militia officers. Concord's schoolmaster was present that morning, and years later he remembered how Davis's face "reddened at the word of command." Davis's cheeks may have been suffused with a flush of pride and resolve, but he may have also been suffering, like his children, from scarlet fever.

Davis's Acton company moved from the left of the line to what became the front of the column. Marching beside Davis were Concord's Major John Buttrick and Westford's Lieutenant Colonel John Robinson. The militia followed behind them in files of two, normally not a fighting formation. In the rear and on horseback, Colonel Barrett repeated to each passing company not to fire first.

Even though men had already been killed at Lexington, many later looked to what was about to happen at the North Bridge as the start of the American Revolution. But, in truth, this was hardly the first time that armed colonists had actively opposed the British military. Back on December 14, the citizens of New Hampshire had attacked Fort William and Mary in Portsmouth and taken the king's gunpowder and artillery. Two and a half years before that, on June 9, 1772, a British customs schooner, HMS *Gaspée*, had been boarded and burned by a group of Rhode Islanders led by the merchant John Brown. In both incidents, American colonists had initiated an attack with the intention of taking or destroying the crown's property.

But the events at the North Bridge were to be different. The militiamen were not out to storm a fort or scuttle a hated customs vessel. They simply wanted to save their town. But first they must cross a river.

The three companies of British regulars at the bridge were commanded by Captain Walter Laurie, who had long since sent a message to Colonel Smith calling for reinforcements. Laurie's hundred or so soldiers were clustered on the west side of the bridge, but when they realized that the militiamen were headed toward them, marching, one of his officers wrote, "with as much order as the best disciplined troops," Laurie ordered his own men back across the bridge. Now most of his force was concentrated in a single group on the east side of the river, with the bridge between them and the approaching militiamen.

Two of Laurie's officers lingered on the bridge and began to pull up some of the planks so as to impede the progress of the militiamen. In the meantime, Laurie tried to assemble two of his companies into what was known as a street-firing formation. After firing, the soldiers kneeling in the front rows would peel off to the sides to reload as those behind moved forward to continue the firing. Maximizing firepower in a confined space, street-firing, if performed properly, might have succeeded in holding the bridge until reinforcements arrived. But as it turned out, Laurie, like Lexington militia captain John Parker before him, hadn't given himself enough time to prepare his men.

As Laurie struggled to get his troops organized, Lieutenant William Sutherland and a handful of men leaped over the wall on the left side of the road leading to the bridge. Sutherland immediately realized that since the road on the other side of the river curved as it approached the bridge, he and his men would have a clear shot of the right flank, or side, of the militia companies before they crossed the river. By this time Concord's Major Buttrick was yelling at the regulars to stop pulling up the planks as Captain Laurie's soldiers did their best to follow their own commander's undoubtedly hurried orders.

Sutherland or one of the men who were with him on the left may have fired the first shot—what seems to have been a warning shot that skipped across the surface of the river. Two more shots were fired, and then came the British volley.

In an engraving based on the testimony of eyewitnesses collected within weeks of the fighting, gray-brown powder smoke billows from the muskets of the regulars bunched on the narrow road to the right. To the left, on the west side of the river, are the militiamen, who have just reached the other side of the bridge, a crude hundred-foot arch of posts and boards. Beneath the bridge, the river flows past, a tranquil strip of blue between the two opposing columns.

The regulars' muskets had a muzzle velocity of approximately a thousand feet per second, meaning that the ball left the barrel at less than a third the speed of a bullet fired by a modern rifle. In an effort to offset the effects of gravity and increase the musket's range, the regulars tended to fire high. At the North Bridge, many of them fired too high.

Militiaman Amos Barrett of Concord remembered that "their balls whistled well." Isaac Davis's brother Ezekiel's head was grazed when a bullet passed through his hat. Virtually the same thing happened to Joshua Brooks of Lincoln. The many high, slashing wounds prompted one militiaman to conclude that "the British were firing jack-knives."

But some of the regulars had better aim. A ball that passed under the arm of Lieutenant Colonel Robinson grazed the side of fifer Luther Blanchard before it hit the Concord minuteman Jonas Brown. Acton private Abner Hosmer was shot through the face and killed instantly. Captain Isaac Davis, marching in the front row beside Major Buttrick and Lieutenant Colonel Robinson, was hit in the chest, and the musket ball, which may have driven a shirt button through an artery and out his back, opened up a gush of blood that extended at least ten feet behind him, drenching David Forbush and Thomas Thorp and covering the stones in front of the North Bridge with a slick of gore.

Captain David Brown had never uttered a profanity in his life, but when he realized that the regulars were firing with deadly intent, he could not help himself. "God damn them," he cried, "they are firing balls!"

Reverend William Emerson's house was on the east side of the river and overlooked the bridge. Just as Punkatasset Hill had become a gathering point for the women and children of Concord, so had his parsonage attracted a large number of the town's inhabitants. He'd spent much of the morning attending to these people—until his wife had huffily tapped on the windowpane and motioned for him to come inside and pay attention to *her*.

By the time the militiamen began to march toward the North Bridge, Emerson had walked from his house toward the river. When the first shots were fired, he was closer to the regulars than the nearest provincials, which meant that he had a clear view of the devastating volley that killed Isaac Davis and Abner Hosmer.

A month before, on March 13, Emerson had delivered a sermon in which he assured his parishioners that "a consciousness of having acted up to the principles of our religion . . . when we go forth to battle will be a most comfortable antidote against fear and cowardice, and serve to stimulate us to the most heroic actions." He believed every word of that sermon but still could not help but wonder how these farmers and artisans would respond to the volley. Later, he admitted to his fellow clergyman William Gordon that he was "very uneasy until he found that the fire was returned."

Major John Buttrick leaped into the air and cried, "Fire, fellow soldiers, for God's sake fire!" According to Thaddeus Blood, "The cry of fire, fire was made from front to rear. The fire was almost simultaneous with the cry."

Lieutenant Sutherland and the men on the British left flank soon discovered that they were dreadfully exposed to the militiamen's musket balls. Sutherland got spun around by a hit to the chest, and two privates fell beside him dead or mortally wounded. Captain Laurie's attempts to maintain a blistering rate of fire were stymied by the almost immediate loss of four of eight officers. As the militia and minutemen made their way across the bridge, those in front kneeling so that those behind could fire over their heads, British resistance crumbled, and the regulars, despite Laurie's protestations, turned and fled. "The weight of their fire was such," Lieutenant Jeremy Lister wrote, "that we was obliged to give way, then run with the greatest precipitance." According to militiaman Amos Barrett, "There were eight or ten that were wounded and a running and a hobbling about, looking back to see if we were after them."

The provincials streamed across the bridge but seemed unwilling to continue the fighting. Part of the problem was that the regulars' commanding officer, Colonel Smith, had arrived from the center of Concord with reinforcements. The militiamen may have also realized by this point that Concord was not in fact burning. The shocking loss of Captain Isaac Davis could have also contributed to the sudden absence of resolve. But perhaps the biggest reason the militia stopped firing on the British was the realization that something truly momentous had just occurred. They had done much more than fire on British troops; they had forced three companies of light infantry to retreat. It was a victory, of sorts, but for what purpose? The town, it turned out, was not in flames. The British had fired the first shot, but the provincials had clearly forced the issue by marching on the bridge, and people had died on both sides. The only directive the Provincial Congress had provided was the necessity of not firing the first shot. Now that the shot had been fired, should the militiamen continue to fight? Or should they return to waiting for the other side to make the next move? Instead of iron resolve, hesitation and confusion reigned in the aftermath of the confrontation at the North Bridge.

Colonel James Barrett and roughly half his force backtracked to the other side of the river and eventually returned to Punkatasset Hill. Major Buttrick and a few hundred minutemen continued across the bridge and climbed into the ridge of hills that overlooked the road leading into Concord, where they took up a position behind a stone wall. Below them on the road, about 250 yards away, Colonel Smith and the grenadiers met up with the remnants of Captain Laurie's three companies. "There we lay," the militiaman Amos Barrett remembered, "behind the wall, about 200 of us, with our guns cocked expecting every minute to have the word—fire; . . . if we had fired, I believe we would have killed almost every officer there was in front. . . . They stayed there about 10 minutes and then marched back and we after them."

No provincial officer seemed willing to take charge after the fighting at the North Bridge. According to Thaddeus Blood, "everyone appeared to be his own commander." In this vacuum of leadership, Private Ammi White, in his early twenties, came upon one of the infantrymen who had fallen on the British left flank. Like several others, the regular had been left behind in the chaotic retreat from the North Bridge. Exactly what happened next is difficult to determine. The soldier was injured but still very much alive, and he may have tried to defend himself with his bayonet. Whether it was out of anger or fear, Ammi took up his hatchet and struck the wounded soldier repeatedly in the head. The Reverend Emerson watched the attack and seems to have been more disturbed by the incident than Ammi, who years later confided that he simply did what he thought was expected of a soldier in the midst of battle.

Unfortunately, Ammi did not succeed in immediately killing the infantryman. For more than an hour the soldier lay on the ground, his head chopped into a mess of splintered bone and brains, as both the British and the provincials waited for the return of Captain Parsons from Barrett Farm. Neither side knew what to do next. Smith apparently feared that any attempt on his part to cover Parsons's retreat across the bridge might incite yet another attack from the provincials. So he returned to Concord's village center and did nothing, which meant that Colonel Barrett on Punkatasset Hill was free to annihilate the British detachment when it returned to the North Bridge. But would Barrett be willing to resume hostilities?

In this strange netherworld of paralysis and doubt, Parsons and his men finally made their way back toward the river. They knew nothing of what had occurred just an hour or so before and were disturbed to see that there were no longer any British troops at the bridge. As Parsons and his men glanced worriedly from hill to militia-covered hill, they inevitably picked up the pace until they were virtually running by the time they crossed over the river. The speed of their retreat did not prevent them from noticing, however, the horribly injured soldier, whom they assumed had been scalped.

By noon, when Colonel Smith finally ordered the regulars to begin the march back to Boston, a rumor was working its way up and down the column: instead of just one, four soldiers had been "scalped, their eyes gouged, their noses and ears cut off." What's more, the colonists were likely to do the same to anyone else "they get alive, that are wounded and cannot get off the ground."

As far as the regulars were concerned, the militiamen were no longer fellow Englishmen. By butchering the soldiers' fallen comrade beside the North Bridge, the provincials had revealed themselves to be anything but civilized members of the British Empire; they were, one soldier angrily insisted, "full as bad as the Indians."

Gone was the uncertainty of the morning's march to Concord. From here on in, this was war.

Throughout what proved to be a very long, if only six-mile, march back to Lexington, Colonel Smith made use of flank guards—groups of between eighty and one hundred light infantrymen—who were sent out on either side of the road in an attempt to rid the countryside of militiamen who might threaten the column. As long as the country was relatively open, the flank guards proved quite effective. The trouble came when stone walls, swamps, rocky hills, and especially woodlands hindered the flank guards' passage even as these natural features provided their enemies with the cover they needed to fire upon the column. Houses were both a threat and a lure. Not only could the provincials use them for cover but they were also a source of temptation for the flank guards, since each house contained food and drink as well as valuables that could be pawned in Boston to augment the soldiers' meager pay.

About a mile outside Concord, the British troops were approaching Meriam's Hill, the same hill from which the local militia had watched them in the morning. So far the flanking parties had succeeded in keeping the surrounding countryside fairly free of snipers. At Meriam's Hill, however, an intervening brook required that the light infantrymen on the left flank temporarily return to the road so that they could pass over a bridge.

By this time, militia companies from several nearby towns, including Billerica (the home of Thomas Ditson, who had been tarred and feathered by the

regulars back in March and was there that day, eager for revenge), Tewksbury, and Reading had recently arrived and taken up positions overlooking
the road.

Unlike the morning, when the regulars had arrived in Concord accompanied by fife and drum, no music was played that afternoon. Edmund Foster
was serving as a volunteer with a minuteman company from Reading, and
he remembered how "silence reigned on both sides" as the light infantrymen
of the left flank guard returned to the road "without music or word being spoken that could be heard."

The regulars marched across the bridge. Somewhere a musket fired. The
soldiers wheeled to their left and unleashed a volley. Their muskets fired high
and missed their mark. The militiamen, having had time to take up positions
behind stone walls and rocks, fired with more effectiveness, and Foster
watched as "two British soldiers fell dead at a little distance from each other,
in the road near the brook." Lieutenant Jeremy Lister, one of the handful of
officers to remain unscathed during the encounter at the North Bridge, took
a musket ball in the right elbow. "The battle now began," Foster remembered,
"and was carried on with little or no military discipline and order, on the part
of the Americans."

The provincials may have been improvising as they took up positions
along the sometimes winding road to Lexington, but that did not prevent
them from maintaining a deadly volume of fire. "We were fired on from
houses and behind trees . . . [and] from all sides," Lieutenant John Barker recorded in his diary, "but mostly from the rear, where people had hid themselves in houses till we had passed then fired." What had seemed like just
another country road in New England as they marched toward Concord earlier in the morning was now bristling with the muskets of militiamen that the
regulars could not even see. Safely hidden behind walls, trees, and rocks, the
provincials were revealed only by the telltale cloud of powder smoke as their
musket balls rained down on the grenadiers with fatal effect.

The militiamen used the stone walls to their advantage, but so did the
British. These rugged partitions of granite boulders were often chest-high
and topped with the trunks and branches of trees, and whenever the regulars
marching along the road found themselves besieged on either side, they
would, one Woburn militiaman remembered, "stoop for shelter from the
stone walls as they ran by the ambush."

For the flanking parties, the fighting was less anonymous. Several times, the light infantrymen were able to surprise the militiamen, who were either too inexperienced to anticipate their presence or too preoccupied with firing at the column to notice that the soldiers were coming at them with their bayonets fixed. One New Englander later said it was the sound of the infantrymen running through the fresh spring grass, a predatory "swish, swish," that he remembered most vividly about that terrible day. Some militiamen were able to escape the flankers with their lives, but others were less lucky. Bedford's Captain Jonathan Wilson had predicted, "We'll have every dog of [the British] before night." Near the Hartwell farm (where a few hours before Mary Hartwell had admired the beauty of the passing column in the early morning light), Wilson was surprised from behind by some flankers and killed, as was Daniel Thompson from Woburn. By the time the fighting reached the Fiske farm outside Lexington, Isaac Davis's Acton friend James Hayward had fired so many times that he had almost finished off an entire pound of gunpowder. Desperate for something to drink, he ran for a well, only to discover that a regular had the same idea. Both raised their muskets and fired. The regular was killed, but not before his musket ball fractured Hayward's nearly empty powder horn into deadly splinters that pierced his abdomen and left him mortally wounded.

It was a ruthless kind of fighting that even the experienced soldiers on both sides found profoundly troubling. Instead of a proper battlefield to contain the horror, they were fighting amid homes and farms. Both sides felt violated, and both sides found it necessary to regard the other as brutal and inhuman. Ever since the atrocity at the North Bridge, the regulars had viewed the provincials as tomahawk-wielding savages. For the New Englanders, this was King Philip's War redux. "The people say," the Reverend William Gordon reported, "that the soldiers are worse than the *Indians*."

Sergeant John Ford of Chelmsford had fought in the French and Indian War; so had Charles Furbush of Andover. At one point they came upon a regular stealing valuables from a roadside home, and together they rushed into the house and killed the soldier. Ford would kill a total of five regulars that day, but the fighting brought neither him nor Furbush any joy or satisfaction. "Our men seemed maddened with the sight of British blood and infuriated to wreak vengeance on the wounded and helpless," Furbush later told his grandson. At one point they came upon a fallen grenadier who'd been

"stabbed again and again" by passing militiamen. "Remembering the day
when they had called these men companions-in-arms," the two veterans
lifted up the dying soldier and gave him a drink of water.

On a hill outside Lexington, Captain John Parker and the remnants of his
militia company waited for the British column. Earlier that morning their
town, which had a total of 208 males over the age of sixteen in 1775, had lost
18 to death or injury. By this point, Colonel Smith and his regulars had been
reduced to a similar state of suffering. They had just endured a series of am-
bushes that had killed and wounded more than two dozen men. They had
long since given up any hope of reinforcements coming from Gage in Boston.
They were running out of ammunition. It was on this hill that Parker's company let forth their own devastating volley. "We were totally surrounded with
such an incessant fire," Lieutenant Barker wrote, "as it's impossible to con-
ceive." Captain Parsons, the leader of the battalion that had searched the Barrett farm in Concord, was wounded, as was Colonel Smith, who was shot in
the thigh. The regulars eventually cleared the hill, costing fifty-four-year-old
militiaman Jedidiah Munroe, who'd been wounded on Lexington Green, his
life. But the damage to Colonel Smith's little army had been done. In the minutes ahead, during which Major Pitcairn was thrown from his horse amid yet
another provincial onslaught, the British column fell into serious disarray. Today the rocky rise of land where the company from Lexington helped to initi-
ate the collapse of Smith's command is known as Parker's Revenge.

Soon after, at what was known as Concord Hill and is the last piece of
high ground before Lexington Green, the British officers lost control of their
men. "Our ammunition began to fail," Ensign DeBerniere explained, "and the
light companies were so fatigued with flanking they were scarce able to act,
and a great number of wounded scarce able to get forward, made a great confusion." With Smith and Pitcairn injured and with the bodies of the British
dead strewn along the bloody road behind them, the soldiers started to run
for the town green. The triangle of grass where the events of this long and
disquieting day had begun was now looked to as a possible sanctuary. At
least there were no stands of trees out of which yet another ambush might
erupt. Perhaps here, on this wide stretch of open grass, they might be able to
surrender. "We began to run rather than retreat in order . . . ," DeBerniere
remembered, "[the officers] attempted to stop the men and form them two
deep, but to no purpose, the confusion increased rather than lessened."

Just as Lieutenant Barker, one of the few uninjured officers, resigned himself to either laying "down our arms or [being] picked off by the rebels at their pleasure," the miraculous occurred. Up ahead, beyond the Lexington Meetinghouse, stretching across the road to Boston, was a long line of British regulars—more than 1,350 members of Hugh Percy's First Brigade, assembled in what the weary and bleeding Lieutenant Sutherland claimed was "one of the best dispositions ever I saw." What's more, they had artillery with them, and as Smith's ragged and exhausted column made its way toward Percy's brigade, a cannonball ripped through the walls of the Lexington Meetinghouse and sent the provincials scurrying for cover. Sutherland remembered, "We began to entertain very sanguine hopes of our returning in safety to Boston."

But as they were soon to discover, the fighting had just begun.

Before leaving Boston, Percy's brigade of almost fifteen hundred men had assembled on Tremont Street. The long line of regulars stretched all the way from the common's elm-lined mall to the Queen Street Writing School, at least a quarter mile away, where thirteen-year-old Benjamin Russell was in his final year. The entire city, Russell remembered, was "in agitation." For the boys of the Queen Street School, which was the poor man's alternative to Boston Latin, these were tremendously exciting times, especially when Master Carter dismissed class that morning with the phrase, "Boys, the war's begun, and you may run."

They were words that Russell and his compatriots took literally. When Percy's brigade left Boston around nine that morning, the Queen Street boys followed close behind. Once in Roxbury, Percy's fifers started playing "Yankee Doodle," a song from the French and Indian War that mocked the provincials' lack of social sophistication. But as it turned out, the boys would get the last laugh.

As the British fifers had their fun with "Yankee Doodle," a boy (who may or may not have been part of Russell's entourage) began "jumping and laughing" to the point that Percy asked "at what he was laughing so heartily." "To think," the boy responded, "how you will dance by and by to 'Chevy Chase.'" For hundreds of years, "Chevy Chase" had been one of the most popular ballads in Britain, and as it so happened, the song had a disturbing connection to Lord Percy's family. In the ballad, Percy, Earl of Northumberland, leads an ill-advised hunting trip across the Scottish border that results in a bloody clash between Percy and his Scottish counterpart the Earl of Douglas, both of whom are ultimately killed. What had begun as a lighthearted march into the New England countryside had been darkened by the mention of an ancient act of bloodshed. According to the Roxbury minister William Gordon, the boy's "repartee stuck by his lordship the whole day."

Earlier that morning, a messenger arrived at Joseph Warren's house on Hanover Street and told him of what had happened at Lexington. "His soul beat to arms," a contemporary remembered, "as soon as he learned the intention of the British troops." He woke up his medical assistant William Eustis and announced that it was time for him to take over the practice. By eight o'clock Warren had mounted his horse and was on his way out of Boston.

Instead of going by way of the Neck, Joseph Warren went by boat to Charlestown accompanied by his friend the printer Isaiah Thomas. While boarding the boat, Warren was overheard telling another acquaintance, "Keep up a brave heart! They have begun it—that either party can do; and we'll end it—that only one can do."

A meeting had been scheduled of the Committee of Safety at the Black Horse Tavern in Menotomy, where earlier that morning committee members Orne, Lee, and Gerry had evaded the British troops by lying in a cornfield. Warren came upon Percy's brigade in Cambridge as the troops made their way to Menotomy. The provincials had pulled up the planks of the bridge across the Charles in an attempt to prevent the regulars from entering the town. However, they'd left the planks stacked in plain sight, enabling Percy's soldiers to quickly repair the bridge, and the brigade had marched unhindered into Cambridge.

The road was filled with British regulars, and after helping drive away two soldiers who were attempting to confiscate a townsman's horse, Warren managed, with some difficulty, to make his way to the tavern in Menotomy. Also in attendance at the meeting that morning was William Heath, a thirty-eight-year-old farmer from Roxbury. As a boy, Heath had been, in his own words, "remarkably fond of military exercises," and had subsequently devoted himself to "the *theory* of war," and had bought and read "every military treatise in the English language which was obtainable." By 1772 he was colonel of the Suffolk County Militia; by the winter of 1775, he'd been appointed a general in the new provincial "army of observation."

There were generals who outranked Heath, but they all lived too far away to reach the scene of the fighting that day, and Heath resolved that he must get himself to Lexington as soon as possible. To avoid the British troops on the road to that town, he took the indirect route via Watertown, and at some point he met up with Joseph Warren. Given Warren's ambition to one day serve in a "high military capacity," he'd decided, an early biographer wrote, "that he should share the dangers of the field as a common soldier with his fellow citizens, that his reputation for bravery might be put beyond the possibility of suspicion." Heath was willing to let Warren accompany him as a volunteer, and over the course of the afternoon to come, the two seem to have been almost inseparable. For both men war was more a theoretical undertaking than a thing of blood and horror, but that was about to change.

Earlier that morning, the women of Acton had put together provisions for their husbands. It fell to their teenage sons to get the food to Concord. Francis Faulkner, sixteen, was one of these young men, but when he and his friends arrived at the North Bridge, they learned that not only had three of their townsmen been killed, but the British regulars—and the fighting—had moved east toward Boston. So the boys started down the road to Lexington. Not far from Meriam's Hill, they saw a man, wounded or dead, they couldn't tell for sure, lying beside a wall in a field. "That is my father!" Francis cried and, slipping off his horse, ran toward the fallen militiaman. "It was," his grandson later wrote, "a dreadful sight. . . . He had never seen death in such a bloody and ghastly form before. But it was not his father."

The boys from Acton continued on. The houses were all deserted. The bodies of dead soldiers littered the road. As the boys approached the town of Lexington they were filled with "fear and trembling." And then they heard the boom of a cannon.

Militiamen from towns all over New England had gathered on Lexington Green, their sweaty faces blackened by powder blasts, their knees and elbows stained by the mud and grass. The boys went from group to group, looking for their fathers, and finally they found them. To their astonishment, the Acton men were "in the highest spirits." They proudly informed their sons that they had avenged the deaths of their fellow Acton men "tenfold and would destroy all [the regulars] before they could get to Boston." Instead of being terrorized, these middle-aged husbands and fathers were having the time of their lives.

Faulkner was relieved, in a way, to see his father so "full of confidence and fight." But he was also troubled by the determination of the Acton men. "Indignation," Faulkner remembered, "filled every heart."

Not content with sending a cannon ball through the Lexington meetinghouse, General Percy ordered that several houses just to the east of the green be set on fire. The militiamen were shooting at his regulars from those houses, and the structures must be destroyed. "We set [the houses] on fire," one soldier wrote, "and they ran to the woods like devils." The stone walls were also harboring militiamen, and during the next hour the regulars pushed over more than one thousand yards of Deacon Joseph Loring's wall.

About a quarter mile behind Percy's front line was the Munroe Tavern, which in addition to providing the officers with food and drink served as a hospital. It was here that surgeon's mate Simms extracted a musket ball from Lieutenant Jeremy Lister's elbow. By the time the brigade began to head back to Boston, Lister was suffering from both a loss of blood and a lack of food. Too faint to walk, he asked Colonel Smith if he might borrow his horse. The previous night on Boston Common, when one of Smith's officers claimed to be too sick to participate in the expedition, Lister had volunteered to take his place. Back then, Smith had urged Lister to "return to town . . . and not go into danger for others," but Lister had felt that the honor of the regiment depended on his participation. Now that Lister's life appeared to be in the balance, Smith gladly gave him his horse, even though the colonel was suffering from a painful leg wound and was, in the words of Lieutenant Barker, "a very fat heavy man." A soldier offered Lister a bit of biscuit; another offered him a hatful of water from a horse pond. Feeling much better, Lister and the approximately two thousand men under General Percy's command left Lexington at about three in the afternoon. Now that the column stretched for almost half a mile, it took a full thirty minutes before they were all under way. The march back to Boston would take all the discipline and courage the British regulars could muster. About two miles to the southeast lay the town of Menotomy.

Heath and Warren arrived at Lexington just about the same time as Percy's brigade. Heath did what he could to pull together the scattered companies of militia into the makings of a proper regiment. The plan—if it could be called a plan—was to surround the British column with what Percy later described as "a moving circle . . . of incessant fire [that] followed us wherever we went."

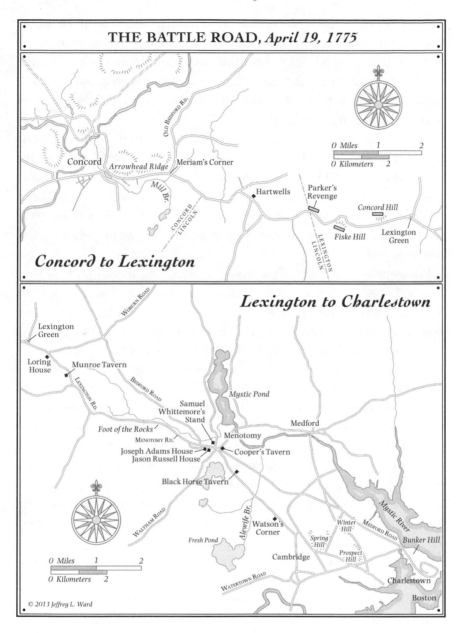

THE BATTLE ROAD, *April 19, 1775*

Concord to Lexington

Concord *Arrowhead Ridge* Meriam's Corner

OLD BEDFORD RD.

Mill Br.

CONCORD LINCOLN

Hartwells Parker's Revenge Concord Hill

Fiske Hill Lexington Green

LEXINGTON LINCOLN

0 Miles 1 2
0 Kilometers 2

Lexington to Charlestown

WOBURN ROAD

Lexington Green

Loring House Munroe Tavern

LEXINGTON RD. BEDFORD ROAD

Mystic Pond

Samuel Whittemore's Stand

Foot of the Rocks Medford

MENOTOMY RD. Menotomy

Joseph Adams House Cooper's Tavern
Jason Russell House

Black Horse Tavern

WALTHAM ROAD Alewife Br. Watson's Corner Winter Hill MEDFORD ROAD Bunker Hill

Mystic River

Fresh Pond Spring Hill

Cambridge Prospect Hill

0 Miles 1 2
0 Kilometers 2

WATERTOWN ROAD Charlestown

Boston

© 2013 Jeffrey L. Ward

Given the danger of the flank guards, the best place for the militiamen to harass the column was from behind, and in anticipation of this, Percy appointed a battalion from one of his most experienced regiments, the Welch Fusiliers, to be the rear guard. Adding to the difficulties encountered by the rear guard as they turned to defend the column from the militiamen gathered behind was the direction of the ever-increasing wind. Since it was blowing out of the west and they were headed east toward Boston, the regulars were continually blanketed in the powder smoke generated by their own muskets, "covering them," one colonist wrote, "with such a cloud that blinded them yet [still left them] . . . a plain mark for the militia."

As the fighting raged on and the fusiliers ran out of ammunition and men, Percy was forced to replace them with another battalion; over the course of the next fifteen miles, three different battalions served as the rear guard. In the meantime, the exhausted men of Colonel Smith's original expeditionary force marched in what was supposed to be the relative safety of the head of the column. But as they discovered, "the fire was nearly as severe [there] as in the rear."

Lieutenant Jeremy Lister, the wounded officer who'd been given Colonel Smith's horse, soon learned that a saddle was also not the best place to be. "I found the balls whistled so smartly around my ears," he wrote, "I thought it more prudent to dismount." Lister then used the horse as a shield, shifting from side to side so as to put the animal between him and the militiamen's fire. When a nearby horse with one wounded man on the saddle and three men cowering beside it was shot dead, Lister offered his horse to the now defenseless soldiers and decided to take his chances with the rest of the column. Other wounded soldiers hitched rides on the two fieldpieces, which were towed by horses. Whenever Percy ordered the cannons to be put to use, the soldiers who had been clinging to the weapons were sent tumbling to the ground as the fieldpieces were turned toward the column's rear and fired.

Some have claimed that, based on Heath's own account of his activities, he provided important tactical leadership during this portion of the fighting. However, given the chaotic realities of that afternoon, the effectiveness of the provincial fire had more to do with there being close to four thousand militiamen on the field that day than anything else. If an organizational element was responsible for the success of the provincials, it had been provided that winter by the Committee of Safety. What was happening that afternoon on what came to be known as the Battle Road was, for the most part, highly fluid and spontaneous. It also didn't hurt that many of the militia companies contained veterans of the French and Indian War who, unlike Heath, had experience in just this kind of guerilla-style fighting.

"Whoever looks upon them as an irregular mob," Percy later begrudgingly admitted, "will find himself much mistaken. They have men amongst them who know very well what they are about, having [been] employed as rangers against the Indians and Canadians and this country being much covered with wood and hills is very advantageous for their method of fighting." But what most impressed Percy was the personal courage these militiamen demonstrated as they methodically hunted the British officers in the column. Unlike the enlisted men, whose cheaply dyed red coats quickly faded to a pinkish orange, the officers' coats were made with a more expensive and long-lasting crimson dye and were easily distinguished from the washed-out uniforms of the rank and file. For the militiamen, the vivid red of the officers' coats presented a target that was too tempting to resist. "Many of [the provincials] . . . advanced within ten yards to fire at me and the other officers," Percy marveled, "though they were morally certain of being put to death themselves in an instant."

Lieutenant Mackenzie of the Welch Fusiliers made special note of those provincials who used horses to increase their effectiveness against the British column. "Numbers of them were mounted," he wrote, "and when they had fastened their horses at some little distance from the road, they crept down near enough to have a shot. As soon as the column had passed, they mounted again, and rode round until they got ahead of the column and found some convenient place from whence they might fire again." Just as the colonial veterans of the French and Indian War were relying on their own considerable experience and judgment as they joined in on the fighting, so were these lone riders acting on their own initiative.

What Heath provided that afternoon and evening was not tactical and strategic brilliance but legitimacy. Simply by being there, he, as a general in the provincial army, made what happened along the road to Boston something more than a backyard skirmish between some irate farmers and the regulars of the British Empire. With Heath and his companion Dr. Joseph Warren standing there on the hip of the column's rear guard, the provincials were beginning to have, in a very crude and inchoate form, the trappings of a command structure.

They were a most unlikely pair. Heath was fat and bald. Warren was tallish and handsome, his hair pinned up on the sides of his head in stylish horizontal rolls. There is no mention of Heath taking any extraordinary risks that day, but Warren was, according to one contemporary, "perhaps the most active man in the field." At a section of Menotomy known as Foot of the Rocks,

Warren put himself so squarely in harm's way that a British musket ball struck out one of the pins that was holding up his curled hair. "The people were delighted with his cool, collected bravery and already considered him as a leader," one commentator wrote.

As a military novice, Warren clearly didn't have much expertise to offer. What he did have was a charismatic talent for inspiring people. And he was learning.

Warren wasn't the only one who tried to look his best that day. Before leaving Acton, many of the town's militiamen carefully powdered their hair with flour. Jotham Webb was a brickmaker from Lynn. He'd recently gotten married, and before leaving that morning, he put on the wedding suit he'd worn just a few days before. "If I die," he told his new wife, "I will die in my best clothes."

That afternoon Jotham and the rest of his company from Lynn decided to position themselves ahead of the British column near the house of Jason Russell in Menotomy. Russell, fifty-eight, had been about to reshingle his house, and using the bales of cedar shingles to create a kind of breastworks in his front yard, he, with the help of the militiamen, resolved to defend his property against the approaching British. Some of the militiamen were posted behind the shingles; others assembled on the hillside behind the house, where an orchard provided some cover. On the other side of the road, Gideon Foster and some militiamen from Danvers put together the makings of what they hoped would be an ambush. As the vanguard of the British column became visible coming down the road from Lexington, Russell's neighbor Ammi Cutter warned him that he was much too close to the road for his own safety. Russell, who was lame and apparently quite stubborn, waved him off with the words, "An Englishman's home is his castle."

The British hit them like a thunderbolt—not from the road, but from behind. As the militiamen looked eagerly for the column, flankers came at them from seemingly nowhere, flushing the provincials out of the orchard and toward the house. Since the column was coming at them from the road, they were trapped between the hammer and anvil of the flankers and the advance guard. The would-be ambushers had been outflanked, and one of the first killed was Jotham Webb in his new bridal suit, soon followed by his twenty-five-year-old friend Abednego Ramsdell.

The desperate survivors of the initial British onslaught fled for the safety of Jason Russell's house. Russell was killed on his own doorstep, shot twice and stabbed an estimated eleven times by British bayonets. The Russell house was a typical, very humble colonial structure—two rooms on the ground floor and two rooms upstairs, with a cellar down below. Anything but a castle, the home of Jason Russell was about to become a slaughterhouse.

Eight men from Danvers, Beverly, and Lynn hurried into the darkness of the cellar. They proved to be the lucky ones. By blasting away at any regular who dared to approach the cellar entrance, they were able to hold off the soldiers even as they filled the beams of the house with bullet holes that can still be seen today. The militiamen who remained up above found themselves in the greatest trouble as the regulars poured into the house. Soon the rooms were filled with the ear-splitting boom of muskets and choking clouds of powder-smoke. In desperation, Daniel Townsend and Timothy Munroe jumped through the windows. Townsend took out the entire window sash and was dead when he hit the ground. Somehow Munroe was still alive when he tumbled from the window; he staggered to his feet and began to run. Regulars fired at him repeatedly but to no effect. "Damn him!" one was heard to cry. "He is bullet proof, let him go." Munroe, who received just a wound in the leg, later found thirty-two bullet holes in his clothes and hat; even his buttons had been shot off. Outside the house Dennison Wallis was taken captive. He quickly realized that the British were executing their prisoners. So he decided to run for it. He ultimately received twelve wounds and was left for dead, but somehow he survived.

A total of twelve provincials and two regulars were killed at the Jason Russell house. Later that day the dozen bodies were laid out in the south room. According to Jason Russell's wife, the blood was "almost ankle deep" when she returned to find her husband dead and her house "riddled with bullets." Two days later, the bodies were piled on a sled and dragged by oxen to the cemetery. The townspeople dug a trench and laid the bodies "head to point" in a single grave.

Several more harrowing incidents occurred along the road through Menotomy, all of them within hearing, if not seeing, distance of each other. Seventy-eight-year-old Samuel Whittemore decided to make a stand not far from his house. After killing several regulars, he took a musket ball to the jaw and was bayoneted repeatedly before being left for dead. He lived for another eleven years. Prior to Whittemore's encounter, Deacon Joseph Adams had run for the safety of the hay barn, leaving his wife and children (among them a newborn baby) hiding in his house's bedroom. Fortunately, Adams's nine-year-old son showed a bit more pluck than his father, and after admonishing the regulars for stealing the family silver, the boy used some newly brewed beer to put out a fire that might have otherwise destroyed the house.

At Cooper's Tavern, two townspeople insisted on enjoying a rum drink known as a flip even as the regulars approached. The tavern keeper and his wife fled for the cellar, leaving their customers to have their brains literally bashed out by the soldiers. Just outside Menotomy in the outskirts of Cambridge, at a house on Watson's Corner, yet another group of novice militiamen, many of them from the town of Brookline, were "scooped up" by the British flank guard and killed. It's estimated that approximately half the total deaths that occurred that day (forty-nine for the provincials, sixty-eight for the British) happened in and around Menotomy.

Soon after the incident at Watson's Corner, with sunset approaching, General Percy made the decision that saved his command. Rather than push on through Cambridge and return to Boston via the bridge, he veered left and headed for Charlestown, just a few miles away on the other side of a narrow, defensible neck and under the protective guns of the navy. This seems to have caught General Heath completely by surprise. In his memoirs Heath was quite proud of the fact that prior to heading for Lexington, he instructed the Watertown militia to dismantle, once again, the bridge. He appears to have also sent instructions to prepare an ambush for the British. What he had not anticipated was this last-minute decision on the part of Percy to make what was, in retrospect, a quite predictable move given what Percy had earlier encountered when crossing the bridge into Cambridge.

But as it turned out, the provincials had, unknown to Heath, a trick up their sleeve. Marching south from Salem were militia captain Timothy Pickering Jr. and several hundred men. Instead of taking the road through Menotomy, the Salem men were well to the east in Medford. If they pushed on, they just might cut off the British before they reached Charlestown.

As Pickering marched south and the British continued to fight their way, house by house, toward Charlestown, John Andrews looked out from the hills of Boston. He could see, he wrote, "the engagement very plain. It was very bloody for seven hours." Benjamin Franklin's sister Jane Mecom later wrote to her brother of "the horror the town was in when the battle approached within hearing," especially since it was expected that the fighting "would proceed quite in to town." Similar fears were felt in communities throughout the region. Like Andrews in Boston, the Reverend Samuel West watched the fighting from Needham. "We could easily trace the march of the troops from the smoke which arose over them," he wrote, "and could hear from my house the report of the cannon and the platoons [i.e., volleys] fired by the British." Even worse for the residents of Needham, who lost five that day, were "the infinitely more distressing scenes which we expected would follow. We even anticipated the enemy enraged as they were at our doors and in our houses acting over all the horrors which usually attend the progress of a victorious exasperated army especially in civil wars like this."

In Menotomy, where the women and children had gathered in houses safely removed from the firing, the rumor began to circulate that the town's slaves were about to launch a revolt of their own and "finish what the British had begun by murdering the defenseless women and children." When Ishmael, an enslaved man belonging to the Cutler family, approached the house of George Prentiss, one of the many terrified women gathered inside asked, "Are you going to kill us, Ishmael?" No, Ishmael replied; he wasn't there to kill them; he was there to see whether his owner's wife, Mrs. Cutler, was safe.

A similar fear overtook the women of Framingham, who armed themselves with "axes and pitchforks and clubs" and assembled in the Edgell house, convinced that "the Negroes were coming to massacre them all." One resident later attributed this "strange panic" to "a lingering memory of the earlier Indian alarms . . . , aided by the feeling of terror awakened by their defenseless condition and the uncertainty of the issue of the pending fight."

Whatever the source of this terrible fright might have been, it marked a disturbing transformation among the citizens of Massachusetts. Reverend West of Needham claimed that prior to Lexington and Concord, his parishioners had been "mild and gentle." Once their loved ones began to die, however, these same parishioners became "ferocious and cruel—at least towards all those they suspected as unfriendly to their cause." In town after town, the battle lines were being drawn.

Around seven in the evening, Percy and his column reached the safety of Charlestown, where a height of land known as Bunker Hill provided the defensive ground they needed to convince the provincials to discontinue the pursuit. It was dusk, dark enough, William Heath remembered, "as to render the flashes of the muskets very visible."

Heath later came to the conclusion that there could have been a very different result that evening. If only Captain Timothy Pickering and his men from Salem had "arrived a few minutes sooner," Heath wrote, "the left flank of the British must have been greatly exposed and suffered considerably; perhaps their retreat would have been cut off." In other words, if Pickering had only shown the proper spirit, April 19, 1775, might have ended with a decisive American victory.

In his defense, Pickering claimed that he had marched his men from Salem as quickly as was reasonably possible. But like James Nichols, the Englishman from Lincoln who decided that he could not fire a musket in anger at the North Bridge in Concord, Pickering had his reasons to avoid a confrontation. Even though he had been instrumental in organizing the militia not only in Salem but throughout New England, he was not part of the patriot inner circle. For one thing, his father, Timothy Pickering Sr., was an outspoken loyalist. But Timothy Pickering Jr. was too "assuming . . . and headstrong" to let even his own father influence what he decided to do. In the future, Pickering would become one of George Washington's most trusted officers, and he eventually served as secretary of state under both Washington and John Adams. But on the evening of April 19 he still believed, he wrote a friend, that "a pacification upon honorable terms is practicable."

Rather than charging into Cambridge and cutting Percy off, Pickering lingered on Winter Hill, more than a mile away, where he stood at the head of his men and looked toward Charlestown in the deepening twilight. Pickering was so nearsighted that if he didn't wear his glasses, "the smallest object he could discern . . . was a regiment." One of his officers later remembered seeing him "riding along at night with the light of the campfires flashing on his spectacles." Playing across the lenses of his glasses that evening on Winter Hill were the muzzle flashes of British and provincial muskets. Pickering looked through those pieces of glittering glass and saw not a war to be won but a reason to talk.

He was, it turned out, in the minority.

CHAPTER EIGHT

No Business but That of War

By the morning of Thursday, April 20, hundreds if not thousands of militiamen had flooded into Cambridge and Roxbury, with thousands more on the way from towns across Massachusetts. With the exception of the harbor, which was dominated by Admiral Graves's warships, British-occupied Boston had been effectively surrounded by militiamen from the country. All the while, terrified noncombatants began to put as much distance as possible between themselves and the British regulars stationed inside Boston.

That morning, after a day and a night listening to the distant firing of guns, the Bostonian Sarah Winslow Deming was shaking so uncontrollably that she had trouble standing, as did her two female houseguests, one of whom she expected to "fall into hysteric fits every minute," while the other clung desperately to "anything she could grasp." They must, Deming wrote in a diary account of her ordeal, flee this "city of destruction" and take their chances in the country. Deming's husband insisted on remaining, at least temporarily, in Boston, but he was willing to drive his wife and her companions out of the city in a chaise before he returned to make sure their home and personal effects were safe. Soon the Demings had joined a long line of carriages and carts waiting to exit the city. After making it past four different British sentries, they were finally on the road to Roxbury. Deming's husband asked where she wanted to go next; Sarah told him to let the horse decide. The horse followed the road up to Meetinghouse Hill, which was crowded, Deming wrote, with militiamen "old, young, and middle-aged." She was struck by the "pleasant sedateness on all their countenances." Instead of being encouraged by the provincials' presence, Deming was reminded of "sheep going to the slaughter."

Harvard professor John Winthrop and his wife Hannah had spent the night in a house in Fresh Pond, about a mile from their home in Cambridge, with between seventy and eighty anguished wives and their children. As Cambridge filled up with militiamen from as far away as Worcester, they and three others decided to head to Andover. They took turns riding and then walking beside "one poor tired horse chaise" as they made their way through what Hannah described as "the bloody field at Menotomy . . . strewn with mangled bodies." "We met one affectionate father with a cart," she wrote, "looking for his murdered son and picking up his neighbors who had fallen in battle." Another New Englander traveling in the opposite direction noted that the houses "were all perforated with balls and the windows broken. Horses, cattle and swine lay dead around. Such were the dreadful trophies of war for twenty miles." It was no wonder "all [was] confusion," Deacon William Tudor of Brighton reported. "The rumor was that if the soldiers came out again they would burn, kill, and destroy all as they marched." Like Sarah Deming, who spent the night with the Reverend William Gordon in Roxbury before traveling to Rhode Island and then to Connecticut, they must turn their backs on the city that had once been the center of their lives.

Panic and confusion had also gripped the British soldiers in Boston. It was close to midnight by the time Lieutenant Jeremy Lister, his right arm swollen and caked in blood, crossed the harbor and staggered up the crooked street to the house where he lived with several officers. As he sat on a chair, stunned and famished, waiting for a pot of tea to brew, he was besieged by people wanting to know about the events of that terrible day. By his own estimation, he had marched "about sixty miles in [the] course of twenty-four hours," almost half of those miles "after I was wounded and without a morsel of victuals." It was no wonder, then, that when someone asked about Lieutenant Sutherland, who had received a musket ball in the chest at the North Bridge, Lister dispensed with all tact and said exactly what he assumed to be the case. "I replied [that] I supposed by that time he was dead." Unknown to Lister, Sutherland's wife was standing behind him, and she "immediately dropped down in [a] swoon."

That night Admiral Graves urged General Gage to allow his warships to blast Charlestown and Roxbury to pieces so that the British army could seize the high ground to the north and south. Gage insisted that his army was not strong enough to undertake such a bold move. The best that they could do was to dig in and prepare for the attack that they all assumed was about to come from the provincials.

On the morning of Thursday, April 20, Captain Timothy Pickering was asked to attend a meeting in Cambridge. In addition to key militia officers, the group included members of the Committee of Safety, most notably Dr. Joseph Warren. The topic for discussion that morning was nothing less than *what to do next*.

After watching Percy's retreat into Charlestown the night before, Pickering had assumed that the fighting at Lexington and Concord was the equivalent of the Stamp Act Riots of 1765 and the Boston Massacre of 1770: an eruption of violence that was soon to be followed by a gesture of British forbearance. There was no need to assemble an army until after they had first seen whether General Gage wanted to negotiate. Some of those present agreed with Pickering, but only some. "Others thought that now was the time to strike," he wrote, "and cut off the troops before they were reinforced; and then, said they, the day will be our own." Pickering believed such talk was recklessly unrealistic. "I do not see," he wrote, "what mighty advantage can accrue to us by getting possession of Boston; none, I am sure, which can countervail the loss of thousands in storming the town, which will immediately be beat to pieces by the men-of-war."

But what troubled Pickering the most about the meeting was not the wildness of the rhetoric; it was the motives of the more radical patriot leaders. Up until that moment, Pickering had assumed they were driven by an honest love of country; but now he had the unsettling suspicion that "*ambition . . . was as powerful a stimulus as the former.*" And with John Hancock and Samuel Adams soon to depart for Philadelphia, Joseph Warren had emerged as the de facto leader of what Pickering described as "the intended revolution."

That day Warren issued a circular letter for distribution throughout the colony under the auspices of the Committee of Safety, urging men to enlist in the provincial army. It was not a moderate document. "Our all is at stake," he wrote. "Death and devastation are the instant consequences of delay. Every moment is infinitely precious. An hour lost may deluge your country in blood, and entail perpetual slavery upon the few of your posterity who may survive the carnage. We beg and entreat, as you will answer to your country, to your own consciences, and, above all, as you will answer to God himself, that you will hasten and encourage by all possible means the enlistment of men to form the army, and send them forward to headquarters at Cambridge."

Warren took a different tone when he turned his attention to what he referred to as "my ever-adored town." Since the first tumultuous hours after Lexington and Concord—during which Sarah Deming and her friends had been lucky enough to escape—Boston had been almost completely sealed off from the surrounding countryside. Across from the fortifications at Boston Neck, Roxbury had quickly become a town populated chiefly by militiamen, making it impossible for Gage and his army to receive any provisions or supplies from the city's only access point to the mainland. Before the many patriots trapped inside Boston could get out and the loyalists outside the city could get in, some kind of agreement had to be reached with Gage. That day, Warren wrote the general a letter about the need to settle on a policy regarding Boston. Instead of the hysteria and bluster of the earlier call for recruits, Warren addressed his counterpart as a leader he both respected and was willing to trust. "Your Excellency, I believe, knows very well the part I have taken in public affairs," he wrote. "I ever scorned disguise. I think I have done my duty. Some may think otherwise; but be assured, sir, as far as my influence goes, everything which can reasonably be required of us to do shall be done, and everything promised shall be religiously performed." Warren was just thirty-three years old and hardly a career politician. A doctor who had been raised on a farm in Roxbury, he had first assumed elective office less than a year before, yet he apparently had no qualms about writing the man at the apex of political and military power in British North America as an equal. Perhaps Timothy Pickering was right; perhaps there was more than a modicum of ambition behind Warren's commitment to the patriot cause. But exactly this kind of ambition was to become the driving force—both for good and for bad—behind the United States.

The next day, Friday, April 21, the Committee of Safety determined to raise an army of eight thousand Massachusetts soldiers to serve until the end of the year, even though no one was yet sure how the soldiers were going to be paid. By that time the provincial army had a new leader, General Artemas Ward, forty-seven, from Shrewsbury. A veteran of the French and Indian War and a former member of the upper chamber of the General Court, Ward had been languishing in bed with an attack of kidney stones when he received word of Lexington and Concord. That had not prevented him from riding almost forty miles to Cambridge, where he presided over his first council of war on the night of April 20. Over the course of the next few days, Ward began to organize his rudimentary army.

General John Thomas, fifty-one, a doctor from Kingston who had served with distinction in the French and Indian War, was put in charge of the provincials stationed in Roxbury. Israel Putnam was the already mythologized warrior from Connecticut who had visited Boston the year before. He had been plowing his fields on April 20 when, at a little before noon, he received word of Lexington and Concord. He handed the plow over to his son and was in Cambridge by the following day. He was soon ranging restlessly up and down the lines stretching from the ridge of hills overlooking the Mystic River to the inner reaches of the Charles River.

In the days to come, militiamen arrived from towns in not only Massachusetts and Connecticut but Rhode Island, New Hampshire, and Maine. The Provincial Congress eventually decided to raise a New England–wide army of as many as 30,000 men, with Massachusetts's quota increased to 13,600. Having raised armies in the past for the many wars against the French and Indians, the region's leaders had considerable experience in recruiting soldiers. Traditionally, the officers did the actual recruiting, with the officer's rank based on how many soldiers he could convince to enlist (a captain, for example, had to raise fifty men; a lieutenant, twenty-five). Since officers typically recruited in their hometowns, each company tended to be made up of neighbors, friends, and relatives, all of whom looked with considerable suspicion on anyone whom they didn't already know. And yet with companies of militiamen already beginning to arrive from towns throughout the colony and beyond, Cambridge and Roxbury were rapidly becoming the chaotic centers of what was, for New England, a remarkably diverse gathering of humanity. Included in this new army would be farmers, sailors, artisans, merchants, doctors, lawyers, some free African Americans (the Provincial Congress quickly determined that the recruitment of slaves was "inconsistent with the principles that are to be supported and reflect dishonor on this colony"), and Native Americans from western Massachusetts and Connecticut.

It was an exciting time—the kind of time when no one knew what was going to happen next. Benjamin Russell was the thirteen-year-old student at Boston's Queen Street School who had followed Percy's brigade out of Boston. Once in Cambridge he and his classmates had decided to spend the afternoon playing games on the town's common, only to discover on the evening of April 19 that they were now trapped outside Boston with no way to communicate with their parents. Instead of despairing, they volunteered to serve as errand boys for the officers of the emerging army. Russell would not hear from his parents for another three months.

Around sunset on Friday, April 21, as a meeting of the Committee of Safety drew to a close in Cambridge, Benjamin Church announced, "I am determined to go into Boston tomorrow." The other committee members were dumbfounded. "Are you serious, Dr. Church?" Joseph Warren asked. "They will hang you if they catch you in Boston." Church was insistent. "I am serious," he said, "and am determined to go at all adventures."

The discussion continued, and when Church, who like many of them had family in the city, insisted that he was willing to risk possible capture, Warren said, "If you are determined, let us make some business for you." The provincial army was in desperate need of medical equipment to tend to the wounded, which included several British prisoners, and Church was given the mission to secure whatever Gage and his medical staff might be willing to give.

Church appears to have prepared the way for this announcement by providing what he hoped was incontrovertible proof that he was a man to be trusted. Paul Revere was serving as the committee's messenger, and the morning after Lexington and Concord, Church had shown him "some blood on his stocking," claiming that it had "spurted on him from a man who was killed near him as he was urging the militia on." "I argued with myself," Revere later remembered, "if a man will risk his life in a cause, he must be a friend to that cause."

Still, the decision to cross the British lines was a bold one, even by the standards of Benjamin Church, who would have the audacity to meet with Gage the next day at the governor's residence in Province House. But as Church knew better than anyone, Warren and the other patriot leaders were too preoccupied with trying to stay ahead of each new and potentially catastrophic development to question his motivations. For now at least, they were willing to give him the benefit of the doubt.

Gage had been reluctant to do anything more than hunker down for a siege—with one notable exception. On Thursday, April 20, he launched a rescue mission. Back in January, he had sent a force of about a hundred regulars under the command of Captain Nesbitt Balfour to Marshfield, where they had based themselves at the estate of Nathaniel Ray Thomas (a distant relative of provincial general John Thomas). Balfour and his men had enjoyed a quiet winter and spring (even finding the time to construct an elaborate wine cabinet in the cellar of Thomas's house) until the fighting at Lexington and Concord inspired more than a thousand militiamen from the towns surrounding Marshfield to descend on the loyalist stronghold.

On the morning of April 20, Gage ordered Admiral Graves to provide the vessels needed to extract Balfour and his men from Marshfield. Soon the schooner *Hope* and two recently confiscated wood sloops were on their way to the rugged piece of coastline at the mouth of the Cut River known as Brant Rock. Despite having an overwhelming numerical advantage, the militiamen surrounding the Thomas estate were reluctant to engage the British regulars. A message was sent to General Thomas in Roxbury requesting that he lead them in what might prove to be a battle that put the previous day's fighting to shame. Although General Ward needed him in Roxbury, Thomas was able to provide the militia forces in Marshfield with "eleven hundred brave men and cannon." By the time the provincial reinforcements arrived, Balfour's detachment, along with a hundred or so loyalists, had bluffed their way onto the three rescue vessels and were headed for Boston. The lesson was clear: even the most enthusiastic and well-meaning militiamen were military amateurs who needed competent officers to lead them.

Back on the morning of April 19, Committee of Safety member Joseph Palmer had given a professional post rider named Isaac Bissell a letter with a brief description of the engagement at Lexington Green. Paul Revere may have helped spread the word that the regulars were coming on the night of April 18, but Bissell helped to spread the news of the fighting at Lexington across the Atlantic seaboard. According to tradition, he was in Worcester by early that afternoon, his exhausted horse falling down dead in front of the town's meetinghouse. From there, Bissell went to Hartford, Connecticut, and by the evening of the next day, Thursday, April 20, another rider had carried the message to New London. By the evening of April 21 the message had reached New York City; by 5:00 p.m. of April 24, it had reached Philadelphia.

Everywhere the news was received, it caused a sensation. At Brunswick, North Carolina, word of the fighting at Lexington was forwarded to Charleston, South Carolina, with the note, "I request, for the good of our country and the welfare of our lives and liberties and fortunes, you will not lose a moment's time." By the first week in May the news had spread south to Georgia and west across the Blue Ridge into the Shenandoah Valley. When a group of frontiersmen camped on the middle fork of Elkhorn Creek heard about the militiamen's deaths in Massachusetts, they decided to name their outpost for the historic event. That is why what was then a part of Virginia is known today as Lexington, Kentucky.

On Saturday, April 22, the Provincial Congress of Massachusetts convened for the first time since the outbreak of violence, meeting briefly at Concord before adjourning to Watertown so as to be closer to what was becoming the center of provincial activity in Cambridge. That afternoon the Congress formed a committee to take depositions "from which a full account of the transactions of the troops, under General Gage, in their route to and from Concord, on Wednesday the last, may be collected, to be sent to England, by the first ship from Salem." General Gage was already preparing his own official account, which would soon be on its way to London. Massachusetts must prove that the British not only had fired the first shot but were now waging a most brutal and inhumane war against innocent New England citizens.

Even though the next day was a Sunday, Congress convened at 7:00 a.m. With John Hancock about to head for Philadelphia, they needed a new president. That afternoon an election was held for a "president *pro tempore*," and the committee appointed to count the ballots reported that "the vote was full for Doctor Warren."

That same day, even as Admiral Graves oversaw the construction of a battery of cannons amid the cemetery stones of Copp's Hill in the North End, the fate of many of Boston's still-remaining patriots was being decided at an emergency town meeting. Gage had offered the town's inhabitants a proposal that had been approved by Warren and the Committee of Safety. If the Bostonians agreed to surrender their weapons, he would allow anyone who was so inclined to exit the city with whatever baggage they could take with them. It was humiliating to have to hand over their guns, but after a day-long town meeting in Faneuil Hall, they reluctantly agreed. In the days ahead a staggering 1,778 muskets, 634 pistols, 973 bayonets, and 38 blunderbusses were collected and labeled for eventual return.

Gage appears to have initially offered the proposal in good faith. With no more foodstuffs coming into Boston from the country, the fewer mouths to feed the better. The loyalists in the city, however, saw it differently. They were convinced that the presence of a sizable number of patriots in Boston had prevented their rebellious brethren from mounting an attack. They needed what were in effect hostages to ensure that the ever-increasing hordes in Roxbury and Cambridge did not come rampaging across the Neck and kill them all. Bowing to the loyalists' demands, Gage ultimately refused to honor the agreement he had made with the town's inhabitants, one of the few instances during his tenure in Boston when he did not keep his word.

Eventually Gage settled on a kind of compromise. A limited number of people were allowed to leave as long as they did not take any of their possessions with them. Those who were prepared to depart at all costs, such as John Andrews's wife, Ruthy (who was as incapacitated by fear as Sarah Deming had been), eventually left the city. Her husband, however, decided to stay. If he left, there would be no one to watch over their home and personal effects, and he was, at least for now, unwilling to lose everything. Reverend Andrew Eliot was the minister of the New North Meeting; his wife and children and most of his congregation had already left the city, as had almost every other Congregational minister, but he resolved to stay. Someone, he decided, needed to look after the spiritual life of those few remaining residents. "I have been prevailed with to officiate to those who are still left to tarry," he explained, "but my situation is uncomfortable to the last degree—friends perpetually coming to bid me adieu, much the greater parts of the inhabitants gone out of town—the rest following as fast as the general will give leave." Patriots and loyalists alike found it both sad and terrifying to watch as the city was, in the words of Peter Oliver, "reduced to a perfect skeleton."

Over the course of the next few months more than nine thousand people left Boston as the provincial army that surrounded the city grew to the point that it came close to approaching Boston's former population of fifteen thousand. A city had been turned inside out: flushed of its inhabitants and artificially stuffed, as if by a taxidermist, with a British army that, as military transports continued to arrive in Boston Harbor, eventually approached nine thousand men.

With the economic life of the city having come to a standstill, Boston quickly became a ragged ghost of what it had once been. "Grass growing in the public walks and streets of this once populous and flourishing place," the Reverend Andrew Eliot wrote, "shops and warehouses shut up. Business at an end and everyone in anxiety and distress. The provincial army at our doors. The [British] troops absolutely confined in this town which is almost an island and surrounded with ships which [are] its greatest security. . . . These things . . . keep us in perpetual alarm and make this a very unquiet habitation. I cannot stand it long."

As Eliot observed, Boston was "almost an island," actually one of dozens of islands dotting a huge harbor that was in many places dangerously shallow and difficult to navigate. And as he also observed, the British warships that lay anchored around the city were "its greatest security." However, the sheer size of these ships meant that while their cannons provided plenty of protection, their depth of draft curtailed their mobility in this harbor of mudflats and lurking rocks to the point that smaller vessels—in particular those indigenous American watercraft such as schooners and the even smaller and rowable whaleboats—could literally sail circles around these ponderous men-of-war. The British were quick to see the advantage of the close-winded schooner, and Graves had added several of these vessels to his fleet, highlighted by the new and well-equipped *Diana*, commanded by Graves's nephew, Lieutenant Thomas Graves.

The provincials realized that if they were ever going to mount an assault on Boston, they must do it primarily by water. General Putnam had come up with the idea of storming Boston Neck behind bales of tightly packed hay, but most of the assault force must approach by boats—and small boats at that, given the shallowness of the immense Back Bay, which lay between Cambridge and Boston's western shore. And so the call had gone out throughout coastal Massachusetts for whaleboats. Over the course of the next few weeks dozens upon dozens of these canoelike craft—some of them confiscated from the largely loyalist whaling port of Nantucket—headed toward Boston Harbor like a flock of migrating birds. Paul Litchfield lived in the coastal town of Scituate, and one day that spring he stopped to watch as "a number of whaleboats went along the shore from the southward for the use of our army." Boat-building operations were begun in Cambridge to add to the fleet that was to include what were known as "fire boats," raftlike vessels designed to transport an explosive blaze of devastating fire to the men-of-war anchored around Boston. When Gage learned of the provincials' plans (a spy report claimed that as many as three hundred whaleboats had already been collected), he ordered Admiral Graves to take any small craft his officers might come across as they patrolled the reaches of Boston Harbor.

Besides preparing for a possible provincial invasion, the most immediate concerns Gage had were not only providing his army with food but also procuring hay, which was used as bedding for his men. Since he no longer had access to the surrounding countryside, he was forced to look to the harbor's grass-covered islands, many of which were dotted with unguarded herds of sheep and cattle. In the weeks to come, as the size of the army grew and the quantity of provisions diminished, the British forces found themselves in a kind of nautical chess game as they competed with the provincials for access to these resource-rich islands.

By Friday, April 28, the maritime focus of the provincial army had temporarily shifted to a single vessel—a little schooner of sixty or so feet named the *Quero*, captained by thirty-four-year-old John Derby of Salem. On Monday, April 24, Gage had sent his official account of Lexington and Concord to London aboard the *Sukey*. Since then the provincials had been hard at work collecting depositions that had been condensed into a report written, in part, by none other than Benjamin Church. Warren had addressed the cover letter to Benjamin Franklin (who, unknown to the patriots, had already left London for Philadelphia), and now the package was ready for transport to England. Four years before, a loyalist account of the Boston Massacre had been the first to reach London, putting the patriots at an immediate disadvantage. This time, the provincials vowed, their account would be the one to reach London first, even though Gage already had a four-day head start. The *Quero* might be less than a third of the displacement of the *Sukey*, but she was fast. To get the absolute most out of her performance, she was "in ballast," which meant that instead of a cargo she carried nothing but ballast stones in her hold, carefully positioned by Captain Derby so as to optimize the schooner's trim and speed through the water. In the early hours of Saturday, April 29, the *Quero* sneaked out of Salem Harbor, beginning a race that might very well change the course of history.

Almost lost in this furious rush of events was the arrival just three days before of a vessel from England bearing Josiah Quincy Jr. After his months in London observing the workings of the ministry and Parliament, combined with his many conversations with Benjamin Franklin and other Americans with a deep understanding of British policy, he felt he had information that was of immense importance to the future of Massachusetts. He must speak directly with either Samuel Adams or Joseph Warren.

The passage had been long and miserable, made all the more agonizing by Quincy's rapidly deteriorating health. By the time the vessel came within sight of land, Quincy knew he did not have long to live and expressed his last wishes to one of the ship's sailors, who dutifully wrote a transcript of the young lawyer's dying soliloquy. Quincy was convinced that what he had to tell Adams and Warren might have been of "great service to my country," but he dared not commit his message to paper. We will never know what Quincy wanted to say. However, given the drastic changes that had occurred since Lexington and Concord, Quincy's almost two-month-old insights were probably no longer relevant. In the end, Quincy, like virtually everyone who had attempted to improve relations between Great Britain and her rebellious colonies, was defeated by the sea.

The following day, April 27, Joseph Warren wrote to their mutual friend Arthur Lee in London. "Our friend Quincy just lived to come on shore to die in his own country," he wrote. "He expired yesterday morning. His virtues rendered him dear, and his abilities useful, to his country." And that was it.

Without a paragraph break, Warren launched into a description of New England at this critical juncture. "I think it probable," he wrote, "that the rage of the people . . . will lead them to attack General Gage, and burn the ships in the harbor. . . . The next news from England must be conciliatory, or the connection between us ends, however fatal the consequences may be."

Despite the posturing that had so troubled Timothy Pickering on the day after Lexington and Concord, Warren still felt that a reconciliation was possible. "If anything is proposed that may be for the honor and safety of Great Britain and these colonies," he wrote, "my utmost efforts shall not be wanting." Warren ended this brief, hurriedly dashed-off expression of grief, resolve, anger, and hope—which appears to have been personally delivered to Lee by Captain Derby of the *Quero*—with a glimpse of himself amid the provincial army in Cambridge. He was, he wrote Lee, "in the utmost haste, surrounded by fifteen or twenty thousand men."

Even before the outbreak of fighting, the provincial forces realized that the secret to ousting the British from Boston required something they did not have: a suitable number of cannons. They also realized that they needed officers with the artillery skills required to fire these cannons. Two Boston men fit the bill perfectly: Colonel Richard Gridley, sixty-five, a hero of the 1745 Siege of Louisbourg, and Lieutenant Colonel William Burbeck, fifty-nine, who had been serving at the Castle for a number of years. Both officers had already worked extensively with the British army; in fact, Gridley was one of the handful of Americans with a commission in that army—a prize that not even George Washington had been able to win. To secure these two valuable officers, the Provincial Congress offered Gridley and Burbeck not only salaries but lifetime annuities. But if the provincial army now had two experienced artillery officers, it still did not have a sufficient number of cannons.

On Sunday, April 29, a new arrival from New Haven, Connecticut, named Benedict Arnold told Joseph Warren and the Committee of Safety exactly what they wanted to hear. At the poorly defended British stronghold of Fort Ticonderoga at the southern end of Lake Champlain there were "80 pieces of heavy cannon, 20 brass and 4 18-pounders and 10–12 mortars." In retrospect it was an almost eerie moment of historical synchronicity. The weekend after the spy Benjamin Church had met not-so-secretly with General Gage in Boston, the man destined to become the Revolution's most notorious traitor was in Cambridge convincing Joseph Warren to finance his genuinely patriotic bid to take Fort Ticonderoga.

In 1775, Captain Benedict Arnold was a long way from betraying his country. A successful and self-made merchant captain with a specialty in trading horses, he had forced the New Haven selectmen, at virtual gunpoint, to provide his "Governor's Footguards" with the powder and weapons they needed from the town's arsenal and then marched his men to Cambridge. At thirty-four, he was almost exactly Warren's age; he was bright, charismatic, and ambitious, and the two men seem to have struck up an almost instant friendship. Within a few days Warren had ordered Arnold to mount an attack on Fort Ticonderoga.

Unknown to both Warren and Arnold, another group from Connecticut was at that very moment enlisting the aid of Ethan Allen and his Green Mountain Boys to do exactly the same thing, thus making the Massachusetts effort instantly redundant. There was also the question of jurisdiction. What gave Massachusetts—or Connecticut, for that matter—the right to attack a fort outside their colony, let alone confiscate the cannons from that fort? But the most serious strike against this misguided mission into the New York wilderness had to do with what was already a well-known deficiency in Massachusetts. More than anything else—more than cannons and mortars—the province needed gunpowder. On May 1, as Warren considered Arnold's proposal, he wrote Committee of Supplies member Elbridge Gerry on this very issue. Without more powder, they might very well "trifle away this only moment we have to employ for the salvation of our country." Even knowing this, Warren equipped Arnold with two hundred pounds of this valuable substance for his mission to Fort Ticonderoga.

As it turned out, Arnold had no use for the gunpowder. Soon after learn-
ing of the rival expedition, he raced toward Lake Champlain and presented
Ethan Allen with his orders from the Committee of Safety of Massachusetts.
Since Allen had no official orders of his own, he reluctantly agreed to allow
Arnold to serve with him as a coleader, and unopposed, the two men strode
side by side through the entrance of the British fort.

The two hundred pounds of Massachusetts gunpowder proved unnecessary at Fort Ticonderoga but might have changed the course of the Battle of
Bunker Hill. Instead of an example of farsighted strategic planning, the decision to send Benedict Arnold to the Champlain Valley was the mistake that
may have cost Joseph Warren his life.

By the first week of May, Warren had learned that Connecticut was sending a
delegation to talk to General Gage about the possibility of "a cessation of hostilities." Warren had been able to marginalize Timothy Pickering and the
other equivocators among the provincial officer corps, but a rival colony from
New England was something else altogether. If Connecticut should break
ranks and negotiate its own separate agreement with the British, it would
mean the end to a New England–wide army. Unlike Massachusetts, Connecticut had in Jonathan Trumbull a governor elected by the people of his colony
rather than appointed by the king, making Connecticut's potential defection
all the more damaging. If a reconciliation was to happen, it had to be initiated
not by the Americans but by the British. Until then, they must all agree to
prepare for war. "We fear our brethren in Connecticut are not even yet convinced of the cruel designs of Administration against America . . . ," Warren
wrote Trumbull. "We have lost the town, and we greatly fear, the inhabitants
of Boston, as we find the general is perpetually making new conditions, and
forming the most unreasonable pretenses for retarding their removal from
the garrison. . . . Our people have been barbarously murdered by an insidious
enemy, who under cover of the night, have marched into the heart of the
country, spreading destruction with fire and sword. No business but that of
war is either done or thought of in this colony."

The Connecticut delegation met with Gage, who was quite persuasive in
pointing out that with thousands of militiamen surrounding Boston, the
British, not the provincials, were the ones on the defensive. In the end, however, Gage's decision to renege on his original agreement with the townspeople of Boston was what brought Connecticut over to Massachusetts's way of

thinking. Having misled the poor beleaguered people of Boston, Gage was, a Connecticut officer in Cambridge wrote, "wicked, infamous, and base without parallel." Governor Trumbull ultimately decided that he must stand by Massachusetts, and on May 4 he wrote Warren, assuring him of his colony's support.

As Warren moved from crisis to crisis, he was unable to fulfill his obligations to both the Committee of Safety and to the Provincial Congress, which often required him to be in two places at once. At one point, the Provincial Congress was forced to adjourn several times in a single day as its members impatiently waited for a report from the Committee of Safety "respecting the inhabitants of Boston." Frustrations reached the point that on May 2, the Congress elected a new president—James Warren of Plymouth (no close relation to Joseph Warren). When that same day James Warren declined to serve, a committee was formed to go to Hastings House, home of the Committee of Safety, to see if Joseph Warren "can now attend the Congress." On the back of a letter he'd just received from the Boston selectmen, Warren hurriedly drafted his reply, "Doct. Warren presents his respects to the honorable Provincial Congress; informs them that he will obey their order, and attend his duty in congress in the afternoon." Despite the fact that he was spread dangerously thin, the consensus appeared to be that there was no one better suited to serve as president than Joseph Warren.

Tensions among provincial leaders reached a crescendo during the beginning of the second week in May. Many of the militiamen who had arrived in Cambridge in the days immediately following Lexington and Concord had begun to drift back to their homes. Some never returned. Others only needed to make arrangements with their loved ones and perhaps plant their spring crops before they enlisted in the provincial army for the next eight months. If the officers were going to recruit new men, they, too, had to return to their hometowns. All of this meant that there was an alarming, if temporary, drop in the number of soldiers in the lines around Boston. When word reached headquarters in Cambridge that Gage was planning to attack the undermanned American forces, General Ward was deeply concerned. By May 10, fears of an imminent British initiative prompted the Provincial Congress to consider evacuating Cambridge. Instead, they decided to put out the call to the local militias with the hope of hurriedly assembling as many as two thousand men to come to General Thomas's aid in Roxbury.

During this anxious and desperate time, Benjamin Church committed an act that might have had disastrous consequences. On May 10 letters were sent out by the Committee of Safety over Church's signature requesting that officers "repair to the town of Cambridge with the men enlisted under your command." This was all well and good except for the fact that one of these letters was sent to General John Thomas in Roxbury. If Thomas had obeyed the order, there would have been no one left to oppose a British advance out of Boston. Thomas had the good sense to check directly with Joseph Warren, who was initially baffled by how such an order could have been made in the first place. Once he'd figured out that Thomas's letter was one of many that had been sent out on the same day, he attempted to put the embarrassing gaffe in the best possible light. "Sending the order to your camp was certainly a very great error . . . ," he wrote Thomas. "Your readiness to obey orders does you great honor, and your prudence in sending to headquarters upon receiving so extraordinary an order convinces me of your judgment."

Once again, Warren seems to have given Church the benefit of the doubt. One has to wonder, however, whether the letter to Thomas had really been an honest mistake. Shortly before May 10, Church had been given reason to fear that the provincials were on to him. He sent Gage a garbled, scribbled-over description of an incident in which someone "mentioned distrust of me, that he suspected my going into Boston." What's more, the accuser had made something of a spectacle of himself. "All this uttered with the fury of a demon before the whole camp," Church wrote. "I do not perceive that he made any great impression upon the people. I left him abruptly . . . [and] destroyed my papers. . . . Caution on my part is doubly necessary as instant death would be my portion should a discovery be made. . . . Secrecy respecting me on the part of [General Gage] is indispensable to rendering him any services, and . . . necessary to the preservation of my life." Whether or not Church sent the letter to General Thomas on purpose, he wanted, more than anything else, a resolution of the present crisis before he was discovered to be a spy. "May I never see the day when I shall not dare to call myself a British American . . . ," he wrote Gage. "Oh for peace and [honor] once more."

As it turned out, Gage was not planning an assault on the American lines, and in the days ahead, as more and more provincials returned from their visits home, the size of the army once again began to increase. Thursday, May 11, the day following the mix-up initiated by Church, had been designated a provincewide day of public humiliation, fasting, and prayer. The

Provincial Congress adjourned at four that afternoon, and at some point Joseph Warren was on his way to Dedham.

Boston was a city under siege, but its hills still provided views of stunning beauty. Captain George Harris and his regiment had just left their winter quarters and were now living in tents on the common, where they dug fortifications to defend the town from an assault from the Back Bay. He was, he wrote his cousin in England, "twenty yards from a piece of water, nearly a mile broad, with the country beyond most beautifully tumbled about in hills and valleys, rocks and woods, interspersed with straggling villages, with here and there a spire peeping over the trees, and the country of the most charming green that delighted eyes ever gazed on. Pity these infatuated people cannot be content to enjoy such a country in peace. But, alas, this moment their advanced sentinels are in sight."

On the evening of May 11, Joseph Warren made his way through this green, rural world. According to the diary of Dr. Nathaniel Ames, the owner of the tavern in Dedham where Sally Edwards, now seven and a half months pregnant, was staying, the day was sunny and cloudless. Ames also recorded that Warren made an appearance at the tavern that day, undoubtedly to see his "fair *incognita pregnans.*" Secrets were nothing new to Warren. Just the day before, he had written Gage in confidence, urging him to ignore the loyalists, who "care not if they ruin you or this empire," and honor his agreement with the people of Boston. In a postscript, he wrote, "As no person living knows or ever will know from me of my writing this, I hope you will excuse a freedom which I very well know would be improper in a letter which was exposed to general view." A secret between himself and General Gage was one thing; the paternity of a baby delivered by an unwed teenage girl was quite another.

For more than a century the people of New England had been using the ceremony of the fast to repent for their sins even as they girded their loins for the battle to come—that was what they had done during King Philip's War and the many conflicts that followed it, and that was what they were doing now as they spent this lovely spring day abasing themselves before God so that they and their country might enjoy better days to come. How much Warren took these traditions to heart as he visited the girl who was now the living embodiment of, if not his own personal failings, at least someone else's, will never be known. We do know that by the following day, he was back in

Watertown and presiding over the discussion of whether the time was right to assume "a civil government for Massachusetts." The army they had worked so assiduously to assemble was proving to be a most unruly and dangerous invention, and something had to be done to control it.

From the first, the patriots had feared that the provincial army might ultimately destroy the liberties it was supposed to protect by establishing a military dictatorship. That was what had happened in Rome when Caesar became emperor, and that was what had happened during the English Revolution when Oliver Cromwell became Lord Protector of the British Commonwealth.

Civil leaders in Massachusetts in May 1775 were in an especially precarious position. The First Continental Congress had instructed them not to establish a formal government, since the other colonies would view this as an unnecessarily provocative repudiation of British sovereignty. But now, after Lexington and Concord, with an army of thousands assembling in Cambridge and Roxbury, a recognized civil authority must be allowed to assert some sort of control. Otherwise this army—already fidgety for something to do after the excitement of April 19—might take matters into its own hands.

By all accounts, the soldiers were eating well—feasting on what food and alcohol they could pillage from the abandoned homes of the loyalists and the stream of provisions that flowed in from the country. Hygiene, however, was a problem. The dormitory at Harvard and other buildings in Cambridge and Roxbury had been turned into barracks, and one loyalist claimed that the soldiers were not only dirty but "lousy." There were not enough latrines, and the growing number of recruits who died of typhus, or "putrid fever" (as many as two or three a day by early June), suggests that as spring turned to summer, a most unpleasant smell had arisen in Cambridge and Roxbury.

That these primarily young men from the country were not accustomed to taking orders from anyone made the enforcement of discipline difficult. Not only did the members of a typical company all know each other (indeed, many were related by blood), they were accustomed to making decisions by consensus at town meetings. This meant that the soldiers, not their officers, decided any issues that might have a direct impact on their welfare. On May 10, Private James Stevens complained in his diary that Captain Thomas Poor "spoke very rash concerning our choosing a sergeant and said that we had no right." Taking umbrage, the soldiers decided to "do no duty that day." Captain

Poor had no choice but to apologize to his men, and after his "recantation," Stevens and the others returned to duty. This army was a dangerous thing— a budding democracy of young men with firearms.

Inevitably adding to the surliness of the recruits was the availability of large quantities of rum. Muskets kept going off—sometimes accidentally, sometimes for the fun of it, injuring and, in at least one instance, killing American soldiers. "Four guns were discharged in camp and endangered men's lives," David Avery recorded in his diary on May 8. "One out of our window, one at the picket guard. Two others hurt. An awful day!" The New Englanders could be raucous, but they also tended to be exceedingly religious, attending prayers on an almost daily basis and listening to one, sometimes two sermons each Sunday. The diary kept by Private Amos Farnsworth is as much a record of his spiritual life as it is an account of his experiences in the provincial army. "I was filled with love to God. . . . ," he wrote at one point, "and lifted up my soul to God in ejaculation, prayers, and praise." These men were fighting for liberty, but they also believed that the Lord was, in his own inscrutable way, working through each and every one of them.

Spiritual, ornery, and clannish, the New Englanders defined their struggle in profoundly local terms. They refused to serve under an officer they did not know or like. They also seemed intent on having a good time. Ezekiel Price of Stoughton visited Roxbury in early June and found the soldiers "in high spirits and healthy; being mostly young men and many of them persons of wealth and reputable yeomen." That was not the impression of a surgeon from a man-of-war who had been given permission to cross the provincial lines to attend to wounded British prisoners. He found the streets of Cambridge "crowded with carts and carriages, bringing them rum, cider, etc., from the neighboring towns, for without New England rum, a New England army could not be kept together. . . . They drink at least a bottle of it a man a day." The surgeon had his obvious biases, but there was more than a little truth in his description of an army that was barely under anyone's control: "nothing but a drunken, canting, lying, praying, hypocritical rabble, without order, subjection, discipline, or cleanliness; and must fall to pieces of itself in the course of three months. They are . . . the descendants of Oliver Cromwell's army, who truly inherit the spirit which was the occasion of so much bloodshed in [England]."

When the Provincial Congress and Committee of Safety proved slow in providing commissions not only for General Ward's officers but for Ward himself, there was much grumbling within the army about the inefficiency of what passed for civil government in Massachusetts. One of Gage's spies reported that he heard the provincial soldiers "complaining much of the private men having the superiority over the officers, rather than the officers over the men. I plainly saw there was no kind of subordination observed among them." Jonathan Brewer was a well-respected veteran of the French and Indian War, and when the Provincial Congress turned down his request to lead an expedition to Quebec (something George Washington would in fact decide to do in just a few months' time), there were those in the provincial army who were not happy. "By God," one soldier was overheard to say, "if this province is to be governed in this manner, it is time for us to look out; and it is all owing to the Committee of Safety, a pack of sappy-headed fellows; I know three of them myself." In Waltham, Lieutenant Colonel Abijah Brown insisted that the Provincial Congress should not be allowed to take the gunpowder from the town's arsenal, claiming "that the Congress had no power to do as they did; for all the power was and would be in the army; and if the Congress behaved as they did, that within 48 hours the army would turn upon the Congress, and they would settle matters as they pleased."

Some in Massachusetts blamed General Ward for the army's lack of discipline, but Warren realized that they could not impose, at this early stage, too much restraint. "Subordination is absolutely necessary in an army," he admitted; "but the strings must not be drawn too tight at first . . . amongst men who know not of any distinction but what arises from some superior merit. . . . Our soldiers . . . will not be brought to obey any person of whom they do not themselves entertain a high opinion." Given the unsettled and tentative state of civil government in Massachusetts, the time was not right to impose stricter discipline among the troops. Indeed, too much oversight on the part of the Provincial Congress might instigate a wholesale mutiny. Before there could be a proper army, there had to be a proper government; otherwise, Warren wrote Samuel Adams in Philadelphia, "a military government must certainly take place."

Legitimacy was the real issue. How could a self-created legislative body of questionable legal authority expect to impose its will on a group of soldiers who had the power to overthrow it? And besides, who were these soldiers fighting for—for Massachusetts, for the Continental Congress, for the king? No matter what the British regulars might call them, the soldiers of the provincial army refused to consider themselves "rebels," claiming that they

remained loyal to their still beloved monarch. It was his advisers and legislators with whom they had an issue. Liberty—not independence—was what
they were fighting for, and as proud Englishmen they still flew the British
flag.

Their counterparts in Boston regarded such claims as patently absurd.
On May 1, Lieutenant John Barker recorded in his diary, "The Rebels have
erected the standard at Cambridge; they call themselves the King's Troops
and us the Parliament's. Pretty burlesque!" Even the provincial leaders had to
admit that the logic of their position was more than a little tortured, and to
provide at least some clarity in this time of uncertain allegiances, Warren felt
that the Continental Congress must allow Massachusetts to form its own civil
government. He also insisted that the Congress in Philadelphia should appoint "a generalissimo" to take control of the provincial army.

Warren was greatly concerned about the threat of a military coup, but he
wanted to make sure that Samuel Adams understood that he was not "angry
with my countrymen." Unlike many revolutionaries, including Adams himself, whose commitment to the cause could be disturbingly cold-blooded,
Warren continued to have an abiding affection for even the most unruly of
Massachusetts's citizens. "I love—I *admire* them," he wrote. He might be president of the Provincial Congress, but that did not prevent him from spending
as much time as possible with these men. "He mingled in the ranks . . . ," one
commentator wrote, "and succeeded in a most wonderful manner in impart-
ing to them a portion of the flame which glowed in his own breast." But he
was more than just a cheerleader. Warren's contemporary John Eliot (son of
the Boston minister Andrew Eliot) claimed that he "did wonders in preserving order among the troops" and was "perhaps the man who had the most
influence."

As a kind of surrogate civilian general, Warren came to have a deep sympathy for the men who comprised what was optimistically referred to as the
Grand American Army. "The errors they have fallen into are natural and
easily accounted for," he explained to Samuel Adams. "A sudden alarm
brought them together, animated with the noblest spirit. They left their
houses, their families, with nothing but the clothes on their backs, without a
day's provision and many without a farthing in their pockets." Much of the
current problem lay with the fact that all of them—soldiers and civil office
holders alike—were traveling in uncharted territory. "It is not easy for men,
especially when interest and the gratification of appetite are considered, to

know how far they may continue to tread in the path where there are no landmarks to direct them." That said, a dangerous metamorphosis was occurring among the recruits in Cambridge and Roxbury. "It is with our countrymen as with all other men, when they are in arms, they think the military should be uppermost." If something was not done quickly, "what was not good at first will be soon insupportable . . . as the infection is caught by every new corps that arrives. . . . For the honor of my country, I wish the disease may be cured before it is known to exist."

In a consummate irony, Joseph Warren entrusted the delivery of the letter communicating this desperate plea to Benjamin Church. But this was not another instance in which Warren proved remarkably obtuse as to Church's true character. On the contrary, by sending Church to Philadelphia, Warren was getting someone who had proved to be both erratic and, on occasion, incompetent as far away from Cambridge as possible. "I am appointed to my vexation to carry the dispatches to Philadelphia," Church complained in a dispatch to Gage on May 24, "and must set out tomorrow which will prevent my writing for some time unless an opportunity should be found thence by water."

As it turned out, Church did not return to New England until the day of the Battle of Bunker Hill.

Israel Putnam was the provincial army's most beloved officer. Grizzled and battle-scarred as an old whale, he exuded an aura of rustic belligerence. While his superior General Ward wanted to do nothing that might endanger a possible reconciliation with Britain, Putnam was impatient for action. On May 13, he led two thousand men on what could only be taken as a brazen taunt when he and his soldiers marched across the Neck at Charlestown, up Bunker Hill, where according to Lieutenant Barker, watching from Boston, "they kept parading a long time" before they marched into the virtually abandoned village of Charlestown on the Boston side of the peninsula. Once at the waterfront, with the British man-of-war *Somerset* anchored less than a quarter mile away, the soldiers gave "the war-whoop" and, Barker wrote, "returned as they came." Putnam's boyish love of adventure had made for a strange and most unmilitary display. "It was expected the body of [soldiers] in Charlestown would have fired on the *Somerset*, at least it was wished for," Barker mused, "as she had everything ready for action and must have destroyed great numbers of them, besides putting the town in ashes."

The march to Charlestown may have been foolish but was no doubt good for morale as the siege appeared to be settling into an unsatisfactory stalemate. With no clear military objective except for keeping the British bottled up in Boston, the men had little to do other than build earthen fortifications (known as "fatigue" duty) and serve as sentries. For the New Englanders watching from the hills of Roxbury and Cambridge, any activity on the part of the British, no matter how inconsequential, provided a welcome distraction from the growing tedium. On the night of May 17, fire erupted in Boston's Dock Square when, it was reported, a spark from a candle fell among a pile of cartridges of gunpowder. The regulars refused to allow the town's inhabitants to help put out the fire, and by 3:00 a.m. the barracks and an estimated thirty warehouses, at least some of which undoubtedly contained goods owned by patriot merchants, had burned to the ground.

On Saturday, May 21, Gage ordered four sloops to sail to tiny Grape Island near the town of Weymouth to pick up some recently harvested hay. The appearance of this little British fleet along the shores of Braintree and Weymouth immediately created concern among the local inhabitants. Thinking this might be the prelude to a full-scale invasion, people living along the coast south of Boston began to flee into the countryside. General Thomas dispatched three companies from Roxbury, and once they, along with President Joseph Warren, had arrived at the Weymouth shore, the first skirmish of the post–Lexington and Concord era was under way.

Although many shots were fired, the distance to the island was too great for those onshore to do much more than watch as the regulars on the island gathered the hay and prepared to load it on the sloops. Finally the tide came in enough to float several boats that had been stranded along the Weymouth shore, and the provincials raised sail and set off for the island. The regulars loaded what hay they could and quickly departed, but not without trading fire with the provincials who made sure to burn what they estimated to be eighty tons of abandoned hay.

To the east of Charlestown were two contiguous islands, Hog and the much larger Noddle's Island, which together formed a peninsula that reached southwest from the town of Chelsea toward Boston to the southwest, with the town of Winnisimmet on the opposite shore directly to the north. Hundreds of sheep, cattle, and horses grazed on both Hog and Noddle's islands, and the provincials decided that before the British could get their hands on the

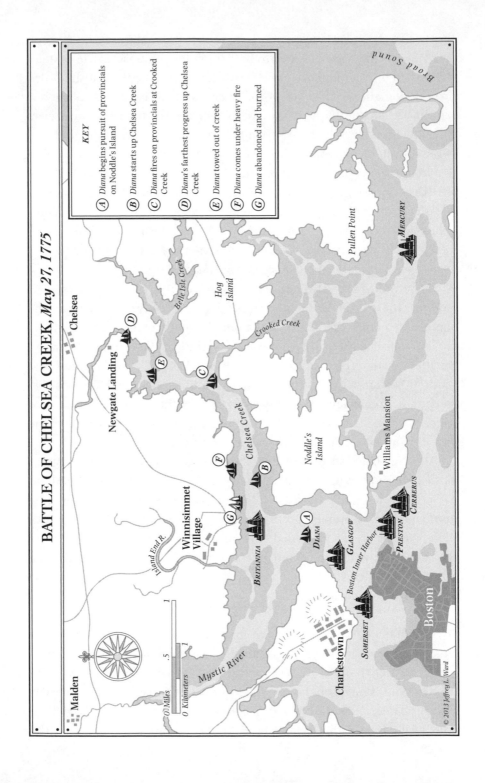

BATTLE OF CHELSEA CREEK, *May 27, 1775*

KEY

(A) *Diana* begins pursuit of provincials on Noddle's Island

(B) *Diana* starts up Chelsea Creek

(C) *Diana* fires on provincials at Crooked Creek

(D) *Diana's* farthest progress up Chelsea Creek

(E) *Diana* towed out of creek

(F) *Diana* comes under heavy fire

(G) *Diana* abandoned and burned

Broad Sound

Chelsea

Belle Isle Creek

Hog Island

Crooked Creek

Pullen Point

MERCURY

Newgate Landing

Noddle's Island

Williams Mansion

Chelsea Creek

Island End R.

Winnisimmet Village

BRITANNIA

DIANA

GLASGOW

Boston Inner Harbor

PRESTON

CERBERUS

Malden

Mystic River

Charlestown

SOMERSET

Boston

0 Miles   .5   1

0 Kilometers   1

© 2013 Jeffrey L. Ward

livestock and hay, they must drive the animals off the islands, which were separated from one another and the mainland by creeks that were only knee-high at low tide.

On the evening of May 26, Colonel John Nixon of Sudbury and Colonel John Stark of Dunbarton, New Hampshire, led a party of about six hundred men to the town of Chelsea, where on the morning of May 27 they waded across Belle Isle Creek to Hog Island. As the provincials surreptitiously rounded up the sheep and cattle, Admiral Graves happened to be celebrating his promotion to vice admiral of the white squadron. At precisely 8:00 a.m. his new white flag was raised to the masthead of the *Preston*, followed by a thir-teen-gun salute. Soon after, his nephew Lieutenant Thomas Graves, com-mander of the schooner *Diana*, sailed into Boston Harbor after a cruise to Maine. The lieutenant promptly anchored near his uncle's flagship and had joined in the festivities when around 2:00 p.m., the admiral was notified that smoke could be seen rising from Noddle's Island. By that time, Nixon's and Stark's men had moved on to that most outlying of the two islands and be-sides killing some of the livestock had set a barn full of hay on fire.

Graves ordered his nephew to sail the *Diana* up the narrow waterway that lay between the islands and the shore to the north, known as Chelsea Creek, so as "to prevent [the rebels'] escape," while approximately 170 marines were sent to pursue the provincials by foot on Noddle's Island. By about five in the afternoon, the provincials were hurrying back across the creek to Hog Island with the marines in close pursuit and the guns of the *Diana* blasting away at them from Chelsea Creek to the north. Half the provincials continued on with the livestock as the other half jumped into a ditch and commenced a rear-guard action designed to keep both the schooner and the marines at bay. "We had a hot fire," Amos Farnsworth recorded in his diary. Two marines were wounded before the British commander gave the order to retreat, allowing the provincials to direct all their fire at the *Diana*, which continued sailing up the ever-narrowing creek until she'd reached the confines of Haley's Landing. Under heavy fire from the provincials and with an outgoing tide threatening to leave his schooner high and dry, Lieutenant Graves sought the aid of a dozen or so longboats, which began towing him back down the creek in the dying breeze. In hopes of ambushing the *Diana* before she reached the safety of the harbor, the provincials rushed down the north shore of Chelsea Creek toward Winnisimmet. By 9:00 p.m., reinforcements led by General Putnam had joined the provincials stationed at the mouth of Chelsea Creek, only to discover that the British marines had transported several cannons to a hill on Noddle's Island. Soon cannonballs were whistling down at them out of the deepening darkness as the provincials waded into the creek and fired at the longboats towing the schooner past the Winnisimmet shore.

Through it all, General Putnam was his usual adventurous self, leading his men, one witness recounted, "up to his middle in mud and water." Putnam later boasted that "there was nothing between them and the fire of the enemy but pure air" as he and his men, who were joined by President Joseph Warren, did their best to disable the schooner and the longboats. They fired with such deadly effectiveness that the longboat crews were forced to abandon the *Diana*, which, with her crew huddling belowdecks to escape the unceasing rain of musket balls, soon drifted toward shore, grounding itself on the wooden rails extending from the ferry dock around 10:00 p.m. Lieutenant Graves and his men attempted to use their anchor to drag the schooner to deeper water, but as the tide continued to ebb and the vessel began to roll onto her side, they had no choice but to abandon her for the sloop *Britannia*, which had been waiting in the deeper water to the south. The firing continued as the provincials plundered the schooner of her guns, rigging, and equipment and, with the help of some strategically placed hay, set her on fire. Around 3:00 a.m. the flames reached the vessel's powder magazine, and the *Diana* exploded.

For the newly promoted vice admiral of the white and his nephew, the former commander of the *Diana*, what came to be known as the Battle of Chelsea Creek was a humiliating defeat. For the provincials, however, the encounter was nothing short of "astonishing." Not only had they taken their first British vessel; they had put Graves's marines on the run. At least two marines had been killed in the action (although the provincials remained convinced that they had killed dozens more), while the Americans suffered just four wounded. "Thanks be to God that so little hurt was done us," the ever-devout Amos Farnsworth wrote, "when the balls sung like bees round our heads." That night Putnam and Warren returned to Cambridge to report to General Ward. "I wish we could have something of this kind to do every day," Putnam crowed. "It would teach our men how little danger there is from cannonballs."

Ward countered with the concern that the engagement might provoke the British to launch a sortie from Boston they would all come to regret, but Putnam remained unrepentant. Turning to the president of the Provincial

Congress, he said, "*You know*, Dr. Warren, we shall have no peace worth anything till we gain it by the sword."

The skirmish at Chelsea Creek had been a clear provincial victory, but it had also consumed a worrisome amount of gunpowder. Since those first overheated days after Lexington and Concord, when Joseph Warren had been in favor of an assault on Boston, he now had a more realistic view of his army's preparedness for a major offensive against the British. Rather than agree with Putnam, Warren demurred. "I admire your spirit and respect General Ward's prudence," he said diplomatically. "Both will be necessary for us, and one must temper the other."

CHAPTER NINE

The Redoubt

The next day, May 28, Captain John Derby was guiding the *Quero* along the southern coast of England when he sighted the Isle of Wight. Once he'd found a safe place to leave his schooner, he hired a boat to row him to nearby Portsmouth, and after passing the docks of the massive naval shipyard, he was in a coach headed for London. By Monday, May 29, as Derby's account of the fighting at Lexington and Concord circulated throughout the city, Lord North and his fellow ministers were, according to one writer, "in total confusion and consternation." Secretary of State Dartmouth issued a statement insisting that the provincial account was not to be believed, but former governor Thomas Hutchinson, who knew Derby to be a reliable man, insisted that there was in all likelihood a disturbing amount of truth behind the captain's claims.

They called him the "accidental captain." He seemed to have appeared out of thin air with his typeset account of the fighting, along with a sheaf of depositions from not only Massachusetts militiamen but a handful of British prisoners. Some claimed that Derby had first arrived in Southampton, the point of departure 155 years before of the Pilgrims' *Mayflower*, but there was no sign of his vessel along that port's docks. Edward Gibbon, then at work on his monumental *History of the Decline and Fall of the Roman Empire* (which is as much about the British Empire as it is about Rome), wrote that "it is pretty clear [Derby] is no imposter" and theorized that his schooner was probably hidden "in some creek of the Isle of Wight."

Derby let it be known that he had left Salem four days after the departure of the vessel carrying General Gage's account of Lexington and Concord. But the *Quero* had not only managed to pass the much larger *Sukey*, she had put twelve days between her and the British vessel. This meant that for almost two weeks, the king's ministers were unable to refute the patriot version of events. Lord Dartmouth grew so frustrated by the seemingly endless wait that on June 1 he penned a letter to Thomas Gage in Boston: "It is very much to be lamented that we have not some account from you of this transaction. . . . We expect the arrival of that vessel with great impatience, but till she arrives I can form no decisive judgment of what has happened."

Gage's account turned out to be quite similar to the provincial version of events. There was the unresolved question of who fired first, but that did not change the fact that men, on both sides, had been killed. Contrary to the ministry's expectations, the Americans had proved themselves to be more than willing to fight.

Even as the schooner *Quero* was approaching England with word of Lexington and Concord, Major Generals William Howe, Henry Clinton, and John Burgoyne were headed to Boston on the man-of-war *Cerberus*. Somewhere in the Atlantic, the *Quero* (with her report of Lexington) and the *Cerberus* (with the commanders sent to bolster Gage) passed each other. The irony of three well-known British generals sailing to America on a vessel named for the mythical three-headed dog that guarded the gates of hell was simply too obvious to escape comment in the English press:

Behold the *Cerberus* the Atlantic plow,
Her precious cargo—Burgoyne, Clinton, Howe.
Bow, wow, wow!

General John Burgoyne, the first named in this little ditty, had both an ego and a way with words. In addition to being a military officer who'd established a reputation for bravery in Europe, he was a playwright, whose *The Maid of the Oaks* had been produced recently in London by David Garrick, and Burgoyne, for one, wasn't going to let the name of the ship crimp his notorious flair for the dramatic. As the *Cerberus* approached Boston Harbor, she came upon a packet bound for Newport. The two vessels luffed into the wind so that their crews could speak, and Burgoyne shouted out to the packet's captain, "What news?" The captain responded that Gage's army in Boston was surrounded by ten thousand country people. Burgoyne cried out in astonishment. "What! Ten thousand peasants keep five thousand king's troops shut up! Well, let *us* get in, and we'll soon find elbowroom." Burgoyne was to regret the boast, to which Gage (when he later heard of it) must have responded with a knowing and weary smile.

As Gage was well aware, sending Howe, Clinton, and Burgoyne (who arrived in Boston on May 25, just in time to witness the debacle at the Battle of Chelsea Creek) was hardly a vote of confidence on the part of the king and Lord North. What's more, their arrival required him to recount, in all its dreary detail, the even more embarrassing debacle at Lexington and Concord.

Burgoyne was the showman (and a classmate of Gage's at Westminster), but it was William Howe who had the reputation as a fighter. When Wolfe led the victorious assault on Quebec during the French and Indian War, he had looked to Howe to find a way to scale the near-vertical cliffs fronting the Plains of Abraham. A year earlier, Howe's greatly admired older brother George had died in the arms of Israel Putnam at the failed assault at Fort Ticonderoga; indeed, George had been so beloved by the soldiers from Massachusetts that the colony had paid for a memorial in Westminster Abbey. Given both his own and his brother's legacies in America, William Howe was an inspired choice on the part of the British ministry.

Henry Clinton was a bit of a mystery to his fellow officers. Although he'd been born in New York, his professional reputation had been made fighting in the European theater of the Seven Years' War. Intelligent and ambitious, he was also socially awkward (he described himself in a letter written during the passage to Boston as a "shy bitch") and had a reputation for working badly with his peers—an unfortunate characteristic given that the British army in Boston now had more than its share of major generals.

By early June, Gage had determined that there was no longer any "prospect of any offers of accommodation" from the provincials. It was therefore time, he decided, to issue a proclamation instituting martial law in Massachusetts. Given Burgoyne's reputation as a wordsmith, Gage requested that his old Westminster schoolmate ghostwrite a proclamation that offered clemency to all patriot leaders who promptly surrendered, with the exceptions of Samuel Adams and John Hancock. Written with an arrogant, overblown pomposity (at one point, Burgoyne ridiculed the provincials as rebels "who with a preposterous parade of military arrangement, affected to hold the army besieged"), the proclamation only strengthened the provincials' resolve to oppose the ministry's forces.

When these three officers weren't writing their friends and patrons back in England about the commander in chief's incompetence and their own dismal prospects (Burgoyne complained of a "motionless, drowsy, irksome medium, or rather vacuum, too low for the honor of command, too high for that of execution"), they were in discussions with Gage about the best way to break out of their current dilemma. Howe, who was the senior of the major generals and could be expected to lead whatever plan was finally put into action, appears to have had a key role in coming up with a strategy that he, at least, felt could turn the tables on the provincial army. In a letter written on June 12 to his brother Richard, an admiral in the British navy, he outlined how it was to be done.

On Sunday, June 18, when a significant portion of the provincial forces were attending religious services, Burgoyne would begin cannonading Roxbury from Boston Neck as Howe led a detachment to Dorchester Heights, to the east of Roxbury, and Clinton led the attack in "the center." Once Howe had thrown together two redoubts on Dorchester Heights, he'd attack General Thomas's army in Roxbury. As Thomas's force fled in retreat, Howe would turn his attention to Charlestown on the other side of Boston. After he'd secured the hills overlooking that town, it was on to Cambridge. "I suppose the rebels will move from Cambridge," he wrote his brother confidently, "and that we shall take and keep possession of it."

And so they agreed. In six days the British would break out of Boston and become the masters of Roxbury, Charlestown, and most important of all, Cambridge, the headquarters of the provincial army.

About the time Howe wrote his brother of their plan to move against the rebels, Joseph Warren set out in a small boat, its oars muffled so that he might row undetected past the many warships anchored between Charlestown and Boston. For the president of the Provincial Congress to be on a boat headed for the Boston waterfront was extremely ill advised, but Warren had spent the last sixty days putting himself at risk. Whether he was rallying the men at Menotomy, Grape Island, or Chelsea Creek, he had made sure to be wherever the danger was greatest. In addition to the musket-ball-whizzing thrills of the skirmishes, Warren had come to enjoy the daily hustle from one make-or-break meeting in the Provincial Congress or the Committee of Safety to another as all of Massachusetts wavered on the edge of chaos and confusion. Warren appears to have thrived under conditions that most found overwhelming. Indeed, his addictive love of life in the balance may have led him to carry on a dalliance with Sally Edwards even as he courted the woman who seems to have been his soul mate, Mercy Scollay. Now, in early June, not only his own life but the lives of everyone in New England were teetering on the brink, and Warren was in his element.

So it should come as no surprise that on a night in the middle of June he was headed to a secret rendezvous in British-occupied Boston. Mitigating the risk was the location of the meeting at Hudson's Point in the North End, described in a spy report to General Gage as "a nest of very wicked fellows, ship carpenters and caulkers" who used red signal flags to pass messages to the provincial troops on the other side of the harbor. Yet another spy report claimed that so many "rebels get out [of Boston] without passes" because the men who ran the two ferries that docked in the North End "let them go." Given the alternatives, the North End was the safest portion of the Boston waterfront for a clandestine meeting.

Warren needed a doctor to serve as the army's surgeon general. Dr. Benjamin Church, now in Philadelphia, was the obvious choice, but Warren's confidence in Church appears to have been badly shaken over the course of the last month. With Church conveniently out of town, Warren had decided to seek out an alternative. Dr. John Jeffries had an excellent professional reputation and was a fellow member of the St. Andrew's Masonic Lodge at the Green Dragon; both he and Warren had served their apprenticeships under Dr. James Lloyd. Indeed, Dr. John Jeffries was the perfect candidate, except for the fact that he was, by all accounts, a loyalist. Warren, however, believed he had an offer that Jeffries, who was waiting for him on the docks, could not refuse.

In his dual roles as leader of the Congress and the Committee of Safety, Warren was the one to whom prospective officers appealed when they were angling for a commission in the provincial army. John Adams later recalled how Warren "often said that he never had till then any idea or suspicion of selfishness of this people, or their impatient eagerness for commissions." In the British army, an officer came from the English upper class and had to purchase his commission. In the new American army, however, no such social and financial qualifications existed. Instead of paying for a commission, an officer was expected to earn it by recruiting the sufficient number of men. This meant that, in the words of John Adams, "the lowest can aspire as freely as the highest." And as Warren now knew from firsthand experience, "there is no people on earth so ambitious as the people of America."

But when he offered Jeffries one of these coveted commissions, he received an unexpected response. "I thought, Warren, that you knew me better," the doctor said.

"Don't be so quick, Jeffries," Warren replied, "*I* have a general's commission in my pocket. We want you to be at the head of the medical service." But even this was not enough, and the offer was declined.

Jeffries, it turned out, was not interested in making it to the top of the provincial pecking order; he was a loyalist and therefore wanted to be a member of the British upper class in the larger imperial realm. In the years to come, he moved to London and did his best to work the English patronage system, attaching himself to anyone who might further a career that ultimately included being a part of the two-man crew that completed the first balloon flight across the English Channel in 1785. It was a fundamentally different approach to life from what was emerging in America, where the absence of a deeply rooted aristocracy meant that ambition had replaced deference as the way to get ahead.

A few weeks before, Warren had written to Samuel Adams about just these issues. Soldiers searching Thomas Hutchinson's house in Milton had come across a trunk of letters that revealed, Warren claimed, what had gone wrong with the former governor. Like Jeffries, Hutchinson was not content with what was available to him in provincial Massachusetts; he aspired to use his political office as a stepping-stone to greater glory that could only be found in England. The fault was not necessarily with Hutchinson, who, like all of them, was ambitious; the fault was with a government that required him to go against the wishes of his own people if he was to attain the ultimate prize of a lordship or some other royal preferment. "It is probable," Warren wrote Samuel Adams, "that [Hutchinson] would have remained firm in [the people's] interest . . . had there not been a higher station to which his ambitious mind aspired . . . ; in order to obtain this, he judged it necessary to sacrifice the people." What was needed in America was a government in which "the only road to promotion may be through the affection of the people." Instead of attaining membership in a group that existed above the people, the highest office in government should require an official to serve those people. "This being the case," he wrote, "the interest of the governor and the governed will be the same."

Warren was describing a government whose leaders were beholden to what we have come to call "the will of the people." An eight-year war and many additional years of compromise and struggle would be required to create a political system that approximated the ideal described in Warren's letter to Samuel Adams. But as it turned out, Warren, caught in the paroxysms of a revolution even as he searched for his own place in that revolution, had seen the future.

Jeffries's refusal to accept the surgeon generalship put Warren in a temporary bind, especially when Congress offered the post to *him*. Even before Lexington and Concord, Warren had "fully resolved that his future service should be in the military line." Like General John Thomas, a doctor who had spurned the medical corps during the French and Indian War and become one of America's finest officers, he wanted to fight. Congress dutifully submitted to their president's will, and on June 14, he was chosen by ballot to be a major general. Warren might have complained to John Adams about the overweening ambitions of his countrymen, but that had not prevented him from claiming a rank that put him ahead of William Heath, the officer to whom he had attached himself during the fighting in Menotomy just two months before.

On June 16, Ezekiel Price of Stoughton recorded in his diary that "Dr. Warren was chosen a major general" and that "Heath was not chosen any office, but it was supposed that no difficulty would arise from it." This may have been wishful thinking on Price's part. If the last surviving letter Warren ever wrote is any indication, he had to work very hard to make sure that Heath was not put out by his own good fortune. We'll never know the exact nature of the deal that was finally agreed upon, but Warren was careful to assure Heath in this June 16 letter that "everything is now going agreeable to our wishes." That said, Warren made sure to remind Heath that he needed to submit the required paperwork to Congress "without a moment's delay." One gets the sense that Heath had been sullenly dragging his feet in the wake of Warren's sudden rise past him. It was just the beginning of the jockeying and infighting that was to plague the new army's officer corps for months to come.

Before Warren was officially a major general, he had to be formally commissioned by Congress. Up until that point, Warren was the one who delivered the oath to the new officers—"a harangue in the form of a charge in the presence of the assembly," John Adams remembered, "[that] never failed to make the officer, as well as the assembly, shudder." If Warren were to become a major general, the Provincial Congress must select a new president. But before that particular bridge could be crossed, yet another new and desperate crisis had arisen. "A gentleman of undoubted veracity," who had "frequent opportunity of conversing with the principal officers in General Gage's army," had revealed that on June 18, the British planned to take Dorchester Heights and Bunker Hill.

Even before the skirmish at Chelsea Creek, General Israel Putnam had been impatient for some kind of action, claiming "that the army wished to be employed, and the country was growing dissatisfied at the inactivity of it." It was time, he declared in a council of war on May 12 attended by not only Artemas Ward and the other generals but also the members of the Committee of Safety, to occupy the high ground at Charlestown so as to "draw the enemy from [Boston], where we might meet them on equal terms." Joseph Palmer of the Committee of Safety agreed with Putnam, but both Ward and Warren felt that it was too risky, especially since there was "no powder to spare and no battering cannon." Putnam insisted, his son Daniel remembered, that no matter how the British responded to a move to the hills above Charlestown, "We will set our country an example of which it shall not be ashamed." Years later, Daniel Putnam recounted how Warren had paced the room in Hastings House, considering Putnam's proposal. "Almost thou persuadest me, General Putnam," he said, leaning over the back of the general's chair, "but I must think the project a rash one. Nevertheless, if it should ever be adopted and the strife becomes hard, you must not be surprised to find me with you in the midst of it."

By June 15, with the British about to strike at Dorchester and Charlestown, Warren and the others were finally convinced that the provincial army must make a preemptive move of its own. After determining that General Thomas's forces in Roxbury were not strong enough to take and hold nearby Dorchester Heights, the Committee of Safety decided to implement a plan along the lines first proposed by Putnam. In the early-morning hours of June 17—a day before the British were to begin their assault on Dorchester Heights—the provincial army would seize the currently unoccupied high ground above Charlestown.

At 6:00 p.m. on Friday, June 16, about one thousand provincial soldiers under the command of Colonel William Prescott assembled on the common in Cambridge, opposite Hastings House—the headquarters of General Ward and the Committee of Safety. Clutching an odd assortment of muskets and dressed in homespun clothes with sweat-stained hats on their disheveled heads, they

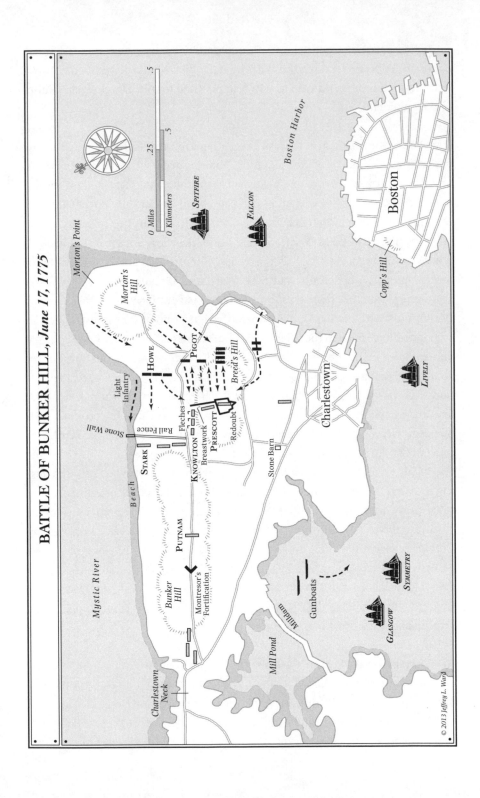

BATTLE OF BUNKER HILL, *June 17, 1775*

© 2013 Jeffrey L. Ward

looked just like the militiamen who had fought at Lexington and Concord. The only difference was that after almost two months away from home, much of it spent digging fortifications and marching up and down Cambridge Common, they were much dirtier than the farmers who had rushed to action on April 19. None of them knew what lay ahead that night, but once they'd gathered around the Reverend Samuel Langdon in prayer and headed out toward Charlestown in the deepening dusk accompanied by a wagon full of entrenching tools and several horse-drawn fieldpieces, they must have known that they were about to get dirtier still.

Soon after leaving Cambridge, they paused to meet up with about two hundred soldiers from Connecticut under the command of Captain Thomas Knowlton. At some point during the march, which took them past the common in Charlestown where the body of the slave Mark had once hung in chains, they were joined by General Israel Putnam. Also accompanying them was Lieutenant Colonel Richard Gridley, the noted engineer and commander of the artillery regiment.

Soon they were crossing Charlestown's narrow neck—only thirty feet wide in some places at high tide, with the Mystic River to their left and the shallows of a tidal mill pond to their right—before they mounted the gentle rise of Bunker Hill. They were without a moon that night, with only the stars to reveal the contours of the 110-foot-high hill that just two months before had provided General Percy's men with the protection they so desperately needed on the evening of April 19. Gage had decided to abandon these heights, but not until after his engineer Captain John Montresor had thrown up a fortification, and this hastily built, arrow-shaped wall still stood on the rounded and otherwise empty summit of Bunker Hill.

Colonel Prescott's orders told him to fortify this hill, which overlooked the roads from Cambridge to the west and from Medford to the north, as well as the waters of the Mystic River to the east. A fort built here would go a long way to stymieing a British attempt to take Charlestown to the south and then Cambridge. What's more, the British had given Colonel Gridley a head start by constructing a defensive wall. And since it was already well past 10:00 p.m. when they reached the heights overlooking Charlestown, with dawn set to arrive a little past 4:00 a.m., time was of the essence if they were to have any chance of building a fort before the morning light revealed their efforts to the British in Boston.

But instead of remaining on the grassy summit of Bunker Hill, they continued along the road toward Charlestown, following a ridge that led them to the smaller, seventy-five-foot-high Breed's Hill, almost half a mile to the southeast. Directly to the south lay the almost completely abandoned settlement of Charlestown. In the days after Lexington and Concord, General Gage had delivered an ultimatum to the selectmen of this little city of approximately three hundred houses, dozens of commercial structures, and wharves. If any provincial soldiers should venture onto the Charlestown peninsula, he would do as Admiral Graves had wanted to do on April 19 and consign the city to the flames. Since then almost all of Charlestown's residents had sought refuge elsewhere, and the streets and homes of the community that had been settled a year before Boston in the early seventeenth century were now quiet, dark, and strangely empty.

Just a quarter mile to the south lay the wharves of Boston, with Admiral Graves's fleet of warships anchored in the waters in between and, even more menacing, the mammoth cannons of the Copp's Hill battery pointed in their direction. To place a fort overlooking Charlestown on Breed's Hill—right in the figurative face of the British—was an entirely different undertaking than had been ordered by the Committee of Safety. Instead of a defensive position, this was an unmistakable act of defiance. A fort built here, especially one equipped with provincial cannons that could rake British shipping and the Boston waterfront, invited a forceful response from the British army. Given the provincials' almost nonexistent reserves of gunpowder, this was not what the Committee of Safety had in mind. But this was where Prescott, Putnam, and Gridley began to build the fort.

We will never know exactly why they arrived at this decision. According to the only account we have of what transpired among the three officers that night, Gridley, the engineer, and one of the other officers wanted to begin by fortifying Bunker Hill, but "on the pressing importunity" of the third officer, they started with Breed's Hill instead. Given Putnam's aggressive personality—he was the one, after all, who led the brazen march down to the Charlestown waterfront back in May—many have assumed that he browbeat the others into disregarding Ward's orders and building the fort in a place that General Gage could not ignore. But as the events of the following day revealed, Prescott was just as forceful, if not more so, than Putnam, who appears to have been there only as a volunteer. No matter whose idea it was, Prescott was in charge of the operation and was therefore the one who assumed ultimate responsibility for the location of the fort. In the day to come he would fight with a ruthless, often inspiring ferocity, but that did not change the fact that dysfunction came to define a battle that was ultimately named—perhaps appropriately, given its befuddled beginnings—for the wrong hill. As John Pitts later wrote to Samuel Adams, "Never was more confusion and less command."

And so they began. Around midnight, with only four hours between them and the approach of morning, Gridley began to sketch out the contours of a quadrangular fort on Breed's Hill. In addition to pickaxes and shovels, the men had been provided with fascines (cylindrical bundles of brushwood), gabions (cages filled with rocks or soil), and empty barrels that were used to build the fort's earthen walls, the two longest of which stretched approximately 132 feet and met to form a west-facing V. A ditch surrounded the roofless, fully enclosed fort, known technically as a redoubt, which could be accessed from the rear, east-facing wall by what was called a sally port.

The redoubt (which means, ironically enough, "place of retreat") was about as simple a structure as could be designed but still required hours of backbreaking labor to build. They wanted their efforts to remain a secret for as long as possible. Unfortunately, only a few hundred yards away were several men-of-war, floating cities of sailors whose watches stood on the decks gazing across the warm, unruffled harbor. The absence of wind meant that the sounds of shovels and pickaxes banging against rocks and pebbles echoed unimpeded across the dark emptiness toward Boston. Fearful that they were about to be discovered, Prescott sent a group of sixty men, which included that devout veteran of the Battle of Chelsea Creek, Amos Farnsworth, down into the empty village of Charlestown to act as sentinels. Those who were not patrolling the waterfront were told to wait in the town house and, Farnsworth recorded, "not to shut our eyes." Prescott's concern was so great that he descended the hill several times that night to make sure they were still undetected. He later told his son about how relieved he felt when he heard the watch aboard the sloop-of-war *Lively* report, "All's well."

As it turned out, they *were* detected. General Henry Clinton, living in John Hancock's house on Beacon Hill, was having trouble sleeping that night. So he went for a walk along the northern margins of Boston and quickly realized that something was going on in the direction of Charlestown. He could hear it—the unmistakable sounds of digging. He stood either on a wharf or, more likely, on a well-positioned hill and stared into the darkness through his spy-glass. Sure enough, he "saw them at work."

He rushed to Province House and awakened Thomas Gage. In an early-morning meeting with Gage and Howe, Clinton urged "a landing in two divisions at day break." Howe appeared to think it was a good idea, but as he so often did when presented with a plan for immediate action, Gage demurred. They would wait to see what the light of day revealed.

It came gradually—the brightening of the sky in the east toward the islands of Boston Harbor, the fading of the stars overhead into a gray, increasingly bluish sky, and then the sudden realization that they were digging a fortification that might very well become their collective grave. When the provincial soldiers paused to look around, they could now see that instead of being set back on the distant height of Bunker Hill, they were here, on the little knoll of Breed's Hill, overlooking Charlestown. Peter Brown of Westford, Massachusetts, was appalled. He estimated that they were surrounded by eight cannon-equipped ships, along with "all Boston fortified against us." "The danger we were in," he wrote to his mother in Newport, Rhode Island, "made us think . . . that we were brought there to be all slain, and I must and will venture to say that there was treachery, oversight, or presumption in the conduct of our officers."

In front of them was Charlestown, tucked into the side of the hill and the harbor. To the east was the sweep of an easy slope that ran down to a thirty-five-foot shoreside bump known as Morton's Hill. There were some fences, some swampy ground, and the clay pits of a brick kiln, but nothing of any substance to prevent an army of regulars from landing at the tip of the peninsula and attacking from their unprotected left. Here they were—all by themselves, already exhausted and sleep-deprived, with no one to support them.

Just as this terrifying realization began to settle in, they saw a bud of flame erupt from the side of one of those nearby warships, followed by a soul-shattering roar and the hissing smack of a cannonball as it buried itself in the dirt. It was the sloop-of-war *Lively*, and soon enough, another cannonball was flying through the air in their direction. It was mesmerizing, the way you could see the black dot arc lazily through the cloudless sky, all the while knowing that it was going to land somewhere near where you were standing. The officers assured the men that while the cannons made plenty of noise, they were, in actuality, surprisingly ineffective when it came to killing soldiers. It was time to get back to work and finish the fort.

On the third, perhaps the fourth, shot one of those black dots proved the officers wrong. Thirty-five-year-old Asa Pollard of Billerica was working in front of the redoubt when a four-inch-diameter cannonball weighing nine pounds divided his head from the rest of his body. This was more than many of these young recruits could stand. They asked Colonel Prescott what they should do with their friend's headless corpse. A minister offered to say a few words before Pollard was committed into the ground, but Prescott insisted that he be buried immediately and that they continue to work on the fort. The minister seems to have succeeded in conducting an impromptu service, but it was Prescott who soon had his men's attention.

He leaped onto the parapet of the redoubt, and as cannonballs continued to sizzle through the air, he urged the men on. He had a three-cornered hat on his head, and "strutting backward and forward" with a long evening coat (known as a banyan) swirling about him like a colorful cape, he pulled the hat off his head and, waving it in the air, shouted at the British warships below them, "Hit *me* if you can." It was a most inspiring display of courage, and yet what one veteran later remembered was how all the hat-waving had somehow displaced Prescott's pigtail so that "it hung over his right shoulder, giving him a quite ludicrous appearance."

Prescott had fought with such distinction during the French and Indian War that he had been offered a commission in the British army—an offer he was quite happy to refuse. An anger smoldered inside Prescott, who appears to have had no patience with Israel Putnam's nostalgic fondness for the British officers with whom he had fought in Canada. A few months earlier, his brother-in-law Abijah Willard, a loyalist, had warned him "that his life and estate would be forfeited for treason" if he took up arms against Britain. "I have made up my mind on that subject," Prescott replied, "I think it probable I may be found in arms, *but I will never be taken alive.*"

Prescott could see that they were dreadfully open to attack on the left. They needed to build an earthen wall that ran more than 150 feet to the east, where it would connect with a virtually impassable swamp. If men were posted behind that wall, the British would have a much harder time surrounding them.

By this point, Gridley, the engineer, had, in Prescott's words, "forsook me." A brief lull in the firing from the *Lively* gave Prescott the chance to draw out the dimensions of the wall in the dirt, and soon his men were at it once again—digging a deep ditch and piling up the dirt into what came to be known as "the breastwork."

But as the cannon fire resumed and the sun climbed in the sky and exhaustion and thirst began to erode what little enthusiasm Prescott had been able to muster, the men started to wonder once again about what they'd gotten themselves into. In addition to artillery fire from the *Lively* and the other men-of-war, the battery on Copp's Hill, less than a mile away and with cannons that fired balls that, at twenty-five pounds, were more than twice as heavy as those from the *Lively*, now had its big guns trained on Prescott's redoubt. "Some of our country people [started to] desert," Peter Brown wrote, "apprehending the danger in a clearer manner than the rest, who were more diligent in digging and fortifying ourselves against the [enemy]. We began to be almost beat out, being tired by our labor and having no sleep the night before, but little victuals, no drink but rum."

Some of Prescott's officers insisted that it was time to request reinforcements. After building the fort, these men could not be expected to defend it. They must send a messenger to General Ward in Cambridge. But Prescott was adamant. They were the ones who had built these walls, "and they should have the honor of defending them." No reinforcements were necessary.

There may have been more than a little defensiveness in Prescott's refusal to seek aid. If they had been where they were supposed to be—on Bunker Hill—there would have been no need for reinforcements. They would have been beyond the effective range of the British battery. They would have also been much closer to the relative safety of Cambridge. There would have been none of this drama and angst—just a lot of digging. That was why General Ward had made no apparent preparations for a possible battle on June 17. But Prescott had changed everything. Whether it was a result of, as Private Peter Brown wrote, "treachery, oversight, or presumption," Prescott had stirred up a hornet's nest by building this lonely redoubt, and he was reluctant to admit that he now needed help.

Finally it was decided; they must seek assistance. But there was a problem. No one had a horse. And so, just after 9:00 a.m., Major John Brooks, a twenty-three-year-old doctor from Medford, began the three-and-a-half-mile walk to Cambridge.

By that time the British had a plan. Soon after daybreak, Gage had conducted a meeting with Clinton, Howe, and Burgoyne in Province House to discuss the best way to deal with the new patriot fort. Clinton was for mounting a two-pronged attack. While Howe led a frontal assault against the redoubt, he would venture up the Mystic River by boat with five hundred regulars, and after landing at Charlestown Neck, attack from the rear. If Gage had agreed to this plan, Clinton would have, a fellow officer later claimed, "shut them up in the peninsula as in a bag. . . . They must have surrendered instantly or been blown to pieces." But as Gage pointed out, this would have placed Clinton in an exceedingly risky position. All it would take was a provincial assault from Cambridge to trap him and his small force between two armies.

Howe had what Gage considered to be a far less risky plan. As they could all plainly see, the redoubt was almost totally exposed to an assault from the American left. By capitalizing on this glaring vulnerability, Howe proposed to envelop the redoubt and attack it from several sides simultaneously. With the exception of Clinton (who lamented that "my advice was not attended to"), the other officers agreed that Howe's plan was a sound one.

Before it could be put in place, the regulars had to be assembled at Long Wharf and the North Battery for transportation across the harbor to Morton's Point on the eastern tip of the peninsula. With high tide scheduled for around three in the afternoon, they would aim to coordinate the assault with the tide.

At some point that morning, Howe met with Admiral Graves. It was essential that the ships' cannons provide the troops with an effective covering fire; they also wanted to be sure to pound the redoubt as unmercifully as possible, even as they did everything in their power to prevent provincial reinforcements from crossing the Neck onto the Charlestown peninsula. Graves's largest vessels, the *Boyne* and *Somerset*, could not elevate their guns high enough to fire on the heights of Breed's Hill, and they were too big to approach Charlestown Neck. This left the *Lively*, whose guns had begun the fighting, the *Glasgow*, the *Symmetry*, and the much smaller *Falcon* and *Spitfire*, which were all positioned around the southern and western sides of the peninsula. The causeway of a milldam provided a barrier to the vessels approaching the Neck from the Charles River, but with the aid of two raftlike gondolas, each equipped with a twelve-pound cannon, they should be able to make the Neck a very hot place for any provincial reinforcements.

Gage would spend most of the day in Province House, but that morning he ventured out to inspect the American fort for himself. With the help of his spyglass he could see a man standing on the parapet of the redoubt, about a thousand yards away as the cannonball flies. Beside Gage was the loyalist Abijah Willard. Handing Willard his telescope, Gage asked if could recognize the man standing so promiscuously on the fort. The distance was probably too great to see his face, but the banyan may have tipped Willard off. By God, it was his brother-in-law, William Prescott.

"Will he fight?" Gage asked.

"Yes, sir," Willard replied. "He is an old soldier and will fight as long as a drop of blood remains in his veins."

Around 10:00 a.m. Major John Brooks arrived in Cambridge after the long walk from Charlestown. He immediately reported to General Ward at Hastings House. The ever-cautious commander in chief found himself in an impossible position. Prescott had disobeyed orders and built a fort within easy cannon shot of the British, and now he needed reinforcements in anticipation of a British attack. But who was to say the British were not going to stay with their original plan and move on Dorchester and Roxbury on the other side of Boston? And then there was the possibility of an amphibious assault not on Charlestown but on Cambridge. He must wait to see what the British were up to before he could send a sizable force to support Prescott.

But no matter what the British did, the Americans had to face a most distressing reality. The army had very little gunpowder. The Committee of Safety was then in session at Hastings House, and they sent out a desperate plea to David Cheever on the Committee of Supplies. Although they had just received thirty-six half barrels of powder from Connecticut, there were only twenty-seven half barrels in the provincial magazine. There was apparently no more powder available from the towns. And as John Brooks had recently discovered, horses were also very difficult to come by. The Committee of Safety (the entity that functioned as the province's executive body) was without the express riders required to communicate effectively with its own army, which was scattered across a ten-mile perimeter around Boston.

Making matters even worse, the committee's chairman, Dr. Joseph Warren, was nowhere to be found. The night before, Warren had frightened many of his colleagues with wild words about joining Prescott and his men on Bunker Hill. But that was before one of the headaches he had been known to suffer required him to retire to a darkened room and await the passing of the incapacitating pain. Warren had done a heroic job of holding the province together over the last two months, but even he, apparently, had his limits. Delegating responsibility had never been his forte, and with Warren out of commission, no one seemed willing to act.

Finally, Committee of Safety member Richard Devens made a decision. They must reinforce Prescott. With Ward's reluctant approval, they would send all, not just some, of the New Hampshire regiments led by James Reed and John Stark to the Charlestown peninsula. Reed's men were housed near Charlestown Neck and Stark's were in Medford, and with luck they would reach Prescott by the middle of the afternoon.

One of the few provincials with a horse was General Israel Putnam. Already, he had ridden at least twice from Bunker Hill to Cambridge and back. Having participated in the discussion the night before about where to build the redoubt, he was now obsessed with the need to build a fortification on Bunker Hill. Otherwise Prescott's men would have nowhere to fall back to in the event of a British attack. What Putnam did not have, however, were entrenching tools.

By about noon, it seemed as if Prescott had finally finished his redoubt and breastwork. Putnam decided it was time that he and some of Prescott's men carry the tools up to Bunker Hill. But Prescott would have none of it. Already, he had lost a significant number of men to desertion. The British cannon fire had been unremitting. In fact, one of his most trusted officers, Captain Ebenezer Bancroft, a fellow French and Indian War veteran, had been blinded in one eye by the shock wave of a cannonball that had narrowly missed his head. Prescott told Putnam that "if he sent any of the men away with the tools, not one of them would return." Putnam assured him that "every man [shall] return" and left with the tools and a considerable number of soldiers, none of whom, it turned out, ever made their way back to Breed's Hill.

Not long after Putnam's departure, an artillery captain belatedly arrived at the redoubt with several fieldpieces. Unfortunately, Colonel Gridley had made no provision for cannons in the redoubt. Normal procedure was to build embrasures—openings for cannons in the fort's earthen walls—but that had apparently escaped Gridley's attention during the tense discussions the night before. Making it even worse, they were now without any digging tools.

Prescott ordered Captain Bancroft and his men to dig an embrasure by hand. They went at it with a will, but soon realized that their bleeding fingers were not up to the task. But Bancroft had an idea. He ordered the artillery captain to load his fieldpiece and blast a hole through the wall of the redoubt, and soon enough a cannon could be seen protruding from the redoubt on Breed's Hill.

By 1:30 p.m., the first wave of British boats had been loaded with regulars at Long Wharf and the North Battery and had begun to row across the harbor toward the Charlestown peninsula. Generals Clinton and Burgoyne had positioned themselves at the battery on Copp's Hill. They were not the only spectators that day. All around them, on the top of every hill, roof, and steeple, the inhabitants of Boston looked to the north.

They were a community in the sky, their eyes trained across a quiet and, except for the warships, empty harbor in the boiling sun, looking toward a hilly peninsula and an unoccupied town that was almost the mirror image of their own. Cannons boomed from the battery and the surrounding ships, and now they could see the boats, twenty-eight of them, rowing across in two parallel lines of fourteen each, with brass fieldpieces in the forwardmost boats and between thirty and forty regulars in each one of the others, their musket barrels glittering in the sun.

The fighting at Lexington and Concord had been fierce, but one could claim, as Timothy Pickering Jr. had done, that April 19 amounted to nothing more than yet another misunderstanding between Britain and her American colonies that had gotten out of hand. The fighting at Lexington and Concord had occurred, by and large, offstage, only visible to the Bostonians as a distant cloud of dust and powder smoke moving across the countryside to Charlestown. But the fighting today was going to be different. Already the big guns of the warships and the battery on Copp's Hill had been filling the air with sound and smoke, but that was just a prelude. Much more than a skirmish, this was going to be a true battle, unfolding with a painstaking deliberation before their very eyes as Howe's red-clad army rowed slowly across the blue and sparkling harbor toward a green hill where the provincials were, the Reverend Andrew Eliot wrote, "up to their chins entrenched."

Colonel Jones of the Fifty-Second Regiment appears to have been standing with Clinton and Burgoyne on Copp's Hill. "I have seen many actions," he wrote, "but the solemn procession preparative to this, in embarking the troops in the boats, the order in which they rowed across the harbor, their alertness in making good their landing, their instantly forming in front of the enemy and marching to action, was a grand sight to all concerned."

Hovering over the awful beauty of the scene was a most disturbing question. What if Howe and his regulars were defeated? The question would have seemed laughable just a few months before, but after the humiliation of April 19 and the equally embarrassing loss of the *Diana* at the mouth of Chelsea Creek, the shade of a doubt had entered the minds of more than a few British officers. Despite his bold talk about "elbowroom" back in May, Burgoyne could not help but speculate that a loss today might mean "a final loss to the British Empire in America."

Somehow it had come to this: a battle that could very well determine the fate of the English-speaking world. And here they now were, on rooftops and on hills—a city of loyalists, patriots, soldiers, and refugees—awaiting the outcome.

CHAPTER TEN

The Battle

Captain John Chester of Wethersfield, Connecticut, had just finished his midday dinner in Cambridge. It was about 1:00 p.m. "I was walking out from my lodgings," he remembered, "quite calm and composed and all at once the drums beat to arms and bells rang and a great noise in Cambridge." Suddenly Putnam's son Israel Jr. rode up "in a full gallop." Chester asked, "What is the matter?" "Have you not heard?" Putnam cried. "Why the regulars are landing in Charlestown, and father says you must all meet and march immediately to Bunker Hill."

Amid the shouts and ringing bells and beating drums, Chester ran back to his quarters and retrieved his musket and ammunition. Then it was on to the Anglican church that served as a barracks for his men, who were "mainly ready to march." But they had a problem. Unlike virtually all the other provincial soldiers, Chester's company from Wethersfield had uniforms; in fact, they looked so good in their red-trimmed blue coats that a week before they'd been given the honor of accompanying Warren and Putnam on a prisoner exchange that had involved several convivial hours with a group of equally well-dressed British officers and their men. But now the uniforms were a liability. Wearing a bright blue coat amid an army of slovenly farmers was tantamount to having a target on your back. So before they headed for Bunker Hill, they put "our frocks and trousers on over our other clothes . . . for we were loath to expose ourselves."

Provincial officials now knew that the British were about to attack the redoubt, but what about Roxbury and Cambridge? The Committee of Safety sent a desperate message to General Thomas. "The troops are now landing at Charlestown from Boston," it read. "You are to judge whether this is designed to deceive or not. In haste [we] leave you to judge of the necessity of your movements." Handwringing and paralysis had gripped the command center in Cambridge. Making this hesitancy all the more frustrating was the ambiguity of many of the orders issued from Hastings House. A series of three entrenchments had been built beginning at the Cambridge shore of the Charles River. For some reason, Putnam's second-in-command, Lieutenant Colonel Experience Storrs, was sent up the river to Fort No. 1, the farthest from the action at Charlestown. By the time Storrs realized where he was needed most, it was too late to be of any help. To the bafflement of the provincial soldiers already stationed there, Colonel James Scammon and his men from Maine ended up at Lechmere's Point. Not till three that afternoon would Captain John Chester and his soldiers, already overheated in their double-layered clothes, be on their way to Charlestown.

Howe had ordered his troops to land at the tip of Morton's Point, far to the east of Prescott's position atop Breed's Hill. There were only enough boats to transport half the regulars, and Howe and Brigadier Robert Pigot, who was to command the left wing, arrived with the second wave of troops, which brought the total to about sixteen hundred soldiers. Standing atop Morton's Hill, Howe could see the earthen redoubt and breastwork to his left, but there was also something else. To the right, back a bit from the American fort, was a new line of provincial soldiers.

It was as if they had read his mind. Anticipating a British flanking movement from their own left, they were now busily constructing an obstruction of some sort that would extend their lines across the width of the peninsula to the Mystic River. This was disturbing. Howe decided to call up his seven-hundred-man reserve. The regulars already assembled on the Charlestown peninsula broke ranks, sat down to eat some dinner, and waited for the reserves.

Soon after Howe's troops set out by boat from Boston, Prescott decided to make an attempt, even if it was a halfhearted one, to oppose the enemy's landing—and the way to do that was with cannons. So far, however, the provincial artillery had proven to be shockingly ineffectual.

Firing a cannon was an admittedly complex operation. It took at least seven trained men to fire one of these carriage-mounted fieldpieces. You had to jam the cartridge (a flannel bag full of powder) down the bore with a long-handled rammer and compress it with a clump of cotton rags known as the wad; then came the iron cannonball, which had to be free of any dust or dirt; otherwise it might jam in the barrel and blow the fieldpiece to smithereens. But that was only the beginning. Powder had to be poured in the vent at the rear of the gun, known as the touchhole, before another man shoved a pick down the vent and pierced the cartridge to ensure that it would ignite. Only then did the artillery officer introduce a burning match to the touchhole with a long stick known as a linstock, firing off the cannon.

The provincial army's lack of gunpowder meant that there had been precious few opportunities for rehearsing this complicated procedure. As a consequence, the rudiments of actually firing a cannon remained a challenge for the provincial artillerymen, especially since the cartridges contained in the cannons' side boxes proved to be too large to fit down the bore. The gunners had to tear open the cartridges and transfer the powder from the bag to the cannon barrel with an elongated ladle. And then there was the just as tricky matter of aiming the fieldpiece with any accuracy. The few balls successfully fired had buried themselves inoffensively in the side of Copp's Hill. Peter Brown recounted how after this pitiful display of marksmanship, during which the cannon was "fired but a few times," the artillery officer "swang his hat round three times to the enemy, then ceased fire."

Prescott undoubtedly felt that he had little use for the fieldpieces at the redoubt and even less for the artillery officers and their men. For as had also become clear, being able to fire a cannon did not necessarily mean that you had any familiarity with being fired *at* by a cannon. After several hours of enduring the British artillery onslaught, Prescott's men had become relatively inured to the cannonballs that kept raining down on them, even the ones that skipped menacingly along the hillside, sometimes veering in unexpected directions (one man lost a leg to one of these erratically bouncing balls of iron) before they buried themselves in the dirt or simply rolled to a gradual stop. Since the earthen walls of the redoubt and breastwork were able to absorb the impact of the cannonballs, the structures provided surprisingly good protection from the onslaught, and by the early afternoon, the men had developed a routine whenever they knew another cannonball was headed in their direction. "We could plainly see them fall down," a spectator in Boston wrote, "and mount again as soon as the shot was passed, without appearing to be the least disconcerted." This did not apply, apparently, to the artillery officers and their men, most of whom had already fled for the relative safety of Bunker Hill.

One artillery officer, however, was eager for action. Unlike the others—whose chief qualification, in at least two instances, was that they were related to the artillery regiment's commander Colonel Gridley—Captain Samuel Trevett appears to have known what he was about. Prescott ordered

Trevett to move two of his fieldpieces in the direction of Morton's Hill and fire on the British soldiers as they disembarked from the boats. He also ordered Captain Thomas Knowlton and his two hundred soldiers from Connecticut to provide Trevett with whatever protection he might need as he opened up on the regulars.

Once they had left the redoubt, Prescott never saw Trevett and Knowlton again and assumed that, like the men who had accompanied Putnam with the entrenching tools, they had abandoned him for the high ground to the north. This, however, was anything but the case. Instead of deserting his commander, Knowlton hit upon a way to fix, at least in part, the mess Prescott had created by building his redoubt on Breed's Hill.

About two hundred yards behind the fort, Knowlton came across a ditch. Just ahead of the ditch was a fence made of stone at the bottom and rails of wood at the top that ran parallel to the ditch as it extended across the width of the peninsula to the Mystic River. All it took were a few modifications to make the fence at least look like a sturdy, if hardly bulletproof, defensive structure. The surrounding field had been divided by the residents of Charlestown into a series of thin east-to-west-running strips. Fences had been built along each property line, so that the southeastern-facing slope of the hill was ribbed with wooden rails, and Knowlton and his men used these rails to build a second fence just ahead of the one that ran alongside the ditch. Stuffing some recently mowed and still-green grass in between the two fences, along with whatever rocks and pieces of wood they could find, they made a stout and serviceable barricade—a kind of wood-and-grass sandwich—that became known as the rail fence.

All of this took time, but thanks to Howe's decision to wait for the reserve, Knowlton and his men had the opportunity they needed to build a structure that looked, at least to Howe's eye, "cannon proof." What they didn't have, however, were enough soldiers to man this new expanse of fence. But help was on the way.

If ever there was a man who embodied the flinty frontier spirit of backwoods New Hampshire, it was Colonel John Stark. At forty-six, he was a lean, less voluble version of Israel Putnam. Two decades earlier, while trapping in the northern wilderness, he had been taken captive by the Abenakis, who had been so impressed by his bravery that they'd adopted him into the tribe.

During the French and Indian War, he'd fought with Rogers's Rangers along-side British regulars, so he knew their ways well. Now he was fighting against the New Hampshire legislature, whose members were outraged by his refusal to curry favor for a commission. But no matter what the politicians thought, his men adored him, and with thirteen companies, Stark had the largest regiment in the provincial army. His major, Andrew McClary, was six foot six and "of an athletic frame." McClary was now marching proudly with Stark, whose bushy eyebrows seemed locked in a perpetual scowl, toward the Charlestown Neck.

The fire of the gunboats and warships clustered around the causeway of the Mill Pond had turned the Neck into a terrifying war zone. Cannonballs kept flying across this narrow strip of land, some of them tearing the dirt into ragged furrows. The ships were also firing bar shot, evil-looking dumbbells of metal designed to take down the rigging of a sailing vessel but which also did devastating things to a human body. A soldier recounted how one of these murderous projectiles "cut off three men in two." What with the smoke, dust, and bloody chunks of torn flesh—not to mention the deafening roar—it was hardly a surprise that a crowd of fearful provincial soldiers was now blocking the approach to the Neck. In his deep and booming voice, Major McClary requested that the officers and their men immediately step aside so that Colonel Stark and his regiment could march across to Bunker Hill.

Captain Henry Dearborn was twenty-three and a doctor, and he was at the head of the column beside Colonel Stark. Despite the fact that cannonballs and bar shot were tearing up the ground all around them, they were marching, Dearborn remembered, "at a very deliberate pace." He made the mistake of suggesting to his commander that they might march a little faster. "With a look peculiar to himself," Dearborn wrote, "[Stark] fixed his eyes upon me, and observed with great composure, 'Dearborn, one fresh man in action is worth ten fatigued ones.'" Needless to say, they did not pick up the pace.

Stark was not impressed by what he found on Bunker Hill. Putnam sat atop his white horse in what was called his "summer dress": a sleeveless waistcoat (as opposed to the long-sleeved coat an officer was expected to wear) that was more in keeping, one soldier claimed, with the leader of "a band of sicklemen or ditchers, than musketeers." Putnam seems to have devoted most of his energies that afternoon to fulminating at the crowd of more than a thousand mostly idle soldiers that had assembled around the peak of

Bunker Hill. Part of the problem was that no one seemed sure what Putnam wanted them to do. Were they to build the fortifications he had started, or were they to march to the rail fence and fight? Instead of prioritizing what needed to be done to support Prescott and the line of defense that was emerging to the left of the redoubt, Putnam seems to have bounced from distraction to distraction with increasing futility. All agreed that Putnam was as brave and inspiring a fighter as you could find, but focus and strategic thinking had never been his strong suits. He was, an observer wrote, "one to whom constant motion was almost a necessity," and the Battle of Bunker Hill was not to be his finest hour. "Had Putnam done his duty," Stark was reputed to say, "he would have decided the fate of his country in the first action."

Stark led his regiment into the valley to the south. The British had begun directing their artillery fire toward the swarm of provincial soldiers atop Bunker Hill, and as a consequence, the march south proved to be almost as hot as anything Stark's men had encountered on the Neck. Up ahead and to his right, Stark could see the redoubt and the breastwork; directly in front, he could see Knowlton and his men building the rail fence; to the left was the Mystic River. Beyond this jagged, uncertain line, about half a mile to the south, were more than two thousand British regulars. Stark could not understand what Prescott had been thinking when he built what looked to be a very puny and poorly sited redoubt and was heard to speak of "the want of judgment in the works," which he dismissively referred to as "the pen." Knowlton's rail fence provided the beginning of a solution to the problem created by Prescott's redoubt, but it was only a beginning. There were still two glaring weaknesses. Between the end of the breastwork and the beginning of the rail fence was a diagonal gap of several hundred yards. Luckily, the ground in this section was quite swampy, which provided something of an obstacle to the regulars, but more needed to be done. Whether or not Stark suggested it, someone began building three fleches—Vs made of either fence rails or a combination of rails, fascines, and dirt—positioned along the space between the breastwork and the rail fence. In addition to plugging the gap, the fleches would allow provincial soldiers and even Captain Trevett's cannons to fire on the left flank of any regulars who tried to attack the rail fence.

It was the other end of the rail fence to which Colonel Stark turned most of his attention. The fence went as far as it had to go to keep a sheep or a cow from straying into the fields above and below it, but it did not extend all the way to the water's edge, where a steep bank went down to a narrow beach. All

General Howe had to do was send a column of soldiers along the beach (where they would be hidden from the provincials by the bank), and he would have rendered useless all their efforts with the breastwork and rail fence. Stark later walked over this same ground with a fellow officer and told how "he cast his eyes down upon the beach and . . . thought it was so plain a way that the enemy could not miss it; he therefore ordered a number of *his boys* to jump down the bank and with stones from the adjacent walls, they soon threw up a strong breastwork to the water's edge behind which he posted triple ranks of his choice men." As Stark plugged up this gap, his subordinates worked to fortify the rail fence to the west with fistfuls of hay. Each soldier made sure to create "an aperture in the grassy rampart, through which . . . he could take deliberate aim" with his musket.

Stark, Prescott, and Putnam were part of the same army, but as far as all three of them were concerned, they were each going to fight this particular battle on their own. With Prescott confined to the redoubt, Putnam preoccupied with building a fortification atop Bunker Hill, and Stark supervising at least the eastern portion of the rail fence, there was no one to synchronize the three of them into a single cohesive unit. Adding to the difficulty of getting these three commanders to work together were preexisting personal animosities. Stark didn't like Putnam—a feeling that was probably mutual—and as had already been made clear by the interchange about the entrenching tools, Prescott and Putnam didn't exactly see eye to eye.

It also didn't help that the three of them were from different colonies. At this point a continental army did not yet exist, and in the absence of a unifying "generalissimo," a quite considerable intercolonial rivalry had developed. General Ward might be the head of the provincial army, but only the soldiers from Massachusetts and New Hampshire were officially a part of that army; Connecticut had not yet formally placed its soldiers under Ward's control. What had been true in Cambridge a few hours before was true now on the hills overlooking Charlestown: no one seemed to be in charge.

But that wasn't necessarily all bad. There might be, in essence, three different commanders on the American lines, but as far as General Howe was concerned they amounted to a single, very difficult-to-read enemy. In just the last hour he had watched as the provincial fortifications organically evolved in ways of which not even he was entirely aware. Howe wasn't up against a leader with a plan to implement; he was watching three different leaders try to correct the mistakes of the other two. The workings of this strange amalgam of desperation and internal one-upmanship were baffling and a bit bizarre, but as Howe was about to discover, the end result was surprisingly formidable.

Around three in the afternoon, David Townsend arrived at Hastings House in Cambridge. Townsend, twenty-two, was one of Joseph Warren's apprentices, and while visiting the Carnes family, formerly of Boston and now living in Brighton, he'd learned that the British "were firing very heavy on our men at Bunker Hill." Townsend announced that he "must go and work for Dr. Warren," and set out on foot for Cambridge.

As he approached the town common, he could hear the distant firing from the battery in Boston and from the ships positioned around the Charlestown peninsula. Cambridge, however, was "quiet as the Sabbath—all the troops gone, and no one at Hastings House," except, he soon learned, for Dr. Joseph Warren.

"[He] was sick with one of his oppressive nervous headaches," Townsend remembered, "and had retired to rest and taken some chamomile tea for relief." Chamomile was recognized in the eighteenth century as a way to dissipate the black bile and thus reduce melancholy. No doubt rubbing his eyes, Warren said that if Townsend would wait to have a cup of tea with him, they could go together to Bunker Hill.

The night before, Warren had told his roommate and fellow Committee of Safety member Elbridge Gerry that he intended to join the soldiers on Bunker Hill. "As sure as you go," Gerry had said, "you will be slain." Warren admitted that Gerry was probably right but insisted that it would be impossible for him to remain in Cambridge "while my fellow citizens are shedding their blood for me."

We know that Townsend found Warren in Hastings House in the middle of the afternoon on June 17, but Warren's whereabouts earlier in the day are unknown. He may have, as Townsend seems to suggest, spent the morning holed up at Hastings House. According to another account, he "pretended that he was going to Roxbury" so as "to deceive" his colleagues into thinking that he had decided not to go to Bunker Hill. But there is another possibility. Instead of Roxbury, he may have gone all the way to Nathaniel Ames's tavern in Dedham.

Decades later, a woman made an extraordinary claim to the son of Warren's brother John. Like his father and his uncle, Edward Warren was a doctor, and one of his patients told of how she had been born in Dedham around the time of the Battle of Bunker Hill and that Joseph Warren had been her mother's doctor. The woman claimed that on the morning of the battle, Warren visited her mother in Dedham "and finding she had no immediate occasion for his services, told her that he must go to Charlestown to get a shot at the British and he would return to her in season." We'll never know for sure whether or not Warren visited Sally Edwards on June 17, but we do know that eleven days after the battle, Dr. Nathaniel Ames delivered her a baby girl, which meant that Edward Warren's patient might have been Joseph Warren's illegitimate daughter.

Once Warren and Townsend had shared a cup of chamomile tea in Hastings House, they set out for Charlestown. Townsend later remembered that Warren was dressed exquisitely in "a light cloth coat with covered buttons worked in silver, and his hair was curled up at the sides of his head and pinned up." All signs of his headache had vanished, and "he was very cheerful and heartily engaged in preparations for the battle." They were approaching Charlestown Neck when they learned that several wounded provincial soldiers had been taken to a nearby house. Warren told his apprentice that he "had better remain and dress their wounds," and with only a cane in his hand, Warren continued walking toward Bunker Hill.

William Howe was a handsome man, about six feet tall, with dark hair, black eyes, and a majestic reticence that did not prevent him from having a very good time when not on the battlefield. Politically he was a Whig, and as a member of Parliament he had spoken against the advisability of a war with Britain's American colonies. But that was before King George had requested his presence in Boston, with the understanding that he would be next in line should General Gage's services no longer be required.

When it came to maneuvering infantry regiments across a battlefield, Howe was considered a master tactician. Over the course of the last five years, he had introduced a new system by which light infantry companies increased the mobility of the British army, and just a few months before he had been stationed on the Salisbury Plain near Stonehenge, conducting drills. In an age before the machine gun, lines of infantry could march boldly up to the enemy and once within musket range—about a hundred yards or so—charge ahead with their seventeen-inch-long bayonet blades thrust forward. The trick was to get the enemy to fire early enough that the first volley did minimal damage while the terrifying sights and sounds of a line of bellowing soldiers emerging from the powder smoke made the opposing force turn and run. One favorite tactic was to make it look as if you were launching an attack on one segment of the line when you were really concentrating your forces in an entirely different direction. That was what Howe hoped to do today.

Over on the left, General Pigot was to lead his men in a great show against the redoubt and breastwork while on the right Howe focused on the rail fence. But the real work was to be done by the light infantry on the beach beside the Mystic River. With the famous Welch Fusiliers leading the way, a long column of light infantry was to overwhelm whatever resistance they encountered on the beach and, in Howe's words, "attack them in flank." Unfortunately, Howe had not been able to perform any significant reconnaissance of this crucial portion of the battlefield. Ever since the loss of the *Diana*, Admiral Graves had been reluctant to expose his fleet to unnecessary risk, and he had been unwilling to move any of his ships up the Mystic River. Not only could a vessel on the Mystic have provided Howe with some useful eyes and ears, her cannons could have directed a devastating stream of fire on the rear of the rebel line. Graves's concerns about losing one of his ships in the shallows of the river did not apply to the gunboats, and Howe requested that they be rowed around the peninsula from the Charlestown milldam to the Mystic River. The tide, however, was against them, and by the time they took up their positions on the Mystic, the battle was essentially over.

Since the right-most column of light infantry was hidden behind the bank of the Mystic River, this critical movement was to remain largely unappreciated by those watching in Boston, while all attention was directed to the forces in the middle and on the left, where Howe and Pigot each had a line of ten companies, or about three hundred soldiers, with a second line following close behind. According to John Burgoyne, then standing on Copp's Hill, the deployment of these troops was "exceedingly soldierlike; in my opinion it was perfect."

But just as the attack was about to begin, trouble arose on the left. Colonel Prescott had sent a detachment of provincials down into Charlestown, where they were now occupying empty buildings and firing on Pigot's regulars.

As it so happened, Admiral Graves had just arrived at Morton's Point. Ever since the night of April 19, he'd been eager to burn this troublesome town, and he now saw his chance. He asked if Howe wanted Charlestown destroyed. The general gave his consent.

Two types of projectiles were used to fire on and burn a town from without: superheated cannonballs known as hotshot and circular metal baskets full of gunpowder, saltpeter, and tallow that looked so much like the ribcages of the dead that they were called carcasses. The first carcass fell short near the ferry dock, but the second fell in the street and was soon spewing molten fire among the surrounding houses. Just to make sure, Graves dispatched a group of sailors from the *Somerset* to help "fire the town," and in short order, Charlestown's several hundred buildings, tinder dry after several weeks with little rain, had erupted into flame. "A dense column of smoke rose to great height," Henry Dearborn wrote, "and there being a gentle breeze from the southwest it hung like a thundercloud over the contending armies." In the hours to come, the cinders of Charlestown were scattered as far as Chelsea, more than two miles away.

As the inferno raged to the west, General Howe turned to address his troops one last time. "I shall not desire one of you to go a step farther than where I go myself at your head," he assured them. "Remember, gentlemen, we have no recourse to any resources if we lose Boston but to go on board our ships, which will be very disagreeable to us all." Howe's artillery of six field-pieces, two light twelve-pounders, and two howitzers were lined up along the crest of Morton's Hill, and in addition to the growing plume of smoke, "innumerable swallows" could be seen dancing above the heads of the British soldiers.

Prescott estimated that there were only about 150 men left in the redoubt. They were exhausted, hungry, and nearly driven mad with thirst. The fort's earthen walls, once moist and cool, had been baked dry by the sun. With the regulars about to begin the assault, Prescott's men were desperate for assistance from the mass of provincials they could see lingering around General Putnam on Bunker Hill. "Our men turned their heads every minute to look on the one side for reinforcements," remembered Captain Bancroft.

But none were forthcoming—except for one man, who could be seen making his solitary way toward the redoubt. Instead of wearing a brown floppy hat or red worsted wool cap like the rest of them, he was, a witness remembered, "dressed . . . like Lord Falkland, in his wedding suit." It was Dr. Joseph Warren, and the "soldiers received him with loud hurrahs."

Since leaving his apprentice on the outskirts of the Charlestown Common, Warren had crossed the Neck, and after borrowing a musket from a doctor who was tending to the wounded at a tavern on the west side of Bunker Hill, he'd found General Putnam. Warren made it clear that despite recently being named a major general he'd come not to command but to serve as a volunteer. He also wanted to know where the fighting was going to be the hottest, and Putnam had directed him to the redoubt.

Like Putnam before him, Prescott asked whether Warren was to act as his superior officer. "No, Colonel," he replied. "But to give what assistance I can, and to let these damn rascals see that the Yankees will fight."

From the start, the British advance was plagued by unanticipated complications. Many of the cannon had been provided with the wrong size of cannonballs; as a last resort, the artillerymen took to firing alternative projectiles—clusters of smaller balls known as grapeshot—but the mix-up stalled the initial momentum of the attack. The worst impediment came, however, from the terrain. Most of the hay on the hillside had not yet been harvested, requiring that the regulars march through a sea of waist-high grass that concealed the many rocks, holes, and other obstacles that lurked at the soldiers' feet. The fences that Captain Knowlton and his men had cannibalized to such good effect in building the rail fence provided an unforeseen hindrance to the regulars' advance. Every hundred yards or so, the soldiers encountered yet another one of these solidly built fences, requiring that they pause to take down the rails before they could push on ahead. Adding to the soldiers' torment was the heat of the afternoon sun, augmented by the swirling bonfire of Charlestown and the smothering warmth of their wool uniforms. It also didn't help matters that they were loaded down with packs and other equipment.

But gradually, Howe's and Pigot's long, increasingly straggling lines of soldiers made their inevitable way up the hill as beside them a city burned and above them an army waited. For those watching in Boston, the regulars made for an unforgettable sight, what John Burgoyne called "a complication of horror and importance beyond anything that ever came to my lot to be witness to." The movement of the troops amid the unceasing cannonade from the ships and the hilltop battery were impressive, but it was the destruction of "a large and noble town" that transfixed the eye, particularly the church steeples, which had become, Burgoyne wrote, "great pyramids of fire" as entire blocks of houses collapsed in crashes of flame and smoke.

The provincials were equally impressed, especially those stationed in the redoubt, who had, one officer wrote, "the conflagration [of Charlestown] blazing in their faces." Few of them had ever confronted such a daunting display of military power and resolve. Joseph Warren had always insisted that there were limits to how far Britain was willing to go when it came to opposing her colonies, claiming "that they never would send large armies" into battle against the Americans. Now, with Charlestown burning and an army of more than two thousand soldiers marching in his direction, he must have realized that he'd been wrong. He also must have begun to wonder whether all the destruction and death that lay ahead would be justified by the ultimate result.

Prescott, however, had more immediate concerns. He must convince his exhausted, awe-struck soldiers that they had a fighting chance. He told them that "the redcoats would never reach the redoubt if they would observe his directions: withhold their fire until he gave the order, take good aim, and be particularly careful not to shoot over their heads; aim at their *hips*." Ebenezer Bancroft remembered that Prescott also told them to "take particular notice of the fine coats," meaning that they should do their best to shoot at the scarlet, as opposed to red, coats of the British officers.

To the east, at the rail fence, Colonel Stark told his men to hold their fire until they "could see the enemy's half-gaiters," the heavy linen splash guards that were secured to a regular's foot by a strap below the instep and reached halfway up the calf. At the beach Stark provided the men clustered behind the stone wall with a visual aid, positioning either a rock or a piece of wood about fifty yards away to indicate the place that the enemy must cross before they could open fire. In every instance, the message was the same: to maximize the effectiveness of their very limited supplies of gunpowder, they must wait till the last possible moment before they unleashed a volley. Perhaps one provincial officer even used an expression that had been in common usage for decades and told his men to hold their fire until they could see the whites of the enemy's eyes.

Howe marched bravely at the head of his line of grenadiers toward the rail fence, his staff, including a servant clutching a bottle of wine, clustered about him. As they approached the rebel line, the cannonading of the enemy suddenly ceased so as to prevent any injury to the British forces during the attack. In the unnatural, smoke-filled quiet, the regulars prepared for the assault.

Over on the right, on the beach between the bluff and the river, in their own narrow corridor of sand, the light infantry of the Welch Fusiliers approached the provincial stone wall, "as if," a provincial wrote, "not apprised of what awaited them." The soldiers' uniforms were faced in royal blue. At the Battle of Minden in northern Germany in 1759, the Fusiliers had been part of an army that had proven its valor against a French force that was estimated to be 54,000 strong. Up ahead, there could not have been many more than one hundred provincials behind that stone wall. They would punch through with their bayonets fixed. It seemed strange that the enemy had not yet begun to fire; perhaps they had already turned and run.

Suddenly the provincial muskets erupted in flame and smoke. Packed in three deep behind the wall, the New Englanders took turns firing. As one man reloaded his musket, which took a little less than thirty seconds, another was blasting away at the British. As long as their powder held out, the provincials could sustain what was described as "a continued sheet of fire." Unfortunately, the Welch Fusiliers, with a steep nine-foot bank to their left and the river to their right, had nowhere to hide. Musket balls slammed into their torsos and legs with a sickening slap, cutting bloody gouges into their flesh and splintering bones. (A British surgeon later wondered whether the Yankees purposely aimed low so as to add to the regulars' sufferings, since leg wounds almost always required amputation.) Every man in the front group dropped to the ground, either dead or wounded; others came up from behind and were also cut down. Over and over again, the scenario was repeated. According to Stark, "The dead lay as thick as sheep in a fold." Finally, with close to a hundred bodies lying lifeless on the beach, the remnants of Howe's light infantry turned and fled. A minister watching from the opposite shore of the Mystic River reported that they "retreated in disorder and with great precipitation to the place of landing, and some of them sought refuge even within their boats. Here the officers were observed . . . to run down to them, using the most passionate gestures and pushing men forward with their swords."

It was almost as bad on the high ground to the west when the provincials opened up on the line of grenadiers. Already frustrated by the fences and the terrain, many of the grenadiers disobeyed orders and paused to fire at the entrenched enemy instead of charging ahead. Not only did this stop the advance in its tracks, Howe's picture-perfect formation was ruined as the second line found itself stumbling into the grenadiers ahead of them. "They began firing," Howe wrote, "and by crowding fell into disorder and in this state the second line mixed with them." This confused jumble of soldiers provided the enemy with an excellent target. "There was no need of waiting for a chance to fire," one provincial soldier wrote, "for as soon as you had loaded, there was always a mark at hand, and as near as you pleased."

But if all seemed confusion, there was, among the provincials at least, a definite agenda. "Our men were intent on cutting down every officer . . . ," Henry Dearborn wrote, "[shouting,] 'there,' 'see that officer,' 'let us have a shot at him.' When two or three would fire at the same moment . . . , [resting] their muskets over the fence, they were sure of their object." The grenadiers, on the other hand, who were without the benefit of a barricade and were firing desperately from a standing position, were less effective with their muskets and inevitably shot too high. After the fighting, Dearborn noticed that an apple tree behind the rail fence "had scarcely a ball in it from the ground as high as a man's head while the trunk and branches above were literally cut to pieces."

According to Marine Lieutenant John Clarke, one provincial soldier did particular damage to the ranks of the British officers. Standing on a platform that put him close to three feet higher than those around him, the rebel sharpshooter would see a British officer, fire, hand over his spent musket, get handed a loaded weapon, and fire again. Over the course of ten to twelve minutes, the sharpshooter killed or wounded, Clarke estimated, "no less than 20 officers" until a grenadier from the Welch Fusiliers finally shot him down.

About this time Captain John Chester and his company, their blue uniforms hidden beneath their shabbiest of clothes, had made it across the Neck to Bunker Hill. Chester was horrified by what he found. All around them, provincial soldiers were doing their best to avoid the fighting, "some behind rocks and haycocks and 30 men perhaps behind an apple tree and frequently 20 men round a wounded man, retreating, when not more than three or four could touch him to advantage. Others were retreating, seemingly without any excuse." Putnam was providing anything but inspirational leadership. "The plea was," Chester wrote, "the artillery was gone, and they stood no chance for their lives in such circumstances, declaring 'they had no officers to lead them.' "

Chester and his company pushed on toward Breed's Hill, "the small as well as cannon shot . . . incessantly whistling by us." Samuel Webb was marching beside Chester. "Descending into the valley from off Bunker Hill . . . ," Webb wrote, "I had no more thought of ever rising the hill again than I had of ascending to heaven as Elijah did, soul and body together. But after we got engaged, to see the dead and wounded around us, I had no feelings but that of revenge; four men were shot dead within five feet of me."

After the first disastrous attack on the rail fence, Howe reformed his ranks and tried once again. With reinforcements, however slight, from Bunker Hill, the provincial line once again held firm, making Howe's hoped-for bayonet charge impossible. According to a British officer, "an incessant stream of fire poured from the rebel lines . . . for near 30 minutes. Our light infantry were served up in companies against the grass fence, without being able to penetrate—indeed how could we penetrate? Most of our grenadier and light infantry, the moment of presenting themselves lost three-quarter and many nine-tenths of their men. Some had only eight and nine men a company left; some only three, four, and five." One provincial soldier claimed that the regulars were reduced to piling the bodies of their dead compatriots "into a horrid breastwork to fire from." A British officer ruefully wrote, "We may say with Falstaff . . . that 'They make us here but food for gunpowder.' "

The fire from the three arrow-shaped fleches between the breastwork and the rail fence proved particularly lethal to the grenadiers, especially since Captain Trevett, the only American artillery officer to distinguish himself that day, was there with a cannon. Several Connecticut soldiers insisted that at one point General Putnam was also in the vicinity with a cannon of his own. Having watched in outrage as two artillery officers abandoned their fieldpieces on Bunker Hill, Putnam convinced Captain John Ford, the same officer who had killed five regulars on the Battle Road on April 19, to help haul one of the cannons down to the front lines. There, Putnam assisted in firing the fieldpiece, using a ladle to jam powder from the oversize cartridge down the barrel. When a particularly effective shot tore into the regulars' ranks, one provincial soldier was heard to shout, "You have made a furrow through them!"

Up until this point, the fighting at the redoubt had been relatively light. The provincial sharpshooters who had formerly occupied houses in Charlestown had moved to a stone barn farther up the hill, and not until General Pigot had eliminated this annoying threat on his left could he turn his full attention to the redoubt. However, Prescott's men, standing behind the fort's earthen walls, had already fired enough times to cause deep concern about the supply of gunpowder. Prescott resolved that the next time the regulars attacked, he would wait until they were within just thirty yards before he allowed his men to fire.

As the muskets inside the redoubt ceased firing, Pigot may have become convinced that Prescott's men had abandoned the fortification, an impression that was reinforced the closer his soldiers approached without any enemy fire. Inside the redoubt, the tension mounted as the regulars threatened to surround them in an annihilating rush. According to one account, Prescott and his officers ran across the top of the redoubt, knocking up the muzzles of the men's muskets to prevent them from firing too early. "[The regulars] advanced toward us in order to swallow us up," Peter Brown wrote, "[but] they found a choky mouthful of us."

When Prescott finally gave the order to fire, the regulars were almost upon them. "We gave them such a hot fire," he wrote, "that they were obliged to retire nearly 150 yards before they could rally and come again to the attack." A British officer put it another way: "On the left Pigot was staggered and actually retreated."

But it was Howe, standing all alone at the rail fence, who felt the full devastating brunt of what had just transpired in the hills overlooking the still raging flames of Charlestown. His aide-de-camp had been killed at his side; by the time he reached the provincial line, every member of his staff was either dead or wounded; even the bottle of wine held by his servant had been shattered by a musket ball. Both the provincials and Howe's own regulars looked on in astonishment as he stood there, resplendent in his scarlet uniform, a seemingly unmissable target for the rebel sharpshooters. Given the effectiveness of the provincial fire, one can only wonder how the British leader managed to remain unhurt. "For a near minute," one of his officers marveled, "he was quite alone."

Surrounded by the dead and the dying, having learned that the light infantry who were to have assured him of a victory had been, in his own words, "repulsed," Howe experienced what proved to be a life-altering sensation. Writing to a friend in England, he admitted, "There was a moment I have never felt before."

For an officer of Howe's experience and temperament, it was a startling revelation. Staggered by grief, anger, shock, and embarrassment, he turned and started down the hill, picking his way through the bodies of the dead, considering what to do next.

Howe had a decision to make. Should he try it once again—*could* he try it once again? Additional reinforcements must be ordered from Boston. A change of strategy was also required. Instead of a line, he would attack in columns. Instead of focusing on the rail fence, he would direct his energies against the redoubt and breastwork. The fleche-punctuated gap provided the opportunity to position his artillery so that the cannons raked the men behind the breastwork. He must act quickly before the provincial soldiers gathered on Bunker Hill had a chance to reinforce the rebel lines. As a final touch, the regulars were ordered to dispense with their packs and other unnecessary equipment.

Despite all that they had so far suffered, the British soldiers were impatient for one last try at the provincials. "Push on! Push on!" was the cry among the grenadiers. And so they began once again, with Howe at their head, "distinguished . . . by his figure and gallant bearing." Instead of a long line across the hillside, they advanced toward the breastwork and redoubt in a column of eight men across. One provincial soldier estimated that there was about twelve feet between each man at the head of the column while behind them the soldiers were "very close after one another in extraordinary deep files." The depth of the column meant that no matter how many British soldiers the provincials killed, there always seemed to be more to replace them. "As fast as the front man was shot down," a provincial wrote, "the next stepped forward into place, but our men dropped them so fast they were a long time coming up. It was surprising how they would step over their dead bodies, as though they were logs of wood."

The discipline and bravery of the British soldiers—who were heard to shout, "Fight, conquer, or die!"—was a terrifying wonder to behold, but the artillery, repositioned on the right and firing grapeshot, was what began to change the course of the battle. The minister over on the eastern shore of the

Mystic River was well placed to see the devastation wreaked by the British cannons on the provincials standing behind the breastwork, who were forced, he wrote, "to retire within their little fort."

Prescott's force inside the redoubt gained by this sudden inflow of desperate men, but as the breastwork was abandoned, the grenadiers were given the toehold they needed to begin to work their way around the fort from the east. Stark at the rail fence was tempted to move his men toward the redoubt in an attempt to thwart this portion of the British advance, but soon realized that given the cannonading of the breastwork, such a move would be virtual suicide. Instead, Stark decided to reposition his men, who had at that moment no British to fight, to help cover what was beginning to look like an inevitable provincial retreat.

In the meantime, the grenadiers led by General Pigot were working their way toward the other side of the redoubt. Even though they were in danger of becoming surrounded, Prescott's men remained in high spirits. "The regulars were no longer invincible in their eyes," Prescott's son wrote. Their biggest concern was their low supplies of ammunition. Somewhere on the dirt floor of the redoubt someone found an abandoned artillery cartridge. They ripped it open and began distributing the powder to the men positioned at the walls as Prescott exhorted them "not to waste a kernel of it, but to make it certain that every shot should *tell*." A few of the provincials had bayonets, and Prescott positioned them "where he considered the wall most likely to be scaled."

Not until the British were within fifteen yards did Prescott allow his men to fire. "The fire on our left wing was so hot that our troops broke," a British officer later wrote. But unlike the previous time, there was no wholesale retreat. Once again the officers received the highest losses. One company of grenadiers lost both its captain and a lieutenant. As his men lay on the grass, musket balls blasting the dirt all around them, the sergeant turned to the remaining privates and said, "You now see, my lads, that our brave captain is greatly wounded and the lieutenant killed; now I have the honor to command you; therefore let us get into the trenches as fast as possibly we can, for we must conquer or die."

Every officer of any experience said that the rebel fire was the worst they'd ever known. One marine captain turned to Major Pitcairn, the officer who had watched helplessly as the firing had begun on Lexington Green two months before, and said that "of all the actions he had been in this was the hottest: first from the burning of the houses of Charlestown; next the heat of the day, and thirdly from the heat of the enemy's fire." Pitcairn told him to quit talking about the heat and to attack the redoubt.

Pinned down by the provincial fire behind a stone wall and some trees, Adjutant John Waller, "half mad with standing in this situation and doing nothing," tried to organize his men for a final assault on the redoubt. "We were now in confusion after being broke several times in getting over rails, etc.," he wrote. He needed to get his men to stop firing their muskets and prepare for a bayonet charge. "I ran from right to left and stopped our men from firing," he wrote. "[And] when we had got in tolerable order, we rushed on, leaped the ditch, and climbed the parapet, under a most sore and heavy fire." During this mad dash toward the redoubt Major Pitcairn took a musket ball to the chest. It proved to be a mortal wound, and Waller later wrote of "the irreparable loss of poor Major Pitcairn."

Waller wasn't the only one leading the charge onto the parapet. Captain George Harris of the Fifth Foot had spent much of May and early June tending a vegetable garden he and his servant had planted beside their tent on Boston Common. In just six weeks, the garden had produced what he described to his cousin in England as "such salads." He was particularly enthusiastic about the "excellent greens the young turnip-tops make. Then the spinach and radishes, with the cucumbers, beans, and peas so promising." Now Harris was at the base of the fort, trying to get his men to follow him up onto the top of the parapet. After two tries, he finally succeeded in getting them to come with him as he mounted the wall, only to be met by the muzzle of a musket. "The ball grazed the top of my head," he wrote, "and I fell deprived of sense and motion into the arms of Lord Rawdon." Lieutenant Rawdon, twenty, an Irish lord dressed in a circular cap made of cat fur, ordered four soldiers to carry their commander to safety despite Harris's mumbled plea to "let me die in peace." As soon as the soldiers carrying Harris ventured beyond the wall of the redoubt, they found themselves back in the provincials' line of fire, and three of them were wounded (one mortally) by the time they'd carried their captain down the hill.

Repeating the mantra "Conquer or die," the grenadiers continued to climb up onto the redoubt. "At the first onset," Henry Dearborn wrote, "every man that mounted the parapet was cut down by the troops within who had formed on the opposite side not being prepared with bayonets to meet a charge." For the regulars it was a terrible and very personal loss of life. "Archy

Campbell . . . fell," John Waller wrote, "poor Ellis also on this fatal spot . . . Shea received also his mortal wound here and Chudleigh Ragg and Dyer were also wounded." Only after the fighting did Waller begin to grieve; "In the heat of the action," he wrote, "I thought nothing of the matter." Lieutenant Rawdon had difficulty believing that the Yankees had not yet begun to retreat. "There are few instances of regular troops defending a redoubt till the enemy were in the very ditch of it," he wrote, "and [yet] I can assure you that I myself saw several pop their heads up and fire even after some of our men were upon the berm," the point between the ditch and the rampart.

Eventually, however, Prescott's men ran out of powder. "We fired till our ammunition began to fail," one provincial remembered, "then our firing began to slacken—and at last it went out like an old candle." The floor of the redoubt was filled with stones, which the men took up and hurled at the regulars, who were now coming over the rampart, one provincial remembered, "with their guns in their left hand and their swords in their right." Ebenezer Bancroft had a single charge left, but before he could get off what he estimated to be his twenty-seventh shot, "an officer sprang over the breastwork and presented his piece." Bancroft had just finished loading his musket. He threw away the rammer and, in his own words, "instantly placed the muzzle . . . against [the regular's] right shoulder, a little below the collarbone, and fired, and he fell into the trench." Bancroft was convinced that he had killed Major Pitcairn, but that honor appears to have been won by Salem Poor, a free African American.

As the redoubt filled up with a chaotic mixture of British and American soldiers, Prescott realized that he must order a retreat. At this point Joseph Warren was said to have demonstrated great bravery, exhibiting, one provincial wrote, "a coolness and conduct which did honor to the judgment of his country in appointing him a major-general." With their gunpowder expended, some of the provincials grabbed the still-warm barrels of their muskets and began swinging them like clubs. The roiling dust and smoke inside the redoubt made it difficult to see, and one provincial told how he was "obliged to feel about for the outlet." Those who couldn't find the sally port simply climbed over the redoubt's walls and did their best to flee. Those who were unable to escape quickly fell victim to what Adjutant Waller described as the grenadiers' "rage and ferocity." "I cannot pretend to describe the horror of the scene within the redoubt . . . ," he continued, " 'twas streaming with blood and strewed with dead and dying men, the soldiers stabbing some and dashing out the brains of the others. . . . We tumbled over the dead to get at the living, who were crowding out of the gorge of the redoubt."

After shooting the British officer with his last charge of gunpowder, Ebenezer Bancroft realized it was time to get out of the fort. He was particularly proud of his musket, "a venerable one," that he'd "taken from the French" during the war in Canada. Holding the musket "broadside before my face," he rushed into the mass of regulars ahead of him and then "leaped upon the heads of the throng in the gateway." Punching and kicking his way out of the redoubt, he finally broke free and with "a shower of shot falling all around me . . . ran down the hill." He lost a forefinger to a musket ball but eventually made it back to Cambridge alive.

Watching from Boston's Beacon Hill, the loyalist Samuel Paine "heard the shouts of the British army whom we now saw entering the breastworks and soon they entered and a most terrible slaughter began upon the rebels who now were everyone shifting for himself." Thomas Sullivan wrote that the provincial forces were "so thick and numerous in the works that they maybe justly compared to a swarm of bees in a beehive. Our brave men ran through with their bayonets, such of them as had not time to run away."

Colonel Prescott was one of the last out of the redoubt. Surrounded by the enemy, he had, his son wrote, "several passes with the bayonet made at his body, which he parried with his sword." By the time he exited the redoubt, his banyan and waistcoat had been "pierced in several places, but he escaped unhurt."

Warren may have left the fort even after Prescott, who had no knowledge of what eventually happened to the provincial leader. Some later claimed that not wanting to be taken alive, Warren actively sought death. But if that were the case, it's difficult to understand why he died with several incriminating letters in his pocket from Bostonians sympathetic to the provincial cause. It's just as likely that, caught up in the considerable heat of the moment, he took it upon himself to cover, as best he could, the retreat of his compatriots. By this time in the battle he'd acquired a sword, which he waved in the air as he "endeavored to rally the militia." About sixty yards from the redoubt, he was "bravely defending himself against several opposing regulars" when he was recognized by an officer. The officer's servant impulsively took up a pistol and "in a cowardly manner" shot Warren in the face, the ball entering just below his left eye and exiting through the back of his head.

Not until the next morning did General Howe discover that Joseph Warren was dead. By that time the British had succeeded in flushing the provincials from the Charlestown peninsula. Israel Putnam, so unsuccessful at digging an entrenchment on Bunker Hill, had spent the night overseeing work on nearby Prospect Hill to the west. Prescott, after bitterly asking Putnam why he had not provided the promised support, assured the ever fretful General Ward that "the enemy's confidence would not be increased by the result of the battle." The Americans had lost 115 killed and had 305 wounded, with most of the casualties occurring during the retreat. Of the approximately 2,200 British soldiers in the battle, close to half—1,054—had been killed or wounded. The British had been victorious, but as Howe wrote, "The success is too dearly bought."

Despite the heavy losses, Howe's men still held their leader in high esteem. "All the soldiers are charmed with General Howe's gallant behavior," an officer wrote. Only slightly injured in the foot, he somehow managed to survive a battle that by all rights should have killed him. And yet he had not emerged unscathed from the bloody carnage on Breed's Hill. As Charles Lee later wrote, "The sad and impressive experience of this murderous day sunk deep into the mind of Sir William Howe."

When he learned on the morning of June 18 that Joseph Warren had been killed, Howe expressed disbelief that a man of Warren's political stature had dared to subject himself to the risks of this terrible battle. He asked John Jeffries, the doctor who had met with Warren on the docks of the North End just a week before, to verify that the body, which had been stripped of its beautiful clothes, did indeed belong to Warren. Jeffries remembered that Warren had "lost a fingernail and wore a false tooth," and after examining the body, he confirmed that this was indeed Joseph Warren. Howe shook his head in wonder and said that "this victim was worth five hundred of their men." For a general who had just suffered more than a thousand casualties in less than an hour and a half, this was high praise indeed.

Part III
THE SIEGE

In sieges, as in all undertakings, it is necessary [and] timely to consider every . . . circumstance that may happen during the execution of the design, and to provide in the best manner against every seeming obstacle. Not only the general's character, the reputation of the army, and the glory of his country are concerned, but a prodigious expense must unavoidably attend such an enterprise, all [of] which are entirely lost in case of a miscarriage, besides the lives of a number of men, a more sensible loss to the nation.

—John Muller, *The Attack and Defense of Fortified Places*, 1757

It is a military maxim that "fortune may fail us, but a prudent conduct never will." At the same time, some of the most brilliant victories have been obtained by a daring stroke.

—William Heath, 1798

The history of this war down to the present day . . . will be little else than a detail of marvelous interpositions of providence.

—the Reverend William Gordon, April 1, 1776

CHAPTER ELEVEN

The Fiercest Man

Even before the end of the battle, boats filled with British casualties began arriving at the wharves of Boston. All that night and well into Sunday morning the town's streets were crowded with "coaches, chariots, single-horse chaises, and even handbarrows" full of bleeding soldiers. "To see the carts loaded with those unfortunate men," the loyalist Peter Oliver wrote, "and to hear the piercing groans of the dying . . . extorted the sigh from the firmest mind."

At one point Oliver saw an officer he knew "advancing towards me, his white waistcoat, breeches and stockings being very much dyed of a scarlet hue." Oliver called out, "My friend, are you wounded?" "Yes, sir!" he replied. "I have three bullets through me." "He then told me the places where," Oliver remembered, "one of them being a mortal wound. He then with a philosophical calmness began to relate the history of the battle, and in all probability would have talked till he died, had I not begged him to walk off to the hospital, which he did in as sedate a manner as if he had been walking for his pleasure."

Typically, the church bells tolled during a funeral. So many soldiers were dying from their wounds in the days following the battle—the army had suffered casualties approaching fifty percent—that Gage ordered that the bells be stilled. Otherwise they would be tolling all day. But it wasn't just wounded soldiers who were dying. Many of the city's inhabitants, especially the poor and elderly, had been weakened by months without fresh meat and vegetables and were beginning to die in startling numbers. The Bostonian Rufus Greene had a relative with the inauspicious name of Coffin. When Coffin died in early July, Greene was one of his pallbearers, and no bells rang. "It seemed strange," he wrote.

"Death has so long stalked among us," Jonathan Sewall wrote, "that he is become much less terrible to me than he once was. . . . Funerals are now so frequent that for a month past you meet as many dead folks as live ones in

Boston streets, and we pass them with much less emotion and attention than we used to pass dead sheep and oxen in days of yore when such sights were to be seen in our streets."

Within a week of the battle, General Gage had reluctantly decided, at the prodding of Henry Clinton, that he must proceed with the original plan and take Dorchester Heights. Now that Howe had possession of Bunker Hill, it only made sense to assume control of this last remaining piece of strategically placed high ground, especially since the provincials clearly lacked the gunpowder and artillery needed to defend it. But after going through the motions of putting together a detachment of two thousand regulars for the assault, Gage, fearful that the provincial force in Roxbury was larger than it actually was, abandoned the operation.

In the weeks to come, Howe's troops on Bunker Hill constructed an elaborate, virtually impenetrable fort atop the peninsula that had cost the British so many lives to obtain. But Dorchester Heights, even though it overlooked both the Castle and Boston's South End, remained empty and neglected: a kind of monument to the deathblow that the Battle of Bunker Hill had dealt to the ambitions of Thomas Gage.

He had arrived in Boston with hopes of snuffing out an insurrection. He now knew that Britain was in for a protracted war—a war against her own subjects for which it was difficult for a British soldier to have much enthusiasm. "We shall soon be driven from the ruins of our victory . . . ," an officer predicted. "Our three generals [Howe, Clinton, and Burgoyne] came over in high spirits and expected rather to punish a mob than fight with troops that would look them in the face; there is an air of dejection through all our superiors which forebodes no good, and does not look as things ought to after a victory." Before Lieutenant Colonel James Abercrombie died of the wounds he received on Breed's Hill, he delivered a deathbed speech of sorts. "My friends," he was reputed to have said, "we have fought in a bad cause, and therefore I have my reward."

On the Sunday after the fighting, Margaret Gage went walking with a female friend. As they stood gazing across Boston Harbor at the smoky remnants of Charlestown, Margaret recited some lines from Shakespeare's *King John*:

> The sun's o'ercast with blood; fair day, adieu!
> Which is the side that I must go withal?

I am with both; each army hath a hand,
And in their rage—I having hold of both—
They whirl asunder, and dismember me.

A few days later, her husband penned a letter to secretary of war Lord Barrington. "The loss we have sustained is greater than we can bear . . . ," he wrote. "I wish this cursed place was burned."

Joseph Warren's twenty-two-year-old brother John was in Salem on June 17 when around sunset "a very great fire was discovered" in the direction of Boston. He soon learned that a battle had been fought in Charlestown and that his brother had been in it. After just a few hours of sleep, he left Salem around two in the morning. By sunrise he was in Medford, where he "received the melancholy and distressing tidings that my brother was missing." He rushed to Cambridge, where each person he talked to seemed to have a different story. Some said his brother was alive and well; others said that he'd been killed. "This perplexed me almost to distraction," he wrote. "I went on inquiring, with a solicitude which was such a mixture of hope and fear as none but one who has felt it can form any conception of. In this manner I passed several days, every day's information diminishing the probability of his safety."

He knew that the only ones who could provide definitive word were the enemy, so he went to the British line at Charlestown Neck and requested to speak with someone who knew what had happened to his brother. When the sentry refused to help, Warren desperately tried to push his way past until the sentry stabbed him with a bayonet. Bleeding from a wound that would eventually harden into a jagged scar, John Warren returned to Cambridge, where he became one of the army's senior surgeons.

By this time even Warren had become convinced that his brother Joseph was in fact dead. "The loss of such a man," John Eliot wrote, "in addition to our defeat, and at a time when the distracted state of our affairs greatly needed his advice, threw a gloom upon the circumstances of the people, and excited the most sincere lamentation and mourning." One of the most strongly moved was Warren's mentor and friend Samuel Adams. Writing from Philadelphia, Adams admitted to his wife that the death "of our truly amiable and worthy friend Dr. Warren is greatly afflicting. The language of friendship is, how shall we resign him! But it is our duty to submit to the dispensations of heaven." For John Adams, Warren's life and death served as a kind of cautionary tale. As head of the Committee of Safety, the Provincial Congress, and as a major general, the good doctor had taken on "too much for mortal." "For God's sake . . . ," he wrote, "let us be upon our guard against too much admiration of our greatest friends." But Adams's wife, Abigail, took a different view. "We want [i.e., need] him in the senate, we want him in his profession, we want him in the field. We mourn for the citizen, the senator, the physician and the warrior."

The delegates of the Provincial Congress proceeded to elect a new president and argue over the meaning of the battle that had just robbed them of the leader upon whom they'd come to depend. Some claimed that the fighting at Breed's Hill represented a failed military opportunity that should have "terminated with as much glory to America as the 19th of April." Others claimed that the encounter had done more for the provincial cause than anyone could have legitimately expected. "This battle has been of infinite service to us," one observer insisted. Another recalled how the New England soldiers had returned from Charlestown "like troops elated with conquest [rather] than depressed with defeat . . . saying that a few such victories would restore America her liberty." Or, as the Rhode Islander Nathanael Greene wrote, "I wish [we] could sell them another hill at the same price."

By the end of June, the commander of the provincial forces in Cambridge, General Artemas Ward, had learned that he was about to be replaced. In response to Massachusetts's pleas back in May, the Continental Congress had not only addressed the issue of formalizing the province's civil government by sanctioning the election of a new General Court; it had also assumed control of the army. To facilitate the provincial army's transformation from a regional army into a truly continental force, Congress had decided to put the Virginia planter and former army officer George Washington at its head.

Washington had accepted his new position with great trepidation, insisting from the start that "I do not think myself equal to the command I am honored with." Not until he had left Philadelphia for Cambridge did he hear about the Battle of Bunker Hill. According to one account, he immediately asked the messenger if "the provincials stood the British fire." When he was assured that they had, he responded, "Then the liberties of our country are safe."

As Washington perhaps sensed, the Battle of Bunker Hill had been a watershed. What he didn't realize was that the battle had convinced the British that they must abandon Boston as soon as possible. Now that the rebellion had turned into a war, the British knew they must mount a full-scale invasion if they had any hope of making the colonists see the error of their ways. Unfortunately, from the British perspective, Boston—hemmed in by highlands and geographically isolated from the colonies to the south—was not the place to launch a knockout punch against the enemy. Rather than become mired in an unproductive stalemate in Boston, the British army had to resume the fighting in a more strategically feasible location—either in New York or even farther to the south in the Carolinas. That was what Gage suggested in his correspondence that summer, and that was what the British ministry decided to do within days of learning of the battle on July 25. But, of course, Washington had no way of knowing what Gage and the ministers in London intended.

When he arrived in Cambridge on July 2, Washington was a long way from becoming the stoic icon that stares at us each day from the dollar bill. He might have impressed his fellow delegates at the Continental Congress as "sober, steady, and calm," but as the painter Gilbert Stuart came to recognize, lurking beneath Washington's deceptively placid exterior were "the strongest and most ungovernable passions." "Had he been born in the forest," the painter claimed, "he would have been the fiercest man among the savage tribes."

Washington, forty-three, with reddish hair and fair skin that burned in the sun, had assumed his duties as commander in chief with reluctance. Within weeks of his arrival in Boston, however, he had decided that he must end the siege with one dramatic stroke. Unaware of the enemy's decision to evacuate, he was determined to destroy the British army before it had another opportunity to venture out of Boston. Washington was perfectly aware of the consequences of such a decision. By attacking the city itself, he would, in all likelihood, consign Boston to the flames.

Against all odds, Boston had so far endured. What remained to be seen was whether she would survive George Washington.

Even though they were an old and prominent family, the Washingtons were not rich enough to be considered genuine Virginia aristocracy. Washington's father had died when he was eleven. The teenager's best hope for achieving the social standing he craved was in the military, and in 1754, at the age of twenty-two, he was sent into the wilderness of modern western

Pennsylvania to retake the fort at the confluence of the Allegheny and Monongahela rivers that the French had seized from the British and renamed Fort Duquesne. With the help of a group of Iroquois warriors led by Tanacharison, also known as the Half-King, Washington's band of approximately forty soldiers attacked a smaller detachment of French. What happened next will never be completely known, in large part because Washington did his best to downplay the brutal horror of the encounter. It seems likely that despite their best efforts to surrender, the French, who claimed to be on a diplomatic mission, were slaughtered by Washington's combined Indian and English force. According to one account, Washington was attempting to communicate with the enemy's wounded leader Jumonville when Tanacharison clove the Frenchman's skull in two with a tomahawk and proceeded to wash his hands in Jumonville's mangled brains.

Washington later tried to depict the encounter as a kind of backwoods brawl. In truth, he had lost control of a situation that ultimately sparked the beginning of the French and Indian War. Several weeks later, by which time Washington's native allies had abandoned him, the roles were reversed when the Virginians, now holed up at the Great Meadows, several miles from the skirmish scene in what Washington called Fort Necessity, were attacked by a large French force led by Jumonville's brother. By nightfall, close to a third of Washington's men were killed or wounded. Convinced that they were about to be massacred, the remnants of Washington's force broke open the rum supply and proceeded to drink themselves into oblivion. Luckily, the French leader allowed the English to surrender the next morning on the condition that they not return to the region for a year. Somehow Washington survived this catastrophe with his reputation intact (a talent he would display throughout his life), and the following year he found himself in the midst of yet another slaughter when he and a young British officer named Thomas Gage were part of General Braddock's disastrous attempt to take Fort Duquesne in 1755.

What remained of the first phase of Washington's military career was devoted to righting the wrongs committed during this bloody baptism in the wilds of western Pennsylvania. Disgusted with the inadequacies of the undisciplined colonial militia, he wanted, more than anything else, an officer's commission in the British army. The British army, however, did not want him, and in the years after the failed Braddock Expedition, he did his best to create his own provincial version of the regular army.

Paul Revere's 1768 depiction of the arrival of British troops at Long Wharf, the event that ultimately led, a year and a half later, to the Boston Massacre.

An engraving of Boston Common based on a 1768 watercolor by Christian Remick. The tents of the newly arrived British regulars are bracketed by the elm-lined Mall below and John Hancock's mansion above.

An 1801 depiction of the Old State House, known as the Town House in pre-revolutionary Boston and the seat of the province's General Court.

The Old South Meeting on the corner of Milk and Marlborough streets, where as many as five thousand people gathered prior to the Boston Tea Party on December 16, 1773.

Province House, the official residence of the colony's governor, originally built in 1679 by Peter Sargent.

The copper weathervane atop Province House depicting an Indian archer. It was crafted by Shem Drowne and probably based on Massachusetts's colonial seal.

Two wagons from Pope Night, Boston's version of Guy Fawkes Day, the November 5 celebration during which rival gangs from the North and South Ends battled for supremacy. Included in this 1767 sketch by the Swiss artist Pierre Eugène du Simitièrc are caricatures of the devil and the pope.

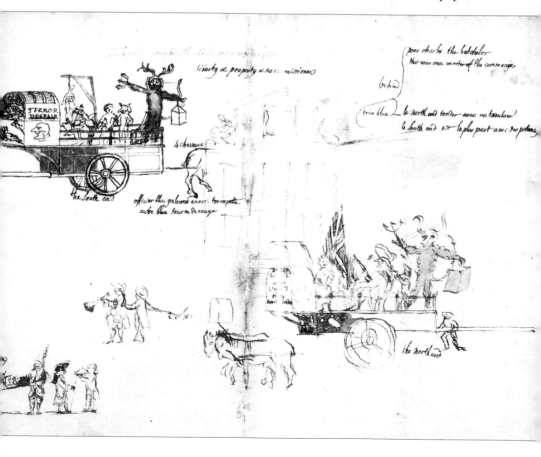

The BOSTONIAN'S Paying the EXCISE-MAN, or TARRING & FEATHERING

Plate I.

London, Printed for Rob.t Sayer & J.Bennett, Map & Printseller, N.o53, Fleet Street as the Act directs 31 Oct.r 1774.

The tarring and feathering of John Malcom in 1774 as depicted by the British artist Philip Dawe. The patriots are pouring tea down Malcom's throat as a noose dangles menacingly from the branch of the Liberty Tree.

During the winter of 1774, the poet Phillis Wheatley described the patriots' insistence on liberty and their tolerance of African American slavery as a "strange absurdity."

Published according to Act of Parliament, Sept. 1, 1773 by Arch.d Bell, Bookseller N.o 8 near the Saracens Head Aldgate.

Fanueil Hall, where Boston town meetings were traditionally held, was described by the patriot Thomas Young as a "noble school" of democracy.

The home of Dr. Joseph Warren on Hanover Street; it was from this house that Warren dispatched Paul Revere to alert the countryside that British regulars were on their way to Concord.

A satirical cartoon of Charles Lee, the eccentric British officer whose admiration for the patriot cause was almost as strong as his love for his Pomeranian dog, Spado.

Israel Putnam, known as "Old Put," was a hero of the French and Indian War who played a prominent if controversial role in the Battle of Bunker Hill.

Lord Percy was the young, impeccably bred British officer who led the mission to rescue Colonel Francis Smith's regulars as they fought their way back to Boston from Concord.

Thomas Flucker was the provincial secretary of Massachusetts; his daughter Lucy married the patriot bookseller Henry Knox, who reported that his loyalist father-in-law was in possession of information that could only have been communicated by a British spy.

Benjamin Church, the famous Indian fighter whose 1716 narrative of King Philip's War was reissued in the 1770s. This engraving by Paul Revere, who was a patriot colleague of Church's great-grandson, Dr. Benjamin Church, may bear a distinct resemblence to the controversial doctor, who proved to be a British spy.

ABOVE: Francis Smith in 1764, eleven years before he led the British regulars to Lexington and Concord.

William Heath was the only provincial general on the scene during the British retreat from Lexington to Charlestown in April 1775. During the Siege of Boston, he vehemently opposed Washington's plans to invade Boston.

General John Thomas was a physician from Kingston, Massachusetts, who commanded the American forces in Roxbury.

William Howe had a reputation as a master tactician in the British army; he was to meet his match at the Battle of Bunker Hill.

Henry Clinton's considerable strategic abilities were marred by a nervous, often irascible temperament; he was, he admitted in a letter to a friend, "a shy bitch."

John Burgoyne bragged about making "elbow room" for the British forces trapped in Boston; they were words he came to regret.

Dr. John Jeffries claimed that Joseph Warren offered him a position as the head of the provincial army's medical corps, despite the fact that Jeffries was a self-proclaimed loyalist. After the Battle of Bunker Hill, he would identify Warren's corpse.

The British regulars storm the redoubt on Breed's Hill in a panel from a modern cyclorama by the artist Leonard Kowalsky.

A 1775 satirical cartoon depicting the sufferings of a British regular during the Siege of Boston. As the drawing points out, the average soldier fighting in America was paid less than a chimney sweep back in London.

OPPOSITE: Bostonians watch the Battle of Bunker Hill from the city's rooftops in an engraving by Howard Pyle.

A 1776 British cartoon mocking the American soldiers who manned the entrenchments during the Siege of Boston. Each one wears a cap that reads "Death or Liberty."

The discovery of this coded letter in September 1775 revealed Dr. Benjamin Church, head of the provincial army's medical department, to be a British spy.

General Howe supervises the evacuation of Boston in March 1776.

A sketch by the British engineer Archibald Robertson of the burning of Castle William.

John Quincy Adams in 1843, the same year that the Bunker Hill Monument was completed. Adams was haunted by his memories of the battle he'd watched as a seven-year-old boy.

In 1755, Virginia governor Robert Dinwiddie named Washington colonel of the Virginia Regiment. It was an unparalleled opportunity for an aspiring twenty-three-year-old American officer—a chance to organize a group of a thousand full-time soldiers, their salaries paid by the colony. Washington proved to be a tough disciplinarian, whipping malcontents and hanging deserters at a rate that equaled, if not exceeded, what prevailed in the British army. He designed his own distinctive uniforms that ultimately led to the regiment being called "the Blues." After just a year of defending the colony's frontier, the Blues had become the toughest, best-trained group of soldiers in America. "If it should be said," he wrote Governor Dinwiddie, "that the troops of Virginia are irregulars, and cannot expect more notice than other provincials, I must beg leave to differ and observe in turn that we want nothing but commissions from His Majesty to make us as regular a corps as any upon the continent."

By that time, the focus of the French and Indian War had shifted to the north, and Washington and his regiment toiled in relative obscurity. But in 1758 he finally got his chance to step into the limelight. General John Forbes had been ordered to venture to the region where Washington's military career had begun and take Fort Duquesne. Forbes proved surprisingly receptive to almost all of Washington's ideas and suggestions; unfortunately, the young colonel's frustrations with the British military establishment had reached the point that he was unable to contain his resentment. Surly and recalcitrant throughout the planning of this arduous campaign, he seemed almost disappointed when after hacking their way through the wilderness the British army discovered that the French had burned and fled the fort, thus giving Forbes a well-deserved, if anticlimactic, victory. Soon after, Washington announced his retirement from the military.

Some have speculated that Washington's petulant behavior during the Forbes campaign could be attributed to something besides the hurt he felt at being denied a commission in the British army. In 1758 he was on the verge of marrying the wealthiest widow in Virginia, Martha Custis. Unfortunately, he'd also managed to fall in love with his best friend's wife, Sally Fairfax. But just as he had helped to assuage his frustrations with the regular army by creating a regiment that was "more British than the British," he contained his unruly passions for the beautiful and aristocratic Sally by marrying the woman who enabled him to attain the wealth and social standing to which he'd always aspired.

In the years ahead, the New York statesman Gouverneur Morris came to know Washington well. Like the painter Gilbert Stuart, Morris recognized that "boiling in his bosom [were] passion[s] almost too mighty for man." Washington was destined to become one of the foremost generals of his age, but "his first victory," Morris maintained, "was over himself."

As was to become clear in the months after his arrival in Boston, that victory had not yet been entirely won.

On July 20, 1775, James Thacher, a twenty-one-year-old physician from Plymouth, got his first glimpse of the army's new commander. "I have been much gratified this day with a view of General Washington," he recorded in his journal. "His Excellency was on horseback, in company with several military gentlemen. It was not difficult to distinguish him from all others; his personal appearance is truly noble and majestic; being tall and well proportioned. His dress is a blue coat with buff-colored facings, a rich epaulette on each shoulder, buff under dress, and an elegant small sword; a black cockade in his hat."

All agreed. No one looked better than Washington on a horse. He was six foot two, large-boned with thigh muscles that gave him, one observer remembered, "such a surpassing grip with his knees, that a horse might as soon disencumber itself of the saddle, as of the rider." If there was a visceral power about Washington, there was also an undeniable elegance. The Philadelphia physician Benjamin Rush claimed that Washington had "so much martial dignity in his deportment that you would distinguish him to be a general and a soldier from among ten thousand people. There is not a king in Europe that would not look like a valet de chamber by his side."

Washington had spent most of the last two decades as one of Virginia's wealthiest plantation owners, managing several hundred slaves, experimenting with crops, and gradually expanding his home at Mount Vernon into one of the most impressive residences on the Potomac. He was accustomed to living with a sophistication and grace that was difficult for the average Yankee to comprehend. Underwhelmed by the first house selected for him by the Massachusetts authorities, he quickly found a grander and more appropriate alternative—the Vassall house on Cambridge's Tory Row, about a mile from the town common. Here he installed what he called his "family," surrounding himself with a staff that tended to be from just about anywhere but New England. One of the exceptions was his commissary general Joseph

Trumbull, from Connecticut, who was joined briefly by his younger brother
John, the future painter, who served as one of Washington's aides. "I suddenly found myself in the family of one of the most distinguished and dignified men of the age," the younger Trumbull remembered; "surrounded at his
table by the principal officers of the army, and in constant intercourse with
them."

A year before, Boston's patriots had spoken disparagingly of the aristocratic opulence of the loyalists of Tory Row. Now their new general, whom
everyone referred to as His Excellency, was living in one of the neighborhood's grandest houses in a style befitting the home's original owners. A revolution that had begun when several dozen yeomen farmers decided to linger
defiantly at Lexington Green was now being led by a general who looked and
acted suspiciously like the enemy. But whereas the provincial soldiers appear
to have been for the most part pleasantly surprised by their new commander,
the feeling was hardly mutual. Washington was not just disappointed by the
New Englanders who had begun this war with the mother country; he was
disgusted by them.

He had been led to believe by the Continental Congress that he would find
twenty thousand battle-tested soldiers. What he found instead was a northern version of the undisciplined militiamen who had made his first command
in the western wilderness a nightmare. This was not a proper army; this was
a mob of puritanical savages that included seventeen actual Indians from the
Massachusetts town of Stockbridge as well as Native Americans from New
Hampshire, Connecticut, and Rhode Island. Even worse, from the perspective
of a slaveholder from Virginia, was the presence of a significant number of
African Americans in the ranks.

Rather than tents, these soldiers lived in hovels or, in the case of the Stockbridge Indians, wigwams. "Some are made of boards," the minister William
Emerson wrote, "some of sailcloth and some partly of one and partly of the
other. Others are made of stone and turf and others again of brick and others
brush. Some are thrown up in a hurry and look as if they could not help it—
mere necessity—others are curiously wrought with doors and windows,
done with wreathes and withes in manner of a basket." Emerson thought
"the great variety of the American camp is upon the whole rather a beauty
than a blemish to the army," but Washington thought otherwise, describing
the New Englanders in a letter to his cousin in Virginia as "an exceeding
dirty and nasty people." But there was more. He detected "an unaccountable

kind of stupidity in the lower class of these people, which believe me prevails but too generally among the officers of the Massachusetts part of the army, who are nearly of the same kidney with the privates."

The extremity of Washington's reaction to the army he had inherited is curious. Generals Charles Lee and Horatio Gates, two former British officers whose military experience was much more extensive than Washington's, came to recognize that the militia model upon which this New England army was based had great potential in the peculiar kind of war that lay ahead. These farmers might lack the rigid training of the British regulars, but they knew how to fight. As Gates was overheard to say that fall, "he never desired to see better soldiers than the New England men made." By reacting so negatively, Washington was in danger of irreparably damaging his relationship with the army before he had a chance to rebuild it.

The problem, as Washington saw it, was in how these soldiers had been originally assembled. Since an officer's rank was based on how many men from his hometown he could convince to serve under him, it was almost impossible for him to get these soldiers to do something they didn't want to do. Making a bad situation even worse was the fact that the men's enlistments ended in December, just five months away. If these churlish, unkempt Yankees weren't happy with how they were being treated, they would undoubtedly refuse to reenlist for another year and leave for home at the end of December. He needed to do here in Massachusetts what he had done in Virginia twenty years ago. He needed to create an American version of the British army.

As had been proven on April 19, the militia, which could be assembled in the proverbial blink of an eye, was the perfect vehicle with which to begin a revolution. But as Joseph Warren had come to realize, an army of militiamen was not built for the long haul. Each company was loyal to its specific town; given time, an army made up of dozens of competing loyalties would tear itself apart—either that, or turn on the civil government that had created it and form a military dictatorship. An army that was to remain loyal to the Continental Congress could not be based on local affiliation.

Twenty years ago, Washington had experienced firsthand the dangerous volatility of an army made up of citizen soldiers. He knew how bad things could get when all control was lost. A war fought along the lines of what had happened only three months earlier during the British retreat through Menotomy might turn the Revolution into a ferocious orgy of bloodshed out of which America's liberties might never emerge intact. The ultimate aim of an army was, in Washington's view, not to generate violence but to curtail it.

He might have recognized the dangers of an undisciplined army, but Washington was also driven by a desperate need to prove himself. Even though it might not be justified militarily by what he'd found in Cambridge and Roxbury, he wanted to attack. This meant that the Siege of Boston had entered a new phase that was as much about the conflict raging within Washington as it was a standoff between two armies. Half of him wanted to create an altogether different kind of army—a painstaking process that required time and patience. The other, more impulsive half wanted to "destroy" the British army with one cataclysmic thrust and be done with it. Boston's fate, it turned out, depended on whether Washington could be saved from himself.

For the time being, Washington directed his energies to overhauling the provincial army. He pushed forward the courts-martial that had accumulated in the wake of the Battle of Bunker Hill, making, he bragged, "a pretty good slam among such kind of officers as the Massachusetts government abound[s] in." He issued order after order, insisting that the sentries no longer fraternize with the enemy, and that anyone swimming in the Charles River be sure to hide his nakedness—particularly when a genteel lady was crossing the bridge into Cambridge; he detailed what an officer must wear (a colorful sash across his chest or an epaulette on his shoulder or a cockade in his hat) to distinguish him from his men; perhaps most important, the men must begin using the latrines, or the dysentery that had already begun to spread through the camp would only get worse. "There is great overturning in camp," the Reverend William Emerson wrote, "as to order and regularity. New lords new laws. . . . The strictest government is taking place. . . . Everyone is made to know his place and keep in it or be tied up and receive . . . 30 or 40 lashes. . . . Thousands are at work [digging entrenchments] every day from four till eleven in the morning. It is surprising how much work has been done."

Almost immediately, Washington was forced to confront a crisis among his own officers. Back in June, the Continental Congress had granted commissions that did not reflect the pecking order already established by the colonies. When Connecticut's General Spencer learned that General Putnam now outranked him, he left for home. General Thomas of Massachusetts was outraged when he discovered that his subordinate William Heath now outranked *him*. After several weeks of soothing ruffled feathers and applying for new commissions from Congress, Washington eventually worked things out to just about everyone's satisfaction. This was not possible, however, when it came to the army's regiment of artillery, whose failings at the Battle of Bunker Hill had brought about many of the courts-martial proceedings. The real problem was the regiment's commander, Colonel Gridley, whose insistence on promoting the fortunes of his incompetent relatives had disaffected what few good officers remained. The medical corps was in an even worse state, with little or no coordination among the many hospitals scattered along the lines. In an attempt to apply some order to this mess, the Continental Congress had appointed Dr. Benjamin Church to be the equivalent of the army's surgeon general, but the controversial doctor had already angered and alienated a significant number of his fellow physicians.

And then there was the issue of the riflemen from Pennsylvania, Virginia, and Maryland, who the Continental Congress had believed were going to wreak havoc with the British sentries. Thanks to their weapons' grooved barrels (which imparted a stabilizing spin to the bullet), the riflemen could reputedly hit a tiny target two hundred yards away—more than twice the range of the average musket. Unfortunately, the riflemen proved to be even more undisciplined than the Yankees. When they weren't threatening mutiny, they were deserting to the British. At one point a fight broke out between a group of riflemen from Virginia and a regiment of fishermen from Marblehead. Years later, Israel Trask, who was just a boy of ten at the time, remembered seeing Washington suddenly appear with his black slave Billy Lee at his side, both of them mounted on big, noble horses.

> With the spring of a deer [Trask remembered], he leaped from his saddle, threw the reins of his bridle into the hands of his servant, and rushed into the thickest of the melee [and] with an iron grip seized two tall, brawny, athletic, savage-looking riflemen by the throat, keeping them at arm's length, alternately shaking and talking to them. In this position the eye of the belligerents caught sight of the general. Its effect on them was instantaneous flight at the top of their speed in all directions from the scene of the conflict. Less than fifteen minutes had elapsed from the commencement of the row before the general and his two criminals were the only occupants of the field of action.

But the misbehavior of the riflemen was nothing compared to the challenge Washington faced in supplying his army with gunpowder. When he first arrived in July, he had been assured that the army had 308 barrels of the precious substance. Three weeks later he learned that there were, in actuality, only 90 barrels, meaning that each man in this army of fourteen thousand (as opposed to the advertised twenty thousand) had enough gunpowder for just nine cartridges. General Sullivan from New Hampshire reported that when Washington heard this stunning news, he was rendered speechless for the next half hour. Without powder, Washington could not attack the British. "Could I have foreseen what I have, and am like to experience," he complained, "no consideration upon earth should have induced me to accept this command."

For the most part, Washington seems to have kept his frustrations to himself. The persona he had labored to create over the years—that of a dignified, modest, physically magnificent, and exquisitely dressed American nobleman—provided him with a shield to hide behind. If privately he fumed, he impressed almost everyone he met with his equanimity and willingness to listen, even if that too was an act. "[He] has so happy a faculty of appearing to accommodate and yet carrying his point," Abigail Adams wrote, "that if he was really not one of the best-intentioned men in the world, he might be a very dangerous one."

And besides, this summer of disappointments had its occasional moments of promise. In hopes of quickly securing some more gunpowder, he began to look to the possibility of sending out a fleet of armed schooners that might prey on the British supply ships that continued to stream into Boston Harbor. It would take months before the schooners came up with any tangible results, but at least the creation of what was, in essence, an American navy provided Washington with a diversion from the tedium of this unrelenting siege.

In August he decided to send Benedict Arnold, just back from Fort Ticonderoga, on an expedition first proposed by Jonathan Brewer back in May. Working his way up the Kennebec River, Arnold would eventually arrive at the Saint Lawrence River, link up with yet another advance toward Canada from New York being led by General Richard Montgomery, and take Quebec. The plan—aimed at "liberating" Canada from the British Empire—proved almost impossible to implement, but like the initiative with the schooners, the Arnold Expedition demonstrated an early willingness on Washington's part to explore potentially innovative solutions to seemingly intractable problems.

Closer to home, Washington was relieved to discover that not all of the officers in the army he had inherited from General Ward were the spineless, self-serving imbeciles he initially took them to be. General Nathanael Greene from Rhode Island, a thirty-three-year-old lapsed Quaker who walked with a limp, was cool, thoughtful, and refreshingly forceful for a man of his tender years. It also didn't hurt matters that Greene had a beautiful wife from Block Island.

Just when Washington had begun to think that he was without any competent engineers, he came upon the lumbering former bookseller Henry Knox of Boston. Knox had overseen the design and construction of the most impressive works Washington had come across so far in Roxbury. Knox was big and imposing in the manner of Washington, but there was also an almost cherubic fleshiness and good humor about him. He freely admitted that almost everything he knew about engineering and artillery had come from the books he had sold in his store. A few years earlier he had lost several fingers of his left hand when his fowling piece exploded on Noddle's Island, and he concealed the injury by wrapping his hand in a stylish silk scarf. Although only twenty-five years of age, he might be just the one to make sense of the army's artillery regiment. And like Nathanael Greene, he had a fetching wife, the ebullient and raven-haired former Lucy Flucker, daughter of the province's secretary, Thomas Flucker. Washington, it seems, had a weakness for charismatic but physically damaged officers, particularly ones with beautiful spouses.

Back on the morning of April 19, thirteen-year-old Benjamin Russell and his schoolmates from the Queen Street Writing School had followed General Percy's brigade out of Boston. Events quickly left them marooned in Cambridge with no way to communicate with their parents back in Boston. Since then, Russell had become an errand boy for the army, picking up his company's provisions at the commissary in Cambridge and returning to the lines laden with drink and foodstuffs. He and four soldiers were making their way through the town's streets when they came upon Russell's father and uncle, who had "just escaped from Boston."

Throughout the summer and fall Bostonians kept finding ways to get out of the city. Some were lucky enough to receive permits to pass across the lines. At least one inhabitant—a barber named Richard Carpenter—swam his way to freedom, only to return to Boston, once again by swimming, and get thrown into jail, where he languished for the duration of the siege as a suspected spy. The boats that daily departed from the town wharves to fish in Boston Harbor provided another way to sneak out of the city; that was how

George Hewes, the shoemaker who had gotten caned by the customs agent John Malcom a year and a half before, managed to make his escape.

Whatever method Benjamin Russell's father used, he showed little joy at finally finding his long-lost son. Instead of wrapping the boy in a hug, Mr. Russell grabbed him by the shoulders and began to berate him "for not writing." One of the soldiers came to Russell's defense. "Don't shake that boy, Sir," he said. "He is our clerk."

Russell's days with the army were numbered. His father took him to see General Putnam, who agreed to discharge the boy into his father's custody. Soon Russell was in Worcester and indentured to the newspaper editor Isaiah Thomas.

Around this same time in August, Mercy Scollay and two of Joseph Warren's young daughters traveled from Worcester to the seat of the newly reinstituted General Court at Watertown. As might be expected, Scollay had been devastated by the news of Warren's death. "For a time," she wrote, "[I was] incapable of writing or feeling any animating sensations." What made it particularly difficult was what she described as "my uncertain situation." Although she and Warren had agreed to marry and she had been acting as his children's surrogate parent for the last four months, she had no legal claim to Warren's offspring. The Continental Congress in Philadelphia was then in recess, and with John Hancock, Samuel Adams, and John Adams back in New England, she had sought them out for advice as to what she should do. "[I] find nothing can be done respecting the children," she reported to her friend Mrs. Dix in Worcester, "till a judge is appointed and I cannot hold them one moment after the relations claim *their right*."

She also reported that her fellow New Englanders appeared to have already forgotten about her beloved Joseph Warren. "Instead of seeing people look dejected with the dire calamities that are impending over our heads, they appear like frolic coming to [a Harvard] commencement. My melancholy countenance is a novelty in this place. . . . Everything appears with a different affect to me now and the sight of my friends gives a keener edge to my grief." She still had trouble believing that Warren was dead—especially since she could find no one who had actually seen his body. "Pray heaven," she wrote, "I may some time or other be able to acquiesce in the received opinion or else be confirmed in my own hopes and ardent wishes [that he is alive]."

But the most devastating blow had come from Warren's own family. His brother John, she had just learned, had sold Warren's "every feather bed" to

George Washington. Another man—and not just any other man—was literally sleeping in her dead fiancée's bed. She poured out her heart to John Hancock, who "appeared," she wrote to Mrs. Dix, "much affected by my relation
[and] said his brother had no right to do those things without proper authority."

What, if anything, Hancock ever did to appease Mercy Scollay is unknown. There is evidence, however, that she found a way, if indirectly, to
stake her claim to Warren's legacy. Later that year an elegy to Joseph Warren
appeared as a broadside. This poem by an anonymous author is not about a
noble warrior dying heroically on the battlefield; it is about a loving father
and friend, "faithful, gentle and sincere," whose "orphan babes" deserve the
sympathy and support "of every parent through the extensive land." More
significantly, the poem, almost certainly penned by Scollay, contains a rhetorical question:

> Nor were the duties of a friend and sire
> Neglected midst those busy scenes of life:
> Speak, speak thou spark of bright immortal fire,
> Who claimed on Earth the tender name of wife?

A conjecture haunted Mercy Scollay for the rest of her life, and still has import today: What if Joseph Warren had survived the Battle of Bunker Hill?
Would the course of American history have been any different? One person,
at least, believed he knew the answer to that question. If Joseph Warren had
lived, the loyalist Peter Oliver maintained in 1782, Washington would have
been "an obscurity."

Siege warfare dates back to before 3000 BC, by which time settlements in the
Middle East had begun to defend themselves from attack by building large stone
walls, ditches, towers, and other protective structures. Sieges were conducted
by the ancient Chinese, Greeks, and Romans; in the Middle Ages, siege warfare
led to the construction of castles throughout Europe and beyond. Although the
development of heavy artillery rendered these once impregnable structures ob-
solete, engineering advances in the seventeenth and eighteenth centuries led to
the creation of a new breed of fortifications that proved surprisingly durable
even in the face of severe cannon fire. Despite all these technological advances,
the basics of a siege were the same in 1775 as they'd been at the Battle of

Jericho: an army surrounds a city with the intent of conquering its inhabitants through a combination of attrition, intimidation, and, if necessary, force.

By the fall, Washington's army had succeeded in creating what was known as a line of contravallation: a ring of earthworks that encircled Boston. But there was a fatal flaw. As long as the British maintained control of the harbor, their supply ships from Canada and England could provide the regulars with food. Gage's army could no longer get any fresh provisions from the country, but as long as their warships succeeded in keeping the entrance to Boston Harbor open, they were not going to starve.

Washington had to somehow force the issue, either by an outright assault on the city or, as had occurred at Breed's Hill, by luring the British soldiers out from behind their defensive walls and engaging them in a pitched battle. But here too Washington was stymied by a lack of gunpowder and artillery. As a consequence, he could do little to displace the more than eight thousand British troops who remained in Boston.

Occasional bursts of activity broke the monotony—when, for example, New Hampshire's General John Sullivan advanced the American lines to Plowed Hill near Charlestown Neck in an operation that had all of the discipline and rigor that had been missing from the Battle of Bunker Hill. For the most part, however, the summer and fall of 1775 settled into a militarily listless stalemate. The Continental forces would launch an annoying jab at the British that was inevitably answered by a cannonade. "At one time a horse would be knocked in the head, and at another time a man would be killed," a loyalist wrote; "it seemed to be rather in jest than in earnest. At some times, a shell would play in the air like a sky rocket, rather in diversion, and there burst without damage; and now and then, another would fall in the town, and there burst to the terror or breaking of a few panes of glass. . . . Little else was done but keeping both armies out of the way of idleness, or rather the whole scene was an idle business." According to a British officer stationed on Bunker Hill, "The regulars and the provincials squint at one another like wild cats across a gutter."

By September Washington's frustrations had reached the point that he had decided he must launch an assault on Boston. He didn't have much gunpowder, but his already meager supplies were dwindling every day. If he didn't attack soon, he might lose forever the chance to engage the enemy. As was quickly becoming apparent, maintaining an army of this size was extraordinarily expensive. The Continental Congress was issuing paper currency, but who knew how much longer the people would be willing to pay for a war—especially if it did not yield significant results. And besides, by the new year, Washington might not have an army to command when the soldiers' terms of enlistment came up in December.

He also had to consider the British army, which continued to grow with the arrival of each new transport full of troops. Perhaps Gage had been waiting all this time, gathering steam before launching one last, furious assault. Washington did not have enough soldiers to cover almost ten miles of fortifications; those that he did have were still so poorly equipped that spears—spears!—had been provided in the event of another British sortie. If Gage managed to find one of the many weak points in the Continental lines, his regulars might send the American army reeling. Better to attack now, before the British had a chance to break out of Boston.

But perhaps Washington was most powerfully motivated by the expectations that had surrounded his arrival in early July. He had inherited an army that had a fighting reputation, a reputation, he was convinced, it did not deserve. And yet so far he had done nothing that could compare to the achievements of Bunker Hill and Lexington and Concord. Ready or not, he must act.

But he could not act alone. The Continental Congress had insisted that he must consult his council of war, made up of Generals Ward, Lee, Gates, Putnam, Thomas, Heath, Sullivan, and Greene. On September 8 he proposed "to make a successful attack upon the troops in Boston, by means of boats, cooperated by an attempt upon their lines at Roxbury." They would use the small boats that had been assembled in Cambridge to launch an amphibious assault on Boston. Given Washington's reservations about the fighting capabilities of his army and the lack of arms and ammunition, it was an extraordinarily imprudent proposal. These New Englanders were reliable enough when fighting from behind a wall; to expect them to assault the many entrenchments surrounding Boston was another matter altogether. Even if they did somehow manage to make it past the entrenchments, the assault would transform Boston's crooked streets into a horrifying labyrinth of house-to-house fighting. By attacking now, Washington stood a good chance of destroying his own army and handing the British yet another undeserved victory. Three days later, the council of war, which met at Washington's headquarters in Cambridge, unanimously decided that "it was not expedient to make the attempt at present, at least."

On October 18, in anticipation of the arrival of a committee of three delegates from the Continental Congress, which included Benjamin Franklin,
Washington once again proposed that they attack. Once again the council
voted unanimously against the proposal, but this time there were some qualifications. Nathanael Greene said it might work "if 10,000 men could be
landed at Boston." John Sullivan said that "winter gives a more favorable opportunity," while Charles Lee claimed that he was "not sufficiently acquainted with the men to judge—therefore thinks it too great a risk."

At the end of October, after a nearly week-long summit with the congressional committee, during which guidelines were drawn up for creating a
more "regular" continental army (one of which required that even free African Americans be excluded), Washington formally asked for guidance on the
all-important issue of attacking Boston: "The general wishes to know how far
it may be deemed proper and advisable to avail himself of the season to destroy the troops who propose to winter in Boston by a bombardment, when
the harbor is blocked up, or in other words whether the loss of the town and
the property therein are to be so considered."

Franklin and the other committee members decided that this was "a matter of too much consequence to be determined by them" and that they must
first "refer it to the Honorable Congress." For now, Washington would have to
wait.

In the meantime, his predecessor General Artemas Ward was of the opinion that instead of attacking Boston, Washington should be more concerned
with the strategic importance of Dorchester Heights. As early as August 25,
Ward advised, "We . . . ought carefully to consider what steps may be taken,
consistent with prudence and safety should an enemy in part gain such an
ascendency. . . . I beg Your Excellency to give me some instructions relative to
my duty in that case." It was a theme Ward would return to in the months
ahead.

By the end of October, Washington was facing a new and completely unexpected crisis. Evidence had come forward that Benjamin Church, the controversial head of the army's medical corps, was a British spy. In September,
Church's mistress confessed that the coded letter she had unsuccessfully attempted to deliver to British authorities in Newport, Rhode Island, had been
authored by Church. The letter, written in cipher, had been quickly decoded.
It was hardly the kind of document one would have expected from a spy.

Instead of revealing any secrets, it overstated the strength of Washington's army in a way that seemed helpful to the Continental cause. According to Church, he had written the letter "to impress the enemy with a strong idea of our strength and situation . . . and in hopes of effecting some speedy accommodation of the present dispute." He wasn't a traitor, he insisted; instead, he was using his loyalist family connections (the letter had been addressed to his brother-in-law in Boston) to bring about peace.

A court-martial found him guilty "of holding a criminal correspondence with the enemy." Unfortunately, the Continental Congress had not yet contemplated the possibility of treason, and the worst punishment a court-martial could inflict was a whipping and expulsion from the service—hardly a sufficient sentence, given the nature of the crime. But was Church truly guilty of treason? According to Massachusetts law, treason was defined as a crime against the king, and no one claimed that anything Church had done had been intended to undermine George III. Massachusetts might be in a state of armed rebellion, but even the most ardent patriots still claimed loyalty to their sovereign; that's why Washington referred to his adversaries as the "ministerial" (as opposed to king's) troops. To find Church guilty of treason was, in effect, to declare independence. And no one, at this point, was willing to do that. This meant that there was no legitimate way to punish Church for his crime. Indeed, under the law as currently written, Church, the spy, was the most loyal patriot of them all.

He spent the following weeks confined to his quarters in a house on Tory Row (where he carved "B. Church, Jr." in a closet door). Finally, on October 27, he was brought before the House of Representatives in Watertown. "The galleries being opened upon the occasion," he wrote in his own account of the proceedings, "were thronged with a numerous collection of people of all ranks, to attend so novel and important a trial."

For years Church had been at the forefront of the patriot movement. To think that a man of his standing and obvious abilities (even Washington admitted that Church had already done much to overhaul the army's hospitals) was capable of betraying everything that he claimed to stand for was difficult to comprehend. In Philadelphia, John Adams responded, "Good God! What shall we say of human nature? What shall we say of American patriots?" Many tried to attribute Church's betrayal to a personal failing. If a man had been unfaithful to his wife, it was natural then that he would be unfaithful to his country. At least that's how Abigail Adams and Mercy Otis Warren saw it.

But as became clear, most of Church's male compatriots had long since known about his infidelities. And Church was by no means the first noted patriot to be guilty of moral turpitude. One of England's most cherished friends of America, John Wilkes, an outspoken member of Parliament and the current mayor of London, made no secret of his sexual profligacy, and he was still looked to as an inspiration by almost all New Englanders.

Church was at his audacious best before the House of Representatives on October 27. So far, he explained, he had been denied the benefit of counsel. He hadn't learned that he was going to appear before the House until that morning. How could a people who claimed to be fighting for liberty and freedom deny him due process?

> It has been frequently objected to us by our adversaries, [he pointed out,] that we were struggling to establish a tyranny much more intolerable than that we meant to oppose. Shall we justify the prediction of our enemies . . . ? Am I impertinent in claiming the rights of Magna Carta, and bill of rights; have I no title to a trial by jurors, or the benefit of the Habeas Corpus act . . . ? Why are the rules and articles framed by the Continental Congress for the government of the army violated in every letter to accumulate distress on me?

On November 11 the House voted that Church be "utterly expelled," even though he had long since offered his resignation. Neither the Massachusetts General Court nor the Continental Congress wanted anything to do with the case, and Church was eventually transported to Norwich, Connecticut, where he was placed under the custody of Governor Trumbull, who had been a classmate of Church's father at Harvard. There Church would remain for the rest of the siege, a troubling reminder that when it came to the question of loyalty all of them were, in a sense, guilty.

On September 26, Thomas Gage learned that he had been recalled to London. Margaret had preceded him by a month and a half, leaving Boston on August 21 in a ship loaded with 170 sick and wounded survivors of the Battle of Bunker Hill. When the *Charming Nancy* stopped briefly at Plymouth before continuing on to London, the locals were horrified by the handful of officers and men who came ashore, "some without legs and others without arms and their clothes hanging on them like a loose morning gown." Back in Boston, Gage was no doubt relieved to learn that it was William Howe's turn to, in

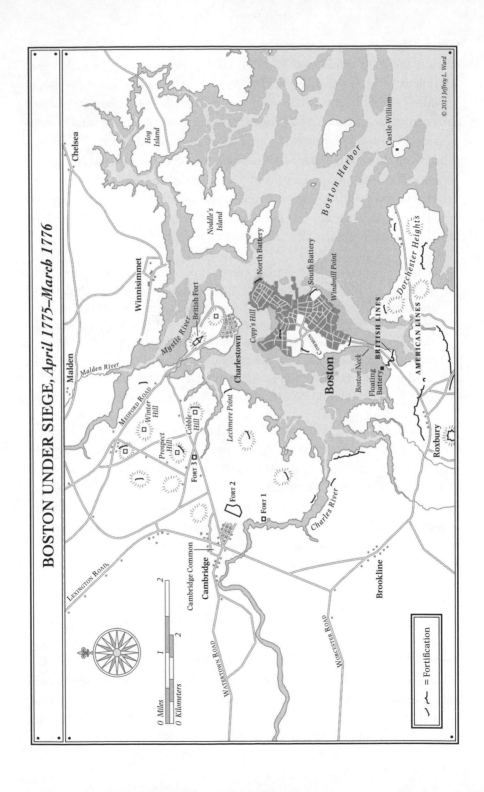

BOSTON UNDER SIEGE, *April 1775–March 1776*

© 2013 Jeffrey L. Ward

Chelsea

Hog Island

Noddle's Island

Winnisimmet

Malden

Malden River

Mystic River

British Fort

MEDFORD ROAD

Winter Hill

Cobble Hill

Prospect Hill

FORT 3

Charlestown

Copp's Hill

North Battery

South Battery

Windmill Point

Boston Harbor

Castle William

Dorchester Heights

AMERICAN LINES

BRITISH LINES

Boston

Common

Boston Neck

Floating Battery

Roxbury

Lechmere Point

FORT 2

FORT 1

Charles River

Cambridge Common

Cambridge

LEXINGTON ROAD

WATERTOWN ROAD

WORCESTER ROAD

Brookline

0 Miles   1   2

0 Kilometers   1   2

⌣ = Fortification

words Gage had used to the ministry, "take the bull by the horns," and on October 11 Gage departed on the *Pallas*, accompanied by Lucy Knox's father, Secretary Thomas Flucker.

In November, Howe received orders to evacuate the troops from Boston before the arrival of winter. He regretted to inform the ministry that there were not enough ships in Boston Harbor to handle all his army, as well as the artillery and "stores of all denominations, [and] the well-disposed [i.e., loyalist] inhabitants with their effects and such merchandise as it may be thought prudent to remove." They must wait until spring. But not to worry. "We are not under the least apprehension of an attack upon this place . . . ," he assured Lord Dartmouth; "on the contrary it were to be wished that they would attempt so rash a step and quit those strong entrenchments to which alone they may attribute their present security."

A poisonous languor settled upon the British army in Boston. With no military objective left to achieve other than simple survival, the officers and their men settled in for a long, futile winter. Dysentery and smallpox ravaged soldiers and civilians alike, to the point that twenty to thirty people were reported to be dying a day. Howe's confidence in his army's security was apparently not shared by his own officers. "Boston . . . may very justly be termed the grave of England," one of them wrote, "and the slaughterhouse of America. . . . If we hear a gun fired upon the Neck, we are all under arms in a moment and tremble least the provincials should force their way into the town and put us all to the sword for our cruelty at Lexington and setting fire to the large, ancient and flourishing town of Charlestown . . . But the glorious expedition we are upon is approved of by an all-wise, all-merciful ministry; and therefore all must be right." Wrote another, "Our barracks are all hospitals and so offensive is the stench of the wounds that the very air is infected with the smell. What, in God's name are ye all about in England? Have you forgot us?"

And in fact, many back in Britain had done exactly that. The boycott of British goods that the colonials hoped would bring the mother country to her knees was having no visible effect. After the conclusion of the Russo-Turkish War in 1774, Great Britain enjoyed what Edmund Burke described as the "most astonishing market." "The poor are industrious," one observer wrote from London, "and the manufacturers have full employment. . . . And were it not for the newspapers, the people at large would hardly know there was a civil war in America." By the fall, the ministry had decided to do what Gage had proposed the year before and mount an army of twenty thousand British soldiers and mercenaries for the war in America. These military preparations also helped to stimulate the economy. "War, indeed," Burke wrote, "is become a sort of substitute for commerce."

But while Britain prospered, her army in Boston was in danger of freezing to death. Howe ordered that the city's older structures be torn down and used as fuel. In the months ahead, the Old North Meetinghouse and the parsonage of the Old South Meetinghouse, which had been built in the seventeenth century by Governor John Winthrop, were demolished, along with dozens of other buildings. Boston was, in fact, being burned by the British, one historic structure at a time.

Back in August some regulars had cut down that revered patriot icon, the Liberty Tree. In October the Old South Meetinghouse was taken over by the British light dragoons and converted into a riding school. The soldiers ripped out the pulpit, pews, and seats (one particularly finely carved pew was turned into a hog sty) and laid down a layer of tanbark cloth and manure. The sacred place where patriots such as Josiah Quincy Jr. and Joseph Warren had once spoken before crowds of thousands had become an echoing barn full of horses.

At the direction of Massachusetts lieutenant governor Thomas Oliver, the Green Dragon Tavern, yet another patriot shrine, was turned into a hospital. But perhaps the ultimate indignity came when Faneuil Hall, Boston's hallowed seat of town government, was turned into a theater—an institution that proper Bostonians had shunned as immoral since the town's founding.

Gage was gone, but his counterpart in the British navy, Admiral Graves, remained, despite the fact that no one seemed to have anything good to say about him. Indeed, if there was anyone who embodied the venality and corruption of the British Empire, it was Graves. During the summer, when all of Boston's inhabitants—civilians and regulars alike—were desperate for fresh foodstuffs, Graves added to their miseries by refusing to grant fishing permits unless his secretary was paid "a dollar for each boat." "You may guess what execrations were poured forth," an officer wrote. That summer, Graves refused to grant customs commissioner Benjamin Hallowell permission to harvest his own hay from Gallup's Island. During the Battle of Bunker Hill, Hallowell had suggested that Graves place his ships where they could have done some good on the Mystic River; the admiral angrily refused and "from thence sprang a dislike." "Are we not sufficiently oppressed by the enemies without," Hallowell wrote Graves on July 20, "but must suffer by those who are sent for our protection?" In August Hallowell confronted Graves in the streets of Boston; Graves drew his sword on the unarmed commissioner, who proceeded to snap the blade in half and pummel the admiral until his face was black and blue. Graves responded by sending one of his young nephews after Hallowell, who was blindsided by a bludgeon as he walked on Cornhill near School Street. The nephew was eventually court-martialed and found guilty of nothing more than "an error in judgment."

Throughout the summer and fall, Graves suffered humiliation after humiliation as packs of provincial whaleboats managed to elude his many warships stationed throughout Boston Harbor. A fleet of thirty boats led by Major Benjamin Tupper attacked and burned the Boston lighthouse on Little Brewster Island not once but twice. Finally, in response to a hint from Lord Sandwich that "you may be blamed for doing too little but can never be censured for doing too much," Graves was moved to act. In October he gave Captain Henry Mowat of the *Canceaux* orders to put towns up and down the New England coast to the torch as a demonstration of the fearsome might of the British navy. After determining that the houses in Gloucester were spread too far apart to allow him to burn the settlement, Mowat settled on Falmouth (modern Portland, Maine), whose patriots had a few months before briefly kidnapped him. At first, the town's inhabitants did not appear to take the British captain's threats seriously, and they were thrown into a panic when he finally began to bombard the town. It took a while for Mowat's two fourteen-gun vessels to lay the town to waste, but by 6:00 p.m. of October 18, about two thirds of the town—almost all of its waterfront—was "one flame."

The burning of this particular town at the edge of the Massachusetts wilderness did more to unite the opposition than it did to support the king's cause. The British were experiencing the dilemma that afflicts any empire—ancient or modern—that is reduced to attacking an essentially defenseless civilian population. Even the successes are viewed as moral failures.

But Admiral Graves's ultimate indignity was yet to come. By the end of November, Washington's nascent navy of armed schooners was beginning to have an impact on British attempts to supply the troops in Boston. "We are now almost as much blocked up by the sea," one officer complained, "as we have been for these eight months by the land."

John Manley of Marblehead had received his commission directly from Washington and was captain of a schooner that had been recently renamed the *Lee* in honor of General Charles Lee. On November 29, Manley and his crew, pretending to be a Boston pilot boat, captured the British ordnance ship *Nancy*. Stored inside the *Nancy*'s hold was a virtual armory of artillery and munitions. "There was on board," William Heath enthused in his diary, "one 13-inch brass mortar, 2,000 stand of arms, 100,000 flints, 32 tons of leaden ball, etc. A fortunate capture for the Americans!" Washington's army had been provided with exactly what it needed if it were to have any hope of successfully attacking Boston.

Within a few days, word of the *Nancy*'s capture had reached the British in Boston. "There is nothing to prevent the rebels taking every vessel bound for this port," an officer lamented. "For though there are near twenty pendants flying in this harbor, I cannot find that there is one vessel cruising the bay. Surely our admiral cannot be allowed to remain here much longer [as] a curse upon the garrison."

But Graves was not entirely to blame for the ineffectiveness of his squadron. The British government had failed to provide him with enough sailors to operate his ships, given the inevitable effects of disease and desertion. One naval officer estimated that if you took all the sailors in all the ships presently stationed in Boston Harbor, there wouldn't be enough to "man one half of the ships, which are likewise in want of all sorts of stores and necessaries." The Admiralty, under the incompetent leadership of Lord Sandwich, was the real source of the problem, this officer insisted. "You may depend on it," he wrote, "the remissness complained of did not arise from the admiral, who frequently left his own ship in too defenseless a state (in my opinion) in order to keep his cruisers at sea. . . . [He] has been cruelly used."

At the end of December, with the arrival of the fifty-gun *Chatham*, Graves learned that, like Gage before him, he had been recalled and that Admiral Molyneux Shuldham was the new commander of the British navy in Boston.

Washington spent much of December peering at Boston through his spyglass, as often as not from the heights of Prospect Hill overlooking the Charlestown peninsula, the Mystic River, the harbor, and Boston itself. He could see the British soldiers preparing for the winter ahead, building barracks both in the town and on the Charlestown peninsula. The British appeared to be there to stay. But when Washington ordered successful advances at Cobble Hill and then Cambridge's Lechmere Point, Howe's army barely responded. Washington was dumbfounded. "[I am] unable," he wrote, "upon any principle whatever to account for their silence, unless it be to lull us into a fatal security."

Rather than playing a complex game of psychological warfare, William Howe had simply lost the will to fight. His experience at Bunker Hill had certainly stunned him, but there were other factors contributing to his lassitude. In Europe, winter was a time for armies to rest and recoup. This was not the case, however, in New England, where the ice and snow actually increased an army's mobility. A hundred years before during King Philip's War, an intercolonial army had marched across the frozen wetlands of Rhode Island and surprised a huge village of Narragansett Indians in what became known as the Great Swamp Fight. Washington was hopeful of using the ice around Boston to facilitate an attack later that winter. But for Howe the coming cold provided an opportunity to attend plays at Faneuil Hall and gamble with his officers, often attended by the beautiful blond wife of Joshua Loring, a loyalist who'd been appointed the town's sheriff, at his side.

Some have blamed the distractions provided by Howe's affair with Elizabeth Loring for his lack of initiative during the winter of 1775–76. But perhaps the real reason Howe could not bring himself to venture out of Boston was that, like Gage before him, he did not know how to proceed against an enemy composed of British subjects, many of them from a colony that had built a memorial in Westminster Abbey to his beloved older brother. Howe's ambivalence is revealed in the letter he sent Lord Dartmouth in January. Washington's army was not "by any means to be despised," he wrote, "having in it many European soldiers, and all or most of the young men of spirit in the country." Rather than launching a full-scale attack, might it not be "better policy," he continued, "to withdraw entirely from the delinquent provinces, and leave the colonists to war with each other for sovereignty." That Howe was probably correct in his assessment does not change the fact that this was a general who had little interest in a war.

Washington tried to be philosophical about the approaching reenlistment crisis, reassuring both a fellow general and himself that "order and subordination in time will take place of confusion, and command be rendered more agreeable." He knew that many of the soldiers were unhappy about the changes he had put in place for the new Continental Army. As former militiamen, they were used to serving with soldiers from their own colony, but that was not how it necessarily was going to be in the future. "Connecticut wants no Massachusetts man in their corps," Washington wrote; "Massachusetts thinks there is no necessity for a Rhode-Islander to be introduced amongst them; and New Hampshire says, it's very hard, that her valuable and experienced officers . . . should be discarded because her own regiments under the new establishment, cannot provide for them."

Some of the regiments from Connecticut had decided that they were technically free to depart as early as December 1, and that day the excitable and blasphemous General Lee ordered them to form into what Simeon Lyman described as "a hollow square." Lee, no doubt followed by his black Pomeranian dog Spado, stepped into the square's center. "He flung and curst and swore at us," Lyman wrote, "and said if we would not stay he would order us to go on Bunker Hill and if we would not go he would order the rifleman to fire at us." Lee's tantrum did little to change the soldiers' minds. On December 10, Nathanael Greene reported that the "Connecticut men are going home in shoals this day." As anyone from Massachusetts, New Hampshire, or Connecticut knew, this was the way the region's militia had worked for more than a century. "'Tis the cast of the New Englanders to enlist for a certain time," Reverend William Gordon wrote, "and when the time is expired to quit the service and return home, let the call for their continuance be ever so urgent."

Nathanael Greene understood the phenomenon but could not help but share in his commander's frustration and anger. "If neither the love of liberty nor dread of slavery will rouse them from the present stupid state they are in," he wrote, "and they obstinately persist in quitting the service, they will deserve the curses of the present and future generations to the latest ages. . . . What can equal such an infamous desertion . . . ? We that have boasted so loud of our private virtue and public spirit, do not have the very vital principles of liberty."

Greene admitted, however, that Washington bore part of the blame for the reenlistment crisis by expecting too much of the army he had inherited. "His Excellency has been taught to believe the people here a superior race of mortals and finding them of the same temper and disposition . . . of the common people of other governments, they sink in his esteem." As Greene rightly pointed out, "you cannot expect [to make] veterans [from] a raw militia [after] only a few months' service."

Not surprisingly, the army's first commander in chief, Artemas Ward, was even more critical of Washington and his lack of appreciation for the soldiers from New England. At one point, Ward wrote of his great concern about the raising [of] a new army, for the genius of this people is different from those to the southward. Our people are jealous and are not inclinable to act upon implicit faith; they choose to see and judge for themselves. They remember what was said of them by some that came from the southward last summer, which makes them backward in enlisting or manifesting a willingness to enlist. . . . Some have said hard things of the officers belonging to this colony and despised them, but I think as mean as they have represented them to be, there has been no one action with the enemy, which has not been conducted by an officer of this colony.

One can only wonder what would have happened if at the outset Washington had had a New England general with the polish and empathy of Joseph Warren on his staff. Warren might have provided the perspective that allowed Washington to recognize the provincial army's considerable strengths. At least one biographer has criticized Washington for not taking a direct role in addressing the recruitment problem. With someone such as Warren (as opposed to the excitable, foulmouthed Charles Lee) exhorting the men to reenlist, the conversion from the old into the new army might have gone much more smoothly.

There is evidence that Washington had begun to recognize the error of his ways. By December, his highly valued secretary Joseph Reed had returned to Philadelphia. In the months ahead, Reed served as his epistolary confidant, and on December 15, Washington responded to a letter in which Reed apparently reported that some of the general's negative comments about the New Englanders had caused grumblings among the delegates in Congress. "I am much obliged to you for the hints . . . ," he wrote. "I will endeavor a reformation, as I can assure you my dear Reed that I wish to walk in such a line as will give most general satisfaction." In the weeks to come, Washington continued to thank Reed for passing along anything he heard about him—good or bad. "I can bear to hear of imputed or real errors," he wrote; "the man who wishes to stand well in the opinion of others must do this, because he is thereby enabled to correct his faults . . . for as I have but one capitol object in view, I could wish to make my conduct coincide with the wishes of mankind as far as I can consistently."

Washington had spent his life attempting to control his emotions. He was accustomed to adjusting his behavior in ways that were more congenial to the wishes of those he sought to impress. In the past, he had succeeded in winning an honorable reputation among his peers in Virginia. Now it was the delegates of the Continental Congress whose expectations he sought to fulfill. This meant that he was no longer just a Virginian; he was attempting to be something that did not yet exist—an American. But already he had taken steps toward achieving that possible future. Through the creation of an army representative of the "continent," he had provided a tangible, if admittedly imperfect, example of how thirteen autonomous colonies might one day become a new nation.

Washington had long since come to the conclusion that a reconciliation with the mother country was a virtual impossibility, and in this he was not alone. As early as October 19, after having dinner with a group of Continental officers, the minister Jeremy Belknap recorded in his journal, "I found that the plan of *independence* was become a favorite point in the army, and that it was offensive to pray for the king." Finally, after more than a decade of clinging to the fiction that the king remained America's most stalwart friend, the colonists were beginning to see the truth. The policies of King George and his ministers were one and the same. The only alternative left was what Nathanael Greene termed, in a letter written on December 20, "a declaration of independence."

By the end of the month, Washington had decided to reverse himself on the issue of African American soldiers and allow free blacks into the army. Back in Virginia, royal governor John Murray, Earl of Dunmore, had offered the colony's slaves freedom if they fought on the side of the British, and this may have contributed to Washington's change of heart. But the most compelling reason he decided to put aside the prejudices of his southern upbringing had to do with what had transpired six months before at the Battle of Bunker Hill.

On December 5, thirteen of Washington's officers filed a petition to the Massachusetts General Court, requesting that the African American Salem Poor be rewarded for his bravery on June 17, 1775. Poor had "behaved," the petition read, "like an experienced officer as well as an excellent soldier." It had been Poor, many claimed, who had shot Major Pitcairn as the British officer mounted the wall of the redoubt, shouting "The day is ours!"

The New Englanders in Washington's army were making a statement: If during a battle when so many white officers had displayed irresolution and outright cowardice, an African American private had fought with such distinction, then certainly such a man should not be denied the ability to fight for his country. Washington appears to have taken this kind of testimony to heart, and by the beginning of the new year Salem Poor, who had purchased his freedom for the price of twenty-seven pounds in 1769, was a soldier in the Continental Army.

On December 22, the Continental Congress responded to Washington's query about whether he could attack Boston even if it meant the total destruction of the city. His Excellency, Congress informed him, was free to make an assault on the British "in any manner he may think expedient, notwithstanding the town and property in it may thereby be destroyed."

Washington was going to need every soldier—white or black—that he could get.

CHAPTER TWELVE

The Clap of Thunder

O n January 1, 1776, a British officer approached the American lines in Roxbury under a flag of truce. After more than fifteen months of continual expansion, the fortifications around Boston had been pushed to the farthest portion of the Neck, where massive earthen walls (which a Connecticut soldier compared to the fabled fortress of Gibraltar) had been augmented by the guns of a floating battery in the Back Bay as well as lines of abatis—obstacles made from the trunks and sharpened branches of trees that served the same purpose as modern-day barbed wire—to prevent the enemy from storming the bulwarks by foot. At the old town gate, well within these outer lines, a moat had been dug across the Neck, meaning that Boston, surrounded by its "chain of forts," was now an actual island.

Between the British and American lines was a flat marshy sweep of bottomland punctuated by the charred remnants of several burned-out buildings. Waving a white flag, the British officer, probably accompanied by one or two others, walked across the fire-scorched no-man's-land.

At least one of the men was carrying copies of a broadside for distribution among the soldiers of the Continental Army. This was more than the usual proclamation from General Howe; this was the King's Speech, delivered before Parliament back on October 27. It had been published by "the Boston gentry" with the hope of putting the fear of God into the rebel army.

Once and for all, the king had called the colonists' bluff, declaring that their "strongest protestations of loyalty to me" were both absurd and offensive given that they were presently engaged in a "rebellious war . . . carried for the purpose of establishing an independent Empire." The colonists could no longer pretend that they still remained loyal to their sovereign; they must either return to the British fold or admit that they were engaged in a war of independence. The loyalists felt confident that once the rebels realized that they were on the verge of permanently alienating themselves from their beloved king, they would begin to rethink this deluded adventure and plead for a reconciliation.

As it so happened, Washington had already acted to strengthen the solidarity and resolve of his troops. January 1 was the first day of the new Continental Army, and to help celebrate this historic event, he replaced the large red flag previously raised by Israel Putnam on the heights of Prospect Hill with the "Union flag," the red, white, and blue British standard that combined the crosses of St. George and St. Andrew. Created by King James in 1606 to symbolize his role as ruler of both England and Scotland, the Union flag had become, in recent years, a symbol of colonial unity in the face of British oppression. By raising the Union flag, Washington was announcing his army's transition from a provincial to a truly continental army, and the ceremony was accompanied by the firing of thirteen guns and "the like number of cheers."

The works at Prospect Hill were the equal of any fortification in Boston and had the advantage of being situated on a broad outcropping with a commanding view of the Mystic River and all of Boston Harbor. Soon after the fighting at Noddle's Island, Israel Putnam's men had transformed the schooner *Diana*'s seventy-six-foot mainmast into a flagpole, and it was from this towering section of tar-stained pine that the Union flag of the Continental Army proudly waved.

Washington soon learned that the "redcoats" on Bunker Hill and in Boston construed the raising of the Union flag not as a "compliment to the United Colonies," but as "a token of the deep impression the speech had made upon us, and as a signal of submission." "I presume," he wrote, "they begin to think it strange that we have not made a formal surrender of our lines." In actuality, the King's Speech had the opposite effect on the American soldiers. When the broadsides eventually made their way from Roxbury to Cambridge, they "excited," it was reported, "the greatest degree of rage and indignation . . . as proof of which, [a copy of the speech] was publicly burnt in the camp."

Washington was amused by the "farcical" nature of the confusion over the Union flag, but it also spoke to the uncomfortable ambiguity that still lingered over their cause. They might prefer to interpret the flag as representing unity among the colonies, but that did not change the fact that what we call today the Union Jack was a British flag. At some point, the Americans, if that was what they intended to call themselves, must have a flag of their own.

On the night of January 8, Faneuil Hall was jammed with playgoers. Present that evening were the cream of the British army, including commander in chief General William Howe. Although the siege had devolved into a stalemate and no orders had been received from the ministry since the fall, there were signs that military operations against the rebels might soon move in other and more productive directions. Back in December, General Burgoyne had departed for London, intent on finding a new role for himself that might bring about a decisive British triumph. In a few weeks' time, General Clinton was to depart on a secret mission to the south. For now, the officers and their wives were gathered for the premiere of a play Burgoyne had completed before leaving for England: a comedy titled *The Blockade of Boston*.

The curtain rose to thunderous applause as out stepped the figure of George Washington "in an uncouth gait, with a large wig, a long rusty sword, attended by a country servant with a rusty gun." Before General Washington could get a word in edgewise, a sergeant suddenly appeared on the stage and shouted, "The Yankees are attacking our works on Bunker Hill!" This inspired more laughter and applause as the audience "clapped prodigiously."

Not until General Howe himself stood up and shouted, "Officers to your alarm posts!" was it realized that the sergeant was no actor. "A general scene of confusion ensued," a playgoer recounted, "[officers] immediately hurried out of the house to their alarm posts; some skipping over the orchestra, trampling on the fiddles; and in short, everyone making his most speedy retreat, the actors (who were all officers) calling out for water to get the paint and smut off their faces; women fainting, etc." The story of *The Blockade*'s premiere soon made its way across enemy lines. To the minister William Gordon of Roxbury, it seemed almost providential that a play "designed to ridicule us" had been so comically interrupted. "Thus the ridicule," Gordon wrote, "was turned upon themselves."

The rebels, it was soon discovered, had not attacked the British works on Bunker Hill; they had instead sent a detachment of several hundred men under the command of Thomas Knowlton of Connecticut on a raid across the milldam that connected Cambridge to the Charlestown peninsula. The mission's aim was to destroy what houses still remained in Charlestown so that the British soldiers stationed on the peninsula could no longer use the structures either as barracks or as a source of firewood. Under heavy fire from the guns atop Bunker Hill, Knowlton and his men retreated with five prisoners after torching eight of the houses.

This operation had been made possible by the ice that had finally begun to form along the edges of the Charles River and would, if the cold persisted, extend across the entire river and Back Bay. With Boston surrounded by ice,

Washington might finally be able to launch his long-hoped-for attack. As far as he was concerned, they should have assaulted Boston with the help of boats back in the fall—before the reenlistment crisis reduced his already undermanned army by half. "Could I have foreseen the difficulties which have come upon us," he wrote Joseph Reed on January 14, "could I have known that such a backwardness would have been discovered in the old soldiers to the service, all the generals upon earth should not have convinced me of the propriety of delaying an attack upon Boston till this time. When it can now be attempted I will not undertake to say, but this much I will answer for, that no opportunity can present itself earlier than my wishes."

All December and January—despite the arrival of his wife, Martha, and her son and daughter-in-law—the tension had been building within Washington. So far his efforts to create a larger and more disciplined regular army had been a failure, forcing him to rely increasingly on the local militias. But it wasn't only the lack of men; there was the lack of gunpowder as well as a paucity of weapons—problems that had been exacerbated by the Continental Congress's failure to come forth with the funds he needed to purchase muskets and pay his army. In a rare moment of candor, Washington revealed the extent of his despair to Joseph Reed:

> The reflection upon my situation and that of this army produces many an uneasy hour, when all around me are wrapped in sleep. Few people know the predicament we are in, on a thousand accounts—fewer still will believe, if any disaster happens to these lines, from what causes it flows. I have often thought how much happier I should have been if, instead of accepting of a command under such circumstances, I had taken my musket upon my shoulder and entered the ranks or, if I could have justified the measure to posterity and my own conscience, had retired to the backcountry and lived in a wigwam. If I shall be able to rise superior to these and many other difficulties, which might be enumerated, I shall most religiously believe that the finger of Providence is in it, to blind the eyes of our enemies. For surely if we get well through this month, it must be for want of their knowing the disadvantages we labor under.

At a council of war two days later, attended by his generals as well as John Adams and the president of the Massachusetts legislature, James Warren (from Plymouth, and no relation to Joseph Warren), Washington was finally able to get his generals to unanimously agree that "a vigorous attempt ought to be made upon the ministerial army in Boston, as soon as practicable." Toward that end, it was decided to almost double the size of the existing army of about nine thousand soldiers with the temporary addition of thirteen regiments of militia from Massachusetts, New Hampshire, Rhode Island, and Connecticut, a process that would take at least a month.

But there was more. Expected any day was a bonanza even greater than the windfall of armaments provided by Captain Manley's capture of the *Nancy.* Back on November 15, Henry Knox, the former bookseller with an interest in artillery and a talent for building fortifications, had left Cambridge with his nineteen-year-old brother, William, on a mission to Fort Ticonderoga at the western edge of New England, on the southern end of Lake Champlain. After a journey of more than three hundred miles over the ice and snow, the Knox brothers and a primarily horse-drawn train of forty-two sledges bearing fifty-nine iron and brass cannons, howitzers, and mortars—more than sixty tons of artillery—were about to arrive in Framingham.

At first they had prayed for warm weather. The plan was to transport the armaments by boat from the northern tip of Lake George (only a few miles from Fort Ticonderoga) to Fort George on the lake's southern end—a distance of about thirty-two miles. As soon as they began rowing the guns down the lake in early December, contrary winds and dropping temperatures slowed their progress, forcing them at some points to hack their way through the newly formed ice. Knox decided to push ahead of what he called his "little fleet" so that he could make preparations for the guns' arrival at Fort George. As evening approached on December 10, he and his boat crew were making good progress down the lake, but "knowing [the men] to be exceedingly weary," he decided it was time he allowed them to go ashore to rest. Using "very large quantities of dry wood ready cut," they made a roaring fire. "We warmed ourselves sufficiently," Knox recorded in his diary, "and took a comfortable nap—laying with our feet to the fire." About a half hour before daylight, they set out once again, and after more than six hours "of excessive hard pulling against a fresh head breeze," they finally arrived at Fort George.

One of the scows fetched up on a rock and filled with water, but eventually all the deeply laden boats reached Fort George. Knox had made arrangements to build a group of "exceeding strong sleds" for the intended journey south over the frozen Hudson River to Albany, where they would begin to make

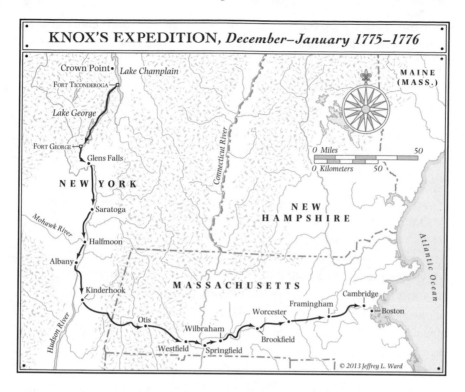

KNOX'S EXPEDITION, *December–January 1775–1776*

their way east across the breadth of Massachusetts. On December 17 he wrote Washington that he hoped for "a fine fall of snow, which will enable us to proceed further and make the carriage easy. If that shall be the case I hope in 16 or 17 days' time to be able to present to your Excellency a noble train of artillery."

But it was not to be. On December 28, the man who was to provide him with sleds walked off in a huff after General Philip Schuyler complained that he was charging too much for his services. Knox took some consolation in knowing that it had actually snowed too much for his cannons to have begun their journey, since the heaping drifts made it impossible for the horses and oxen to make any headway. As his brother remained at Fort George waiting for the sleds to be provided by another source, Knox ventured ahead to the Hudson River, where he took steps to strengthen the ice in anticipation of the cannons' arrival, "getting holes cut in the different crossing places in the river" so that water flowed up through the holes and, upon freezing, added to the thickness of the ice.

Soon they had the sleds they needed, and the cannons had begun to make their way south toward the Hudson from Fort George. But now there was a different problem. From Albany on January 5, Knox wrote Washington,

> I was in hopes that we should have been able to have had the cannon at Cambridge by this time. The want of snow detained us some days, and now a cruel thaw hinders from crossing Hudson River, which we are obliged to do four times from Lake George to this town. The first severe night will make the ice on the river sufficiently strong, till that happens the cannon and mortars must remain where they are. . . . These inevitable delays pain me exceedingly, as my mind is fully sensible of the importance of the greatest expedition in this case. . . . My utmost endeavors have been and still shall be used to forward them with the utmost dispatch.

Logistical practicalities required Knox to break up his caravan into several smaller groups of sleds, and in early January a sled bearing one of the largest of his cannons broke through the ice of the Hudson River. After successfully getting most of the other sleds across the river, Knox was able to save "the drowned cannon" with the help of the local citizenry, and from that day forward the piece of artillery was known as "The Albany."

Crossing and recrossing the Hudson had proven difficult, but the hills and mountains of western and central Massachusetts were just as challenging—especially on the down slopes, when the huge sleds threatened to run ahead of the teams that were pulling them. They were also plagued by a frustrating lack of snow, and when another "cruel thaw" left them temporarily stranded in the town of Westfield, Knox took the opportunity to show the country people, many of whom had never before seen a cannon, what one of these "big shooting irons" could do, repeatedly firing a mortar that came to be known as "Old Sow." By this time Knox had learned that with the help of Washington and John Adams—both of whom had come to believe that the embarrassing failures of the artillery regiment during the Battle of Bunker Hill required new leadership—the Continental Congress had named Knox as Richard Gridley's replacement.

That night in Westfield an appreciative crowd gathered around the twenty-five-year-old colonel at the town's inn. Many of the men were members of the Westfield militia and, like most town militias throughout New England, there were a disproportionate number of officers. This imbalance had made it necessary for Washington to reduce the officer corps in the

Continental Army, a move that had inevitably angered many former officers and contributed to the reenlistment crisis. Now in Westfield, as Knox was introduced to officer after officer, he could appreciate firsthand one of the many difficulties his commander in chief had been forced to confront while he had been overseeing the transportation of cannons from Fort Ticonderoga. Once the introductions had been completed in the Westfield tavern, Knox smiled broadly and said, "What a pity it is that our soldiers are not as numerous as our officers."

By January 25 Knox was back in Cambridge, having completed his mission. Not only had his journey made possible this windfall of artillery, it had provided the officers of Washington's army—particularly those in the artillery regiment—with time to reconcile themselves to the fact that a twenty-five-year-old with minimal military experience had ascended to the rank of colonel. There had been more than a little outrage—Thomas Crafts, who had hoped the appointment might have gone to him, wrote John Adams of the "astonishment, mortification, and disappointment I was thrown into"—but at least Knox had not been around to experience it. By the time he did return to Cambridge, he had achieved a significant success that helped put Washington's decision to promote the young artilleryman in its proper perspective. Officers might continue to grumble, but events were about to unfold that soon commanded everyone's attention.

Washington had much more on his mind than the siege of Boston. By the end of January, he had decided to send General Lee to New York. Convinced that General Clinton was headed for that city, he wanted one of his generals there to prepare for the possibility of a future British attack. Word had also reached Washington of a major setback in Canada. Montgomery and Arnold's attempt to take Quebec had failed. Montgomery was dead and Arnold injured, and the prospects were not good. The arrival of a delegation of Mohawks from the north provided a different approach to influencing the balance of power along the Canadian border, but by the beginning of February, Washington's focus had returned to attacking Howe's army in Boston.

On February 16, he convened yet another council of war. Three days before he had visited the works at Lechmere Point, where the engineer Jeduthan Baldwin had been laboring since December to construct a fortification that might accommodate some of the cannons Knox had secured from Ticonderoga. The problem was the frost—which extended almost two feet below the ground—making the earth, in Baldwin's words, "as hard as a rock." In a single night in January, the ground had frozen an additional eight inches down, and the next morning Baldwin and his men "pried up cakes of frozen earth nine feet long and three feet broad." As Baldwin could attest, building an adequate redoubt in these conditions was almost impossible.

Somehow, however, Baldwin was close to achieving the unachievable, and during an inspection of the site on February 13, Washington saw that the bitter cold had finally reached the point that the ice might help rather than hinder his plans. As Baldwin recorded in his diary, they "found a good bridge of ice to Boston." The time had come, Washington decided, to launch an attack on Boston.

At the council of war in Cambridge on February 16, Washington made his case before his generals. They now had cannons, but they still did not have enough gunpowder to bombard the British regulars in Boston with any effectiveness. The only way to dislodge the troops, given the lack of powder, was to rely on "small arms" through "a general assault upon the town" across the ice. "[A] stroke well aimed at this critical juncture," he insisted, "might put a final end to the war and restore peace and tranquility." And since they had no way of knowing how long the cold might last, they had to launch the attack as soon as possible.

According to the minister William Gordon, who appears to have spoken to Artemas Ward and perhaps others who attended the meeting on February 16, Ward "opposed the idea, saying, 'The attack must be made with a view of bringing on an engagement, or of driving the enemy out of Boston and either end will be answered much better by possessing Dorchester Heights.' " This, of course, was what Ward had been saying since August, and it was not what Washington wanted to hear now that the harbor was frozen in February. Even worse, Washington's trusted adjutant, General Horatio Gates, agreed with Ward, maintaining that "our present army has neither the numbers, the arm[s] nor the discipline necessary to secure success in the assault of Boston" and that "our defeat may risk the entire loss of the liberties of America forever." The vote of Washington's generals was unanimous; instead of attacking Boston across the ice, they should occupy Dorchester Heights.

According to Gordon, "the commander-in-chief could not refrain from showing that he was greatly dissatisfied." Stifling his anger and frustration, he agreed to support Ward's plan to "possess Dorchester Heights, with a view of drawing the enemy out." As it so happened, Ward, "unknown to General

Washington . . . had been for some time collecting fascines, gabions, etc., . . . in expectation that the same would be wanted for this purpose." Gordon recounted how Washington, no doubt somewhat sullenly, left "the conducting of the business [at Dorchester Heights] . . . to General Ward."

Washington, however, refused to wholly abandon his plan to attack and destroy the British in Boston. If after the Americans occupied Dorchester Heights, the British should do as they did on June 17, 1775, and launch an assault on the hastily constructed fortifications, Washington proposed that they then launch a backdoor assault of their own on the western side of Boston, using boats to transport soldiers from Roxbury and Cambridge. Since a significant portion of the British force would be engaged in the attack on Dorchester, the odds would now be in the Americans' favor. With luck, they would have succeeded in taking the city before the British troops had a chance to return from Dorchester Heights.

Even Ward and Gates appear to have believed that this modified plan to take Boston had merit, but there was one general who insisted that such an attack "would most assuredly produce only defeat and disgrace to the American army." William Heath had been there with Joseph Warren during the British retreat from Lexington, and he now maintained that even if the enemy was "induce[d] to make a sally" from Boston, General Howe could be counted on to "provide for the defense of the town." The Americans in Cambridge would not simply row across the Back Bay to the shores of an undefended city; they would most assuredly face stiff and potentially devastating opposition. To expect these soldiers to cross a mile and a half of open water in the face of British artillery was ludicrous; to expect them to "effect a landing . . . under such a tremendous fire" was madness. Washington's unnecessarily aggressive plan would in all likelihood turn a victory into a humiliating defeat.

Whether or not Washington's unceasing six-month campaign to oust the British by force had finally worn down his council of war, the majority of the generals voted in support of his latest proposal. At long last, a committee was formed to draw up a detailed plan for attacking Boston.

Washington had gotten at least a portion of what he wanted, but he remained resentful that his original plan to attack the city across the ice had been rejected. As late as February 26, he wrote Joseph Reed, "But behold! though we had been waiting all the year for this favorable event, the enterprise was thought too dangerous!" But even Washington had to admit that he might have allowed his own mounting frustrations to interfere with his better judgment. In one of the most confiding letters he ever wrote to a member of the Continental Congress, he acknowledged to John Hancock that "the irksomeness of my situation . . . might have inclined me to put more to hazard than was consistent with prudence." The immense pressures of conducting a siege without the resources required to win it had, he confessed, taken a toll. "To have the eyes of the whole continent fixed with anxious expectation of hearing of some great event and to be restrained in every military operation for want of the necessary means of carrying it on, is not very pleasing; especially as the means used to conceal my weakness from the enemy conceals it also from our friends, and adds to their wonder." In the meantime, he would do his best to embrace the plan "to take post on Dorchester" and see whether, he wrote Reed, "the enemy will be so kind as to come out to us."

Nathanael Greene was Washington's youngest general, but no one on the council of war had a better appreciation of the dilemma facing their commander in chief. An attack on Boston, Greene wrote his brother, "would be horrible if it succeeded and still more horrible if it failed." And yet, he continued, "the advantage that America would derive from making ourselves masters of the garrison at this time would be inconceivable. It would damp the spirits of Great Britain and give ours a new spring. In a word, it would put a finishing stroke to the war; it would heal all the divisions among ourselves, silence the Tories and work a general reformation throughout the continent." No wonder Washington yearned to attack Boston.

Artemas Ward may have been the earliest and most forceful proponent of the plan to take Dorchester Heights, but Washington acted quickly to give the operation his own personal stamp. As he had witnessed during the construction of the fortifications at Lechmere Point, the freezing temperatures meant that building a redoubt atop the bare, wind-swept hills of Dorchester was going to be no easy matter. By this time a self-taught engineer of unusual promise, thirty-eight-year-old Rufus Putnam of Braintree (and a cousin of General Israel Putnam), had come to his attention. Unlike Henry Knox, everything Putnam knew about the subject of fortifications came not from books but from practical experience, which was admittedly slight. Despite having worked beside several British engineers during the French and Indian War, he "pretended no knowledge of laying works" and had been reluctant to volunteer his services at the beginning of the siege. At the insistence of William Heath, he agreed to try his hand at building the fortifications at Roxbury, and he was soon overseeing the construction of works at Cobble Hill and other critical locations.

Around the time of the February council of war, Washington invited Putnam to dine at his headquarters, asking that he "tarry after dinner." Once the two of them were alone, the general "entered in a free conversation on the subject of storming the town of Boston." By this point, Washington was at least publicly stating that it would be best to begin such an operation by occupying Dorchester; what he wanted Putnam to figure out was how to quickly build a fortification on ground that was frozen solid. "If I could think of any way in which it could be done," Putnam wrote, "[I was] to make a report to him immediately."

That evening, Putnam was on his way back to his quarters in Roxbury when he decided to stop by the residence of General Heath and "pay my respects." Heath happened to be in, and the officers were soon enjoying a companionable chat when Putnam noticed a book on Heath's table by the noted British military engineer John Muller. "I immediately requested the general to lend it me," he wrote. But Heath refused, claiming that "he never lent his books." "I then told him," Putnam related, "that he must recollect that he was the one who at Roxbury in a measure compelled [me] to undertake a business of which at the time I confessed I never had read a word about and that he must let me have the book." After "some more excuses on his part," Heath finally allowed Putnam to borrow the book.

Not until the next morning did Putnam finally open John Muller's *Attack and Defense of Fortified Places*. On page 4 he discovered an engineering term he had never heard before: "chandelier." Upon reading the definition, he quickly realized that he had found the solution for building a fort on Dorchester Heights.

A chandelier (the fortification frame, not the lighting ornament) is a double-ended wooden scaffold that sits on the ground; when it is placed beside another chandelier, the open space between the two frames is then filled up with fascines, bundles of tree branches that when covered with dirt form the basis of a cannon-proof bulwark. With the help of dozens of precut chandeliers and many more fascines, the Americans could almost instantly create the beginnings of a fort atop Dorchester Heights. With the addition of some of the cannons that had been brought down from Ticonderoga, they would be able to present the British with the illusion, if not the reality (since they still lacked the gunpowder required to do any significant damage with their artillery), of an armed fortress capable of bombarding into oblivion both Boston and the many men-of-war in the harbor. The British would have only two alternatives: launch a desperate sortie against the fort or evacuate.

Once Washington heard of Rufus Putnam's plan, he directed both Henry Knox and the man whom Knox had superseded as head of the artillery regiment, Richard Gridley, to consult with Putnam and determine whether chandeliers might provide a feasible solution to the problem. According to Putnam, "They fell in with my plan." The general approved their report, and "preparations [were] immediately set on foot to carry it into effect."

Plenty of challenges still remained. The road from Roxbury to Dorchester traversed a neck of lowland that was in plain view of the British sentries stationed in Boston. The darkness would help, but some sort of blind needed to be built on the city side of the road that somehow managed to conceal both the sights and the sounds of hundreds of ox-driven carts carrying materials to the Heights. Rufus Putnam initially recommended using stones, since the surrounding terrain was crisscrossed by so many walls, but eventually decided to go with seven-hundred-pound bundles of compressed hay.

In addition to preparing chandeliers and other materials typically used in constructing a fortress, such as fascines and gabions, the Americans built, at the suggestion of the Boston merchant William Davis, barrels. Once filled with stone, gravel, and sand, the barrels could be used to shore up the fort's walls. However, in the event of a British attack, the barrels had yet another, potentially devastating use. As the regulars climbed up the steep, almost treeless hillside, the barrels could be, in the words of William Heath, "rolled down the hill [and] must have thrown the assailants into the utmost confusion and have killed and wounded great numbers." Even as the barrels and other materials were being prepared in and around Roxbury, carpenters in Cambridge were building forty-five flat-bottomed bateaux—each capable of carrying eighty men—along with two floating batteries, in anticipation of an American amphibious assault on Boston.

The Americans might not have much powder, but all agreed that some kind of cannonade of Boston was necessary on the night they took Dorchester Heights. With cannons blazing in Cobble Hill, Lechmere Point, and Roxbury, the British might be too preoccupied to notice what was happening to the southeast in Dorchester. Knox had already begun to install some of his newly acquired cannons in these three sites, and plans were put in place to begin firing on the British several days prior to the move on Dorchester. Not only would this provide Knox's artillery teams with some practice prior to the main event, it would further the illusion that the Americans had finally secured ample stores of powder. The trick was to fire as few shots as possible while still engaging the British army's attention.

All that remained to be decided was the date of the move on Dorchester. For the first time, Quartermaster Thomas Mifflin was invited to a council of war—no doubt because the operation was proving to be as much a logistical as a military challenge. During the meeting, Mifflin related how a friend had suggested that the night of March 4 would be the most appropriate for the move to the Heights. If, as hoped, the British attacked the next day, what might be the battle to end all battles would occur on March 5, the anniversary of the Boston Massacre. Mifflin said that this "would have a wonderful effect upon the spirits of the New Englanders." For some reason, Horatio Gates "deemed it an improper time," but after a spirited debate the council decided, "by a majority of one," to launch the operation on the night of March 4.

Washington's great fear was that the British might learn of the intended advance and seize Dorchester Heights before the Americans could make their move. The near-constant arrival of militiamen and the cutting of trees for fascines and abatis (the Warren family apple orchard in Roxbury was soon sacrificed to the cause) meant that just about everyone living in the towns surrounding Boston knew that something significant was about to happen. On the night of February 26, what Washington described as "a rascally rifleman" deserted to the British. Convinced that the enemy now knew of their plans, Washington ordered Artemas Ward in Roxbury to station "six or eight trusty men by way of lookouts" while preparing several regiments "to be ready to march at a moment's warning to the heights of Dorchester; for should the enemy get possession of those hills before us they would render it a difficult task to dispossess them."

On February 27, he issued an order intended to prepare the army for the impending confrontation while making it clear that instances of cowardice similar to those that had marred the Battle of Bunker Hill were not to be tolerated:

As the season is now fast approaching, [he wrote,] when every man must expect to be drawn into the field of action, it is highly necessary that he should prepare his mind, as well as everything necessary for it. It is a noble cause we are engaged in; it is the cause of virtue and mankind. Every temporal advantage and comfort to us and our posterity depends upon the vigor of our exertions; in short, freedom or slavery must be the result of our conduct. There can therefore be no greater inducement to men to behave well. But it may not be amiss for the troops to know that if any man in action shall presume to skulk, hide himself, or retreat from the enemy, without the orders of his commanding officer, he will be *instantly shot down* as an example of cowardice, cowards having too frequently disconcerted the best formed troops by their dastardly behavior.

In anticipation of the confrontation that might win or lose the siege and perhaps even the war, Washington began to clear his desk of the considerable paperwork that had accumulated over the last eight months. Back in October, the African American poet Phillis Wheatley had sent a poem she had written praising him. "Not knowing whether it might not be considered rather as a mark of my own vanity than as a compliment to her," he explained in a letter to Joseph Reed, "I laid it aside till I came across it . . . while searching over a parcel of papers the other day in order to destroy such as were useless." On February 28, in the midst of the feverish preparation for the move on Dorchester, he wrote the poet a letter, apologizing for the delay and praising her poem as "striking proof of your great poetical talents." Then Washington, the owner of several hundred slaves in Virginia, did something remarkable. He invited the young black woman to pay him a visit. "If you should ever come to Cambridge or near headquarters, I shall be happy to see a person so favored by the muses."

He attended to personal business as well, writing to his wife's brother-in-law, Burwell Bassett, about "my landed affairs on the Ohio." Washington had originally purchased this vast tract of land as an investment. He was now beginning to look to the property as a possible refuge. If "the worst event" should occur on March 5—if the war should be lost and he was stripped of his estate at Mount Vernon—this land along the Ohio River "will," he explained to Bassett, "serve for an asylum."

On the night of March 2, cannons in Lechmere Point began lobbing in both shot (solid cannonballs) and shells (hollow projectiles containing explosives) into Boston. Archibald Robertson, a thirty-year-old British engineer stationed at the newly constructed battery on what he and his fellow countrymen called Mount Whoredom, just beside Beacon Hill, estimated that the rebels fired "11 shots and 13 shells without hurting anybody." He also noted that a few equally harmless shells had been fired from Roxbury.

The next morning Washington was chagrined to learn that the only significant damage sustained that night had been self-inflicted. Three American mortars had split open, probably because they had been improperly bedded on the frozen ground. On the following night, the much-ballyhooed "Congress"—the cannon that had come with the taking of the *Nancy*—split open after firing only its third shell. The American artillery regiment's already limited ability to cannonade Boston had been severely curtailed. Apparently Knox and his officers still had much to learn.

But on the night of March 4, Knox's regiment exonerated itself. At 7:00 p.m. the firing began from Roxbury, Lechmere Point, and Cobble Hill at almost ten times the rate of the previous nights as the British responded with a furious cannonade of their own. One observer reported that there were instances when the fiery trails of as many as seven shells could be seen crisscrossing the night sky. In Braintree, Abigail Adams arose from bed around one in the morning. "I could no more sleep," she wrote her husband, "than if I had been in the engagement. The rattling of the windows, the jar of the house and the continual roar of 24-pounders, the bursting of shells . . . realize a scene to us of which we could scarcely form any conception." Samuel Webb on Cobble Hill reported that "our shell raked the houses terribly, and the cries of poor women and children frequently reached our ears." According to Archibald Robertson in Boston, the American artillery succeeded in killing or wounding six British regulars, with one officer writing, "it is agreed on all hands that their artillery officers are at least equal to our own."

The preparations for the advance to Dorchester Heights had begun the previous morning as Quartermaster Mifflin supervised the organization of more than 350 oxen carts. Sunset was at 5:35, and it soon proved to be the perfect night: a low-lying haze prevented the British from seeing much of anything beyond Boston as a full moon provided the Americans with the light they needed to find their way to Dorchester, and a southerly wind blew whatever noise the soldiers made "into the harbor between the town and the Castle."

At 7:00 p.m., two "covering parties" of four hundred soldiers each crossed the Neck into Dorchester and, after mounting the heights, took up positions where they could watch for the British soldiers both in Boston and at the Castle. Next came General Thomas with a work party of approximately twelve hundred soldiers, followed by the wagons, each driver urging his oxen "in a whispering tone." Soon a total of three thousand of what Thomas described as "picked men" were at work, laying huge bundles of hay along the Neck to act as a screen, and once on the Heights, assembling two different forts—one facing the Castle, the other facing Boston. The chandeliers were quickly arranged and the fascines put in place as the men went to work with their picks and shovels, digging ditches and hurling the frozen clods of dirt onto the breastworks. They labored with astonishing speed and efficiency, and after only a couple hours' work, as the carts continued to go back and forth in silence, General Thomas was pleased to note that "they had got two forts, one upon each hill, sufficient to defend them from small arms and grape shot." He took out his pocket watch and was amazed to discover that it was only ten o'clock. As it so happened, at almost precisely the same time, the British sentinels in Boston relayed word to Brigadier General Francis Smith (who had received a promotion since leading his troops to Concord a little less than a year before) that "the rebels were at work on Dorchester Heights." As on the night before the Battle of Bunker Hill, no one within the British leadership chose to act on the information.

The next morning the British were astounded to see two towering forts atop the hills of Dorchester. "They were all raised during the night," an awestruck officer wrote, "with an expedition equal to that of the Genii belonging to Aladdin's wonderful lamp." Thanks to the magnifying effect of the haze that lay on the land and water, the American works "loomed to great advantage and appeared larger than the reality." The minister William Gordon later learned that "Howe was seen to scratch his head and heard to say by those that were about him, that he did not know what he should do, that the provincials . . . had done more work in one night than his whole army would have done in six months." The engineer Archibald Robertson estimated that the fortifications must have been the work of between fifteen thousand and twenty thousand men.

The rumor among the Americans was that Howe had long since vowed that should they dare to "break ground" on Dorchester Heights he would "sally on us [even] if he was sure of losing two-thirds of his army." As the soldiers atop Dorchester Heights waited to see whether Howe was as good as his supposed word, the British batteries began firing at the new forts. The surgeon James Thacher was with the soldiers on the Heights. "Cannon shot are continually rolling and rebounding over the hill," he wrote in his diary, "and it is astonishing to observe how little our soldiers are terrified by them." But the British artillerymen had a problem. Dorchester Heights was simply too high for them to fire at it effectively. "They endeavored to elevate their cannons so as to breach our works by sinking the hinder wheels . . . into the earth," General John Sullivan wrote, "but after an unsuccessful fire of about two hours, they grew weary of it and desisted."

Even before the cessation of artillery fire, onlookers began to make their way to Dorchester. "The hills and elevations in this vicinity are covered with spectators," James Thacher reported, "to witness deeds of horror in the expected conflict." All of Boston lay before them. "Nothing could take place at the wharves or next to the water," one observer wrote, "but we could note it by the help of glasses." It certainly looked as if Howe were preparing to attack. "The wharf was thronged with soldiers," wrote William Gordon, who along with Thacher was "looking upon the adjacent hills for a bloody battle." As the regulars boarded transports and were taken to the Castle, the natural staging ground for an attack, the Americans on Dorchester Heights "rejoiced at seeing it, clapped their hands and wished for the expected attack."

Their British counterparts were not as enthusiastic. A Boston resident later recounted how the regulars lined up along the town's streets "looked in general pale and dejected and said to one another that it would be another Bunker's Hill affair or worse." In anticipation of scaling the American bulwarks, they collected ladders and cut them into ten-foot lengths.

The optimum time for a British attack was at high tide, which was at two that afternoon, and the Americans watched with mounting excitement to see whether Howe dared to go through with it. By this time Washington had appeared on the Heights and was overheard exhorting, "Remember it is the fifth of March!" and "Avenge the death of your brethren!" "It was immediately asked," William Gordon wrote, "what the general had said by those that were not near enough to hear, and as soon answered; and so from one to another through all the troops, which added fresh fuel to the martial fire before kindled."

All the while, on the other side of the Boston peninsula, four thousand

American soldiers under the commands of Generals Putnam, Sullivan, and Greene were waiting at the mouth of the Charles River, ready to climb into their boats and begin the assault of the city. Greene and half the troops were to land just to the south of Barton's Point at the northwestern tip of Boston; Sullivan was to come ashore at the Boston Common; both were to fight their way through the city until they reached the town gate and joined their compatriots coming in from Roxbury.

But as it turned out, Howe had decided to delay the move on Dorchester Heights until the following morning. That night the surgeon James Thacher's regiment, which had been on station for the last twenty-four hours, was allowed to return to their barracks in Roxbury for some rest. "I bade adieu to Dorchester Heights," he recorded in his journal in the early morning hours of March 6, "without being called to dress a single wound."

For William Howe and his officers, it proved to be a most tension-filled evening and night. Archibald Robertson, for one, believed that the general was making a terrible mistake by even considering an attack. The American works atop the Heights were simply too formidable. Instead of mounting an assault, "we ought immediately to embark" and leave Boston. "The fate of this whole army and the town is at stake," he wrote in his diary at four that afternoon, "not to say the fate of America." After communicating his concerns to every superior officer he could find, he went to Province House, where at 7:00 p.m. Howe and his generals were in the midst of a council of war. Robertson waited outside the door for more than an hour until his commanding officer, the engineer Captain John Montresor, stepped out of the room. Montresor also believed that they had no choice but to evacuate, and he told Robertson that he had said as much during the council of war. He also recounted how "Lord Percy and some others seconded him," and only then did Howe confess that evacuation had been "his own sentiment from the first" and that it was "the honor of the troops" that had moved him to order an attack. Howe had "agreed immediately," Montresor continued, "to embark everything." As Washington's council of war had done three weeks before, Howe's officers had prevented their commander from making a decision that might have destroyed both his army and Boston.

If Howe had any lingering doubts when he went to bed that night, the weather decided the matter for all of them. A storm that some judged to be a hurricane blew up out of the south, knocking down buildings and blowing two of the troop transports moored off the Castle onto the shore of nearby Governors Island. Even if Howe had wanted to, he could not have launched an attack on Dorchester Heights.

At eleven the next morning, Howe called together the army's commanding officers and "acquainted them with his intentions of evacuating this place and going to Halifax." Washington did not get the chance to attack Boston. Signals had been prepared at the meetinghouse in Roxbury to mark the moment when the amphibious assault was to be launched. "But kind heaven," William Heath wrote, "which more than once saved the Americans when they would have destroyed themselves, did not allow the signals to be made."

On March 8, a British officer bearing a letter from the Boston town selectmen approached the American lines at Roxbury under a flag of truce. General Howe, the selectmen indicated, would not burn the town if the Americans allowed the British to evacuate. This was hopeful news to be sure, but Washington remained fearful that Howe was in fact stalling for time so that he could launch one final thrust against the American forces. As the days passed and Howe's army remained in Boston, Washington attempted to hurry the British along by building a fortification at Dorchester Heights that was even closer to Boston. Howe responded to each new move on the Americans' part with artillery fire (in one instance killing several Continental soldiers), and as the day of departure approached, the British general was terrifyingly close to torching the town, a prospect that kept the Bostonians in an unremitting state of apprehension and alarm.

All the while, chaos reigned in the city as the British soldiers struggled to collect as many of their stores as possible for transportation to Halifax. Due to the Admiralty's almost criminal undermanning of the naval vessels, there was a severe lack of sailors to operate the evacuation fleet. This wasn't the only problem thrust upon General Howe by his superiors in London. "When the transports came to be examined," an officer wrote, "they were void of both provisions and forage. . . . Never troops in so disgraceful a situation, and that not in the least to their own fault or owing to any want of skill or discretion in our commanders, but entirely owing to Great Britain being fast asleep. I pity General Howe from my soul." Dozens of perfectly serviceable sailing vessels were tied up to the wharves, but without the needed sailors and provisions Howe was unable to use them.

The departing British army had no choice but to leave behind a vast amount of heavy armaments and other supplies. To prevent the artillery pieces from being used against them, the soldiers hammered metal rods into the cannons' touchholes, a procedure known as spiking the guns. As preparations to leave extended into the second week, marauding gangs of soldiers and sailors plundered stores and houses. Howe issued orders that looters be shot on sight, but the stealing continued.

For the region's loyalists, who had sought sanctuary from patriot reprisals, the decision to evacuate Boston was overwhelming. "The Tories . . . carried death in their faces," one inhabitant wrote, "some run distracted." Washington reported that "by all accounts there never existed a more miserable set of beings than these wretched creatures now are. . . . When the order [was] issued for embarking the troops in Boston, no electric shock—no sudden clap of thunder—in a word the last trump—could not have struck them with greater consternation. They are at their wit's end."

Howe did what he could to accommodate all those who wanted to accompany his army to Halifax, but once again, there was not enough room for all their furnishings and possessions. In the brigantine *Unity* was the family of Adino Paddock, the former commander of Boston's artillery company, along with seven other loyalist households. The outspoken customs commissioner Benjamin Hallowell, the owner of two mansions—one in Boston, the other in Roxbury—found himself sleeping in a cabin with thirty-six others, "men, women, and children; parents, masters, and mistresses, obliged to pig together on the floor, there being no berths." The province's treasurer, Harrison Gray, who two and a half years before had admonished Josiah Quincy Jr. for his treasonous words in the Old South Meetinghouse, boarded the *Francis*, along with thirty-seven others. A total of eleven hundred loyalists divided among thirty vessels ultimately left the wharves of Boston, first sailing past the Castle to the Nantasket Roads at the western end of the harbor, five miles from the city, where they anchored near Paddock and Hull islands and waited for the arrival of the fifty transports bearing the nine thousand soldiers of Howe's army.

Many of the loyalists would settle in Canada; others went to England. Neither place seemed like home. Some, such as the lawyer Daniel Leonard, who was named chief justice of Bermuda, established new and flourishing careers. A few, such as Dr. John Jeffries, to whom Joseph Warren had offered the position of surgeon general of the provincial army, eventually returned to Boston and through a combination of personal charm and professional ability once again became respected members of the community. But that was decades in the future, and an exception to the rule of forgiveness. Bostonians, like their Puritan forebears, would prove to have long and exacting memories.

By purging itself of loyalists, Boston had, in a sense, reaffirmed its origins. The town's first settlers had put an ocean between them and their king so that they could worship as they pleased. They were unafraid of risk; otherwise they never would have left England for a new and unknown land. Over the course of the next century and a half, Boston had grown from a settlement of a few hundred Puritans to a diverse and thriving port with a strong commercial connection to London. Many Bostonians, particularly the merchants, had come to cherish their ties to Great Britain. In the last decade, however, a new generation of risk takers had staged a revolution, and those who refused to disavow the mother country were about to sail to Halifax, never to return. Boston was, once again, its own "city on a hill."

The engineer Archibald Robertson was one of the last to leave. He had spent the two previous days throwing up barriers across the streets and wharves of Boston to impede the progress of any American soldiers who might try to harass the evacuating regulars. Howe had ordered the town's citizens to remain confined in their homes so they didn't interfere with his army's final preparations to depart. Robertson walked the empty, weirdly quiet waterfront. More than twenty-five brigs, schooners, sloops, and ships had been abandoned, some still full of stores, all of them scuttled. General Gage's chariot lay broken on Long Wharf. The dragoons had left 110 horses in the stables at the rope walks, along with ten tons of hay. "There seems a vast deal of confusion in every department," Robertson recorded in his diary, "and no settled plan of operations."

By 9:00 a.m. on March 17, a Sunday, "all the regiments but the rear guard were embarked." Robertson, Captain Montresor, and three others lingered on Long Wharf, ready to set fire to a few houses if the enemy should prematurely storm the city, "but none appeared and we went all off in the greatest order." By ten o'clock he was at the Castle and could see "the rebels on the heights of Charlestown and making a great parade on Dorchester Heights." As it so happened, March 17 was St. Patrick's Day, a date celebrated by Irish Protestants in Boston since 1737. Now Bostonians had yet another reason to celebrate March 17, a date that became known as Evacuation Day.

A young officer named James Wilkinson from Maryland was one of the first into the city. Wilkinson had come via the Charlestown peninsula, where the British had delayed the arrival of the American troops by leaving several "effigies" that looked like regulars with their muskets shouldered. Only after General John Sullivan had determined that the fortress at Bunker Hill was "defended by lifeless sentries" had Wilkinson and the others been allowed to cross the Neck. Near "the ruins of Charlestown . . . now buried in its own ashes," he'd found a canoe in which he and several others paddled to Boston "on the *presumption* the enemy had taken their departure." After disembarking at the waterfront, they'd followed "a long narrow winding street" but were unable to find a living soul to talk to. "The town presented a frightful solitude in the bosom of a numerous population . . . ," he remembered; "a death-like silence pervaded an inhabited city, and spectacles of waste and spoil struck the eye at almost every step."

Even days later, the three thousand or so Bostonians who had lasted out the siege had a muted, exhausted air about them. James Thacher marched into the city three days after the evacuation. "The inhabitants appeared at their doors and windows," he wrote; "though they manifested a lively joy on being liberated from a long imprisonment, they were not altogether free from melancholy gloom which ten tedious months' siege has spread over their countenances." Two days later, Thacher watched as "a concourse of people from the country crowd[ed] into town, full of friendly solicitude. It is truly interesting to witness the tender interviews and fond embraces of those who have been long separated."

One of those left pining for a reunion was John Andrews, whose beloved wife Ruthy was not able to return to Boston for several weeks. He missed her terribly, but to his brother-in-law in Philadelphia he asserted that despite all he'd suffered over the course of the last five months, he'd "never suffered the *least* depression of spirits . . . for a *persuasion* that my country *would eventually* prevail, kept up my spirits, and never suffered my *hopes* to *fail*." Andrews's good mood was no doubt reinforced when at the end of March none other than George Washington, accompanied by Martha and her son and daughter-in-law, came to his house for dinner "with no earlier notice," he wrote his brother-in-law, "than half past eleven the same day."

Two days after the evacuation, the British saw fit to destroy the fortifications at the Castle with a spectacular series of explosions. The resulting fire raged throughout the night with such intensity that a lieutenant from Connecticut discovered that even though he was several miles away he was able to read a letter from his wife by the light of the burning fortress. The fate of the Castle served as a fresh reminder of the devastation that had been avoided through the occupation of Dorchester Heights. Washington, however, continued "lamenting the disappointment" of not having been able to implement what he described in a letter to a friend in Virginia as his "premeditated plan" to attack Boston, "as we were prepared for them at all points."

Even though he still wished he had been given the chance to attack Boston—an assault that would have surely laid much of the city to waste and probably destroyed his army—Washington was now perceived as the general who had rescued Boston from ruin. On March 28, the day after the British evacuation fleet finally departed the Nantasket Roads for Halifax, the Boston selectmen formally thanked him for having "saved a large, elegant, and once populous city from total destruction." His Excellency responded in kind, claiming that "what greatly adds to my happiness [is] that this desirable event has been effected with so little effusion of human blood."

There is no reason to doubt the genuineness of Washington's remarks. One of his greatest gifts was his ability to learn from a situation, and by the end of March—three weeks after the taking of Dorchester Heights—he had, with considerable reluctance, started to reconcile himself to the fact that what he wanted to happen in any given situation was ultimately beside the point. "I will not lament or repine at any act of Providence," he wrote Reed, "because I am in a great measure a convert to [the poet] Mr. Pope's opinion that whatever is, is right." This did not prevent him from once again rehashing in his letter all the reasons why his plan to attack the city would have worked, but the evidence was nonetheless clear: Washington had begun to recognize that his role as commander in chief was not all about winning glory on the battlefield. If he had failed to head off a coming war with one brilliant and bloody stroke, he had accomplished something far more difficult. He had forged the beginning of an army that might—just might—lay the groundwork for a new American society.

On the morning of April 4, Washington left his headquarters in Cambridge and began what proved to be a ten-day march to New York. Soon after, John Warren and his brother Eben located their older brother's body in its shallow grave on Breed's Hill. The remains were badly decomposed, but the same false teeth that had allowed Dr. Jeffries to make the identification soon after the Battle of Bunker Hill also enabled John and Eben to verify that this was indeed their brother. A funeral service was held at King's Chapel, which, being an Anglican church and made of stone, had suffered no damage during the British occupation.

Warren was buried with all the honors due a former grand master of the St. Andrew's Masonic Lodge. One prominent mason, however, was unable to attend the service. The merchant John Rowe had spent much of the last year and a half not sure of where he stood when it came to the tug-of-war between patriot and loyalist interests. But when Rowe arrived at King's Chapel on April 8 "to attend and walk in procession with the lodges under my jurisdiction with our proper jewels and clothing," he was—to his "great mortification"— "very much insulted by some furious and hot persons without the least provocation." One of his fellow masons thought it "most prudent for me to retire." That evening, Rowe was plagued by "some uneasy reflections in my mind as I am not conscious to myself of doing anything prejudicial to the cause of America either by will or deed."

In June, Benjamin Church was returned to Boston from his confinement in Connecticut. The General Court's plans to exchange him for an American prisoner inspired what Church's wife described as "a riot." The town's inhabitants wanted to see the hated spy suitably punished. Once tempers eventually cooled, Church was allowed to board a ship for Martinique in January 1778. When the ship was lost in a storm with all hands, Bostonians could rest assured that justice had finally been served.

For a variety of reasons, hundreds of loyalists had decided to remain in Boston. The Reverend Mather Byles, sixty-nine, was the minister of the Hollis Street Meeting. When a member of his congregation asked how he could possibly remain a "brainless Tory," he replied, "Tell me, which is better, to be ruled by one tyrant 3,000 miles away, or by 3,000 tyrants not a mile away?" By the time Byles had been stripped of his ministry and confined to his house under an armed guard (a noted punster, he referred to the sentinel as his "observe-a-Tory"), Boston had been revisited by the legendary Joyce Junior, the fabled "chairman of the committee for tarring and feathering." In an advertisement in the *Boston Gazette*, Joyce announced that he had returned "after almost two years absence" to rid the city of "those shameless brass faced Tories, who have the audaciousness to remain among this much abused and insulted people." A few days later, Joyce Junior and his minions rounded up five loyalists and, after loading them in a cart, proceeded out of town. Joyce was, according to Abigail Adams, "mounted on horseback with a red coat, a white wig, and a drawn sword, with drum and fife following. A concourse of people to the amount of 500 followed." Once over the Roxbury line, Joyce "ordered the cart to be tipped up," Adams recounted, "then told them if they were ever caught in town again it should be at the expense of their lives."

George Washington had little patience with the loyalists, but during the Siege of Boston he had acted decisively to stop the kind of tribal acts of intolerance that were Joyce Junior's stock-in-trade. On November 5, 1775, the day when Bostonians traditionally held anti-Catholic demonstrations, the general had issued an order forbidding what he called "that ridiculous and childish custom of burning the effigy of the Pope." Now that Canada and all its French Catholics were their potential allies, it was "void of common sense . . . to be insulting their religion." With the help of Washington (who had already begun to rethink his relationship to African Americans), the New Englanders in his army could not help but begin to reconsider some of their old prejudices.

It was perhaps not surprising that the new Continental Army was almost devoid of the Bostonians who had been at the forefront of the revolutionary movement over the course of the last decade. As Paul Revere observed to a friend in New York, "I find but few of the Sons of Liberty in the army." Men who had relished dumping tea into Boston Harbor and tarring and feathering reprobate loyalists like John Malcom apparently had trouble fitting into the army of His Excellency George Washington.

The Revolution had begun as a profoundly conservative movement. The patriots had not wanted to create something new; they had wanted to preserve the status quo—the essentially autonomous community they had inherited from their ancestors—in the face of British attempts to forge a modern empire. Enlightenment rhetoric from England had provided them with new ideological grist, but what they had really been about, particularly when it came to the yeoman farmers of the country towns, was defending the way of life their forefathers had secured after more than a century of struggle with the French and Indians. But something had shifted with the arrival of the new general from Virginia. As Washington had made clear in his orders of

November 5, 1775, his army was already moving in directions that would have been unthinkable to the New Englanders of old.

With the approach of the summer of 1776, Bostonians began to emerge from the dark doldrums of the siege. Howe's fleet of almost 150 vessels had sailed for Halifax at the end of March, but a few naval warships continued to linger near the Boston lighthouse to warn supply ships arriving from Britain that the army had removed to Nova Scotia. On June 13, the last of the men-of-war was finally forced to depart when cannons were installed on one of the harbor's outlying islands. By the middle of July, word had reached the city of the signing of the Declaration of Independence.

They were no longer fighting simply to preserve their ancient liberties; they were fighting to create a new nation. The officers of Washington's army had begun to talk in these terms as early as the fall of 1775, but not until the publication of Thomas Paine's *Common Sense* in January 1776 did the goal of independence begin to look like an inevitability. "We have it in our power to begin the world over again," Paine wrote. "A situation similar to the present, hath not happened since the days of Noah until now. The birthday of a new world is at hand."

On July 18, the Declaration of Independence was made public for the first time in Boston. As sheriff, William Greenleaf was supposed to read all official proclamations. But the fifty-six-year-old Greenleaf had a weak voice. So he asked Thomas Crafts, the same man who had objected to the promotion of Henry Knox to colonel of the army's artillery regiment, to "act as his herald." A big man with a fiery red face, Crafts was now a colonel in Massachusetts's artillery regiment, and he and Greenleaf stood together on the balcony of the Town House. Ahead of them was not only a large crowd but an unobstructed view of Long Wharf, where more than two years before General Gage and his regulars had first disembarked.

Greenleaf read a passage from the declaration; Crafts repeated the words in his own booming voice, and so it went. According to Abigail Adams, who was in the crowd that day, "great attention was given to every word." As soon as Crafts had finished, "the cry from the balcony was," Abigail wrote, "God Save our American States and then three cheers which rended the air, the bells rang, the privateers fired, the forts and batteries, the cannon were discharged, the platoons followed and every face appeared joyful."

Later that evening the ornate figures of the lion and the unicorn (representing England and Scotland) that bracketed the gable at the front of what Adams now called the State House were taken down and burned in a bonfire along with the king's arms from the courthouse. Boston had survived, but "every vestige" of the king was destroyed that night. "Thus ends royal authority . . . ," Abigail wrote, "and all the people shall say Amen."

Epilogue—Character Alone

O n the evening of June 17, 1843, the seventy-five-year-old John Quincy Adams stood in front of his son's house in Quincy (formerly a part of Braintree), Massachusetts. It was the sixty-eighth anniversary of the Battle of Bunker Hill, and despite the fact that an immense celebration had occurred in Charlestown honoring the completion of a new 221-foot-high granite obelisk, Adams had as always spent the day at home, where he "visited my seedling trees" and attended to his correspondence.

The festivities had begun early that morning on Boston Common, where soldiers, veterans, freemasons, firemen, and many others had assembled for a parade that extended for two miles as it made its way through the city and across the Warren Bridge to Charlestown. The hundred or so veterans of the American Revolution had traveled in twenty-six different carriages, one of which had even contained a "miniature monument" in tribute to what was called the Battle of Lexington. Also present was no less a personage than the president of the United States, John Tyler, who traveled with his two sons in a barouche drawn by six black horses and flanked by a detachment of lancers.

But perhaps the most noted attendee was the legendary Daniel Webster, the U.S. senator and renowned speaker. By all accounts it was a stirring scene in Charlestown once Tyler and the other dignitaries had settled in their seats and Webster had begun to speak. "In front of the orator and upon either side of him was a dense and countless mass of human beings . . . ," a reporter for the *Daily Atlas* wrote. "Crowning all, and raising its lofty head to the clouds in calm sublimity, stood the majestic monument, glistening in the rays of the bright sun."

But John Quincy Adams, the sixth president of the United States and now a lowly but very active member of the U.S. House of Representatives, was having none of it. "What a name in the annals of mankind is Bunker Hill?" he recorded in his diary. "What a day was that 17th June 1775? And what a burlesque upon both is an oration upon them by Daniel Webster, and a pilgrimage of John Tyler . . . to desecrate the solemnity by their presence!"

Now, in the twilight of a long political career, Adams had emerged as what one Virginia legislator described as "the acutest, the astutest, the archest enemy of Southern slavery that ever existed." Two years before, Adams had argued before the U.S. Supreme Court on the behalf of the slaves who had led a bloody revolt aboard the schooner *Amistad*. Much as the lawyer James Otis had done back in 1761, when he insisted that the writs of assistance violated the British constitution (the legal case that John Quincy's father had claimed initiated the series of events that became the American Revolution), he had insisted before the Supreme Court that maritime law and property rights did not apply when a human being's fundamental freedoms had been violated. And unlike Otis, John Quincy had won his case.

Just the winter before he had so infuriated his congressional colleagues from the South with his insistence that all petitions regarding slavery must be read before the House that they had moved to censure him. The resulting two-week hearing had given Adams exactly the forum he wanted (it is "a trial," he rather immodestly wrote at the time, "[in] which the liberties of my country are enduring in my person"), and best of all, the ouster attempt had failed. When his family and friends suggested it might be time for him to retire, he responded, "The world will retire from me before I shall retire from the world."

From Adams's perspective, both Webster and Tyler were guilty of turning their backs on the all-important issue of slavery. Webster was, he wrote in his diary, "a heartless traitor to the cause of human freedom," while the president was "a slave monger." Adams's sixty-eight-year-old memories of the Battle of Bunker Hill were too personal, too vivid, to be contaminated by the politicians' presence. In his diary he imagined the scene in front of the monument with "Webster spouting with a Negro holding an umbrella over his head and John Tyler's nose with a shadow outstretching that of the monumental column." "How could I have witnessed all this," he wrote, "without an unbecoming burst of indignation or of laughter?" No, it was best that he had remained at home.

John Quincy Adams had a history of refusing to attend celebrations associated with the Battle of Bunker Hill, which had proven to be the bloodiest engagement of the eight years of fighting that followed. In 1786, as a student at Harvard, he had not accompanied his fellow classmates on a trip to Breed's Hill to enjoy a memorial dinner where the head of the table was "placed on the very spot where the immortal Warren fell." "I passed the day in the solitude of my study," he remembered, "and dined almost alone in the hall." He owed the fact that he could hold a pen with his once-broken right hand to Dr. Warren, and for John Quincy, who, like his father, had kept a diary for almost all his life, the act of writing was essential to his very being.

Other Adams family members shared his reverence for the memory of Joseph Warren. In 1786, the same year that John Quincy declined to attend the dinner at Breed's Hill, his mother had seen a new painting by George Washington's former aide John Trumbull titled *Death of General Warren at the Battle of Bunker's Hill*. Although full of historical inaccuracies, the painting, in which Warren is shown dying in the arms of a fellow provincial soldier as a British regular threatens to stab him with a bayonet, had an immense impact on Abigail Adams when she first saw it in London. "I can only say," she wrote, "that in looking at it, my whole frame contracted, my blood shivered and I felt a faintness at my heart." She predicted that Trumbull's painting "will not only secure his own fame, but transmit to posterity characters and actions which will command the admiration of future ages and prevent the period which gave birth to them from ever passing away into the dark abyss of time whilst he teaches mankind that it is not rank or titles, but character alone, which interests posterity."

This, according to Abigail, was the meaning of the Revolution—that it was "character alone" that mattered. It was a conviction that as early as March 1776 prompted her to insist that her husband in his capacity as a delegate to the Continental Congress "remember the ladies and be more generous and favorable to them than your ancestors. Do not put such unlimited power into the hands of the husbands . . . [since]," she wrote, "your sex are naturally tyrannical." It was a conviction that also prompted her to wonder, despite her immense respect for the slave owner George Washington, whether "the passion for liberty cannot be equally strong in the breasts of those who have been accustomed to deprive their fellow creatures of theirs. Of this I am certain that it is not founded upon that generous and Christian principle of doing to others as we would that others should do unto us."

Abigail Adams had hit upon the unappreciated radicalism that lay within the Declaration of Independence—"that all men are created equal." For most Americans in 1776 this was largely a rhetorical flourish, a claim of innate equality that did not apply to women and enslaved African Americans. But as the years unfolded and the words of the Declaration acquired a renewed and largely unanticipated relevance, many Americans began to realize that the work of the Revolution was far from over.

And so on the evening of June 17, 1843, as John Quincy Adams looked toward Charlestown, his appreciation of what he'd witnessed sixty-eight years earlier was accompanied by an invigorating sense of righteous anger. In the distance, he could see the monument's pyramid-shaped top rising out of the smoke that wafted from "the cannonade salute of the closing day." Then came, he wrote, "in forcible impulse to my memory the cannonade and the smoke and the fire of the 17th of June 1775."

It was not for him to spout purple platitudes about men like Joseph Warren who had died so that they could all be free. It was up to him, who as a seven-year-old boy had watched and wept beside his thirty-year-old mother, to continue what the doctor had helped to begin.

"My life must be militant to its close," he wrote, and on that evening in June 1843, as he turned to walk back to the home he had inherited from his father, he was still spoiling for a fight.

Acknowledgments

Researcher and friend Michael Hill has been an immense help during the three years it took to write this book. I am indebted to the descendants of two historical personages who figure large in this narrative: Lord Nicholas Gage, who spoke with me over a glass of sherry at his ancestral home of Firle in Sussex, England, and Paul Revere Jr., with whom I had lunch at Spanky's Clam Shack in Hyannis, Massachusetts. My thanks to Robert Pasley-Tyler in London and John Ross on Cape Cod for making the interviews possible. Thanks to writer Adam Nicolson for his insights into the British gentry. Peter Drummey at the Massachusetts Historical Society was extremely generous with his time and expertise; it was Peter who first told me that Dr. Samuel Forman was at work on a biography of Dr. Joseph Warren, and I have benefited greatly from Dr. Forman's recently published book and the correspondence we have conducted over the course of several months. J. L. Bell's blog *Boston 1775* has been a daily source of inspiration and research advice. Special thanks to Victor Mastone of the Massachusetts Board of Underwater Archaeological Resources, Craig Brown of the Department of Anthropology of the University of Massachusetts at Boston, and Christopher Maio of the Department of Earth, Environmental and Ocean Sciences of the University of Massachusetts at Boston for sharing the results of their research into the Battle of Chelsea Creek and for the tour of East Boston. Ever since as editor of the *New England Quarterly* he published my first article of history, Professor William Fowler has provided me with essential advice and encouragement; many thanks, Bill, for all your help. Professor Paul Lockhardt's writings about the Revolution include an important book about the Battle of Bunker Hill; many thanks, Paul, for your input. Former British Consul General of Boston Philip Budden helped me appreciate the British perspective on the events described in this book. Judge Hiller Zobel, author of the still-definitive *Boston Massacre* (1970), is, in addition to being a noted legal scholar and colonial historian, a master of the English language; thanks, Hiller, for making this a better book. William Gow

Harrington spent many hours on my behalf at the Dedham Historical Society; his father, Peter Gow, has been reading my manuscripts for more than twenty-five years; thanks, Peter and Will. Elizabeth Mansfield provided a seemingly endless supply of research leads. Thanks to Emily Stover, Carolyn Paris, and Penny Scheerer, who accompanied my wife, Melissa, and me on a research sail to Statia, the Caribbean island from which revolutionary New Englanders secured Dutch tea and gunpowder; Penny (distantly related to militiaman Nathaniel Page of Bedford, Massachusetts) also directed me to information concerning the famous Bedford flag. Special thanks to Erik Goldstein, curator of Mechanical Arts and Numismatics at Colonial Williamsburg, for his late-inning input; thanks to Gregory Whitehead for asking the right questions.

I also want to thank Caroline Keinath at the Adams National Historic Site in Quincy, Massachusetts; Elizabeth Watts Pope at the American Antiquarian Society, in Worcester, Massachusetts; the staffs of the many sites of the Boston National Historical Park, but especially Sean Hennessey and Marty Blatt at the Charlestown Navy Yard; Richard Spiver and Richard Tourangeau at the Bunker Hill Monument and Museum; and William Barlow for his "tower tour" of historic Boston. Thanks also to Brian Lemay, Elizabeth Roscio, Nathaniel Sheidley, and Marieke Van Damme at the Bostonian Society; to Peter Harrington at the Brown University Library; and to Leslie Tobias-Olsen at the John Carter Brown Library, both in Providence, Rhode Island; to Gavin W. Kleespies at the Cambridge Historical Society; to Barbara DeWolfe, Brian Dunnigan, Clayton Lewis, and Janet Bloom at the Clements Library in Ann Arbor, Michigan; to Andre Ashby of the Independence National Historic Site in Philadelphia, Pennsylvania; to the staffs of the many sites operated by the Lexington Historical Society; to Peter Drummey, Anne Bentley, Anna Cook, and Liz Francis at the Massachusetts Historical Society; to the staffs of the sites associated with Minute Man National Park in Concord, Massachusetts; to Tal Nadan and Thomas Lannon at the New York Public Library; to Jane Hennedy and Andrew Boisvert of the Old Colony Historical Society in Taunton, Massachusetts; to the staffs of the Old North Church and of the Paul Revere House, both in Boston; to the staff of the Royall House and Slave Quarters in Medford, Massachusetts; to the staff of the Jason Russell House in Arlington, Massachusetts; to Emily Curran at the Old South Meetinghouse; and to James Shea, Anita Israel, and David Daly at Washington's Headquarters/ Longfellow House in Cambridge, Massachusetts.

For reading and commenting on the manuscript I am indebted to J. L. Bell, Philip Budden, Dr. Samuel Forman, William Fowler, Erik Goldstein, Peter Gow, Michael Hill, Paul Lockhardt, Jennifer Philbrick McArdle, Bruce Miller, Melissa D. Philbrick, Marianne Philbrick, Samuel Philbrick, Thomas Philbrick, Gregory Whitehead, and Hiller Zobel. All errors of fact and interpretation are mine and mine alone.

At Viking Penguin, I have been privileged to work, once again, with the incomparable Wendy Wolf. Thanks also to Clare Ferraro, Nancy Sheppard, Margaret Riggs, Francesca Belanger, Katherine Griggs, James Tierney, Andrew Duncan, Louise Braverman, Meghan Fallon, and Carolyn Coleburn. Thanks to Miranda Ottewell for the copyediting and to Margaret Moore Booker for the index. Thanks also to Jeffrey Ward for the maps.

My agent, Stuart Krichevsky, has been showing me the way for more than fourteen years; thanks again, Stuart, for your friendship and guidance. Thanks also to his associates Shana Cohen and Ross Harris. Thanks to Meghan Walker of Tandem Literary for keeping me connected to my readers through my Web site and social media.

Finally, a special thanks to my wife, Melissa, and to all our family members for your support and patience.

Notes

Abbreviations

AAS—American Antiquarian Society

AA4—*American Archives*, 4th series, edited by Peter Force

BAR—*The Beginnings of the American Revolution*, edited by Ellen Chase

CHS—Cambridge Historical Society

CKG—*The Correspondence of King George the Third*, vol. 3, edited by John Fortescue

DAR—*Documents of the American Revolution*, edited by K. G. Davies

DJW—*Dr. Joseph Warren*, by Samuel Forman

EIHC—*Essex Institute Historical Collections*

FYAR—*The First Year of the American Revolution*, by Allen French

HSOB—*History of the Siege of Boston*, by Richard Frothingham

JEPC—*The Journals of Each Provincial Congress of Massachusetts in 1774 and 1775*, edited by William Lincoln

LAR—*Letters of the American Revolution*, edited by Margaret Willard

LJA—*Letters of John Andrews*

LJW—*The Life of Joseph Warren*, by Richard Frothingham

MHS—Massachusetts Historical Society

NDAR—*Naval Documents of the American Revolution*, edited by William Bell Clark

NEHGR—*New England Historical and Genealogical Register*

NEQ—*New England Quarterly*

NYPL—New York Public Library

OPAR—*Origin and Progress of the American Rebellion*, by Peter Oliver

PGW—*The Papers of George Washington: Revolutionary War Series*, edited by Philander Chase

PIR—*Province in Rebellion: A Documentary History of the Founding of the Commonwealth of Massachusetts, 1774–1775*, edited by L. Kinvin Wroth

PNG—*Papers of Nathanael Greene*, vol. 1, edited by Richard Showman

SHG—*Sibley's Harvard Graduates*, by Clifford Shipton

SSS—*The Spirit of Seventy-Six*, edited by Henry Steele Commager and Richard Morris

WMQ—*William and Mary Quarterly*

An immense amount has been written about the American Revolution, especially as it relates to its beginnings in Boston, and I am indebted to all the authors and editors referred to in the notes and bibliography. Several late-breaking (and, in one instance, ongoing) additions to the scholarly canon have provided information and insights that would have not been available if I had attempted to write this book just a few years earlier. Samuel Forman in his biography *Dr. Joseph Warren* (2011) has brought a much-needed physician's perspective to the life of his subject while unearthing all sorts of new connections and associations, particularly when it comes to Warren's relationship with his fiancée, Mercy Scollay. Two books about the Battle of Bunker Hill, Paul Lockhardt's *The Whites of Their Eyes* (2011) and James Nelson's *With Fire and Sword* (2011), have provided different but complementary perspectives on the battle, while Nelson's earlier publication *George Washington's Secret Navy* (2008) helped put the maritime side of the story in a fresh context. Although the Boston Tea Party is only briefly touched on in what follows, Benjamin Carp's *Defiance of the Patriots* (2010) arrived just in the nick of time, as did Ron Chernow's monumental *George Washington* (2010), Vincent Carretta's *Phillis Wheatley* (2011), Jack Rakove's *Revolutionaries* (2010), T. H. Breen's *American Insurgents, American Patriots* (2010), Neil Longley York's *Henry Hulton and the American Revolution* (2010), and Ray Raphael's *Founders* (2009), which expanded on the view originally presented in Raphael's New England–specific *The First American Revolution* (2002). Most recently, the publication of J. L. Bell's *General George Washington's Headquarters and Home—Cambridge, Massachusetts* (2012) by the U.S. Park Service has given the story of the Siege of Boston a depth and scholarly rigor that had not previously existed. Bell's blog *Boston 1775* continues to provide an informative and highly entertaining window into the history and scholarship of revolutionary Boston.

Two final points: First, I have adjusted the spelling and punctuation of quotations to make them more accessible to a modern audience—something that had already been done by the editors of several collections cited below. Second, even though provincial Boston was technically a town (since it was governed by a board of selectmen instead of a mayor), I refer to it on occasion as a city. Not only does this help to distinguish Boston from the much smaller towns in the province; it reflects the usage of those in the seventeenth and eighteenth centuries, for whom the term "city" applied to any community, large or small, as in John Winthrop's biblically inspired reference to Boston as a "city on a hill."

Preface—**The Decisive Day**

The description of John Quincy Adams's response to the Battle of Bunker Hill is based primarily on the notes provided in Abigail Adams's June 18, 1775, letter to her husband, in *Adams Family Correspondence*, edited by L. H. Butterfield, pp. 222–24. My thanks to Caroline Keinath at the Adams House National Historic Site in Quincy, Mass., for showing me the hill on which John Quincy Adams and his mother watched the battle. In a February 13, 1818, letter to Hezekiah Niles, John Adams writes, "But what do we mean by the American Revolution? Do we mean the American war? The Revolution was effected before the war commenced. The Revolution was in the minds and hearts of the people; a change in their religious sentiments of their duties and obligations" (*Works*, 10:282–89). On the ways that interpersonal relationships determined political beliefs, see the quotation from Henry Laurens cited by Gordon Wood in *The Radicalism of the American Revolution* in which Laurens claimed that personal animosities "did more to make him a patriot . . . than all the whig pamphlets he might have read" (p. 63); Wood also cites the claim by a Philadelphian that he had known "every person, white and black, men, women, and children in the city of Philadelphia by name," even though that city was considerably larger than Boston (p. 59). John Adams claimed that only about a third of the population was dedicated to the patriot cause at the beginning of the Revolution in an August 1813 letter to Thomas McKean (*Works*, 10:63); according to Robert Calhoon ("Loyalism and Neutrality," in *A Companion to the American Revolution*, edited by Jack Greene and J. R. Pole, p. 235), about 20 percent of the colonists were loyalists, with at least half the population wanting to avoid a conflict altogether and with the patriots gaining the support of between 40 and 45 percent of the population. Walter McDougall in *Freedom Just Around the Corner* writes that the American colonists were the "least taxed people on earth" and also enjoyed the "highest per capita standard of living of any people on earth" (pp. 118, 123). Gene Sharp's *From Dictatorship to Democracy: A Conceptual Framework for Liberation* was first published in Bangkok in 1993 by the Committee for the Restoration of Democracy in Burma; since then it's been translated into thirty-one languages and counting; it's now in its fourth U.S. edition and is published, perhaps suitably given the city's revolutionary history, in East Boston by the Albert Einstein Institution. See Sheryl Gay Stolberg, "Shy U.S. Intellectual Created Playbook Used in a Revolution," *New York Times*, February 16, 2011.

Chapter One—**The City on the Hill**

My description of Josiah Quincy Jr.'s speech in Old South Meetinghouse on December 16, 1773, is based primarily on Josiah Quincy's *Memoir of Josiah Quincy*, which cites Daniel Greenleaf's memory of Quincy's dramatic words (pp. 124–25); Greenleaf had been a student of the Lovells at Boston Latin School and was in the gallery that day. Edward Randolph's letter to King Charles II concerning the claims made by Massachusetts governor Leverett is cited in Michael Hall's *Edward Randolph and the American Colonies*, pp. 24–25. Leverett's bloody leather battle jacket is at the MHS. On the aftereffects of King Philip's War, see my *Mayflower*, pp. 345–46, and Stephen Saunders Webb's *1676: The End of American Independence*, pp. 409–16. On the overthrow and jailing of Governor Edmund Andros, see G. B. Warden's *Boston, 1689–1776*, pp. 3–14. On the 1745 Siege of Louisbourg, see J. Revell Carr's *Seeds of Discontent: The Deep Roots of the American Revolution, 1650–1750*, pp. 186–262.

On Britain's economic policies during the first half of the eighteenth century, see James Henretta's *"Salutary Neglect": Colonial Administration Under the Duke of Newcastle*, pp. 323–25, 344. On the debt generated by the end of the French and Indian War, see Alvin Rabushka's *Taxation in Colonial America*, pp. 568–69. L. Kinvin Wroth describes the trade patterns and other economic activities of Massachusetts in the mid-1700s in an interpretive essay in *Province in Rebellion* (*PIR*), 1:1–3. My thanks to former British consul general in Boston Philip Budden for pointing out the Puritan roots of the slogan "No taxation without representation," in a private correspondence. Oliver Dickerson analyzes the effects of the various acts in *The Navigation Acts and the American Revolution*; according to Dickerson, the customs officers were "paid out of the revenue collected" (p. 203). Ray Raphael provides a good synopsis of James Otis's arguments on the writs of assistance in *Founders*, pp. 13–17. On the details of what happened in the Boston Massacre, see Hiller Zobel's *The Boston Massacre*, pp. 180–205, and Richard Archer's *As if an Enemy's Country*, pp. 182–206. John Greenwood writes of the comet and the fears of an apocalypse in *The Revolutionary Services of John Greenwood*, pp. 3–4. The comet that appeared in the night sky over New England during the summer of 1773 was much commented on at the time and is now known as Lexell's Comet (for Anders Johan Lexell, who computed its orbit); modern-day astronomers have estimated that Lexell's Comet passed closer to Earth than any other comet in recorded history.

John Tyler's *Smugglers and Patriots* is an excellent examination of the complex role merchants played in the controversies leading up to the Revolution, particularly when it came to the impact Dutch smugglers had on the Boston Tea Party (pp. 171–210). My account of the Tea Party depends largely on Benjamin Carp's *Defiance of the Patriots*, pp. 118–40, and Benjamin Labaree's *The Boston Tea Party*, pp. 140–45. According to Edward Byers in *Nation of Nantucket*, whale oil exports constituted almost 53 percent of all pounds sterling earned by New England's exports to Great Britain in the years prior to the Revolution (p. 144). On Hancock's attempts to corner the whale oil market, see Eric Jay Dolin's *Leviathan: The History of Whaling in America*, pp. 132–35; see also W. T. Baxter's *The House of Hancock*, especially pp. 243–46, on Hancock's final disastrous 1766 campaign to corner the market, which resulted in the loss of 3,600 pounds sterling and effectively ended Hancock's attempts to compete with the Nantucketers. Also adding to the anti-Nantucket feeling among the Boston patriots was the fact that one of the leading customs officials in Boston, Nathaniel Coffin Sr., came from a family with deep island connections, a point made by James Grieder in "The Boston Tea Party Unmasked: Nantucket's Real Role in the Start of the American Revolution," *Historic Nantucket*, vol. 62, no. 1, p. 12.

Joyce Junior's broadsides and other announcements appeared in the January 17 and 31, March 28, and April 4, 1774, issues of the *Boston Gazette*; an advertisement for John Winthrop Junior's latest shipment of "Baltimore Flour" also appears in the April 4 issue. My description of Joyce Junior's back history is based in part on two articles by Albert Matthews, "Joyce Junior" and "Joyce Junior Once More." The identity of Joyce was revealed by a loyalist commentator in a listing of various patriot leaders from 1775 in the James Bowdoin papers at the MHS; see MHS *Proceedings*, 2nd ser., 12 (1897–8): 139–42. A physical description of Joyce Junior appeared in the November 9, 1821, *Boston Daily Advertiser*: "A man used to ride on an ass, with immense jack boots, and his face covered with a horrible mask, and was called Joyce, Jr. His office was to assemble men and boys in mob style, and ride in the middle of them, and in such company to terrify adherents to royal government, before the Revolution. The tumults which resulted in the massacre, 1770, was excited by such means. Joyce Junior was said to have a particular whistle, which brought his adherents, etc. whenever they were wanted." Esther Forbes writes insightfully about the hazy genealogy of Joyce Junior and its connection to Pope Night in *Paul Revere*, pp. 96, 127, 189, 211, 326–29, 471–72. On Pope Night, see J. L. Bell, "Du Simitiere's Sketches of Pope Day in

Boston 1767." Alfred Young describes Joyce Junior as "an all-powerful figure who would mobilize the people against their enemies but would not countenance mob action," in the chapter "Tar and Feathers and the Ghost of Oliver Cromwell," in *Liberty Tree: Ordinary People and the American Revolution*, p. 164; elsewhere Young speaks of the "conservative backlash" that followed the Tea Party in the spring of 1774, p. 121. A version of Joyce Junior appears in Nathaniel Hawthorne's short story "My Kinsman, Major Molineux." On John Winthrop Jr. see Clifford Shipton's biographical essay in *SHG*, 16:294–95.

My account of Boston in 1774 is based largely on Nathaniel Shurtleff, *A Topographical and Historical Description of Boston*; Shurtleff refers to the Nathaniel Hawthorne short story collection, *Legends of Province House*, that talks about how the Indian atop Province House appeared to be aiming at the weathercock of the Old South Meetinghouse, p. 601; see also Walter Muir Whitehill's *Boston: A Topographical History*. On the Liberty Tree at the corner of Essex and Newbury streets, see Arthur Schlesinger, "The Liberty Tree: A Genealogy." Richard Frothingham in *History of the Siege of Boston* (*HSOB*) writes of the flagstaff that rose out of the top of the Liberty Tree, p. 27. See *Deacon Tudor's Diary* for an account of the deep snow in Boston in late January; on January 31 he wrote: "Still cold, fine sledding for 200 miles to the westward as travelers tell us and snow in general 3 feet deep. This January for the most part has been very cold" (p. 45). My description of the tarring and feathering of John Malcom is based largely on Frank Hersey's "Tar and Feathers: The Adventures of Captain John Malcom," which reprints accounts of the incident that appeared in Boston newspapers, as well as Benjamin Irvin's "Tar, Feathers, and the Enemies of American Liberties, 1768–1776" and Walter Watkins's "Tarring and Feathering in Boston in 1770." In old age, George Hewes provided two accounts of his encounter with John Malcom, first in James Hawkes, *A Retrospect of the Boston Tea Party*, pp. 33–35, and then in Benjamin Thatcher, *Traits of the Tea Party*, pp. 127–34. See also Alfred Young's *The Shoemaker and the Tea Party*, pp. 46–51.

Benjamin Carp writes about the relationship between colonial firefighters and the patriot cause in "Fire of Liberty: Firefighters, Urban Voluntary Culture and the Revolutionary Movement," pp. 781–818. On January 20, 1766, John Adams recorded in his diary Daniel Leonard's comments on the destruction of Thomas Hutchinson's house: "Thought Hutchinson's History did not shine. Said his house was pulled down, to prevent his writing any more by destroying his materials" (1:300). According to Pauline Maier in "Revolutionary Violence and the Relevance of History," "Mobs were too easily transformed into corporate organs of their communities to be considered explosive repositories of dissent. The rioters of one night might serve the next evening as posse, military company or . . . fire company" (p. 131). See also Maier's "Popular Uprisings and Civil Authority in Eighteenth Century America" and her seminal *From Resistance to Revolution: Colonial Radicals and the Development of American Opposition to Britain, 1765–1776*. On William Russell, see Francis Drake, *Tea Leaves*, p. 159. According to an account that received wide distribution in England in the fall of 1774, Malcom was forced by the crowd to toast the king and his family and drink a large amount of tea, which was ultimately forced down his throat with a funnel—an anecdote that inspired a well-known engraving. However, none of the Boston newspapers makes any mention of the tea-drinking episode, and even more significantly, Malcom himself never refers to it in his own detailed account of his sufferings, in which he is careful to enumerate all the outrages committed by the Bostonians. I have, therefore, chosen not to include the tea-drinking episode in my account of Malcom's tarring and feathering. See R. T. H. Halsey, *The Boston Port Bill as Pictured by a Contemporary London Cartoonist*, pp. 82–86, 93, for both the engraving and the newspaper accounts. The story of John Malcom's patriot brother Daniel is told in George Wolkins's "Daniel Malcom and Writs of Assistance." In a January 31, 1774, letter, the loyalist Ann Hulton writes in detail about the tarring and feathering of John Malcom and reports, "The doctors say that it is impossible this poor creature can live. They say his flesh comes off his back in steaks." *Letters of a Loyalist Lady*, p. 71.

John Singleton Copley's April 26, 1774, letter to Isaac Clarke telling of how he was threatened with a visit from Joyce Junior is in *Letters and Papers of John Singleton Copley and Henry Pelham*, p. 218. Jules David Prown in *John Singleton Copley in American Art* writes of the "stunning immediacy" of Copley's portraits and the "sense of presence, of the physical entity and personality of the sitter, which is conveyed across the span of 200 years. The subject of the portrait appears as a distinct, knowable human being" (p. 53). The statistic that one in five Boston families owned slaves in the second quarter of the eighteenth century comes from Gordon Wood, *The Radicalism of the American Revolution*, p. 51. An advertisement for Phillis Wheatley's new book of poems appears in the January 24, 1774, issue of the *Boston Gazette*. On Wheatley and how she had become a "political hot potato," see David Waldstreicher, "The Wheatleyan Moment," pp. 540–41. Her February 11, 1774, letter to Samson Occom is reprinted in William H. Robinson's *Phillis Wheatley and Her Writings*, p. 332. See also Vincent Carretta's *Phillis Wheatley: Biography of a Genius in Bondage*, pp. 159–60. Abner Goodell writes about the execution and gibbeting of Mark in "The Trial and Execution . . . of Mark and Phillis," pp. 28–30. In his account of his famous ride, Paul Revere refers to the place "where Mark was hung in chains," in "A Letter from Col. Paul Revere to the Corresponding Secretary," p. 107. On the advertisements for slaves in Boston newspapers, see Robert Desrochers Jr.'s "Slave-for-Sale Advertisements and Slavery in Massachusetts, 1704–1781." On the legislative attempts to end slavery in colonial Massachusetts, see George Moore's *Notes on the History of Slavery in Massachusetts*, especially pp. 138–40, and "Negro Petitions for Freedom," pp. 432–37. F. Nwabueze Okoye writes passionately about the reality of slavery in American colonial society in "Chattel Slavery as the Nightmare of the American Revolutionaries." The October 31, 1768, petition signed by John Hancock and John Rowe accusing a British officer of inciting Boston's slaves to revolt is in *Boston Under Military Rule, 1768–1769*, edited by Oliver Morton Dickerson, p. 16.

On the impact of both Joyce Junior and the tarring and feathering of John Malcom on the English press, see R. T. H. Halsey, *The Boston Port Bill as Pictured by a Contemporary London Cartoonist*, pp. 82–143; Halsey reprints the account of Malcom being forced to drink large quantities of tea as well as the engravings it inspired, pp. 82–86, 92. The March 28, 1774, description of Americans as a "strange set of people" by a member of the House of Commons was reprinted in the *Boston Gazette* on May 16, 1774. Benjamin Thatcher refers to how John Malcom took a piece of his own tarred-and-feathered skin to London with him in *Traits of the Tea Party*, p. 133. Frank Hersey in "Tar and Feathers" quotes from John Malcom's petition to the king in which he asks to be made "a single Knight of the Tar," p. 463.

Chapter Two—**Poor Unhappy Boston**

On Thomas Gage's background and his wife Margaret Kemble Gage, see John Richard Alden's *General Gage in America*, pp. 19–204. For a less sympathetic portrayal of Gage, see John Shy's "Thomas Gage: Weak Link of Empire," pp. 3–38, in vol. 2 of *George Washington's Generals and Opponents*, edited by George Athan Billias. David Hackett Fischer in *Paul Revere's Ride* quotes Gage's letter comparing London to Constantinople or "any other city I had never seen" (p. 40). Carl Van Doren provides a detailed account of Franklin's experience in the Cockpit in *Benjamin Franklin*, pp. 461–77. Gage's comments about Franklin are in a note in Alden's *General Gage in America*, p. 200. King George's description of his meeting with Gage is in no. 1379—"The King to Lord North," in *CKG*, p. 59. Gage describes America as "a bully" in a November 12, 1770, letter to Lord Barrington, cited in Alden's *General Gage in America*, p. 188. On navigating the islands of Boston Harbor, I have relied on Nathaniel Shurtleff, *A Topographical and Historical Description of Boston*, pp. 416–578. Bernard Bailyn provides a probing portrait of Thomas Hutchinson in *The Ordeal of Thomas Hutchinson*; I am also indebted to several unpublished manuscripts by John Tyler, who is editing a new edition of Hutchinson's letters. Andrew Walmsley's *Thomas Hutchinson and the Origins of the American Revolution* is a succinct analysis of how the governor served as a scapegoat for the patriots.

For the text of the Port Act, see *Province in Rebellion* (subsequently referred to as *PIR*), edited by L. Kinvin Wroth et al., 1:44–51. For the text of Josiah Quincy Jr.'s "Observations on . . . the Boston Port-Bill," see Josiah Quincy's *Memoir*, pp. 359–469. Gage speaks of giving the Port Bill "time to operate" in a May 19, 1774, letter to Lord Dartmouth, *Correspondence of Thomas Gage*, p. 355. On Faneuil Hall, see Abram Brown's *Faneuil Hall and Market*, pp. 123–30. Thomas Young describes Faneuil Hall as "a noble school" in a March 22, 1770, letter cited by Ray Raphael in *Founders*, pp. 80–81. Peter Oliver speaks of a meeting of the House of Representatives as "a pandemonium" in *OPAR*, p. 67. Peter Shaw in *American Patriots and the Rituals of Revolution* writes about conscience patriotism (pp. 23–24); he also writes insightfully about the psychic toll of the Revolution on such patriots as James Otis (pp. 77–108); John Adams (pp. 109–30); Joseph Hawley (pp. 131–52); and Josiah Quincy Jr. (pp. 152–75). John Adams tells of his uncontrolled outburst in an entry in his diary made in late December 1772 in *Diary and Autobiography of John Adams*, 2:75–76. In his *Autobiography* (vol. 3 of his *Writings*), Adams describes a revealing exchange between himself and Joseph Warren regarding the psychological cost of the patriot movement. According to Adams, Warren frequently and unsuccessfully urged him to "harangue" at Boston town meetings. "My answer to him always was, 'that way madness lies.' The symptoms of our great friend Otis, at that time, suggested to Warren a sufficient comment on these words at which he always smiled and said, 'it was true' " (p. 291). Henry Adams's reference to his Boston ancestors being "ambitious beyond reason to excel" is cited by Walter McDougall in *Freedom Just Around the Corner*, p. 147. Gillian Anderson in the "The Funeral of Samuel Cooper" cites the references to "silver-tongued Sam" and to his "ductility," p. 657. Clifford Shipton cites the reference to Cooper's eventual mental breakdown being attributed to "the inordinate use of Scotch snuff," *SHG*, 11:211. In a March 15, 1773, letter to Benjamin Franklin, Cooper refers to having spent the winter "confined to my house . . . by my valetudinary state, and been little able to see and converse with my friends," *The Papers of Benjamin Franklin*, 20:110.

On Samuel Adams, see the biographies by John Miller, William Fowler, Ira Stoll, and Mark Puls. Adams seems to have been a "revolutionary ascetic," of the type described in Bruce Mazlish's book of the same name. In an April 4, 1774, letter to Arthur Lee, Adams writes of the future he sees for America and England: "It requires but a small gift of discernment for anyone to foresee that providence will erect a mighty empire in America, and our posterity will have it recorded in history, that their fathers migrated from an island in a distant part of the world, [the inhabitants of which] were at last absorbed in luxury and dissipation; and to support themselves in their vanity and extravagance they coveted and seized the honest earnings of those industrious emigrants. This laid a foundation of distrust, animosity and hatred, till the emigrants, feeling their own vigor and independence, dissolved every former band of connection between them and the islanders sunk into obscurity and contempt" (p. 82). On the population and number of towns in Massachusetts, see L. Kinvin Wroth's interpretive essay in *PIR*, 1:1–3. Richard D. Brown's *Revolutionary Politics in Massachusetts* is an excellent study of the Boston Committee of Correspondence and the towns; for the beginnings of the committee, see pp. 38–122. G. B. Warden also provides a useful account of the committee's activities in *Boston, 1689–1776*, pp. 241–74. Brown cites the town of Gorham's January 7, 1773, letter to the Boston Committee of Correspondence in *Revolutionary Politics*, p. 118. For the exchange between Hutchinson and the House of Representatives in early 1773, see *The Briefs of the American Revolution*, edited by John Phillip Reid, pp. 7–102. On the May 13, 1774, town meeting, see the minutes in *Boston Town Records, 1770–1777*, pp. 171–74.

Charles Bahne calculates the cost of the East India Tea lost on December 16, 1773, in the Friday, December 18, 2009, entry of J. L. Bell's blog *Boston 1775*, http://boston1775.blogspot.com/2009/12/how-much-was-tea-in-tea-party-worth.html. Stephen Patterson writes of Samuel Adams's political maneuvering at the expense of John Rowe and other merchants in *Political Parties in Revolutionary Massachusetts*, pp. 74–83. Gage's arrival and reception at Straight Wharf on May 17 is detailed in the May 23, 1774, issue of the *Boston Gazette*. On John Hancock, see Herbert Allan's *John Hancock: Patriot in Purple*, William Fowler's *The Baron of Beacon Hill*, and Harlow Giles Unger's *John Hancock: Merchant King and American Patriot*. John Andrews details the falling out between Hancock and Gage in entries written on August 16 and 17, 1774, in "Letters of John Andrews" (subsequently referred to as LJA): 342–43. Reverend Gad Hitchcock's May 25, 1774, sermon preached before General Gage is in *PIR*, 1:299–322. Gage's rejection of the patriot councillors is described in an article in the

May 30, 1774, *Boston Gazette*, which also reprints the speech Gage gave before both houses of the General Court.

John Rowe tells of where the British naval ships were stationed around Boston Harbor in the May 29, 1774, entry of his *Diary*, pp. 272–73; his reference to "Poor unhappy Boston" is made on June 1, 1774 (p. 273). Francis Drake in *Tea Leaves* recounts how John Rowe asked, "Who knows how tea will mingle with salt water?" at the Old South Meetinghouse prior to the night of the Tea Party (p. 63). Rowe expresses regret for the Tea Party as well as criticism of the ministry's response in a June 2, 1774, entry in his *Diary*, p. 274. In a May 30, 1774, letter to Charles Thomson, Samuel Adams writes of how the "yeomanry . . . must finally save this country" (*Writings*, 3:99). A transcript of the Solemn League and Covenant is in *PIR*, 1:453–59. John Andrews voices his disapproval of the League and Covenant in a June 12, 1774, entry in LJA, p. 329. John Rowe tells of the arrival of the Fourth and Forty-Third Regiments on June 14 and 15, 1774, in his *Diary*, p. 275. Captain Harris writes of the sentries on the common hurling stones at the cows and of the lushness of the grass in an August 7, 1774, letter, in S. R. Lushington, *The Life and Services of General Lord Harris*, p. 34. John Andrews complains of the inconvenience and cost of shipping goods overland from Salem to Boston in letters written on August 1, 20, and November 9 (pp. 336, 344, 383). John Rowe describes Boston's "distressed situation" in a June 12, 1774, entry of his *Diary*, p. 275.

Chapter Three—**The Long Hot Summer**

I am indebted to Kinvin Wroth and his fellow editors for the title of this chapter; part 3 of volume 1 of their compilation of primary sources in *PIR* is entitled "Long Hot Summer: June 18–Sept. 28, 1774." The reference to "an attack upon one colony was an attack upon all" is in Edmund Burnett, *The Continental Congress*, p. 20. Robert Treat Paine, in a 1795 note in the Robert Treat Paine Papers, MHS, recounts how in June 1774 he contributed to Samuel Adams's plan to prevent Daniel Leonard from interfering with the selection of delegates for the Continental Congress. William Hanna includes an account of the Paine-Leonard incident in his *History of Taunton*, pp. 100–101. Ralph Davol in *Two Men of Taunton* tells the story of Daniel Leonard, Thomas Hutchinson, and the Tory pear tree, pp. 208–9. On Daniel Leonard, see the biography in James Henry Stark, *The Loyalists of Massachusetts*, pp. 325–32. Gage's proclamation dissolving the General Court on June 17, 1774, is in *Journals of the House of Representatives of Massachusetts*, vol. 5 (1773–74,) p. 291. Thomas Young describes the gathering of "very important and agreeable company" at Joseph Warren's house in a June 19, 1774, letter cited by Richard Frothingham in his *Life of Joseph Warren* (*LJW*), p. 325. In addition to Frothingham's biography of Warren, there is John Cary, *Joseph Warren: Physician, Politician, and Patriot*, and Samuel A. Forman, *Dr. Joseph Warren* (*DJW*). As in many matters relating to Joseph Warren, I am indebted both to Forman's book and to my correspondence with Forman since his book's publication; Forman provided me with input on Warren's eye color in a March 1, 2012, e-mail. In *Paul Revere* Esther Forbes writes of Warren, "He had a mobile face . . . and the 'fine color' so much admired. In his portrait his hair is powdered, but his coloring and even the shape of his face suggest he was very blond" (p. 66). Warren's account and ledger books (the first for 1763–68, the second running from May 3, 1774, to May 8, 1775) are at the MHS. The ledger book provides almost a daily record of the patients he saw and what he prescribed for each of them; his first mention of "Miss Mercy Scollay" is on May 30, 1774.

Forman analyzes Warren's medical practice in *DJW*, pp. 107–8, 335–44; he also provides a physician's perspective on Warren's possession of "the touch": "that ephemeral human quality enabling [a physician] to connect with patients in a way that, quite aside from treatments we would view as archaic, made people feel at ease, confident and healed. It is much more than the placebo effect of a sugared pill, rather a human and humane interaction depending on communication, compassion, and a transmittable confidence that a health condition, no matter how grave, could be dealt with in the best possible way" (pp. 88–89). J. P. Jewett in *The Hundred Boston Orators* refers to the position of Warren's pew ("opposite the old southern door, in the body of the house") at the Brattle Street Meetinghouse; he also mentions that in 1835, when the site of Warren's house on Hanover Street was excavated, "wired skulls, from his anatomical room, were discovered" (p. 48). Forman in *DJW* cites William Gordon's claim that Warren was "judged handsome by the ladies," p. 179; he also speculates that Warren and Hooten's first child was conceived out of wedlock, p. 182.

Samuel Forman hypothesizes that the John Singleton Copley painting titled *Lady in a Blue Dress* at the Terra Foundation for American Art in Chicago is that of Mercy Scollay at age twenty-two (*DJW*, p. 379). Edward Warren, the son of Joseph Warren's younger brother John, describes Mercy Scollay as "a woman of great energy and depth of character" in his *Life of John Warren, M.D.*, p. 87. The poem "On Female Vanity" appears in the June 1774 issue of Isaiah Thomas's *Royal American Magazine*. In an introduction that precedes the poem, Thomas explains how he came to publish the poem: "I was lately in a company, where the conversation turned to the nonconsumption agreement. . . . One of the company desired a lady to give him a list of the necessaries of life for a fine lady, and she soon sent him an elegant copy of verses; which falling into my hands I enclose to you." "On Female Vanity" appears under the title "To the Hon. J. Winthrop, Esq." in Mercy Otis Warren's 1790 collection *Poems, Dramatic and Miscellaneous*. My thanks to J. L. Bell for identifying Mercy Otis Warren as the poem's author. In a September 27, 1774, letter to Mercy Otis Warren, Hannah Winthrop repeats the rumor that the poem was written by Mercy Scollay and that Joseph Warren was "the gentleman who requested it" (in *Warren-Adams Letters*, 1:33).

The June 27–28, 1774, town meeting minutes are in *Boston Town Records, 1770–1777*, pp. 177–80. Richard D. Brown in *Revolutionary Politics in Massachusetts* includes a detailed account of the town meeting and cites Jonathan Williams's letter describing the meeting's first day and the fact that there were "many people just idle enough to attend"; Brown writes, "The test revealed the limits of the Boston committee's capacity for political leadership . . . always resting on continuous public consent rather than any formal, institutionalized authority" (pp. 196–99). John Andrews's account of the meeting is in a July 22, 1774, entry in *LJA*, pp. 330–32. See also Stephen Patterson, *Political Parties in Revolutionary Boston*, pp. 83–85. John Rowe writes of the overwhelming vote in favor of the Committee of Correspondence in the June 28 entry of his *Diary*, p. 277. Gage complains of the "timidity and backwardness" of the loyalists in a July 5, 1774, letter to Dartmouth, in *Correspondence of Thomas Gage*, p. 359. The June 1774 propaganda sheet inviting the soldiers to desert is in the Gage Papers at the Clements Library. Thomas Hutchinson writes of Gage's unsettling letter to his wife in an August 20, 1774, entry in his *Diary*, 1:223–24. John Rowe records the arrival of Admiral Graves, General Percy, and the Fifth and Thirty-Eighth regiments in his *Diary*, p. 277. One of the best portraits of Percy during his time in Boston, even if heightened by more than a few fictional flourishes, is provided by Harold Murdock's *Earl Percy's Dinner Table*. Of note to J. K. Rowling fans, the Percy ancestral estate known as Alnwick Castle in Northumberland served as Hogwarts in the first two Harry Potter films. Lieutenant Williams of the Twenty-Third Regiment writes of the large number of prostitutes in Boston in a June 12, 1775, entry in his *Journal*: "Perhaps no town of its size could turn out more whores than this could. They have left us an ample sample of them" (p. 5). Mount Whoredom appears on several British maps of Boston made during the siege. John Andrews refers to the incident at Mrs. Erskine's and the violent encounter after that, as well as to Percy's attempts to see that justice was done, in an August 1, 1774, entry in LJA, pp. 333–35.

The many letters chronicling the donations to Boston are contained in "Correspondence, in 1774–1775, between a committee of the town of Boston and contributors of donations for the relief of the sufferers by the Boston Port Bill," in MHS *Collections*, 4th ser., 4:1–275. John Andrews mentions the donations from South Carolina, Marblehead, and Connecticut and the public works projects in an August 1, 1774, letter in LJA, p. 337; he complains of how "middling people" are the ones on whom "the burthen falls heaviest," in an August 20 letter, p. 344. The Massachusetts Government and Justice Acts as they were received by Gage are reprinted in *PIR*, 1:506–19; in a postscript to Gage (also in *PIR*, 1:519–22), Lord Dartmouth appended the recently passed (on June 2, 1774) Quartering Act. On the Quebec Act, see chapter 6, "The Problem of Quebec," in Peter Thomas's *Tea Party to Independence: The Third Phase of the American Revolution*, pp. 88–117. John Andrews describes how Parliament's punitive acts "encouraged the sons of freedom to persevere . . . and confirmed the lukewarm that were staggering" in an August 25 letter; he tells how "every denomination of people" disapproved of Lord North in an August 11 letter; both in LJA, pp. 347, 341. Thomas Young's August 19, 1774, letter to Samuel Adams about the huge volume of correspondence being received by the committee is cited by Richard Frothingham in *LJW*, p. 343.

Joseph Warren's reference to the "glorious stands" appears in the October 7, 1765, issue of the *Boston Gazette* under the byline "B. W." Following up on an identification provided by Warren's contemporary Harbottle Dorr, Warren biographer John Cary finds "stylistic characteristics" that confirm the piece as Warren's, especially the "inordinate number of imperative sentences charging the people to action," in *Joseph Warren*, p. 43. Frothingham in *LJW*, p. 405, reprints Warren's "A Song of Liberty," which was sung to the tune of "The British Grenadier." The loyalist Peter Oliver in *OPAR* claims that Warren's earlier financial problems were solved by marrying "a tolerable sum of money; he also took administration on part of a gentleman's estate which he appropriated to his own use" (p. 128). This is a reference to Warren's curious role as court-appointed administrator of the estate of the merchant Nathaniel Wheelwright, whose bankruptcy in 1765 proved the financial undoing of many Boston merchants, including John Scollay, father to Mercy. Wheelwright left Boston and died of yellow fever in Guadeloupe in 1766, and in 1767, Warren became administrator of the Wheelwright estate; see J. L. Bell, "A Bankruptcy in Boston, 1765," *Massachusetts Banker*, fourth quarter, 2008, pp. 14, 16, 18, 23. Peter Oliver also makes the claim that by 1774, Warren's devotion to the patriot cause "had reduced his finances to a very low ebb. He was now forced to strike any bold stroke that offered" (*OPAR*, p. 128). According to Edward Warren, in *Life of John Warren*, p. 33, Joseph Warren "was of a free and liberal disposition, and never acquired any rigid notions of economy"; Edward Warren also describes Joseph Warren's copartnership with James Latham, "surgeon in the King's or 8th Regiment of foot" to erect a smallpox hospital at Point Shirley in Chelsea (p. 21), adding, "It is certainly curious to see Joseph Warren at this time, July 1774, forming a partnership for 21 years with a surgeon in his majesty's regiment of foot. . . . It is very certain that [he did not have] any idea or wish at this time for a separation from the mother country" (pp. 40–41). In a letter written to John Hancock on May 21, 1776, Mercy Scollay refers to Warren's partnership in the hospital as a possible source of income for his now orphaned children, who "might be benefited by their father's part of the profits" (at CHS). Joseph Warren insists "that nothing is more foreign from our hearts than a spirit of rebellion" in an early June letter to Charles Thompson cited by Richard Frothingham in *LJW*, p. 332. Mercy Scollay's sister Priscilla and her husband, Thomas Melvill, were destined to become the grandparents of the novelist Herman Melville, whose father added a final *e* to the family name.

John Andrews writes of the financial help Samuel Adams received to prepare him for the Continental Congress and the departure of the delegates in the entries for August 10 and 11 in LJA, pp. 339–40. On Charles Lee and his visit to Boston in August 1774, see John Richard Alden's *General Charles Lee, Traitor or Patriot?* pp. 1–60. Samuel Adams Drake in *Old Boston Taverns* writes that the young George Washington stayed at the Cromwell's Head Tavern in Boston, the same place where decades later Charles Lee stayed (pp. 44–45). Lee's August 6, 1774, letter to Gage is in *PIR*, 1:593–95. William Cutter writes of the legendary exploits of Israel Putnam in *The Life of Israel Putnam*, pp. 33–127. Alden in *General Charles Lee* cites Thomas Young's letter to Samuel Adams about Lee's discussions with British officers and his leave-taking from Boston (p. 59).

John Andrews refers to the Government Act as "a blank piece of paper" while chronicling the news from the western portion of the province during August 1774 in LJA, pp. 343–49. Richard Brown also writes of the increasing political activity in the western counties that summer in *Revolutionary Politics in Massachusetts*, pp. 212–20. Ray Raphael provides an excellent account of Massachusetts's response to the Government Act during the summer and fall of 1774 in *The First American Revolution*, insisting that "it was the Massachusetts Government Act, not the Boston Port Act, which led common people throughout the colony to take decisive action" (p. 222). John Andrews writes of Daniel Leonard's problems in Taunton and Gage's standoff with the Salem Committee of Correspondence over the town meeting issue, as well as the town of Danvers's outrageous challenge to his authority in the August 24, 25, 26, and 29 entries of LJA, pp. 346–48. Gage writes that "conciliating, moderation, reasoning [are] over" in a September 2, 1774, letter to Dartmouth; see *Gage Correspondence*, pp. 369–72. Robert Gross describes the divisions and resource challenges faced by the towns of Massachusetts in the first half of the eighteenth century and how resistance to Great Britain brought an unprecedented consensus to the region in *The Minutemen and Their World*, pp. 60–108. On Joseph Hawley's role in the Northampton controversies in the aftermath of the Great Awakening, see Peter Shaw's *American Patriots and the Rituals of Revolution*, pp. 131–52. Samuel Quincy's June 1, 1774, letter to his brother Josiah is in Josiah Quincy's *Memoir of the Life of Josiah Quincy Junior*, pp. 160–64. John Andrews's description of Gage and his entourage near the common is in his letter of August 31, LJA, pp. 349–50.

Chapter Four—**The Alarm**

On the history of the militia system in New England, see Fred Anderson, *A People's Army*, pp. 26–28. Peter Oliver writes of the Indian scalps "waving in the wind" and of "savage" being "convertible" in *OPAR*, pp. 132–33. John Adams and James Otis represented the Marblehead fisherman who harpooned a British officer; see Adams's *Diary*, 1:348; see Hiller Zobel's *Boston Massacre* for a detailed discussion of the case, pp. 113–31. David Hackett Fischer writes of New Englanders within twenty miles of the sea bringing their weapons with them to meeting every Sunday in *Albion's Seeds*, p. 120. On the importance of gunpowder to the colonies see the chapter "The Value of Gunpowder" in Robert Richmond's *Powder Alarm 1774*, pp. 37–45. The search for alternative supplies of gunpowder may have been why the patriot merchant John Winthrop Jr. (aka Joyce Junior) was reported to be "strolling in the West Indies" in the spring of 1775; see MHS *Proceedings*, 2nd ser., 12 (1897–98): 142. In addition to Richmond's *Powder Alarm*, Patrick Johnston provides a helpful analysis of the importance of the Alarm to the events preceding Lexington and Concord in "Building to a Revolution: The Powder Alarm and Popular Mobilization of the New England Countryside, 1774–1775."

On William Brattle, see Clifford Shipton's biographical essay in *SHG*, 7:10–23. John Andrews describes how by "chance or design" Brattle's letter slipped from Gage's pocket and the repercussions of the letter (which he quotes from) becoming public knowledge in a September 1 letter in LJA, pp. 350–51. Richmond reprints Brattle's letter in *Powder Alarm*, pp. 51–52. John Andrews writes of the "conjectures" about the troop activity in the September 1 entry of LJA, p. 350. On the history of Ten Hills Farm, see C. S. Manegold's *Ten Hills Farm*, pp. 3–101. Accounts of the British operation to take the powder from the Quarry Hill arsenal and what came to be called the Powder Alarm appear in the September 5, 1774, *Boston Gazette* and John Andrews's September 1, 2, and 3 letters in LJA, pp. 350–53. Benjamin Hallowell's September 5, 1774, letter to Grey Cooper, as well as Thomas Gage's September 2, 1774, letter to

Lord Dartmouth and Thomas Oliver's September 3, 1774, letter to Dartmouth, are in *DAR*, 8:187–91, 179–82, 182–84. McNeil's firsthand account of the Alarm is in *Ezra Stiles' Literary Diary*, 1:476–83. Thomas Young's September 4, 1774, letter to Samuel Adams is in the Adams Papers at the Manuscripts and Archives Division, NYPL, Astor, Lenox, and Tilden Foundations. Joseph Warren's September 4, 1774, letter to Samuel Adams is reprinted in Frothingham's *LJW*, pp. 355–57.

Peter Oliver writes of Joseph Warren's youth as "a bare legged milk boy to furnish the Boston market" (*OPAR*, p. 128). Joseph Warren's youngest brother John was two years old at the time of their father's death; John's son Edward writes in *The Life of John Warren, M.D.*, "The sight of his father's body borne home to the house, made an impression upon his mind at this early age which was never effaced" (p. 4). Edward Warren even claims that "the fearful scene which he witnessed in childhood" later motivated John Warren to become a doctor (p. 12). Nathaniel Ames records three different performances of *Cato* "acted at Warren's Cham[ber]": on July 3, 1758; on July 6 ("to perfection"); and on July 14 ("Cato more perfect than before"); Ames, *Diary*, p. 14. Samuel Forman in *DJW* writes of Warren's speculative involvement with the militia company at Harvard (pp. 40–41). J. P. Jewett in *The Hundred Boston Orators*, pp. 47–48, recounts the rainspout incident, as does Samuel Knapp in *Biographical Sketches of Eminent Lawyers, Statesmen, and Men of Letters*; Knapp claims he was told of the incident by "a spectator of this feat" who "related this fact to me in the college yard, nearly half a century afterwards, and the impression it made on his mind was so strong, that he seemed to feel the same emotion, as though it happened but an hour before" (pp. 107–8). Samuel Forman in *DJW* writes about the Spunkers and cites the November 17, 1773, letter of William Eustis (who was one of Joseph Warren's apprentices) to John Warren, describing how he and fellow Spunkers competed with another group of medical students for the body of Levi Ames (pp. 35–36). Forman believes that Warren's rainspout incident may have been related to his Spunkers activities; while I'm not sure the evidence warrants that specific speculation, I agree with Forman that Warren's association with the Spunkers "suggests . . . a tolerance of illegality and secrecy, if such is in the service of a higher good" (p. 39). John Cary in *Joseph Warren* writes in detail about Warren's activities during the 1764 smallpox epidemic (pp. 21–23); as does Forman, pp. 55–61, who also describes Warren's activities with the masons (pp. 109–25). John Eliot in his *Biographical Dictionary* writes of how the North End Caucus was "guided by the prudence and skillful management of Dr. Warren"; he also writes of "the secret springs that moved the great wheels" (p. 472). See William Tudor, *The Life of James Otis*, for yet another account of Warren's involvement in this secret political group (pp. 461–62). Samuel Knapp in *Biographical Sketches of Eminent Lawyers, Statesmen, and Men of Letters* writes of how Warren had "the wisdom to guide, and the power to charm"; he also writes that Warren "could discern the signs of the times, and mold the ductile materials to his will, and at the same time seem only to follow in the path of others" (p. 111).

In a July 25, 1773, letter to Samuel Danforth, Benjamin Franklin writes of Danforth's supposed discovery of the Philosopher's Stone: "I rejoice . . . in your kind intentions of including me in the benefits of that inestimable stone, which curing all diseases (even old age itself) will enable us to see the future glorious state of our America. . . . I anticipate the jolly conversations we and twenty more of our friends may have in a hundred years hence on this subject," *Memoirs of the Life and Writings of Benjamin Franklin*, vol. 2 (London: Colburn, 1818), pp. 13–14. The pronunciation of Danforth as "Danfurt" is mentioned by Clifford Shipton in his biographical essay in *SHG*, 14:250. On Benjamin Hallowell, see Sandra Webber's "Benjamin Hallowell Family and the Jamaica Plain House." In addition to the previously cited letter to Grey Cooper, Hallowell describes being chased back to Boston in a detailed September 8, 1774, letter to Gage (*PIR*, 1:609–12). John Andrews relates that Hallowell, one of the two customs commissioners "born among ourselves," was responsible for the unnecessarily harsh interpretation of the Boston Port Bill in an August 2 letter in LJA, pp. 336–37. On Thomas Oliver, see Clifford Shipton's essay in *SHG*, 13:336–44. Joseph Warren writes of "the little matters in which we are engaged" in his September 4, 1774, letter to Samuel Adams in Frothingham's *LJW*, p. 356; Frothingham also reprints Adams's September 25, 1774, letter to Warren in which he refers to the suspicions concerning New England at the Continental Congress and the fear that Massachusetts wants "a total independency" (pp. 377–78).

My account of the effect of the Powder Alarm and the Suffolk Resolves on the first Continental Congress in Philadelphia is based in large part on Edmund Cody Burnett, *The Continental Congress*, pp. 39–46, which cites the quotations from Silas Deane and John Adams. Jack Rakove writes insightfully about the Congress's response to the Suffolk Resolves and the move toward moderation after their endorsement in *The Beginnings of National Politics*, pp. 45–49. The text of the Suffolk Resolves appears in *PIR*, 2:914–20. On Paul Revere's role as "the Mercury of the American Revolution," see David Hackett Fischer, *Paul Revere's Ride*, pp. 26–28; as Fischer states, Revere, whom a loyalist described as a patriot "ambassador," was "less than an ambassador, but more than merely a messenger" (p. 28). John Andrews provides a day-by-day account of the measures Gage took to defend Boston from a possible incursion from the country that includes the anecdotes about the marksmen and giant from the country; Andrews also writes of the outflow of weapons and the stealing of cannons, both by land and water, and Gage's frustrations with building barracks for his soldiers (LJA, pp. 355–74), and of the decision of Admiralty Court that the navy "had no right . . . to stop or molest any boats carrying merchandise," in a November 21 letter (p. 386).

Walter McDougall in *Freedom Just Around the Corner* writes of Americans being on average two inches taller than Europeans (p. 124). Vincent Kehoe in *We Were There!* points out that "there were few [among the regulars] who were old soldiers enough to be called veterans," and that it had been more than twelve years since any of them had seen action (p. 9). Nathaniel Appleton recounts the conversation between two Louisbourg veterans about the fortifications on the Neck in a November 15, 1774, letter to Josiah Quincy Jr., in *Memoir of Josiah Quincy Jr.*, pp. 202–3. As John Galvin writes in *The Minute Men*, the concept of the minuteman dated back to the French and Indian War (p. 33). The incident involving William Dawes, the cannon, and Joseph Warren was told by Dawes's granddaughter and is in Henry Holland's *William Dawes and His Ride with Paul Revere*, p. 37. William Tudor also speaks of the theft of two cannon from the gun house beside the common in *The Life of James Otis*, pp. 452–55. John Andrews chronicles the sufferings and death of large numbers of British soldiers, specifically commenting on how fatal the rum distilleries proved to be when used as barracks: "the smell of the lees in the cisterns added to their urine, has caused an infectious distemper among 'em, whereby two or three have dropped down dead of a day," in LJA, pp. 389–93. Major John Pitcairn writes that rum "will destroy more of us than the Yankees will" in a March 4, 1775, letter to Lord Sandwich, printed in *Naval Documents of the American Revolution* (subsequently referred to as *NDAR*), edited by William Bell Clark, 1:125. Andrews writes of the execution of the soldier on the common and of how repeated whippings meant that "their ribs are laid quite bare," as well as of the fieldpiece in the center of town "to be fired in case of a mutiny," in LJA, pp. 357, 397, 393. Gage tells of his difficulties throughout the fall in letters to Dartmouth, which climax with his plea for an army of twenty thousand men in an October 20, 1774, communication in *Correspondence*, p. 383.

Joseph Warren compares the delegates at the Provincial Congress to "an assembly of Spartans or ancient Romans" in a November 21, 1774, letter in Frothingham's *LJW*, pp. 346–49. In an October 16, 1774, letter to Samuel Adams, John Pitts writes that he is "informed by a member of the congress that the Boston Committee are by far the most moderate men," Samuel Adams Papers, Manuscripts and Archives Division, NYPL, Astor, Lenox, and Tilden Foundations. Joseph Warren's letters to and from Samuel Adams, in which he seeks his advice about the best course to take that fall (and refers to being "rapacious for the intelligence"), are reprinted in Frothingham's *LJW*, pp. 355–58, 375–78, 381–82. Forman in *DJW* writes of Warren witnessing Josiah Quincy Jr.'s last will and testament (p. 100). In his description of Dr. Thomas Young's exit from Boston, Ray Raphael in *Founders* cites Young's letter to Samuel Adams in which he describes his wife's "terrors" (pp. 146–49). J. L. Bell outlines the shadowy circumstances surrounding William Molineux's death in "A Bankruptcy in Boston, 1765," in *Massachusetts Banker*, fourth quarter, 2008, p. 26. John Rowe describes Molineux as the "first leader of dirty matters" in an October 24 entry in his *Diary*, p. 286. In a letter of January 1, 1798, to "the Corresponding Secretary," Paul Revere writes of his memories of Benjamin Church (pp. 106–12). John Boyle tells of the bells ringing in Boston to celebrate the return of the delegates from the Continental Congress on November 9, 1774, in his *Journal*, p. 381.

Chapter Five—**The Unnatural Contest**

On the taking of the powder and armaments at Portsmouth, see Elwin Page, "The King's Powder, 1774," pp. 83–92; Charles Parsons, "Capture of Fort William and Mary, December 14 and 15, 1774," pp. 18–47; and Thomas Kehr's "The Seizure of . . . Fort William and Henry," http://nhssar.org/essays/FortConstitution.html. As David Hackett Fischer writes in *Paul Revere's Ride*, "Revere's intelligence was not entirely correct" (p. 54). Fischer rightly points out that the incident was an embarrassment to Gage. Ultimately, however, it may have worked in Gage's favor in that the attack came to be perceived by many colonists as an overreaction given that Gage had not yet decided to send troops to Fort William and Mary. As Gage writes to Dartmouth on

January 18, 1775, "We hear from New Hampshire that the people who were concerned in the rash action against Fort William and Mary . . . are terrified at what they have done, and only anxious to obtain pardon for their office" (*Correspondence*, p. 390). John Andrews writes of the extraction of Plymouth Rock in an October 6 letter in LJA, pp. 373–74; see also my *Mayflower*, pp. 350–51. William Hanna in *A History of Taunton* writes of how a flag with the slogan "Liberty and Union" was raised on a 112-foot liberty pole on Taunton Green on October 21, 1774, pp. 104–5. On Jesse Dunbar and the ox, see Justin Winsor's *History of Duxbury*, pp. 123–46. Peter Oliver provides a stirring overview of the abuses suffered by the loyalists in the countryside in his *OPAR*, pp. 152–57. See also the article in *Rivington's Gazette*, March 9, 1775. On Timothy Ruggles, see James Stark, *The Loyalists of Massachusetts*, pp. 225–29.

For the Daniel Leonard–John Adams newspaper exchange during the winter of 1775, see *Tracts of the American Revolution*, edited by Merrill Jensen, pp. 277–349. Gage's January 18, 1775, letter to Dartmouth is in *Correspondence*, p. 390; Gage writes of the encouraging developments in Marshfield in a January 27, 1775, letter, p. 391. Ray Raphael in *The First American Revolution* writes insightfully about the loss of momentum suffered by the patriots in the winter of 1775: "Once local Tories had been defeated, the patriots . . . began to show signs of division," p. 187, and quotes from Ephraim Doolittle's March 21, 1775, letter to John Hancock, p. 189. In a November 25, 1774, letter to Josiah Quincy Jr., James Lovell writes of how the fortifications at the Neck have been whitewashed and how "'tis boasted they are as strong as those of Gibraltar," in *Memoir of Josiah Quincy*, pp. 478–79. On Frederick Haldimand, see Alan French's "General Haldimand in Boston," MHS *Proceedings*, pp. 80–95. John Andrew provides a detailed account of Haldimand's encounter with the coasting boys of Boston and Gage's response in a January 29 letter in LJA, pp. 398–99. John Andrews reports that Gage's own officers refer to him as "an old woman," in a March 18 letter in LJA, p. 401; he writes of Gage's coolness to the refugee loyalists in a November 19 letter, p. 386; he writes scathingly of the British marines in a December 30 letter, p. 392.

Gage and Graves's feuding over the marines is chronicled in *NDAR*, pp. 123–27; Gage's March 6, 1775, letter to Graves complaining of how his naval blockade turned away provisions intended for the troops is also in *NDAR*, p. 128. A December 13, 1775, letter published in the January 17, 1776, issue of London's *Morning Post and Daily Advertiser* claims that the feud between Gage and Graves "first originated with their wives; both of whom led their husbands," in *Letters on the American Revolution* (*LAR*), edited by Margaret Willard, p. 238. Major James Wemyss claimed that Gage "was governed by his wife, a handsome American," in "Character Sketches of Gage, Percy and Others," Sparks Papers, Harvard University, xxii, 214. In his *Diary*, Lieutenant John Barker tells of Margaret Gage's subscription "scheme" for the ball in January as well as the February ball attended by both the Gages and the Graveses, pp. 19–24; he also writes of the Gage-Graves squabble over the marines, p. 15. Hannah Mather Crocker writes nostalgically of "The Last Queen's Ball" in *Observation on the Real Rights of Women and Other Writings*, pp. 161–62.

Frothingham writes of Joseph Warren's role on the Committee of Safety in *LJW*, pp. 389–91. The huge numbers of supplies deposited in Concord are listed in *Diaries and Letters of William Emerson*, edited by Amelia Forbes Emerson, p. 60. John Andrews reports on how the "quantities that are barreled up" have contributed to the "dearness of provisions among us" in Boston, in LJA, pp. 394–95. Edward Warren in *Life of John Warren* claimed that Joseph Warren "induced his brothers Eben and John to appropriate a large portion of their small paternal estate" to help purchase gunpowder for the provincial army (p. 33); he includes the letters between Joseph and John during January and February 1775 in which Joseph attempts to convince his younger brother to take out a note of 200 pounds to Dr. Greenleaf (pp. 34–36, 41–42), and comments, "Like other people of ardent disposition, [Joseph Warren] does not look forward to what might happen even within six months" (p. 42). Samuel Forman in *DJW* documents Warren's April 4, 1775, purchase of medical supplies from Greenleaf with 20 percent in cash (p. 266). Paul Revere tells of "a gentleman who had connections with the tory part but was a whig at heart" and who acquainted him with the existence of a spy, in "A Letter . . . to the Corresponding Secretary," p. 106. On Henry Knox and his involvement in patriot spying efforts, see Mark Puls, *Henry Knox*, pp. 20–23. The January 3, 1775, letter in which Josiah Quincy writes to his son Josiah Jr. in England recounting the intelligence concerning the miserable morale of the British soldiers and sailors is in *Memoir of Josiah Quincy*, pp. 212–15. Paul Revere writes of the spy network he was involved with that met regularly at the Green Dragon Tavern in "A Letter . . . to the Corresponding Secretary," p. 106.

Joseph Warren describes Gage being of "honest, upright principles" in a November 21, 1774, letter to Josiah Quincy Jr. in Frothingham's *LJW*, p. 395. Samuel Forman writes of how Warren formed an alliance with British traveling masonic lodges so that his own St. Andrew's could achieve grand lodge status (*DJW*, pp. 116–25). Joseph Warren's April 20, 1775, letter to Gage, in which he wishes he had "told you all I knew or thought of public affairs," is in *PIR*, 3:1925–26.

On Benjamin Church, see Clifford Shipton's essay in *SHG*, 13:380–98; and Revere's "Letter to . . . the Corresponding Secretary," pp. 110–11. In just about every issue of the *Boston Gazette* in 1774 Benjamin Church's auctioneer father ran an advertisement. On Benjamin Church as the Indian fighter in King Philip's War, see my *Mayflower*, especially p. 358. Alan French was the first to document Dr. Benjamin Church's role as a spy; see *General Gage's Informers*, pp. 147–201. French writes that when it came to Gage's decision to send troops to Salem in February, he "was strongly influenced by his secret information" (p. 25). Although Church does not identify himself as the source of each specific report, his role as a delegate in the Provincial Congress and stylistic similarities to his earlier and later writings have led me to identify him as the author of the reports that are attributed to him in the text. The March 4, 1775, "Intelligence of Military Preparations in Massachusetts" is reprinted in *DAR*, 8:63–66. The report filed by Brown and DeBerniere is in an appendix to "The Diary of Lieutenant John Barker," in *Journal of the Society of Army Historical Research*, pp. 170–74. George Nash, in "From Radicalism to Revolution: The Political Career of Josiah Quincy, Jr.," writes of Quincy's ever-changing views when in London during the fall and winter of 1774–1775 (pp. 266–85), as do Daniel Coquillette and Neil Longley

York in *Portrait of a Patriot* (1:35–76), which contains the edition of Quincy's *London Journal* from which I quote in the text (1:223–69). Concerning North's "Conciliatory Proposition," Peter Thomas in *Tea Party to Independence* writes that "North evidently believed that he had found a permanent solution to the imperial crisis" (pp. 199–200); Thomas also cites Thomas Hutchinson's optimistic letter to his son (p. 218). Dartmouth's January 27, 1775, letter to Gage is in *DAR*, 3:37–41.

My account of Joseph Warren's Massacre Day Oration is based on the following sources: two letters written by Samuel Adams on March 12 and 21, 1775, in *Writings*, 3:154–55, 160–62; Thomas Hutchinson's conversation with Colonel James, who attended the oration, as recorded in Hutchinson's *Diary* for Sept. 6, 1775, 1:528–29; Lieutenant John Barker's *Diary*, March 6, 1775, pp. 25–26; Frederick Mackenzie's *Diary*, March 6, 1775, pp. 36–39; the March 16, 1775, issue of *Rivington's New York Gazetteer*; and J. P. Jewett's biography of Joseph Warren in *The Hundred Boston Orators*, pp. 59–60. Eran Shalev's "Dr. Warren's Ciceronian Toga: Performing Rebellion in Revolutionary Boston" provides a useful analysis of the classical resonances of Warren's oration; the manuscript version is in the John Collins Warren Papers at MHS. The reference to Warren's "true puritanical whine" is in Thomas Bolton's "Oration." Samuel Forman in *DJW* writes that Warren's description of the fallen husband and father was "recalled for him from his father's untimely death" (p. 62); Forman also points out that the dramatic paragraph in which Warren refers to "fields of blood" was "written as an insertion on a separate piece of paper" (p. 234). According to David Hackett Fischer in *Paul Revere's Ride*, "In the New England dialect with its lost postvocalic r's, 'Fie! Fie!' sounded like 'Fire! Fire!' " (p. 70).

Thomas Ditson's account of the events leading up to and including his tarring and feathering by the soldiers appears as a footnote in *JEPC*, pp. 131–33. When it came to the complaints about Ditson, John Andrews recorded that Gage was "greatly disgusted with their remonstrance (being a very spirited one) but finally dismissed them with every assurance of protection from danger"; March 18, 1775, letter in LJA, p. 400, which also contains Andrews's description of Bolton's oration. A manuscript version of Bolton's "Oration" is at MHS. Bolton wasn't the only one pointing out the moral duplicity of the patriots; in *Bodies Politics: Negotiating Race in the American North*, John Wood Sweet cites a British play performed during the Boston occupation in which a black prostitute named Fanfan "rebukes ostensibly chaste Sons of Liberty, for their hypocrisy: 'Tho' in public you scoff, / I see many a spark, / Would tink me sweet pretty / Girl in the Dark' " (p. 149). John Rowe complains of being mentioned in Bolton's "Oration" in a March 15, 1775, entry of his *Diary*, p. 290. John Andrews writes of his "irascibility rising" in a March 18, 1775, letter in LJA, p. 401. Sanborn C. Brown writes about Mary Dill Thomas's affair with Benjamin Thompson and quotes her claim that "she would roast in hell rather than give him up" in *Benjamin Thompson, Count Rumford*, pp. 35–36.

Robert Brand Hanson, editor of Nathaniel Ames's *Diary*, published in 1998, was the first to make the link between Warren's "*incognita pregnans*" and Sally Edwards (p. 278). Samuel Forman in *DJW* expands upon that identification by noting that Mercy Scollay later referred to Sally Edwards as a "little hussy" and "vixen" in letters written to Mrs. Dix on July 27, 1776, and November 26, 1776 (CHS, pp. 185, 189). Having independently identified that a Sally Edwards who turned thirteen in 1774 later married the eldest son of Paul Revere (which is not mentioned in Forman's book), I asked Forman if he had explored that connection, and he generously shared with me that he had indeed made the possible identification, in a personal communication, February 23, 2012. Whether or not she was the same Sally Edwards who eventually married a son of Paul Revere, it appears almost certain that at some point in September 1774, Joseph Warren got a young woman named Sally Edwards pregnant. An alternative explanation could be that Warren had arranged obstetrical care for a friend. Maintaining the unwed mother and child on Warren's account after his death might have been a way to shield the identity of the true father, who was not Warren. My description of medical practices in the colonial era depends on Lester King, *The Medical World of the Eighteenth Century*, and Forman in *DJW*, pp. 45–53. Forman points out that ipecac had uses in the eighteenth century beyond treatment for poisoning, since it was "a common prescription for reducing pathologic levels of the humor choler by way of the gastrointestinal tract" (p. 49). When it comes to why Warren prescribed ipecac to Scollay in September 1774, he writes, "I cannot identify the disease entity in modern terms, though it involved close follow-up and hands-on care" (p. 394), including the application of a neck plaster the day after Scollay visited Warren twice in a single day.

John Barker writes of the March 30 expedition with Percy's brigade in his *Diary*, pp. 27–28. Frothingham tells of the reaction to Percy's expedition in *LJW*, pp. 446–47. Joseph Warren tells of the incident in an April 3, 1775, letter to Arthur Lee, *LJW*, pp. 447–48. The Provincial Congress's March 30 resolve regarding "artillery and baggage" is cited in John H. Scheide, "The Lexington Alarm," p. 60. As early as March 30, 1775, Gage was receiving intelligence reports about "several grand debates . . . in this committee such as fixing a criterion for assembling the militia together, the manner how the alarm is to be given, and the place where the counties are to assemble" (*PIR*, 3:1976); on April 3 he learned that "should any body of troops, with artillery and baggage march out of Boston, the country would instantly be alarmed and called together to oppose their march to the last extremity" (p. 1977).

Chapter Six—**The Trick to See It**

Joseph Warren's April 8, 1775, letter to Arthur Lee, in which he recounts how he used the information in Lee's December 21, 1774, letter to shake the Provincial Congress out of the "state of security into which many have endeavored to lull them," is in *LJW*, pp. 447–48. Samuel Knapp in *Biographical Sketches* writes of how Warren had been preparing himself "for several years . . . to take a conspicuous rank in the military" (pp. 115–16). Edward Warren in *Life of John Warren* tells of how Warren's father insisted that his son Joseph not be "a coward" (p. 2). Knapp writes of Warren choosing "to be where wounds were to be made rather than where they were to be healed," in *Biographical Sketches*, p. 117; Knapp also writes of Warren's "versatility" (p. 111). J. P. Jewett in *Boston Orators* relates William Eustis's account of Warren's outraged response to the taunts of the British soldiers as well as their nighttime visit to Cornhill (pp. 48–49). Thomas Hutchinson writes of Warren's ambition to "become the Cromwell of North America" in "Additions to Thomas Hutchinson's 'History of Massachusetts Bay,' " edited by Catherine Barton Mayo, *Proceedings of the AAS* 59, pt. 1 (1949): 45. Peter Oliver in *OPAR* writes of Warren's determination to "mount the last round of the ladder or die in the attempt" (p. 128). General Hugh Percy tells of the provincials' determination "either to set [Boston] on fire . . . or to . . . starve us out" in an April 8, 1775, letter to Thomas Percy, in his *Letters*, p. 48.

John Andrews writes of how Boston's residents were "afraid, mad, crazy, or infatuated" and began leaving the city in droves in LJA, p. 402. Thomas Hutchinson records the account of Samuel Cooper's tense meeting with Joseph Warren during a Sunday service in April 1775 (which had been told him by Harrison Gray) in the August 15, 1777, entry of his *Diary*, 2:156. According to Cooper's own *Diary*, he was in Weston by April 10, "having received several menaces and insults, particularly at Mrs. Davis, having a scurrilous song offered me by an officer," cited by Charles Akers in *The Divine Politician*, p. 195. Clifford Shipton writes of Joseph Warren "knowing that a warrant for his arrest was in Gage's pocket" in *SHG*, 14:521; Shipton also writes of how Warren assisted Isaiah Thomas in getting his printing press and type out of Boston (p. 520). A transcript of Warren's brief April 10, 1775, letter about moving his family and personal effects to Worcester appeared in a lot description in a June 9, 1999, Christie's auction cited by Samuel Forman in *DJW*, pp. 394–95. Robert Hanson in a note to *The Diary of Dr. Nathaniel Ames* records that Ames began billing Joseph Warren's account on April 8, 1775 (p. 278). Daniel Leonard's comparison of patriot leaders to a "false guide" who leads a traveler to the brink of an abyss first appeared in December 19, 1774, and is reprinted in *Tracts of the American Revolution*, edited by Merrill Jensen, p. 279. King George's November 18, 1774, letter to Lord North insisting that "blows must decide" whether the American colonies "are to be subject to this country or independent" is in *CKG*, p. 153. As Peter Thomas writes in *Tea Party to Independence*, both sides read each other incorrectly when it came to the outbreak of the American Revolution: "Congress was bluffing, confident that Britain would again back down, as in 1766 and 1770. . . . This time Britain did not do so, and called the colonial bluff. . . . The War of Independence was not a heroic enterprise but the result of a political miscalculation" (pp. 174–75). John Andrews tells of General Percy's praise of his wife's drawing in an April 11, 1775, letter in LJA, p. 403. Percy writes of the weather in Boston in an April 8, 1775, letter in *Letters*, p. 49.

The April 7, 9, 15, and 18, 1775, espionage reports addressed to General Gage appear in *PIR*, 3:1978–83. Allen French discusses the contents of these letters and the fact that they were written by an insider in the Provincial Congress (who was proven to be Benjamin Church by subsequent letters he wrote to Gage), as well as how the letters influenced the general's decision making relative to the expedition to Concord, in *General Gage's Informers*, pp. 18–33. Many historians cite an account by the British spy John Howe (*History of Middlesex County*, vol. 2, edited by D. Hamilton Hurd, pp. 579–84), who claimed to have advised Gage to send troops to Concord instead of Worcester, but I have doubts about the reliability of the Howe narrative and have therefore not cited it; see D. Michael Ryan's argument that the Howe account is nothing but an "embellished 'plagiarism' " in *Concord and the Dawn of Revolution*, p. 53. Admiral Samuel Graves writes of moving the *Somerset* "exactly in the ferry way between the two towns," in his "Narrative" in *NDAR*, 1:179. Dartmouth's January 27, 1775, letter to Gage is in *DAR*, 8:37–41. Allen French carefully analyzes Gage's orders to Colonel Francis Smith, the originals of which (including an early draft) are at the Clements Library in Ann Arbor, Michigan, and concludes that "Gage did not plan to seize Hancock and Adams," in *General Gage's Secret Informers*, p. 33. Lieutenant Barker writes of Gage's April 15 orders to the grenadiers and light infantry being "by way of a blind" in his *Diary*, p. 29. Paul Revere writes of how on the "Saturday night preceding the 19 April, about 12 o'clock at night, the boats belonging to the transports were all launched, and carried under the sterns of the men of war," as well as other events preceding and including his famous ride to Lexington, in "A Letter . . . to the Corresponding Secretary," pp. 106–10. Ellen Chase in *The Beginnings of the American Revolution* (*BAR*), vol. 2, lists the height of the steeple of Christ Church as 191 feet (p. 326). The detailed description of the military stores in Concord made on April 18, 1775, is in *PIR*, 3:1982–83.

According to William Gordon, Warren learned of Gage's expedition to Concord "by a mere accident . . . just in time to send messengers over the neck and across the ferry," in his *History of the American Revolution*, p. 477; Gordon's reference to "a daughter of liberty, unequally yoked in point of politics" (p. 476) is often cited as a possible reference to Margaret Gage as Warren's informer; however, the unnamed female informant Gordon refers to sent a message not to Warren but to Samuel Adams— several days before April 19. Charles Stedman tells of Percy overhearing the townspeople gathered on Boston Common talking about the impending expedition to Concord in his *History of the American War*, 1:119. In an interview with me at the Gage estate in Firle, Sussex, in March 2011, Lord Nicholas Gage (a direct descendant of Thomas and Margaret Gage) insisted that there was no family tradition concerning an estrangement between the Gages—an assertion that seems borne out by the portraits of Thomas and Margaret, painted after their return to England from Boston in 1775, that still bracket a fireplace mantel at the Gage estate. J. L. Bell in his blog "Boston 1775" does a masterful job of demonstrating why it's highly unlikely that Margaret Gage revealed any secrets about her husband's planned expedition to Concord; see postings for April 12 and 13, 2011, http://boston1775.blogspot.com/2011/04/marriage-of-thomas-and-margaret-gage.html. Another possibility is that Warren's informant was none other than Benjamin Church. In the weeks ahead, Warren would turn a blind eye to some highly suspicious behavior on the part of Church, perhaps because the doctor had earned Warren's trust by acting as a double agent on the night of April 18.

In an October 25, 1775, entry in his journal, Jeremy Belknap records various accounts he'd heard of events in Boston on the evening of April 18, including the appearance of a light infantryman in a shop and the conversation between two officers on Long Wharf (pp. 84–86). Ellen Chase includes this evidence as well as Samuel Drake's account of the man who spoke with the groomer in the stables of Province

House, along with an account of the officers dispatched to guard the roads to Concord, in *BAR*, 2:320–31. The essential illegality of Warren's decision to send out the alarm on the night of April 18, 1775, is discussed by John Scheide in "The Lexington Alarm," pp. 59–61; by John Cary in *Joseph Warren*, p. 183; and by Clifford Shipton in his biography of Warren in *SHG*, 14:520–21. Seemingly in his own defense, Warren writes Joseph Reed on May 15, 1775: "I verily believe that the night preceding the barbarous outrages committed by the soldiery in Lexington, Concord, etc. there were not 50 people in the whole colony that ever expected any blood would be shed in the contest between us and Great Britain" (*LJW*, p. 486). This statement appears to be at complete odds with what Warren knew to be the truth, especially since as recently as April 3, 1775, he had written to Arthur Lee that if Percy's March 30 foray into the countryside had resulted in the destruction of any military stores "not a man of them [Percy's brigade] would have returned to Boston" (*LJW*, p. 448). "Was he," as Clifford Shipton so rightly asks concerning Warren's decision to send out the alarm, "deliberately creating an incident which would assure war?" (p. 521). We'll never know for sure, especially since, according to some accounts, many of Warren's papers were destroyed after his death. Did these papers include incriminating documents that might have indicated just how deliberate Warren's decision to send out the alarm really was? Once again, we'll probably never know for sure.

William Munroe describes Paul Revere's arrival at the Jonas Clarke house on the night of April 18 in an affidavit recorded on March 7, 1825, in Elias Phinney's *History of the Battle of Lexington* (subsequently referred to as Phinney), p. 33; Phinney provides the detail about Hancock responding, "Come in, Revere. We are not afraid of you" (p. 17). William Gordon appears to have spoken in great detail with Samuel Adams about the night of April 18 and morning of April 19; in his *History of the American Revolution*, vol. 1, he records, "Mr. Adams inferred from the number [of British regulars] to be employed that [the stores in Concord] were the objects, and not himself and Mr. Hancock, who might be more easily seized in a private way by a few armed individuals, than by a large body of troops that must march, for miles together, under the eye of the public" (pp. 476–77). Probably the best way to visualize Lexington Common or Green (both terms were used in eighteenth-century accounts) in 1775 is by looking at the relevant engraving in the series by Amos Doolittle, all of which are based on sketches made at the sites within weeks of the events in 1775. My description of John Parker is based on Elizabeth Parker's "John Parker," pp. 47, 60–61, and *BAR*, 2:345–46. Lexington militia company clerk Daniel Harrington reported that 130 militiamen answered the first call that night in William Gordon's "Account of the Commencement of Hostilities" in *AA4*, 2:627. The number of Munroes, Harringtons, Smiths, Reeds, and Tidds on the Lexington militia rolls is in *BAR*, 2:380.

As explained in Mary Babson Fuhrer's "The Revolutionary Worlds of Lexington and Concord Compared," Lexington had not experienced the divisions that had plagued Concord primarily because it was a younger town and had a history of strong and open-minded ministers. Fuhrer writes of how liberty in the eighteenth century had an entirely different meaning than it would have in the nineteenth century, citing the example of John Parker's abolitionist grandson Theodore Parker, who believed "that liberty is an inalienable right of personhood, not as his forefathers had believed, of property" (p. 118). Levi Preston was the militiaman who said, "We always had been free, and we meant to be free always"; Mellen Chamberlain, "Why Captain Preston Fought," pp. 68–70, and cited in *BAR*, 3:56, and David Hackett Fischer, *Paul Revere's Ride*, p. 164. For information on Prince Estabrook, see George Quintal's *Patriots of Color*, pp. 97–98; also present on the Lexington Common that morning were two more "men of color," Eli Burdoo and Silas Burdoo (pp. 69–71). The reference to the coercive tactics of the patriots ("everyone bends") was made by General Frederick Haldimand, second in command to Gage in Boston; in Allen French's "General Haldimand in Boston," pp. 90–91. Lieutenant Frederick Mackenzie writes in his *Diary* of how the militiamen frequently called out "King Hancock forever" during the British retreat to Boston that day (p. 57). On November 21, 1822, William Sumner recorded Dorothy Quincy's memories of the morning of April 19 in the Clarke parsonage, which included Adams's insistence that "we belong to the cabinet" ("Reminiscences by Gen. William H. Sumner," p. 187).

David Hackett Fischer provides an excellent description of the uniforms and equipment of the British grenadiers and light infantrymen in *Paul Revere's Ride*, pp. 118–23. According to Samuel Abbot Smith, *West Cambridge 1775*, a townsman from Menotomy was awakened that night "by the rattle of the pewter plates on his dresser, jarred, as they were, by the measured tramp of the soldiers" (p. 17); Smith also relates Deacon Ephraim Cutter's account of how he heard later in the day "the measured tread of the soldiers as of one man" (pp. 26–27). According to Frank Coburn in *The Battle of April 19, 1775*, "the moon was shining sufficiently bright" for the soldiers to read signs along the road; Coburn also recounts how Mrs. Timothy Tufts looked out her window in Cambridge's Beech Street and "saw from her bed the gun-barrels shining in the moonlight" (pp. 48–50), and how the widow Rand and her bullet-casting neighbor saw the soldiers' footprints in the dirt of the road through Cambridge (p. 49). Lieutenant Jeremy Lister writes of how "the country people began to fire their alarm guns, light their beacons" as the regulars marched out of Menotomy in Vincent Kehoe, *We Were There!* (subsequently referred to as Kehoe), p. 115. Lieutenant Sutherland writes of hearing "several shots being fired . . . between 3 and 4 in the morning (a very unusual time for firing)" in Kehoe, p. 140. Colonel Smith's account of how they "found the country had intelligence or strong suspicion of our coming, and fired many signal guns, and rung the alarm bells repeatedly" is also in Kehoe, p. 73. Samuel Abbot Smith relates how the Committee of Safety members fled the Black Horse Tavern in *West Cambridge 1775*, pp. 16–17.

My description of the approach of the British advance guard to Lexington Common is based, in large part, on the accounts of Sutherland, Smith, Pope, Pitcairn, and Marr, all of which are in Kehoe (pp. 73, 76, 110, 138–89, and 155). *BAR*, vol. 2, contains descriptions of the capture of Porter, Richardson, and Wellington (pp. 360–61). Paul Revere writes in detail of his conversation with Major Mitchell and his officers in "A Letter . . . to the Corresponding Secretary," p. 109. For a description of the dress and training of the provincial militiamen, see David Hackett Fischer's *Paul Revere's Ride*, pp. 149–62; Doolittle's engravings clearly indicate the differences in dress between the militiamen and the regulars. William Munroe testified to seeing two hundred cartridge papers lying on the ground in Phinney, p. 34. According to Reverend Jonas Clarke, *A Brief Narrative*, "After all this precaution, we had no notice of [the regulars'] approach, till the brigade was actually in the town" (p. 4). Paul Revere recounts overhearing John Parker's order to "let the troops pass by and don't molest them, without they being first," in a deposition taken April 24, 1775, in *Paul Revere's Three Accounts of his Ride*, p. 22. Robert Douglass's account of hearing a militiaman say, "There are so few of us, it would be folly to stand here" (to which Parker replied, "The first man who offers to run shall be shot down"), is in Ezra Ripley's *A History of the Fight at Concord*, p. 52. John Robbins's testimony that one of the British officers cried out, "Throw down your arms, ye villains, ye rebels," is in *A Narrative of the Excursion and Ravages of the King's Troops*, p. 8. Ezra Stiles records a secondhand description of Major Pitcairn's activities at Lexington, in which Stiles recounts how Pitcairn "struck his . . . sword downwards with all earnestness as the signal to forbear or cease firing," in his *Diary*, 1:604–5. Paul Revere describes "a continual roar of musketry," in "A Letter . . . to the Corresponding Secretary" (p. 110). The testimonies of John and Ebenezer Monroe concerning what happened that morning, including how Joshua Simons was prepared to blow up the open cask of powder in the attic of the Lexington Meetinghouse with his gun, are in Phinney, pp. 35–37. The death of Jonathan Harrington is recounted in *BAR*, 2:370. In an October 8, 1775, letter to R. Donkin, Colonel Smith writes of how he prevented the regulars from attacking the provincials inside the buildings on Lexington Common, in Kehoe, pp. 75, 141–42. Lieutenant Barker writes in his *Diary* that the light infantrymen "were so wild they could hear no orders" (p. 32).

John Galvin discusses the problems created by Gage's decision to go with a "motley mixture of units"—specifically "a loose command structure" that required company commanders "to operate with new procedures under unfamiliar leaders"—in *The Minute Men*, p. 103. Lieutenant Mackenzie in his *Diary* tells how Colonel Smith's officers tried to convince him "to give up the idea of prosecuting his march and to return to Boston" (p. 63). William Heath's criticism of the Lexington militia is in his *Memoirs*, p. 6. Harold Murdock in *The Nineteenth of April 1775* argues that Samuel Adams must have been the one pulling the strings at Lexington that morning (pp. 23–25), as does Arthur Bernon Tourtellot in *Lexington and Concord* (originally titled *William Diamond's Drum*), 79, 112, 125–27. But as the testimony of William Munroe makes clear (in which he recounts Hancock's insistence that "if I had my musket, I would never turn my back upon these troops"), it was Hancock they were listening to (Phinney, p. 34). See J. L. Bell's May 19, 2008, entry, "Who Really Wanted to Fight at Lexington?" in his blog *Boston 1775*, http://boston1775.blogspot.com/2008/05/who-really-wanted-to-fight-at-lexington.html, for a balanced assessment of Adams's and Hancock's influence (if any) on what happened at Lexington Green. William Gordon recounts the exchange between Samuel Adams and John Hancock, in which Adams describes the day as "glorious," in his *History*, 1:478–79. Hancock's description of the

Lexington militia being only "partially provided with arms, and those they had were in most miserable order" is in "Reminiscences by Gen. William Sumner," p. 187.

Chapter Seven—**The Bridge**

　　Mary Hartwell's account of the regulars passing her house on the way to Concord is in A. E. Brown's *Beneath Old Roof Trees*, p. 221. Colonel Smith writes of how his column marched "with as much good order as ever troops observed in Britain or any friendly country," in his October 8, 1775, letter to R. Donkin, cited in Vincent Kehoe, *We Were There!* p. 75. Thaddeus Blood's account of the Concord fight is in the *Boston Daily Advertiser*, April 20, 1886 (subsequently referred to as his Narrative). D. Michael Ryan in *Concord and the Dawn of Revolution* cites an article in the July 16, 1888, *Boston Transcript* that tells of an Emerson family tradition that "an English banner with 'Union and Liberty' inscribed in white letters" flew from the Concord liberty pole (p. 71). Lemuel Shattuck in *A History of Concord* quotes Reverend Emerson as saying, "Let us stand our ground" (pp. 105–6). Ezra Ripley in *A History of the Fight at Concord* describes how Colonel Barrett ordered the provincials to march over the North Bridge to Punkatasset Hill (p. 16). *BAR* contains an account of the activities at the Barrett farm in anticipation of the arrival of the British soldiers (3:6–7); some of this account is drawn from the interview Benson J. Lossing had with Colonel Barrett's grandson James in 1848, which is referred to in Lossing's *Pictorial Field-book of the Revolution*, 1:551. Parson's search of the Barrett farm under the watchful eyes of Mrs. Barrett is described in *BAR*, 3:23–24, 46. Robert Gross in *The Minutemen and Their World* writes of Lieutenant Joseph Hosmer's prickly personality and his role as Concord's "most dangerous man" (pp. 64–65). On the history of the Bedford flag, see Sharon Lawrence McDonald's *The Bedford Flag Unfurled*, pp. 8–13, 33–39, 52–58. On the New Englanders' uneasy relationship with their region's native history and how "a white man in Indian costume could envision himself as an American ideal, both civilized and free," see Benjamin Carp's *Defiance of the Patriots*, pp. 147–57, as well as my *Mayflower*, pp. 357–58. In 1850 Amos Baker (then known as "the last survivor" of the Concord fight) described James Nichols's conversation with the regulars at the North Bridge and his decision not to participate in the fight in his "Affidavit of the Last Survivor," printed in Joel Parker's *Address to the Students of the University of Cambridge*, pp. 133–35. See also Michael Ryan's "Mysterious Militia Man Deserts at Old North Bridge," *Concord Magazine*, March/April 2001, available at http://www.concordma.com/magazine/marapr01/mysteryman.html.

　　Affidavits about Isaac Davis's actions on April 19 are in Josiah Adams, *Letter to Lemuel Shattuck*, pp. 14–20; Ellen Chase provides a useful distillation of this material in *BAR*, 3:24–28. See also Michael Ryan's "The Concord Fight and a Fearless Isaac Davis," *Concord Magazine*, May 1999, available at http://www.concordma.com/magazine/may99/davis.html. Ryan also writes about the tune the fifer in Davis's company was reputedly playing in "White Cockade: A Jacobite Air at the North Bridge?" available at https://www2.bc.edu/~hafner/lmm/music-articles/white_cockade_ryan.html. Lemuel Shattuck tells of Joseph Hosmer "earnestly" inquiring, "Will you let them burn the town down?" in *History of Concord*, p. 111. In Gage's official account of April 19, 1775, the townspeople of Concord are described as "sulky"; *JEPC*, p. 680. Martha Moulton's testimony appears in Richard Frothingham's *HSOB*, p. 369; Ellen Chase provides a good account of the activities of the British regulars in Concord in *BAR*, 3:19–21. George Bancroft writes that the Concord schoolmaster "could never afterwards find words strong enough to express how [Davis's] face reddened at the word of command"; Bancroft also repeats Davis's famous words, "I have not a man that is afraid to go," in his *History of the United States*, 2:302. Lieutenant Jeremy Lister's claim that the militiamen marched "with as much order as the best disciplined troops" is in Kehoe, p. 116. John Galvin describes how Laurie's street-firing maneuver *should* have worked in *The Minute Men*, pp. 150–51. Lieutenant Sutherland's description of what happened at the North Bridge is in Kehoe, pp. 142–43. Amos Doolittle's engraving of the scene is titled "The Engagement at the North Bridge in Concord." My thanks to William Fowler for his input regarding the muzzle velocity of a musket in a personal communication. Amos Barrett's memory of how "their balls whistled well" is in his Narrative in *Journal and Letters of Henry True*, p. 33. Amos Baker's statement that "we concluded they were firing jack-knives" can be found in his "Affidavit of the Last Survivor." D. Hamilton Hurd in *History of Middlesex County* describes the death of Isaac Davis: "The ball passed quite through his body, making a very large wound, perhaps driving in a button of his coat. His blood gushed out in one great stream, flying, it is said, more than 10 feet, besprinkling and besmearing his own clothes . . . and the clothes of Orderly Sergeant David Forbush and a file leader, Thomas Thorpe" (1:261). Captain David Brown is credited with crying out, "God damn them, they are firing balls!" in Frederic Hudson, "The Concord Fight," p. 797.

According to Reverend Emerson's great-granddaughter Phebe Ripley Chamberlin, Emerson's wife told her "that she felt hurt because [her husband] did not stay more with her [on April 19] and once when he was feeding the women and children with bread and cheese she knocked on the widow and said to him that she thought she needed him as much as the others," in *Diaries and Letters of William Emerson*, p. 73. According to William Gordon in a May 17, 1775, letter, Emerson "was nearer the regulars than the killed" when the firing began at the North Bridge; Gordon also writes that Emerson was "very uneasy till he found that the fire was returned," *AA4*, 2:630. Emerson's March 13, 1775, sermon is in his *Diaries and Letters*, p. 65. Frederic Hudson writes that Major Buttrick cried, "Fire, fellow soldiers, for God's sake, fire!" in "The Concord Fight," p. 797; Thaddeus Blood tells how "the fire was almost simultaneous with the cry" in his Narrative. Lieutenant Lister's description of how the regulars crumbled before the provincial fire is in Kehoe, p. 116. Amos Barrett's memory of how the regulars retreated, "running and a hobbling about," as well as how he and other provincial soldiers lay behind a stone wall on the hill overlooking the North Bridge with their "guns cocked expecting every minute to have the word—fire," is in *Journal and Letters of Henry True*, p. 33. Thaddeus Blood's account of how after crossing the North Bridge "everyone appeared to be his own commander" is in his Narrative. William Gordon records the Reverend Emerson's account of the Ammi White incident: "A young fellow coming over the bridge in order to join the country people, and seeing the soldier wounded and attempting to get up, not being under the feelings of humanity, very barbarously broke his skull, and let out his brains with a small axe" (*AA4*, 2:630). See also Michael Ryan's "Senseless Act Begets Rage and Propaganda" in February 1999 *Concord Magazine*; also available at http://www .concordma.com/magazine/feb99/scalping.html. Jeremy Lister's account of the rumor instigated by Ammi White's attack on the wounded regular is in Kehoe, p. 116. The regulars' claim that the provincials would scalp any soldier "they get alive, that are wounded and cannot get off the ground," along with the additional claim that the militiamen are "full as bad as the Indians," is in an April 28, 1775, letter in *AA4*, 2:439.

On the importance of the flank guards, see Douglas Sabin's *April 19, 1775*, p. 125. Edmund Foster's account of how the fighting started on the road back to Lexington is in Ezra Ripley's *History of the Fight at Concord*, p. 33. Lister's account of how a musket ball "effectually disabled" his right arm is in Kehoe, p. 117. Barker writes of how the regulars were fired on "from all sides" in his *Diary*, p. 35. Samuel Thompson's account of how the regulars "stooped for shelter from the walls" is in *BAR*, 3:70. Ellen Chase writes that "50 years later eye-witnesses recalled the peculiar 'swish, swish' made by the grass as the regulars brushed through it" in *BAR*, 3:28. Douglas Sabin in *April 19, 1775*, provides a detailed account of the deaths of Jonathan Wilson and Daniel Thompson in the vicinity of the Samuel Hartwell house, pp. 134–35; Sabin also tells of James Hayward's fatal encounter with a regular at the well near the Fiske house (p. 149). William Gordon writes of how "the people say that the soldiers are worse than the *Indians*" in his May 17, 1775, letter in *AA4*, 2:630. Sarah Bailey writes of Ford and Furbush and the dying grenadier in *Historical Sketches of Andover*, pp. 307–8; see also *BAR*, 3:63–64. Lieutenant Barker writes of being "totally surrounded by such an incessant fire" in his *Diary*, p. 35. David Hackett Fischer in *Paul Revere's Ride* writes that the hill on which the Lexington militia ambushed Colonel Smith's column is called today Parker's Revenge (p. 229). Douglas Sabin in *April 19, 1775* points to Concord Hill as the place at which the column began to collapse, p. 151. Ensign DeBerniere's account of how the regulars were thrown "into confusion" and "began to run rather than retreat in order" is in Kehoe, p. 122. Lieutenant Barker's insistence that if Percy's brigade had not appeared "we must soon have laid down our arms or been picked off by the rebels at their pleasure" is in his *Diary*, p. 37. Lieutenant Sutherland's description of Percy's brigade as "one of the best dispositions ever I saw" and of their "sanguine hopes" is in Kehoe, p. 144.

Joseph Tinker Buckingham in *Specimens of Newspaper Literature*, vol. 2, tells of Benjamin Russell and his classmates at the Queen Street Writing School on April 19 and how they followed Percy's brigade to Cambridge (pp. 2–3). William Gordon in his *History*, vol. 1, recounts the anecdote about Percy's fifers playing "Yankee Doodle" and the boy's teasing remark about the ballad "Chevy Chase" (p. 481). John Eliot in *Brief Biographical Sketches* tells how Warren's "soul beat to arms" when he heard the news from Lexington (p. 473). Frothingham in *LJW* describes how Warren turned over his medical practice to Eustis, then took the ferry to Charlestown, on which he told a compatriot to "keep up a brave heart!" (pp. 456–57). Isaiah Thomas in *The History of Printing in America* says he accompanied Warren to Charlestown (p. 168). Frothingham relates an account from a Dr. Welch, who claimed to have accompanied Warren out of Charlestown, as well as how Warren drove off the two soldiers trying to steal a horse, in *LJW*, p. 457. William Heath tells of his military studies in his *Memoirs*, pp. 1–4. Samuel Knapp in *Sketches* writes of how Warren felt it was "indispensable" that he get sufficient military experience that "his reputation for bravery might be put beyond the possibility of suspicion" (p. 119).

Cyrus Hamlin writes of Francis Faulkner's youthful experiences on April 19 in *My Grandfather, Colonel Francis Faulkner*, pp. 5–6. In an April 28, 1775, letter in *AA4*, a regular tells of how the militiamen "ran to the woods like devils" when the British lit the houses on fire (2:440). Joseph Loring in *JEPC* lists "200 rods of stone wall thrown down" in an account of damages inflicted by the British troops (p. 686). Lieutenant Lister recounts his conversation with Smith on the night of April 18 in Kehoe, as well as how Smith later offered him his horse as the column left Lexington (pp. 115, 117–18). Lieutenant Barker's description of Smith as a "fat heavy man" is in his *Diary*, p. 34. William Heath writes in his *Memoirs* of how he "assisted in forming a regiment, which had been broken by the shot from the British fieldpieces," as well as how Joseph Warren "kept with him" throughout that afternoon and evening (pp. 7–8). General Percy writes of how the militiamen clustered around the column "like a moving circle" in an April 20, 1775, letter to General Harvey in his *Letters*, p. 52. The description of how the westerly wind created "such a cloud that blinded" the regulars yet left them "a plain mark for the militia" is in Box 1, Folder 1, U.S. Revolution Collection, 1754–1928, AAS. Lieutenant Mackenzie writes of the fire being as bad in the front of the column as it was in the rear in his *Diary*, p. 57. Lieutenant Lister describes how he used a horse as a shield in Kehoe, p. 118. A summary of Ensign Martin Hunter's account of "men clinging in numbers [to the carriages of the fieldpieces] and tumbling off when the cannon halted to fire," is in Kehoe, p. 150. John Galvin writes of how "Heath's firm grasp of the tactics of the skirmish line and his tendency to see any battle as a series of isolated little fights was just what the provincials needed" in *The Minute Men*, p. 206. I find it interesting that, except for Heath's own memoirs, there are virtually no contemporary accounts describing Heath's leadership role during the afternoon of June 19; if a person is singled out, it's inevitably Joseph Warren, but more as a charismatic cheerleader than a strategist or tactician. If anything, the fighting during Percy's march from Lexington to Charlestown seems to have been even wilder and less controlled than it had been during Smith's retreat from Concord, when all agreed the militiamen fought "with little or no military discipline and order." Whatever leadership was being exerted on the side of the provincials was coming from the company captains with previous military experience in the French and Indian War, most of whom had little or no contact with General Heath—a point that Percy makes when he says in his *Letters*, "They have men amongst them who know very well what they are about" (p. 53).

David Hackett Fischer in *Paul Revere's Ride* writes about the differences between the scarlet uniforms of the British officers and the faded red coats of the rank and file (p. 122). Lieutenant Mackenzie writes of the effectiveness of the provincials who used their horses to ride ahead of the column and then wait in ambush in his *Diary*, p. 67.

In my account I have resisted the temptation to describe the legendary activities of one Hezekiah Wyman, a long-haired old man on a white horse, who reputedly killed many a regular on that bloody afternoon, and who does not appear in the literature until the publication of a widely reprinted article titled "The White Horseman," which first appeared in the August 22, 1835, *Boston Pearl and Literary Gazette*. See J. L. Bell's series on the subject in his blog *Boston 1775*, which begins with his May 29, 2010, entry "Hunting for Hezekiah Wyman"; http://boston1775.blogspot.com/2010/05/hunting-for-hezekiah-wyman.html. If there was a miraculous warrior on a white horse that day, it was General Percy, whom even the understated Lieutenant Mackenzie described in his *Diary* as behaving "with great spirit throughout this affair and at the same time with great coolness" (p. 59). John Eliot in *Brief Biographical Sketches* describes Warren as "perhaps the most active man in the field" (p. 473). William Heath in his *Memoirs* tells of how "a musket ball came so near to the head of Dr. Warren, as to strike the pin out of the hair of his earlock" (p. 8). Samuel Knapp writes of how "the people were delighted with his cool, collected bravery" (p. 116).

Thomas Thorp describes how the Acton militiamen "were putting powder (flour) on their hair" before heading out to Concord in a deposition appended to Josiah Adams's *Letter to Lemuel Shattuck*, p. 15. J. W. Hanson in *History of Danvers* writes of Jotham Webb's determination to "die in my best clothes" (p. 297; cited by Ellen Chase in *BAR*, 3:128). Chase provides a useful synthesis of accounts from Hanson, Hurd's *History of Middlesex County*, and other sources in *BAR*, 3:130–35. See also Samuel Abbot Smith's *West Cambridge 1775*, in which he repeats Mrs. Russell's claim that the south room was "almost ankle deep" in blood and describes the burial of the bodies "head to point," pp. 37–39, 52. My summary of the other incidents that occurred in Menotomy is based on *BAR*, 3:122–24, 145–47, 157–59, and Smith's *West Cambridge 1775*, pp. 34–37, 42–44. William Heath tells in his *Memoirs* how he had instructed the Watertown militia to go to Cambridge "to take up the planks, barricade the south end of the bridge, and there to take post; that, in case the British should, on their return, take that road to Boston, their retreat might be impeded" (p. 7). John Andrews writes of watching the progress of the British column down the Battle Road from the hills of Boston in an April 19, 1775, letter in LJA, p. 405. Jane Mecom in *The Letters of Benjamin Franklin and Jane Mecom* describes "the horror the town was in" on that day in a May 14, 1775, letter to her brother Benjamin Franklin (p. 154). The Reverend Samuel West's description of watching the fighting from his house in Needham as he and his parishioners feared the worst, as well as his troubling portrayal of a once "mild and gentle" people turned "ferocious and cruel," are available online at http://www2.needham.k12.ma.us/eliot/technology/lessons/primary_source/lex_con/memoir.htm. Samuel Abbot Smith recounts in *West Cambridge 1775* how the women gathered at the house of George Prentiss in Menotomy feared that the slave Ishmael had come "to kill us" (p. 50). J. H. Temple in *History of Framingham* describes the women's fear of a slave revolt (p. 275). William Heath writes of how "the flashes of the muskets [were] very visible" as the British approached Charlestown; he also speculates that "their retreat would have been cut off" if Pickering and his men from Salem had marched with a little more fortitude, in his *Memoirs*, pp. 8–9. Clifford Shipton provides an insightful sketch of Timothy Pickering Jr. in *SHG*, vol. 15, describing Pickering's nearsightedness and the way the light reflected on his spectacles at night (pp. 453–54). Timothy Pickering writes of believing "that a pacification upon honorable terms is practicable" in an April 26, 1775, letter in Octavius Pickering, *The Life of Timothy Pickering*, 1:80–82.

Chapter Eight—**No Business but That of War**

Sarah Winslow Deming writes of her departure from Boston in a journal she addressed to her niece at MHS. She describes Boston as a "city of destruction" in her April 20, 1775, entry, in which she recounts how she and her two friends left the city and spent the night in Roxbury. Hannah Winthrop tells of her travels with her husband John in an undated letter to Mercy Otis Warren, pp. 29–31. David McClure writes of "the dreadful trophies of war" in his *Diary*, pp. 155–61. Deacon Tudor tells of the rumor "that if the soldiers came out again they would burn, kill, and destroy," in the April 20, 1775, entry in his *Diary*. Jeremy Lister describes his return to Boston after the march back from Concord in his *Narrative*, pp. 33–35. Admiral Graves recounts how he suggested that Gage allow him to cannonade Charlestown and Roxbury in his *Narrative* in *NDAR*, 1:193. Timothy Pickering writes about his April 20 meeting in Cambridge with militia officers and members of the Committee of Safety in an April 26, 1775, letter in Octavius Pickering, *The Life of Timothy Pickering*, 1:80–82, and in a June 26, 1807, letter cited in Allen French's *FYAR*, in which Pickering states, "I had no previous information of the plans of *patriotism* or *ambition* (and I now believe the latter was as powerful a stimulus as the former) of the *leaders* in the intended revolution" (pp. 26–27). Frothingham cites Joseph Warren's April 20, 1775, circular letter in which he claims, "Our all is at stake," as well as his April 20, 1775, letter to Gage, in *LJW*, pp. 466–67.

Charles Martyn describes Artemas Ward's arrival in Cambridge in his biography of the general, pp. 89–90. For information on General John Thomas, I have relied on Charles Coffin's *Life and Services of Major General John Thomas*, pp. 3–8. On recruitment in Massachusetts during the French and Indian wars, see Fred Anderson, *A People's Army*, pp. 39–48. The resolution that the recruitment of enslaved African Americans reflected "dishonor on this colony" is in the May 20, 1775, minutes of the Committee of Safety, *JEPC*, p. 553. Joseph Tinker Buckingham in *Specimens of Newspaper Literature*, vol. 2, tells of how Benjamin Russell and his classmates found themselves marooned in Cambridge and how they attached themselves to the officers of the provincial army (p. 4). Paul Revere relates the conversation that followed Benjamin Church's announcement that he had decided to pay a visit to Boston, as well as how Church pointed out the stain of blood on his stockings, in "A Letter . . . to the Corresponding Secretary," pp. 110–11. Lysander Salmon Richards in his *History of Marshfield* tells of the wine closet Nesbitt Balfour built in the cellar of the Thomas house during the winter of 1775 (pp. 117–18). Allen French provides a detailed account of the militia's tentative and ultimately unsuccessful attempts to prevent Balfour's detachment from escaping from Marshfield in *FYAR*, pp. 28–30. My thanks to J. L. Bell in a personal communication for pointing out that Isaac Bissell's first name was changed to Israel as the result of a copyist's mistake as the message about the fighting at Lexington was carried from town to town. For an account of Bissell's ride from Boston to New York and the spread of news of the fighting at Lexington throughout the colonies, see John Schiede, "The Lexington Alarm," pp. 47–50, 62–75. For the activities of the Provincial Congress on April 22 and 23, 1775, see *JEPC*, pp. 147–50.

On Gage's negotiations with the town and the April 27 surrender of thousands of firearms on the part of the Boston residents as well as the loyalists' insistence that the agreement not be honored, see Frothingham's *History of the Siege of Boston (HSOB)*, pp. 94–96. John Andrews tells of his decision to stay in Boston despite his wife's decision to flee in an April 24, 1775, letter in LJA, pp. 405–6. Andrew Eliot writes of his intention to stay in Boston in a May 31, 1775, letter at MHS, in which he also writes of the "grass growing in the public walks and streets"; Eliot writes of "more than nine thousand" Bostonians having left the city in a June 19, 1775, letter to Isaac Smith, in MHS *Proceedings*, 1878, p. 287. Peter Oliver describes the town as "a perfect skeleton" in *OPAR*, p. 124. By March 1776 the British army in Boston had reached 8,906 men, including officers: see *DAR* 10:246. An April 25, 1775, intelligence report to Gage states that "Colo. Putnam proposes [attacking Boston from the Neck] by advancing large bodies of screwed hay before them"; the report also claims that "flat boats" are being built by the provincials in Watertown and Cambridge, in *PIR*, 3:1984–85; an April 30 intelligence report claims "that they had returns last evening from Wellfleet, upon the Cape Cod shore, that three hundred whale boats were ready, and they still talk of burning the ships," *PIR*, 3:1987; a May 28 intelligence report claims that there is a provincial plan to "make their way good into town by boats, numbers of which of the whale boat kind are provided, from Nantucket, Cape Cod and all that coast to the amount of 500," in *PIR*, 3:1994. Paul Litchfield writes of the whaleboats passing along the Scituate shore in a June 10, 1775, entry of his *Diary*, p. 378. On May 27, 1775, fifty whaleboats were confiscated from Nantucket by provincial forces and taken to Cape Cod for ultimate delivery to the Boston area, as described in Edouard Stackpole's *Nantucket in the American Revolution*, p. 15.

My account of the race between the *Quero* and *Sukey* depends on Robert Rantoul, "The Cruise of the *Quero*," pp. 1–4, and James Duncan Phillips, *Salem in the Eighteenth Century*, pp. 364–67. Josiah Quincy Jr.'s final wishes are recorded in the end of his *London Journal* in *Portrait of a Patriot*, vol. 1, edited by Daniel Coquillette and Neil Longley York, pp. 267–69. Joseph Warren's April 27, 1775, letter to Arthur Lee appears in Frothingham's *LJW*, p. 471. The resolves providing annuities for artillery officers William Burbeck and Richard Gridley are in *JEPC*, pp. 153, 157. Allen French provides a good summary of Benedict Arnold's activities in Boston as well as during the taking of Ticonderoga in *FYAR*, pp. 149–52; the evolution of the Committee of Safety's decision to employ Arnold in this "secret service" can be traced in *JEPC*, pp. 531, 532, 534. Samuel Forman points out that the powder Warren gave to Arnold's expedition to Ticonderoga "could have made all the difference if made available to Prescott's beleaguered Americans" on Bunker Hill in *DJW*, p. 298. Joseph Warren's letter to Connecticut governor Trumbull is in *LJW*, pp. 475–76; Frothingham discusses Gage's dealings with the delegation from Connecticut in *HSOB*, pp. 104–5; see also Allen French's *FYAR*, pp. 132–34, which includes Jedediah Huntington's claim that Gage was "wicked, infamous, and base without a parallel." Frothingham in *LJW* tells of the committee from the Provincial Congress appointed to "wait on Warren, to know whether he could serve them as their president"; he also quotes Warren's note in which he replies that "he will obey their order," p. 475. The minutes from May 2, 1775, of the Second Provincial Congress indicate that frustrations with Warren's lack of attendance led to the election of Colonel James Warren of Plymouth (husband of Mercy Otis Warren) to the presidency, but after James Warren declined to serve that same day ("after offering his reasons for excuse"), a committee was selected to talk to Joseph Warren about retaining the presidency, an office he held until his death (*JEPC*, p. 178).

Fears concerning an imminent British attack around May 10 are evident in the congressional minutes, in *JEPC*, pp. 210–15; see also Frothingham in *HSOB*, p. 107. The best account of Church's role in the mix-up with General Thomas in Roxbury is in Charles Martyn's *Life of Artemas Ward*, pp. 102–4. The most helpful transcription of what is evidently Benjamin Church's espionage report to Gage written about May 10, 1775, is in *PIR*, 3:1988–90; see also French's *Gage's Informers*, pp. 151–53. The resolution for "a day of public humiliation, fasting, and prayer" on May 11, 1775, is in the April 15 minutes of the second Provincial Congress; citizens were instructed to "humble themselves before God, under the heavy judgments felt and feared, to confess the sins that have deserved them, to implore the forgiveness of all our transgressions, a spirit of repentance and reformation, and . . . that America may soon behold a gracious interposition of Heaven for the redress of her many grievances, the restoration of all her invaded liberties, and their security to the latest generations" (*JEPC*, p. 145). Captain George Harris's May 5, 1775, letter describing the beauty of what he sees from his tent door on Boston Common is in *The Life and Services of General Lord Harris*, edited by Stephen Lushington, p. 39. Nathaniel Ames records "Public Fast for the times. Dr. Warren here" in the May 11, 1775, entry of his *Diary*, p. 280; Ames also indicates that the weather was fair on that day.

Warren's confidential May 10, 1775, letter to Gage in which he says "no person living knows, or ever will know from me of my writing this," is in *PIR*, 3:2076. On the significance of the ceremony of the fast to New England and America in general in the eighteenth century, see Perry Miller's "The Moral and Psychological Roots of American Resistance"; according to Miller, "New England clergy had so merged the call to repentance with a stiffening of the patriotic spine that no power on earth . . . could separate the acknowledgment of depravity from the resolution to fight" (p. 256). The May 12, 1775, reference to Congress debating "where there is now existing in this colony a necessity of taking up and exercising the powers of civil government, in all its parts" is in *JEPC*, p. 219. On May 10, 1775, the Congress considered accusations of disloyalty against Samuel Paine, who was accused of claiming "that those quartered in the colleges were lousy" (*JEPC*, p. 214). James Stevens tells of the difficulty Captain Thomas Poor had with his men in a May 10 entry in his *Journal*, p. 44. David Avery refers to the muskets being fired, "one out of our window," in the May 8 entry of his *Diary*, p. 27. Amos Farnsworth's reference to "ejaculation, prayers, and praise" is in the June 5–6, 1775, entry of his *Diary*, p. 82. Ezekiel Price speaks of the "high spirits" of the provincial soldiers in Roxbury in the June 7, 1775, entry of his *Diary*, p. 188. The unnamed British surgeon's description of the provincial encampment in Cambridge is in a May 26, 1775, letter in *LAR*, p. 120. A June espionage report speaks of hearing officers "complaining much of the private men having the superiority over the officers, rather than the officers over the men," in *PIR*, 4:2779. Allen French in *FYAR* includes the quote (from Benjamin Edwards) describing the Committee of Safety as "a pack of sappy-headed fellows," p. 70. Abijah Brown's complaints against the Provincial Congress are in *AA4*, 2:720–21. Joseph Warren's May 17, 1775, letter to Samuel Adams, in which he talks about how "the strings must not be drawn too tight at first" when it comes to applying discipline to the provincial army, is in Frothingham's *LJW*, p. 485.

John Barker's May 1, 1775, reference to the "Pretty Burlesque!" of the provincial claims of loyalty to the king is in his *Diary*, p. 40. Joseph Warren writes of the need for a "generalissimo" in his May 17, 1775, letter to Samuel Adams in Frothingham's *LJW*, p. 485. Warren writes of his affection for the provincial soldiers in a May 26, 1775, letter to Samuel Adams in Frothingham's *LJW*, pp. 495–96. John Eliot writes of Warren's "influence" with the army and how "he did wonders in preserving order among the troops" in *Brief Biographical Sketches*, p. 473. Joseph Warren speaks of the "errors [the soldiers] have fallen into" in a May 26, 1775, letter to Samuel Adams in *LJW*, p. 496. Frothingham, in *HSOB*, cites an article in the June 8, 1775, issue of the *Essex Gazette* that refers to "the grand American army" (p. 101). Benjamin Church's espionage report to Gage, in which he speaks of the "vexation" he feels at having been chosen to go to Philadelphia at the end of May, is in *PIR*, 3:1992–93. On Church's return to the Boston area on the day of the Battle of Bunker Hill, see Clifford Shipton's "Benjamin Church," *SHG*, 13:388. John Barker describes Israel Putnam's brazen march into Charlestown in front of the guns of the *Somerset* in the May 13 entry of his *Diary*, p. 46. For an account of the incident at Grape Island on Sunday, May 21, 1775, see the article, probably written by Joseph Warren, that appeared in the *Essex Gazette* and is reprinted in Frothingham's *LJW*, pp. 492–93, as well as Abigail Adams's May 24, 1775, letter to John Adams in *Adams Family Correspondence*, edited by L. H. Butterfield, pp. 204–6. For my account of the Battle of Chelsea Creek, I have depended on *Chelsea Creek: First Naval Engagement of the American Revolution*, by Victor Mastone, Craig Brown, and Christopher Maio; and Vincent Tentindo's and Marylyn Jones's *Battle of Chelsea Creek, May 27, 1775: Graves' Misfortune*. Both studies contain extensive amounts of primary source material from contemporary diaries, letters, logs, and newspapers. See also *NDAR*, 1:544–46. Amos Farnsworth writes about his experiences during the skirmishes associated with the battle in the May 27, 1775, entry of his *Diary*, pp. 80–81. Charles Chauncy, in a July 8, 1775, letter to Richard Price, writes, "I heard General Putnam say, who had the command of our detachment, that the most of the time he and his men were fighting there was nothing between them and the fire of the enemy but pure air"; Tentindo and Jones, *Battle of Chelsea Creek*, p. 102. The account of the conversation among Putnam, Ward, and Joseph Warren after the Battle of Chelsea Creek is in "Colonel Daniel Putnam's Letter Relative to the Battle of Bunker Hill and General Israel Putnam," p. 285.

Chapter Nine—**The Redoubt**

My account of the *Quero*'s arrival in England is based on Robert Rantoul's "The Cruise of the *Quero*," which includes Walpole's reference to John Derby as the "Accidental Captain," as well as the letter referring to the "total confusion and consternation" of the ministers, along with Gibbon's remarks on the incident, and Dartmouth's frustrated letter to Gage, pp. 4–30. I've also consulted James Phillips, *Salem in the Eighteenth Century*, pp. 367–69, and George Daughan, *If by Sea*, pp. 14–16. Richard Frothingham quotes the doggerel about the three British generals from *The Gentleman's Magazine* in HSOB, p. 8. Frothingham quotes a contemporary newspaper report describing the meeting of the *Cerberus* and a packet bound for Newport during which Burgoyne made the comment about "elbowroom" in HSOB, p. 114. On Burgoyne I have consulted Edward De Fonblanque's *Life and Correspondence* and George Athan Billias's "John Burgoyne: Ambitious General," in *George Washington's Generals and Opponents*, edited by George Athan Billias, pp. 142–65; on Howe I have looked to Bellamy Partridge, *Sir Billy Howe*, pp. 1–25; Troyer Anderson, *The Command of the Howe Brothers*, pp. 42–84; Ira Gruber, *The Howe Brothers and the American Revolution*, pp. 3–71; and Maldwyn Jones, "Sir William Howe: Conventional Strategist" in *George Washington's Generals and Opponents*, edited by George Athan Billias, pp. 39–50. On Clinton, I have consulted William Willcox's *Portrait of a General*, pp. 40–50 (which contains Clinton's description of himself as a "shy bitch"); and Willcox's "Sir Henry Clinton: Paralysis of Command," in *George Washington's Generals and Opponents*, edited by George Athan Billias, pp. 73–76. Gage's June 12, 1775, Proclamation (ghostwritten by Burgoyne) is in PIR, 4:2769–72; Gage's letter of the same date to Lord Dartmouth, in which he explains that there is no longer any "prospect of any offers of accommodation," is in DAR, 9:171. Burgoyne complains of the "vacuum" that surrounds him in a June 25 letter to Rochford in E. D. de Fonblanque, *Political and Military Episodes*, p. 143. Howe's June 12, 1775, letter to his brother Richard, in which he explains the plan to take Dorchester Heights, Charlestown, and ultimately Cambridge, is in *Proceedings of the Bunker Hill Monument Association*, 1907, pp. 112–17.

The meeting between Joseph Warren and John Jeffries is described in a May 22, 1875, letter written by Jeffries's son and "derived from statements of my father," titled "A Tory Surgeon's Experiences," pp. 729–32. J. L. Bell, in the October 18, 2007, entry of his blog *Boston 1775* (http://boston1775.blogspot.com/2007/10/dr-joseph-warrens-body-first.html), expresses his doubts that the meeting between Warren and Jeffries ever happened—quite rightly describing Jeffries as a "slippery character" and pointing out that when Jeffries later returned to Boston after years away in England, it was useful to have been once sought after by Joseph Warren. I am inclined, however, to believe Jeffries's account. Given Warren's difficulties with Benjamin Church and his willingness to communicate directly with the supposed enemy (as attested to by his correspondence with Gage), as well as his obvious love of risk, this sounds like just the kind of thing he would have done when circumstances required him to find a surgeon general. Also, Jeffries's account as reported by his son gets corroboration of sorts in Samuel Swett's *History of Bunker Hill*, which includes a reference to Warren's visit to Jeffries (p. 58). Another intriguing reference comes from the loyalist Peter Oliver, who writes of "a gentleman who was tampered with by . . . Major Genl. Warren. . . . Warren was in hopes to take this gentleman into their number, and laid open their whole scheme. He told him that 'Independence was their object; that it was supposed that Great Britain would resent it and would lay the town of Boston in ashes, from their ships; that an estimate had accordingly been made of the value of the estates in town; and that they had determined to pay the losses of their friends from the estates of the loyalists in the country.' The gentleman refused to join with them, but Warren replied that they would pursue their scheme" (*OPAR*, p. 148). Was Jeffries the "gentleman" referred to by Oliver? If he was, the midnight conversation between the two men appears to have been in line with the earlier impression Timothy Pickering had of Warren after the post–Lexington and Concord meeting on April 20 in Cambridge.

The May 30, 1775, espionage report to Gage describing the North End as "a nest of very wicked fellows" is in *PIR*, 3:1994–95. The espionage report claiming that "the men that go in the ferry-boats are not faithful" is in *PIR*, 4:2776–77. John Adams's memory of how Joseph Warren spoke of "the selfishness of this people, or their impatient eagerness for commissions" is in a February 18, 1811, letter to Josiah Quincy in his *Works*, 9:633; in the same letter Adams also makes the claim that "there is no people on earth so ambitious as the people of America . . . the lowest can aspire as freely as the highest." John Bell's July 30, 2006, entry to his blog *Boston 1775* describes how John Jeffries worked the British patronage system once he moved to London after the evacuation of Boston (http://boston1775.blogspot.com/2006/07/dr-john-jeffries-physician-loyalist_30.html). Edmund Morgan in *Inventing the People* writes of how the "decline of deference and emergence of leadership signaled the beginnings . . . [of] a new way of determining who should stand among the few to govern the many" (p. 302). Joseph Warren's May 14, 1775, letter to Samuel Adams in which he writes of his hope that in the future "the only road to promotion may be through the affection of the people. This being the case, the interest of the governor and the governed will be the same" is reprinted in Frothingham's *LJW*, pp. 483–84.

The statement that Warren had "fully resolved that his future service should be in the military line" is also in *LJW*, p. 510, as is the statement that Warren was "proposed as a physician-general; but preferring a more active and hazardous employment, he accepted a major-general's commission" (p. 504). Allen French writes that the "choice of Joseph Warren [as major general] was strange. . . . Not one high office had yet been given to an inexperienced man. . . . But such were his enthusiasm and magnetism, and so great was the confidence felt in his talents and devotion, that the position was given him, with tragic results" (*FYAR*, pp. 72–73). French claims that Warren's only relevant experience was his time with the Committee of Safety but makes no reference to his conspicuous role on April 19 and his presence at the skirmishes at Grape Island and Chelsea Creek. French also writes of Heath's less than enthusiastic reaction to Warren's elevation to major general despite Warren's letter to him "urging him to apply for his colonelcy. . . . Stubbornly, perhaps, Heath made no move" (p. 73). Warren's June 16, 1775, letter to Heath is reprinted in *LJW*, p. 507. In his June 16 diary entry Ezekiel Price writes, "Colonel Richmond from the Congress says that Dr. Warren was chosen a major-general; that Heath was not chosen any office, but it was supposed that no difficulty would arise from it" (p. 190). John Adams's statement that Joseph Warren "made a harangue in the form of a charge . . . to every officer, upon the delivery of his commission, and that he never failed to make the officer as well as all the assembly shudder" is in *Works*, 3:12.

Allen French writes of the June 13 warning from the New Hampshire Committee of Safety about a report from "a gentleman of undoubted veracity" concerning an attack on Dorchester Heights on June 18 in *FYAR*, p. 209. Daniel Putnam recounts the conversation that Joseph Warren had with Putnam and others about Putnam's early proposal to entrench Bunker Hill in his "Letter Relative to the Battle of Bunker Hill," pp. 248–49. Allen French relates the process by which provincial leaders came to the decision to reinforce Bunker Hill on June 17 in *FYAR*, pp. 211–14; French repeats the claim that portions of Charlestown Neck were only thirty feet wide (p. 220). According to Francis Parker in *Colonel William Prescott: The Commander in the Battle of Bunker's Hill*, "a serious engagement was neither intended nor expected as a result of the entrenching expedition," adding that the decision to build on Breed's Hill "was to change the whole character of the expedition" (p. 11). Samuel Gray, writing from Roxbury on July 12, 1775, makes the claim that "one general and the engineer were of opinion we ought not to entrench on Charlestown [i.e., Breed's] Hill till we had thrown up some works on the north and south ends of Bunker Hill, to cover our men on their retreat . . . but on the pressing importunity of the other general officer, it was consented to begin as was done," in the appendix to *HSOB*, p. 394. Ebenezer Bancroft, in John Hill's *Bi-Centennial of Old Dunstable*, believed it was Putnam who voted to go with Breed's instead of Bunker Hill: "The dispute which delayed the commencing of the work was probably on the part of Prescott insisting that his orders were to fortify Bunker's Hill, and Putnam and Gridley insisting that Breed's Hill was the proper place" (p. 66). Prescott's son, however, saw it differently: "Colonel Prescott conferred with his officers and Colonel Gridley as to the place intended for the fortification; but Colonel Prescott took on himself the responsibility of deciding, as well he might, for on him it would rest"; Frothingham, *The Battle Field of Bunker Hill*, p. 29. In an August 25, 1775, letter to John Adams, William Prescott makes the technically inaccurate statement "I received orders to march to Breed's Hill. . . . The lines were drawn by the engineer and we began the entrenchment about 12 o'clock," in the appendix to *HSOB*, p. 395. The Committee of Safety's account of the battle, in which they refer to the placement of the redoubt on Breed's Hill being "some mistake," is also in the appendix to *HSOB*, p. 382. In a July 20, 1775, letter to Samuel Adams, John Pitts wrote in French, *FYAR*, "Never was more confusion and less command," adding, "No one appeared to have any but Col. Prescott whose bravery can never be enough acknowledged and applauded" (p. 228). French also describes the dimensions of the redoubt in *FYAR*, p. 216.

Amos Farnsworth recounts how he and the others had "orders not to shut our eyes" as they waited in the Charlestown town house as sentries patrolled the waterfront and those on Breed's Hill dug the redoubt in the early morning of June 17 in his *Diary*, p. 83. In Frothingham, *The Battle-Field of Bunker Hill*, William Prescott's son tells of his father's being "delighted to hear 'All is well,' drowsily repeated by the watch on board the king's ships" (p. 19). Henry Clinton's claim that "in the evening of the 16th I saw them at work, reported it to Genls Gage and Howe and advised a landing in two divisions at day break" is quoted in French, *FYAR*, pp. 209–10. According to Howe, Clinton wasn't the only one who heard the provincials digging that night: "The sentries on the Boston side had heard the rebels at work all night without making any other report of it, except mention it in conversation" (*CKG*, p. 221). Peter Brown's June 28, 1775, letter to his mother is quoted in *Literary Diary of Ezra Stiles*, 1:595–96. On the death of Asa Pollard, see Samuel Swett's *History of Bunker Hill Battle*, p. 22; Swett also cites a claim that Pollard's heart "continued beating for some time after it was cut out of him by the cannonball" (p. 52). Prescott's son tells in Frothingham's *Battle-Field of Bunker Hill* how his father "mounted the parapet, walked leisurely backwards and forwards . . . It had the effect intended. The men soon became indifferent to the fire of the artillery" (pp. 19–20); Prescott's son also wrote of his father's determination to *"never be taken alive"* (p. 26). Prescott tells of how Gridley "forsook me" in an August 25, 1775, letter to John Adams in the appendix to *HSOB*, pp. 395–97. John Brooks, the twenty-three-year-old doctor who carried Prescott's call for reinforcements to General Ward, later became governor of Massachusetts, and in 1818 he along with several of his staff walked Breed's Hill, where he told William Sumner about Prescott's histrionics on the redoubt wall; William Sumner, "Reminiscences of Gen. Warren and Bunker Hill," p. 228. Prescott's son recounts his father's stubborn insistence that the men who had built the redoubt "should have the honor of defending [it]"; Frothingham, *Battle-Field of Bunker Hill*, p. 19.

The claim that if Gage and Howe had followed Clinton's advice they would have "shut [the provincials] up in the peninsula as in a bag" appears in a July 5, 1775, letter from an anonymous British officer in *SSS*, p. 135; this same account discusses the lack of reconnaissance on Howe's part and its tragic consequences. In a June 20, 1775, letter, Lord Rawdon writes in *SSS* that the "men-of-war in the harbor could not elevate their guns sufficiently to bear upon [the redoubt]" (p. 130). Prescott's son told of Gage's conversation with Prescott's brother-in-law Abijah Willard in Frothingham's *Battle-Field of Bunker Hill*, p. 26–27. Paul Lockhardt in *The Whites of Their Eyes* is justifiably skeptical that this interchange ever occurred, claiming that "the idea that Willard could have seen and recognized Prescott, given the primitive optics of the day and the amount of gunsmoke that must have hung in the air, seems implausible at best" (footnote, p. 227). However, given that Prescott was dressed in a much-commented-on banyan (a loose-fitting coat), facial recognition probably was not required, and I'm inclined to believe the anecdote, particularly given the source and my own experience with telescopes from the eighteenth century.

The activities of the Committee of Safety on June 17 can be traced to a limited extent in its minutes in *JEPC*, p. 570. Charles Martyn provides a useful analysis of the activities at Hastings House involving General Ward and the Committee of Safety in *The Life of Artemas Ward*, pp. 125–27, as does Paul Lockhardt in *The Whites of Their Eyes*, pp. 231–33. According to Samuel Swett, soon after the arrival of Major Brooks, Richard Devens's "importunity with the general and the Committee [of Safety] for an ample reinforcement was impassioned and vehement, and his opinion partially prevailed; the committee recommended a reinforcement, and the general consented that orders should be dispatched immediately to Colonels Reed and Stark"; *History of Bunker Hill Battle*, p. 25. There are several accounts of Warren stating that it was his intention to join the fighting at Bunker Hill. Warren's roommate Elbridge Gerry later told his biographer that Warren "entrusted to Mr. Gerry alone the secret of his intention to be on the field"; James Austin, *The Life of Elbridge Gerry*, 1:79. Warren's apprentice David Townsend tells of Warren being "sick with one of his oppressive nervous headaches and, as usual, had retired to rest" in Hastings House on the morning of June 17; "Reminiscence of Gen. Warren," p. 230. William Heath writes of Putnam and Prescott's interchange about the entrenching tools in his *Memoirs*, p. 13. Ebenezer Bancroft's account of using a cannon to blast out an embrasure is in his *Narrative* in John Hill's *Bi-Centennial of Old Dunstable*, pp. 59–60. Bancroft later learned that the two cannonballs he had fired through the redoubt sailed all the way into Boston, with one landing harmlessly in Brattle Square, the other on Cornhill (p. 60). In a June 19, 1775, letter to Isaac Smith Jr., Andrew Eliot describes the provincials being "up to the chin entrenched" (p. 288). Colonel Jones's June 19, 1775, account of what he appears to have seen while watching with Generals Burgoyne and Clinton on Copp's Hill is in Frothingham's *Battle-Field of Bunker Hill*, pp. 45–46. Burgoyne tells of his concern that the battle might result in "a final loss to the British Empire in America" in his June 25, 1775, letter to Lord Stanley in *SSS*, pp. 133–34.

Chapter Ten—**The Battle**

John Chester's account of the alarm in Cambridge and of how he and his men hid their uniforms beneath their civilian clothes is in the appendix to *HSOB*, pp. 390–91. A transcript of Azor Orne's June 17, 1775, letter to General John Thomas in which he tells Thomas to "judge whether this is designed to deceive or not" is in a February 7, 2012, auction lot description, http://www.nhinsider.com/press-releases/2012/2/7/rare-documents-artifacts-of-new-hampshire-representative-up.html. On the confusion emanating from Ward's headquarters in Cambridge, see French's *FYAR*, pp. 246–47. On the mechanics of firing a cannon, I have looked to Michael McAfee's *Artillery of the American Revolution*, p. 16, and S. James Gooding's *An Introduction to British Artillery*, p. 38. Peter Brown writes of the artillery officer swinging his hat around his head in his June 28, 1775, letter to his mother in *Diary of Ezra Stiles*, 1:595–96. Richard Ketchum in *Decisive Day* cites a June 22, 1775, letter that describes how the rebels fell to the ground when they saw the flash of the British cannon (p. 250); Ketchum also cites James Thacher's account of how cannon balls "are clearly visible in the form of a black ball in the day, but at night they appear like a fiery meteor with a blazing tail," and how "When a shell falls, it whirls around, burrows, and excavates the earth to a considerable extent" (p. 249). Prescott recounts how he "ordered the train, with two field-pieces" to go and oppose the landing of the British in his August 25, 1775, letter to John Adams in the appendix to *HSOB*, p. 395. French provides an excellent summary of the various descriptions of the rail fence in a footnote in French's *FYAR*, p. 227. Howe describes the rail fence as "cannon proof" in his June 22–24, 1775, letter in *CKG*, p. 221.

My account of John Stark is based on Caleb Stark's *Memoir and Correspondence of General John Stark*, pp. 11–29, and Ben Rose's *John Stark*, pp. 9–51. Frothingham in *HSOB* describes Andrew McClary as "of an athletic frame," p. 186. Peter Brown tells of three men being cut in half by a single cannonball in his letter in *Diary of Ezra Stiles*, 1:595–96. Henry Dearborn tells of Stark's insistence that they maintain a "very deliberate pace" across Charlestown Neck in "An Account of the Battle of Bunker Hill," pp. 6–7. The description of Putnam's "summer dress" is in Henry Dawson's *Gleanings*, pt. 4, p. 157. Francis Jewett Parker describes Putnam as "one to whom constant motion was almost a necessity" in *Colonel William Prescott*, p. 18. James Wilkinson walked the battlefield with John Stark after the evacuation and his account, not published until 1816, was based on notes taken during that interview; in Charles Coffin's *History of the Battle of Breed's Hill*, Wilkinson describes how Stark directed "his boys" to build the stone wall at the Mystic River beach (pp. 9–17). Samuel Swett cites a Dr. Snow's claim that "rivalry and jealousy" existed not only between Stark and Putnam but also between Stark and Reed in *History of Bunker Hill Battle*, supplement, p. 9; Swett also cites Reverend William Bentley's claim that Stark said that if Putnam had "done his duty, he would have decided the fate of his country in the first action," as well as Stark's description of the redoubt as "the pen" and "the want of judgment in the works" (supplement, p. 9). Allen French discusses how "localism" was a persistent problem during the early days of the provincial army in *FYAR*, pp. 60–61. Francis Parker in *Colonel William Prescott* writes of the presence of "too much intercolonial jealousy" among the provincial ranks (p. 20).

David Townsend recounts his finding Joseph Warren at Hastings House in "Reminiscence of Gen. Warren," p. 230. As Samuel Forman points out in a personal communication, Townsend, like William Eustis, was one of Warren's medical apprentices, and in the months after Warren's death, both Townsend and Eustis ended up paying Sally Edwards's bills at the Ames tavern. Since Townsend's is the only account we have of Warren at Hastings House on June 17, the possibility exists that Townsend was, in Forman's words, "covering for Warren, who *maybe* did go to Dedham that morning." Warren's claim that he "should die were I to remain at home while my fellow citizens are shedding their blood for me" is in Samuel Swett's *History of Bunker Hill Battle*, p. 25. Jeremy Belknap was told by Joseph Henderson, who was a clerk of "the board of war" during the battle, about how Warren "was very desirous to go" to Breed's Hill and how he deceived his associates when "he pretended that he was going to Roxbury," in "Extracts from Dr. Belknap's Note-books," pp. 91–98. Edward Warren writes about his conversation with a woman who claimed that Joseph Warren visited her pregnant mother on the day of the Battle of Bunker Hill, in *The Life of John Warren*, pp. 22. Allen French discusses Howe's strategy and quotes the oft-cited words of Howe's mentor James Wolfe on how to attack an entrenchment, in *FYAR*, pp. 234–35; French also cites Clinton's account of how the floating batteries were unsuccessfully moved over to the Mystic River, p. 230. Burgoyne describes Howe's deployment of troops as "perfect" in his June 25, 1775, letter to Lord Stanley in *SSS*, pp. 133; Burgoyne also describes how he and Clinton on Copp's Hill received the order to burn Charlestown. The detail that one British carcass "fell short near the ferry way;

a second fell in the street, and the town was on fire" is in Samuel Swett's *History of Bunker Hill Battle*, p. 38, as is the mention of the detachment of men from the *Somerset*. Henry Dearborn writes in "An Account of the Battle of Bunker Hill" of how the smoke from Charlestown "hung like a thundercloud" (p. 9). According to John Clarke, who quotes Howe's speech to his officers and soldiers in Samuel Drake's *Bunker Hill: The Story Told in Letters*, Howe made his remarks as Charlestown went up in flames beside them (p. 43). The presence of "innumerable swallows" is mentioned in a footnote in Samuel Swett's *History of Bunker Hill Battle*, p. 33. William Prescott in his August 25, 1775, letter writes of being left with "perhaps 150 men in the fort" in the appendix to *HSOB*, p. 396. Ebenezer Bancroft in his Narrative, in John Hill's *Bi-Centennial of Old Dunstable*, writes of how "our men turned their heads every minute to look on the one side . . . for the reinforcements" (p. 60).

A June 26, 1775, letter from an unnamed American tells of the provincials being "arrayed in red worsted caps and blue great coats, with guns of different sizes," in *LAR*, p. 150; this same writer speaks of Joseph Warren having "dressed himself like Lord Falkland in his wedding suit and distinguished himself by unparalleled acts of bravery during the whole action" (p. 151). Falkland was a royalist during the English Civil War who, growing increasingly disillusioned with the conflict, reputedly courted death and was killed in the Battle of Newbury in 1643. On Warren's activities after leaving Townsend prior to crossing Charlestown Neck, see Frothingham's *LJW*, pp. 513–15. Samuel Swett tells how Warren was greeted in the redoubt "with loud hurrahs," p. 32. James Wilkinson is the source for Warren's words to Prescott, reported to Wilkinson by Warren's apprentice William Eustis, who was at the redoubt that day, in *History of the Battle of Breed's Hill*, p. 15. John Jeffries's claim that the younger son of John Lovell, loyalist master of the Boston Latin School, was responsible for the improperly sized cannonballs is in Samuel Swett's *History of Bunker Hill Battle*, supplement, p. 24. The terrain through which the regulars advanced toward the provincial forces is described in "The Criticism of the Battle . . . , August 3, 1779" in the appendix to *HSOB*, p. 399. Henry Clinton's description of Howe's troop formation as "one long straggling line two deep" is cited by Allen French in *FYAR*, p. 235. Burgoyne's description of Charlestown burning is in his June 25, 1775, letter to Lord Stanley in *SSS*, pp. 133–34. Henry Lee writes of "the conflagration of a town . . . blazing in their faces," in "Reflections on the Campaign of Sir William Howe," in Charles Coffin's *History of the Battle of Breed's Hill*, p. 8. John Eliot's claim that Joseph Warren believed Britain "never would send large armies" is in *Brief Biographical Sketches*, p. 472.

Prescott's son recounts how his father told the men in the redoubt to hold their fire and "aim at their *hips*," in Frothingham's *Battle-Field of Bunker Hill*, p. 20. Ebenezer Bancroft recounts how Prescott instructed them "to take particular notice of the *fine coats*" in John Hill's *Bi-Centennial of Old Dunstable*, p. 61. James Wilkinson recounts how Stark had made a mark in the bank along the Mystic to indicate when the provincials should open up on the British; Stark also recounted how he had told his men to hold their fire till they saw the enemy's "half-gaiters" in Charles Coffin's *History of the Battle of Breed's Hill*, p. 13. Philip Johnson remembered Putnam saying,

"Don't fire till you see the whites of their eyes," in Samuel Swett's *History of Bunker Hill Battle*, supplement, p. 17. Wilkinson describes how the Fusiliers advanced "as if not apprised of what awaited them," in Charles Coffin's *History of the Battle of Breed's Hill*, p. 13. On the formation of the provincials behind the stone wall, John Elting writes, "Most of the American infantry originally seems to have been formed in the usual three ranks behind their defenses, each rank to fire in turn on order and then drop back to reload so that a steady fire could be maintained," in *The Battle of Bunker's Hill*, p. 31. The description of "a continued sheet of fire" from the provincials is in a July 5, 1775, letter from an unnamed British officer quoted by French in *FYAR*, p. 239. A British surgeon named Grant writes in a June 23, 1775, letter that given the large number of men "wounded in the legs, we are inclined to believe it was their design, not wishing to kill them, but leave them as burdens on us, to exhaust our provisions and engage our attention, as well as intimidate the rest of the soldiery," in *LAR*, p. 141; Grant also complains that the provincials charged their muskets "with old nails and angular pieces of iron." Stark's description of the dead at the beach being as "thick as sheep in a fold" is in Wilkinson's account in Charles Coffin's *History of the Battle of Breed's Hill*, p. 13. Peter Thacher was the minister watching from the opposite shore of the Mystic River; his observations became the basis of the Committee of Safety's account in the appendix to *HSOB*, pp. 382–83.

Howe tells how the grenadiers disobeyed orders and stopped to fire at the provincial lines in his June 22–24, 1775, letter in *CKG*, p. 222. A provincial soldier's claim that "there was no need of waiting for a chance to fire" comes from an account in the August 3, 1775, *Rivington Gazette* in the Appendix to *HSOB*, p. 397. Henry Dearborn tells how the provincials sought out the British officers in "An Account of the Battle of Bunker Hill," p. 11. John Clarke's account of the rebel sharpshooter who killed or wounded "no less than 20 officers" is in Samuel Drake's *Bunker Hill*, pp. 48–49. John Chester writes of the disorder they found on Bunker Hill in a July 22, 1775, letter in the appendix to *HSOB*, p. 391. Samuel Webb writes of the terrifying scene as they descended "into the valley from off Bunker Hill," in a July 11, 1775, letter in Frothingham, *The Battle-Field of Bunker Hill*, p. 33. The description of "an incessant stream of fire" from the provincials and of the futility of attempting to advance is from a July 5, 1775, letter from an unnamed British officer, quoted by French in *FYAR*, p. 239. Samuel Swett in *History of Bunker Hill Battle* writes of how the regulars piled the bodies of their dead into a "horrid breastwork," claiming that his information came from "Mr. Smith of Salem," and was "unquestionable" (p. 37). An unnamed officer in a June 19, 1775, letter writes "we may say with Falstaff . . . that 'they make us here but food for gunpowder,' " in *LAR*, p. 136. Samuel Swett writes about how Captain Ford brought up an abandoned cannon to the American lines in *History of Bunker Hill Battle*, p. 31; in the supplement to this work he also includes the testimony of several men who saw Putnam firing one of the abandoned fieldpieces (pp. 6, 16) as well as Amos Foster's account of Hill, "a British deserter," shouting "You have made a furrow through them!" (p. 14).

According to Samuel Swett's *History of Bunker Hill Battle*, Prescott was assisted by both Colonels Robinson and Buttrick (both of whom were at the North Bridge on

April 19) when it came to running "round the top of the parapet and [throwing] up the muskets," p. 34. Peter Brown writes of how the regulars "found a choky mouthful of us" in his June 28, 1775, letter to his mother quoted in *Diary of Ezra Stiles*, 1:595–96. Prescott writes in an August 25, 1775, letter of how he "commanded a cessation till the enemy advanced within 30 yards, when we gave them such a hot fire that they were obliged to retire nearly 150 yards," in the appendix to *HSOB*, p. 396. The reference to Pigot's force being "staggered" is in a July 5, 1775, letter from an unnamed British officer quoted by French in *FYAR*, p. 239. Frothingham in *HSOB* quotes an article in a British journal that recounts that Howe's servant (a "Mr. Evans") "attended the whole time with wine and other necessaries . . . during which, Evans had one of the bottles in his hand dashed to pieces, and got a contusion on one of his arms at the same time, by a ball from some of the provincials," p. 199. In a June 23, 1775, letter an unnamed officer writes that "for near a minute [Howe] was quite alone," in *LAR*, p. 144. Howe tells of experiencing "a moment I have never felt before" in his June 22–24, 1775, letter in *CKG*, p. 222.

Lord Rawdon recounts how the men "at last grew impatient and all crying out, 'Push on! Push on!' advanced" in a June 20, 1775, letter in *SSS*, pp. 130. Prescott's son writes of Howe marching at the head of his troops, "distinguished . . . by his figure and gallant bearing," in Frothingham, *The Battle-Field of Bunker Hill*, p. 22. A provincial soldier whose letter appeared in the August 3, 1775, *Rivington Gazette* writes of the "extraordinary deep files" of the British column during the third and final advance and how the regulars "pushed over the walls with their guns in their left hand and their swords in their right," in the appendix to *HSOB*, p. 398; this same soldier writes of how the dust and smoke in the redoubt made it "so dark in the square that he was obliged to feel about for the outlet." In a July 11, 1775, letter Samuel Webb writes that "Fight, conquer, or die was what [the British] officers was plainly heard to say very often," in Frothingham, *The Battle-Field of Bunker Hill*, p. 32. Samuel Swett recounts how the British used artillery to "turn the left of the breastwork [and] to enfilade the line," in *History of Bunker Hill Battle*, p. 41. Thacher's account of how those behind the breastwork were forced to "retire within their little fort" is in the Committee of Safety's Account in the appendix to *HSOB*, p. 383. Wilkinson tells of Stark's decision to "retreat reluctantly" in Charles Coffin's *History of the Battle of Breed's Hill*, p. 14. Prescott's son recounts how his father told his men to make "every shot . . . *tell*" and how they broke open an abandoned cartridge in Frothingham's *Battle-Field of Bunker Hill*, pp. 21–22. John Clarke recounts the inspiring words a grenadier sergeant delivered to the surviving privates in his company, as well as the testimony of a marine captain as to how this was on three accounts the "hottest" action he'd ever experienced, in Samuel Drake's *Bunker Hill*, pp. 46, 49–50.

Adjutant John Waller's account of the fighting comes from two different accounts: the first written on June 21, 1775, at MHS, and the second written on June 22, 1775, and in Samuel Drake's *Bunker Hill*, pp. 28–30. Captain George Harris writes of his vegetable garden in a June 12, 1775, letter printed in Stephen Lushington, *The Life and Services of General Lord Harris*, p. 40, which also includes his account of being wounded on the parapet of the redoubt (pp. 41–42). Henry Dearborn tells of how every regular who first mounted the parapet was shot down in "Account of Bunker Hill," p. 8. Allen French quotes from an August 3, 1775, letter written by Lord Rawdon in which he describes the tenacity of the provincials in the redoubt, in *FYAR*, pp. 247–48. Needham Maynard's account of how the provincial fire "went out like an old candle" is in J. H. Temple's *History of Framingham*, p. 291. Ebenezer Bancroft writes of firing his last shot at a British officer and his struggle to escape the redoubt in "Bunker Hill Battle" in John Hill's *Bi-Centennial of Old Dunstable*, pp. 61–62. On the possibility that Major Pitcairn was killed not by Bancroft but by the African American Salem Poor, see the evidence presented by J. L. Bell in *Washington's Headquarters*, pp. 279–81. Samuel Paine's June 22, 1775, account of what he saw from Beacon Hill is in AAS *Proceedings* 19 (1908–9):435–38. Thomas Sullivan compares the provincial soldiers to "bees in a beehive" in "The Common British Soldier—from the Journal of Thomas Sullivan 49th Regiment of Foot," p. 233. Prescott's son describes his father's sword-wielding exit from the redoubt in Frothingham's *Battle-Field of Bunker Hill*, p. 22.

Mercy Otis Warren claims that Joseph Warren chose "rather to die in the field than to grace the victory of his foes by the triumph they would have enjoyed in his imprisonment," in *History of the . . . American Revolution*, p. 122. As Samuel Forman points out in *DJW*, given that he died with several important letters in his pocket, it's highly unlikely that he sought death (p. 305). On the possible circumstances surrounding Warren's death, see Frothingham's *LJW*, pp. 517–20. Based on a photograph that survives of Warren's skull, in which the entry wound of the bullet is clearly visible, Samuel Forman has determined that Warren must have been killed by an officer's pistol instead of a regular's musket, thus making one of the accounts collected by Frothingham (in which an officer's servant seizes his pistol and shoots Warren in the face) the likeliest of the many scenarios that have been attributed to Warren's death, in Forman's *DJW*, pp. 303–4, 365–66. Samuel Swett cites the Reverend Daniel Chaplin and John Bullard's claim that Prescott asked Putnam, "Why did you not support me?" in *History of Bunker Hill Battle*, supplement, p. 9. Prescott's son relates that his father assured Ward that "the enemy's confidence would not be increased by the result of the battle," in Frothingham's *Battle-Field of Bunker Hill*, p. 23. Howe writes that the victory at Bunker Hill was "too dearly bought" in his June 22–24, 1775, letter in *CKG*, p. 223. The reference to the soldiers being "charmed with General Howe's gallant behavior" is in a June 19, 1775, letter written by an unnamed British naval officer, in *LAR*, p. 137. Swett attributes the detail that Howe "at last received a ball in the foot" to Dr. John Jeffries, in *History of Bunker Hill Battle*, p. 42. Charles Lee writes of the effect of this "murderous day" on Howe in Charles Coffin's *History of the Battle of Breed's Hill*, p. 8. Dr. John Jeffries's account of identifying Warren's body and Howe's response are given in Samuel Swett's *History of Bunker Hill Battle*, p. 58.

Chapter Eleven—**The Fiercest Man**

The reference to the vehicles used to transport dead and wounded British soldiers is from "Clarke's Narrative," in Samuel Drake's *Bunker Hill: The Story Told in Letters*, p. 49. Peter Oliver's description of the mortally wounded officer is in *OPAR*, pp. 127–28. Rufus Greene writes of the funeral of "Uncle Coffin" in a July 3, 1775, letter in *Journal of Mrs. John Amory*, p. 82. Jonathan Sewall writes of the omnipresence of death in Boston in a July 15, 1775, letter cited in French's *FYAR*, pp. 337–38; French also discusses Clinton's unsuccessful attempt to convince Gage to take Dorchester Heights, p. 260. The letter from the British officer who writes of how they "shall soon be driven from the ruins of our victory" is in *LAR*, pp. 140–41. Allen French in *FYAR* relates the account of the dying Lieutenant Colonel Abercrombie claiming that "we have fought in a bad cause," p. 318. In a November 1, 1775, letter that appeared in the *Calendar of Home Office Papers, 1773–1775*, edited by Richard Arthur Roberts, an unnamed correspondent in Perth Amboy, New Jersey, recounts a conversation with Margaret Gage "the day after that dreadful one, when you thought the lines so expressive," then quotes the relevant passage from Shakespeare's *King John*, p. 479. Gage writes of his wish that "this cursed place was burned" in a June 26, 1775, letter to Lord Barrington in *Correspondence of Thomas Gage*, pp. 686–67. John Warren writes of his desperate attempts to find out his brother's fate at Bunker Hill in his diary, which is quoted in Edward Warren's *Life of John Warren*, pp. 45–46; according to his son, the sentry's bayonet thrust gave John Warren a scar "which he bore through life." John Eliot writes of the "sincere lamentation and mourning" after Joseph Warren's death in *Brief Biographical Sketches*, p. 473. Frothingham in *LJW* quotes Samuel Adams's letter to his wife about the "greatly afflicting" news of Warren's death (p. 521). John Adams writes of Warren taking on "too much for mortal" in a July 6, 1775, letter to James Warren in *Warren-Adams Letters*, 1:74; Adams continues in that letter: "This accumulation of admiration upon one gentleman, which among the Hebrews was called idolatry, has deprived us forever of the services of one of our best and ablest men. We have not a sufficient number of such men left to be prodigal of their lives in future." Abigail Adams writes of the profound sense of loss felt in the wake of Joseph Warren's death in a July 5, 1775, letter in *Adams Family Correspondence* 1:240.

In a June 20, 1775, letter to John Adams (also in *Warren-Adams Letters*), James Warren claims that "had a Lee or a Washington instead of a general destitute of all military ability [i.e., Artemas Ward]" been in command at Bunker Hill, the battle "would have terminated with as much glory to America as the 19th of April," p. 63. Samuel Gray writes of the battle being of "infinite service to us" in a July 12, 1775, letter in *HSOB*, p. 394. The reference to the provincial soldiers returning to Cambridge "like troops elated with conquest" is in a June 23, 1775, anonymous letter in *LAR*, p. 142. Nathanael Greene writes of wishing to sell the British "another hill at the same price" in a June 28, 1775, letter in *PNG*, p. 92. George Washington's insistence that he did not "think myself equal" to commanding the American army is from a June 16, 1775, "Address to the Continental Congress," in *PGW*, 1:1. Allen French describes Washington's positive response to the news of Bunker Hill ("Then the liberties of our country are safe") in *FYAR*, p. 267. Peter Thomas in *Tea Party to Independence* describes how the ministry quickly decided after hearing about Bunker Hill on July 25 that New York, not Boston, should "become the seat of the war," p. 270. Eliphalet Dyer describes Washington as "sober, steady, and calm" in a June 17, 1775, letter in *PGW*, 1:3. Ron Chernow cites Gilbert Stuart's description of Washington as "the fiercest man among the savage tribes" in *Washington: A Life*, p. xix.

My account of Washington's early military experience is indebted to Chernow's biography, Joseph Ellis's *His Excellency George Washington*, David Clary's *George Washington's First War*, Edward Lengel's *General Washington: A Military Life*, and Fred Anderson's *Crucible of War*, as well as his article "The Hinge of the Revolution: George Washington Confronts a People's Army." Washington's letter to Governor Dinwiddie claiming that his "troops of Virginia" were "as regular a corps as any upon the continent" is cited by Ellis in *His Excellency George Washington*, p. 26; Ellis also argues that Washington was in "emotional turmoil" during the Forbes campaign "because he had fallen in love with one woman and was about to marry another," p. 35. Fred Anderson writes of Washington's effort to "become more British than the British," in "The Hinge of the Revolution," p. 42. Gouverneur Morris's description of Washington having passions that were "almost too mighty for man" is in an "Oration upon the Death of General Washington," in *Eulogies and Orations on the Life and Death of General George Washington*, pp. 44–45. James Thacher's description of first seeing Washington is in his *Military Journal*, p. 30. Washington's stepson George Custis's description of the general's "surpassing grip with his knees" is cited by Richard Brookhiser in *George Washington: Founding Father*, p. 111; Brookhiser also cites Benjamin Rush's claim that the typical European king would "look like a valet de chamber by his side," 114. John Trumbull's description of being temporarily part of "the family of one of the most distinguished and dignified men of the age" is in his *Autobiography*, p. 23. On daily life at Washington's headquarters, see J. L. Bell's *General George Washington's Headquarters and Home*, especially pp. 163–84.

Fred Anderson writes insightfully about Washington's reaction to the provincial army in "The Hinge of the Revolution," commenting that in "the New Englanders' squalid camps . . . Washington saw the symbol of a mixed multitude in peril of becoming a mob" (p. 29). On the Native American composition of the provincial army, particularly the "Stockbridge Indians," see Colin Calloway's *The American Revolution in Indian Country*, pp. 85–94. William Emerson's account of the soldiers' living quarters, including his description of a meal with the Stockbridge Indians in their wigwams, is in a July 7, 1775, letter included in his *Diary*, pp. 80–81. Washington calls the New Englanders "exceeding dirty and nasty people" and describes their "unaccountable kind of stupidity" in letters to Lund Washington on August 20, 1775, and Richard Henry Lee on August 29, 1775, both in *PGW*, 1:336, 372. On Charles Lee's differing reaction to the typical American militiaman, see John Shy's "Charles Lee: The Soldier as Radical" in *George Washington's Generals and Opponents*, edited by George Billias; according to Shy, "Washington and Lee looked at the same troops but where the Virginia planter saw only surliness and disobedience, the British radical saw alertness and zeal" (p. 34). In an October 21, 1775, entry in his journal, Jeremy Belknap records that Horatio Gates "said he never desired to see better soldiers than the New England men made" (p. 83). My statement that Washington believed the "ultimate aim of an army was . . . not to generate violence but to curtail it" is based in large part on Fred Anderson's assertion in "The Hinge of the Revolution" that "the control, not the propagation, of violence was for him the core of military service. . . . To allow war to become the engine of revolution—would be to imperil the social order, together with all the laws, rights, and liberties that he hoped to preserve"; Anderson also discusses Washington's concerns about recruitment and tour-of-duty as well as his realization that "local sympathies could tear an army to shreds" (pp. 31–34, 44, 45).

Washington writes of making "a pretty good slam" among the officers from Massachusetts in an August 29, 1775, letter to Richard Henry Lee in *PGW*, 1:373. William Emerson writes of the "great overturning in camp" in a July 7, 1775, letter contained in his *Diary*, p. 79. J. L. Bell in *General George Washington's Headquarters* describes how Washington dealt with the difficulties created among his officers by the commissions granted by the Continental Congress in the chapter "Generals Old and New," pp. 87–128; Bell provides an overview of how Washington went about reinventing the provincial army in the chapter "Remaking the Troops into a Continental Army," pp. 219–59; see also his "Engineering a New Artillery Regiment," pp. 287–314. Israel Trask's account of Washington's handling of the two combative riflemen is in John Dann, *The Revolution Remembered*, p. 409. John Sullivan's August 5, 1775, letter in which he tells of Washington's stunned reaction to the lack of gunpowder is in Thomas Amory's *John Sullivan*, p. 16. Washington writes of how "no consideration upon earth should have induced me to accept this command" in a November 28, 1775, letter to Joseph Reed, in *PGW*, 2:449. Abigail Adams's comment that if Washington wasn't "one of the best-intentioned men . . . he might be a very dangerous one" is cited by Richard Brookhiser in *George Washington*, p. 115. On Washington's efforts to create the beginnings of a navy, see James Nelson's *George Washington's Secret Navy* and Chester Hearn's *George Washington's Schooners*. Allen French provides an account of the beginnings of the Arnold campaign up the Kennebec River to Quebec in *FYAR*, pp. 431–35. On Washington's advocacy of the young Nathanael Greene and the even younger Henry Knox, Ron Chernow in *Washington* writes of how his "meritocratic bent . . . clashed with his aristocratic background and grew more pronounced with time. With Greene and Knox, he encouraged two aspiring young men who bore psychological scars from their childhood" (p. 205).

J. L. Bell describes the various ways that Bostonians, including the swimming barber Richard Carpenter, managed to get in and out of the city in *Washington's Headquarters*, pp. 361–66. Joseph Tinker Buckingham in *Specimens of Newspaper Literature* recounts Benjamin Russell's adventures in Cambridge during the Siege (2:4–5); see also Francis Baylies's *Eulogy on the Honorable Benjamin Russell*, pp. 8–12. Mercy Scollay writes of how the death of Joseph Warren "rendered me for a time incapable of . . . feeling any animating sensations" in a May 21, 1776, letter to John Hancock at CHS. She writes of her "uncertain situation" and her distress at discovering that John Warren had sold his brother's "every feather bed to General Washington" in an August 17, 1775, letter to Dr. Dix in Worcester, also at CHS. Samuel Forman was the first to identify Mercy Scollay as the probable author of "An Elegy, Occasioned by the Death of Major-General Joseph Warren," which he reprints in *DJW*, pp. 376–78. Peter Oliver makes the claim that "Had [Warren] conquered, Washington had remained in obscurity" in *OPAR*, p. 128.

On the history of siege warfare, I have consulted several books by Christopher Duffy—*Siege Warfare*, vols. 1 and 2, and *Fire and Stone: The Science of Fortress Warfare*,

1660–1860—as well as Paul Davis's *Besieged*. Allen French in *FYAR* compares the taking of Plowed Hill to that of Breed's Hill, "but better ordered," p. 481. Peter Oliver describes the "idle business" of the siege in *OPAR*, p. 131. The description of the armies squinting at each other "like wild cats across a gutter" is in a December 4, 1775, letter in *LAR*, p. 231. Nathanael Greene mentions the spears that had been provided in lieu of bayonet-equipped muskets in a November 15, 1775, order: each regiment was to appoint thirty men "to stand ready to push the enemy off the breastwork if they should attempt to get over the parapet into the lines," in *PNG*, 1:151. Washington mentions the many factors contributing to his proposal to attack in his September 8, 1775, "Circular to the General Officers," in *PGW*, 1:432–34. The September 11, 1775, council of war decision that "it was not expedient to make the attempt at present at least" is in *PGW*, 1:450–51. The proceedings of October 18, 1775, are in *PGW*, 2:183–84. The minutes of the conference with the committee from the Continental Congress, in which Washington asks for advice about whether it is "advisable . . . to destroy the troops who propose to winter in Boston," are in *PGW*, 2:190–203. Artemas Ward's August 25, 1775, letter to Washington about Dorchester Heights is in *PGW*, 1:362–63. See Charles Martyn's *Artemas Ward* for a discussion of Ward's largely unacknowledged advocacy of the strategy that ultimately won the Siege and prevented "the hotheaded Virginian . . . [from] wrecking the careful work of Massachusetts patriots" through what would have surely been a disastrous attack on Boston (pp. 171–72).

Benjamin Church's October 3, 1775, letter to Washington, in which he claims he wrote the coded letter "to impress the enemy with a strong idea of our strength and situation," is in *PGW*, 2:85–87. David Kiracofe discusses the philosophical dilemma of both the Massachusetts House of Representatives and the Continental Congress when it came to dealing with Church in "Dr. Benjamin Church and the Dilemma of Treason in Revolutionary Massachusetts," pp. 443–50. Church describes his appearance before the House in "Account of the Examination of Doctor Benjamin Church," pp. 84–94. Clifford Shipton, in his biography of Church in *SHG*, recounts that when Church was confined in the Vassall House (a different house from Washington's headquarters), he carved "B. Church, Jr." in a closet door (12:390). Allen French in *General Gage's Informers* provides a detailed account of the proceedings surrounding Church's arrest and quotes John Adams's comment, "Good God! What shall we say of human nature?" (p. 195). Kiracofe in his "Dilemma of Treason" writes of how Mercy Otis Warren and Abigail Adams felt that a man's personal sins "undermine the very bonds of society," as well as the recognition among many patriots, including Samuel Adams, that Church's infidelities were "notorious" (pp. 455–56). Church's claim that his liberties had been violated by the House of Representatives is in his "Examination," p. 87.

Allen French in *FYAR* quotes the account of the "shocking spectacle" of the Bunker Hill survivors on the *Charming Nancy*, pp. 323–24. Gage writes of "taking the bull by the horns, attacking the enemy in their strong parts," in his June 26, 1775, letter to Barrington in *Correspondence*, p. 687. In a November 26, 1775, letter to Dartmouth, Howe explains that he'll have to delay the evacuation until at least the spring with the assurance that "we are not under the least apprehension of an attack" (*DAR*,

9:191). Boston is described as "the grave of England" in an August 18, 1775, letter in *LAR*, pp. 190–91, which describes as many as thirty bodies being "thrown into a trench at a time, like those of so many dogs." An August 27, 1775, letter, also in *LAR*, asks the question, "Have you forgot us?" (p. 205). Peter Thomas in *Tea Party to Independence* includes Edmund Burke's reference to "the most astonishing market" and the fact that "war . . . is become a sort of substitute for commerce," as well as the remark that were it not for the newspapers, the British people "would hardly know there was a civil war in America" (pp. 270–71). The Old North Meetinghouse, which was demolished and burned by the British, should not be confused with Christ Church of Paul Revere fame, which is often referred to today as "Old North." In his *Diary*, Boston selectman Timothy Newall writes of the many old houses being burned for fuel as well as "the most savage manner" with which the regulars have turned the Old South Meetinghouse into "a riding school," pp. 269–70. Allen French writes of Faneuil Hall's transformation into a playhouse in *FYAR*, p. 537.

My account of the confrontation between Benjamin Hallowell and Admiral Graves is based largely on French's "The Hallowell-Graves Fisticuffs, 1775," pp. 41–45. An August 19, 1775, letter in *LAR*, speaks of Graves's "black eye," p. 195; a December 13, 1775, letter, also in *LAR*, describes how Graves's secretary extorted bribes for fishing permits, p. 238. Ezekiel Price writes of American whaleboat attacks on the Boston lighthouse in his diary on July 20, p. 198, and on July 31, p. 201. John Tilley cites Sandwich's letter telling Graves that he "can never be censured for doing too much" in *The British Navy and the American Revolution*, p. 48. Allen French tells of the burning of Falmouth, Maine (and includes the reference to the town being "one flame"), in *FYAR*, p. 540–43; see also James Nelson's *George Washington's Secret Navy*, pp. 139–47. The outrage created by the burning of Falmouth was so extensive that the incident is even referred to in the catalogue of complaints contained in the Declaration of Independence. The comment that the British were "almost as much blocked up by the sea as we have been . . . by land" is in a December 4, 1775, letter in *LAR*, p. 231. For an account of John Manley's capture of the *Nancy*, see James Nelson's *Washington's Secret Navy*, pp. 207–15. William Heath's November 30, 1775, diary entry about the armaments taken with the *Nancy* is in his *Memoirs*, p. 24. The reference to Graves being a "curse upon the garrison" is in a December 13, 1775, letter in *LAR*, p. 237. The claim that Graves had been "cruelly used" is in a January 20 letter in *LAR*, p. 256. John Tilley agrees with this assessment in *The British Navy and the American Revolution*, claiming that "it is difficult to suggest how any other admiral could have done substantially better [than Graves]. The oafish performance of the North American Squadron was no more than a manifestation of a colossal ineptitude that the next five years were to expose throughout the British naval and military establishments" (p. 66).

Washington writes of being "unable upon any principle to account" for the lack of response on the part of the British in a December 15, 1775, letter to Joseph Reed, in *PGA*, 2:553. According to Maldwyn Jones in "Sir William Howe: Conventional Strategist," in *George Washington's Generals and Opponents*, edited by George Billias, in keeping with common practice in Europe, "Howe closed his mind to the possibility of winter campaigns" (p. 49). I describe the Swamp Fight of 1675 in *Mayflower*, pp. 265–80. Howe's relationship with Joshua Loring Jr.'s wife is described in Bellamy Partridge's *Sir Billy Howe*, pp. 32–34. Maldwyn Jones in "Sir William Howe" cites the letter to Dartmouth in which Howe proposes that the British army "withdraw entirely . . . and leave the colonists to war with each other" and comments, "For a man newly appointed to put down the rebellion, this was an astonishing statement. . . . [A] situation in which he had both to conquer and to pacify appears to have made him uncertain what measure of coercion was to be used" (p. 50). Washington makes the assurances that "order and subordination in time will take place of confusion" in a December 5, 1775, letter to General Philip Schuyler in Albany, N.Y., who was experiencing his own reenlistment and discipline issues and was thinking about resigning, in *PGW*, 2:498. Washington complains of the unwillingness of the soldiers to serve with those from another colony in a November 8, 1775, letter to Joseph Reed in *PGW*, 2:335. Allen French in *FYAR* cites Simeon Lyman's description of Charles Lee's blasphemous recruitment efforts (pp. 514–15). Nathanael Greene in a letter of December 10, 1775, to Samuel Ward tells of the Connecticut soldiers leaving "in shoals" (*PNG*, 1:160). William Gordon in his "Apr. 6, 1776, Letter to Samuel Wilson" writes of it being "the cast of New Englanders . . . to quit the service . . . when the time is expired" (p. 360). Nathanael Greene writes in a November 29, 1775, letter of the "infamous desertion" of the New England soldiers, and in a letter of December 18, 1775, of Washington's unrealistic expectations regarding the provincial army he inherited (*PNG*, 1:154, 163–64). Artemas Ward's letter defending the New Englanders from the criticisms of those "from the southward" is cited by Clifford Shipton in his biography of Ward in *SHG*, 12:335–36. Douglas Southall Freeman in *George Washington* faults Washington for having "devoted too much of his own time to 'paper work' " during the siege and not enough time involving himself in the even more vital recruitment process; given his experience twenty years before in Virginia, it was clear Washington "knew how to make an army out of a congeries of jealous colonial contingents"; therefore he was guilty of a "failure to exercise the full functions of a command-in-chief" while in Cambridge in the fall of 1775 (4:69). Joseph Warren seems to have been guilty of the opposite extreme during the spring of 1775, when the time he spent with the army prevented him from keeping up with the paperwork associated with the Committee of Safety and the Provincial Congress.

Washington writes of giving "most general satisfaction" and of making "my conduct coincide with the wishes of mankind" in a December 15, 1775, letter to Joseph Reed in *PGW*, 2:551–52, and in a January 14, 1776, letter, also to Reed, in *PGW*, 3:87. In a February 10, 1776, letter to Reed (*PGW*, 3:288), Washington reveals, "I have never entertained an idea of an accommodation since I heard of the measures which were adopted in consequences of the Bunkers Hill fight," meaning that he had resigned himself to war back in the fall. This is borne out by Jeremy Belknap's October 19, 1775, observation in his journal that "*independence* was become a favorite point in the army" (p. 78). Nathanael Greene's December 20, 1775, letter speaking of "a declaration of independence" is in *PNG*, p. 167. J. L. Bell discusses Washington's decision to reverse himself on the issue of allowing free blacks to serve in the army in

Washington's Headquarters, pp. 272–76. George Quintal Jr., in *Patriots of Color*, pp. 170–80, cites the petition concerning Salem Poor. As Quintal states, attributing the character and skills of a gentleman officer to an African American was "extraordinary"; Quintal also includes a copy of Poor's manumission document; in addition, he cites a tradition from Andover that Poor shot General Abercromby (as opposed to Pitcairn). J. L. Bell in *Washington's Headquarters* cites the claim by Samuel Swett that Poor shot Major Pitcairn, p. 280. The December 22 resolve from the Continental Congress that Washington could attack Boston "notwithstanding the town . . . be destroyed," is in a footnote in *PGW*, 2:590. Washington did not receive this resolve until early January (as he states in his January 4, 1776, letter to John Hancock in *PGW*, 3:18), but he was clearly operating in anticipation of a congressional blessing to attack Boston when he decided to reverse himself on the issue of free African Americans in the army. On December 31, 1775, Washington wrote to John Hancock and the Continental Congress that "it has been represented to me that the free negroes who have served in this army are very much dissatisfied at being discarded—as it is to be apprehended, that they may seek employ in the ministerial army—I have presumed to depart from the resolution respecting them, and have given license for their being enlisted, if this is disproved of by Congress, I will put a stop to it" (*PGW*, 2:623).

Chapter Twelve—**The Clap of Thunder**
My account of the raising of the Union flag on Prospect Hill is based largely on Peter Ansoff's "The Flag on Prospect Hill," which debunks the legend that Washington raised the horizontally striped Continental Colors on January 1, 1776, on Prospect Hill. As Ansoff writes, the Union Jack had become "a symbol of resistance to British policies" in the colonies (p. 78). Probably the best depiction of the fortifications at Boston Neck are in Lieutenant Page's "A Plan of the town of Boston with entrenchments, etc." Sir Thomas Hyde's "A Plan of the Town of Boston and its Environs with the Lines, Batteries, and Encampments," is also extremely helpful. Samuel Webb in a March 1 diary entry in *Correspondence and Journals*, p. 129, makes the claim that "even the strong fortifications of Gibraltar is said not to equal them, they have cut a canal through the Neck by which Boston is now an island, on the south and west sides they are strongly fortified by a chain of forts." Washington writes of the events of the first of the year in a January 4, 1776, letter to Joseph Reed in *PGW*, in which he says that the broadsides of the speech were "sent out by the Boston gentry"; he also writes of the "farcical" belief on the part of the British soldiers that the Union flag had been raised "as a signal of submission" (3:23–25). Ansoff cites the report of an anonymous ship captain who claimed that the rebels burned a copy of the speech (pp. 84–85), as well as the report of British lieutenant William Carter, who wrote that the rebels "fired 13 guns and gave the like number of cheers" (p. 85).

Richard Frothingham in *HSOB* provides an account of the interrupted performance of *The Blockade of Boston* (p. 27), as does Allen French in *FYAR*, p. 635. The performance is also described in letters written on January 15, and January 20, 1776, in which one correspondent reports how the audience "clapped prodigiously," and the actors called out "to get the paint and smut off their faces" (*LAR*, pp. 255 and 259).

William Gordon writes of how "the ridicule was turned upon themselves" in "Apr. 6, 1776, Letter to Samuel Wilson" (p. 361). Gordon writes of Knowlton's mission crossing "the mill-dam upon the ice" to burn the buildings on the Charlestown peninsula in his *History*, 2:18. Washington writes that "all the generals upon earth should not have convinced me . . . of delaying an attack" in a January 14, 1776, letter to Joseph Reed in *PGW*, 3:90; in the same letter he writes of wishing he had retreated "to the backcountry and lived in a wigwam" rather than taken this command (p. 89). The minutes of the January 16, 1776, council of war in which it was decided that "a vigorous attempt" against the regulars in Boston should be attempted "as soon as practicable" is in *PGW*, 3:103–4.

Henry Knox describes how he and his men "took a comfortable nap" around a roaring fire on Lake George in the December 10 entry of his *Diary*, the original copy of which is at the MHS. Knox's December 17, 1775, letter to Washington in which he describes his efforts to secure forty-two "exceeding strong sleds" and his hope for "a fine fall of snow" is in *PGW*, 2:563–64. Knox writes of Schuyler's refusal to pay the price the original manufacturer of the sleds demanded as well as of the snow being "too deep for the cannon to set out even if the sleds were ready" in a December 28, 1775, entry in his *Diary*, in which he also writes in a January 1–4 entry of "getting holes cut . . . in the river in order to strengthen ice." According to an article in the February 20, 1915, *Albany Evening Journal*, "upward pressure on the ice would cause water to flow through the holes...[and] the clear water would freeze to add thickness to the ice." Knox's January 5, 1775, letter to Washington is in *PGW*, 3:29. Knox writes of the cannon breaking through the ice at Albany and of the eventual rescue of the "drowned cannon . . . , owing to the assistances [of] the good people of the city . . . in return for which we christened her The Albany," in the January 7 and 8, 1776, entries of his *Diary*. The account of Knox's experiences at Westfield is in John Becker, *The Sexagenary: or Reminiscences of the American Revolution*, pp. 34–35. J. L. Bell provides an excellent account of Knox's ascendancy to colonel of the artillery regiment in *Washington's Headquarters*, in which he cites Thomas Crafts's December 16, 1775, letter of outrage (pp. 302–9).

Jeduthan Baldwin writes of his efforts to build a fortification at Lechmere Point in his *Diary*, pp. 18–28, including his observation on February 13 that Washington "found a good bridge of ice to Boston." The minutes of the February 16, 1776, council of war are in *PGW*, 3:320–22. William Gordon's account of how Ward opposed Washington's proposal with a counterproposal to take Dorchester Heights is in his *History*, 2:24–25. Horatio Gates's notes on the meeting are reprinted in a footnote in *PGW*, 3:323. William Heath recounts how he opposed Washington's proposal to attack Boston in the event Howe decided to attack the fortifications on Dorchester Heights in his *Memoir*, p. 31. The "Plan for Attacking Boston" drawn up by Putnam, Sullivan, Greene, and Gates is in *PGW*, 3:332–33. Washington's February 26, 1776, letter to Joseph Reed complaining of the council of war's rejection of his original proposal to attack Boston and his hope that the British "will be so kind as to come out to us" once he occupies Dorchester Heights is in *PGW*, 3:370. Washington's February 18, 1776, letter to John Hancock in which he admits that "the irksomeness of my situation" may have put too much "to hazard" is in *PGW*, 3:335–36. Nathanael Greene's summation of what an attack on Boston might accomplish can be found in *PNG*, 1:194. Rufus Putnam describes how he came up with the idea of using chandeliers to build a fortification atop Dorchester Heights in his *Memoirs*, pp. 54–58. Although Putnam claims the book he borrowed from Heath was John Muller's *Field Engineer*, it was, in all probability, Muller's *Attack and Defenses of Fortified Places*, which contains both a definition and a picture of a chandelier in its early pages, which is not true of his *Field Engineer*, which is a translation of a work by M. le Chevalier De Clairac. Rufus Putnam's early proposal of creating a stone and timber blind along Dorchester Neck is described in his February 11, 1776, letter to Washington, in *PGW*, 3:295–98.

Heath writes of how William Davis was responsible for the idea of filling barrels with earth for rolling down onto the attacking British in his *Memoirs*, p. 33. William Gordon writes of the building of the forty-five bateaux and two floating batteries and of Quartermaster Mifflin's proposal to occupy Dorchester Heights on March 4, the day before the anniversary of the Boston Massacre, in his *History*, 2:25. Washington writes to Ward about the desertion of the "rascally rifleman" in a February 27, 1776, letter in *PGW*, 3:384. Washington's February 27, 1776, "General Order" is in *PGW*, 3:379–80. He writes to Joseph Reed of stumbling upon Phillis Wheatley's poem of praise in his pile of correspondence in a February 10, 1776, letter to Joseph Reed in *PGW*, 3:290. Washington's February 28, 1776, letter to Wheatley is in *PGW*, 3:387. Washington's February 28, 1776, letter to Burwell Bassett about using his lands along the Ohio as a possible "asylum" is in *PGW*, 3:386.

Archibald Robertson writes of the number of rebel "shot and shells" fired on the night of March 2, 1776, in his *Diary*, p. 73. Heath records in his diary entry for March 2 that the American cannons split because they "were not properly bedded, as the ground was hard frozen" (*Memoir*, p. 32). Samuel Webb records in a March 4 journal entry that "some conjecture 'tis want of knowledge in the bombardiers, some one thing and some another, but 'tis hinted—treachery, if the latter I hope it may come to light" (*Correspondence and Journals*, p. 134). Frothingham reprints Knox's tally of the total number of shot and shell fired by his artillery regiment on the night of March 4: "Lamb's Dam [in Roxbury]: five 13-inch shells, six 10-inch shells; 42 24-pound shot, 38 18-pound shot; Lechmere's Point: 32 24-pound shot, 14 18-pound shot; two 10-inch shells; Cobble Hill: 18 18-pound shot; total: 144 shot, 13 shells" (*HSOB*, p. 298). Douglas Southall Freeman in *George Washington*, 4:34, cites the reference to seeing as many as seven shells "in the air at the same instant" on the night of March 4. Abigail Adams writes of the roar of the cannons on the night of March 4 in a letter to her husband John started on March 2, in *Adams Family Correspondence*, vol. 1, edited by L. H. Butterfield, pp. 354–55. Samuel Webb records hearing "the cries of poor women and children" in a March 5 journal entry in *Correspondence*, p. 134. Archibald Robertson writes of the British casualties inflicted by the American cannonade in a March 4 entry in his *Diary*, p. 73. A March 4, 1776, letter from a British officer in *LAR* includes the statement that "it is agreed on all hands that their artillery officers are at least equal to our own" (p. 277).

William Gordon describes the weather conditions ("hazy below the height . . .

bright moonlight night above the hills") in his *History*, 2:27; he records the fact that the wind carried the noise of the American advance onto Dorchester Heights "into the harbor between the town and the castle" in his "Apr. 6, 1776 Letter to Samuel Wilson," p. 362. John Thomas describes how he led "3,000 picked men beside 360 ox teams" onto Dorchester Heights in a March 9 letter to his wife Hannah in Charles Coffin's *Life and Services of . . . Thomas*, pp. 20–21; Coffin includes a brief note to Hannah, also written on March 9, in which Thomas reports that their ten-year-old son John "is well and in high spirits. He ran away from Oakeley privately, on Tuesday morning, and got by the sentries came to me on Dorchester Hills, where he has been most of the time since" (p. 21). William Gordon reports that General Thomas "told me that he pulled out his watch and found that by ten o'clock at night, they had got two forts . . . sufficient to defend them from small arms and grapeshot" in his "Apr. 6, 1776 Letter to Samuel Wilson," pp. 362–63. Archibald Robertson records in the March 4 entry of his *Diary* that "about 10 o'clock Lt. Col. Campbell reported to Brig. Smith that the rebels were at work on Dorchester Heights" (p. 73). The reference to the works atop Dorchester Heights being raised "with an expedition equal to that of the genii belonging to Aladdin's wonderful lamp" is in a letter from a British officer in *LAR*, p. 278. James Thacher in his *Journal* claims that due to the fog the American fort atop Dorchester Heights "loomed to great advantage" (p. 40). William Gordon's account of Howe claiming the Americans had done more in a single night than "his whole army would have done in six months" can be found in his "Apr. 6, 1776 Letter to Samuel Wilson," p. 363. Archibald Robertson's estimate that it must have taken fifteen to twenty thousand men to erect the two forts is in his *Diary*, p. 74. Samuel Webb records the rumor that Howe had vowed to attack any fort built on Dorchester Heights even "if he was sure of losing two thirds of the army" in a March 1 entry in his *Diary*, p. 131.

Thacher writes of the cannon balls "rolling and rebounding over the hill" in his *Journal*, p. 39. John Sullivan writes of how the British attempted to "elevate their cannons . . . by sinking the hinder wheels" in a March 15, 1776, letter to John Adams, in C. James Taylor, *Founding Families*. James Thacher writes of the spectators covering the hills of Dorchester in his *Journal*, p. 39. William Gordon describes the ease with which the Americans atop Dorchester Heights could see what was happening on the wharves of Boston "by the help of glasses" and how the spectators and soldiers "clapped their hands and wished for the expected attack" in his "Apr. 6, 1776 Letter to Samuel Wilson," p. 363; Gordon also writes of how the regulars were "not hearty in the matter," and how ladders were collected in anticipation of an attack on the American fort (pp. 364–65). Gordon writes of how Washington's exhortation, "Remember it is the fifth of March," was repeated along the lines in his *History*, 2:28. Gordon writes of the preparations in place for the amphibious assault on Boston in the event that the British attack Dorchester Heights in "Apr. 6, 1776 letter to Samuel Wilson," p. 363. Thacher writes of leaving Dorchester Heights without having "to dress a single wound" in his *Journal*, p. 39. Archibald Robertson recounts the tense meetings that preceded Howe's decision to abort the attack on Dorchester Heights as well as Howe's March 6 meeting at 11:00 a.m. with his officers, announcing his decision to evacuate, in his *Journal*, pp. 74–75. Heath's judgment that the combination of "almost a hurricane" and Howe's decision to evacuate "saved the Americans when they would have destroyed themselves" is in his *Memoirs*, p. 33.

Frothingham in *HSOB*, describes how the letter from the town selectman was carried across the lines under a flag of truce (p. 301). Town selectman Timothy Newall provides an excellent on-the-scene account of the mixture of bedlam and fear in Boston as the Americans continued to move their fortifications ever closer along the ridge of Dorchester Heights in his *Journal*, pp. 273–76. The reference to "Great Britain being fast asleep" is in a March 7 letter in *LAR*, p. 279. The reference to the loyalists carrying "death in their faces" comes from a March 21 letter from Caleb Adams to General Folsom cited in Allen French's *FYAR*, p. 664. Washington writes of the loyalists being "at their wit's end" in a March 31, 1776, letter to John Augustine Washington in *PGW*, 3:568. Allen French in *FYAR* writes of the travails of the loyalists Adino Paddock, Benjamin Hallowell, and Harrison Gray, pp. 665–66. Lieutenant Governor Thomas Oliver estimated in French, *FYAR*, that of the 3,500 inhabitants in Boston toward the end of the Siege, "The loyal and their connections may amount to 2,000 and upwards. . . . There are, I suppose, 60 or 70 persons with their families who could never make their peace with the rebels" (p. 651). This means that only about half of those whom Oliver considered loyalists chose to sail to Halifax. My thanks to Gregory Whitehead for his insights regarding Boston's "second culling" in a personal communication. Archibald Robertson describes his last day in Boston in his *Journal*, p. 79. Inventories of "British Stores Left in Boston" and "British Ordnance Stores Left in Boston" are in *PGW*, 3:525–27, 549–50. My thanks to Philip Budden for pointing out the significance of March 17 for Boston's Irish population in a personal communication.

John Sullivan in a March 19 extension of a letter started on March 17, 1776, to John Adams describes the "lifeless sentries" guarding the British fortress at Bunker Hill, in Taylor, *Founding Families*. James Wilkinson writes of Boston on evacuation day in his *Memoirs*, p. 32–33. James Thacher writes of the "melancholy gloom" of the Bostonians in his *Journal*, pp. 41–42. John Andrews writes of how his longing for his wife Ruthy has not prevented him from feeling a sense of optimism throughout the siege in *LJA*, p. 411. Archibald Robertson describes assisting John Montresor in the destruction of the Castle in his *Diary*, pp. 80–81. Washington writes of "lamenting the disappointment" of not having been allowed to attack Boston in a March 27, 1776, letter to Landon Carter, in *PGW*, 3:545. The "Address from the Boston Selectmen" thanking Washington for "the recovery of this town" is in *PGW* (3:571–72), as is Washington's "Address to the Boston Selectmen and Citizens" (3:572–73) and his March 7 installment of a letter started on February 26 to Joseph Reed, in which he claims, "I will not lament or repine at any act of Providence because I am in a great measure a convert to Mr. Pope's opinion that whatever is, is right" (3:373–74).

John Warren writes of retrieving his brother's body from Breed's Hill in his journal, which is quoted in Edward Warren's *Life of John Warren*, p. 74. John Rowe writes of being insulted at Joseph Warren's funeral in his *Diary*, p. 307. Clifford Shipton details the demise of Benjamin Church in *SHG*, 13:395–97. A. W. H. Eaton in *The Famous Mather Byles* writes about the minister losing his congregation in 1776; he recounts Byles's comment about being ruled by "one tyrant 3,000 miles away" instead of "3,000 tyrants not a mile away" (pp. 146–47), as well as Byles's pun about his "observe-a-Tory" (p. 173). Albert Mathews in "Joyce, Junior" quotes from the advertisement in the March 17, 1777, *Boston Gazette* in which Joyce Jr. refers to taking action against the "shameless brass-faced Tories who have the audaciousness to remain" (p. 94). Abigail Adams describes Joyce Junior's carting of the loyalists across the town line in an April 20, 1777, letter in Taylor, *Founding Families*. Washington's General Orders forbidding the observance of "that ridiculous and childish custom of burning the effigy of the Pope" can be found in *PGW*, 2:300. Esther Forbes in *Paul Revere* cites Revere's April 1777 letter to John Lamb in which he writes, "I find but few of the Sons of Liberty in the army" (p. 323). Ruth Bloch in *Visionary Republic* cites Thomas Paine's claim that the "birthday of a new world is at hand" (p. 75). J. L. Bell in his July 4, 2007, *Boston 1775* blog entry, "Sheriff Greenleaf and Col. Crafts Read the Declaration," cites Greenleaf's son's account of his father and Crafts declaiming the Declaration of Independence, http://boston1775.blogspot.com/2007/07/sheriff-greenleaf-and-col-crafts-read.html. Abigail Adams's account of the event is in a July 21, 1776, letter to John Adams in Taylor, *Founding Families*.

Epilogue—**Character Alone**

John Quincy Adams's account of what he did on June 17, 1843, can be found in his *Diary* at the MHS; my thanks to Mike Hill for providing me with a transcript. My account of the festivities surrounding the sixty-eighth anniversary of the Battle of Bunker Hill is based on articles in the June 19, 1843, issue of the *Daily Atlas* and the June 22, 1843, issue of the *Emancipator and Free American*. My account of John Quincy Adams's late career in the U.S. House of Representatives is based largely on Paul Nagel's *John Quincy Adams*, in which he details Quincy's role in the *Amistad* trial (pp. 379–80) and the House censure trial (pp. 386), in which Nagel quotes the description of Quincy as "the acutest, the astutest, the archest enemy of Southern slavery that ever existed." Nagel cites Quincy's claim that "the world will retire from me before I shall retire from the world" (p. 381). Concerning Joseph Warren's saving Quincy's forefinger from amputation, Nagel writes, "JQA often considered how brief his diary and letters might have been if his writing hand had been maimed" (p. 8). Abigail Adams's account of seeing Trumbull's painting *The Death of General Warren at the Battle of Bunker's Hill*, in which she refers to "character alone," is in a March 4, 1786, letter to Elizabeth Smith Shaw in *Adams Family Correspondence*, 7:82. She writes of curbing the "unlimited power" a husband has over a wife and of how "the passion of liberty cannot be equally strong" in a slaveholder in a March 31, 1776, letter to John Adams, in *Adams Family Correspondence*, 1:569–70. Paul Nagel cites John Quincy Adams's insistence that "My life must be militant to its close" in *John Quincy Adams*, p. 328. As Nagel writes in his biography, John Quincy Adams died on February 23, 1848, from the effects of a stroke he suffered while rising to speak on the House floor.

Bibliography

Abercrombie, Lt. Col. James. Letter to Colden, May 2, 1775. MHS *Proceedings* 2, no. 11 (1897): 306.

Adair, Douglass. *Fame and the Founding Fathers.* Indianapolis: Liberty Fund/W. W. Norton, 1974.

Adams Family Correspondence. Edited by L. H. Butterfield et al. Cambridge, Mass.: Harvard University Press, 1963–93.

Adams, Charles F. "Battle of Bunker Hill from a Strategic Point of View." AAS *Proceedings*, n.s., 10 (1895): 387–98.

Adams, John. *Works.* Edited by Charles Francis Adams. Boston: Little, Brown, 1850–56.

———. *Diary and Autobiography of John Adams.* Edited by L. H. Butterfield et al. 4 vols. New York: Atheneum, 1964.

Adams, Josiah. *Letter to Lemuel Shattuck . . . in Vindication of the Claims of Isaac Davis.* Boston: Damrall and Moore, 1850.

———. *An Address Delivered at Acton, July 21, 1885, Being the First Centennial Anniversary of the Organization of that Town.* Boston: J. T. Buckingham, 1835.

Adams, Samuel. *The Writings of Samuel Adams.* Edited by Harry Alonzo Cushing. Vol. 3. New York: G. P. Putnam's, 1904.

Adelson, Bruce. *William Howe: British General.* Philadelphia: Chelsea House, 2002.

Akers, Charles. "The Lost Reputation of Samuel Cooper." *NEHGR* 80 (1976): 23–34.

———. *Called unto Liberty: A Life of Jonathan Mayhew, 1720–1776.* Cambridge, Mass.: Harvard University Press, 1964.

———. *The Divine Politician: Samuel Cooper and the American Revolution in Boston.* Boston: Northeastern University, 1982.

Alden, John E. "John Mein: Scourge of Patriots." *Publications of the Colonial Society of Massachusetts* 34 (1942): 583–86.

Alden, John Richard. *General Charles Lee: Traitor or Patriot?* Baton Rouge: Louisiana State University Press, 1951.

———. "Why the March to Concord?" *American Historical Review* 49 (1944): 446–54.

———. *General Gage in America.* New York: Greenwood Press, 1969.

Alexander, John K. *Samuel Adams: America's Revolutionary Politician.* Lanham, Md.: Rowman and Littlefield, 2002.

Allan, Herbert S. *John Hancock: Patriot in Purple.* New York: Beechhurst Press, 1953.

Allen, Thomas. *Tories: Fighting for the King in America's First Civil War.* New York: HarperCollins, 2010.

Allis, Frederick S. Jr., ed. *Seafaring in Colonial Massachusetts.* Boston: Colonial Society of Massachusetts, 1980.

Allison, Robert J. *The Boston Massacre.* Beverly, Mass.: Commonwealth, 2006.

Ames, Nathaniel. *Diary, 1756–1821.* Edited by Robert Brand Hanson. Rockport, Maine: Picton Press, 1998.

Alline, Henry. Letter, July 1776. MHS.

Ammerman, David. *In the Common Cause: American Response to the Coercive Acts of 1774.* New York: Norton, 1974.

Amory, Mrs. John. *The Journal of Mrs. John Amory with Letters from Her Father Rufus Greene.* Edited by Martha Codman. Boston: privately printed, 1923.

Amory, Thomas. *John Sullivan.* Boston: Wiggin and Lunt, 1868.

Anderson, Fred. "The Hinge of the Revolution: George Washington Confronts a People's Army, July 3, 1775." *Massachusetts Historical Review* 1 (1999): 21–48.

———. *A People's Army: Massachusetts Soldiers and Society in the Seven Years' War.* Chapel Hill: University of North Carolina Press, 1984.

———. *Crucible of War: The Seven Years' War and the Fate of Empire in British North America, 1754–1766.* New York: Knopf, 2000.

Andrews, Joseph. "Letters of John Andrews, Esq., of Boston, 1772–1776." Edited by Winthrop Sargent. MHS *Proceedings*, 1st ser., 8 (1866): 316–412.

Ansoff, Peter. "The Flag on Prospect Hill." *Raven* 13 (2006): 77–100.

Anthony, Katharine. *First Lady of the Revolution: A Life of Mercy Otis Warren.* Garden City, N.Y.: Doubleday, 1958.

Appleby, Joyce. "The Social Origins of American Revolutionary Ideology." *Journal of American History* 64 (1978): 935–58.

Archer, Richard. *As If in an Enemy's Country: The British Occupation of Boston and the Origins of Revolution.* New York: Oxford University Press, 2010.

Arendt, Hannah. *On Revolution.* New York: Viking, 1965.

Armitage, David, and Michael J. Braddick, eds. *The British Atlantic World, 1500–1800.* New York: Palgrave, 2002.

Austin, James T. *The Life of Elbridge Gerry.* Boston: Wells and Lilly, 1828.

Avery, David. "A Chaplain of the American Revolution." *American Monthly Magazine* 17 (1900): 342–47.

Bacon, Edwin M. *Rambles around Old Boston.* Boston: Little Brown, 1914.

Bailey, Sarah Loring. *Historical Sketches of Andover.* Boston: Houghton Mifflin, 1880.

Bailyn, Bernard. "The Index and Commentaries of Harbottle Dorr." MHS *Proceedings*, 3d ser., 85 (1973): 21–35.

———. "Religion and Revolution: Three Biographical Studies." *Perspectives in American History* 4 (1970): 85–169.

———. *The Peopling of British North America: An Introduction.* New York: Knopf, 1986.

———. *Voyagers to the West: A Passage in the Peopling of America on the Eve of the Revolution.* New York: Knopf, 1986.

———. *The Ideological Origins of the American Revolution.* Cambridge, Mass.: Harvard University Press, 1990.

———. *The Ordeal of Thomas Hutchinson.* Cambridge, Mass.: Harvard University Press, 1974.

———. *Faces of Revolution: Personalities and Themes in the Struggle for American Independence.* New York: Vintage, 1992.

———. *To Begin Anew: The Genius and Ambiguities of the Founding Fathers.* New York: Knopf, 2003.

Bailyn, Bernard, and John B. Hench, eds. *The Press and the American Revolution.* Boston: Northeastern University Press, 1981.

Baker, Amos. "Affidavit of the Last Survivor." In Joel Parker, *Address to the Students of the University at Cambridge*, pp. 133–35. Cambridge, Mass.: John Bartlett, 1853.

Baker, James. *Diary*, 1775. MHS.

Bakeless, John. *Traitors, Turncoats, and Heroes: Espionage in the American Revolution.* 1959; reprint, New York: Da Capo Press, 1998.

Balderston, Marion, and David Syrett, eds. *The Lost War: Letters from British Officers During the American Revolution.*

Baldwin, Jeduthan. *The Revolutionary Journal of Col. Jeduthan Baldwin, 1775–78.* Edited by Thomas Williams Baldwin. Bangor, Maine: DeBurian, 1906.

Bamford, William. "Bamford's Diary." *Maryland Historical Magazine* 27 (1932): 240–314.

Bancroft, Ebenezer. "Colonel Bancroft's Narrative." In *Bi-Centennial of Old Dunstable*, ed. John B. Hill, pp. 59–60. Nashua, N.H.: 1878.

Bancroft, George. *History of the Colonization of the United States.* Vol. 3. Boston: Little, Brown, 1854.

Bangs, Isaac. *Journal.* 1776. MHS.

Barber, Daniel. "Diary, June 1775." *Historical Magazine* 7 (1863): 82–88.

Barker, John. *The British in Boston: The Diary of Lt. John Barker.* Edited by Elizabeth Ellery Dana. Cambridge, Mass.: Harvard University Press, 1924.

Barone, Michael. *Our First Revolution: The Remarkable British Upheaval That Inspired America's Founding Fathers.* New York: Three Rivers Press, 2008.

Barrett, Amos. *Journals and Letters.* Edited by Henry True. Marion, Ohio: Henry True, 1906.

Barrow, Thomas C. *Trade and Empire: The British Customs Service in America, 1660–1775.* Cambridge, Mass.: Harvard University Press, 1967.

Bass, Henry. Letter to Samuel Savage, December 19, 1765. MHS *Proceedings* 44 (1911): 688.

Batchelder, Samuel F. *The Washington Elm Tradition: Is It True?* Cambridge, Mass.: privately printed, 1925.

Baxter, W. T. *The House of Hancock.* Cambridge, Mass.: Harvard University Press, 1945.

Baylies, Francis. *Eulogy on the Honorable Benjamin Russell.* Boston: The Freemason's Magazine, 1845.

Becker, John. *The Sexagenary; or, Reminiscences of the American Revolution.* Albany, N.Y.: J. Munsell, 1866.
Belknap, Jeremy. "Extracts from Dr. Belknap's Note-books and a Correspondence between Dr. Belknap and Ebenezer Hazard." MHS *Proceedings* 14 (1875–76): 91–98.
———. "Answers to Queries Respecting the Slavery and Emancipation of Negroes in Massachusetts." MHS *Collections* 4 (1795): 191–211.
———. "Journal of My Tour to the Camp. . . ." MHS *Proceedings* 4 (1858): 77–86.
Bell, J. L. *General George Washington's Headquarters and Home—Cambridge, Massachusetts.* National Park Service: U.S. Department of the Interior, 2012.
———. *Boston 1775.* Blog. www.boston1775.net.
———. "Du Simitière's Sketches of Pope Day in Boston, 1767." In *The Worlds of Children, 1620–1920,* Dublin Seminar for New England Folklife Annual Proceedings 2002, 209–17. Boston: Boston University, 2004.
———. "A Bankruptcy in Boston, 1765." *Massachusetts Banker,* 4th quarter 2008, pp. 14, 16, 18, 23.
———. "The Talented Mr. Bradlee: From Rioter to Proper Bostonian." *Bostonian Society News,* Spring 2000, pp. 6–7.
———. "From Saucy Boys to Sons of Liberty: Politicizing Youth in Pre-Revolutionary Boston." In *Children in Colonial America,* edited by James Marten, pp. 204–16. New York: New York University Press, 2007.
Benes, Peter. "Night Processions: Celebrating the Gunpowder Plot in England and New England." In *New England Celebrates: Spectacle, Commemoration, and Festivity,* Dublin Seminar for New England Folklife Annual Proceedings 2000, pp. 9–28. Boston: Boston University, 2002.
Berkin, Carol. *Jonathan Sewall: Odyssey of an American Loyalist.* New York: iUniverse, 2000.
Berniere, Henry de. "Account of Reconnaisances, 1775." *Journal of the Society for Army Historical Research* 7 (1928): 170–74.
Berthoff, Rowland. *An Unsettled People: Social Order and Disorder in American History.* New York: Harper and Row, 1971
Billias, George Athan, ed. *General Washington's Generals and Opponents.* New York: William Morrow, 1969.
Birnbaum, Louis. *Red Dawn at Lexington.* Boston: Houghton Mifflin, 1986.
Bixby, Samuel. "Diary, 1775." MHS *Proceedings* 14 (1875–76): 285–98.
Blake, John B. *Public Health in the Town of Boston, 1630–1822.* Cambridge: Harvard University Press, 1959.
Bloch, Ruth H. *Visionary Republic: Millennial Themes in American Thought, 1756–1800.* New York: Cambridge University Press, 1985.
Blood, Thaddeus. "Narrative." *Boston Daily Advertiser,* April 20, 1886.
Boardman, Benjamin. "Diary, 1775." MHS *Proceedings* 2, no. 7 (1891–92): 400–413.
Bobrick, Benson. *Angel in the Whirlwind.* New York: Penguin, 1997.
Bolton, Charles K. *The Private Soldier under Washington.* London: Kessinger, 2006.
Bolton, Dr. Thomas. "An Oration Delivered March 15, 1775, at the Request of a Number of the Inhabitants of the Town of Boston." MHS.
Boorstin, Daniel J. *The Americans: The Colonial Experience.* New York: Random House, 1958.
———. *Hidden History: Exploring Our Secret Past.* New York: Vintage, 1989.
Boston Gazette 1774. Barre, Mass.: Imprint Society, 1972.
Bourne, Russell. *Cradle of Violence: How Boston's Waterfront Mobs Ignited the American Revolution.* New York: John Wiley and Sons, 2006.
Bowen, Ashley. *Autobiography.* Edited by Daniel Vickers. Peterborough, Ontario: Broadview Press, 2006.
Bowen, Catherine Drinker. *John Adams and the American Revolution.* Boston: Little, Brown, 1950.
Bowler, Arthur A. *Logistics and Failure of the British Army in America.* Princeton, N.J.: Princeton University Press, 1975.
Bowne, William L. *Ye Cohorn Caravan: The Knox Expedition in the Winter of 1775–1776.* Schuylerville, N.Y.: NaPaul, 1975.
Boyle, John. "Journal of Occurrences in Boston, 1759–1778." NEHGR 84 (1930): 142–71, 248–72, 357–82; 85 (1931): 5–28, 117–33.
Boynton, Thomas. "Journal, April 19, 1775." MHS *Proceedings* 15 (1877): 254–55.
Bradford, Charles H. *The Battle Road: Expedition to Lexington and Concord.* Philadelphia: Nimrod Press, 1988.
Breck, Samuel. *Recollections of Samuel Breck.* Edited by Horace Elisha Scudder. London: Sampson, Low, 1877.
Breen, T. H. *The Marketplace of Revolution: How Consumer Politics Shaped American Independence.* New York: Oxford University Press, 2004.

———. *American Insurgents, American Patriots.* New York: Hill and Wang, 2010.

Brennan, Ellen E. *Plural Office Holding in Massachusetts, 1760–1780: Its Relation to the "Separation" of Departments of Government.* Chapel Hill: University of North Carolina Press, 1945.

Bridenbaugh, Carl. *Cities in the Wilderness: The First Century of Urban Life in America, 1625–1742.* New York: Oxford University Press, 1971.

———. *Cities in Revolt: Urban Life in America, 1743–1776.* New York: Oxford University Press, 1955.

Brinton, Crane. *The Anatomy of Revolution.* New York: Vintage, 1965.

Brooke, John L. *The Heart of the Commonwealth: Society and Political Culture in Worcester County, Massachusetts, 1713–1861.* Amherst: University of Massachusetts Press, 1993.

Brookhiser, Richard, ed. *George Washington's Rules of Civility.* New York: Free Press, 1997.

———. *Founding Father: Rediscovering George Washington.* New York: Free Press, 1997.

Brooks, Noah. *Henry Knox.* New York: Putnam, 1900.

Brooks, Victor. *The Boston Campaign, April 1775–March 1776.* Conshohocken, Pa.: Combined, 1999.

Brown, Abram English. *Beneath Old Roof Trees.* Boston: Lee and Shepard, 1896.

———. *Faneuil Hall and Faneuil Hall Market.* Boston: Lee and Shepard, 1901.

———. *Beside Old Hearthstones.* Boston: Lee and Shepard, 1891.

Brown, M. L. *Firearms in Colonial America.* Washington, D.C.: Smithsonian Institution, 1980.

Brown, Moses. "Account of Journey to Distribute Donations 12th Month 1775." Introduction by Mack E. Thompson. *Rhode Island History* 15, no. 4 (1956): 97–121.

Brown, Rebecca Warren. *Stories about General Warren in Relation to the Fifth of March Massacre and the Battle of Bunker Hill.* Boston: James Loring, 1835.

Brown, Richard D. *Revolutionary Politics in Massachusetts: The Boston Committee of Correspondence and the Towns, 1772–1774.* New York: Norton, 1976.

Brown, Robert E. *Middle-Class Democracy and the Revolution in Massachusetts, 1691–1789.* Ithaca, N.Y.: Cornell University Press, 1955.

Brown, S. C. *Benjamin Thompson, Count Rumford.* Cambridge, Mass.: MIT Press, 1981.

Brown, Wallace. *The King's Friends: The Composition and Motives of the American Loyalist Claimants.* Providence, R.I.: Brown University Press, 1965.

———. *The Good Americans: The Loyalists in the American Revolution.* New York: Morrow, 1969.

Brumwell, Stephen. *Redcoats: The British Soldier and War in the Americas, 1755–1763.* Cambridge, Mass.: Harvard University Press, 2002.

Buchanan, John G. "The Justice of America's Cause: Revolutionary Rhetoric in the Sermons of Samuel Cooper." *NEQ* 50, no. 1 (1977): 101–124.

Buckingham, Joseph Tinker. *Specimens of Newspaper Literature, with Personal Memoirs.* Boston: Redding, 1852.

Buel, Jr., Richard. *In Irons: Britain's Naval Supremacy and the American Revolutionary Economy.* New Haven, Conn.: Yale University Press, 1998.

Bullock, Steven C. *Revolutionary Brotherhood: Freemasonry and the Transformation of American Social Order, 1730–1840.* Chapel Hill: University of North Carolina Press, 1996.

Bumsted, J. M. " 'Things in the Womb of Time': Ideas of American Independence, 1633–1763." *WMQ* 31 (1974): 533–64.

Burnett, Edmund C. *The Continental Congress.* New York: Norton, 1964.

Burnham, John. "Narrative, May 1775–January 1784." *Magazine of History*, extra no. 54 (1917): 119–33.

Burns, Eric. *Infamous Scribblers: The Founding Fathers and the Rowdy Beginnings of American Journalism.* New York: Public Affairs, 2001.

Burstein, Andrew. *Sentimental Democracy: The Evolution of America's Romantic Self-Image.* New York: Hill and Wang, 1999.

Bushman, Richard L. *King and People in Provincial Massachusetts.* Chapel Hill: University of North Carolina Press, 1992.

———. *From Puritan to Yankee: Character and the Social Order in Connecticut, 1690–1765.* New York: Norton, 1970.

Butler, Jon. *Becoming America: The Revolution Before 1776.* Cambridge, Mass.: Harvard University Press, 2000.

———. *Awash in a Sea of Faith: Christianizing the American People.* Cambridge, Mass.: Harvard University Press, 1992.

Butterfield, Herbert. *The Whig Interpretation of History.* New York: Norton, 1965.

Byers, Edward. *Nation of Nantucket.* Boston: Northeastern Press, 1987.

Cadbury, Henry. "Quaker Relief During the Siege of Boston." *Colonial Society of Massachusetts Transactions* 34 (1943): 39–149.

Calhoon, Robert M. *The Loyalists in Revolutionary America, 1760–1781*. New York: Harcourt Brace, 1973.

Callahan, North. *Henry Knox: General Washington's General*. New York: Rinehart, 1958.

Calloway, Colin. *The American Revolution in Indian Country: Crisis and Diversity in Native American Communities* New York: Cambridge University Press, 1995.

Carbone, Gerald M. *Nathanael Greene: A Biography of the American Revolution*. New York: Palgrave Macmillan, 2009.

Carp, Benjamin. "Fire of Liberty: Firefighters, Urban Voluntary Culture and the Revolutionary Movement. *WMQ*, 3rd ser., 58 (2001): 781–818.

———. *Rebels Rising: Cities and the American Revolution*. New York: Oxford University Press, 2007.

———. *Defiance of the Patriots: The Boston Tea Party and the Making of America*. New Haven, Conn.: Yale University Press, 2010.

Carp, E. Wayne. *To Starve the Army at Pleasure: Continental Army Administration and American Political Culture, 1775–1783*. Chapel Hill: University of North Carolina Press, 1984.

Carr, Jacqueline Barbara. *After the Siege: A Social History of Boston, 1775–1800*. Boston: Northeastern Press, 2005.

Carr, J. Revell. *Seeds of Discontent: The Deep Roots of the American Revolution, 1650–1750*. New York: Walker, 2008.

Carretta, Vincent. *Phillis Wheatley*. Athens: University of Georgia Press, 2011.

Cary, John. *Joseph Warren: Physician, Politician, Patriot*. Urbana: University of Illinois Press, 1961.

Cash, Arthur H. *John Wilkes: The Scandalous Father of American Liberty*. New Haven, Conn.: Yale University Press, 2006.

Cash, Philip. *Medical Men at the Siege of Boston*. Philadelphia: American Philosophical Society, 1973.

Chamberlain, Allen. *Beacon Hill: Its Ancient Pastures and Early Mansions*. Boston: Houghton Mifflin, 1925.

Chamberlain, Mellen. *A Documentary History of Chelsea*. Vol. 2. Boston: MHS, 1908.

———. "Why Captain Preston Fought." *Danvers Historical Collections* 8 (1920): 68–70.

Chamberlin, William. "Diary, April 19, 1775." MHS *Proceedings*, 2d ser., 10 (1895–96): 490–504.

Chase, Ellen, ed. *The Beginnings of the American Revolution: Based on Contemporary Letters, Diaries, and Other Documents*. 3 vols. New York: Baker and Taylor, 1910.

Cheever, William. "William Cheever's Diary, 1775–1776." MHS *Proceedings* 60 (1926–27): 91–97.

Chernow, Ron. *Washington: A Life*. New York: Penguin, 2010.

Chidsey, Donald Barr. *The Siege of Boston*. New York: Crown, 1966.

Child, Lydia Maria. *The Rebels; or, Boston Before the Revolution*. Boston: Cummings, Hilliard, 1825.

Christie, Ian R. *Crisis of Empire: Great Britain and the American Colonies, 1754–1783*. New York: Norton, 1966.

Christie, Ian R., and Benjamin W. Labaree. *Empire or Independence, 1760–1776: A British-American Dialogue on the Coming of the American Revolution*. New York: Norton, 1976.

Church, Benjamin. "Account of the Examination of Doctor Benjamin Church." MHS *Collections* 1 (1792): 86.

Cipolla, Carlo M. *Guns, Sails and Empires: Technological Innovation and the Early Phases of European Expansion, 1400–1700*. New York: Pantheon, 1965.

Clark, J. C. D. *The Language of Liberty, 1660–1832: Political Discourse and Social Dynamics in the Anglo-American World*. New York: Cambridge University Press, 1994.

Clark, William Bell, ed. *Naval Documents of the American Revolution*. Vols. 1 and 2. Washington, D.C.: U.S. Office of Naval Operations, 1964.

Clarke, Jonas. *Opening of the War of the Revolution, 19th of April, 1775*. Lexington, Mass.: Lexington Historical Society, 1901.

Clarke, Richard. "Selections from the Papers of Richard Clarke." Colonial Society of Massachusetts *Transactions* 8 (1906): 78–90.

Clinton, Henry. *The American Rebellion: Sir Henry Clinton's Narrative of His Campaigns, 1775–1782*. New Haven, Conn.: Yale University Press, 1954.

Coburn, Frank Warren. *The Battle of April 19, 1775 in Lexington, Concord, Lincoln, Arlington, Cambridge, Somerville and Charlestown, Massachusetts*. Lexington, Mass.: privately printed, 1912.

———. *Fiction and Truth about the Battle on Lexington Common*. Lexington, Mass.: privately printed, 1918.

Coffin, Charles. *The Life and Services of Major General John Thomas*. New York: Egbert, Hovey, King, 1844.

———, ed. *History of the Battle of Breed's Hill, by Major-Generals William Heath, Henry Lee, James Wilkinson, and Henry Dearborn*. Saco, Maine: William J. Condon, 1831.

Colbourn, H. Trevor. *The Lamp of Experience: Whig History and the Intellectual Origins of the American Revolution*. Chapel Hill: University of North Carolina Press, 1965.

Commager, Henry Steele. *The Empire of Reason: How Europe Imagined and America Realized the Enlightenment*. Garden City, N.Y.: Anchor Books, 1978.

Commager, Henry Steele, and Richard B. Morris, eds. *The Spirit of 'Seventy-Six: The Story of the American Revolution as Told by Its Participants*. Edison, N.J.: Castle, 2002.

Conroy, David. *In Public Houses: Drink and the Revolution of American Authority in Colonial Massachusetts*. Chapel Hill: University of North Carolina Press, 1995.

Conser, Walter H., et al. *Resistance, Politics, and the American Struggle for Independence, 1765–1775*. Boulder, Colo.: Lynne Rienner, 1986.

Cook, Edward. *The Fathers of the Towns: Leadership and Community Structure in Eighteenth Century New England*. Baltimore: Johns Hopkins University Press, 1976.

Cooper, Samuel. "Diary." Edited by Ferderic Tuckerman. *American Historical Review* 6 (1901): 301–41.

———. " 'A Place for My People Israel': Samuel Cooper's Sermon of 7 April 1776." *NEHGR* 132 (1978): 123–39.

———. "Letters of Samuel Cooper to Thomas Pownall, 1769–1777." Edited by Frederic Tuckerman. *American Historical Review* 8, no. 2 (January 1903): 301–30.

———. Letters to Benjamin Franklin. *The Papers of Benjamin Franklin*. Vol. 20. New Haven, Conn.: Yale University Press, 1976.

Copley, John Singleton. *Letters and Papers of John Singleton Copley and Henry Pelham*. Boston: MHS, 1914.

"Correspondence between the Boston Sons of Liberty and John Wilkes." MHS *Proceedings* 47 (1913–14): 190–215.

Craft, Benjamin. "Craft's Journal of the Siege of Boston." Edited by S. P. Fowler. *Historical Collections of the Essex Institute* 3, no. 2 (1861): 51–57, 133–40, 167–74, 219–28.

Cray, Robert Jr. "Bunker Hill Refought: Memory Wars and Partisan Conflicts, 1775–1825." *Historical Journal of Massachusetts* 29 (Winter 2001): 22–52.

Crocker, Hannah Mather. *Observations on the Real Rights of Women and Other Writings*. Lincoln: University of Nebraska Press, 2011.

Crowley, John. *The Invention of Comfort: Sensibilities and Design in Early Modern Britain and Early America*. Baltimore: Johns Hopkins University Press, 2001.

Cummings, Abbott Lowell. "The Foster-Hutchinson House." *Old-Time New England* 54, no. 3 (1964): 59–76.

Curwen, Samuel. *The Journal and Letters of Samuel Curwen, 1775–1783*. Edited by George Atkinson Ward. Boston: Little, Brown, 1864.

Cutter, William. *The Life of Israel Putnam, Major-General in the Army of the American Revolution*. New York: George F. Cooledge & Brother, 1847.

Daniel, Jere R. *Experiment in Republicanism: New Hampshire Politics and the American Revolution, 1741–1794*. Cambridge, Mass.: Harvard University Press, 1970.

Dann, John C., ed. *The Revolution Remembered*. Chicago: University of Chicago Press, 1980.

Darling, Anthony D. *Red Coat and Brown Bess*. Ottawa: Museum Restoration Service, 1970.

Daughan, George. *If by Sea: The Forging of the American Navy*. New York: Basic Books, 2008.

Davidson, Philip. *Propaganda and the American Revolution, 1763–1783*. Chapel Hill: University of North Carolina Press, 1941.

Davies, K. G., ed. *Documents of the American Revolution*. Vols. 2–12. Shannon, Ireland: Irish University Press, 1972–76.

Davis, Paul. *Besieged: 100 Great Sieges from Jericho to Sarajevo*. New York: Oxford University Press, 2003.

Davis, Thomas. "Emancipation Rhetoric, Natural Rights and Revolutionary New England: A Note on Four Black Petitions in Massachusetts, 1773–77." *NEQ* 62 (1989): 248–63.

Davol, Ralph. *Two Men of Taunton*. Taunton, Mass.: Davol, 1912.

Dawson, Henry. *Gleanings from the Harvest Field of American History*. Pt. 4. Morrisania, New York, 1860.

Dearborn, Henry. "An Account of the Battle of Bunker Hill." *The Port Folio*, 4th ser., 5 (1818): 181–82.

Dederer, John Morgan. *War in America to 1775: Before Yankee Doodle*. New York: New York University Press, 1990.

Degler, Carl N. *Out of Our Past: The Forces That Shaped Modern America*. 3d ed. New York: Harper, 1984.

Deming, Sarah Winslow. Journal, 1775. MHS.

Desrochers, Robert E. Jr. "Slave-for-Sale Advertisements and Slavery in Massachusetts, 1704–1781." *WMQ*, 3rd ser., 59, no. 3 (2002): 623–64.

Diamond, Sigmund. "Bunker Hill, Tory Propaganda, and Adam Smith." *NEQ* 25, no. 3 (1952): 363–74.

Dickerson, Oliver Morton. "British Control of American Newspapers on the Eve of the Revolution." *NEQ* 24 (1951): 453–68.

————, ed. *Boston Under Military Rule: As Revealed in a Journal of the Times.* Boston: Chapman and Grimes, 1936.

————. *The Navigation Acts and the American Revolution.* Philadelphia: University of Pennsylvania Press, 1951.

Dirst, Tara, and Allan Kulikoff. "Was Benjamin Church a Traitor?" *Common-Place* 6, no. 1 (October 2005). http://www.common-place.org/vol-06/no-01/tales/.

Dolin, Eric Jay. *Leviathan: The History of Whaling in America.* New York: Norton, 2007.

Donkin, Robert Major. *Military Collections and Remarks.* New York: Gaine, 1777.

Donoughue, Bernard. *British Politics and the American Revolution: The Path to War, 1773–1775.* New York: St. Martin's Press, 1964.

Douglas-Lithgow, R. A. "Governor Hutchinson's House on Milton Hill." *Massachusetts Magazine* 3 (April 1910): 121–24.

Drake, Samuel Adams. *History of Middlesex County, Massachusetts.* Boston: Estes and Lauriat, 1880.

————. *History of Roxbury.* Boston: City of Boston, 1908.

————. *Life and Correspondence of Henry Knox.* Cambridge, Mass.: Wilson and Son, 1873.

————. *The History and Antiquities of Boston.* Boston: Luther Stevens, 1856.

————, ed. *Bunker Hill: The Story Told in Letters from the Battlefield.* Boston: Nichols and Hall, 1875.

————. *Tea Leaves: Being a Collection of Letters and Documents.* Boston: Crane, 1884.

————. *Old Landmarks and Historic Personages of Boston.* Boston: Little, Brown, 1900.

Drake, Samuel Adams, and Walter Kendall Watkins. *Old Boston Taverns and Tavern Clubs.* Boston: W. A. Butterfield, 1917.

Draper, Theodore. *A Struggle for Power: The American Revolution.* New York: Random House, 1996.

Drew, Bernard. *Henry Knox and the Revolutionary War Trail in Western Massachusetts.* Jefferson, N.C.: McFarland, 2012.

Duffy, Christopher. *Fire and Stone: The Science of Fortress Warfare: 1660–1860.* Edison, N.J.: Castle Books, 2006.

————. *Siege Warfare, Volume 1: The Fortress in the Early Modern World.* London: Routledge, 1987.

————. *Siege Warfare, Volume 2: The Fortress in the Age of Vauban and Frederick the Great, 1680–1787.* London: Routledge, 1985.

Dunn, Jr., Walter S. *People of the American Frontier: The Coming of the American Revolution.* Westport, Conn.: Praeger, 2005.

Earle, Alice Morse. *Home Life in Colonial Days.* Stockbridge, Mass.: Berkshire House, 1993.

Eaton, A. W. H. *The Famous Mather Byles.* 1914; reprint, Boston: Gregg Press, 1972.

Edes, Henry H. "Memoir of Dr. Thomas Young, 1731–1777." *Publications of the Colonial Society of Massachusetts Transactions, 1906–1907* 11 (1910): 2–54.

Edes, Peter. *Diary kept in Boston Gaol,* June 19–October 3, 1775. MHS.

————. "Letter." MHS *Proceedings* 12 (1871): 175.

Edes, Peter, ed. *Orations Delivered at the Request of the Inhabitants of the Town of Boston. . . .* Boston: Peter Edes, 1785.

Egnal, Marc, and Joseph Ernst. "An Economic Interpretation of the American Revolution." *WMQ,* 3rd ser., 29 (1972): 3–32.

Eliot, Andrew. "Letter to Thomas Hollis, September 27, 1768." MHS *Collections,* 4th ser., 4 (1858): 398–461.

————. "Letters to Thomas Hollis and others, April 25, 1775, to February 19, 1776." MHS *Proceedings* 16 (1878): 281–306.

Eliot, John. "Letters to Jeremy Belknap." MHS *Collections,* 6th ser., 4 (1891): 74–209.

————. "Memoirs of Major-General Warren." *Boston Magazine,* 1784, pp. 221–22.

————. *Biographical Dictionary.* Boston: Cushing and Appleton, 1809.

Ellis, George E. *History of the Battle of Bunker's [Breed's] Hill.* Boston: Lockwood, Brooks, 1875.

————. *March 17th, 1876: Celebration of the Centennial Anniversary of the Evacuation of Boston by the British . . . and a Chronicle of the Siege of Boston.* Boston: City Council, 1876.

Ellis, Joseph J. *His Excellency George Washington.* New York: Vintage, 2005.

Elting, John. *The Battle of Bunker's Hill.* Monmouth, N.J.: Philip Freneau Press, 1975.

Emerson, William. *Diary and Letters, 1743–1776.* Edited by Amelia Forbes Emerson. Madison: University of Wisconsin, 1972.

Endicott, Charles M. "Leslie's Retreat or the Resistance to British Arms at the North Bridge in Salem, etc." *Essex Institute Proceedings* 1 (1859): 89–126.

Eulogies and Orations on the Life and Death of George Washington. Boston: Manning and Loring, 1800.

Evelyn, Capt. W. Glanville. *Memoir and Letters.* Edited by G. D. Scull. Oxford, England: James Parker, 1879.

Everett, Alexander H. "Joseph Warren." In *American Biography*, edited by Jared Sparks. Boston: Hilliard, Gray, 1838.

Farnsworth, Amos. *Diary.* Edited by S. A. Greene. MHS *Proceedings* 12 (1873): 74–107.

Farrell, James M. "The Writs of Assistance and Public Memory: John Adams and the Legacy of James Otis." *NEQ* 79 (2006): 533–66.

Fay, Bernard. *Revolution and Freemasonry, 1680–1800.* Boston: Little, Brown, 1935.

Fen, Elizabeth A. *Pox Americana: The Great Smallpox Epidemic of 1775–82.* New York: Hill and Wang, 2001.

Ferguson, Robert A. "The Commonalities of Common Sense." *WMQ* 57 (2000): 465–504.

———. *The American Enlightenment, 1750–1820.* Cambridge, Mass.: Harvard University Press, 1994.

Ferling, John. *First of Men: A Life of George Washington.* New York: Oxford University Press, 2010.

———. *The Ascent of George Washington: The Hidden Political Genius of an American Icon.* New York: Bloomsbury Press, 2009.

Finkenbine, Roy E. "Belinda's Petition: Reparations for Slavery in Revolutionary Massachusetts." *WMQ* March 2007: 95–102.

Fischer, David Hackett. *Albion's Seed: Four British Folkways in America.* New York: Oxford University Press, 1989.

———. *Paul Revere's Ride.* New York: Oxford University Press, 1994.

———. *Liberty and Freedom: A Visual History of the America's Founding Ideas.* New York: Oxford University Press, 2005.

———. *Washington's Crossing.* New York: Oxford University Press, 2006.

Fitch, Jabez. Diary. MHS *Proceedings* 2, no. 9 (1894–95): 41–91.

Flavell, Julie. *When London Was the Capital of America.* New Haven, Conn.: Yale University Press, 2010.

———. "British Perceptions of New England and the Decision for a Coercive Policy, 1774–1775." In *When Britain and America Go to War: The Impact of War and Warfare in Anglo-America,* edited by Julie Flavell and Stephen Conway, pp. 95–115. Gainesville: University Press of Florida, 2004.

Flavell, Julie, and Stephen Conway, eds. *When Britain and America Go to War: The Impact of War and Warfare in Anglo-America.* Gainesville: University Press of Florida, 2004.

Fleming, Thomas. *The First Stroke: Lexington, Concord, and the Beginning of the America Revolution.* Washington, D.C.: National Park Service, 1978.

———. *Now We Are Enemies: The Story of Bunker Hill.* Washington, D.C.: American History Press, 2010.

———. *1776: Year of Illusions.* New York: Norton, 1975.

Flexner, James Thomas. *John Singleton Copley.* New York: Fordham University Press, 1993.

Flick, Alexander C. "General Henry Knox's Ticonderoga Expedition." *Quarterly Journal* (New York State Historical Association) 9 (April 1928): 119–35.

Fliegelman, Jay. *Declaring Independence: Jefferson, Natural Language, and the Culture of Performance.* Sanford, Calif.: Stanford University Press, 1993.

Florence, Justin. "Minutemen for Months: The Making of an American Revolutionary Army before Washington, April 20–July 2, 1775." AAS *Proceedings* 113 (2005): 59–101.

Fonblanque, E. D. de. *Political and Military Episodes . . . Derived from the Life and Correspondence of the Right Hon. J. Burgoyne.* 2 vols. London: Macmillan, 1876.

Foner, Eric. *Tom Paine and Revolutionary America.* New York: Oxford University Press, 1976.

Forbes, Esther. *Paul Revere and the World He Lived In.* Boston: Mariner, 1999.

Force, Peter, ed. *American Archives,* 4th ser. (*AA4*). Washington, D.C., 1837–53.

Ford, W. C. "Henry Knox—Bookseller." MHS *Proceedings* 6 (1927–28): 227–303.

———, ed. *The Warren-Adams Letters.* 2 vols. Boston: MHS, 1917–25.

Forman, Samuel. *Dr. Joseph Warren: The Boston Tea Party, Bunker Hill, and the Birth of American Liberty.* New Orleans: Pelican, 2011.

Fortescue, John E., ed. *The Correspondence of King George the Third from 1760 to December, 1783.* 6 vols. London: Macmillan, 1927–28.

Fowler, William M. *The Baron of Beacon Hill: A Biography of John Hancock.* Boston: Houghton Mifflin, 1980.

———. *Samuel Adams: Radical Puritan.* New York: Longman, 1997.

———. *Rebels Under Sail.* New York: Scribner's, 1976.

Fox, Ebenezer. *The Revolutionary Adventures of Ebenezer Fox.* Boston: Charles Fox, 1847.

Franklin, Benjamin. *The Autobiography of Benjamin Franklin.* New Haven, Conn.: Yale University Press, 1964.

Freeman, Douglas Southall. *George Washington.* Vols. 3 and 4. New York: Scribner's, 1951.

Freiberg, Malcolm. "Thomas Hutchinson and the Province Currency." *NEQ* 30 (1957): 190–208.

———. "Thomas Hutchinson: The First Fifty Years, 1711–1761." *WMQ* 15 (1958): 35–55.

French, Allen. "First George Washington Scandal." MHS *Proceedings* 65 (1932–36): 460–74.

———. "The Hallowell-Graves Fisticuffs, 1775." MHS *Proceedings* 63 (1929–30): 23–48.

———. "General Haldimand in Boston." MHS *Proceedings* 66 (1942): 80–95.

———, ed. *A British Fusilier in Revolutionary Boston: Being the Diary of Lieutenant Frederick Mackenzie. . . . January 5–April 30, 1775.* Cambridge, Mass.: Harvard University Press, 1926.

———. *The First Year of the American Revolution.* New York: Octagon, 1968.

———. *General Gage's Informers.* New York: Greenwood Press, 1968.

———. *The Day of Concord and Lexington.* Boston: Little, Brown, 1925; reprint, Philadelphia: Eastern National Park and Monument Association, 1984.

———. *The Colonials: Being a Narrative of the Events Chiefly Associated with the Siege and Evacuation of the Town of Boston in New England.* New York: Doubleday, 1902.

———. *The Siege of Boston.* New York: Macmillan, 1911.

———. *The Historic Concord and Lexington Fight.* Cambridge, Mass.: Harvard Common Press, 1978.

Frese, Joseph R. "Smuggling, the Navy, and the Customs Service, 1763–1772." In *Seafaring in Colonial Massachusetts*, edited by Frederick S. Allis Jr., pp. 199–212. Boston: Colonial Society of Massachusetts, 1980.

Frey, Sylvia. *Water from the Rock: Black Resistance in a Revolutionary Age.* Princeton, N.J.: Princeton University Press, 1991.

Fritz, Jean. *Cast for a Revolution: Some American Friends and Enemies, 1728–1814.* Boston: Houghton Mifflin, 1972.

Frothingham, Richard, ed. "Correspondence in 1774–1775." MHS *Collections*, 4th ser., 4 (1863): 1–275.

———. *Life and Times of Joseph Warren.* Boston: Little, Brown, 1865.

———. *The History of the Siege of Boston.* Boston: Little Brown, 1873.

———. *The Battle-field of Bunker Hill.* Boston: Richard Frothingham, 1876.

Fuhrer, Mary Babson. "The Revolutionary Worlds of Lexington and Concord Compared." *NEQ* 85, no. 1 (2012): 78–118.

Gage, Thomas. "Response to Queries from George Chalmers." MHS *Collections*, 4th ser., 4 (1858): 369–70.

———. "Circumstantial Account of an Attack that Happened on the 19th April, 1775. . . ." MHS *Collections*, 2nd ser., 2 (1814): 224–7.

———. *The Correspondence of General Thomas Gage . . . 1763–1775.* Edited by Clarence E. Carter. 2 vols. New Haven, Conn.: Yale University Press, 1931–33.

Gale, R. R. *"A Soldier-Like Way": The Material Culture of the British Infantry, 1751–1768.* Elk River, Minn.: Track of the Wolf, 2007.

Galvin, John R. *The Minute Men: The First Fight; Myths and Realities of the American Revolution.* Washington, D.C.: Potomac, 2006.

———. *Three Men of Boston.* New York: Crowell, 1976.

Gannet, Caleb. "The Diary of Caleb Gannet for the Year 1776." *WMQ*, 3rd ser., 3, no. 1 (1946): 117–22.

Garden, Alexander. *Anecdotes of the American Revolution.* Brooklyn: Union Press, 1865.

Gates, Henry Louis. *The Trials of Phillis Wheatley: America's First Black Poet and Her Encounters with the Founding Fathers.* New York: Basic Civitas, 2000.

Gavett, William. "Account of the Affair at North Bridge." *Essex Institute Proceedings* 1 (1859): 126–28.

Gilje, Paul A. *Rioting in America.* Bloomington: Indiana University Press, 1996.

———. *Liberty on the Waterfront: American Maritime Culture in the Age of Revolution.* Philadelphia: University of Pennsylvania, 2007.

Gilje, Paul A., and William Pencak, eds. *Pirates, Jack Tar, and Memory: New Directions in American Maritime History.* Mystic, Conn.: Mystic Seaport: 2007.

Gipson, Lawrence H. *The Coming of the Revolution, 1763–1775.* New York: Harper Torchbook, 1962.

Goldfeld, Alex. *The North End: A Brief History of Boston's Oldest Neighborhood.* Boston: History Press, 2009.

Goldstein, Erik. "A British Grenadier's Button from a Bunker Hill Grave." *Military Collector and Historian* 60 (Spring 2008): 70–78.

Goodell, Abner Cheney Jr. *The Trial and Execution, for Petit Treason, of Mark and Phillis.* Cambridge, Mass.: John Wilson, 1883.

Gooding, S. James. *An Introduction to British Artillery in North America.* Bloomfield, Ontario: Museum Restoration Service, 1980.

Gordon, William. "Apr. 6, 1776, Letter to Samuel Wilson." MHS *Proceedings* 60 (1926–1927): 361–64.

———. "An Account of the Commencement of Hostilities Between Great Britain and America . . ." In *AA4*, 2:625–31. Washington, D.C., 1837–53.

———. *The History of the Rise, Progress, and Establishment of the Independence of the United States of America*. 1788; reprint, Freeport, N.Y: Books for Libraries Press, 1969.

Goss, Elbridge Henry. *The Life of Colonel Paul Revere*. 2 vols. Freeport, N.Y.: Books for Libraries, 1891.

Gould, Eligia H. *The Persistence of Empire: British Political Culture in the Age of the American Revolution*. Chapel Hill: University of North Carolina Press, 2000.

Grant, James. Letters to Edward Harvey. James Grant Papers, LOC.

Greene, George Washington. *The Life of Nathanael Greene*. Vol. 1. New York: Putnam, 1867.

Greene, Jack P. *Pursuits of Happiness: The Social Development of Early Modern British Colonies and the Formation of American Culture*. Chapel Hill: University of North Carolina Press, 1988.

Greene, Jack P., and J. R. Pole, eds. *A Companion to the American Revolution*. Malden, Mass.: Blackwell, 2004.

Greene, Joshua. Diary, 1775, extracts. MHS.

Greene, Nathanael. *Papers of General Nathanael Greene*. Vol. 1, edited by Richard Showman. Chapel Hill: University of North Carolina Press, 1976.

Greenwood, Isaac J., ed. *Revolutionary Services of John Greenwood of Boston and New York, 1775–1783*. New York: De Vinne Press, 1922.

Grieder, James. "The Boston Tea Party Unmasked: Nantucket's Real Role in the Start of the American Revolution." *Historic Nantucket* 62, no. 1 (2012): 11–15.

Gross, Robert A. *The Minutemen and Their World*. New York: Hill and Wang, 1976.

Gruber, Ira. *The Howe Brothers and the American Revolution*. New York: Norton, 1975.

Gustafson, Sandra. *Eloquence Is Power: Oratory and Performance in Early America*. Chapel Hill: University of North Carolina Press, 2000.

Hale, Edward E. *One Hundred Years Ago*. Boston: Lockwood Brooke, 1875.

———. "The Siege of Boston." In *The Memorial History of Boston*, edited by Justin Winsor, pp. 67–118. Boston: Osgood, 1881.

Hall, Michael Garibaldi, *Edward Randolph and the American Colonies, 1676–1703*. Chapel Hill: University of North Carolina Press, 1960.

Hallahan, William H. *The Day the American Revolution Began*. New York: Perennial, 2001.

Halsey, R. T. Haines. *The Boston Port Bill as Pictured by a Contemporary London Cartoonist*. New York: Grolier Club, 1904.

Hamilton, Edward Pierce. "General John Thomas." MHS *Proceedings* 84 (1972): 44–52.

Hamlin, Cyrus. *My Grandfather, Colonel Francis Faulkner*. Boston: Stanley and Usher, 1887.

Hanna, William F. *A History of Taunton, Massachusetts*. Taunton, Mass.: Old Colonial Historical Society, 2008.

Hanson, John Wesley. *History of the Town of Danvers*. Danvers, Mass.: J. W. Hanson, 1848.

Harris, John, ed. *Lexington-Concord Alarm: Our Revolutionary War Begins*. Boston: Globe, 1975.

Haskell, Caleb. *Caleb Haskell's Diary*. Edited by Lothrop Withington. Tarrytown, N.Y.: W Abbatt, 1922.

Haslewood, Captain William. "A Journal of a British Officer During the American Revolution." *Mississippi Valley Historical Review* 7 (June 1920–March 1921): 51–58.

Hassam, John T. "King's Arms Tavern." *NEHGR* 34 (1880): 41–48.

———. "Castle Tavern." *NEHGR* 33 (1880): 400–403.

Hatch, Nathan O. "The Origins of Civil Millennialism in America: New England Clergymen, War with France, and the Revolution." *WMQ*, 3rd ser., 31 (1974): 407–30.

———. *The Democratization of Christianity*. New Haven, Conn.: Yale University Press, 1989.

———. *The Sacred Cause of Liberty: Republican Thought and the Millennium in Revolutionary New England*. New Haven, Conn.: Yale University Press, 1977.

Hawes, Samuel. "The Journal of Samuel Hawes." Edited by Richard Brigham Johnson. *NEHGR* 130 (1976): 208–19, 273–83; 131 (1977): 40–50.

Hawkes, James. *A Retrospect of the Boston Tea-Party: With a Memoir of George R. T. Hewes*. New York, 1834.

Hawthorne, Nathaniel. *Legends of Province House*. Boston: Joseph Knight, 1897.

Hearn, Chester. *George Washington's Schooners: The First American Navy*. Annapolis, Md.: Naval Institute Press, 1995.

Heath, William. *Memoirs of Major-General Heath*. Boston: Thomas and Andres, 1798.

Heimert, Alan. *Religion and the American Mind from the Great Awakening to the Revolution*. Cambridge, Mass.: Harvard University Press, 1966.

Henretta, James. *The Evolution of American Society, 1700–1815*. Lexington, Mass.: Heath, 1973.

———. *Salutary Neglect*. Princeton, N.J.: Princeton University Press, 1972.

———. "Economic Development and Social Structure in Colonial Boston." *WMQ*, 3rd ser., 22 (1965): 75–92.

Henriques, Peter. *Realistic Visionary: A Portrait of George Washington*. Charlottesville: University of Virginia Press, 2008.

Henshaw, William. *The Orderly Book of Colonel William Henshaw of the American Army*. Boston: A. Williams, 1881.

Hersey, Frank W. C. *Heroes of the Battle Road*. Boston: Perry Walton, 1930.

———. "Tar and Feathers: The Adventures of Captain John Malcom." *Colonial Society of Massachusetts Publications* 8 (1903): 89–104.

Hibbert, Christopher. *George III: A Personal History*. New York: Basic Books, 2000.

Higginbotham, Don. *The War of American Independence*. Boston: Northeastern University Press, 1983.

———. *George Washington: Uniting a Nation*. Lanham, Md.: Rowman and Littlefield, 2004.

Hill, John B. *Bi-Centennial of Old Dunstable*. Nashua, N.H.: E. H. Spaulding, 1878.

Hoerder, Dirk. *Crowd Action in Revolutionary Massachusetts, 1765–1780*. Ann Arbor, Mich.: Academic Press, 1977.

———. "Boston Leaders and Boston Crowds, 1765–1776." In *The American Revolution: Explorations in the History of American Radicalism*, edited by Alfred F. Young, pp. 233–72. DeKalb: Northern Illinois University Press, 1976.

Hoffman, Ronald, and Peter J. Albert, eds. *The Transforming Hand of Revolution*. Charlottesville: University Press of Virginia, 1995.

———, eds. *Women in the Age of the American Revolution*. Charlottesville: University Press of Virginia, 1992.

Hogeland, William. *Declaration: The Nine Tumultuous Weeks When America Became Independent*. New York: Simon and Schuster, 2010.

Holbrook, Stewart Hall. *The Story of the Boston Post Road*. New York: McGraw Hill, 1962.

Holland, Henry W. *William Dawes and His Ride with Paul Revere*. Boston: John Wilson and Son, 1878.

Holton, Woody. *Abigail Adams*. New York: Free Press, 2009.

Hosmer, James K. *Samuel Adams*. Boston: Houghton Mifflin, 1888.

———. *The Life of Thomas Hutchinson . . .* Boston: Houghton Mifflin, 1896.

How, David. *Diary of David How, a Private in Colonel Paul Dudley Sargent's Regiment of the Massachusetts Line*. Morrisania, N.Y., 1865.

Howard, Bret. *Boston: A Social History*. New York: Hawthorne, 1976.

Howe, John. *Journal*. In *History of Middlesex County, Massachusetts*, by D. Hamilton Hurd, 579–84. Philadelphia: J. W. Lewis, 1890.

Howe, William. *General Sir William Howe's Orderly Book*. Edited by Benjamin Franklin Stevens. London: Benjamin Franklin Stevens, 1890.

Hudson, Frederic. "The Concord Fight." *Harper's New Monthly Magazine* 50, no. 300 (May 1875): 801.

Hull, Lt. Edward. *Narrative*. MHS *Proceedings* 16 (1878): 155–58.

Hulton, Ann. *Letters of a Loyalist Lady*. Cambridge: Harvard University Press, 1927.

Hunter, Phyllis Whitman. *Purchasing Identity in the Atlantic World: Massachusetts Merchants, 1670–1780*. Ithaca, N.Y.: Cornell University Press, 2001.

Hurd, D. Hamilton. *History of Middlesex County, Massachusetts*. Philadelphia: J. W. Lewis, 1880.

Hutchinson, Thomas. *The Diary and Letters*. Edited by Peter Orlando Hutchinson. 2 vols. Boston: Houghton and Mifflin, 1894.

———. *History of the Province of Massachusetts Bay*. Vol. 3. London: John Murray, 1828.

Ingalls, Phineas. "Revolutionary War Journal, April 19, 1775–December 8, 1776." *Historical Collections of the Essex Institute* 53 (1917): 81–92.

Irvin, Benjamin H. "Tar, Feathers, and the Enemies of American Liberties, 1768–1776." *NEQ* 76 (2003): 197–238.

———. *Clothed in Robes of Sovereignty: The Continental Congress and the People Out of Doors*. New York: Oxford University Press, 2011.

———. *Samuel Adams: Son of Liberty, Father of Revolution*. New York: Oxford University Press, 2002.

Jaffe, Eric. *The King's Best Highway: The Lost History of the Boston Post Road, the Route That Made America*. New York: Scribner, 2010.

Jameson, J. Franklin. *The American Revolution Considered as a Social Movement*. Princeton, N.J.: Princeton University Press, 1940.

Jeffries, John. "A Tory Surgeon's Experiences, June 17, 1775." *Boston Medical and Surgical Journal* 92, no. 24 (June 17, 1875): 729–32.

Jehlen, Myra. *America Incarnation: The Individual, the Nation, and the Continent*. Cambridge, Mass.: Harvard University Press, 1986.

Jensen, Merrill, ed. *Tracts of the American Revolution, 1763–1776.* Indianapolis: Bobbs-Merrill, 1967.

Johnson, Claudia Durst. *Daily Life in Colonial New England.* Westport, Conn.: Greenwood Press, 2002.

Johnson, Paul. *A History of the American People.* New York: HarperCollins, 1998.

Johnston, Patrick. "Building to a Revolution: The Powder Alarm and Popular Mobilization of the New England Countryside, 1774–1775." *Historical Journal of Massachusetts* 37, no. 1 (2009): 123–40.

Jones, Douglas Lamar. *Village and Seaport: Migration and Society in Eighteenth-Century Massachusetts.* Hanover, N.H.: University Press of New England, 1981.

Jones, E. Alfred. *Loyalists of Massachusetts.* 1930; reprint, Baltimore, Md.: Clearfield, 1995.

Jones, Howard Mumford. *O Strange New World: American Culture: The Formative Years.* New York: Viking, 1964.

Jones, Thomas Morton. "Ballad of Boston Ministers, 1774." *NEHGR* 13 (1839): 131–33.

Kammen, Michael. *Empire and Interest: The American Colonies and the Politics of Mercantilism.* Philadelphia: Lippincott, 1970.

———. *A Rope of Sand: The Colonial Agents, British Politics, and the American Revolution.* New York: Vintage, 1974.

Keegan, John. *Fields of Battle: The Wars for North America.* New York: Vintage: 1997.

Kehoe, Vincent J. R., ed. *We Were There! April 19, 1775: The British Regulars.* Chelmsford, Mass.: Vincent Kehoe, 1975.

Kehr, Thomas. "The Seizure of His Majesty's Fort William and Mary." http://nhssar.org/essays/FortConstitution.html.

Kelly, Alfred, et al. *Leadership in the American Revolution.* Washington, D.C.: Library of Congress, 1974.

Kemble, Lt. Col. Stephen. *Journals of Lieutenant-Colonel Stephen Kemble, 1773–1789.* Boston: Gregg Press, 1972.

Kerber, Linda. *Women of the Republic: Intellect and Ideology in Revolutionary America.* New York: Norton, 1986.

Kerr, Lowell. "Benedict Arnold and the Warrens." *Americana,* 30, no. 2 (April 1936): 324–34.

Ketchum, Richard M. *Decisive Day: The Battle for Bunker Hill.* New York: Henry Holt, 1999.

Kettle, John. Diary, 1775. MHS.

Kidder, Frederic. *History of the Boston Massacre, March 5, 1770.* Albany, N.Y.: Joel Munsell, 1870.

King, Lester. *The Medical World of the Eighteenth-Century.* Chicago: University of Chicago Press, 1958.

Kiracofe, David James. "Dr. Benjamin Church and the Dilemma of Treason in Revolutionary Massachusetts." *NEQ* 70, no. 3 (1997): 443–62.

Knapp, Samuel. *Biographical Sketches of Eminent Lawyers, Statesmen and Men of Letters.* Boston: Richardson and Lord, 1821.

Knollenberg, Bernhard. "Bunker Hill Reviewed: A Study in the Conflict of Historical Evidence." MHS *Proceedings* 72 (1963): 84–100.

———. "John Adams, Knox, and Washington." AAS *Proceedings* 56, pt. 2 (1947): 207–38.

Knox, Dudley. *The Naval Genius of George Washington.* Boston: Houghton Mifflin, 1932.

Knox, Henry. Diary, 20 November 1775–13 January 1776. MHS.

———. "Letter to John Adams, Sept. 25, 1776." AAS *Proceedings* 56, pt 2 (1946): 217.

Kolchin, Peter. *American Slavery, 1619–1877.* New York: Hill and Wang, 2003.

Krieger, Alex, and David Cobb. *Mapping Boston.* Cambridge, Mass.: MIT Press, 2001.

Kulikoff, Alan. "The Progress of Inequality in Revolutionary Boston." *WMQ,* 3rd ser., 28 (1971): 375–412.

Kurtz, Stephen G., and James H. Hutson, eds. *Essays on the American Revolution.* Chapel Hill: University of North Carolina Press, 1973.

Labaree, Benjamin W. *Colonial Massachusetts: A History.* Millwood, N.Y.: KTO, 1979.

———. *The Boston Tea Party.* Boston: Northeastern University Press, 1979.

Labaree, Leonard W. *Royal Government in America: A Study of the British Colonial System Before 1783.* New York: Frederick Ungar, 1958.

Lambert, Frank. *Pedlar in Divinity: George Whitefield and the Transatlantic Revivals, 1737–1770.* Princeton, N.J.: Princeton University Press, 1994.

Langford, Paul. *A Polite and Commercial People: England, 1727–1783.* Oxford: Clarendon, 1989.

Laurie, Walter S., "Letter to John Roebuck, June 23, 1775." *NEQ* 25, no. 3 (1952): 366–74.

Lax, John, and William Pencak. "The Knowles Riot and the Crisis of the 1740s in Massachusetts." *Perspectives in American History* 10 (1976): 161–214.

Leach, John. "Journal Kept . . . During His Confinement by the British in Boston Gaol, in 1775." *NEHGR* 19 (1865): 255.

Lechmere, Richard. Letters. MHS *Proceedings,* 2d ser., 16 (1902): 285–90.

Lee, Richard Henry. *Life of Arthur Lee*. Boston: Wells and Lilly, 1829.

Leehey, Patrick M. *Paul Revere: Artisan, Businessman, and Patriot: The Man Behind the Myth*. Boston: Paul Revere Memorial Association, 1988.

Lemisch, Jesse. "Radical Plot in Boston (1770): A Study in the Use of Evidence." *Harvard Law Review* 84 (1970): 485–504.

———. "Jack Tar in the Streets: Merchant Seamen in the Politics of the Revolutionary America." *WMQ*, 3rd ser., 25 (1968): 371–407.

Lengel, Edward G. *General George Washington: A Military Life*. New York: Random House, 2007.

"Leslie's Retreat." *EIHC* 17 (1880): 190–92.

"Letters of John Hancock, Joseph Warren, Thomas Gage, James Warren and Governor Trumbull." *MHS Collections*, 5th ser., 10 (1888): 283–312.

Lincoln, William, ed. *Journals of Each Provincial Congress of Massachusetts*. Boston: Dutton and Wentworth, 1838.

Linebaugh, Peter, and Marcus Rediker. *The Many-Headed Hydra: Sailors, Slaves, Commoners and the Hidden History of the Revolutionary Atlantic*. Boston: Beacon, 2000.

Lister, Jeremy. *Narrative*. Cambridge, Mass.: Harvard University Press, 1931.

Litchfield, Paul. *Diary*. MHS *Proceedings* 19 (1882): 377–79.

Litchfield, Israel. "Diary." *NEHGR* 129 (1975): 150–71.

Longley, R. S. "Mob Activities in Revolutionary America." *NEQ* 6 (1933): 98–130.

Longmore, Paul. *The Invention of George Washington*. Charlottesville: University of Virginia Press, 1999.

Lord, Arthur. "A Soldier of the Revolution, General John Thomas." *Bostonian Society Publications* 12 (1915): 1–35.

Loring, J. S. "Reminiscence of General Warren." NEHGS *Register* 12, no. 3 (1858): 230.

———. *The Hundred Boston Orators*. Boston: J. P. Jewett, 1852.

———. "The Relics of General Warren." *Historical Magazine* 1 (1857): 363–68.

Lossing, Benson J. *The Pictorial Field-Book of the Revolution*. Vol. 1. New York: Harper, 1851.

Lothrop, Samuel Kirkland. *History of the Church in Brattle Street*. Boston: Crosby and Nichols, 1851.

Lovell, James. "Letter to Josiah Quincy, Jr., 3 November 1774." MHS *Proceedings* 50 (1916–17): 472–73.

Lukens, Jesse. "Incidents of the Siege of Boston, in 1775." *American Historical Record* 1 (1872): 546–50.

Lunt, Paul. *Paul Lunt's Diary, May–December 1775*. Edited by Samuel A. Green. Boston, 1872.

Lushington, S. R. *Life and Services of General Lord Harris*. London: Parker, 1840.

Mackenzie, Frederick. *Diary of Frederick Mackenzie*. Edited by Allen French. Cambridge, Mass.: Harvard University Press, 1930.

Maier, Pauline. "Popular Uprisings and Civil Authority in Eighteenth Century America." *WMQ* 28 (1970): 3-35.

———. "Revolutionary Violence and the Relevance of History." *Journal of Interdisciplinary History* 2 (1971): 119–35.

———. "John Wilkes and American Disillusionment with Britain." *WMQ*, 3d ser., 20 (1963): 373-95.

———. "Reason and Revolution: The Radicalism of Dr. Thomas Young." *American Quarterly* 28, no. 2 (1976): 229–49.

———. *American Scripture: Making the Declaration of Independence*. New York: Alfred A. Knopf, 1997.

———. *From Resistance to Revolution: Colonial Radicals and the Development of American Opposition to Britain, 1765–1776*. New York: Norton, 1991.

———. *The Old Revolutionaries: Political Lives in the Age of Samuel Adams*. New York: Alfred A. Knopf, 1980.

Main, Jackson T. *The Upper House in Revolutionary America, 1763–1788*. Madison: University of Wisconsin Press, 1967.

———. "Government by the People: The American Revolution and the Democratization of the Legislatures." *WMQ*, 3d ser., 28 (1966): 391–407.

Mandell, Daniel. *Behind the Frontier: Indians in Eighteenth-Century Eastern Massachusetts*. Lincoln: University of Nebraska Press, 1996.

Manegold, C. S. *Ten Hills Farm: The Forgotten History of Slavery in the North*. Princeton, N.J.: Princeton University Press, 2010.

Manucy, Albert. *Artillery Through the Ages*. Washington, D.C.: U.S. Government Printing Office, 1955.

Martin, Joseph Plumb. *Private Yankee Doodle*. Edited by George F. Scheer. Boston: Little, Brown, 1962.

Martyn, Charles. *The Life of Artemas Ward*. New York: A. Ward, 1921.

Mastone, Victor, Craig Brown, and Christopher Maio. *Chelsea Creek: First Naval Engagement of the American Revolution*. Washington, D.C.: National Park Service, American Battlefield Protection Program, 2011.

Matthews, Albert. "Joyce, Jun." *Colonial Society of Massachusetts Publications* 8 (1903): 89–104.
———. "Joyce Jr. Once More." *Colonial Society of Massachusetts Transactions* 11 (1906–7): 282.
———. "The Solemn League and Covenant, 1774." *Colonial Society of Massachusetts Transactions* 28 (1915–16): 103–22.
Matthews, Albert, and Mary Farwell Ayer. *Check-List of Boston Newspapers, 1704–1780.* Boston: Colonial Society of Massachusetts, 1907.
Mayer, Holly. *Belonging to the Army: Camp Followers and Community During the American Revolution.* Columbia: University of South Carolina Press, 1999.
Mayo, Catherine B., ed. "Additions to Thomas Hutchinson's 'History of Massachusetts Bay.' " AAS *Proceedings* 59, pt. 1 (April 1949): 11–74.
Mazlish, Bruce. *The Revolutionary Ascetic: Evolution of a Political Type.* New York: McGraw Hill, 1976.
McAfee, Michael L., "Artillery of the American Revolution, 1775–1783." Washington, D.C.: American Defense Preparedness Association, 1974.
McClellan, T. K. *Smuggling in the American Colonies at the Outbreak of the Revolution.* New York: Moffat Yard, 1912.
McClure, David. *Diary.* MHS *Proceedings* 16 (1878): 155–61.
McConville, Brendan. *The King's Three Faces: The Rise and Fall of Royal America, 1688–1776.* Chapel Hill: University of North Carolina Press, 2006.
McCullough, David. *John Adams.* New York: Simon and Schuster, 2001.
———. *1776.* New York: Simon and Schuster, 2005.
McDonald, Sharon Lawrence. *The Bedford Flag Unfurled.* Bedford, Mass.: Bedford Free Public Library, 2000.
McDougall, Walter A. *Freedom Just Around the Corner: A New American History, 1585–1828.* New York: Perennial, 2004.
"Memoirs of Major-General Warren." *Polyanthos* 3 (November 1806): 217–24.
Merrill, Lindsay. *The New England Gun.* New Haven, Conn.: Yale University Press, 1975.
Middlekauff, Robert. *The Glorious Cause: The American Revolution, 1763–1789.* New York: Oxford University Press, 2005.
Miller, J. C. *Sam Adams: Pioneer in Propaganda.* Stanford, Calif.: Stanford University Press, 1960.
Miller, Nathan. *Sea of Glory: The Continental Navy Fights for Independence, 1775–1783.* New York: McKay, 1974.
Miller, Perry. "From the Covenant to the Revival." In *The Shaping of American Religion,* edited by James Ward Smith and A. Leland Jamison, pp. 322–68. Princeton, N.J.: Princeton University Press, 1961.
———. "The Moral and Psychological Roots of American Resistance." In *Reinterpretation of the American Revolution,* edited by Jack Greene, pp. 251–74. New York: Harper, 1968.
Mitchell, John Hanson. *The Paradise of All These Parts: A Natural History of Boston.* Boston: Beacon Press, 2008.
Montresor, Capt. John. *The Montresor Journals.* Edited by G. D. Scull. Collections of the New York Historical Society for the Year 1881, vol. 14. New York: New York Historical Society, 1882.
Moore, Frank. *Songs and Ballads of the American Revolution.* New York: D. Appleton, 1855.
———. *Diary of the American Revolution.* New York: Scribner, 1859.
———, ed. *The Patriot Preachers of the American Revolution, with Biographical Sketches, 1766–1783.* N.p., 1860.
Moore, George H. *Notes on the History of Slavery in Massachusetts.* New York: D. Appleton, 1866.
Moore, Warren. *Weapons of the American Revolution and Accoutrements.* New York: Promontory Press, 1967.
Morgan, Edmund S. "Thomas Hutchinson and the Stamp Act." NEQ 21 (1948): 459–92.
———. *Paul Revere's Ride: Three Accounts of His Famous Ride.* Boston: MHS, 2000.
———. *Inventing the People: The Rise of Popular Sovereignty in England and America.* New York: Norton, 1988.
———. "The Puritan Ethic and the American Revolution." WMQ 62, no. 1 (1989): 3–43.
———. *The Birth of the Republic, 1763–1789.* 3rd ed. Chicago: University of Chicago Press, 1992.
———. *American Heroes: Profiles of Men and Women Who Shaped Early America.* New York: Norton, 2009.
Morgan, Edmund S., and Helen M. Morgan. *The Stamp Act Crisis: Prologue to Revolution.* Chapel Hill: University of North Carolina Press, 1995.
Morgan, Nathaniel. "Diary, April 21–July 1775." *Collections of the Connecticut Historical Society* 7 (1899): 99, 101–10.
Morison, Samuel E. *The Maritime History of Massachusetts.* Boston: Houghton Mifflin, 1921.

———. *Three Centuries of Harvard.* Cambridge, Mass.: Harvard University Press, 1986.

Muller, John. *The Attack and Defense of Fortified Places.* 1757; reprint, edited by David Manthey. Woodbridge, Va.: Invisible College Press, 2004.

Murdock, Harold, ed. *Late News of the Excursion and Ravages of the King's Troops on the Nineteenth of April, 1775.* Cambridge, Mass.: Harvard University Press, 1927.

———. *The Nineteenth of April, 1775.* 1923; reprint, Cranbury, N.J.: Scholar's Bookshelf, 2005.

———. *Bunker Hill: Notes and Queries on a Famous Battle.* Boston: Houghton Mifflin, 1927.

———. *Earl Percy's Dinner Table.* Boston: Houghton Mifflin, 1907.

Murray, James. *Letters.* Edited by Nina Moore Tiffany. Boston: n.p., 1901.

Nagel, Paul. *John Quincy Adams.* New York: Knopf, 1997.

Nash, Gary. *The Urban Crucible: The Northern Seaports and the Origins of the American Revolution.* Cambridge, Mass.: Harvard University Press, 1986.

———. *The Unknown American Revolution.* New York: Penguin, 2006.

Nash, George H. III. *From Radicalism to Revolution: The Political Career of Josiah Quincy, Jr.* Worcester, Mass.: American Antiquarian Society, 1970.

Nelson, Craig. *Thomas Paine: Enlightenment, Revolution, and the Birth of Modern Nations.* New York: Penguin, 2006.

Nelson, James. *George Washington's Secret Navy: How the American Revolution Went to Sea.* New York: McGraw Hill, 2008.

———. *With Fire and Sword: The Battle of Bunker Hill and the Beginning of the American Revolution.* New York: Thomas Dunne, 2011.

Nelson, Paul David. *Francis Rawdon-Hastings, Marquess of Hastings: Soldier, Peer of the Realm, Governor-General of India.* Cranbury, N.J.: Farleigh Dickinson University Press, 2005.

Nelson, William H. *The American Tory.* Boston: Beacon Press, 1961.

Newell, Thomas. "Extracts from an Original Diary by Thomas Newell, Boston, 1773, 1774." MHS *Proceedings,* 1st ser., 4 (1860): 261–76.

Newell, Timothy. "A Journal during the Time That Boston Was Shut Up in 1775–76." MHS *Collections* 4, no. 1 (1852): 260–72.

Neyland, James. *Crispus Attucks: Patriot.* Los Angeles: Melrose Square, 1995.

Nicolson, Colin. "Governor Francis Bernard, the Massachusetts Friends of Government, and the Advent of the Revolution." MHS *Proceedings,* 3d ser., 101 (1991): 24–113.

———. " 'McIntosh, Otis & Adams Are Our Demagogues': Nathaniel Coffin and the Loyalist Interpretation of the Origins of the American Revolution." MHS *Proceedings,* 3rd ser., 108 (1996–97): 73–114.

———. "A Plan to 'Banish All the Scotchmen': Victimization and Political Mobilization in Pre-Revolutionary Boston." *Massachusetts Historical Review* 9 (2007): 55–102.

Nobles, Gregory. "Yet the Old Republicans Still Persevere: Samuel Adams, John Hancock, and the Crisis of Popular Leadership in Revolutionary Massachusetts, 1775–90." In *The Transforming Hand of Revolution: Reconsidering the American Revolution as a Social Movement,* edited by Ronald Hoffman and Peter J. Albert, pp. 258–85. Charlottesville: University Press of Virginia, 1995.

Norton, Mary Beth. "Eighteenth Century American Women in Peace and War: The Case of the Loyalists." *WMQ,* 3rd ser., 33 (1976): 386–409.

———. *The British-Americans: The Loyalist Exiles in England, 1774–1789.* Boston: Little, Brown, 1972.

———. *Liberty's Daughters: The Revolutionary Experience of American Women, 1750–1800.* Ithaca, N.Y.: Cornell University Press, 1996.

O'Connor, Thomas H. *Bibles, Brahmins, and Bosses: A Short History of Boston.* Boston: Trustees of the Public Library of Boston, 1976.

Okoye, F. Nwabueze. "Chattel Slavery as the Nightmare of the American Revolutionaries." *WMQ* 37 (January 1980): 3–28.

Olasky, Marvin. *Fighting for Liberty and Virtue: Political and Cultural Wars in Eighteenth-Century America.* Washington, D.C.: Regnery, 1995.

Oliver, Peter. *Origin and Progress of the American Rebellion.* Edited by Douglass Adair and John A. Schutz. Stanford, Calif.: Stanford University Press, 1961.

Page, Edwin L. "The King's Powder, 1774." *NEQ* 18 (1945): 83–92.

Paine, Samuel. Letter, June 22, 1775. AAS *Proceedings* 19 (1908–9):435–38.

Parker, Elizabeth. "John Parker." *Lexington Historical Society Proceedings* 1 (1866–89): 47.

Parker, Francis J. *Colonel William Prescott: The Commander in the Battle of Bunker's Hill.* Boston: Williams, 1875.

Parker, James. "Extracts from the Diary of James Parker of Shirley, Mass." *NEHGR* 69 (1915): 117–27.

Parker, Theodore. *Genealogical and Biographical Notes of John Parker of Lexington and his Descendants.* Worcester, Mass.: C. Hamilton Press, 1893.

Parsons, Charles L. "The Capture of Fort William and Mary, December 14 and 15, 1774." *New Hampshire Historical Society Proceedings* 4 (1890–1905): 18–47.

Partridge, Bellamy. *Sir Billy Howe.* London: Longmans, Green, 1932.

Pasley, Jeffrey L. *The Tyranny of Printers: Newspaper Politics in the Early American Republic.* Charlottesville: University Press of Virginia, 2001.

Patten, Matthew. *The Diary of Matthew Patten of Bedford, N.H: From 1754 to 1788.* Concord, N.H.: n.p., 1903.

Patterson, Stephen. *Political Parties in Revolutionary Massachusetts.* Madison: University of Wisconsin Press, 1973.

Peabody, Robert E. "The Naval Career of Captain John Manley of Marblehead." *EIHC* 45, no. 1 (1909): 1–27.

Pemberton, Thomas. "A Topographical and Historical Description of Boston, 1794." MHS *Collections* 3 (1794): 249–50.

Pencak, William. "The Social Structure of Revolutionary Boston: Evidence from the Great Fire of 1760." *Journal of Interdisciplinary History* 10, no. 2 (1979): 267–78.

———. *War, Politics, and Revolution in Provincial Massachusetts.* Boston: Northeastern University Press, 1981.

Pencak, William, Matthew Dennis, and Simon P. Newman, eds. *Riot and Revelry in Early America.* University Park: Pennsylvania State University Press, 2002.

Percy, Hugh Earl. *Letters.* Edited by Charles K. Bolton. Boston: Goodspeed, 1902.

Perkins, Edward J. *The Economy of Colonial America.* New York: Columbia University Press, 1980.

Philbrick, Nathaniel. *Mayflower: A Story of Courage, Community, and War.* New York: Penguin, 2007.

Phillips, James Duncan. "Why Colonel Leslie Came to Salem." *EIHC* 90 (1953): 313–16.

———. *Salem in the Eighteenth Century.* Salem, Mass.: Essex Institute, 1969.

Phillips, Kevin. *The Cousins' Wars: Religious, Politics, and the Triumph of Anglo-America.* New York: Basic Books, 1999.

Phillips, Leon. *The Fantastic Breed: Americans in King George's War.* Garden City, N.Y.: Doubleday, 1968.

Phinney, Elias. *Battle at Lexington.* Boston: Phelps and Farnham, 1825.

Pickering, Octavius. *The Life of Timothy Pickering.* Vol. 1. Boston: Little, Brown, 1873.

Pomeroy, Seth. *The Journals and Papers.* Edited by Louis E. de Forest. New York: Society of Colonial Wars, 1926.

Porter, Edward G. *Rambles in Old Boston, New England.* Boston: Cupples and Hurd, 1887.

Porter, Joseph W. "Memoir of General Henry Knox." *Bangor Historical Magazine,* February-March 1890, 1–16.

Potter, Israel R. *Life and Remarkable Adventures of Israel R. Potter.* Providence, R.I.: Henry Trumbull, 1824.

Prescott, William. "Judge Prescott's Account of the Battle of Bunker Hill." MHS *Proceedings* 14 (1875–76): 68–83.

Price, Ezekiel. Diary, 1775–76. MHS *Proceedings,* 1st ser., 7 (1863–64): 185–262.

Proctor, Donald J. "John Hancock: New Soundings on an Old Barrel." *Journal of American History* 64, no. 3 (1977): 652–77.

Prown, Jules. *John Singleton Copley in America, 1738–1774.* New York: October House, 1966.

Puls, Mark. *Samuel Adams: Father of the American Revolution.* New York: Palgrave Macmillan, 2006.

———. *Henry Knox: Visionary General of the American Revolution.* New York: Palgrave Macmillan, 2008.

Putnam, Daniel. Letter. *Collections of the Connecticut Historical Society* 1 (1860): 227–50.

Putnam, Rufus. *Memoirs.* Boston: Houghton Mifflin, 1903.

Quarles, Benjamin. *The Negro in the American Revolution.* Chapel Hill: University of North Carolina Press, 1996.

Quincy, Dorothy. Narrative to William Sumner, 1825, in "Reminiscences by Gen. William H. Summer." *NEHGR* 8 (1854): 188–91.

Quincy, Josiah. *A Municipal History of the Town and City of Boston, 1630–1830.* Boston: Little, Brown, 1852.

———. *Memoir of the Life of Josiah Quincy Jun.* Boston: Cummings and Hilliard, 1825.

Quincy, Josiah Jr. *The Major Political and Legal Papers of Josiah Quincy Junior.* Edited by Daniel R. Coquillette and Neil Longley York. Vols. 1–5. Boston: Colonial Society, 2006–10.

Quintal, George, J. *Patriots of Color: A Peculiar Beauty and Merit; African Americans and Native Americans at Battle Road and Bunker Hill*. Boston: National Historical Park, 2002.

Rabushka, Alvin. *Taxation in Colonial America*. Princeton, N.J.: Princeton University Press, 2008.

Rakove, Jack. *Revolutionaries: A New History of the Invention of America*. Boston: Houghton Mifflin, 2010.

———. *The Beginnings of National Politics: An Interpretive History of the Continental Congress*. New York: Knopf, 1979.

Rantoul, Robert S. "The Cruise of the 'Quero': How We Carried the News to the King." EIHC 36, no. 1 (January 1990): 1–30.

Raphael, Ray. *The First American Revolution: Before Lexington and Concord*. New York: New Press, 2002.

———. *Founders: The People Who Brought You a Nation*. New York: New Press, 2009.

Rawley, James A. "The World of Phillis Wheatley." NEQ 50 (1977): 66–70.

Rawlyk, G. A. *Yankees at Louisburg*. Orono: University of Maine, 1967.

Rawson, Michael. *Eden on the Charles: The Making of Boston*. Cambridge, Mass.: Harvard University Press, 2010.

Rebora, Carrie, Paul Staiti, et al. *John Singleton Copley in America*. New York: Metropolitan Museum of Art, 1995.

Record of Streets, Alleys, Places, etc., in the City of Boston. Boston: City Printing Dept., 1910.

"Reminiscence of General Warren." NEHGR 12 (1858): 230.

Revere, Paul. "Letter to Jeremy Belknap, January 1, 1798." MHS *Proceedings* 16 (1878): 371–76.

———. "Revere, Paul to the Corresponding Secretary." MHS *Collections*, 1st ser., 5 (1798): 110.

Richard, Carl J. *The Founders and the Classics: Greece, Rome, and the American Enlightenment*. Cambridge, Mass.: Harvard University Press, 1994.

Richards, Lysander Salmon. *History of Marshfield*. Plymouth, Mass.: Memorial Press, 1901.

Richmond, Robert P. *Powder Alarm, 1774*. Princeton, N.J.: Auerbach, 1971.

Ripley, Ezra. *A History of the Concord Fight*. Concord, Mass.: Allen and Atwell, 1827.

Robertson, Archibald. *His Diaries and Sketches in America*. New York: New York Public Library/Arno Press, 1971.

Robinson, William H. *Phillis Wheatley and Her Writings*. New York: Garland, 1984.

Roche, John F. *Joseph Reed: A Moderate in the American Revolution*. New York: Columbia University Press, 1957.

Rogers, Alan. *Empire and Liberty: American Resistance to British Authority, 1755–1763*. Berkeley: University of California Press, 1974.

Rose, Alex. *Washington's Spies: The Story of America's First Spy Ring*. New York: Bantam, 2007.

Rose, Ben Z. *John Stark: Maverick General*. Waverly, Mass.: Treeline Press, 2007.

Ross, John F. *War on the Run: The Epic Story of Robert Rogers and the Conquest of America's First Frontier*. New York: Bantam, 2009.

Rowe, John. *The Diary of John Rowe, A Boston Merchant, 1764–1779*. Edited by Edward L. Pierce. Cambridge, Mass.: Wilson, 1895.

Royster, Charles. *A Revolutionary People at War: The Continental Army and American Character, 1775–1783*. Chapel Hill: University of North Carolina, 1979.

Rutman, Darrett B. *Winthrop's Boston: A Portrait of a Puritan Town, 1630–1649*. New York: Norton, 1965.

Ryan, Michael. *Concord and the Dawn of Revolution: The Hidden Truths*. Charleston, S.C.: History Press, 2007.

Sabin, Douglas. *April 19, 1775: A Historiographical Study*. Cascade, ID: Sinclair, 2011.

Sabine, Lorenzo. *The Loyalists of the American Revolution*. Springfield, Mass.: Walden Press, 1957.

Sainsbury, John. *Disaffected Patriots: London Supporters of Revolutionary America, 1769–1782*. Montreal: McGill-Queen's University Press, 1987.

Sanger, Abner. *Very Poor and of a Lo Make: The Journal of Abner Sanger*. Edited by Lois K. Stabler. Portsmouth, N.H.: Historical Society of Cheshire County, 1986.

Sawtell, Clement C. *The Nineteenth of April, 1775: A Collection of First Hand Accounts*. Lincoln, Mass.: Sawtells of Somerset, 1968.

Scaife, Lauriston C. *Milton and the Suffolk Resolves*. Milton, Mass: Milton Historical Society, 1921.

Schama, Simon. *Rough Crossings: Britain, the Slaves and the American Revolution*. New York: HarperCollins, 2006.

Scheer, George F., and Hugh F. Rankin, eds. *Rebels and Redcoats*. New York: Da Capo Press, 1957.

Scheide, John H. "The Lexington Alarm." AAS *Proceedings*, n.s., 50, pt. 1 (1940): 49–79.

Schlesinger, Arthur M. "A Note on Songs as Patriot Propaganda, 1765–1776." WMQ, 3rd ser., 11, no. 1 (54): 78–88.

———. "Propaganda and the Boston Newspaper Press." *Publications of the Colonial Society of Massachusetts* 32 (1936): 411–16.
———. "Political Mobs and the American Revolution, 1765–1776." *Proceedings of the American Philosophical Society* 99 (1955): 244–50.
———. *Prelude to Independence: The Newspaper War on Britain, 1764–1776*. New York: Knopf, 1958.
———. "The Liberty Tree: A Genealogy." *New England Quarterly* 25, no. 4 (1952): 435–58.
———. *The Colonial Merchants and the American Revolution*. New York: Ungar, 1957.
Schruth, Jordan, and Susan Fiore. *The Nobel Train of Artillery*. Boston: Commonwealth of Massachusetts, 1976.
Scollay, Mercy, "Letter to John Hancock, May 21, 1776." Warren mss., 2, MHS.
———. Letters to Dr. Dix, August 17, 1775, and Mrs. Dix, July 27, 1776, and November 26, 1776. Mercy Scollay Papers, CHS.
Seasholes, Nancy S. *Gaining Ground: A History of Landmaking in Boston*. Cambridge, Mass.: MIT Press, 2003.
Shain, Barry Alan. *The Myth of American Individualism: The Prostestant Origins of American Political Thought*. Princeton, N.J.: Princeton University Press, 1994.
Shalev, Eran. "Dr. Warren's Ciceronian Toga: Performing Rebellion in Revolutionary Boston." *Common-Place* 7, no. 2 (January 2007). www.common-place.org.
Sharp, Gene. *From Dictatorship to Democracy: A Conceptual Framework for Liberation*. East Boston, Mass.: Albert Einstein Institution, 2002.
Shattuck, Lemuel. *A History of the Town of Concord*. Concord, Mass.: Russell, Odiorne, 1835.
Shaw, Peter. "Fathers, Sons, and the Ambiguities of Revolution . . . ," *NEQ* 49 (1976): 559–76.
———. *American Patriots and the Rituals of Revolution*. Cambridge, Mass.: Harvard University Press, 1981.
———. *The Character of John Adams*. New York: Norton, 1977.
Shurtleff, Nathaniel B. *A Topographical and Historical Description of Boston*. Boston: Rockwell and Churchill, 1891.
Shy, John. *Toward Lexington: The Role of the British Army in the Coming of the American Revolution*. Princeton, N.J.: Princeton University Press, 1965.
———. *A People Numerous and Armed: Reflections on the Military Struggle for American Independence*. New York: Oxford University Press, 1976.
Siebert, Wilbur H. "Loyalist Troops of New England." *NEQ* 4 (1931): 108–47.
Silver, Peter. *Our Savage Neighbors: How Indian War Transformed Early America*. New York: Norton, 2008.
Silver, Rollo G. "Benjamin Edes, Trumpeter of Sedition." *Papers of the Bibliographical Society of America* 47 (1953): 248–68.
Silverman, Kenneth. *A Cultural History of the American Revolution*. New York: Thomas Crowell, 1976.
Simons, D. Brenton. *Boston Beheld: Antique Town and Country Views*. Hanover, N.H.: University Press of New England, 2008.
Slade, Denison Rogers. "Henry Pelham, the Half-Brother of John Singleton Copley." *Transactions of the Colonial Society of Massachusetts* 5 (1897–98): 193–211.
Slocum, Joshua. *An Authentic Narrative of the Life of Joshua Slocum*. Edited by John Slocum. Hartford, Conn.: n.p., 1844.
Slotkin, Richard. *Regeneration Through Violence: The Mythology of the American Frontier, 1600–1860*. Norman: University of Oklahoma Press, 2000.
Smith, Philip Chadwick Foster. *Fired by Manley Zeal*. Salem, Mass.: Peabody Museum, 1977.
Smith, Lt. Col. Francis. Report to General Gage, April 22, 1775. MHS *Proceedings* 14 (1876): 350–51.
Smith, Joshua M. *Borderland Smuggling: Patriots, Loyalists, and Illicit Trade in the Northeast, 1783–1820*. Gainesville: University of Florida Press, 2006.
Smith, M. H. *The Writs of Assistance Case*. Berkeley: University of California Press, 1978.
Smith, Paul H. *Loyalists and Redcoats: A Study in British Revolutionary Policy*. New York: Norton, 1964.
Smith, Samuel Abbot. *West Cambridge on the Nineteenth of April, 1775*. Boston: Mudge and Son, 1864.
Snow, Caleb Hopkins. *History of Boston*. Boston: Abel Bowen, 1825.
Sosin, Jack M. *Revolutionary Frontier, 1763–1783*. Albuquerque: University of New Mexico Press, 1967.
Spring, Matthew H. *With Zeal and with Bayonets Only: The British Army on Campaign in North America, 1775–1783*. Norman: University of Oklahoma Press, 2008.
St. George, Robert Blair. *Conversing by Signs: Poetics of Implication in Colonial New England Culture*. Chapel Hill: University of North Carolina Press, 1998.

Stackpole, Edouard A. *Nantucket in the American Revolution.* Nantucket, Mass.: Nantucket Historical Association, 1976.

Stark, Caleb, ed. *Memoir and General Correspondence of John Stark.* Concord, N.H.: McFarland and Jenks, 1860.

Stark, James Henry. *The Loyalists of Massachusetts and the Other Side of the American Revolution.* Boston: Clarke, 1907.

Stauber, Leland. *The American Revolution: A Grand Mistake.* Amherst, N.Y.: Prometheus, 2009.

Steblecki, Edith. *Paul Revere and Free-Masonry.* Boston: Paul Revere Memorial Association, 1985.

Stedman, Charles. *History of the Origin, Progress, and Termination of the American War.* Vol. 1. London: Stedman, 1788.

Stevens, James. "The Revolutionary Journal of James Stevens of Andover, Mass." *Essex Institute Historical Collections* 48 (1912): 41–71.

Stiles, Ezra. *The Literary Diary of Ezra Stiles.* Vol. 1. Edited by Franklin B. Dexter. New York: Scribner's, 1901.

Stirke, Lieutenant Henry. "A British Officer's Revolutionary War Journal, 1776–1778." Edited by S. S. Bradford. *Maryland Historical Magazine* 56 (1961): 150–75.

Stoll, Ira. *Sam Adams: A Life.* New York: Free Press, 2008.

Storrs, Experience. "Diary of Lieut. Col. Exp. Storrs, of Mansfield." MHS *Proceedings* 14 (1875–76): 84–87.

Stout, Harry S. *The New England Soul: Preaching and Religious Culture in Colonial New England.* New York: Oxford University Press, 1986.

———. "Religion, Communications, and the Ideological Origins of the American Revolution." *WMQ,* 3rd ser., 34, no. 4 (October 1977): 519–41.

Stout, Ned R. *The Royal Navy in America, 1760–1776: A Study of Enforcement of British Colonial Policy in the Era of the American Revolution.* Annapolis, Md.: Naval Institute Press, 1973.

Stow, Nathan. "Orderly Book." *Putnam's Monthly Historical Magazine* 2 (1893): 306–13.

Stuart, Nancy Rubin. *The Muse of the Revolution: The Secret Pen of Mercy Otis Warren and the Founding of a Nation.* Boston: Beacon Press, 2008.

Sullivan, Thomas. *From Redcoat to Rebel: The Thomas Sullivan Journal.* Edited by Joseph Lee Boyle. Westminster, Md.: Heritage Books, 2004.

Sumner, William H. "Reminiscences Relating to General Warren and Bunker Hill." *NEHGR* 12, no. 2 (1858): 225–29.

———. "Reminiscences." *NEHGR* 8 (1854): 187–91.

Sweetser, M. F. *King's Hand Book of Boston Harbor.* Cambridge, Mass.: Applewood, 1882.

Swett, Samuel. *History of Bunker Hill Battle, with a Plan.* Boston: Munroe and Francis, 1826.

Tager, Jack. *Boston Riots: Three Centuries of Social Violence.* Boston: Northeastern University Press, 2001.

Tapley, Harriet Silvester. *Chronicles of Danvers (Old Salem Village), 1632–1923.* Danvers, Mass.: Danvers Historical Society, 1923.

Tatum, Edward H. "Ambrose Serle, Secretary to Lord Howe, 1776–1778." *Huntington Library Quarterly* 2, no. 3 (1939): 265–84.

Taylor, Robert J. *Western Massachusetts in the Revolution.* Providence, R.I.: Brown University Press, 1954.

Taylor, Alan. *American Colonies: The Settling of North America.* New York: Viking, 2001.

———. *Liberty Men and Great Proprietors: The Revolutionary Settlement on the Maine Frontier, 1760–1820.* Chapel Hill: University of North Carolina Press, 1990.

Taylor, C. James, ed. *Founding Families: Digital Editions of the Papers of the Winthrops and the Adamses.* Boston: Massachusetts Historical Society, 2007.

Temple, J. H. *History of Framingham, Massachusetts.* Framingham, Mass.: Town of Framingham, 1887.

Tentindo, Vincent, and Marylyn Jones. *Battle of Chelsea Creek, May 27, 1775: Graves Misfortune.* Revere, Mass.: Revere Historical Commission, 1978.

Thacher, James. *A Military Journal of the American Revolution.* Hartford, Conn.: Hurlbut, Williams, 1862.

Thatcher, Benjamin Bussey. *Traits of the Tea Party: Being a Memoir of George R. T. Hewes.* New York: Harper, 1835.

Thomas, Isaiah. *The History of Printing in America.* Albany, N.Y.: Burt Franklin, 1874.

Thomas, Peter. *Tea Party to Independence: The Third Phase of the American Revolution.* New York: Oxford University Press, 1991.

Thomas, Robert. "A Quantitative Approach to the Study of the Effects of British Imperial Policy upon Colonial Welfare." *Journal of Economic History* 25 (1965): 615–38.

Thornton, J. W., ed. *The Pulpit of the American Revolution.* Boston: Gould and Lincoln, 1860.

Thwing, Annie Haven. *Crooked and Narrow Streets of Boston.* Boston: Charles E. Lauriat, 1925.

Tilley, John A. *The British Navy and the American Revolution*. Columbia: South Carolina University Press, 1987.

Tolman, George. *Events of April Nineteen*. Concord, Mass.: Concord Antiquarian Society, 1902.

Tomlinson, Abraham, ed. *Military Journals of Two Private Soldiers, 1758–1775*. Poughkeepsie, N.Y.: Tomlinson, 1855.

Tourtellot, Arthur B. *Lexington and Concord: The Beginning of the War of the American Revolution*. New York: Norton, 2000.

Triber, Jayne E. *A True Republican: The Life of Paul Revere*. Amherst: University of Massachusetts Press, 1998.

———. "Historical Background on Siege of Boston and Adolescence in Revolutionary Period." Produced for "Bringing History Home," project of the Paul Revere House, Boston, 1999.

True, Henry. *Journal and Letters of Henry True*. Marion, Ohio: Henry True, 1900.

Trumbull, John. *The Autobiography of Colonel John Trumbull*. Edited by Theodore Sizer. New Haven, Conn.: Yale University Press, 1953.

Tuchman, Barbara W. *The First Salute: A View of the American Revolution*. New York: Ballantine, 1988.

Tudor, William, ed. *Deacon Tudor's Diary*. . . . Boston: Wallace Spooner, 1896.

———. *Life of James Otis*. Boston: Wells and Lilly, 1823.

Tyler, John W. *Smugglers and Patriots: Boston Merchants and the Advent of the American Revolution*. Boston: Northeastern University Press, 1986.

Ubbelohde, Carl. *The Vice-Admiralty Courts and the American Revolution*. Chapel Hill: University of North Carolina, 1960.

Ulrich, Laurel Thatcher. " 'Daughters of Liberty'; Religious Women in Revolutionary New England." In *Women in the Age of the American Revolution*, edited by Ronald Hoffman and Peter Albert, 211–43. Charlottesville: University Press of Virginia, 1992.

Unger, Harlow Giles. *John Hancock: Merchant King and American Patriot*. Edison, N.J.: Castle, 2005.

Upham, William P., ed. *Letters Written at the Time of the Occupation of Boston*. Salem, Mass.: Essex Institute Historical Collections, 1876.

Upton, L. F. S. "Proceedings of Ye Body Respecting the Tea." *WMQ*, 3rd ser., 22, no. 2 (1965): 287–300.

Urban, Mark. *Fusiliers: The Saga of a British Redcoat Regiment in the American Revolution*. New York: Walker, 2007.

Van Doren, Carl. *Jane Mecom: Franklin's Favorite Sister*. New York: Viking, 1950.

———, ed. *Letters of Benjamin Franklin and Jane Mecom*. Princeton, N.J.: Princeton University Press, 1950.

———. *Benjamin Franklin*. New York: Viking, 1938.

Vesey, Maud Maxwell. "Benjamin Marston, Loyalist." *NEQ* 15, no. 4 (1942): 622–51.

Volo, James M. *Blue Water Patriots: The American Revolution Afloat*. Latham, Md.: Rowman and Littlefield, 2006.

Vosburgh, Maude B. "The Disloyalty of Benjamin Church, Jr." *Cambridge Historical Society Publications* 30 (1944): 48–71.

Wade, Herbert T., and Robert A. Lively, eds. *This Glorious Cause*. Princeton, N.J.: Princeton University Press, 1958.

Waldstreicher, David. "The Wheatleyan Moment." *Early American Studies*, Fall 2011, 522–51.

Waller, Lt. John. "Letter 21 June 1775." MHS.

Walmsley, Andrew Stephen. *Thomas Hutchinson and the Origins of the American Revolution*. New York: New York University Press, 1999.

Ward, Edward. *Boston in 1682 and 1699*. New York: Burt Franklin, 1970.

Warden, G. B. "Inequality and Instability in Eighteenth-Century Boston: A Reappraisal." *Journal of Interdisciplinary History* 6, no. 4 (Spring 1976): 585–620.

———. *Boston, 1689–1776*. Boston: Little, Brown, 1970.

Warren, Charles. "Samuel Adams and the Sans Souci Club." MHS *Proceedings* 60 (1927): 318–44.

Warren, Edward. *The Life of John Warren, M.D.* Boston: Noyes and Holmes, 1874.

Warren, John Collins. *Genealogy of Warren with Some Historical Sketches*. Boston: privately printed, 1854.

———. "Joseph Warren." In *Rees's Cyclopedia*. London: Longman, Hurst, Rees, Orme and Brown, 1816.

Warren, Mercy Otis. *Poems, Dramatic and Miscellaneous*. Boston: Thomas and Andrews, 1790.

———. *History of the Rise, Progress and Termination of the American Revolution*. Edited by Lester Cohen. Vol. 1. 1805; reprint, Indianapolis: Liberty Classics, 1988.

———. *Selected Letters*. Edited by Jeffrey H. Richards and Sharon M. Harris. Athens: University of Georgia Press, 2009.

Washington, George. *The Papers of George Washington, Revolutionary War Series.* Vols. 1–3. Edited by Philander D. Chase. Charlottesville: University Press of Virginia, 1985, 1987, 1988.

Waters, John J. Jr. "James Otis, Jr.: Ambivalent Revolutionary." *History of Childhood Quarterly* 1 (1973): 142–50.

———. *The Otis Family in Provincial and Revolutionary Massachusetts.* Chapel Hill: University of North Carolina Press, 1968.

Waters, John J., and John A. Schutz. "Patterns of Massachusetts Colonial Politics: The Writs of Assistance and the Rivalry Between the Otis and Hutchinson Families." *WMQ* 24 (1967): 543–67.

Watkins, Kendall. "Tarring and Feathering in Boston in 1770." *Old-Time New England* 20 (1929): 30–43.

Webb, Samuel Blachley. *Correspondence and Journals of Samuel Blachley Webb.* Edited by Worthington C. Ford. Vol. 1. New York: Burnett, 1894.

Webber, Sandra L. "Benjamin Hallowell Family and the Jamaica Plain House." Jamaica Plain Historical Society, January 2007. http://www.jphs.org/colonial/capt-benjamin-hallowell-homestead.html.

Wells, William V. *The Life and Public Service of Samuel Adams.* Boston: Little, Brown, 1865.

Wemyss, James Major. "Character Sketches of Gage, Percy and Others." Sparks Papers, Harvard University, vol. 22, p. 214.

West, Samuel. Memoir. Needham Historical Society. http://www2.needham.k12.ma.us/eliot/technology/lessons/primary_source/lex_con/memoir.htm.

Wheatley, Phillis. "Letters." MHS *Proceedings* 7 (1863–64): 267–78.

Wheeler, Ruth R. *Concord Climate for Freedom.* Concord, Mass.: Concord Antiquarian Society, 1967.

Wheildon, W. H. *Siege and Evacuation of Boston and Charlestown.* Boston: Lee and Shepard, 1876.

———. *Paul Revere's Signal Lanterns.* Boston: Rand, Avery, 1878.

———. *New History of the Battle of Bunker Hill.* Boston: Lee and Shepard, 1875.

Whitehall, Walter Muir, ed. *Boston Prints and Printmakers, 1670–1775.* Boston: Colonial Society of Massachusetts, 1973.

Whitehall, Walter Muir, and Lawrence W. Kennedy. *Boston: A Topographical History.* Cambridge, Mass.: Belknap Press, 1968.

Whitehorne, Joseph. "Shepardstown and the Morgan-Stevenson Companies." *Magazine of the Jefferson County Historical Society* 58 (1992): 16–19.

Wiencek, Henry. *An Imperfect God: George Washington, Slaves and the Creation of America.* New York: Farrar, Straus, and Giroux, 2003.

Wilkinson, James. *Memoirs of My Own Times.* Vol. 1. Philadelphia: Abraham Small, 1816.

Willard, Margaret Wheeler, ed. *Letters on the American Revolution.* 1925; reprint, Port Washington, N.Y.: Kennikat Press, 1968.

Willcox, William. *Portrait of a General: Sir Henry Clinton in the War of Independence.* New York: Knopf, 1964.

Williams, Richard. *Discord and Civil Wars, Being a Portion of the Journal Kept by Lieutenant Williams of His Majesty's Twenty-Third Regiment While Stationed in British North America . . .* Edited by Jane Van Arsdale. Buffalo: Easy Hill Press, 1954.

Wilson, Lisa. *Ye Heart of a Man: The Domestic Life of Men in Colonial New England.* New Haven, Conn.: Yale University Press, 1999.

Winsor, Justin. *The Memorial History of Boston.* 4 vols. Boston: Osgood, 1883.

———. *History of Duxbury.* Boston: Crosby and Nichols, 1849.

Winthrop, Hannah. Letter (n.d.) to Mercy Warren. MHS *Proceedings* 14 (1875): 29–31.

Wolkins, George G. "The Seizure of John Hancock's Ship 'Liberty.' " MHS *Proceedings* 55 (1921–22): 239–84.

———. "Daniel Malcom and Writs of Assistance." MHS *Proceedings* 58 (1924): 5–87.

Wood, Gordon S. "Conspiracy and the Paranoid Style: Causality and Deceit in the Eighteenth Century." *WMQ* 39 (1982): 401–41.

———. "Rhetoric and Reality in the American Revolution." *WMQ*, 3rd ser., 23, 1 (1966): 3–32.

———. "A Note on Mobs in the American Revolution." *WMQ*, 3rd ser., 23, 4 (1966): 635–42.

———. *The Americanization of Benjamin Franklin.* New York: Penguin Press, 2004.

———. *The American Revolution: A History.* New York: Modern Library, 2002.

———. *The Radicalism of the American Revolution.* New York: Vintage, 1991.

———. *The Creation of the American Republic, 1776–1787.* Chapel Hill: University of North Carolina Press, 1969.

Wright, Louis B. *The Dream of Prosperity in Colonial America.* New York: New York University Press, 1965.

Wroth, Lawrence. *The Colonial Printer.* New York: Grolier Club, 1931.

Wroth, L. Kinvin, et al., eds. *Province in Rebellion: A Documentary History of the Founding of the Common-wealth of Massachusetts, 1774–1775.* Cambridge, Mass.: Harvard University Press, 1975.

Wyatt, Thomas. *Life of General Joseph Warren.* Boston: G. R. Graham, 1850.

York, Neil Longley. "Our First 'Good' War: Selective Memory, Special Pleading, and the War of American Independence." *Peace and Change* 15 (1990): 371–90.

———. "Freemasonry and the American Revolution." *Historian* 55, no. 2 (1993): 315.

———. "Rival Truths, Political Accommodation, and the Boston 'Massacre.' " *Massachusetts Historical Review* 11 (2009): 57–95.

———. *Henry Hulton and the American Revolution: An Outsider's Inside View.* Boston: Colonial Society of Massachusetts, 2010.

———. *The Boston Massacre: A History with Documents.* New York: Routledge, 2010.

Young, Alfred F. "George Robert Twelves Hewes (1742–1840): A Boston Shoemaker and the Memory of the American Revolution." *WMQ,* 3d ser., 38 (1981): 561–623.

———. "English Plebeian Culture and Eighteenth-Century American Radicalism." In *The Origins of Anglo-American Radicalism,* edited by Margaret Jacob and James Jacob, pp. 185–212. London: George Allen & Unwin for the Institute for Research in History, 1984.

———, ed. *The American Revolution: Explorations in the History of American Radicalism.* DeKalb: Northern Illinois University Press, 1976.

———. *Beyond the American Revolution: Explorations in the History of American Radicalism.* DeKalb: Northern Illinois University Press, 1993.

———. *The Shoemaker and the Tea Party: Memory and the American Revolution.* Boston: Beacon Press, 1999.

———. *Liberty Tree: Ordinary People and the American Revolution.* New York: New York University Press, 2006.

Zobel, Hiller B. *The Boston Massacre.* New York: Norton, 1996.

Zuckerman, Michael. *Peaceable Kingdoms: New England Towns in the Eighteenth Century.* New York: Knopf, 1970.

Illustration Credits

Page 11 (top): John Trumbull, American, 1756–1843. The Death of General Warren at the Battle of Bunker's Hill, 17 June, 1775, after 1815–before 1831. Oil on canvas. 50.16 × 75.56 cm (19¾ × 29¾ in.). Museum of Fine Arts, Boston. Gift of Howland S. Warren, 1977.853.

Page 12: Peale, Charles Willson (1741–1827). George Washington. Ca. 1779–1781. Oil on canvas, 95 × 61¾ in. (241.3 × 156.8 cm). Gift of Collis P. Huntington, 1897 (97.33) The Metropolitan Museum of Art, New York, NY, U.S.A. Image copyright © The Metropolitan Museum of Art. Image source: Art Resource, NY.

Black-and-white insert

Page 1 (top): Boston Athenaeum.

Page 1 (bottom): I. N. Phelps Stokes Collection, Miriam and Ira D. Wallach Division of Art, Prints and Photographs, The New York Public Library, Astor, Lenox and Tilden Foundations.

Page 2 (top and bottom right), page 5 (top and bottom), page 6 (top), page 13 (top), and page 15 (top): Courtesy of the Bostonian Society, Object Collection.

Page 2 (bottom left) and page 11 (bottom): Author's collection.

Page 3 (top) and page 10 (top): Courtesy of the Massachusetts Historical Society.

Page 3 (bottom): The Library Company of Philadelphia.

Page 4, page 13 (bottom), and page 14 (top): Courtesy of the John Carter Brown Library at Brown University.

Page 6 (bottom): Ritchie, Alexander Hay (1822–1885). Major General Charles Lee. 19th century. Etching and engraving. Image: 6⅛ × 4⁷⁄₁₆ in. (15.5 × 11.3 cm); sheet: 12¹⁄₁₆ × 9½ in. (30.7 × 24.2 cm). The Metropolitan Museum of Art, Bequest of Charles Allen Munn, 1924 (24.90.387). The Metropolitan Museum of Art, New York, NY, U.S.A. Image copyright © The Metropolitan Museum of Art. Image source: Art Resource, NY.

Page 7 (top): Popular Graphic Arts collection, Prints & Photographs Division, Library of Congress, LC-USZ62-5666.

Page 7(bottom): Courtesy of the Osher Map Library, University of Southern Maine.

Page 8 (top): Bowdoin College Museum of Art.

Page 8 (bottom), page 9 (bottom), and page 11 (top left and right): Print Collection, Miriam and Ira D. Wallach Division of Art, Prints and Photographs, The New York Public Library, Astor, Lenox and Tilden Foundations.

Page 9 (top): Lieutenant Colonel Francis Smith (1723–91) 1764 (oil on canvas), Cotes, Francis (1726–70) / National Army Museum, London / The Bridgeman Art Library.

Page 10 (bottom): The Honourable Sir William Howe, 1777 (colour mezzotint), Purcell, Richard (c.1736–c.1766) (after) / Brown University Library, Providence, Rhode Island, USA / The Bridgeman Art Library.

Page 12: Watching the Fight at Bunker Hill, illustration from 'Colonies and Nation' by Woodrow Wilson, pub. in Harper's Magazine, 1901 (litho), Pyle, Howard (1853–1911) (after) / Private Collection / The Bridgeman Art Library.

Page 14 (bottom): Library of Congress, Manuscript Division.

Page 15 (bottom): Spencer Collection, The New York Public Library, Astor, Lenox and Tilden Foundations.

Page 16: John Quincy Adams (1767–1848) 1847 (daguerreotype), American Photographer, (19th century) / Private Collection / Peter Newark American Pictures / The Bridgeman Art Library.

Index

Abercrombie, James, 234
Abercromby, James, 26, 351n
Acton militia, 137–40, 142, 147, 151–52, 156, 330n
Adair, Jesse, 123–24, 126
Adams, Abigail, 236, 245, 252, 279, 289–91, 294
Adams, John, 39–40, 70, 85, 112, 160, 305n, 313n, 336n
 and accused British soldiers, 4, 8
 on American Revolution, 302n, 345n
 on army commissions, 192
 on Benjamin Church, 252
 and Continental Congress, 45, 56, 74, 247, 294
 at council of war, 267
 illness of, 32–33, 68, 307n
 on patriots, 303n
 and Port Act, 36
 promotes Henry Knox, 270
 and Suffolk Resolves, 76
 and Joseph Warren, 194, 236, 307n, 337n, 345n
Adams, John Quincy, 46, 292–95, 356n
Adams, Joseph, 153, 157–58
Adams, Samuel, 28, 52, 57, 90, 95, 123, 163, 190, 247, 322–23n
 on America's future, 308–9n
 and Continental Congress, 44–48, 55–56, 73–74, 113, 130, 312n
 description of, 67, 130
 flees to Lexington, 111–12, 116, 118–19, 122
 and Josiah Quincy, 171–72
 and Lexington fight, 130–31, 325n

 moderates Boston town meetings, 33–34, 48, 96, 99–100, 130
 opposes Government Act, 41–42
 as political leader, 34, 38, 54–55, 66–67, 121
 and Port Act, 36–37
 and Joseph Warren, 81, 110, 180–81, 193–94, 235–36
Administration of Justice Act, 53
African Americans, 51, 65, 71, 121, 159, 324n, 331n
 in army, 165, 228, 241, 262–63, 351n
 casualties of, 128
 exclusion of, 251, 295
 See also slavery; specific names; Washington, George
Allen, Ethan, 173–74
American colonies
 British limit rights of, 44, 55
 desire peace, 98
 founding of, 33
 lack of aristocracy in, 193
 in open rebellion, 112
 rivalry among, 214
 and "salutary neglect," 6
 and "the will of the people," 193–94
 unity of, 76, 262, 265
American navy, 245, 257–58
Ames, Dr. Nathaniel, 101–2, 112, 177, 215–16
ammunition
 bar shot, 212
 bullets, 66, 122, 135
 cartridges, 66, 124, 138, 183, 210
 from Fort Ticonderoga, 268–71

ammunition (*cont.*)
hotshot, 218
lack of, 148, 154, 226
lead balls, 88, 124
on the *Nancy*, 258, 268
See also gunpowder
Amory, John, 48
amphibious assaults, 170, 183, 204, 250,
    276, 282–83
Andover, Mass., 147, 162
Andrews, John, 48–49
on Battle Road, 158, 330n
on Boston, 88, 111, 311n, 315n,
    318n, 321n
on British army, 51–52, 62, 64,
    80, 316n
on Coercive Acts, 58
on Gage, 60, 79, 87, 315n, 317n, 319n
on Government Act, 312n
on Haldimand, 317n
on Massacre Day Oration, 100–1
on patriots, 42, 53
on provincial army, 71, 77–78
on Samuel Adams, 56, 312n
wife of, 113, 169, 286
Andros, Gov. Edmund, 5
Arlington. *See* Menotomy (Arlington)
Arnold, Benedict, 173–74, 245, 271, 332n
artillery, 118, 135, 248, 284
of British army, 78, 103–5, 140, 149,
    210, 213, 218, 225, 273
for continental army, 268–71
lack of, 78, 234, 249–50, 267
on the *Nancy*, 258
officers of, 210–11
regiments of, 197, 244, 246, 270–71,
    276–77, 279, 290, 353n
Attack and Defense of Fortified Places
    (Muller), 273, 353n
Attucks, Crispus, 128
Avery, David, 179

Back Bay, 14, 15, 63, 170, 177, 264, 266
Baldwin, Jeduthan, 271–72
Balfour, Nesbitt, 86, 166–67
Bancroft, Ebenezer, 205–6, 218, 220,
    228–29, 337n, 339n

Barker, John, 102, 116, 128, 148–49, 152,
    181–82, 317n, 325n
Barré, Isaac, 31–32, 94
Barrett, Amos, 141, 143–44, 327n
Barrett, James, 132–36, 138–40,
    143–44, 148
Barrett, Rebeckah, 135–36
Bassett, Burwell, 278
batteries, 168, 254, 264, 276, 279,
    281, 340n
battle at North Bridge. *See* Concord: battle
    at North Bridge
Battle of Bunker Hill
artillery failures at, 244, 270
bloody carnage of, 293, 342n
and breastwork, 217, 223, 225–26, 229
British army/navy and, 213, 230,
    256–57, 343n
and cowardice, 222–23, 277
map of, 196
monument built for, 292–93, 295
and the rail fence, 217, 219–20, 222–27
retreat of provincial army, 222–23,
    228–30
spectators of, 206–7, 210, 217, 219
as watershed event, 236–37
wounded survivors of, 253, 255
See also Breed's Hill
Battle of Chelsea Creek, 183–87, 190, 195,
    199, 207, 336n
Battle Road, 152–60, 223, 330n
bayonets
of British regulars, 124, 132, 157
of infantrymen, 127, 147, 217
of militiamen, 138–39
of provincial army, 221, 226–27, 229
surrendering of, 168
Beacon Hill, 14, 15, 22, 30, 38, 116, 199,
    229, 279
Bedford, Mass., 122, 137–38, 147
Belknap, Rev. Jeremy, 262, 322n
Bernard, Gov. Francis, 68
Beverly militiamen, 157
Billerica, Mass., 99, 145, 201
Bissell, Isaac, 167, 331n
Black Horse Tavern, 118, 123, 150, 153
Blanchard, Luther, 142

Bliss, Daniel, 123
Blockade of Boston, The (Burgoyne), 266
Blood, Thaddeus, 134, 143–44
blunderbusses, 168
Bolton, Dr. Thomas, 100
Boston
    1776 assault on, 278–79, 282–83, 287
    accents of residents, 99
    black community of, 24
    burned by the British, 256, 349n
    casualties arrive in, 233, 349n
    chaos reigns in, 283, 355n
    description of, 177
    economic misery of, 41, 48, 52
    evacuation of, 283–87, 290
    first settlers of, 285
    and food supplies, 88, 233, 256, 318n
    loyalists remain in, 284, 288–89
    maps of, 12–13, 15, 254
    under military occupation, 7, 38, 51, 79,
      96–97, 161–62, 177
    poor of, 52, 57, 70, 233, 311n
    residents die in, 233–34
    residents flee from, 111, 113, 161–62,
      164, 168–69, 246–47, 321n, 332n
    surrounded, 161, 199, 249–50, 351n
    as third-largest port, 31
    topography of, 14, 15, 170, 237
    town gates of, 20, 71, 76–77,
      82, 264
Boston Common, 60, 78–79, 152
    British soldiers encamped on, 42–43,
      56–57, 64, 77, 80, 177, 227
    and Bunker Hill anniversary, 292
    description of, 42–43
    location of, 15, 19
    powderhouse on, 62, 71
"Boston Declaration," 35–36
Boston Gazette, 22, 288
Boston Harbor, 19, 26, 51, 234
    blockade of, 40–41, 87
    British control of, 161, 249
    and British evacuation, 283–85, 290
    description of, 170–71
    maps of, 13, 15, 63, 184, 196, 254
    military transports in, 169
    and the Port Act, 31, 40–41, 43, 70

    and the Powder Alarm, 64–65
    See also Boston Tea Party; British supply
      ships; warships
Boston lighthouse, 13, 257
Boston Massacre, 61, 80, 128, 163
    aftermath of, 4, 8, 129
    anniversary of, 96, 277
    events leading to, 7–8, 11, 24, 37
    loyalist account of, 171
    site of, 19, 39
    and trial for, 4, 8, 32
    See also Massacre Day Oration
Boston merchants, 11, 41–42, 44, 48–49,
    52, 183, 276, 285, 304n, 312n. *See
    also specific names*
Boston Neck, 12, 15, 20, 63, 71, 76–77, 93,
    102, 111, 118, 164, 170, 191,
    254, 264
Boston selectmen, 52, 55, 79–80, 87, 96,
    175, 283, 287
Boston Tea Party, 4, 9–11, 16, 22, 28,
    30–31, 36, 41, 48, 55, 68, 137, 289,
    304–5n
Boylston, Mary. *See* Hallowell, Mary
    Boylston
Braddock campaign, 28–29, 56, 238
Braddock, Edward, 26
Braintree, Mass., 12, 33, 183, 274, 279, 292
Brattle, William, 62, 64–65, 69, 313n
Brattle Street Meeting, 15, 46, 111, 310n
Breed's Hill, 69, 294
    army assembles on, 209, 223
    bloody carnage on, 201, 230, 234
    breastwork on, 196, 201–2, 205, 210,
      213–14
    cannons on, 205–6, 210
    fighting on, 236, 249
    fortifications on, 198–206, 218, 224,
      226, 337n
    location of, 196, 200
    rail fences on, 211, 213–14
    redoubt on, 196, 199, 201–6,
      210–11, 337n
    Warren buried on, 287–88
    See also Battle of Bunker Hill
Brewer, Jonathan, 180, 245
Brighton, 162, 215

Britannia, 184, 186

British dragoons, 256, 285

British goods, boycotting of, 7, 37, 41–42, 44, 47–48, 58, 75, 82–83, 85, 255

British grenadiers, 115–16, 122, 128–29, 144, 146–47, 221–23, 226, 228

British light infantry, 115
  and Battle of Bunker Hill, 196, 223–25
  at battle of North Bridge, 135, 143, 145–48
  at Concord/Lexington, 116, 122–24, 126–29
  established by Gage, 26
  as flank guards, 145–48
  important role of, 216–17
  at Lexington fight, 325n
  See also Welch Fusiliers

British marines, 87, 123, 185–86, 317n

British ministry, 7, 29, 34, 44, 80, 94, 113, 237, 262, 345n
  and account of Concord/Lexington, 188–89
  arrest patriots, 111–12, 115
  calls colonials' bluff, 321n
  colonies' opposition to, 6, 59, 190
  and Government Act, 41–42, 52–53
  military preparations of, 255–56
  repeals acts, 49, 112, 321n

British navy, 31, 43, 61, 78–79, 89, 158, 256–58, 283–84. *See also* warships

British officers, 87, 89, 93, 96, 99–100, 117, 128–29, 143, 208, 282–83. *See also* casualties; commissions; *specific names*

British regular army
  abandons Boston, 237
  arrival of, 7, 42–43, 49, 51
  and Boston Massacre, 7–8, 11
  bravery of, 225
  defeats of, 186, 190
  difficulties faced by, 219, 221–23, 227
  encamped in Boston, 57, 86, 161–62, 169, 177, 183, 189, 249, 255, 257, 332n
  evacuation of, 283–87, 290
  fires first shots, 141–43, 168
  graveyard for, 80, 126
  growing unrest of, 89
  quarters for, 79–80, 87

steals valuables, 145, 147, 158, 284
supplies for, 87, 249, 257–58, 283, 317n
and tensions with Bostonians, 86, 126
during winter of 1775–76, 255–56, 258–59

British supply ships, 87, 245, 249, 258, 268, 290

broadsides, 22, 25, 50, 248, 264–65

Brookline, Mass., 63, 158, 254

Brooks, Joshua, 142

Brooks, John, 202, 204, 338n

Brown, Abijah, 180

Brown, David, 142

Brown, John, 140

Brown, Jonas, 142

Brown, Peter, 200, 202, 210, 224

Buckman's Tavern, 119, 121–22, 125, 127–29

Bunker Hill, 69, 260
  battle named after, 199
  and British army, 182, 215, 234, 249, 265
  fortifications on, 197–98, 205, 213–14, 234, 286
  and gunpowder supplies, 174, 332n
  location of, 196–97
  and Percy's brigade, 159, 197
  and provincial army, 208, 210, 212–13, 215, 218–19, 222–23, 225, 230
  See also Battle of Bunker Hill

Burbeck, William, 172–73

Burdoo, Eli and Silas, 324n

Burgoyne, John, 189–91, 203, 206–7, 217, 219–20, 234, 266, 340n

Burke, Edmund, 255–56

Buttrick, John, 136, 140–44, 342n, 343n

Byles, Rev. Mather, 288

Cambridge, Mass., 14, 67, 116–18, 122, 183
  and Battle of Bunker Hill, 202, 204, 208, 214–15
  and Battle Road, 158
  boatbuilding in, 170, 276, 332n
  bridge leading to, 102–3, 150, 243, 330n
  British plan to attack, 191, 197, 208
  council of war meets in, 164, 272
  description of, 179

headquarters in, 161–65, 168, 172, 175, 186, 191, 208, 250, 287
maps of, 12, 63, 114, 254, 269
militiamen in, 168–69, 173, 175–76, 178–79, 181–82, 236, 246
and taking of Dorchester, 276–77
Tory Row in, 63, 65, 72, 240–41, 252
See also Powder Alarm
Cambridge Common, 63, 65, 69–70, 195, 197, 215, 254
Canada, 5–6, 26–27, 53, 201, 229, 249, 284, 289. See also Quebec, Canada
cannons, 93, 99
of British army, 76, 78–79, 154, 168, 191, 198, 200–3, 205–6, 212, 218–21, 225–26, 249, 339n
and British marines, 186
embrasures for, 205–6
firing of, 209–10, 218, 223, 270, 278
at Fort Ticonderoga, 173
and fortifications, 205–6, 275
and grapeshot, 219, 225, 280
and hotshot, 218
lack of, 78, 172–73, 195
for new Continental army, 268–72, 276–77, 352n
of provincial army, 115–17, 135, 139, 205–6, 209–10, 213, 223, 290
and siege warfare, 248
and "spiking the guns," 284
stolen by patriots, 78–79, 84, 115, 315n
and taking of Dorchester, 276–79
Captain, 39–40
Carlisle militiamen, 138
Carpenter, Richard, 246
Castle, 10, 12, 22, 30–31, 37, 62–63, 65, 68, 234, 254, 279–81, 283, 285–87
Castle William. See Castle
casualties
of African Americans, 128
of British officers, 226–27
of British soldiers, 148, 157, 189, 221–25, 227–30, 233–35, 279, 316n, 342n
of Continental army, 283
of militiamen, 128–29, 140, 142, 148, 156–58, 168, 189
of provincial army, 157, 223, 229–30

Catholic Church, 11, 53, 121, 289
Cerberus, 184, 189
Charles II, King, 5
Charles River, 12, 14, 15, 63–65, 69–70, 103, 116, 118, 122, 150, 165, 209, 243, 266, 282
Charlestown, 23–24, 52, 64, 67, 116, 118, 150, 153
and Battle of Bunker Hill, 195, 197–200, 205, 208–9, 214–15, 217, 292
and Battle Road, 158–60
during British evacuation, 285–86
British march on, 182–83, 198
British plan to attack, 191, 197–98, 206, 208
burned by the British, 218–20, 224, 227, 255, 286, 340n
commons of, 69, 197
description of, 198, 200, 211
location of, 14, 15, 63, 184
raided by Continental army, 266
rail fence built in, 211, 213–14
Charlestown Neck, 196–97, 203, 205, 212–13, 216, 235, 249
Chatham, 258
Chatham, Lord, 94
Cheever, David, 204
Chelmsford militiamen, 138
Chelsea, Mass., 12, 63, 183–85, 191, 218, 254, 312n
Chester, John, 208–9, 222–23
Christ Church, 15, 116, 322n, 349n
Church, Benjamin, 91–92
Church, Dr. Benjamin, 90, 96, 100, 166, 171, 173, 176, 182, 192
court-martial of, 251–53
personality of, 82, 91
and Provincial Congress, 318n, 321n
punishment of, 288
as spy, 91–92, 101, 105, 113, 115, 318n, 321n, 322n
as surgeon general, 244
Clarke, John, 222
Clarke parsonage, 112, 119, 122, 324n
Clarke, Rev. Jonas, 120, 325n
Clinton, Henry, 189–91, 199–200, 203, 206, 234, 266, 271, 338n, 340n

Cobble Hill, 63–64, 254, 258, 275–76, 279, 353n

Coercive Acts, 53, 55, 57–58, 74–75, 95, 120

Coffin, Nathaniel, Sr., 304n

comet, 8, 304n

commissions
and British army, 192, 201, 238–39
of loyalists, 60
and provincial army, 39, 192–93, 243–45

Committee of Correspondence
and "Boston Declaration," 35–36
and boycott of British goods, 37, 41–42, 44
correspondence of, 34–36, 52, 54
and Gage's actions, 79, 84, 103
leaders of, 34, 66–67
meetings of, 58, 69, 103, 310n
members of, 34, 39, 53, 72, 82, 316n
and Solemn League and Covenant, 47–49

Committee of Donations, 52, 54

Committee of Safety, 109–10, 118–19, 121, 123, 126, 150, 176, 331n, 334n
and Battle of Bunker Hill, 195, 198, 204, 208, 215, 337n, 338n, 339n, 342n
and Battle Road, 154
duties of, 88, 104, 204
and Fort Ticonderoga, 173–74
headquarters of, 175, 195
leaders of, 191–92, 236, 336n
meets in Cambridge, 163–64, 166, 175
and provincial army, 164, 179–80

Committee of Supplies, 204

Conciliatory Proposition, 95

Concord, Mass., 62, 75, 81, 88, 91, 96, 109, 111, 113
battle at North Bridge, 133–47, 151, 160, 162, 326n, 327n, 342n, 343n
and Battle Road, 152–54
British expedition to, 114–19, 122–24, 129–30
liberty pole of, 133–35, 139
militia of, 134–36, 141–42
war begins at, 140–43, 145, 189

Concord fight, 132–47, 163, 168, 171, 188–89, 206, 323n

Concord Hill, 148, 153, 328n

Concord River, 133–34, 137, 139–41, 144

Congregational Church, 11, 19, 53, 169

Connecticut, 57, 167, 214, 241, 243, 253, 266, 288
delegates of, 74
and gunpowder, 204
militia/army of, 65, 165, 197, 208, 211, 223, 259–60, 268
supports Massachusetts, 52, 173–75

Continental army, 214, 236, 249, 258
ammunition/artillery for, 268–72
and cowardice, 277–78
devoid of Bostonians, 289
and free African Americans, 251, 262–63
generals/officers of, 262, 270–74
and the King's Speech, 264–65
and reenlistment crisis, 267, 271–72
winter mobility of, 259, 266, 271–72

Continental Congress. See First Continental Congress; Second Continental Congress

Cooper, Rev. Samuel, 33, 46, 96, 100, 111, 308n, 321n

Cooper, William, 42, 96

Cooper's Tavern, 153, 158

Copley, John Singleton, 22–23, 37, 46–47, 68, 306n

Copp's Hill, 14, 15, 21, 168, 196, 198, 202, 206, 210, 217, 254, 340n

Cornhill, 19, 97, 320n, 321n, 339n

council of war, 195, 250–51, 267, 271–75, 277, 282

county conventions, 74–75, 77, 79

couriers/messengers, 54, 75, 204, 322n. See also Revere, Paul

courts-martial, 243–44, 251–53, 257

Crafts, Thomas, 271, 290

Crocker, Hannah Mather, 87–88

Cromwell, Oliver, 178–79

Cromwell's Head Tavern, 56, 312n

Cushing, Thomas, 48, 55–56, 104

customs/customs officers, 7, 14, 16–19, 21, 68, 70, 247, 256, 284, 303–4n, 315n

Daily Atlas, 292

Danforth, Samuel, 69, 72, 314–15n

Danvers, Mass., 40, 58–59, 76, 156–57

Dartmouth, 9

Dartmouth, Lord, 23, 72, 94, 259
    and account of Concord/Lexington,
        188–89
    Gage reports to, 31, 49, 59, 80, 85, 316n
    orders of, 104, 114–15
    and Port Act, 31
Davis, Ezekiel, 141–42
Davis, Isaac, 137–43, 147, 327n
Davis, William, 276
Dawes, William, 78, 118–19, 123
Deane, Silas, 74
Dearborn, Henry, 212, 218, 222, 227
Death of General Warren at the Battle of
    Bunker's Hill (Trumbull), 294
DeBerniere, Henry, 135, 148
Declaration of Independence, 5, 290,
    294–95, 349n
Dedham, Mass., 101–2, 112, 177,
    215–16, 340n
Deming, Sarah Winslow, 161–62, 164,
    169, 331n
Derby, John, 171–72, 188
desertion
    in British army, 50, 80, 311n
    in British navy, 258
    in provincial army, 202, 205
Devens, Richard, 205, 338n
Diana, 170, 184–86, 207, 217, 265
Dinwiddie, Gov. Robert, 239
Ditson, Thomas, 99, 145, 319n
Dock Square, 11, 15, 31, 183
Doolittle, Amos, 323n, 325n, 327n
Doolittle, Ephraim, 86
Dorchester Heights, 12, 14, 15, 63, 191,
    195, 204, 234, 251, 254, 272–83,
    287, 354n, 355n
drummers. See fifers and drummers
Dunbar, Jesse, 84–85
dysentery, 243, 255

East India Company tea, 3–4, 8–9, 11, 37, 52
Edwards, Rev. Jonathan, 59
Edwards, Sally, 101–3, 112, 177, 191–92,
    216, 319n, 320n, 340n
Eliot, John, 181, 235
Eliot, Rev. Andrew, 169–70, 181, 206, 332n
Eliot, Samuel, 48–49

Emerson, Rev. William, 133–34, 142, 144,
    241, 243, 327n
English
    Civil War, 42, 137, 341n
    patronage system, 193
    political system, 94
    Revolution, 4–5, 178
    settlers, 18, 61, 120, 137
Enlightenment, 20, 32, 34, 289
entrenching tools, 205–6, 214
Estabrook, Benjamin, 121
Estabrook, Prince, 121, 128
Eustis, William, 68, 110, 150, 314n, 320n,
    328n, 340n
Evacuation Day, 285

Fairfax, Sally, 239
Falcon, 196, 203
Falmouth (Portland, Maine), 16, 257, 349n
Faneuil Hall, 15, 31–32, 36, 39, 48, 103,
    168, 256, 259, 265–66
farmers, 41, 70, 77, 120, 126, 142, 165,
    197, 208, 241–42, 289, 309n
Farnsworth, Amos, 179, 185–86, 199,
    334n, 337n
Faulkner, Francis, 151–52
fieldpieces, 76, 78, 88, 154, 197, 205–6,
    209–11, 218, 223. See also artillery
fifers and drummers, 124, 128, 132, 138,
    146, 149, 289
fire boats, 170
firefighters, 17, 292, 305n
First Continental Congress, 47, 75, 96,
    110, 247, 253
    and African Americans, 351n
    and army/militia, 181, 236, 241–42, 267
    and civil government, 178, 181, 236
    delegates of, 44–46, 55, 74, 82, 130,
        294, 309n, 312n
    grants commissions, 243–44
    issues paper currency, 250
    militant start of, 76
    replaces Gridley, 270
    resolves of, 82–83, 85
    and Samuel Adams, 73–74, 130
    and Washington, 237, 241, 250–51,
        261–63, 274, 351n

First Meeting, 15, 40

fishery/fishermen, 95, 246, 256, 313n

flags, 30, 137, 192, 264–65, 283, 317n, 326n, 351n

flank guards, 145–48, 153, 156, 158, 160, 209

fleches, 223, 225

Flucker, Lucy. *See* Knox, Lucy Flucker

Flucker, Thomas, 38, 68, 89, 246, 255

Forbes, John, 239

Ford, John, 147–48, 223

Fort Duquesne, 238–39

Fort George, 268–70

Fort Ticonderoga, 26–27, 173–74, 190, 245, 268–69, 271, 276, 332n

Fort William and Mary, 84, 99, 140, 316n, 317n

fortifications, 248, 265
  abatis lines of, 264, 277
  of Boston, 10, 78, 82, 86, 177, 183, 249–50, 254, 351n
  at Boston Neck, 15, 76–77, 93, 164, 317n
  on Breed's Hill, 118, 197–205, 209, 224
  on Bunker Hill, 213–14, 286
  at the Castle, 30, 286–87
  components of, 199, 273, 275–77, 280, 353n
  on Dorchester Heights, 275–76, 280, 282–83
  at Lechmere Point, 271–72, 274

Foster, Edmund, 146

Foster, Gideon, 156

Framingham, Mass., 93, 159, 268–69

France, 5, 221, 238–39, 289. *See also* French and Indian War

Francis, 284

Franklin, Benjamin, 23, 28–29, 36, 53, 64, 93–96, 111, 158, 171, 251, 314n, 315n

freedom, 20, 23, 35, 111, 120–21, 293, 324n

French and Indian War, 38, 60, 194, 315n
  and British soldiers, 61, 132, 190, 212, 239
  and colonial soldiers, 61, 78, 229
  history of, 6, 26–27, 239
  veterans of, 16, 56–57, 67, 70, 85, 120, 134, 154–55, 164–65, 180, 201, 205, 212, 274, 329n

Washington's role in, 238–39
  and "Yankee Doodle," 149

Furbush, Charles, 147–48

Gage, Margaret Kemble, 27, 30, 50, 86–87, 117, 234–35, 253, 317n, 322n, 345n

Gage, Thomas, 29, 60, 109, 162, 164, 237, 250, 311n
  account of Lexington/Concord, 168, 171, 188–89
  army of, 49–51, 73, 79–80, 85–86, 170, 249
  background/family of, 26–28, 38, 50, 86–87, 238, 322n
  and Battle of Bunker Hill, 195, 197–98, 200, 203–4, 216, 233–35
  and Coercive Acts, 57–58
  criticism of, 86–87, 189–90, 317n
  description of, 318n, 333n
  dismisses General Court, 46, 75
  fortifies Boston, 76–80, 82
  and gunpowder supplies, 62, 65, 71–72, 84
  issues martial law, 190
  leads Concord expedition, 115–19, 122–23, 129, 321n, 322n
  and Mass. Government Act, 52–53
  and Massacre Day Oration, 96, 99
  misleads Bostonians, 168–69, 175, 177
  as new governor, 26–27, 30–31, 37–40
  and patriots, 49, 111–12, 121
  and provincial army, 163–64, 166–67, 174–75, 320n
  replacement of, 253, 255–56, 258
  reports to Lord Dartmouth, 31, 49, 59, 80, 85, 316n
  sends regulars to countryside, 102–5
  sends regulars to Lexington, 148–49
  sends sloops to Grape Island, 183
  uses spies, 90–93, 101, 105, 113, 115–16, 135, 173, 176, 180, 182, 192, 318n, 321n

gallows, 15, 20–21

Gaspée, 140

Gates, Horatio, 242, 250, 272–73, 277

General Court, 24, 35, 38–41, 44–46, 75, 81, 164, 236, 247, 253, 288

George III, King, 25, 41, 50, 52, 60, 94,
  103, 190, 252
  1775 speech of, 264–65
  independence from, 262
  and crisis in colonies, 112–15
  loyalty to, 29
  confidence in, 112
  royal authority ends, 291
  and war with colonies, 216, 257,
    264, 321n
Gerry, Elbridge, 123, 150, 173, 215, 339n
Gibbon, Edward, 188
Glasgow, 184, 196, 203
Gordon, Rev. William, 119, 130, 142, 147,
  150, 162, 260, 266, 272–73, 280–81,
  322n, 323n, 327n, 328n, 354n
Gorham, Mass., 35, 41
Government Act. *See* Massachusetts
  Government Act
Governors Island, 12, 63, 283
Grand American Army, 181
Grape Island, 13, 183, 191, 336n
Graves, Samuel, 51, 79, 217–18
  abilities of, 349n
  and Battle of Chelsea Creek, 185–86
  criticism of, 256–58, 317n
  and Fort William and Mary, 84
  and Gage, 87, 162, 170, 198
  orders of, 87, 167–68
  promotion of, 185–86
  ships of, 161, 167, 170, 203
Graves, Thomas, 170, 185–86
Gray, Harrison, 4, 48, 284, 321n
Great Britain
  America's connection to, 34, 55, 74–75,
    93–94, 181, 285
  bans gunpowder export, 62
  defends colonies, 5
  economic prosperity of, 255–56
  loyalty to, 60, 252
  military strength of, 3–5, 93
  opposition to, 54, 58–59, 112, 140,
    190, 257
  reconciliation with, 74, 91, 172, 182,
    262, 264
  right to search premises, 7, 32
  and rights of colonies, 33–34, 44, 55, 134

Green Dragon Tavern, 15, 68, 90, 192,
  256, 318n
Greene, Nathanael, 236, 246, 250–51,
  260, 274, 282, 347n, 348n
Greene, Rufus, 233
Greenleaf, John, 89, 318n
Greenleaf, William, 290
Greenwood, John, 8
Gridley, Richard, 172–73, 197–99, 201–2,
  205, 210, 244, 270, 276, 337n
Griffin's Wharf, 3, 9–10, 15
Groton militiamen, 138
gunboats, 196, 212, 217
gunpowder, 125, 313n, 318n
  of British army, 62, 64–65, 124
  for cannons, 209–10
  explanation of, 62, 64
  lack of, 234, 249–50, 267, 272, 276–77
  needed by provincial army, 78, 173,
    198, 204, 210, 245
  stolen by patriots, 62, 140
  supplies of, 62, 128, 130, 180, 195,
    220–21, 224, 226, 228, 244–45
  See also Powder Alarm
guns, 78, 122, 186, 228, 343n

Haldimand, Frederick, 27, 86, 93, 324n
Halifax, Nova Scotia, 283–85, 287,
  290, 355n
Hallowell, Benjamin, 63, 68, 70–71,
  256–57, 284, 315n
Hallowell, Mary Boylston, 70
Hancock, John, 22, 24, 33, 79–81, 86,
  163, 168, 199, 323n
  alerted by Revere, 123
  chairman of Committee of Safety, 88, 121
  flees to Lexington, 111–12, 116,
    118–19, 122
  and Gen. Gage, 38–40
  as leading politician, 121–22
  and Lexington fight, 130, 325n
  and martial law, 190
  and Massacre Day Oration, 96, 100
  and Mercy Scollay, 247
  official papers of, 125
  personality of, 130
  and secret patriot committee, 90

Hancock, John (*cont.*)
  vessel seized by British, 7, 18
  and Washington, 274, 351n
  and whale oil market, 9
Handley, Charles, 138
Harrington, Jonathan, 119, 127, 323n
Harris, George, 177, 227, 309n
Hartwell, Mary, 132, 134, 147, 153
Harvard College, 11, 40, 63, 67, 97, 178,
  197, 253, 294
Hastings House (Cambridge), 175, 195,
  204, 208, 215–16, 339n, 340n
Hawley, Joseph, 33, 59, 104, 118, 307n
hay, 170–71, 183, 185–86, 214, 219, 256,
  276, 280, 285
Hayward, James, 147
Heath, William, 130, 159–60, 243, 258,
  276, 329n
  background of, 150
  and building fortifications, 275, 353n
  at council of war, 248
  tactical leadership of, 151–52, 154–55,
    158, 330n
  and Joseph Warren, 151–52, 194,
    273, 336n
Hewes, George, 15, 16–17, 21, 247, 305n
History of the Decline and Fall of the Roman
  Empire (Gibbon), 188
Hog Island, 12, 63, 183–85, 254
Hollis Street Meeting, 15, 288
Hooten, Elizabeth. *See* Warren, Elizabeth
  Hooten
horses, 127–28, 140, 150, 152, 154–55,
  173, 204–5, 285
Hosmer, Abner, 142
Hosmer, Joseph, 136, 139, 326n
hospitals, 152, 244, 252, 255–56, 312n
Howe, William, 189, 338n
  ambivalence of, 258–59, 350n
  army of, 206, 209, 218–19, 271, 273
  background of, 190, 216, 259
  and Battle of Bunker Hill, 196, 221–25,
    230, 234, 259
  and Dorchester, 280–83
  and early 1776 raid, 265–66
  evacuates British army, 283–85, 290
  orders Boston burned, 256

orders Charlestown burned, 218
  replaces Gage, 253, 255
  tactics of, 190–91, 200, 203, 211, 214,
    216–17, 225
Hunt, Abra, 51
Hutchinson, Thomas, 32, 39, 68, 72,
  81–82, 95
  aspirations of, 193
  and Boston Massacre, 8
  criticism of, 70, 94
  and Daniel Leonard, 44
  on Derby's account, 188
  on Gage, 50
  home of, 14, 30, 44, 88, 305n
  and John Malcom, 20–21
  and patriot leaders, 90
  removal of, 28, 30, 36, 38
  and Stamp Act, 6, 17–18, 30
  and Tea Act/Tea Party, 3, 9, 34–36
  on Joseph Warren, 110–11

impressment. *See* press gangs
independence, 5, 32, 35, 74, 81, 92, 98,
  110, 112, 262, 264, 290, 315n, 321n,
  336n, 350n
Independent Company of Cadets, 38,
  40, 121
Indians, 35, 57, 61, 66, 121, 137, 159, 211,
  238, 241, 259, 271, 289. *See also* King
  Philip's War; Native Americans

Jeffries, Dr. John, 192–94, 230, 284–85,
  288, 335–36n
Joyce Junior, 10–11, 14, 22–25, 42, 54,
  288–89, 304–5n, 356n

Kemble, Margaret. *See* Gage, Margaret
  Kemble
Kemble, Stephen, 86
King Philip's War, 4–5, 20, 35, 61, 91, 137,
  147, 177, 259
King's Chapel, 15, 288
Knowlton, Thomas, 196–97, 211, 213,
  219, 266
Knox, Henry, 15, 89–90, 246,
  268–71, 274, 277, 279, 290,
  347n, 352n

Knox, Lucy Flucker, 89, 255
Knox, William, 268

Langdon, Rev. Samuel, 197
Laurie, Walter, 140–41, 143–44
Lechmere Point, 12, 63, 209, 254, 258,
    271–72, 274, 276, 278–79, 353n
Lee, 258
Lee, Arthur, 109, 172, 323n
Lee, Charles, 56–58, 72, 100, 230, 242,
    250–51, 258, 260–61, 271, 312n, 346n
Lee, Jeremiah, 123, 150
Lee, Joseph, 69
Leonard, Daniel, 17–18, 44–45, 58, 60,
    62, 85, 112, 284, 305n, 309n
Leslie, Alexander, 93, 99
Leverett, John, 4–5, 32, 303n
Lexington, Mass., 91, 112, 116, 121, 151
    and Battle Road, 152–54
    British army and, 128, 145–49, 273
    first shots at, 189
    militia of, 119–20, 141, 323n
    powderhouse of, 120, 125, 128, 130
Lexington fight, 122–32, 134, 140, 163,
    167, 171, 188–89, 206, 255, 292,
    323n, 325–26n, 328n
Lexington Green, 92, 119, 121–22,
    124–25, 127–30, 134, 148, 151–53,
    226, 241, 323–24n
Lexington Meetinghouse, 119–20,
    125–26, 128, 130, 149, 152
liberty
    defense of, 35, 66, 75, 134
    divinely sanctioned, 120, 134
    meaning of, 323n, 324n
    and patriot cause, 23, 41, 53
    and provincial army, 178–79
    quest for, 32, 34–35, 57, 61, 86, 88,
        130, 181
    and war, 74, 88, 98, 111
Liberty riot, 7, 18
Liberty Tree, 20, 62, 84, 256, 305n
Lincoln, Mass., 132, 137–38,
    142, 160
Lister, Jeremy, 143, 146, 152, 154, 162, 324n
Litchfield, Paul, 170
Littleton militiamen, 138

Lively, 26, 30, 196, 199–200, 202–3
London Bookstore, 15, 89
London, England, 23, 25, 27–28, 36, 41,
    80–82, 93–96, 109, 111, 117, 171,
    188, 253, 255, 285
Long Wharf, 37–40, 42, 64, 117, 203,
    206, 285, 290, 322n
Loring, Joseph, 152
Loring, Joshua and Elizabeth, 259
Lowell, John, 125
loyalists
    in Massachusetts, 170
    number of, 303n
    remain in Boston, 164, 168, 288–89,
        355n, 356n
    resistance movement of, 85
    suppression of, 115, 121, 317n
Lynn militia, 156–57

Mackenzie, Frederick, 97, 129, 155, 324n,
    325n, 330n
Maddison, George, 42, 64
Maine, 16, 34–35, 59, 65, 120, 165, 185,
    209, 257
Malcom, Daniel, 21, 306n
Malcom, John, 14, 15, 16–22, 24, 39, 49,
    53, 86, 247, 289, 305–6n
mandamus councillors, 52–53, 58, 60, 69,
    72, 84–85, 87
Manley, John, 257–58, 268
maps
    Battle of Bunker Hill, 196
    Battle of Chelsea Creek, 184
    Battle Road, 153
    Boston (1774), 12–13, 15
    Boston under siege, 254
    British expedition to Concord, 114
    Concord fight, 133
    Knox's expedition, 269
    Lexington fight, 125
    Powder Alarm, 63
Marblehead, 31, 40–41, 52,
    61, 313n
Mark (slave), 23–24, 197
Marshfield, Mass., 85–86, 166–67
martial law, 78, 190
Maryland, 244, 286

masons, 68, 90–91, 292, 318n. *See also* St.
    Andrew's Lodge of Masons; St. John's
    Masonic Lodge
Massachusetts
    charter of, 5, 41, 81
    civil government for, 59, 95, 178,
        180–81, 236, 242
    deep divisions in, 59, 81, 85–86, 313n
    description of, 34
    founders of, 11
    militia of, 38, 164–65, 214, 242, 260, 268
    open rebellion of, 58–59, 94–95, 109,
        115, 252
    transformation of, 159
Massachusetts Government Act, 41,
    52–53, 58, 74, 312–13n
Massachusetts House of Representatives,
    35, 41, 44–46, 252–53
Massachusetts Spy, 101
Massacre Day Oration, 38, 96–100, 130
McClary, Andrew, 212
Mecom, Jane, 158–59
Medford, Mass., 14, 158, 197, 202, 205, 235
medical corps, 109, 193, 244, 251
medical supplies, 88–89, 109, 166,
    318n, 320n
Melvill, Thomas, 55, 312n
men-of-war. *See specific names*; warships
Menotomy (Arlington), Mass., 118,
    122–23, 150, 152–53, 155–59, 162,
    191, 194, 242, 324n, 330n
Mercury, 184
Meriam's Hill, 133–34, 145, 151
Mifflin, Thomas, 277, 279
military stores
    in Concord, 115–16, 118–19, 130,
        134–35, 138–39, 323n
    funds for, 88
    for provincial army, 88, 109, 115–16,
        118–19, 173–74
militiamen, 58, 175, 188, 242
    and Battle of Bunker Hill, 195, 197
    and Battle Road, 152–60
    and British regulars, 77, 85, 115, 118, 148
    at Concord fight, 132, 134–47, 323n
    and powdering hair, 156, 330n
    at Lexington, 123–31, 134, 326n

loyalties of, 259–60
    organizing of, 73, 77, 152, 160–65
    skillful shooting of, 92
    surround Boston, 174–75, 189
    undisciplined, 178–79, 238, 241,
        243, 329n
    See also farmers; Independent Company of
        Cadets; minutemen; *specific battles*;
        town militias
Mill Pond, 12, 15, 69, 79, 212
Milton, 12, 14, 20, 30, 74
minutemen, 77–78, 136, 144, 315n
Mitchell, Edward, 123, 126
mobs, 6, 11, 17–18, 22, 84, 154, 305n, 346n
Molineux, William, 36, 48, 82, 100, 316n
Montagu, John, 10, 39–40, 51
Montgomery, Richard, 245, 271
Montresor, John, 86, 196–97, 282, 285
Morris, Gouverneur, 240
Morton's Hill, 196, 200, 209, 211, 218
Moulton, Martha, 139
Mount Whoredom, 15, 51, 279, 311n
Mowat, Henry, 257
Muller, John, 275, 353n
Munroe, Ebenezer, 127
Munroe, Jedidiah, 148
Munroe, John, 127
Munroe, Marret, 119
Munroe Tavern, 152
Munroe, Timothy, 157
Munroe, William, 119, 122, 124, 130, 325n
Murray, Gov. John, 262
muskets, 228, 244, 267
    of British army, 141–42, 146, 154,
        217, 222
    loading of, 124
    of provincial army, 78, 129, 135, 179,
        195, 214, 221, 229
    surrender of, 168
Mystic River, 14, 64–65, 116, 184, 197,
    203, 209, 211, 213, 217, 221, 226,
    254, 256, 340n

Nancy, 258, 268, 279
Nantucket Island, 9, 170, 304n, 332n
Native Americans, 61, 165. *See also*
    Indians; King Philip's War

Needham, Mass., 159, 330n
New Hampshire, 65, 84, 101, 165, 205, 211–12, 214, 241, 249, 260, 268, 317n
New York, 8, 27, 44, 48, 56, 82, 167, 237, 271, 287, 345n
Nichols, James, 137, 160, 326n
Nixon, John, 185
Noddle's Island, 12, 63, 183–86, 246, 254, 265
North Administration, 76, 86, 103, 114
North Carolina, 16, 167
North End (Boston), 10, 15, 21, 39, 68–69, 79, 88, 168, 192, 230
North End Caucus, 68–69, 314n
North, Lord, 24, 29, 188, 190, 319n
  and Coercive Acts, 95
  criticism of, 53, 56, 311n
  and Josiah Quincy, Jr., 94
  King George writes to, 112
Northampton, 59
Nova Scotia, 5. See also Halifax, Nova Scotia

Occom, Samson, 23
Old North Meetinghouse, 15, 256, 349n
Old South Meetinghouse, 3–4, 9, 15, 20, 38, 48–49, 96–99, 256, 284
Oliver, Thomas, 63, 72–73, 256, 355n
Oliver, Peter, 61, 111, 169, 233, 248, 311–12n, 314n, 317n, 335–36n
Orne, Azor, 123, 150
Otis, James, 7, 29, 32, 293, 307n, 313n

Paddock, Adino, 78, 284
Paine, Robert Treat, 45, 56, 309n
Paine, Samuel, 229, 333n
Palmer, Joseph, 167, 195
Parker, John, 119–22, 125–27, 129–30, 141, 148
Parker's Revenge, 148, 153, 328n
Parliament, 5–6, 11, 29, 35, 96, 103, 171, 253
  and Conciliatory Proposition, 95
  and King's Speech, 264
  opposition to, 92, 109
  passes Coercive Acts, 53
  and Port Act, 31–32, 37, 40–41
  revokes charter, 41

sovereignty of, 111
  and Tea Party, 25
  and war with colonies, 216
Parsons, Lawrence, 135–36, 138–39, 144–45
patriot movement
  anthems for, 54, 82
  clemency offered to, 190
  demands for unity, 60
  divisions among, 317n
  and moral duplicity, 23, 319n
  motivations of, 8–9
  and preserving status quo, 289
  psychological cost of, 32, 307–8n
  secret activities of, 45, 90, 101, 191–92
Pennsylvania, 8, 29, 44, 53, 56, 76, 238, 244
Percy, Hugh, 52, 104, 197, 282
  and Battle Road, 152–55
  in Boston, 60, 111, 113, 117
  brigade of, 149–50, 152, 165, 246, 323n
  description of, 51, 311n, 330n
  leads expedition to Concord, 114, 117
  leads march into countryside, 102–3
  on provincial army, 154–55, 321n
  retreats to Charlestown, 158–60, 163, 329n
Philadelphia, 44, 48, 54–56, 74–76, 81–82, 113, 163, 167–68, 171, 180, 182, 236, 261
Phipps, David, 64
Pickering, Timothy, 158, 160, 163–64, 172, 174, 206, 330–31n, 336n
Pigot, Robert, 196, 209, 217, 219, 224, 226
pistols, 78, 168
Pitcairn, John, 87, 123–24, 126–28, 139, 148, 226–28, 262, 316n, 325n
Pitts, John, 199, 316n, 337n
Pitts, Samuel, 51
Plymouth, Mass., 84–85, 93, 175, 267
Point Allerton, 13, 15, 31, 40
Pollard, Asa, 201, 338n
Poor, Thomas, 178–79
Poor, Salem, 228, 262–63, 351n
Pope Night, 10–11, 19, 304n
Port Act, 30–31, 36–37, 40–41, 70, 312n

Port Bill, 32, 37, 43, 45, 48, 52, 58, 79, 94, 120, 315n
Porter, Asahel, 123, 127–28
Portsmouth, England, 188
Portsmouth, New Hampshire, 84, 99, 101, 140
Powder Alarm, 62–74, 76–79, 84, 93, 99, 102, 104
Prentiss, George, 159, 330n
Prescott, William, 217, 342–43n
    bravery of, 337–38n
    as fierce fighter, 201
    fires cannons on British, 209–11
    leads provincial army, 195–98
    orders retreat, 228–29
    and redoubt on Breed's Hill, 198–99, 201–2, 206, 213–14, 219–20, 224, 226, 338n
    and reinforcements, 204–5, 218, 230
press gangs, 18, 61
Preston, 51, 184–85
Price, Ezekiel, 179, 194, 336n, 337n
prisoners, 157, 166, 179, 188, 266
Prospect Hill, 64, 230, 254, 258, 265, 351n
prostitution, 46, 51, 68, 311n, 319n
Province House (Boston), 15, 19–20, 32, 40, 51, 87, 117, 166, 200, 203–4, 282
provincial army
    account of, 171, 188–89
    assembling of, 103, 109, 155, 164–65, 175, 178
    bravery of, 262
    cost of, 249–50
    largest regiment of, 212
    make-up of companies, 165, 178
    maritime focus of, 170–72, 183
    "of observation," 150
    overhauling of, 243–46, 251, 259–63, 265, 267
    poor hygiene of, 178
    provisions for, 115–16, 178–79
    recruiting men for, 163–65, 175, 182, 192, 242
    and reenlistment crisis, 259–61
    surrounds Boston, 169, 175
    undisciplined, 146, 178–82, 267

    victories of, 186–87
    See also militiamen
provincial army officers
    artillery skills of, 172–73
    and commissions, 179, 192, 243–44
    infighting among, 194
    lack of, 144, 223
    recruit soldiers, 165, 175, 192
    relationship with soldiers, 178–80
    and Washington, 242–46
    See also specific names
Provincial Congress, 81, 88, 90, 92, 96, 103–5, 109–11, 113, 118–19, 177
    arrest of, 115
    and Battle of Bunker Hill, 236
    delegates of, 316n, 318n
    and first shot, 143
    founding of, 75
    leaders of, 191–92
    meets in Concord, 75, 134, 168
    meets in Watertown, 168
    presidents of, 121, 175, 181, 194, 236, 333n
    and provincial army, 165, 179–80
    and skillful officers, 172–73
    and spies, 321n
provincial resistance movement, 73–75, 77–79, 81, 236
Punkatasset Hill, 133–36, 142–44
Puritan settlers, 4, 6, 10, 23, 34, 121, 132, 137, 285
Putnam, Daniel, 195
Putnam, Israel, 74, 201, 208–9, 247, 334n
    and amphibious assault, 170, 282
    background of, 57
    and Battle of Bunker Hill, 195–98, 213, 337n
    and Battle of Chelsea Creek, 185–87
    at council of war, 190, 250
    criticism of, 212–13, 223
    leads army on Bunker Hill, 182, 205, 212–14, 218–19, 223
    as officer, 165, 182, 243
    personality of, 182, 198
    on Prospect Hill, 230, 265
Putnam, Israel, Jr., 208
Putnam, Rufus, 274–76

Quarry Hill arsenal, 62–64
Quartering Act, 53, 311n
Quebec Act, 53
Quebec, Canada, 26, 180, 190, 245, 271
Queen Street Writing School, 149, 165, 246
Quero, 171–72, 188–89
Quincy, Abigail, 96
Quincy, Dorothy, 122, 324n
Quincy, Josiah, Jr., 33, 60, 72, 90, 256, 284
    death of, 171–72
    illness of, 3, 46, 82, 120, 307n
    in London, 81–82, 93–96, 109, 171, 318n
    and Port Act, 31, 36
    represents British soldiers, 8, 32
    ridicule of, 100
    and Tea Party, 3–4, 48
Quincy, Samuel, 60, 62

Ramsdell, Abednego, 156
Randolph, Edward, 4–5
Reading militia, 146
redoubt
    for Battle of Bunker Hill, 213–14,
        217–20, 224–29, 262, 338n
    on Breed's Hill, 196, 199, 201–6,
        210–11, 337n
    on Dorchester Heights, 191
    at Lechmere Point, 272, 274
Reed, James, 205
Reed, Joseph, 261, 267, 273–74, 278, 287
religion, 4, 59–60, 111, 176–77, 179, 191,
    285, 333n
Revere, Paul, 82, 89, 91, 289, 306n, 316n,
    322n, 349n
    captured by British, 123
    and Green Dragon Tavern, 68, 90, 318n
    at Lexington fight, 125–26, 325n
    as messenger, 76, 116, 118–19, 166, 315n
    on spies, 318n
    and Suffolk Resolves, 74, 76
Rhode Island, 3, 44, 48, 65, 82, 140, 162,
    165, 236, 241, 246, 251, 259, 268
Richardson, Josiah, 123, 127–28
riflemen, 244, 260, 277
Robertson, Archibald, 279–80, 282, 285
Robinson, John, 138, 140, 142, 342n, 343n
Rogers's Rangers, 57, 212

Rotch, Francis, 9
Rowe, John, 24, 36–37, 40–43, 49, 82,
    100–1, 288, 316n
Roxbury, Mass., 71, 112, 116, 149–50,
    254, 266, 353n
    American lines in, 264
    British plan to attack, 191, 204, 208
    fortifications in, 246, 275
    Gen. Thomas's forces in, 195
    location of, 12, 63
    militiamen in, 161–62, 164–65, 167–69,
        175–76, 178–79, 182–83, 234
    and taking of Dorchester, 276–77, 279,
        282–83
Royal American Magazine, 47
Ruggles, Timothy, 85
rum, 80, 179, 202, 238, 316n
Rush, Benjamin, 240
Russell, Benjamin, 149, 165, 246–47, 331n
Russell, Jason, 153, 156–57

Salem, Mass., 31, 40, 43–45, 48, 51–52,
    55, 57–59, 67, 76, 93, 100, 158, 160,
    171, 188, 235, 318n
Salem witch trials, 59, 121
Sandwich, Lord, 257–58, 316n
Scammon, James, 209
schooners, 170
Schuyler, Philip, 269
Scituate, 170, 332n
Scollay, John, 47, 312n
Scollay, Mercy, 47, 55, 70, 101–2, 112,
    192, 247–48, 310n, 312n,
    319–20n, 347n
Scollay, Priscilla, 55
Second Continental Congress, 83, 113
Sewall, Jonathan, 65, 233–34
sharpshooters, 222, 224
Shirley, Gov. William, 31
Shrewsbury, Mass., 65–66, 73, 164
Shuldham, Molyneux, 258
siege
    Boston under, 246–47, 254, 286,
        289–91, 355n
    definition of, 245, 248–49
    devolves into stalemate, 265–66
Siege of Louisbourg, 5, 77, 120

signal flags/lanterns, 116, 192
Simons, Joshua, 128
slavery, 23–24, 121, 159, 165, 197, 240,
    244, 262, 278, 293–95, 306n, 356n
smallpox, 54, 68, 255, 312n, 314n
Smith, Francis, 152, 154, 280
    leads expedition to Concord, 116, 118,
        122–23, 128–29, 132, 136
    marches to Lexington, 145, 148–49
    reinforcements of, 140, 143–44
    searches for supplies, 139
smuggling, 7, 9, 21, 304n
Solemn League and Covenant, 42, 47–49,
    55, 75, 118
Somerset, 182, 184, 203, 218
South Carolina, 3, 52, 167
South End (Boston), 10, 15, 20, 234
spears, 250, 348n
spies, 89–93, 115–16, 135, 170, 180, 192,
    246, 318n, 321n, 334n. See also
    Church, Benjamin; Gage, Thomas
Spitfire, 196, 203
Spunkers, 68, 314n
St. Andrew's Lodge of Masons, 68, 89–90,
    192, 288, 318n
St. James's Palace, 25, 29
St. John's Masonic Lodge, 90
St. Patrick's Day, 285
Stamp Act (1765), 4, 6, 17–18, 20, 30, 163
Stark, John, 185, 196, 205, 211–14,
    220–21, 226, 339–40n
Stevens, James, 178–79
Stiles, Rev. Ezra, 66, 325n
Stockbridge, Mass., 58, 241
Storrs, Experience, 209
Stoughton, Mass., 179, 194
Stow militiamen, 138
street-firing, 141, 327n
Stuart, Gilbert, 237, 240
Stuart kings, 4, 6
Suffolk County militia, 150
Suffolk Resolves, 74–76, 102, 115
Sukey, 171, 188
Sullivan, John, 245, 249–51, 281–82, 286
Sullivan, Thomas, 229
surgeons, 54, 152, 192–94, 235, 244, 281,
    284, 312n, 335n. See also specific names

Sutherland, William, 124, 128, 141, 143,
    149, 162, 324n
swords, 51, 124, 228–29, 325n, 343n
Symmetry, 196, 203

tarring and feathering, 16–22, 24, 32, 39,
    99, 145, 288–89, 305–6n
Taunton, Mass., 44–45, 58, 84–85, 317n
taxation, 6–8, 16, 30, 52, 81, 88, 95,
    111–12, 303n
tea, 7, 10–11, 22, 30, 36, 41, 45, 52–53,
    100. See also Boston Tea Party; East
    India Company tea
Tea Act (1773), 8–10, 34, 120
Ten Hills Farm, 63–64
Tewksbury militia, 146
Thacher, James, 281–82, 286, 339n
Thomas, John, 164–67, 175–76, 183, 191,
    194–95, 208, 243, 250, 280
Thomas, Isaiah, 47, 70, 101, 112, 150,
    247, 310n, 321n
Thomas, Mary Dill, 101
Thomas, Nathaniel Ray, 85–86, 166–67
Thompson, Benjamin, 101
Thompson, Daniel, 147
Thorp, Thomas, 142, 330n
Tories, 71, 86, 274, 284, 288–89,
    317–18n, 356n
Tory Row. See Cambridge: Tory Row in
Town House (Boston), 8, 15, 19–20, 39,
    290–91
town meetings, 32–34, 36, 39, 41, 48–49,
    53, 58, 74, 120, 136, 139, 178, 307n
town militias, 58, 77–78, 81, 93, 119–20,
    136, 242, 267–68, 270. See also
    militiamen; specific towns
Townsend, Daniel, 157
Townsend, David, 215–16, 339–40n
Townshend Act (1766), 7–8
traitors, 89–93
Trask, Israel, 244
treason, 49, 201–2, 252, 284
Trevett, Samuel, 210–11, 213, 223
Trumbull, Gov. Jonathan, 174–75, 253
Trumbull, John, 241, 294
Trumbull, Joseph, 240–41
Tryon, Gov. William, 16

Tudor, William, 162
Tupper, Benjamin, 257
Tyler, John, 292–93

uniforms
    of British officers, 155, 220
    of British regulars, 124, 132, 134, 155,
        219–20, 222, 325n
    of militiamen, 124, 325n
    of provincial army, 208, 243
    of Virginia regiment, 239
Unity, 284

Virginia, 44, 53, 56, 168, 237–40, 244,
    262, 278, 289, 350n
Vose's Tavern, 74–75

Waller, Adj. John, 227–29
Wallis, Dennison, 157
Waltham, Mass., 180
War of Regulation, 16
Ward, Artemas, 167, 182, 198
    advises Washington, 251
    as provincial army's first leader, 164,
        214, 260–61
    and Battle of Bunker Hill, 202,
        204–5, 230
    and Battle of Chelsea Creek, 186–87
    commission of, 179–80
    at council of war, 195, 250–51
    criticism of, 180, 345n
    occupying Dorchester, 272–74, 277
    officers of, 179, 186, 245
    replacement of, 236
Warren, Dr. Joseph, 36, 48, 164, 186–87,
    242, 256, 261, 284, 350n
    background/personality of, 66–69, 89,
        98, 110–11, 155–56, 181, 312n, 314n
    and Battle of Bunker Hill, 195, 208,
        215–16
    and Benjamin Church, 176, 182, 322n
    on the British army, 220
    and the Coercive Acts, 74–75
    and Committee of Correspondence, 52–54
    and Committee of Safety, 109–10, 163,
        166, 168, 173, 175, 191–92, 204–5,
        236, 336n

on Concord/Lexington fight, 323n
death/burial of, 229–30, 235–36,
    247–48, 287–88, 294–95,
    344n, 347n
description of, 46, 164, 309–10n,
    314n, 336n
finances of, 54, 311–12n
and Gov. Gage, 90–92, 177, 318n
house of, 15, 46, 116, 150
and Josiah Quincy, 81–82, 95, 171–72
as major general, 194, 219, 228, 236,
    336n, 337n
Massacre Day Oration of, 96–100,
    130, 319n
medical practice of, 3, 17, 46–47, 53–54,
    78, 102, 216, 310n, 312n, 314n,
    318n, 320n, 328n, 340n
and the Powder Alarm, 70–73, 102
and Provincial Congress, 81, 88, 109,
    110, 168, 175, 181, 191–92,
    316n, 333n
as soldier, 109–10, 150–52, 155–56,
    216, 219, 228, 339n
sounds the alarm, 116–19, 323n
and Suffolk Resolves, 75–76, 102, 115
writes to Samuel Adams, 180–82,
    193–94
See also Adams, John; Edwards, Sally;
    Scollay, Mercy
Warren, Eben, 287–88, 318n
Warren, Edward, 216, 312n, 314n, 318n
Warren, Elizabeth Hooten, 46, 54, 310n
Warren, James, 175, 267–68, 333n
Warren, John, 67, 89, 216, 235, 247–48,
    287–88, 314n, 318n
Warren, Mercy Otis, 47, 252, 310n, 331n,
    333n, 344n
warships, 84, 169, 182
    and Battle of Bunker Hill, 196,
        199–200, 202–3, 212, 215, 217
    and Battle of Chelsea Creek, 183–87
    in Boston Harbor, 26, 76, 89, 114, 116,
        161–62, 172, 184–85, 189–91,
        198–99, 206, 249, 255, 257–58, 276
    and British evacuation, 283, 290
    deep draft of, 170
    plundered by provincials, 186

Washington, George, 53, 160, 172, 180,
    248, 286, 312n
    and African Americans, 241, 262–63,
        289, 351n
    and assault on Boston, 243, 249–51,
        258–59, 263, 267–68, 271–73,
        275–76, 283, 287, 351n
    on cowardice, 277–78
    criticism of, 260–61, 350n
    description of, 237, 240
    and Dorchester, 272–79, 281, 287
    establishes army, 265–68, 287, 289–90
    and gunpowder, 244–45, 249–50, 267
    heads army/navy, 236–37, 240–41,
        245, 257–58
    home of, 240, 278
    and Henry Knox, 268–71
    on the loyalists, 284
    military background of, 26, 56,
        237–40, 242
    negative opinions of, 241–43, 250,
        261, 346n
    overhauls army, 243–46, 251, 259–63,
        267–68
    personality of, 237, 239–40, 245,
        261–62, 274, 346–47n
    and reenlistment crisis, 259–61,
        267, 271
    on war, 350n
Washington, Martha Custis, 239, 267, 286
Watertown, Mass., 14, 69, 72, 103, 151,
    158, 168, 178, 247, 252, 330n, 332n
Watson, George, 22
Watson's Corner, 153, 158
weapons, 78, 115, 124, 168, 172–73, 244,
    267, 315n. *See also* artillery; *specific
    types*
Webb, Jotham, 156
Webb, Samuel, 223, 279

Webster, Daniel, 292–93
Wedderburn, Alexander, 28
Welch Fusiliers, 98, 153–55, 217,
    221–22
Wellington, Benjamin, 124
West, Rev. Samuel, 159, 330n
Westfield, Mass., 269–71
Westford, Mass., 138, 140, 200
Weston, Mass., 93, 111
Weymouth, Mass., 183
whale oil, 9, 304n
whaleboats, 170, 257, 332n
Wheatley, Phillis, 23–24, 278, 306n
Whig party, 89, 104, 216, 318n
White, Ammi, 144, 327–28n
Whitefield, Rev. George, 59
Whittemore, Samuel, 153, 157
Wilkes, John, 253
Wilkinson, James, 286
Willard, Abijah, 201, 204, 338n
Wilson, Jonathan, 147
Winnisimmet, Mass., 63, 183–86, 254
Winter Hill, 63–64, 153, 160, 254
Winthrop, Hannah, 47, 161–62,
    310n, 331n
Winthrop, John, 11, 40, 47, 64,
    161–62, 256
Winthrop, John, Jr., 11, 22, 24, 313n. *See
    also* Joyce Junior
Woburn, Mass., 123, 146–47
Wolfe, James, 26, 190
women, 121, 151, 159. *See also specific
    names*
Worcester, Mass., 58, 65, 77, 86, 93, 109,
    112, 162, 167, 247, 269, 321n

"Yankee Doodle," 149
Young, Dr. Thomas, 48, 54, 57–58, 69–70,
    82, 100, 111